An Open Economy Macroeconomics Reader

D0224882

Over the last two decades, capital mobility and international trade have recorded growth rates that surpass the historically high levels of the last quarter of the nineteenth century. It is therefore crucial that macroeconomic policy takes account of this new openness in trade and capital movements.

An Open Economy Macroeconomics Reader demonstrates how open economy macroeconomics has responded to these new dynamics by combining the seminal contributions to the literature with competent reviews of the most up-to-date research. This combination builds into a stimulating exposition of the topic, as rigorous yet accessible and policy-oriented work is brought together in a way that requires only a basic grounding in quantitative methods.

Consisting of nine themed sections, this book facilitates coherent reading and understanding by way of editorial features, including:

- General and section-specific introductions
- Questions for discussion
- Suggestions for further reading
- Extensive lists of references

An Open Economy Macroeconomics Reader is therefore an essential source of reading and a useful guide to macroeconomic policy-making in open economies, as developed and discussed by distinguished scholars, including Robert A. Mundell, Marcus Flemming, James Meade, Koichi Hamada, Jeffrey A. Frankel and others.

Mehmet Ugur is Jean Monnet Senior Lecturer in the Political Economy of European Integration at the University of Greenwich, UK.

An Open Economy Macroeconomics Reader

Edited by

Mehmet Ugur

London and New York

First published 2002 by Routledge
11 New Fetter Lane, London EC4P 4EE

Simultaneously published in the USA and Canada
by Routledge
29 West 35th Street, New York, NY 10001

Routledge is an imprint of the Taylor & Francis Group

Compilation, original and editorial matter
© 2002 Mehmet Ugur

Typeset in Times by RefineCatch Limited, Bungay, Suffolk
Printed and bound in Great Britain by
The Cromwell Press, Trowbridge, Wiltshire

British Library Cataloguing in Publication Data
A catalogue record for this book is available from the
British Library

Library of Congress Cataloging in Publication Data
Ugur, Mehmet.
    An open economy macroeconomics reader / Mehmet Ugur.
        p.   cm.
    Includes bibliographical references and index.
    ISBN 0–415–25331–4 (alk. paper)—ISBN 0–415–25332–2
        (pbk.: alk. paper)
        1. Macroeconomics.   I. Title.
    HB172.5.U35 2001
    339—dc21   2001048168

ISBN 0–415–25331–4 (hbk)
ISBN 0–415–25332–2 (pbk)

Contents

Acknowledgements

The authors and publishers would like to thank the following for granting permission to reproduce material in this work:

Canadian Political Science Association for permission to reproduce 'Capital mobility and stabilization policy under fixed and flexible exchange rates' by Robert A. Mundell, *The Canadian Journal of Economics and Political Science*, Volume 29, no. 4 (1963), pp. 487–99.

The International Monetary Fund for permission to reproduce 'Domestic financial policies under fixed and under floating exchange rates' by J. Marcus Fleming, *IMF Staff Papers*, Volume 9, no. 3 (1962), pp. 369–79.

Taylor and Francis for permission to reproduce 'The Mundell–Fleming model – its strengths and limitations' by V. Argy, *International Macroeconomics: Theory and Policy*, Routledge, 1994, pp. 73–84.

Edward Elgar Publishing Ltd. for permission to reproduce 'A history of thought on the balance of payments' by Mark P. Taylor, *The Balance of Payments: New Perspectives in Open Economy Macroeconomics*, Chapter 1, Edward Elgar Publishing Ltd., pp. 1–24 and 28–42.

Pearson Education for permission to reproduce 'The current account' by John Williamson and Chris Milner, *The World Economy: A Textbook in International Economics*, Harvester-Wheatsheaf, 1991, pp. 185–218.

The International Monetary Fund for permission to reproduce 'The appropriate use of monetary and fiscal policy for internal and external stability' by Robert A. Mundell, *IMF Staff Papers*, Volume 9, no. 1 (1962), pp. 70–7.

J. E. Meade and the American Economic Association for permission to reproduce 'The meaning of "internal balance"' by James E. Meade, *American Economic Review*, Volume 83, no. 6 (December 1993), pp. 3–9.

The MIT Press for permission to reproduce 'International monetary independence in a Keynesian model' by Koichi Hamada, *The Political Economy of International Monetary Independence*, Koichi Hamada, translated by Charles Yuji Horioka and Chi-Hung Kwan, The MIT Press (1985), pp. 45–65.

Kluwer Academic/Plenum Publishers for permission to reproduce 'International macroeconomic policy coordination: any lessons for EMU? A selective survey of the literature' by Peter Mooslechner and Martin Schuerz, *Empirica: Journal of Applied Economics and Economic Policy*, Volume 26, no. 3 (1999), pp. 171–99.

Springer-Verlag for permission to reproduce 'Global capital movements, exchange rates and monetary policy' by Bernd Braasch and Helmut Hesse, *Trade, Growth and Economic Policy in Open Economies: Essays in Honour of Hans-Jürgen Vosgerau* edited by Karl-Josef Koch and Klaus Jaeger, Berlin, Springer-Verlag, 1988, pp. 249–68.

Blackwell Publishers for permission to reproduce 'What should central banks do? What should be their macroeconomic objectives and operations?' by Charles A.E. Goodhart, *The Economic Journal*, Volume 104 (November 1994), pp. 1425–36.

Blackwell Publishers for permission to reproduce 'Central bank independence and monetary control' by Alex Cukierman, *The Economic Journal*, Volume 104 (November 1994), pp. 1437–48.

The International Monetary Fund for permission to reproduce 'Exchange rate economics: a survey' by Ronald MacDonald and Mark P. Taylor, *IMF Staff Papers*, Volume 39, no. 1 (1992), pp. 1–27.

Jeffrey A. Frankel and the American Economic Association for permission to reproduce 'Recent exchange-rate experience and proposals for reform' by Jeffrey A. Frankel, *American Economic Review*, Volume 86, no. 2 (1996), pp. 153–8.

Sebastian Edwards and the American Economic Association for permission to reproduce 'Exchange rates and the political economy of macroeconomic discipline' by Sebastian Edwards, *American Economic Review*, Volume 86, no. 2 (December 1996), pp. 159–63.

The American Economic Association for permission to reprint 'A theory of optimum currency areas' by Robert A. Mundell, *American Economic Review*, Volume 51, no. 4 (1961), pp. 657–65.

The American Economic Association for permission to reprint 'Optimum currency areas' by Ronald McKinnon, *American Economic Review*, Volume 53, no. 4 (1963), pp. 718–25.

'The theory of optimum currency areas: a critique' © Paul De Grauwe 1992. Reprinted from *The Economics of Monetary Integration* by Paul De Grauwe (1992) by permission of Oxford University Press.

Barry Eichengreen and Oxford University Press for permission to reproduce

'European monetary unification: a *tour d'horizon*' by Barry Eichengreen, *Oxford Review of Economic Policy*, Volume 14, no. 3 (1998), pp. 24–40.

OECD for permission to reproduce *Harmful Tax Competition: An Emerging Global Issue*. Copyright OECD, 1998.

Blackwell Publishers for permission to reproduce 'The case for international tax co-ordination reconsidered' by Peter Birch Sørensen, *Economic Policy*, Volume 31 (October 2000), pp. 431–61 and 466–72.

Economic Council of Sweden for permission to reproduce 'Key lessons for labour market reforms: evidence from OECD countries' experiences' by Jørgen Elmeskov, John P. Martin and Stefano Scarpetta, *Swedish Economic Policy Review*, Volume 5, no. 2 (1998), pp. 207–52.

Cambridge University Press for permission to reproduce 'Labour market regulation and unemployment' by Paul Gregg and Alan Manning, in D.J. Snower and G. de la Dehesa (eds), *Unemployment Policy: Government Options for the Labour Market*, Cambridge, Cambridge University Press (1997), pp. 395–424.

Every effort has been made to contact copyright holders for their permission to reprint material in this book. The publishers would be grateful to hear from any copyright holder who is not here acknowledged and will undertake to rectify any errors or omissions in future editions of this book.

General introduction

The idea for this reader has been brewing for some time. It all started with a simple observation: the great majority of macroeconomic textbooks do not address the need for an accessible but rigorous book on macroeconomic policy in open economies. We make no claim about the originality of this observation. In fact, it has now become an established routine to adopt an open-economy framework in both entry- and intermediate-level textbooks. This is a welcome development in a period of increased commercial and financial integration that, inevitably, is leading to higher levels of interdependence between national economies.

The recent open-economy macroeconomics textbooks, however, do not address the perceived need satisfactorily for two reasons. First, and mainly for didactic reasons, they tend to incorporate an open-economy perspective into key questions that closed-economy macroeconomics has addressed historically. Although such a synthesis is desirable, its effectiveness is reduced by eclecticism and unexplained digressions. Second, the existing textbooks tend to deal with policy design and implementation as a residual determined by the theoretical issue at hand. Obviously, this is justified by the need to provide a theoretical basis for policy discussion. There could be, however, a different way of organisation: why not select the policy issues to be discussed and call on theory to ascertain the policy options available and the relative strengths/shortcomings associated with them?

This reader aims to go beyond the essentially closed-economy framework of the open-economy macroeconomics textbooks and incorporate theory into policy design and implementation rather than the other way round. This aim, however, is hardly sufficient for justifying the trees to be chopped – let alone other resources that could be put to a better use. It also aims to fulfil three other interrelated objectives. First, it will strive to combine the dated yet seminal contributions to open-economy macroeconomics with the most up-to-date research output. Second, it will try to provide a rigorous treatment of the theoretical and policy issues involved without discouraging readers with an entry-level mathematical competence. Finally, it will highlight the significance of micro-level processes for policy design, without necessarily undermining the case for active macroeconomic policy. Given these aims, the book can be described as an attempt to combine rigour, accessibility and policy-relevance in order to make the study of open-economy macroeconomics interesting, engaging and rewarding.

Having stated the overall rationale for the reader, it is now necessary to provide some indications about the extent to which the choice of material is relevant to stated aims and objectives and how it will contribute to their realisation. It must be indicated here that this 'justification exercise' will be kept to a minimum because the contents of each part and the way in which the parts build into an integrated whole are explained in their introductions. What is in order here is a bird's eye view of the book as a whole.

The main message that the reader is seeking to convey is that 'openness' matters. It matters because it alters the environment within which macroeconomic policy is designed and implemented for three reasons. First, financial flows and movement of goods impact upon the way in which macro-economic variables such as output, employment, interest rates, exchange rates and the balance of payments are determined. This impact is examined in Parts I–III, where the framework for macroeconomic policy design and implementation is introduced. Second, openness matters because it gener-ates interdependence between national policies and may make the policy choice endogenous rather than a choice between exogenously given policy options. This issue is examined in Part IV, where it is demonstrated that the spillover effects of national macroeconomic policies could lead the policy-makers to choose suboptimal policies. Finally, openness matters because it bears upon the way in which the private sector interacts with governments. Not only does it increase the ability of the private economic agents to vote with their feet, but it also increases the pressure on governments to adopt macroeconomic policies conducive to increased returns on 'loyalty' to their jurisdictions. This dynamic complicates the policy design/implementation further because it intensifies interdependence and imposes additional domestic constraints on the policy choice. Therefore, the reader incorporates this dynamic into the analysis early in Part III and examines its implications for macroeconomic policies throughout the remaining parts. The following paragraphs will outline the contents of each part and highlight the way in which these parts build into an integrated volume.

Part I examines the achievement of internal balance in open economies. It begins with two seminal articles by Mundell and Fleming, which analyse the use of monetary and fiscal policies for stabilisation purposes in open econ-omies. What Mundell and Fleming demonstrate is that the effect of monetary and fiscal policies on output would depend on the degree of financial integra-tion and the exchange rate regime in place. Therefore, the policy-maker would be faced with two choices: either selecting the effective policy instrument given the degree of financial integration and the exchange rate regime or choosing the latter given his or her preference for the policy instruments. There are two reasons why Mundell's and Fleming's contributions are important. First, they have contributed to the development of open-economy macroeconomics from being a subset of international economics to being an independent area of study in its own right. Second, they constitute a simple but solid foundation upon which further analysis could be developed. The next article by Argy confirms these properties, but it goes on to highlight the limitations of these original works and the way in which the limitations have been addressed. The last article is inspired by classroom experience and tries to demonstrate that the Mundell–Fleming framework can generate Keynesian, neo-Keynesian and classical results – depending on the assumption concerning price determination. What this exercise demonstrates is that the effect of monetary policy on output declines as prices catch up with monetary expansion; and it vanishes if prices increase by the same rate as the increase in money supply.

Part II focuses on the achievement of the external balance, understood as equilibrium in the balance of payments. The perennial question here is whether the government can use the exchange rate as an instrument that would correct external imbalances. The article by Taylor examines the evolution of the debate on this issue, whereas Williamson and Milner provide further explanation about the way in which various approaches analyse the impact of devaluation on the balance of payments. Although there are differences within each group, the debate on balance of payments can be classified into two groups: the expenditure-based approach and the monetary approach. The expenditure-based approach demonstrates that devaluation can lead to improvement in the balance of payments provided that certain conditions are met. The condition in the elasticities approach is that the absolute sum of demand elasticities for exports and imports must be greater than one. In the absorption approach, the condition is that devaluation must be accompanied by absorption-reducing (deflationary) policies. In contrast, the monetary approach (in its specie-flow and global monetarist varieties) argues that balance of payments disequilibria are essentially monetary phenomena. Either they will be rectified when money market equilibrium is achieved (the global monetarist thesis) or they will cause disequilibrium in the money market which, in turn, affects domestic prices and lead to automatic correction (the specie-flow argument).

Having introduced the debate on the achievement of internal and external balance independently, the book proceeds with the debate on the achievement of internal and external balance simultaneously. Therefore, Part III begins with another seminal contribution by Mundell, which analyses the way in which policy instruments should be assigned to targets. Mundell's assignment rule requires that monetary policy should be assigned to the achievement of external balance and fiscal policy should be assigned to the internal balance. The article by Williamson and Milner presents a concise yet rigorous treatment of another seminal contribution by Meade. In Meade's synthesis the exchange rate is assumed to be fixed but adjustable. Therefore, the government has an extra instrument at its disposal. Then, the assignment rule is to assign the exchange rate to the achievement of the external balance and the absorption-regulating policies (i.e. fiscal and monetary policies) to the internal balance. The limitations of this type of policy design have been noted and criticised in the literature. Therefore, the article by Meade in Chapter 9 constitutes not only interesting reading but also an incisive and thought-provoking response. This is followed by yet another classroom exercise, where we examine the implications of rational expectations formation for Mundell's and Meade's policy design.

In a way, the last article in Part III paves the way for further qualifications of the policy design developed in the preceding chapters. What it tries to demonstrate is that it may not be appropriate to treat the government as an efficient social planner trying to maximise a social objective function. This is due to strategic interaction between the government and the private sector. Part IV is devoted to two contributions dealing with another type of strategic interaction: the interaction between governments in the presence of inter-dependence. Again here, we combine a seminal contribution by Hamada who puts the case for policy co-ordination with a recent review of the literature by Mooslechner and Schuerz. The thrust of Hamada's argument is that a policy designed in accordance with the assignment rule may lead to suboptimal outcomes because it does not take into account the strategic reactions of other governments. Therefore, policy co-ordination is necessary to ensure that the externalities generated by independent actions are internalised. Mooslechner and Schuerz introduce the reader into the wide literature that followed and evaluate the scope for policy co-ordination in the European Monetary Union (EMU).

As is well known, monetary unions are radical solutions to monetary and exchange rate policy co-ordination in the sense that they centralise monetary policy and make the exchange rate unavailable. In other words, they consti-tute highly binding arrangements that force the countries involved to internalise the externalities generated by independent policies. Given the move towards monetary union in Europe, the relevance of monetary and exchange rate policy design has increased because of the costs and benefits implied by a highly rigid commitment to co-ordination. Therefore, a detailed evaluation of monetary and exchange rate policies becomes an urgent task. The articles in Parts V and VI are chosen with this consideration in mind. The message conveyed in Part V is that the constraint on monetary policy choice has increased as financial integration has deepened and that the need for credible commitment has become more pressing. In other words, the scope for assigning monetary policy to an output or employment target has dimin-ished and the need for central bank independence has increased as a condi-tion for achieving low inflation. The discussion in Part VI, on the other hand, enables us to derive two conclusions. First, the exchange rate tends to be highly volatile in the short run and a flexible exchange rate regime is more attractive for countries that find it difficult to undertake credible anti-inflationary commitments. Second, a fixed exchange rate is prone to recur-rent crises that may be due to inefficiency in the foreign exchange market or inconsistent macroeconomic policies.

As can be seen from the summary above, the design of macroeconomic policy becomes more complicated as the degree of openness increases. There-fore, it is not surprising to observe that small open countries have become increasingly interested in rules rather than discretion in monetary and exchange rate policies. The most obvious indication of this tendency is the establishment of the EMU. The articles in Part VII are selected with a view to combining the early seminal and the recent contributions to the debate on monetary integration. While the first two articles by Mundell and McKinnon present the optimum currency area (OCA) theory in its original form, the next two articles by de Grauwe and Eichengreen discuss the relevance of the OCA theory and the unresolved issues faced by members of the EMU. What emerges from Mundell's and McKinnon's contributions is that the costs (benefits) of monetary unions are a decreasing (increasing) function of economic convergence and openness to trade. De Grauwe probes the relevance of this conclusion for Europe and points out the need to go beyond the original OCA theory in assessing the costs and benefits of monetary unions. Eichengreen, on the other hand, looks beyond the costs and benefits and highlights the need for further research on unresolved issues such as fiscal policy co-ordination within the EMU, credibility of the European Central Bank, and the implications of the EMU for the rest of the world.

Parts VIII and IX focus on the implications of interdependence for macroeconomic policy in two areas: capital income taxation and the labour market. As is well known, these policy areas stand in contrast to each other in terms of interdependence caused by cross-border mobility. Capital is highly mobile and its mobility has increased as a result of financial liberalisation, whereas labour tends to be immobile. Therefore, it is not surprising to observe a tendency to treat labour market policy as an essentially closed-economy issue. This tendency, however, is becoming increasingly anachronistic for two reasons. First, the convergence towards lower statutory tax rates on capital income has led to an increase in the statutory tax rates on labour. Second, increased capital mobility (hence increased statutory tax rates on labour) has been accompanied by increased labour market de-regulation in all developed countries.

Part VIII presents extracts from a report prepared by the OECD's Committee on Financial Affairs. The Committee identifies the practices that constitute harmful tax competition in capital income taxation and makes recommendations for policy co-ordination. The article by Sørensen is an attempt to quantify the consequences of the tax competition referred to in the OECD report. Sørensen's findings confirm the tendency towards low capital income taxes in Europe, but they also demonstrate that the gains from policy co-ordination are small – less than 1 per cent of GDP. Although this does not invalidate the case for tax policy co-ordination, it is likely to undermine its political feasibility. Another interesting result that can be derived from Sørensen's article is that tax policy co-ordination is beneficial to low-income groups, but it will not be attractive for countries with high levels of income inequality.

These results are highly relevant to the debate on labour market policy represented in Part IX. The article by Elmeskov *et al.* draws on OECD unemployment data and demonstrates that the success of some countries in

Part I

Stabilisation policy in the Mundell–Fleming model

Introduction

The articles in Part I focus on stabilisation policy in the open economy. As is well known, economic thinking on the relevance and effectiveness of stabilisation policy has gone through a full circle. Until the early twentieth century, the classical approach was dominant. The classicals had argued that stabilisation policy is irrelevant due to instantaneous market clearing. It is not surprising, therefore, to observe that the focus of economics during that period was at the micro level – with little attention paid to macroeconomic adjustment in the face of shocks. Then, the 'Keynesian revolution' tipped the balance to the other side and demonstrated that the economy may remain stuck at a suboptimal level of output and employment for a considerable time unless the policy-maker takes corrective action. The suboptimal state of affairs may be due either to rigidities at the micro level or to unintended macro outcomes of what may seem rational micro behaviour (e.g. the 'paradox of thrift'). This 'stabilisation policy optimism' continued to be the dominant view until the early 1970s, when it was realised that stabilisation policy may be ineffective and/or counter-productive – especially in the face of supply shocks.

At this juncture, the monetarist views expressed during the 1950s and 1960s gained added credibility and, more significantly, inspired the 'policy ineffectiveness' thesis of the 'rational expectations revolution'. The new classical school has shifted the attention to the micro level again, but this was not their main contribution. On the one hand, they made rational expectation formation an explicit component of the macroeconomic models. On the other hand, they challenged the assumption that parameters calculated from past data can be held constant in the face of new policy announcements. With this paradigm shift, 'stabilisation policy optimism' left the stage to 'stabilisation policy pessimism' and we returned to square one.

In the meantime, the contribution of Robert Mundell and Marcus Fleming to international macroeconomics added further nuances to the policy effectiveness debate. What Mundell and Fleming did was to demonstrate that the impact of stabilisation policy (monetary, fiscal or exchange rate policies) on output and employment has to be mediated through the exchange rate regime and the degree of financial integration in the world economy.

Thanks to this insight, statements on policy effectiveness had to be qualified in three ways. First, it was realised that monetary policy is ineffective under a fixed exchange rate regime and it becomes increasingly impotent as the degree of financial integration (i.e. capital mobility) increases. Under a flexible exchange rate regime, however, monetary policy is effective and its effectiveness increases as financial integration increases. Secondly, fiscal policy is effective under a fixed exchange rate regime and its effectiveness increases as financial integration increases. Under a flexible exchange rate regime the result is just the opposite: fiscal policy becomes less effective as financial integration increases. Finally, it became apparent that exchange rate policy is effective when it is not available! In other words, exchange rate policy cannot alter the level of output or employment when the exchange rate regime is flexible, but it can be effective when the exchange rate is fixed.

The articles in this part are selected to reflect this contribution to the debate on stabilisation policy. Written at almost the same time, and independently of each other, the articles by Mundell and Fleming (Chapters 1 and 2), demonstrate the way in which these results are derived from an essentially Keynesian model of the open economy. The common assumptions of the models can be listed as follows: a short-run focus, constant wages and prices, static expectations, and a small country case. Both models also follow a similar analytical approach in the sense that they are based on equilibrium conditions in three sectors of the economy: the money market, the goods market and the balance of payments.

The only difference between the models is that domestic interest rate is determined by world interest rate in Mundell, but it is taken as a function of the income velocity of money in Fleming. Despite this difference, the way in which the interest rate is specified enables both Mundell and Fleming to avoid the expectations formation – an issue implied by the uncovered interest rate parity (i.e. the equality of domestic interest rates to foreign interest rates plus the expected rate of depreciation of the domestic currency). But this is an issue that will be discussed later in Part III, where we consider the implications of expectation formation for macroeconomic policy in general.

The point to make here is the following: fiscal expansion leads to current account deficit in both models, but its effect on the overall balance of payments differs. In Mundell's model, fiscal expansion initially leads to a balance of payments surplus due to the wedge between domestic and foreign interest rates. The rise in domestic interest rates after fiscal expansion leads to massive capital inflow, which more than compensates for the current account deficit. In Fleming, fiscal expansion may lead to a surplus or a deficit in the balance of payments – depending on the rise in interest rates, which, in turn, is determined by the income velocity of money. Although this is not necessarily the best way of capturing the extent of variation in domestic interest rates (and hence the extent of foreign capital inflows), Fleming's comments are more in line with later elaborations on the Mundell–Fleming (MF) model that distinguish between different degrees of capital mobility.

What is fascinating in the MF analysis is the careful attention paid to the mechanism of adjustment. Unlike current modelling trends where mathematical sophistication tends to crowd out the narrative on the economic process itself, the MF account is lucid, makes economic sense and is enticing for the ordinary reader. In other words, the reader is kept in touch with the 'economic reality' that the abstract models are trying to explain. For example, Mundell's article begins with a suggestive framework (Table 1.1) reflecting the sectoral and market equilibria, which helps the reader to keep track of the adjustment process involved. In addition, in both articles the change in a particular sector or market is explained and the interaction with other markets or sectors is clarified. Without sounding nostalgic, we would like to indicate that the current tendencies to 'economise' on such explanations may be disenfranchising a significant section of the potential readership.

Although the contributions by Mundell and Fleming are important, we cannot ignore the fact that they are limited for various reasons. First of all, the assumptions concerning constant prices or wages and static expectations are too restrictive. Secondly, the lack of a theory of stock adjustment for capital movements is problematic. Thirdly, the models are about comparative statics rather than dynamic adjustment. Explanations of the dynamic adjustment are necessarily *ad hoc* in the sense that they are based on specifications external to the models.

In addition, the models tend to overlook certain factors that may render stabilisation policy even less effective than what they predict. One such factor is the composition of the balance of payments. A deficit in the current account is considered to be non-problematic as long as it is covered by a surplus in the capital account. Also, the international implications of the current account disequilibria are overlooked. For example, current account surpluses caused by monetary expansion under flexible exchange rates are not tackled – either endogenously or exogenously. However, it is clear that such surpluses enjoyed by the expanding country may well lead to retaliations by its trading partners and the result may be a prisoner's dilemma outcome for all involved.

Finally, the effectiveness of fiscal policy under fixed exchange rate is also taken at face value. From the models, it is clear that fiscal expansion is associated with current account deficits. In addition, it is also clear that such current account deficits in the expanding country imply current account surpluses in its trading partners and must have expansionary effects on the latter. Given these tendencies, would the expanding country not be induced to wait for its trading partners to take the initial step? In other words, can we not envisage another type of co-ordination failure in the international economy? Could this not be a factor that has contributed to the degradation of fiscal policy as a stabilisation instrument in the 1980s and 1990s?

These issues are examined briefly in Argy's article in Chapter 3. Three points can be made about the relevance of Argy's article. First, it strikes a balance between the strengths and weaknesses of the MF model. Secondly, it demonstrates the way in which the MF model can be used as a starting point in tracing the cumulative nature of the literature on open-economy macroeconomics. Finally, it demonstrates that the insights provided by the MF model are still important even though our knowledge of the economy has progressed significantly since the early 1960s.

The final entry in this part is a reflection on the MF model inspired by classroom experience. It is an attempt to strike a balance between encouraging students to think critically and demonstrating to them that we are making progress as far as our understanding of the economy is concerned. This is not an easy task at the undergraduate level, as students tend to adopt a cynical view and treat the emphasis on being 'critical' as a preoccupation with product differentiation. Chapter 4 seeks to demonstrate that synthesis is possible and what seems to be product differentiation is actually a cumulative process that may seem disjointed at times. We hope that the exercise on the MF model and flexible prices rises to this challenge.

1 Capital mobility and stabilization policy under fixed and flexible exchange rates

*Robert A. Mundell**

The Canadian Journal of Economics and Political Science, vol. 29, no. 4 (1963), pp. 487–99

The world is still a closed economy, but its regions and countries are becoming increasingly open. The trend, which has been manifested in both freer movement of goods and increased mobility of capital, has been stimulated by the dismantling of trade and exchange controls in Europe, the gradual erosion of the real burden of tariff protection, and the stability, unparalleled since 1914, of the exchange rates. The international economic climate has changed in the direction of financial integration[1] and this has important implications for economic policy.

My paper concerns the theoretical and practical implications of the increased mobility of capital. In order to present my conclusions in the simplest possible way, and to bring the implications for policy into sharpest relief, I assume the extreme degree of mobility that prevails when a country cannot maintain an interest rate different from the general level prevailing abroad. This assumption will overstate the case but it has the merit of posing a stereotype towards which international financial relations seem to be heading. At the same time it might be argued that the assumption is not far from the truth in those financial centers, of which Zurich, Amsterdam, and Brussels may be taken as examples, where the authorities already recognize their lessening ability to dominate money market conditions and insulate them from foreign influences. It should also have a high degree of relevance to a country like Canada whose financial markets are dominated to a great degree by the vast New York market.

---

* This paper was presented at the annual meeting of the Canadian Political Science Association in Quebec on June 6, 1963. It was written while the author was a member of the staff of the International Monetary Fund, but it does not, of course, necessarily reflect the Fund's official position. [*Canadian Journal of Economics and Political Science*, Vol. XXIX, No. 4 (November, 1963), pp. 475–85. For a generalization of the results of this paper in the context of a world model see R. A. Mundell, "Capital Mobility and Size: Reply," *Canadian Journal of Economics and Political Science*, Vol. XXX, No. 3 (August, 1964), pp. 421–31, especially 424–31.] The author is with the University of Chicago.

I METHOD OF ANALYSIS

The assumption of perfect capital mobility can be taken to mean that all securities in the system are perfect substitutes. Since different currencies are involved this implies that existing exchange rates are expected to persist indefinitely (even when the exchange rate is not pegged) and that spot and forward exchange rates are identical. All the complications associated with speculation, the forward market, and exchange rate margins are thereby assumed not to exist.

In order to focus attention on policies affecting the level of employment, I assume unemployed resources, constant returns to scale, and fixed money wage rates; this means that the supply of domestic output is elastic and its price level constant. I further assume that saving and taxes rise with income, that the balance of trade depends only on income and the exchange rate, that investment depends on the rate of interest, and that the demand for money depends only on income and the rate of interest. My last assumption is that the country under consideration is too small to influence foreign incomes or the world level of interest rates.

Monetary policy will be assumed to take the form of open market purchases of securities, and *fiscal policy* the form of an increase in government spending (on home goods) financed by an increase in the public debt. Floating exchange rates result when the monetary authorities do not intervene in the exchange market, and fixed exchange rates when they intervene to buy and sell international reserves at a fixed price.

It will be helpful, in the following discussion, to bear in mind the distinction between conditions of *sectoral* and *market* equilibria (illustrated in the table). There is a set of sectoral restraints (described by the rows in the table) which show how expenditure in each sector of the open economy is financed: a budget deficit $(G - T)$ in the *government* sector is financed by an increase in the public debt or a reduction in government cash balances (dishoarding); an excess of investment over saving $(I - S)$ in the *private* sector is financed by net private borrowing or a reduction in privately-held money balances; a trade balance deficit $(M - X)$ in the *foreign* sector[2] is financed by capital imports or a reduction in international reserves; and, finally, an excess of purchases over sales of domestic assets of the banking sector is financed by an increase in the monetary liabilities of the banking system (the money supply) or by a reduction in foreign exchange reserves. For simplicity of exposition, I shall assume that there is, initially, no lending between the sectors.

There is also a set of market restraints (described by columns in the table) which refer to the condition that demand and supply of each object of exchange be equal. The *goods and services* market is in equilibrium when the difference between investment and saving is equal to the sum of the budget surplus and the trade balance deficit. The *capital* market is in equilibrium when foreigners and domestic banks are willing to accumulate the increase in net debt of the government and the public. The *foreign exchange* market is in equilibrium when the actual increase in reserves is equal to the rate (which

Table 1.1

Market / Sector	Goods		Securities		Money		International Reserves	
Government	$T - G$	+	Government borrowing	+	Government dishoarding	+	°1	= 0
	+		+		+		+	+
Private	$S - I$	+	Private borrowing	+	Private dishoarding	+	°2	= 0
	+		+		+		+	+
Foreign	$M - X$	+	Capital outflow	+	°3	+	Increase in reserves	= 0
	+		+		+		+	+
Banking	°4	+	Open market sales	+	Monetary expansion	+	Foreign exchange sales	= 0
	‖	+	‖		‖		‖	‖
	0		0	+	0	+	0	= 0

° Negligible or ignored items: (1) would refer to Treasury holdings of foreign exchange; (2) to the non-bank public's holdings of foreign exchange; (3) to foreigners' holdings of domestic money (domestic currency is not a 'key' currency); and (4) to the net contribution of the banking system to goods account. In the analysis government dishoarding will also be assumed zero.

Note that if the entries are defined as *ex ante* or *planned* magnitudes both the horizontal and vertical sums to zero are *equilibrium conditions*, but if they are defined as *ex post* or *realized* magnitudes the sums to zero are *identities*. Note also that the rows could be disaggregated, making special distinctions between households and firms, commercial and central banks, etc., down to each individual spending unit, just as the columns could be multiplied to distinguish between different classes of goods, money, and securites.

may be positive or negative) at which the central bank wants to buy reserves.[3] And the *money* market is in equilibrium when the community is willing to accumulate the increase in the money supply offered by the banking system. I shall also assume that, initially, each market is in equilibrium.

II POLICIES UNDER FLEXIBLE EXCHANGE RATES

Under flexible exchange rates the central bank does not intervene to fix a given exchange rate, although this need not preclude autonomous purchases and sales of foreign exchange.

Monetary Policy. Consider the effect of an open market purchase of domestic securities in the context of a flexible exchange rate system. This results in an increase in bank reserves, a multiple expansion of money and credit, and downward pressure on the rate of interest. But the interest rate is prevented from falling by an outflow of capital, which causes a deficit in the balance of payments, and a depreciation of the exchange rate. In turn, the exchange rate depreciation (normally) improves the balance of trade and stimulates, by the multiplier process, income and employment. A new equilibrium is established when income has risen sufficiently to induce the domestic community to hold the increased stock of money created by the banking system. Since interest rates are unaltered this means that income must rise in proportion to the increase in the money supply, the factor of proportionality being the given ratio of income and money (income velocity).

In the new equilibrium private saving and taxes will have increased as a consequence of the increase in income, and this implies both net private lending and retirement of government debt. Equilibrium in the capital market then requires equality between the sum of net private lending plus debt retirement, and the rate of capital exports, which in conjunction with the requirement of balance of payments equilibrium, implies a balance of trade surplus. Monetary policy therefore has a strong effect on the level of income and employment, not because it alters the rate of interest, but because it induces a capital outflow, depreciates the exchange rate, and causes an export surplus.[4]

It will now be shown that central bank operations in the foreign exchange market ("open market operations" in foreign exchange) can be considered an alternative form of monetary policy. Suppose the central bank buys foreign reserves (gold or foreign currency) with domestic money. This increases bank reserves, causing a multiple expansion of the money supply. The monetary expansion puts downward pressure on the interest rate and induces a capital outflow, further depreciating the exchange rate and creating an export surplus, which in turn increases, through the multiplier effect, income and employment. Eventually, when income has increased sufficiently to induce the community to hold the increased stock of money, the income-generating process ceases and all sectors are again in equilibrium, with the increased saving and taxes financing the capital outflow. This conclusion is virtually the same as the conclusion earlier reached regarding monetary policy, with the single important difference that *foreign* assets of the banks are increased in the case of foreign exchange policy while *domestic* assets are increased in the case of monetary policy. Foreign exchange policy, like monetary policy, becomes a forceful tool of stabilization policy under flexible exchange rates.

Fiscal Policy. Assume an increase in government spending financed by government borrowing. The increased spending creates an excess demand for goods and tends to raise income. But this would increase the demand for money, raise interest rates, attract a capital inflow, and appreciate the exchange rate, which in turn would have a depressing effect on income. In fact, therefore, the negative effect on income of exchange rate appreciation has to offset exactly the positive multiplier effect on income of the original increase in government spending. Income cannot change unless the money supply or interest rates change, and since the former is constant in the absence of central bank action and the latter is fixed by the world level of interest rates, income remains fixed. Since income is constant, saving and taxes are unchanged, which means, because of the condition that the goods market be in equilibrium, that the change in government spending is equal to the import surplus. In turn, the flexible exchange rate implies balance of payments equilibrium and therefore a capital inflow equal to the import surplus. Thus, both capital and goods market equilibria are assured by equality between the rate of increase in the public debt and the rate of capital imports, and between the budget deficit and the import surplus. Fiscal policy thus completely loses its force as a domestic stabilizer when the exchange rate is allowed to fluctuate and the money supply is held constant. Just as monetary policy derives its importance as a domestic stabilizer from its influence on capital flows and the exchange rate, so fiscal policy is frustrated in its effects by these same considerations.

III POLICIES UNDER FIXED EXCHANGE RATES

Under fixed exchange rates the central bank intervenes in the exchange market by buying and selling reserves at the exchange parity; as already noted the exchange margins are assumed to be zero.

Monetary Policy. A central bank purchase of securities creates excess reserves and puts downward pressure on the interest rate. But a fall in the interest rate is prevented by a capital outflow, and this worsens the balance of payments. To prevent the exchange rate from falling the central bank intervenes in the market, selling foreign exchange and buying domestic money. The process continues until the accumulated foreign exchange deficit is equal to the open market purchase and the money supply is restored to its original level.

This shows that monetary policy under fixed exchange rates has no sustainable effect on the level of income. The increase in the money supply arising from open market purchases is returned to the central bank through its exchange stabilization operations. What the central bank has in fact done is to purchase securities initially for money, and then buy money with foreign exchange, the monetary effects of the combined operations cancelling. The only final effect of the open market purchase is an equivalent fall in foreign exchange reserves: the central bank has simply traded domestic assets for foreign assets.

Fiscal Policy. Assume an increase in government spending superimposed on the foreign exchange policy of pegging the exchange rate. The increased spending has a multiplier effect upon income, increasing saving, taxes, and imports. Taxes increase by less than the increase in government spending so the government supplies securities at a rate equal to the budget deficit, whereas the private sector absorbs securities at a rate equal to the increase in saving.

After the new equilibrium is established both the goods and capital markets must be in balance. In the goods market the budget deficit has as its counterpart the sum of the excess of private saving over investment and the balance of trade deficit, which implies that the induced balance of trade deficit is less than the budget deficit. In the capital market the private and foreign sectors must be willing to accumulate the new flow of government issues. But since the excess private saving is equal to the flow of private lending, and since the budget deficit equals the flow of new government issues, capital market equilibrium requires that the import deficit be exactly balanced by a capital inflow, so that there is balance of payments equilibrium after all adjustments have taken place.

There will nevertheless be a change in foreign exchange reserves. Before the flow equilibrium is established the demand for money will increase, at a constant interest rate, in proportion to the increase in income. To acquire the needed liquidity the private sector sells securities and this puts upward pressure on the interest rate, and attracts foreign capital. This improves the balance of payments temporarily, forcing the central bank to intervene by buying foreign reserves and increasing the money supply. The money supply is therefore increased directly through the back door of exchange rate policy. Foreign exchange reserves accumulate by the full amount of the increased cash reserves needed by the banking system to supply the increased money demanded by the public as a consequence of the increase in income.

IV OTHER POLICY COMBINATIONS

Other cases deserve attention in view of their prominence in policy discussions. In the following cases it is assumed that exchange rates are fixed.

Central Bank Financing of Fiscal Deficits. An important special case of combined operations of monetary, fiscal, and exchange policies is central bank financing of budget deficits under fixed exchange rates. As before, the increase in government spending yields a multiplier effect on income. In the new equilibrium there is a budget deficit, an excess of saving over investment, and a balance of trade deficit. The government issues securities at a rate equal to the budget deficit and these are (by assumption) taken up by the central bank. Capital market equilibrium therefore requires that the net flow demand for securities on the part of the private sector be equal to the net capital outflow.

It is easy to see that in the new equilibrium the balance of payments deficit and the consequent rate at which reserves are falling is exactly equal to the budget deficit and to the rate at which the central bank is buying government securities. Since the capital outflow is equal to the excess of saving over investment, and the loss of reserves is equal to the balance of payments deficit, which is the sum of the trade deficit and the capital outflow, reserves fall at a rate equal to the sum of the import deficit and the excess of saving over investment. Then since this sum equals the budget deficit, by the condition of equilibrium in the goods market, it follows that reserves fall at a rate equal to the budget deficit. The budget deficit is entirely at the expense of reserves.

There is, however, in this instance too an initial stock adjustment process. As income increases the demand for money grows, the private sector dispenses with stocks of securities, causing a capital inflow and an increase in reserves. This increase in reserves is a once-for-all inflow equal to the increase in cash reserves necessary for the banks to satisfy the increased demand for money. The rate of fall in reserves takes place, therefore, from a higher initial level.

The Special Case of Sterilization Operations. Sterilization (or neutralization) policy is a specific combination of monetary and exchange policy. When the central bank buys or sells foreign exchange the money supply increases or decreases, and the purpose of sterilization policy is to offset this effect. The mechanism is for the central bank to sell securities at the same rate that it is buying foreign exchange, and to buy securities at the same rate that it is selling foreign exchange. In reality, therefore, neutralization policy involves an exchange of foreign reserves and bonds. The exchange rate is stabilized by buying and selling reserves in exchange for securities.

Suppose the government increases spending during a time when neutralization policy is being followed. The increase in spending would normally have a multiplier effect on income. But this would increase the demand for money and put upward pressure on interest rates as the private sector dispenses with holdings of securities; this would cause a capital inflow and induce a balance of payments surplus. But now the authorities, in their rate-pegging operation, buy foreign exchange and simultaneously sell securities, thus putting added pressure on interest rates and accelerating the inflow of capital without satisfying the increased demand for money. The system has now become inconsistent, for goods market equilibrium requires an increase in income, but an increase in income can only take place if either the money supply expands or interest rates rise. The capital inflow prevents interest rates from rising and the neutralization policy inhibits the money supply from expanding. Something has to give, and it must either be the money supply or the exchange rate. If the central bank sells securities at the same rate as it is buying reserves, it cannot buy reserves at a rate fast enough to keep the exchange rate from appreciating. And if the central bank buys reserves at a rate fast enough to stabilize the exchange rate, it cannot sell securities fast enough to keep the money supply constant. Either the exchange rate appreciates or money income rises.

In a similar way it can be shown that, from an initial position of equilibrium, open market operations (monetary policy) lead to an inconsistent and overdetermined result. A purchase of securities by the central bank would cause a capital outflow, balance of payments deficit, and sales of foreign exchange by the central bank. The restrictive monetary impact of the foreign exchange sales are then offset by further open market purchases which induce further sales of foreign exchange. The process repeats itself at an accelerating speed. There is no new equilibrium because the public wants to hold just so much money, and the central bank's attempt to alter this equilibrium simply results in a fall in reserves. The sterilization procedures merely perpetuate the self-generating process until exchange reserves are exhausted, or until the world level of interest rates falls.

V DIAGRAMMATIC ILLUSTRATION

These results can be illustrated by diagrams similar to those I have used for analysis of related problems.[5] In the top quadrant of both Figures 1.1 and 1.2, *XX* plots the relation between the interest rate and income (given the exchange rate) along which there is no excess demand in the goods and services market (internal balance); *LL* describes a similar relation for the money market; and *FF* gives the external balance condition which is dominated by the world level of interest rates. Analogously in the bottom quadrants, *XX* plots internal balance, and *FF* external balance as a function of income and the exchange rate. The internal balance line in the top quadrant applies only for the given exchange rate represented by π_0 in the bottom quadrant, and the external balance schedule in the bottom quadrant applies only for the initial rate of capital imports (assumed to be zero).

Consider the effects of monetary policy (Figure 1.1). From Q an increase in the money supply shifts LL in the upper quadrant to $L'L'$, implying at the original interest rate and income level (at Q) excess liquidity; this causes a capital outflow. Under flexible exchange rates FF in the lower quadrant shifts downward to $F'F'$, and the improvement in the trade balance increases income and employment as XX in the top quadrant is pushed by the devaluation towards $X'X'$. The new equilibrium is at P, with an improved trade balance and greater capital outflow (or lessened inflow).

With the exchange rate fixed at π_0, however, the increase in the money supply merely creates excess liquidity, an export of capital, a balance of payments deficit, and a reduction in the money supply with no shift in XX in the top quadrant. The line $L'L'$ returns to its original position and Q is restored as equilibrium at a lower level of reserves; Q is the only possible equilibrium consistent with both FF and XX so the money supply will adapt to it if it is allowed to. But if the increase in the money supply is accompanied by *sterilization* operations, that is, if $L'L'$ is maintained, there can be no equilibrium. The central bank buys securities, gold flows out, and the central bank buys more securities. Since the exchange rate is maintained at π_0, XX in the top quadrant is unaffected, as is FF. The attempt of the central bank to maintain $L'L'$ cannot satisfy both the conditions that the interest rate remains at the world level and that the new equilibrium be on XX. Either the exchange

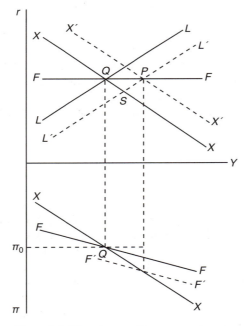

Figure 1.1 Monetary policy

rate must change (shifting XX to $X'X'$) or the attempt to maintain $L'L'$ by sterilization operations must be abandoned.

Consider next the case of fiscal policy (Figure 1.2). An increase in government spending shifts XX to $X'X'$ in both quadrants. At the fixed exchange rate π_0 this increases income and increases the demand for money. Interest rates tend to rise, capital is attracted from abroad, the balance of payments improves and the money supply increases, eventually establishing $L'L'$ as the new money curve. After this instantaneous "stock adjustment," process capital is attracted from abroad sufficiently to establish $F'F'$ as the new foreign balance line, with the equilibrium P in both quadrants.

Under flexible rates, however, the money supply remains constant. The increased spending puts upward pressure on interest rates and appreciates the exchange rate. *FF* therefore shifts downward to $F''F''$ establishing R as the new equilibrium. At R the price of foreign exchange is lower but output and employment are unchanged.

Again, if the exchange rate is fixed *and* the authorities attempt to sterilize the initial gold inflow one of the policies must fail. This is because the new equilibrium (P) on *FF* and $X'X'$ in the upper quadrant is only consistent if the money supply is allowed to expand. Obviously the points J and P cannot be maintained simultaneously.

Certain qualifications or extensions to the analysis should be mentioned. The demand for money is likely to depend upon the exchange rate in addition to the interest rate and the level of income; this would slightly reduce the effectiveness of a given change in the quantity of money, and slightly increase

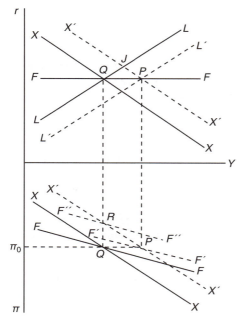

Figure 1.2 Fiscal policy

the effectiveness of fiscal policy on income and employment under flexible exchange rates, while, of course, it has no significance in the case of fixed exchange rates.

Another possible influence is the real balance effect, but this cannot alter in any essential way the final result: income rises, under flexible exchange rates, in proportion to the increase in the money supply, whereas income remains unchanged, in the case of fixed exchange rates, because the quantity of money does not increase.

A further factor that might be considered is the negative effect of changes in the exchange rate upon the level of saving, but again there is no important alteration in the results: although the budget deficit arising from increased government spending under flexible exchange rates is then partly financed by an increase in saving of the private sector the conclusions regarding changes in the level of output and employment are unaltered.

The conclusions of course have not made any allowance for growth. Because of growth the money supply would normally be increased at a rate more or less commensurate with the actual or desired growth of the economy; my conclusions are, so to speak, superimposed on the growth situation. Moreover, many of our actual observations about the economic world are observations of disequilibrium positions; it is clearly possible to alter the money supply (under fixed exchange rates) if there is excess or deficient liquidity, although even this is in practice unnecessary since we can be assured, as we were as long ago as the days of Ricardo, that the money supply would automatically settle down to its equilibrium level. In any case these observations do not vitiate the principles I have been trying to elucidate.

VI CONCLUSIONS

I have demonstrated that perfect capital mobility implies different concepts of stabilization policy from those to which we have become accustomed in the post-war period. Monetary policy has no impact on employment under fixed exchange rates while fiscal policy has no effect on employment under flexible exchange rates. On the other hand, fiscal policy has a strong effect on employment under fixed exchange rates (simple Keynesian conclusions hold) while monetary policy has a strong effect on employment under flexible exchange rates (classical quantity theory conclusions hold).

A further implication of the analysis is that monetary policy under fixed exchange rates becomes a device for altering the levels of reserves, while fiscal policy under flexible exchange rates becomes a device for altering the balance of trade, both policies leaving unaffected the level of output and employment. Under fixed exchange rates, open market operations by the central bank result in equal changes in the gold stock, open market purchases causing it to decline and open market sales causing it to increase. And under flexible exchange rates, budget deficits or surpluses induced by changes in taxes or government spending cause corresponding changes in the trade balance.

Gold sterilization policies make no sense in a world of fixed exchange rates and perfect capital mobility and will ultimately lead to the breakdown of the fixed exchange system. In the absence of gold sterilization, as we have seen, an attempt of the central bank to alter the money supply is frustrated by capital outflows and automatically offsetting monetary changes through the exchange equalization operations; this is running water into a sink that is filled to the brim, causing the water to spill over the edges at the same rate that it is coming out of the tap.[6] But sterilization operations are analogous to trying to prevent the water from spilling out, even though the sink is full and water is still pouring out of the tap.

If my assumptions about capital mobility were valid in Canada,[7] it would mean that expansive fiscal policy under flexible exchange rates was of little help in increasing employment because of the ensuring inflow of capital which kept the exchange rate high and induced a balance of trade deficit: we should have observed a zero or very small multiplier. By the same token, now that Canada has adopted a fixed exchange system, we should not reason from earlier negative experience about the size of the multiplier and conclude that the multiplier is *now* low: while a reduction in the budget deficit under flexible rates would have helped the trade balance without too much damage to employment, a reduction in the budget deficit today could be expected to have a sizable impact on excess demand and unemployment.

Of course the assumption of perfect capital mobility is not literally valid; my conclusions are black and white rather than dark and light grey. To the extent that Canada can maintain an interest rate equilibrium different from that of the United States, without strong capital inflows, fiscal expansion can be expected to play *some* role in employment policy under flexible exchange rates, and monetary policy can have *some* influence on employment and output under fixed exchange rates. But if this possibility exists for us today, we can conjecture that it will exist to a lesser extent in the future.

NOTES

1 See James C. Ingram, "A Proposal for Financial Integration in the Atlantic Community," Joint Economic Committee print, Nov., 1962, for a valuable analysis of financial integration under fixed exchange rates; Harry G. Johnson, "Equilibrium under Fixed Exchange Rates," *American Economic Review*, Vol. LIII (May, 1963), pp. 112–19, for a discussion of some of the advantages of closing the exchange rate margins; C. P. Kindleberger, "European Economic Integration and the Development of a Single Financial Center for Long-Term Capital," *Weltwirtschaftliches Archiv*, Band 90, 1963, Heft 2, pp. 189–210, for a discussion of competition among financial centres as integration proceeds; and A. N. McLeod, "Credit Expansion in an Open Economy," *Economic Journal*, Vol. LXII (Sept., 1962), pp. 611–40, for a theoretical discussion of related topics.
2 The foreign sector refers to all the transactions of the country as a whole with respect to the outside world.
3 For certain purposes it would be more elegant to define a separate market for foreign goods as distinct from domestic goods, but the present approach is satisfactory for the purpose on hand.
4 Richard E. Caves arrives at essentially the same result in his paper, "Flexible Exchange Rates," *American Economic Review*, Vol. LIII (May, 1963), pp. 120–29.

5 "The Appropriate Use of Monetary and Fiscal Policy for Internal and External Stability," *IMF Staff Papers*, Vol. IX, No. 1 (March, 1962); "The International Disequilibrium System," *Kyklos*, Vol. XIV, No. 2 (1961), pp. 153–72; and "Employment Policy under Flexible Exchange Rates," *Canadian Journal of Economics and Political Science*, Vol. XXVII, No. 4 (Nov., 1961), pp. 509–17. In the latter paper (the main purpose of which was to show that commercial policy – import restriction or export promotion – was ineffective under flexible exchange rates) it was argued that *both* monetary and fiscal policies are more effective under flexible exchange rates than under fixed exchange rates. The apparent conflict with the present analysis lies in the different definition of monetary and fiscal policy and in the extreme assumption in the present paper of perfect capital mobility. In the earlier paper fiscal policy was taken to be an increase in government spending with interest rates maintained constant by the central bank, while capital inflows were assumed to be a function of the rate of interest alone; in other words no capital inflow takes place (because the domestic interest rate is constant) while the money supply is allowed to expand in proportion to the increase in income induced by the more expansive fiscal policy. In the present paper, I have defined fiscal policy as an increase in government spending financed by government bond issues with *no* change in the money supply. In both cases the underlying model is (in essence) the same and would yield the same results if the same assumptions were made about capital mobility and the same definitions were used.

It may puzzle the reader why I went to some length to alter the definitions of monetary and fiscal policy and thus to bring about a seemingly artificial difference between the conclusions based purely upon different definitions. The reason is that monetary policy cannot in any meaningful sense be defined as an alteration in the interest rate when capital is perfectly mobile, since the authorities cannot change the market rate of interest. Nor can monetary policy be defined, under conditions of perfect capital mobility, as an increase in the money supply, since the central bank has no power over the money supply either (except in transitory positions of disequilibrium) when the exchange rate is fixed. The central bank has, on the other hand, the ability to conduct an open market operation (which only temporarily changes the money supply) and that is the basis of my choice of this definition of monetary policy for the present analysis.

In an earlier paper I analysed some of the purely dynamic aspects of the adjustment process ("The Monetary Dynamics of International Adjustment under Fixed and Flexible Exchange Rates," *Quarterly Journal of Economics*, May, 1960, pp. 227–57) on varying assumptions regarding capital mobility, but the treatment of the perfect capital mobility case in that paper suffers from the defects I have tried to avoid in this paper by my different definition of "monetary policy." However, the basic conclusions of that paper are not vitiated by the present analysis since the basic problem posed, in the flexible exchange rate case, that "monetary policy" exerts its influence on domestic incomes only indirectly through the exchange rate, still remains, with possibilities of cyclicity and even instability depending on the adjustment speeds; in the present case it can be shown that instability at least would be ruled out if the exchange rate adapted virtually instantaneously.

6 John Exter used a reservoir simile in "The Gold Losses," a speech delivered before the Economic Club of Detroit, May 7, 1962.

7 See the accounts of the Canadian experience by Clarence Barber in his submission to the Royal Commission on Banking and Finance, April, 1962, "The Canadian Economy in Trouble," and by Harry Johnson from his speech to the Canadian Club of Toronto, November, 1962, "Canada in a Changing World." Perhaps the most complete verification of the applicability of the conclusions to the Canadian case is provided in an econometric paper by R. Rhomberg published in the *Journal of Political Economy*.

2 Domestic financial policies under fixed and under floating exchange rates

*J. Marcus Fleming**

IMF Staff Papers, vol. 9, no. 3 (1962), pp. 369–79

The bearing of exchange rate systems on the relative effectiveness of monetary policy on the one hand, and of budgetary policy on the other, as techniques for influencing the level of monetary demand for domestic output, is not always kept in mind when such systems are compared. In this paper it is shown that the expansionary effect of a given increase in money supply will always be greater if the country has a floating exchange rate than if it has a fixed rate. By contrast, it is uncertain whether the expansionary effect on the demand for domestic output of a given increase in budgetary expenditure or a given reduction in tax rates will be larger or smaller with a floating than with a fixed rate. In all but extreme cases, the stimulus to monetary demand arising from an increase in money supply will be greater, relative to that arising from an expansionary change in budgetary policy, with a floating than with a fixed rate of exchange.

THE MODEL

Let us assume a simple Keynesian model[1] in which (a) taxation and private income after tax both vary directly with national income, (b) private expenditure (on consumption and investment) varies directly with income after taxation,[2] and inversely with the interest rate, (c) the interest rate varies directly with the income-velocity of circulation of money (the ratio of national income to the stock of money), (d) the balance of trade (exports *less* imports of goods and services) varies inversely with domestic expenditure[3] and directly with the domestic currency value of foreign exchange, and (e) the balance of payments on capital account varies directly with the rate of interest. All magnitudes are expressed in domestic wage units, and wages are assumed to remain constant in domestic currency. No account is taken of any changes in the propensity to spend from real income changes that result from

* Mr. Fleming, Advisor in the Department of Research and Statistics, is a graduate of Edinburgh University. He was formerly a member of the League of Nations Secretariat, Deputy-Director of the Economic Section of the U.K. Cabinet Offices, U.K. representative on the Economic and Employment Commission of the United Nations, and Visiting Professor of Economics at Columbia University. He is the author of numerous articles in economic journals.

changes in the terms of trade. No account is taken, initially, of the effect of exchange speculation on capital movements.

EFFECTS OF AN EXPANSIONARY SHIFT IN BUDGETARY POLICY

Let us first compare the effects of an expansionary shift in budgetary policy brought about by an increase in public expenditure, without any change in tax rates, under (a) a fixed exchange rate system and (b) a floating exchange rate system, respectively. (A decline in taxation, resulting from a reduction in tax rates, would have effects on expenditure, income, and the balance of payments similar to, though less powerful than, those resulting from an equal increase in public expenditure. No essential feature of the ensuing analysis would be altered if it had been concerned with the former rather than the latter type of budgetary expansion.)

Under fixed exchange rates, an increase in public expenditure will give rise to an increase in income which will be associated—if the economy was previously underemployed—with increases in employment and output.[4] The increase in expenditure will lead to a deterioration in the balance of payments on current account, owing, notably, to a rise in imports. The increase in expenditure and income will also enhance tax revenues, though not to such an extent as to equal the initial increase in public expenditure.[5]

In order to isolate the effect of a change in budgetary policy, it is necessary to assume that monetary policy remains, in some sense, unchanged. In this paper, that is taken to mean that the stock of money is held constant.[6] To keep the money stock constant while the increase in government expenditure is pushing up incomes will necessitate economy in the use of money which is possible only if the interest rate is raised or allowed to rise. The rise in interest in turn will result in (a) a check to the increase in expenditure and income, though some increase will remain,[7] and (b) a favorable shift in the balance of payments on capital account, i.e., a decline in capital exports and/or an increase in capital imports.

Since the increase in public expenditure provokes an unfavorable shift in the current balance and a favorable shift in the capital balance, it is uncertain whether the balance of payments as a whole will deteriorate or improve. It is the more likely to deteriorate, and the less likely to improve, the higher is the marginal propensity to import and the greater the adverse effect on the value of exports as domestic expenditure increases, the less sensitive is the rate of interest to changes in money income and hence in the velocity of circulation, and the less sensitive are capital movements to changes in the rate of interest.[8]

To the extent that the increase in public expenditure gives rise to an improvement or a deterioration, respectively, in the balance of payments, the maintenance of a constant stock of money will call for a decline or an increase, respectively, in the rate of expansion of bank credit. More important is the fact that, if the policy of budgetary expansion results in a deterioration of the balance of payments, shortage of reserves may ultimately compel the authorities to abandon the policy and to renounce the associated expansion in income and employment.[9]

Suppose, now, that the increase in public expenditure takes place in a country where the balance of payments is kept in equilibrium through exchange rate adjustments. Then, if the parameters of our model—notably the sensitivity of capital movements to changes in the rate of interest—are such that a rise in public expenditure would have resulted, with a fixed exchange rate system, in a deterioration in the balance of payments, it will result, with a floating rate system, in a depreciation of the exchange rate, which will bring about a partial restoration of the trade balance. (This restoration will, in general, be only partial since some net deterioration of the trade balance, compared with the situation before the rise in public expenditure, must remain to offset the improvement in the capital balance.) To the extent that the current balance is restored, there will be an increase—over and above that discussed above—in expenditure, income, and output. In other words, the stimulus to income, output, and employment resulting from a given increase in public expenditure will be greater with a floating exchange rate than with a fixed exchange rate.[10] If capital movements were entirely insensitive to the rise in the rate of interest, the exchange rate would depreciate to whatever extent was necessary completely to restore the trade balance, and the stimulus to income and output would be of the same order as would have occurred in a closed economy.

On the other hand, if a rise in public expenditure would, with a fixed exchange rate, have effected an improvement in the balance of payments, it will, with a floating rate, lead to an exchange appreciation; and, to the extent that appreciation intensifies the deterioration in the trade balance, the net stimulus to income, output, and employment will be less than in an open economy with a fixed rate.[11] At first sight, the case in which a rise in government expenditure produces an exchange appreciation would appear to be an academic *curiosum* without practical significance. However, as is shown in a paper prepared by Mr. R.R. Rhomberg, expounding an econometric model of the Canadian economy, the responsiveness of international capital movements to changes in interest rates, and the responsiveness of interest rates to changes in money national income, have probably been sufficiently great in that country over a large part of the postwar period, relative to the marginal propensity to import, for a rise in government expenditure at a constant money stock to have tended to produce just such a result.

It is of interest to note that, if the flow of capital between the country and the outside world were infinitely elastic with respect to the interest rate, the appreciation of the exchange rate resulting from the inflow of capital would bring about a net deterioration in the current balance of payments large enough to offset completely the stimulating effect of the budget deterioration on national income. National income would not increase at all, and the interest rate would remain at the original level.[12]

EFFECTS OF AN INCREASE IN THE STOCK OF MONEY

Now, let us compare the effects on income, output, and employment of increasing the stock of money (a) with fixed exchange rates and (b) with floating exchange rates, respectively.

An increase in the stock of money will entail a decline in the velocity of circulation and lead to a reduction in the rate of interest which will stimulate an increase in private expenditure on investment and consumption, both directly and via the Keynesian multiplier. The rise in expenditure will be associated, as before, with a (smaller) increase in income and output[13] and a deterioration in the balance of payments on current account.[14] The rise in income will moderate the decline in the rate of interest but not to the point of eliminating it; otherwise, neither investment nor income could increase.[15] Since the monetary expansion, even after the rise in expenditure and income, lowers the interest rate, some deterioration will tend to occur in the balance of payments on capital account. In the case of a monetary expansion, therefore, by contrast with that of an increase in public expenditure, a deterioration in the balance of payments as a whole is bound to occur in all circumstances. It follows that the monetary expansion, and the associated expansion of income and output, could only be sustained indefinitely to the extent that in their absence the balance of payments would have been favorable.

It is easy to see that a monetary expansion must always exercise a more powerful effect on income and output when there is a freely floating rate of exchange than when the exchange rate is fixed. The initial tendency toward an adverse shift in the balance of payments will cause a depreciation of the exchange rate to whatever extent may be necessary to keep external transactions as a whole in balance. The favorable influence of the exchange depreciation on the trade balance must come to outweigh the adverse influence of the increase in income to whatever extent may be necessary to produce a net improvement in that balance equal to the deterioration in the capital balance. The stimulus afforded by the depreciation to the trade balance will also act, both directly and via the multiplier, as a stimulus to income, raising it above the level which would have prevailed with a fixed exchange rate.[16]

The expansive effect of a given increase in the stock of money under the floating exchange rate system will be the greater, the greater the responsiveness of the international capital flow to movements in the rate of interest. If there were no responsiveness whatever, the exchange rate would depreciate to the point at which, despite the monetary expansion, no change occurred in the current balance of payments. Income would expand to the same extent as in a closed economy. On the other hand, if the capital flow were infinitely elastic with respect to the interest rate, the exchange rate would depreciate to the point at which the balance of trade became so favorable, and income increased so much, that the rate of interest remained at its original level. This implies that money income would increase by the same percentage as the stock of money.[17]

RELATIVE EFFECTS OF THE TWO KINDS OF FINANCIAL POLICY

It remains to show that the effect on income and output of a given monetary expansion relative to that of a given budgetary expansion will never be less, and will generally be greater, under a floating exchange rate than under a fixed rate, even where budgetary expansion has a tendency to cause a depreciation of the exchange value of the currency.[18] The simplest way to demonstrate this is to compare an increase in the monetary stock (Policy A) and an increase in public expenditure (Policy B) such that, under a fixed exchange rate, the two policies have equal effects in the aggregate on income, output, and employment, and to show that, under a floating rate, the effect of Policy A will never be less, and will in general be greater, than that of Policy B.

Since we have supposed that under a fixed exchange rate the two policies have the same aggregate effect on income and output, they will bring about approximately the same adverse shift in the balance of trade.[19] Since, with incomes the same under the two policies, the money stock will be greater and the velocity of circulation less under Policy A than under Policy B, the rate of interest will be less under the former than under the latter policy. If capital movements were totally insensitive to changes in the interest rate, the two policies would, under a fixed exchange rate, have the same effects on the balance of payments as a whole; and under a floating rate, they would require an equal exchange depreciation to restore external equilibrium. The consequent restoration of the trade balance and the associated further stimulus to income would be the same for the two policies. However, if capital movements respond in any degree to interest changes, the two policies will have different effects. Since Policy A reduces, and Policy B raises, the rate of interest, Policy A under a fixed exchange rate will occasion a more unfavorable capital balance than Policy B. It follows that under a floating rate, Policy A will require, to restore payments equilibrium, a deeper exchange depreciation, and will consequently bring about a greater improvement in the trade balance, and a greater stimulus to income and output, than Policy B.[20] The superiority of Policy A over Policy B as a means of increasing income and output depends notably, as we have seen, on the sensitivity of international capital movements to changes in the rate of interest. At zero sensitivity, there is nothing to choose between the two policies. If the sensitivity is infinite, the level of income resulting from Policy A will exceed that resulting from Policy B in much the same proportion as the money stock under A exceeds that under B.

The nature of the exchange regime has an important bearing not only on the relative effectiveness in influencing income and output of the two types of financial policy—monetary policy and budgetary policy—but also on their relative practicability or sustainability. Thus, under a fixed exchange rate— except to the extent that the external accounts were originally in surplus— monetary expansion can be sustained only as long as reserves hold out, while budgetary expansion, if capital movements are sufficiently sensitive to interest rates, may be sustained indefinitely.[21] Under a floating exchange rate, on the other hand, not only is monetary expansion, while it lasts, likely to generate more additional income than budgetary expansion, relative to what would happen under a fixed exchange rate, but both types of policies can be sustained indefinitely, so far as the balance of payments situation is concerned.

THE EXCHANGE SPECULATIVE ELEMENT IN CAPITAL MOVEMENTS

The foregoing argument has generally assumed the absence of exchange speculation. Under a floating exchange rate, the influence on exchange speculation varies according to whether it is equilibrating or disequilibrating. If it is equilibrating—as was generally the case, for example, in Canada in the 1950's—it will tend to mitigate the exchange rate variations resulting from variations in internal financial policy, whether that policy is budgetary or monetary in character. However, since the greater relative effectiveness which a floating rate gives to monetary policy, compared with budgetary policy, is attributable to the stronger influence that the former exercises on exchange rates, it is to be expected that equilibrating speculation, by damping down exchange rate effects, will tend to reduce the difference in effectiveness between the two kinds of policy. Disequilibrating speculation on the other hand, by exaggerating exchange rate variations, tends to accentuate this difference in effectiveness.[22]

APPENDIX

1. Let Y stand for national income,
    T for taxation,
    N for private income,
    X for private expenditure,
    S for public expenditure,
    Z for total expenditure,
    B for exports *less* imports,
    M for stock of money,
    V for income velocity,
    R for rate of interest,
    C for net capital import, and
    F for domestic currency value of foreign currency.

2. Then

$$Y \equiv X + S + B.$$
$$Z \equiv X + S.$$

$$V \equiv \frac{Y}{M}.$$

$$N \equiv Y - T.$$

$$T = T(Y). \qquad 1 > T_y > 0.$$

$$X = X(N,R). \qquad X_r < 0, \qquad 1 > X_n(1 - T_y) > 0.$$

$$R = R(V). \qquad R_v > 0.$$

$$B = B(Z,F). \qquad 1 > - B_z > 0. \qquad B_f > 0.$$

$$C = C(R).$$

3. Let $\left(\dfrac{dY}{dS}\right)_{00}$ signify $\dfrac{dY}{dS}$ under fixed exchange rates when $dF = 0$, and $dM = 0$.

Let $\left(\dfrac{dR}{dS}\right)_{00}, \left(\dfrac{dT}{dS}\right)_{00}, \left(\dfrac{dC}{dS}\right)_{00}, \left(\dfrac{dB}{dS}\right)_{00}, \left(\dfrac{dC}{dR}\right)_{00}, \left(\dfrac{dB}{dR}\right)_{00}$ be analogously defined.

Then $\left(\dfrac{dY}{dS}\right)_{00} = \dfrac{1 + B_z}{1 - (1 + B_z)\left\{X_n \left(1 - T_y\right) + \dfrac{X_r R_v}{M}\right\}}.$

4. Since $1 > - B_z > 0$,

$$1 > X_n (1 - T_y) > 0,$$

and $X_r < 0$,

$$\therefore \left(\frac{dY}{dS}\right)_{00} > 0.$$

5. For the same reasons,

$$\left(\frac{dT}{dS}\right)_{00} = \frac{T_y(1 + B_z)}{1 - (1 + B_z)\left\{X_n (1 - T_y) + \dfrac{X_r R_v}{M}\right\}} < 1.$$

6. $\left(\dfrac{dX}{dS}\right)_{00} = \dfrac{1}{\dfrac{1}{(1 + B_z)\left\{X_n (1 - T_y) + \dfrac{X_r R_v}{M}\right\}} - 1} \gtreqless 0,$

as $X_n(1 - T_y) + \dfrac{X_r R_v}{M} \gtreqless 0.$

7. $\left(\dfrac{dZ}{dS}\right)_{00} = \dfrac{1}{1 - (1 + B_z) X_n(1 - T_y) + \dfrac{X_r R_v}{M}} > 0.$

8. $\left(\dfrac{dR}{dS}\right)_{00} = \dfrac{R_v}{M}\left(\dfrac{dY}{dS}\right)_{00} > 0.$

$\left(\dfrac{dC}{dS}\right)_{00} + \left(\dfrac{dB}{dS}\right)_{00} = \left(\dfrac{dR}{dS}\right)_{00}\left\{\left(\dfrac{dC}{dR}\right)_{00} + \left(\dfrac{dB}{dR}\right)_{00}\right\}$

$= C_r + \dfrac{MB_z}{R_v(1+B_z)} \gtrless 0,$

as $\dfrac{C_rR_v}{M} \gtrless \dfrac{-B_z}{1+B_z}.$

9. Let $\left(\dfrac{dY}{dS}\right)_{10}$ signify $\dfrac{dY}{dS}$ under floating exchange rates, when

$dB + dC = 0$ and $dM = 0.$

Then $\left(\dfrac{dY}{dS}\right)_{10} = \dfrac{1}{1 - X_n(1-T_y) - (X_r - C_r)\dfrac{R_v}{M}} > 0.$

10. $\left(\dfrac{dY}{dS}\right)_{10} \gtrless \left(\dfrac{dY}{dS}\right)_{00}$ as $\dfrac{-B_z}{1+B_z} \gtrless \dfrac{C_rR_v}{M},$

i.e., as $\left(\dfrac{dC}{dS}\right)_{00} + \left(\dfrac{dB}{dS}\right)_{00} \lessgtr 0.$

11. As $C_r \to \infty,$

$\left(\dfrac{dY}{dS}\right)_{10} \to \dfrac{1}{\infty}$

$\to 0.$

12. Let $\left(\dfrac{dY}{dM}\right)_{01} = \dfrac{dY}{dM}$ at fixed exchange rates when $dF = 0$ and $dS = 0.$

Let $\left(\dfrac{dR}{dM}\right)_{01}, \left(\dfrac{dC}{dM}\right)_{01}, \left(\dfrac{dB}{dM}\right)_{01}$ be analogously defined.

$\left(\dfrac{dY}{dM}\right)_{01} = \dfrac{-X_rR_vY}{M^2}\left[\dfrac{1}{\dfrac{1}{B_z+1} - X_n(1-T_y) - \dfrac{X_rR_v}{M}}\right].$

13. $\left(\dfrac{dB}{dM}\right)_{01} + \left(\dfrac{dC}{dM}\right)_{01} = \dfrac{B_z}{1+B_z}\left(\dfrac{dY}{dM}\right)_0 + C_r\left(\dfrac{dR}{dM}\right)_0 < 0.$

14. $\left(\dfrac{dR}{dM}\right)_{01} = \dfrac{-R_vY}{M^2}\left[\dfrac{1 - X_n(B_z+1)(1-T_y)}{1 - (B_z+1)X_n(1-T_y) + \dfrac{X_rR_v}{M}}\right] < 0.$

15. Let $\left(\dfrac{dY}{dM}\right)_{11} = \dfrac{dY}{dM}$ under floating exchange rates, when $dB + dC = 0$
    and $dS = 0$.

   Then $\left(\dfrac{dY}{dM}\right)_{11} = \dfrac{R_v Y (C_r - X_r)}{M^2}\left[\dfrac{1}{1 - X_n(1 - T_y) + \dfrac{R_v(C_r - X_r)}{M}}\right] > 0.$

16. $\left(\dfrac{dY}{dM}\right)_{11} - \left(\dfrac{dY}{dM}\right)_{01}$

   $= \dfrac{R_v Y}{M^2}\left[\dfrac{C_r - X_r}{1 - X_n(1 - T_y) + \dfrac{R_v}{M}(C_r - X_r)} + \dfrac{X_r}{\dfrac{1}{B_z + 1} - X_n(1 - T_y) - \dfrac{X_r R_v}{M}}\right] > 0.$

17. As $R_v \to \infty$,

   $\left(\dfrac{dY}{dM}\right)_{01} \to \dfrac{Y}{M}.$

   and $\left(\dfrac{dY}{dM}\right)_{11} \to \dfrac{Y}{M}.$

18. As $C_r \to \infty$,

   $\left(\dfrac{dY}{dM}\right)_{11} \to \dfrac{C_r R_v Y}{M C_r R_v} = \dfrac{Y}{M}.$

19. Let $k = \dfrac{\left(\dfrac{dY}{dS}\right)_{00}}{\left(\dfrac{dY}{dM}\right)_{01}} = \dfrac{M^2}{-X_r R_v Y}$

   Then $\dfrac{\left(\dfrac{dY}{dS}\right)_{10}}{\left(\dfrac{dY}{dM}\right)_{11}} = \dfrac{M^2}{(C_r - X_r) R_v Y} < k,$

   unless $X_r = -\infty$

   or $R_v = \infty.$

NOTES

1 See Appendix for a mathematical formulation.
2 It is assumed that the private marginal propensity to spend will always be less than unity with respect to income before tax.
3 It is assumed that the marginal propensity for the balance of trade to decline as expenditure increases is less than unity.

4 Since the marginal propensity to spend out of income is less than unity and since a fraction of each round of expenditure leaks abroad in additional net imports, the increase in income and expenditure will be limited, though possibly large. See Appendix, paragraphs 3 and 4.

5 The rise in tax revenue could exceed the initial rise in government expenditure only if the marginal propensity to spend out of private income after tax were substantially greater than unity. See Appendix, paragraph 5.

6 The only clear-cut alternative would appear to be that of defining constancy of monetary policy as the maintenance of a constant rate of interest. In "Flexible Exchange Rates and Employment Policy," *Canadian Journal of Economics and Political Science* (November 1961), Mr. R. A. Mundell has compared the effects of monetary policy (defined as interest policy), fiscal policy, and commercial policy in a flexible exchange rate system and a fixed exchange rate system, respectively.

7 It is uncertain whether private expenditure, stimulated by the rise in income and depressed by the rise in interest, will increase or decrease. But expenditure as a whole, like income, will increase, except where income velocity is entirely inelastic. See Appendix, paragraphs 6 and 7. In this extreme case, not only expenditure but also income and the balance of trade will remain unchanged.

8 See Appendix, paragraph 8.

9 It is assumed not only that the exchange rate will remain fixed but that there will be no resort to restrictions on international transactions.

10 See Appendix, paragraph 10.

11 *Ibid.*

12 See Appendix, paragraph 11.
   A high sensitivity of the interest rate to changes in velocity of circulation, i.e., a low elasticity of velocity with respect to the interest rate, while it makes for a favorable balance of payments response to government spending, and while it therefore tends to make the income response smaller under floating than under fixed exchange rates, also tends to reduce the magnitude of that response under both exchange systems. If the velocity of circulation were completely inelastic, a change in government expenditure would have no net effect on income under either exchange system.

13 See Appendix, paragraph 12.

14 See Appendix, paragraph 13.

15 See Appendix, paragraph 14.

16 See Appendix, paragraphs 15 and 16. However, in the extreme case where velocity of circulation is completely inelastic, money income will rise proportionately to the money stock under either exchange system. See Appendix, paragraph 17.

17 See Appendix, paragraph 18.

18 To put the same thing in other words, the effect under a floating rate relative to the effect under a fixed rate will never be greater, and will generally be less, in the case of budgetary expansion than in the case of monetary expansion.

19 We have to neglect, as unknown, any effects on trade of the difference in the composition of expenditure under the two policies.

20 See Appendix, paragraph 19.

21 It should be noted, however, that the responsiveness of capital movements to interest rate changes is made up of two components: a relocation of existing capital and a shift in the location of the placement of new savings. Since the former component is nonrecurrent and the latter recurrent in character, it is probable that the sensitivity of capital movements to interest changes will be greater in the short run than in the long run. Consequently, the difference between the two policies with respect to effectiveness and sustainability is also likely to be less in the long run than in the short.

22 Exchange speculation has a bearing not only on the relative effectiveness, but also on the practicability and sustainability of the two policies. Under exchange rates

that are fixed and are expected to remain so, exchange speculation would be absent. But if confidence in the fixed rate were less than complete, the fear of arousing disequilibrating movements of capital would tend to limit the magnitude and duration of the expansionary financial policies, particularly of monetary policy, the effect of which on the balance of payments is in any case the more adverse than that of budgetary policy.

3 The Mundell–Fleming model
Its strengths and limitations

V. Argy
International Macroeconomics: Theory and Policy, Routledge, 1994, pp. 73–84

INTRODUCTION

The MF model, it is worth repeating, is the starting point of all open economy model building and, today, familiar to most intermediate–senior undergraduates.

What we want to do in this chapter, before we extend and build on this important model in the chapters that follow, is to present in a very explicit way its principal strengths and its limitations. The limitations derive in large part from potential weaknesses in the behavioural relations underlying the model, its method of analysis and some general omissions.

ITS STRENGTHS

The model is readily understood and its behavioural equations are simple; it has immediate appeal and is recognisable as a model which captures observable features of the real world.

Its overriding strength is that it offers some insights into the behaviour of an economy, in the wake of a disturbance, policy or otherwise, over a time horizon of something like a year or so. In other words, if after a shock, and all other things being equal, we were to take a snapshot of the economy about a year later, we would recognise many, indeed most, of the outcomes predicted by the model.

Tables 3.1 and 3.2 report various simulations of the effects, after one year, of a 10 per cent increase in the money stock and of a fiscal expansion, taking the form of an increase in government spending by 5 per cent of GNP. The models simulated are the McKibbin–Sachs global model (MSG2), the Multi-Mod (IMF), the MCM (Federal Reserve Board) and the Amps (Murphy) model (for Australia). (See the original sources for a description of the models.)

All these models assume perfect asset substitution. Risk-free perfect arbitrage requires that the excess (shortfall) of the home interest rate over the foreign interest rate reflect, for the relevant time horizon, an expected devaluation (appreciation) of the currency. What this means, importantly, is that

The Mundell–Fleming model 31

Table 3.1 Flexible rates: effect of a monetary expansion of 10 per cent – year 1

	Australia		Canada	UK
	MSG2	NIF	MultiMod	MultiMod
yr	+5.2	+3.6	+3.5	+2.1
e	−14.7	−8.4	−13.3	−13.5
p	+3.5	+2.6	+1.0	+0.5
r_d	−1.9	−2.0	−2.6	−2.3
CAB (or TB) as percentage of GNP	+0.9	+1.2	−2.2	−4.0

Sources: MSG2, McKibbin 1988; NIF, Simes 1991; MultiMod, Masson *et al.* 1990
Notes: Percentage deviations from control with perfect asset substitution.
yr, output; e, exchange rate; p, price level; r_d, interest rate; CAB, current account; TB, trade balance.

Table 3.2 Flexible rates: effect of a fiscal expansion[a] – year 1 (perfect asset substitution)

	Australia		Canada		UK	
	Amps (Murphy)	MSG2	MultiMod	MCM	MultiMod	MCM
yr	+0.6	+0.67 (+2.41)	+1.2	+6.0	+2.7	+3.0
e	+12.2	+2.29 (0)	+4.0	+1.5	+4.7	+1.2
p	+0.35	−0.58 (+0.08)	+0.1	+1.0	+0.5	−0.5
r_d (short)	+3.0	+0.22	−0.4	+2.0	−0.2	+0.5
(long)		(+0.02)	0.0	—	+0.5	—
CAB as percentage of GNP	−1.5	−0.54 (−0.79)	−2.1	−5.5	−0.7	−10.5

Sources: Amps, Martin *et al.* 1987; MSG2, McKibbin 1988, Argy *et al.* 1989; MCM, Edison *et al.* 1986; MultiMod, Masson *et al.* 1990.
Notes: [a] Increase of government spending by 5 per cent of GNP. Results for fixed rates (Australian dollar tied to the US dollar) are given in parentheses.

with perfect asset substitution one should not expect, at least over shorter horizons, the home interest rate to be predetermined by the foreign interest rate. This needs to be kept in mind when interpreting the tables.

What do these tables reveal? A monetary expansion under flexible rates leads to a devaluation, some increase in output, only a 'modest' increase in prices and some fall in the interest rate. A fiscal expansion under flexible rates leads to some appreciation of the currency, some increase in output, some rise in the interest rate (except surprisingly in MultiMod where there is a fall in the short-term interest rate) and a deterioration in the current account.

These outcomes largely confirm the MF predictions. There is one major reservation to be noted, however. The reservation is that a monetary expansion does not necessarily open up a current account surplus, as predicted by the MF model. Indeed, in two of the models there is a current account deficit. At this point, we note that one reason for the ambiguity in a modified MF model is that a monetary expansion *increases* domestic expenditure, which has a negative effect on the current account, but devalues the currency, which has a positive effect on the current account (Boughton 1989).

To test for the effects of a fiscal expansion under fixed rates, we report in Table 3.3 simulations for France and Italy and, as well, one for Australia in Table 3.2 (which allows us to compare outcomes *directly* with those for flexible rates). These appear to confirm that fiscal policy is more effective under fixed than under flexible rates. (Compare for example the effects on output for France and Italy under fixed rates with the effects in Canada and the UK for the same model.) The price effects are again weak, the interest rate rises marginally and there is, predictably, a current account deficit.

ITS LIMITATIONS – SOME GENERAL PRINCIPLES

We intend later in this chapter to present what we consider to be the key assumptions of the MF model.

Before we do this, however, we will illustrate this general proposition by making two 'minor' variations to the MF model and show how even minor variations can make a significant difference to the outcome. This is admittedly 'nitpicking', but it does serve to demonstrate, in a dramatic form, the general truth of the proposition.

The two variations we will make, each independently, are first to modify very slightly the money demand equation used in the MF model and second to extend the capital flow equation by adding one more variable to it.

A variation on the money demand equation

It will be recalled that in the MF model prices do not appear in the money demand equation. If the price level which is relevant to the demand for

Table 3.3 MultiMod simulations: fiscal expansion[a] for France and Italy under narrow exchange rate bands

	France	*Italy*
yr	+3.4	+3.6
e	+0.1	+0.1
p	+1.0	+1.1
r_d	+0.1	+0.1
CAB as percentage of GNP	−2.4	−2.2

Source: MultiMod, Masson *et al.* 1990
Notes: [a] As in Table 3.2.
Perfect asset substitution; monetary policy is completely ineffective.

money balances is the price of home produced goods, such a procedure is legitimate since this price level is assumed fixed in the MF model. If, however, more realistically, the relevant price level is the *consumer* price index, which also includes the price of *imported* goods, then some variation to the model is needed.

Suppose the consumer price index p is a weighted average of the price of home produced goods (p_d) and the price of imported goods in home currency ($p^* + e$), i.e. the foreign price level p^* adjusted by the exchange rate. With p_d and p^* both fixed, we can write the equation for the consumer price as

$$p = (1 - \alpha_{15})e \tag{1}$$

where $1 - \alpha_{15}$ represents the weight attaching to imports in the consumer price index. This clearly assumes that the price of imported goods adjusts more rapidly than the price of home goods, a not unreasonable assumption.

We now modify the MF model, for the flexible rate case, to accommodate an extended money demand equation.

$$\text{mo} = (1 - \alpha_{15})e + \alpha_5 \text{yr} - \alpha_{10}\bar{r}_d \tag{2}$$

Since we are only interested in making one particular point we need only limit ourselves to the case of perfect capital mobility where r_d is exogenously given by the foreign interest rate. It should be noted that the presence of e means that e is now also a *shift* variable in the money demand equation.

Only one additional equation is needed to complete the model here – the demand for goods.

$$\text{yr} = \alpha_1 e - \alpha_4 \bar{r}_d + \alpha_3 \text{gr} \tag{3}$$

Equations (2) and (3) now determine e and yr jointly for a monetary (mo) and fiscal (gr) expansion.

The solutions are simple:

$$\frac{\text{yr}}{\text{mo}} = \frac{\alpha_1}{k_1} \tag{4}$$

$$\frac{e}{\text{mo}} = \frac{1}{k_1} \tag{5}$$

$$\frac{\text{yr}}{\text{gr}} = \frac{\alpha_3(1 - \alpha_{15})}{k_1} \tag{6}$$

$$\frac{e}{\text{gr}} = -\frac{\alpha_3\alpha_5}{k_1} \tag{7}$$

where $k_1 = \alpha_1\alpha_5 + (1 - \alpha_{15})$. These solutions bear comparison with the MF solutions for the special case where $\alpha_{14} = \infty$. The reader can readily demonstrate that the MF results can be reached by setting $\alpha_{15} = 1$.

The real multiplier is smaller for monetary policy and so is the exchange rate effect (i.e. there is now a *smaller* devaluation).

Why is this so? Consider the MF solution which is one where output increases substantially and the currency devalues. At this point now, in this new context, there is an increase in money demand (because the consumer price index will have increased). This is equivalent to a *fall* in the money stock, which in turn at once moderates the increase in output and the devaluation.

The case of a fiscal expansion is more interesting. It will be recalled that in the MF model fiscal policy is completely impotent. (Equation (6) shows that this is the case if $\alpha_{15} = 1$.) Now, it turns out, with the small modification we have made, that fiscal policy has some effectiveness. At the same time, the appreciation is weakened (see equation (7)). Why?

We recall again that in the MF model in equilibrium there is an appreciation of the currency. With both the interest rate and the money stock fixed, output cannot change (see equation (2) with $\alpha_{15} = 1$). Now, however, the appreciation will *reduce* money demand (shift the LM schedule to the right); this is equivalent to an *increase* in the money stock which at once increases output and weakens the appreciation. It is readily seen from (2) that with mo and r_d both fixed yr can increase if e falls.

Extending the capital flow equation

A second modification we might make is to allow the level of real income to influence capital flows, so we now write the capital flow equation as

$$\frac{K}{X_0} = \alpha_{14}(r_d - r^*) + \alpha_{20}\mathrm{yr} \tag{8}$$

There are several ways to rationalise the presence of output in the capital flow equation. At this point and for our purposes, we simply note that it might also capture the positive effect of increased domestic activity on capital flows (reflecting the improved prospects for the economy) (see Helliwell 1969).

We will proceed to show that this small change can also have quite dramatic effects on the outcomes.

For a start it is now no longer evident that the slope of the B schedule is positive. Recalling the equation for the trade balance we have

$$\frac{B}{X_0} = \alpha_{13}e - \mathrm{yr} + \alpha_{14}(r_d - r^*) + \alpha_{20}\mathrm{yr} \tag{9}$$

and the slope (with $B/X_0 = 0$) is now

$$\frac{1 - \alpha_{20}}{\alpha_{14}}$$

which may be positive or negative. It will be negative if $\alpha_{20} > 1$. How is it possible for the slope to be negative?

Consider an increase in output. This now has two opposing effects on the balance of payments. On the one hand there is the conventional negative effect on the trade balance (as in the MF model); on the other hand the increased output is assumed to attract an inflow of capital. If the latter effect dominates then a *fall* in the interest rate is required to restore equilibrium to the balance of payments, implying a negatively sloped B schedule. This particular case is pursued further below. (If the slope is positive the presence of output simply *reduces* the slope.)

Since the slope of the IS schedule is also negative a critical question is the relative slopes of the two schedules. The slope of the IS schedule is $-1/\alpha_4$. The two possibilities are shown in Figure 3.1 as B_1 and B_2.

It needs to be noted that now if the economy were located on the right (left) of the B schedule the balance of payments would be in surplus (deficit), the opposite of the MF case. The reason is that at any given level of the interest rate, if output is above (below) the level required to equilibrate the balance of payments, this must now correspond to an overall surplus (deficit). At the same time, now, if there were a devaluation (appreciation), the B schedule would shift to the *left* (*right*).

To underline the difference between cases B_1 and B_2 we consider rightward shifts in LM and IS. Suppose first that B_1 is the relevant schedule. A shift in LM will now generate an overall surplus (because the income effect on inflows dominates over the continued interest rate and trade effects). If the exchange rate is fixed and there is no sterilisation, the money supply will

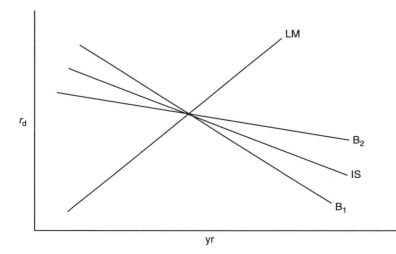

Figure 3.1 The B schedule with output in the capital flow equation

continue to increase. This in turn will only make matters worse, increasing the surplus further. Clearly the situation is unstable. If the exchange rate is flexible the surplus will provoke an *appreciation* of the currency, a bizarre result for a monetary expansion.

If the IS schedule shifts there is again an overall surplus. Allowing the money supply to increase will again generate instability. With flexible rates there is an unambiguous appreciation, whatever the degree of capital mobility.

We turn now to the case where the B schedule is positioned as in B_2. This is the more realistic case, particularly if capital mobility is high.

Now the results are more recognisable. A monetary expansion opens up a deficit (the interest rate effect dominating over the positive output effect) while a shift in IS produces a surplus. This case is stable. If the exchange rate floats the presence of an output term in the capital flow equation *weakens* the exchange rate and output effects for a monetary expansion; for a fiscal expansion the currency will appreciate further while the output effect will be weakened.

ITS KEY LIMITATIONS

We turn now to the key limitations of the model.

1 If we are concerned with the medium-term effects of a permanent disturbance, it is clearly no longer appropriate to assume that wages and prices are fixed. The MF model was in due course extended to accommodate wage and price flexibility. It takes the MF model, as is, and adds to it a wage–price sector. This allows us to focus exclusively on the question of how wage–price adjustment modifies outcomes.

2 The theory underlying capital flows is too simple. In time, the theory was progressively refined. Exchange rate expectations were assigned a role in the capital flow equation. The MF model had implicitly assumed that the expected exchange rate was equal to the current spot rate, thus abstracting from expectations. Argy and Porter (1972) assumed that exchange rate expectations were stationary (i.e. the expected exchange rate was given); this allowed the current spot rate, which was market determined, to depart from the expected rate. This small change, by itself, changes the MF results. Later, exchange rate expectations were assumed to be formed rationally (i.e. the impacts on exchange rates were known) (Dornbusch 1976; Branson and Buiter 1983).

A still more dramatic change came when capital flows were recast in the context of a portfolio balance framework (see Branson and Hill 1971; Hodjera 1973).

It is rewarding, at this point, to take the simplest representation of a portfolio model and to draw out some of its implications for the MF type model.

If the domestic interest rate increased to a new higher level, there would be a permanently higher *flow* of capital into the economy. The alternative (portfolio) representation of capital movements argues, by contrast, that there would be a portfolio readjustment by domestic and foreign residents leading to an inflow of capital in the initial period; at the same time, however, provided wealth is growing, the higher domestic interest rate will provoke a continuing inflow of capital in subsequent periods, but at a much more modest rate.

To illustrate this, suppose domestic residents held foreign assets (but, for simplicity, foreigners did not hold domestic assets). Suppose 'FA' represents the value of foreign assets in foreign currency held by residents, while 'We' represents domestic wealth (and E represents the exchange rate – editor's note). Then, in its very simplest form, we have

$$\frac{EFA}{We} = \alpha_{12}(r^* - r_d) \tag{10}$$

This asserts that the proportion of wealth held in the form of foreign assets (denominated in domestic currency) increases as the foreign interest rate increases relative to the domestic interest rate. Differentiating this equation yields

$$\Delta FA = -K = \alpha_{12}\, We(\Delta r^* - \Delta r_d) + \alpha_{12}\Delta We\,(r^* - r_d) - FA\Delta E \tag{11}$$

The capital inflow following an increase in the domestic interest rate is represented by $\alpha_{12}We$; this inflow, however, is not sustained since Δr_d becomes zero in subsequent periods. The continuing flow is represented by $\alpha_{12}\Delta We$ which says that so long as home wealth is growing, a larger share of the increased wealth will be absorbed in domestic, as against foreign, assets. The sustained flow is therefore $\alpha_{12}\Delta We$, while the initial stock adjustment, by contrast, is $\alpha_{12}We$. The ratio of the flow to the stock adjustment is $\Delta We/We$, which is the rate of growth of wealth. In other words, if wealth grows at 5 per cent the (sustained) flow effect will be 5 per cent of the (initial) stock effect.

For relatively short-term analysis we may disregard the change in wealth, and so $\Delta We = 0$; if we also disregard valuation effects ($FA\Delta E$), this reduces the new capital flow equation to

$$K = \alpha_{12}We(\Delta r_d - \Delta r^*) \tag{12}$$

The implications of this are radical. If we were to use (12) as the capital flow equation, the B schedule becomes vertical after the economy has settled down, *as if capital mobility were zero*. This is because the *level* of the home interest rate no longer has the capacity to generate *permanent* flows.

The portfolio model is elegant and may be better founded in theory and in practice. It is too easy, however, to exaggerate the differences. For *short-term* analysis, there is very little difference. Beyond that, as we have seen, with wealth growing there is a *lasting* flow effect. Moreover, if stock adjustment occurs with a lag the flow effects are *extended*. Finally, perhaps oddly, if capital mobility is perfect the two models have identical implications.

3 The analysis is of a relatively small country. It assumes that the country has no significant impact on the rest of the world and hence that feedback effects from the rest of the world can be disregarded. This holds for the vast majority of economies, including many officially called large by international bodies. The exceptions are the G3 countries: the USA, Japan and Germany.

Mundell himself extended his own model to the large-country case (Mundell 1964). Typically, the large-country case is treated in the context of a world assumed to be composed of two large countries only; interdependence and interactions are then identified and analysed.

In this context the small-country case can be represented as a special case of the two-country framework. In this case the world comprises a huge closed economy entity and a small economy. The small economy cannot impact on the rest of the world but the rest of the world does impact on the small economy (Argy 1990).

In a world where many smaller economies tie their currencies to one larger economy which in turn floats *vis-à-vis* another larger economy, the two-country framework is restrictive. A more flexible and richer framework is one which assumes that the world comprises three countries, two giants and one relatively small.

4 In the money market in the MF model there is a demand for a money *stock*, the only asset explicitly identified in the model. Yet the public is assumed implicitly to hold other assets. Bonds are implicitly in the model since there is an interest rate on *domestic* bonds. There are also transactions in *foreign* bonds since capital flows are also in the model, so *foreign* assets are also held. There is no *unified* system of asset demand within a portfolio, however, which explicitly identifies the assets held by the private sector.

One can take this further. Following up on comments made under (2) above, we can say that in the MF model there appears to be an inconsistency between the money market and the foreign exchange market. If there is a *stock* demand for money, there ought, with consistency, to be a *stock* not a *flow* demand for foreign bonds as part of a unified portfolio.

5 There is no analysis of stock formation. Nor is any role assigned to wealth either in the demand for money or in the real demand for goods. Interest receipts on debt and net foreign assets are also neglected.

In essence, the MF equilibrium is a *flow* not a *stock* equilibrium. The analysis is incomplete in that in true *stock* equilibrium, in a stationary state, the private sector cannot be accumulating new stocks.

This difficult question is addressed in detail [elsewhere]. To anticipate, we conclude that, in a stationary state, stock equilibrium requires that *both* the budget and the current account be zero. We need thus to impose these as *conditions* of longer-run equilibrium.

There is no doubt that this puts a finger on an important deficiency in the MF model but one which is serious only when medium- to longer-run analysis is being undertaken. In the shorter run of a year or so these considerations are of lesser importance and thus again the MF model is essentially upheld.

6 The methodology employed in the MF model is one of comparative statics, i.e. a disturbance is assumed to occur and the new equilibrium is analysed without paying any attention to the dynamics of adjustment.

There were several developments on this front. For a monetary disturbance under flexible rates an important distinction was made between an initial adjustment phase during which only monetary variables – interest rates and exchanges rates – adjust and a later adjustment phase during which the real sector (prices, the current account) adjust. The two 'classic' models that fall in this general category are those of Dornbusch (1976) and Branson (1977).

Subsequently, the adjustment phases were refined. A distinction is made between a short-run MF type adjustment phase and a medium run during which portfolio balance is restored (Frenkel and Razin 1987). In some of these models prices continue to be fixed throughout and only output adjusts, so the only modification made here to the MF model is to accommodate portfolio balance and wealth.

The models were further refined when prices were also allowed to adjust. Now there is, first, a Keynesian phase, during which more refined variations on the MF model are assumed to hold, and second, a more classical medium-run adjustment phase during which prices adjust (with output now returning to its full employment level) and as well portfolio balance constraints are all observed.

7 The MF model assumes away possible J curve effects, supposing a devaluation (appreciation) will improve (worsen) the current account. Perverse exchange rate effects were introduced into an MF framework by Niehans (1975).

As an illustration, we saw that in the MF model under flexible exchange rates with some capital mobility a monetary expansion must provoke a devaluation and a trade surplus sufficient to absorb the net outflow of capital. If a devaluation has perverse effects, an initial deficit on the trade balance is made worse by the devaluation. Thus to restore equilibrium to the balance of payments an *inflow* of capital is needed to offset the deficit in the trade balance, an outcome which is virtually impossible within an MF framework. Moreover, in the presence of a J curve a devaluation now may have deflationary effects on the economy; it also produces more short-run inflation. It is therefore evident that a J curve has the capacity radically to transform MF results.

It is easy, however, to exaggerate the difficulties here for the MF model. Evidence is presented [elsewhere] that J curve effects are most likely to occur in the first nine months after an exchange rate adjustment, but that they tend to disappear beyond that period. Thus, if we reckon the MF model to be relevant for a short run of a year or so, one could argue that this takes us outside the 'contentious' phase. Nevertheless, a radically different approach is needed for analysis over a shorter phase of say up to the first nine months. This is of course a special case of 'dynamic' adjustment, noted earlier.

8 Exchange rate and price expectations are ignored in the MF analysis. These again introduce an element of dynamic analysis.

The New Classical economists were the first to make the important distinction between a disturbance, policy or otherwise, which was anticipated and one which was not. Most of this analysis was conducted in the context of a closed economy. Using relatively simple models, they were led to conclude that any macro policy which was anticipated would be ineffective. They went further and argued that if the authorities followed a predictable stabilisation rule sooner or later the rule would be learned and anticipated and stabilisation policy would thus be ineffective. This in turn led them to propose simple monetary fiscal rules.

The New Classical economists took this analysis a step further. Again using a relatively simple framework, they tried to show that if the monetary authorities were allowed discretion in the implementation of monetary policy they would end up with the worst of all possible worlds: more inflation and a return to the natural rate of unemployment. This further reinforced the case for monetary rules.

Chapter 24 [of my book] introduces an open economy model which explicitly incorporates expected prices as well as exchange rates. It is shown that the analysis of an anticipated policy change can be very complicated. A monetary policy which is anticipated can produce a wage adjustment in the period in which the policy is anticipated to change which can go some way towards nullifying the real effects of such policies. An anticipated change in the currency or in the price level could also produce effects ahead of the anticipated policy change. For example, an anticipated fiscal expansion will create an anticipation of an appreciation of the currency; this in turn affects the current exchange rate and thus may have real effects ahead of the implementation of the fiscal expansion.

Also in the spirit of New Classical economics is the belief in the Ricardian equivalence hypothesis. According to this hypothesis, debt and tax finance are equivalent in their real effects on the economy, because the public will anticipate future tax liabilities if debt finance is undertaken and this will alter their real consumption behaviour in the present. This thesis has radical implications for the workings of fiscal policy.

9 Yet another potential limitation of the MF model is that it assumes that a 'single' base good is produced in the small economy, which good is, in turn, imperfectly competitive with a good produced abroad. An alternative framework assumes that there are two types of goods produced: a traded good (which is perfectly competitive with the good produced abroad) and a non-traded good (e.g. services) which is completely sheltered from competition abroad. A further extension accommodates two traded goods, an import good and an export good, plus a non-traded good.

10 Finally, in the MF model all imports are implicitly assumed to be of consumer goods. Allowing for imports of raw materials and intermediate goods could also modify some of the MF results.

REFERENCES

Argy, V. (1990) 'Choice of exchange rate regime for a smaller economy: a survey of some key issues', in V. Argy and P. de Grauwe (eds), *Choosing an Exhange Rate Regime: The Challenge for Smaller Industrial Countries*, Washington, DC: IMF.

Argy, V. and M.G. Porter (1972) 'The forward exchange rate market and the effects of domestic and external disturbances under alternative exchange rates', *IMF Staff Papers*, XIX (November), pp. 503–32.

Argy, V., W. McKibbin and E. Sieflof (1989) 'Exchange rate regimes for a small economy in a multi-country world', *Princeton Studies in International Finance*, 67 (December).

Boughton, J.M. (1989) 'Policy assignment strategies with somewhat flexible exchange rates', in M. Miller, B. Eichengreen and R. Portes (eds), *Blueprints for Exchange Rate Management*, London: Academic Press.

Branson, W.H. (1977) 'Asset Markets and relative prices in exchange rate determination', *Sozialwissenschaftliche Annalen des Instituts für Höhere Studien*, Reihe A, 1, pp. 69–89 (reprinted in Princeton University *International Finance*, 20 (1980)).

Branson, W.H. and W.H. Buiter (1983) 'Monetary and fiscal policy with flexible exchange rates', in J.S. Bhandari and B.H. Putman (eds), *Economic Interdependence and Flexible Exchange Rates*, Cambridge, Mass.: MIT Press.

Branson, W.H. and R. Hill (1971) 'Capital movements in the OECD area: an econometric analysis', *OECD Occasional Studies* (December).

Dornbusch, R. (1976) 'Expectations and exchange rate dynamic', *Journal of Political Economy*, 84, 6, pp. 1161–76.

Edison, H.J., J.R. Marquez and R.W. Tryon (1986) 'The structure and properties of the FRB multi-country model: part 1: model description and simulation results', *International Finance Discussion Papers* (October), no. 293.

Frenkel, J.A. and A. Razin (1987) 'The Mundell–Fleming model: a quarter century later: a unified exposition', *IMF Staff Papers*, 29 (1), pp. 1–30.

Helliwell, J.F. (1969) 'Monetary and fiscal policies for an open economy', *Oxford Economic Papers*, 21 (March), pp. 35–55.

Hodjera, Z. (1973) 'International short-term capital movements: a survey of theory and empirical analysis', *IMF Staff Papers*, 20 (November), pp. 683–740.

Martin, W.J., C.W. Murphy and D.T. Nguyen (1987), 'Influences on the Australian real exchange rate; an analysis using the AMPS model', Discussion Paper 177, the ANU Centre for Economic Policy Research (August).

Masson, P., S. Symansky and G. Meredith (1990) *Multimod Mark II; A Revised and Extended Model*, Washington, DC: IMF (July).

McKibbin, W.J. (1988) 'Policy analysis with the MSG2 model', *Australian Economic Papers*, supplement, 27 (June), pp. 126–50.

Mundell, R.A. (1964) 'A reply: capital mobility and size', *Canadian Journal of Economics and Political Science*, 30 (August), pp. 421–31.

Niehans, J. (1975) 'Some doubts about the efficacy of monetary policy under flexible exchange rates', *Journal of International Economics*, 5, pp. 275–81.

Simes, R. (1991) 'The Monetary transmission mechanism in macroeconometric models of the Australian economy', in C. Kearney and R. MacDonald (eds), *Developments in Australian Monetary Economics*, Cheshire: Longman.

4 Extensions on the Mundell–Fleming model

Perfect capital mobility and flexible prices

Mehmet Ugur

INTRODUCTION

As Argy indicates in Chapter 3, the strength of the Mundell–Fleming (MF) model lies in the valuable insights it offers into the functioning of an open economy despite its simplicity. That is the main reason why it has become an essential entry in intermediate textbooks on open-economy macroeconomics. It is true that simplicity and the underlying behavioural assumptions have affected the reliability of its predictions. These qualities can be interpreted in two ways.

First, the MF model can be regarded as outmoded and, to some extent, irrelevant. We do not subscribe to this interpretation for the simple reason that its insights still hold. In fact, highly sophisticated models still yield results similar to those predicted by the MF model (see Tables 3.1 to 3.3 in Chapter 3). The second interpretation would be to treat the MF model as a baseline from which different trajectories can be charted by relaxing some of its assumptions and/or by inserting new assumptions about prices, wages, capital mobility, expectations, etc. This is what Argy has demonstrated in Chapter 3. In this chapter, we will focus on only one assumption – namely the assumption concerning price rigidity. We will relax this assumption to demonstrate that the effectiveness of monetary expansion under flexible exchange rates diminishes as the price level increases. Monetary policy becomes totally ineffective if the price level increases proportionately to the increase in money supply. In other words, if inflation is determined by the change in money supply, the MF model yields a classical result. If, however, the time lag between monetary expansion and inflation is long, the MF yields a neo-Keynesian result – implying an increase in output as well as price level. The increase in income, however, will be less significant than what the MF model would predict.

We will proceed by using a simplified version of the MF model under conditions of perfect capital mobility and flexible exchange rates. First, we will solve the model algebraically to establish the impact of monetary expansion on output. Then, we will repeat the exercise diagrammatically to demonstrate the way in which the MF model can be made compatible with the classical, Keynesian and neo-Keynesian analyses.

THE MF MODEL: AN ALGEBRAIC REPRESENTATION

Let the equilibrium in three sectors of the open economy be given by the equations (1)–(3) below.

$$y = a_1(e + p^* - p) + a_2 y^* - a_3 r + a_4 g \tag{1}$$

$$m - p = a_5 y - a_6 r \tag{2}$$

$$r = r^* \tag{3}$$

These equations imply that the model is in log-linear form and, therefore, all variables except interest rates are in logarithms. The interest rate is measured as unity plus the rate of interest as a fraction. For example, a 6 per cent interest rate will be demonstrated as 1.06.

Here:

y = income
e = nominal exchange rate
p^* = foreign prices
p = domestic prices
y^* = foreign income
g = government expenditures
m = nominal money supply
r = domestic interest rate
r^* = foreign interest rate
a_i = parameters with a positive value.

Substituting for interest rates in (1) and (2), the model can be reduced into two simultaneous equations:

$$y = a_1 (e + p^* - p) + a_2 y^* - a_3 r^* + a_4 g \tag{4}$$

$$m - p = a_5 y - a_6 r^* \tag{5}$$

Assuming that all variables except y and e are exogenous, the model can be re-written as follows:

$$y - a_1 e = a_1(p^* - p) + a_2 y^* - a_3 r^* + a_4 g \tag{6}$$

$$a_5 y = m - p + a_6 r^* \tag{7}$$

Bear in mind that the purpose of this exercise is to establish the effect of monetary expansion on output when prices are flexible. Yet, we treat the price level as exogenous. This means that the model above does not specify the way in which the price level is determined. Although this is a weakness, it should not be a serious obstacle because what we are interested in is not price determination but the impact on income when the price level changes. In other words, the price level here should be interpreted as a shift variable.

In matrix form, equations (6) and (7) can be re-written as follows:

$$\begin{bmatrix} 1 & -a_1 \\ a_5 & 0 \end{bmatrix} \begin{bmatrix} y \\ e \end{bmatrix} = \begin{bmatrix} a_1(p^* - p) + a_2y^* - a_3r^* + a_4g \\ m - p + a_6r^* \end{bmatrix} \tag{8}$$

This equation will have a unique solution if the determinant $\begin{vmatrix} 1 & -a_1 \\ a_5 & 0 \end{vmatrix} \neq 0$.

This determinant is $a_1a_5 > 0$. Therefore, a unique solution exists. Applying Cramer's rule, the solution for y is as follows:

$$y = \frac{\begin{vmatrix} a_1 (p^* - p) + a_2y^* - a_3r^* + a_4g & -a_1 \\ m - p + a_6r^* & 0 \end{vmatrix}}{\begin{vmatrix} 1 & -a_1 \\ a_5 & 0 \end{vmatrix}} \tag{9}$$

This yields a solution of

$$y = \frac{a_1(m - p + a_6r^*)}{a_1a_5} = \frac{1}{a_5}(m - p + a_6r^*). \tag{10}$$

Taking total differentials, we can write:

$$dy = \frac{1}{a_5}(dm - dp + a_6dr^*). \tag{11}$$

Assuming foreign interest rate is constant, (11) can be re-written as follows:

$$\frac{dy}{dm} = \frac{1}{a_5}(1 - \frac{dp}{dm}) \tag{12}$$

This result suggests that the impact of monetary expansion on income, for a given level of inflation $dp < dm$, depends on the value of a_5 – which is nothing but the cash-balance ratio (see equation 2). The smaller the cash-balance ratio is, the larger is the part of the increase in money supply spent on goods and services. To the extent that this is the case, the stimulus to the economy will be stronger for two reasons. First, part of the relatively higher level of expenditure will fall on domestically produced goods – leading to relatively higher expansion through what can be visualised as the closed-economy multiplier. Secondly, part of the relatively higher level of expenditure will fall on foreign goods – leading to a relatively higher level of depreciation. As long as $dp < dm$, the relatively higher level of depreciation will have a stronger effect on competitiveness. Then, improved competitiveness will strengthen the expansionary effect resulting from increased foreign expenditure on the expanding country's exports.

Another implication of the result is that these standard MF predictions are now weighted with the ratio of inflation to money supply growth (dp/dm). If, as Mundell and Fleming did, we assume $dp = 0$, monetary policy has a full effect on income – which is equal to $1/\alpha_5$. This is the Keynesian result in the sense that it implies a horizontal aggregate supply curve determined by constant prices (hence wages). Constant prices and wages, in turn, can be explained by the existence of idle resources – i.e. by the fact that national income is below the full-employment level. If $0 < dp < dm$, however, the effect of monetary expansion is dampened by the ratio of inflation to money supply growth. This is what can be described as a neo-Keynesian outcome. We use the 'neo-Keynesian' attribute loosely here to make the point that the economy, initially, may be near or at full-employment equilibrium, but nominal wages tend to be rigid in the short run. Short-run wage rigidity, in turn, may be explained by the time lag for negotiating new wage contracts and/or resistance of the labour force to a fall in nominal wages. Finally, if $dp = dm$, monetary expansion has no effect on income. This is the classical/new-classical result in the sense that the long-run aggregate supply curve is vertical at the full-employment level of income (classical) or rational expectations ensure that the economy is at equilibrium at the non-accelerating inflation rate of unemployment (new classical).

THE MF MODEL: A SYNTHESIS

In what follows, and to elucidate the points made above, we will use a graphical representation of the MF model together with an open-economy aggregate demand (AD)/aggregate supply (AS) model with three different aggregate supply curves. The MF model assumes perfect capital mobility, implying a horizontal balance of payments (BP) schedule drawn at world interest rates. The initial equilibrium at point (a) in the MF model (Figure 4.1, panel 1) is reproduced as the equilibrium point in the AD/AS model in panel 2.

In panel 2, the aggregate demand (AD) schedule is sloping downward to reflect the inverse relationship between prices and aggregate demand. The only difference from the standard closed-economy model is that the AD is drawn at a given exchange rate (e). The exchange rate is a shift variable that determines the position (and not the slope) of the AD schedule. An increase in the exchange rate (a depreciation of the domestic currency) improves competitiveness and causes the AD schedule to shift to the right. A fall in the exchange rate (an appreciation of the domestic currency) has the opposite effect. The horizontal AS_k schedule reflects the Keynesian assumption of constant prices/wages; the upward-sloping AS_n schedule reflects the neo-Keynesian view of flexible prices combined with nominal wage rigidity; the vertical AS_c reflects the classical/new-classical equilibrium at full employment or non-accelerating inflation rate of unemployment.

Monetary expansion leads to a rightward shift in the LM schedule from LM to LM_1 in panel 1. That is because, with fixed prices, income must increase to induce economic agents to hold the extra liquidity. The internal

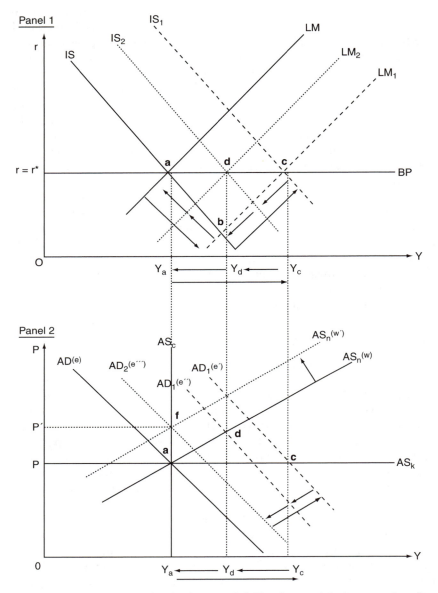

Figure 4.1 Monetary expansion in the Mundell-Fleming model: the case of perfect capital mobility: flexible exchange rates and flexible prices/wages

balance is now at (b), where LM_1 intersects with IS. At b, income is higher and interest rates are lower, leading to deficit in the balance of payments and a depreciation of the domestic currency. Assuming fixed prices, depreciation improves competitiveness and leads to a rightward shift in the IS schedule. The IS schedule will continue to shift to the right until it intersects with LM_1

at c. The economy is now in equilibrium, as both internal balance and external balance are achieved. This is the standard MF result. Monetary policy has a full effect on income because the depreciation of the domestic currency creates a current account surplus large enough to compensate for the capital account deficit caused by capital outflow.

In panel 2, monetary expansion leads to a rightward shift in the AD schedule for two reasons. First, the level of income must increase at each price level to ensure that the demand for money increases in line with the supply of money. Secondly, the depreciation of the domestic currency that is implied by point (b) of panel 1 leads to an improvement in competitiveness, which, in turn, constitutes an additional injection into the system. Then new AD schedule is drawn as $AD_1^{(e')}$ to capture these two effects. If prices are constant, the relevant aggregate supply schedule is AS_k and the depreciation represented by $^{(e')}$ is a real one. Then the equilibrium at (c) in panel 1 corresponds to the equilibrium at (c) in panel 2. This is the standard Keynesian result: monetary expansion has full multiplier effect on income with no effect on prices.

However, the equilibrium at (c) is not sustainable if we allow for price flexibility. Because $Y_c > Y_a$, prices start to pick up. As prices start to increase, the real money supply (real balances) falls and competitiveness decreases. The fall in real balances causes LM_1 to shift to the left (towards LM_2). The decline in competitiveness, on the other hand, causes IS_1 to shift to the left (towards IS_2). The leftward shift will depend on the ratio of price increase to money supply increase (i.e. dp/dm). As long as $dp/dm > 0$, we can assume that the two schedules will shift until they intersect at a point such as d (the intersection between LM_2 and IS_2). The level of income implied by point d, Y_d, is lower than Y_c but is still higher than Y_a. Therefore, monetary policy is effective in changing the level of income, but its effectiveness is dampened by the increase in price level, which leads to a fall in real balances and deterioration in competitiveness. This result is reproduced as Y_d in panel 2, which is determined by the intersection between $AD_1^{(e'')}$ and $AS_n^{(w)}$. $AD_1^{(e'')}$ reflects the appreciation of the domestic currency (and the resulting loss of competitiveness). This is the so-called neo-Keynesian result, which allows for price flexibility in the short run.

One can see clearly that the equilibrium at d is not sustainable in the long run unless wage setters suffer from money illusion. In other words, in the long run, we can no longer expect the nominal wages to remain constant as wage setters demand higher nominal wages at least to maintain the *ex ante* real wage. Once this is the case, higher nominal wages will affect both the AD and AS schedules. As wages increase, the $AS_n^{(w)}$ schedule will start to shift to the left (towards $AS_n^{(w')}$). In other words, higher nominal wages act as an adverse supply-side shock leading to a fall in aggregate supply at each price level. On the other hand, higher wages will affect prices, leading to a further appreciation of the domestic currency. As appreciation renders domestic goods less competitive, the AD schedule will begin to shift leftward. The leftward shift in the AD and AS schedules will continue as long as the income level is above

Y_a. Eventually, equilibrium will be restored when $AD_2^{(e''')}$ and $AS_n^{(w')}$ intersects along the AS_c schedule at point f. At this point, the level of income is the same as before monetary expansion, prices are higher and the domestic currency has appreciated enough to counterbalance the initial depreciation implied by point b above.

We can also trace this process via the MF model in panel 1. As prices continue to increase at point d (because $Y_d > Y_a$), the real money supply falls and LM_2 starts to shift to the left. In the meantime, IS_2 also starts to shift to the left as higher prices undermine competitiveness. These developments have three effects on the balance of payments. First, the current account deteriorates as competitiveness falls. Secondly, the fall in income implied by the leftward shift of IS_2 and LM_2 leads to an improvement in the current account as import falls in line with the marginal propensity to imports. Finally, the capital account improves as the fall in real balances drives a wedge between domestic and foreign interest rates in favour of the former and attracts foreign capital. As a result, we can assume that the leftward shift of IS_2 and LM_2 will be compatible with a balance in the overall balance of payments. Then, the two schedules will continue to shift leftward until they return to their original positions at IS and LM. Consequently, the level of income is again Y_a, implying that monetary policy is ineffective when prices and wages are fully flexible. This is nothing but the classical/new-classical result obtained above.

CONCLUSION

We have demonstrated that the MF model, even if prices and wages are assumed to be flexible, can still be used as an analytical tool to trace the impact of monetary policy on income. It can also enable us to visualise the effect of monetary expansion on the money market, the goods market and the balance of payments. Obviously, it can serve these purposes only if its assumptions are relaxed. Therefore, one can argue that the exercise above represents a move away from the MF model rather than demonstrating its ingenuity. There is an element of truth in this argument, but we also need to remind ourselves of the fact that no theory is better than its assumptions. We also must acknowledge that the MF model's grasp of the open economy is essentially sound – even though some of its behavioural assumptions may be problematic.

Questions

1 Assuming a flexible exchange rate regime and perfect capital mobility, evaluate the Mundell–Fleming model's predictions concerning the effect on income of a monetary expansion based on: (i) domestic open-market operation (OMO); and (ii) foreign exchange market operation (FXO).

2 Assuming imperfect capital mobility and fixed exchange rates, evaluate the Mundell–Fleming model's predictions concerning the effect on income of a fiscal expansion financed by: (i) central bank credits, and (ii) government sale of bonds.

3 Under flexible exchange rates and perfect capital mobility, fiscal policy is completely ineffective because the current account deficit cannot be large enough to ensure that the domestic currency depreciates. Discuss.

4 To what extent is sterilisation (neutralisation) feasible when the stabilisation tool chosen under a fixed exchange rate regime is monetary policy?

5 Explain why the demand for money may be affected by changes in the exchange rate. Assuming perfect capital mobility, discuss the likely implications of your finding for the effectiveness of monetary and fiscal policies under flexible exchange rates.

6 Assuming perfect capital mobility and fixed exchange rates, analyse the impact of a fiscal expansion on output, interest rates, central bank reserves, and the current account of the expanding country. What would you conclude about the desirability of fiscal policy as a stabilisation tool?

7 Assume that the governments of four countries are willing to use either fiscal or monetary policies to increase output. Which policy is more effective in achieving the objective of increased output given the following scenarios:

(a) Country A has a fixed exchange rate regime and is faced with a horizontal aggregate supply (AS) schedule.

(b) Country B has a flexible exchange rate regime and is faced with a positively sloping AS schedule.

    (c) Country C has a fixed exchange rate and is faced with a vertical AS schedule.

    (d) Country D has a flexible exchange rate and is faced with a vertical AS schedule.

For each case, comment on factors that may render the fiscal or monetary policy less effective and/or desirable than what the MF model would suggest.

Further reading and references

FURTHER READING

For the derivation of the MF model and its application in the context of stabilisation policy, consult Dernburg (1989), chapters 5 and 6. For the algebra of the MF model, see Argy (1994), ch. 6 and Williamson and Milner (1991), pp. 273–6. For an empirical assessment of the impact of stabilisation policy, see Bryant *et al.* (1989). Consult Argy (1994), ch. 8, on the MF model with wage and price flexibility. On this, see also Stevenson *et al.* (1988), pp. 257–65. For an introductory, yet rigorous, treatment of the stabilisation policy under the MF model, see Sachs and Larrain (1993), chs 13 and 14.

REFERENCES

Argy, V. (1994) *International Macroeconomics: Theory and Policy*, London: Routledge.

Bryant, R., J. Helliwell and P. Hooper (1989) 'Domestic and cross-border consequences of US macroeconomic policy', in R.C. Bryant, D.A. Currie, J.A. Frenkel, P. Masson and R. Portes (eds) (1989) *Macroeconomic Policies in an Interdependent World*, Washington, DC: IMF.

Dernburg, T.F. (1989) *Global Macroeconomics*, New York: Harper & Row.

Sachs, J.D. and F.B. Larrain (1993) *Macroeconomics in the Global Economy*, New York: Harvester-Wheatsheaf.

Stevenson, A., V. Muscatelli and M. Gregory (1988) *Macroeconomic Theory and Stabilisation Policy*, Hemel Hempstead: Philip Allan.

Williamson, J. and C. Milner (1991) *The World Economy: A Textbook in International Economics*, New York: Harvester-Wheatsheaf.

Part II

Expenditure-switching policy

Devaluation and balance of payments adjustment

Introduction

The two articles in this part examine the theories of balance of payments (BoP) adjustment. Although both articles cover more or less the same ground, they complement each other in a significant way. The contribution by Taylor takes the reader through the evolution of the debate over time and enables him/her to place each theory in a historical context. Williamson and Milner's contribution examines the same issues, but it is more relevant for those interested in the analytical tools that can be used for formalising the theories reviewed by Taylor. Given this complementarity, the reader should be able not only to acquire an insight into the analytical core of each theory, but also to place it in a historical context.

Two conclusions that can be derived readily from Part II are that the debate has a long history and that it is marked with controversy. My reading of the two articles points out another, albeit less apparent, conclusion. Irrespective of the controversy, there is a core issue common to all BoP adjustment theories. This is the link between BoP disequilibria and relative prices, which is shared even by the specie-flow and global monetarist approaches that treat BoP disequilibria as essentially monetary phenomena. Before substantiating this argument, an outline of the two articles is in order.

What is obvious from Taylor's account is the fact that developments in the BoP debate are essentially parallel to the debate in macroeconomics in general. For example, the specie-flow mechanism, which was formalised by Hume and remained intact until the early twentieth century, is in line with the classical tradition. With parities fixed against gold and output determined at the full-employment level, any BoP surplus (deficit) is bound to lead to an increase (decrease) in money supply, which, in turn, leads to a rise (fall) in domestic prices. As domestic prices rise (fall) due to a BoP surplus (deficit), competitiveness deteriorates (improves) and the BoP returns to equilibrium.

The elasticities approach was closely related to another major school in economics – the marginalists. Faced with reservations about the desirability of fixed parities in a period of recessionary pressure, the elasticities approach was concerned about the benefits of relaxing the discipline imposed by the gold standard – i.e. devaluing national currencies against gold. Assuming that the country is a price-taker in the world market and that the elasticities of supply for exports and imports are infinite, a devaluation (i.e. a change in relative prices) would improve the BoP if the absolute sum of demand elasticities for exports and imports is greater than one. This is nothing but the Marshall–Lerner condition of the marginalist school. While Taylor's article sets the historical context and provides an introduction, the article by Williamson and Milner provides an algebraic as well as diagrammatical exposition of how this conclusion can be derived.

The absorption approach to the BoP is also associated with a major development in macroeconomic analysis – the 'Keynesian revolution'. In line with Keynes, the proponents of the absorption approach assume that the national income is determined by expenditures. Therefore, their main concern was about the change in export and import expenditures, which may be caused not only by a change in relative prices but also by a change in income. In other words, they are interested in a general equilibrium analysis of the BoP adjustment. In doing this, they implicitly accept the basic argument of the elasticities approach: a change in relative prices (i.e. devaluation) affects the demand for exports and imports, and hence the BoP. It is on this basis that the absorption approach can proceed to evaluate the effects of the devaluation on income, which are described as the idle resources effect, the resource allocation effect, and the terms-of-trade effect.

It is obvious that the impact of devaluation on the use of idle resources (if any exist) and resource allocation between tradable and non-tradable goods would depend on elasticities. This impact will be positive (negative) if the Marshall–Lerner condition is (not) satisfied. In the case of the terms-of-trade effect, the role of elasticities and the Marshall–Lerner condition may be less obvious, but it is still important. The impact of devaluation on the terms of trade (hence, on income) would depend on relative products of the supply and demand elasticities. If the product of the supply elasticities of exports and imports is larger (smaller) than the product of demand elasticities for exports and imports, devaluation will lead to deterioration (improvement) in income.

Despite this common ground, the absorption approach distances itself from the elasticities approach for a justified reason. It argues that the net effect of the devaluation on the BoP would depend not only on relevant elasticities, but also on the change in income and absorption, which would have repercussions on the BoP. Any increase in income due to an improvement in the BoP (which is brought about by a devaluation) is bound to lead to an increase in imports, and hence a deterioration in the BoP. The net balance, then, must depend on the impact of the devaluation on income and absorption, where the latter is defined as the sum of private- and public-sector expenditures. Therefore, and as long as we are not certain that devaluation leads to a larger change in income compared to absorption, devaluation must be followed by expenditure reducing (absorption-reducing) policies to ensure an improvement in the BoP.

The global monetarist approach is closely related to the monetarist debate in macroeconomics. Yet, in terms of its policy recommendation, it shares common ground with the essentially Keynesian absorption approach. It considers BoP disequilibria as monetary phenomena and treats the BoP adjustment as a stock rather than flow equilibrium. In this respect, the global monetarist approach is also in the tradition of the specie-flow mechanism – albeit the specie-flow mechanism to which it subscribes is put upside down. It begins not with the impact of BoP disequilibrium on money supply and prices, but with the impact of money market disequilibria on prices and the BoP. As long as the domestic credit component of the money supply (the only variable under the policy-maker's control) increases faster than the demand for money, the domestic credit expansion will lead to an increase in demand for foreign assets (due to portfolio adjustment) as well as for foreign goods (to maintain a given cash-balance ratio). Therefore, the BoP will deteriorate. Then, an improvement in the BoP would require monetary tightening (i.e. a reduction in absorption). This is a policy recommendation that the absorption approach would have nothing to quarrel with.

Taylor's article outlines and assesses the various attempts at deriving a synthesis from the global monetarist and absorption approaches (see, for example, Frenkel *et al.*, 1980; Tsiang, 1961). A synthesis may still be elusive, but such attempts have mitigated some of the heat that the debate had generated and induced the students of open-economy macroeconomics to adopt a more eclectic view. In what follows, we will add another reason why eclecticism may be justified – not as a solution to the controversy, but as a basis for further reflection.

As indicated earlier, a thread common to all BoP theories is the issue of relative prices. In the specie-flow and global monetarist approaches, the preoccupation is with the effect of BoP disequilibrium on relative prices. The elasticities and absorption approaches, on the other hand, are concerned with the effect of relative prices on the BoP. Because of their assumptions concerning output determination, the specie-flow and global monetarist approaches arrive at the conclusion that expenditure-switching policies (e.g. devaluation) will lead only to a temporary improvement in the balance of payments. In the case of elasticities and absorption approaches, the improvement in the BoP can be permanent provided that the Marshall–Lerner condition holds or expenditure-switching is followed by expenditure-reducing policies. We would argue that only the elasticities approach can provide a microfoundation for the analysis of the effect of relative prices on the BoP and vice versa. Let us give two examples to demonstrate why this is the case.

Consider the impact of devaluation on income in the absorption approach. Three such impacts have been identified: the idle resource effect, the resource allocation effect and the terms-of-trade effect. In the case of the first two effects, the anticipation is that devaluation would lead to an improvement in the BoP and income. The implicit assumption here is that the Marshall–Lerner condition holds – i.e. the absolute sum of demand elasticities for export and import is greater than one. Unless the Marshall–Lerner condition is satisfied, the recommendation concerning absorption-reducing policies would be disastrous: devaluation will lead to a fall in income and this fall will be exacerbated by absorption-reducing policies. In the case of the terms-of-trade effect, the devaluation's impact on income depends on the products of supply and demand elasticities. If the product of supply elasticities is larger (smaller) than the product of demand elasticities, devaluation will lead to a fall (increase) in income. Therefore, the absorption approach cannot just ignore the elasticities analysis on the grounds that the latter ignores the impact of devaluation on income. The elasticities approach may well be criticised for its partial equilibrium approach focusing only on export and import markets, but any attempt at conducting a general equilibrium analysis must incorporate elasticities. Otherwise, the results will remain suspect and the policy recommendation may well be disastrous.

Now consider the specie-flow and global monetarist approaches. In these approaches, BoP disequilibria are essentially monetary phenomena, constitute only temporary deviations, and have no effect on income. Therefore, one is led to think that the elasticities have no role to play in such models. However, this is misleading. In the case of the specie-flow mechanism, BoP disequilibrium is reflected into the money market and domestic prices, which, eventually, must affect export and import expenditures. In fact, the effect of prices on export and import expenditures is the main channel through which BoP disequilibria are eliminated. Then, the elasticities must be considered to ascertain not only whether the BoP will adjust but also the speed at which the adjustment will take place. If the elasticities of demand for exports and imports are large (i.e. if the Marshall–Lerner condition holds), the adjustment process will work in the predicted direction. In other words, a BoP surplus (deficit) will lead to an increase (decrease) in domestic prices, which, in turn, lead to a deterioration (improvement) in the BoP. In addition, the larger the elasticities are, the faster is the speed of adjustment. If, however, the elasticities are small (i.e. if the Marshall–Lerner condition does not hold), BoP disequilibria will be self-perpetuating. In other words, an increase (decrease) in prices caused by a BoP surplus (deficit) may not eliminate the surplus (deficit) – in fact, it may perpetuate it.

In the case of global monetarism, the scenario is just the other way round. Money market disequilibrium leads to disequilibrium in the BoP, which can be corrected by intervention into the money market. The global monetarist approach argues that such intervention into the money market will affect only portfolios and not expenditures. This argument, however, is problematic. As Currie (1976) has argued, domestic credits can change with no corresponding change in the assets held by the private sector. Therefore, the change in domestic credit (hence the change in money supply) must have 'real' repercussions on expenditures in general and current account expenditures in particular. The effect on current account expenditures can be identified accurately only if the demand elasticities for exports and imports are known.

There are two tentative conclusions that can be derived from the brief analysis above. First, the debate on BoP adjustment has undoubtedly improved our understanding of the open economy. This improvement has essentially been in the form of providing vital pieces that would enable us to complete the jigsaw puzzle. We are now aware of the fact that BoP adjustment must be analysed in both 'real' and monetary terms. Second, the provided pieces do not fit together yet. That is mainly because the designers of a particular piece have not taken into account the contours of the pieces designed by others. Therefore, the task is to refine the shapes of each particular piece (i.e. contribution to the debate) so that the probability of a fit is increased. I think one step in that direction is to incorporate the export and import elasticities explicitly into all models of BoP adjustment. I hope the articles in Part II will inspire fresh ideas in this direction.

REFERENCES

Currie, D. (1976) 'Some criticism of the monetary analysis of balance of payments correction', *The Economic Journal* 86, January, 508–22.

Frenkel, J.A., T. Gylfason and J.F. Helliwell (1980) 'A synthesis of monetary and Keynesian approaches to short-run balance of payments theory', *The Economic Journal* 90, 582–92.

Tsiang, S.C. (1961) 'The role of money in trade-balance stability: synthesis of the elasticities and absorption approaches', *American Economic Review* 51, 912–36.

5   A history of thought on the balance of payments

Mark P. Taylor
The Balance of Payments: New Perspectives in Open Economy Macroeconomics, Edward Elgar (1990), pp. 1–24, 28–42

> He shewed me a very excellent argument to prove, that our importing lesse than we export, do not impoverish the Kingdom, according to the received opinion; which, though it be a paradox, and that I do not remember the argument, yet methought there was a great deal in what he said
>
> (Samuel Pepys, *Memoirs*, 29 February 1663)

INTRODUCTION

International economics is that branch of the discipline which deals with the relationships between distinct economic systems normally identified in the real world with distinct nation states. It may be broadly dichotomized into two areas. The first area, international trade theory, can be seen as an extension of value theory, since its primary concern is with resource allocation and the gains from trade. International monetary economics, as the second branch has become known, may be thought of as an extension of closed-economy macroeconomics, its concern being characterized as the analysis of sets of macro policy targets with respect to external budget constraints. A further subdivision is possible if one wishes to consider both fixed and flexible exchange rate regimes. This chapter will be concerned almost exclusively with international monetary theory developed within the framework of fixed exchange rates, i.e. balance of payments theory.

The idea of an aggregate external budget constraint is encapsulated in the concept of the balance of payments. Since, however, by the conventions of double-entry book-keeping, the balance of payments must always by definition balance, it is necessary to take some subset of the accounts as an indicator of how far constraints are being met; this leads to the distinction between autonomous and accommodating flows. Another problem is that the constraint may not be strictly met in every period – countries may be in 'deficit' or 'surplus'. In what sense then can the constraint be binding? Just like individual households, economies can insert an extra degree of freedom into their current-period financial decisions by borrowing or lending against a future period: the problem is intertemporal. Two points can be made in this connection. The first is that homely maxims such as 'good households balance their books' have spilled over into traditional economic policy, so that analysis has been channelled into correcting one-period imbalances. The second is that the economist's traditional tool in this area, as in much of economics, has been comparative statics rather than intertemporal dynamics. Thus, as we shall see, the literature has traditionally tended to focus on the current account or balance of trade in any one period as a measure of imbalance and, as Krueger notes, has addressed the following question:

> given any situation in which *ex ante* receipts must be increased relative to *ex ante* payments, what are the alternative mechanisms by which this can be accomplished?
>
> (Krueger, 1969)

PRE-KEYNESIAN THEORY

Prior to the 1930s, most questions in the field of international monetary economics were considered as having been settled with a decisiveness unusual even for a discipline which had hitherto displayed an unusual degree of self-confidence. The framework of analysis had been forged mainly by British economists in the eighteenth and nineteenth centuries and was still wearing well without the apparent need for overhaul. But this framework itself had evolved from an earlier system of thought regarding the international monetary mechanism: mercantilism.

Mercantilism

'Mercantile' was the term applied originally by Adam Smith (1776, IV) to a heterogeneous group of pamphleteers active between the late fifteenth and early eighteenth centuries. More generally, Viner has defined 'mercantilist' as applying to 'the doctrine and practices of nation states in [this] period . . . with respect to the appropriate regulation of economic relations' (Viner, 1968). That this term implies a more consistent and self-contained school of thought than was actually the case is certain. Unlike, for example, the physiocrats, the mercantilists never presented a common front and definite school of opinion. Nevertheless, as an indicator of the central tendency of the content of the literature in question, the term is useful, although that content has an undoubtedly high variance.

The dominant strands of thought that together make up the mercantilist outlook are well known: the idea of treasure and bullion as the essence of wealth (an idea inherited from an earlier school – the bullionists, see Seligman, 1930), encouragement of exports, particularly labour-intensive ones, and the idea of international trade as a zero-sum game and so of the general mutual antagonism of nation states. Other important themes were protectionism, an emphasis on population growth and hence low-level wages, a stress on the relationship between economics and power politics, and the idea of supremacy of the State over the individual. But the core of the system, for which it is chiefly remembered, is the so-called balance of trade doctrine: the idea that a surplus on the balance of trade is a measure of the nation's welfare and the consequent advocacy of running a permanent balance of trade surplus.

A major problem in assessing the contribution of this literature is the absence of anything approximating to a disciplined approach to the subject. This is essentially preanalytic economics put forward by practical men of affairs. As a result, we often find terms inconsistently used (often by the same author), arguments rambling in and out and on and off the subject and the copious propagation of fallacies and paradoxes. Nevertheless, Schumpeter has praised this work for introducing one of the first analytic tools into the field – the idea of the balance of trade:

> The balance of trade is not a concrete thing like a price or a load of merchandise. It does not obtrude upon untrained eyes. A definite analytic effort is required to visualise it and to perceive its relation to other economic phenomena, however insignificant that effort may be.
>
> (Schumpeter, 1954, p. 352)

The dominant idea that a positive balance of trade is an index of national welfare is summed up in the title of Thomas Mun's pamphlet: 'England's Treasure by Forraign Trade, or the Ballance of our Forraign Trade is the Rule of our Treasure' (Mun, 1664). And again:

> The ordinary means therefore to encrease our wealth and treasure is by Forraign Trade, wherein wee must ever observ this rule; to sell more to strangers yearly than wee consume of theirs in value.
>
> (Mun, 1664, ch. 2)

Exactly why a balance of trade surplus should be beneficial to the nation has been a source of discussion ever since. The point is that if an inflow of specie concomitant to a trade surplus is not spent in a subsequent period (since the idea is to run a *permanent* surplus) then the only effect will be to increase the money supply. One possibility is that these writers falsely equated money with capital and a favourable balance of trade with the annual balance of income over consumption by incorrectly drawing an analogy between the economics of the individual and of the whole economy (what was later called the anthropomorphic view of economics – see Kaldor, 1983; McCloskey, 1983). This was Smith's line of attack. Some of the best mercantilist writers, Smith conceded,

> do set out with observing, that the wealth of a country consists, not in gold and silver only, but in its lands, houses, and consumable goods of all different kinds; in the course of their reasonings, however, the lands, houses, and consumable goods seem to slip out of their memory, and the strain of the argument frequently supposes that all wealth consists in gold and silver.
>
> (Smith, 1776)

Now, it is true that some writers concentrate on the accumulation of specie as a store of wealth *per se* without reference to the level of consumption or production; or when production is mentioned, it is with reference to the contribution it could make to the further acquisition and retention of treasure. Others, however, saw the acquisition of specie not as an end in itself but as a means to increase the money supply and hence production and employment, stressing the importance of circulation of the surplus rather than mere hoarding. Evidence of this line of thought can be found, for example, in the work of Petty (1662) and later Law (1705). There are essentially two related points being made here. The first is that an increase in the money supply increases general liquidity in the form of working capital or merchant capital and hence is conducive to an increase in economic activity. In terms of the quantity equation, these authors are stressing the relationship between money and output rather than money and prices. A second, closely related point is the increase in the general availability of credit, decline in interest rates and further spur to activity. This is the strand of thought that Keynes picked up in his apologia of the school:

> as a contribution to statecraft which is concerned with the economic system as a whole and with securing the optimum employment of the system's entire resources, the methods of the early pioneers of economic thinking in the early sixteenth and seventeenth centuries may have attained to fragments of practical wisdom which the unrealistic abstractions of Ricardo first forgot and then obliterated.
>
> (Keynes, 1936, ch. 23)

Locke (1691), opposing Petty's advocacy of a maximum rate of interest, had discussed the inverse relationship between the quantity of money and the rate of interest. Thus:

> Mercantilists were conscious that their policy, as Professor Heckscher puts it, 'killed two birds with one stone'. 'On the one hand the country was rid of an unwelcome surplus of goods, which was believed to result in unemployment, while on the other the total stock of money in the country was increased', with the resulting advantages of a fall in the rate of interest.
>
> (Keynes, 1936, quoting from Heckscher, 1931)

Now, according to Keynes, 'The weakness of the inducement to invest has been at all times the key to the economic problem' (ibid.), and so he argues that the policy prescriptions of the mercantilists were correct insofar as an inflow of specie would depress the interest rate and stimulate investment. Since the economic problem in Keynes's era, as he perceived it, was too large a capital stock relative to labour, so that the marginal efficiency of investment was below the market rate of interest, a fall in the interest rate would give the required fillip to the economic system; and this could be achieved by allowing the money supply to drift upwards. In Hicksian terms (Hicks, 1937) the initial impact of a balance of trade surplus will be a rightward shift of the IS curve, as the injection drives up both income and interest rates. But as the surplus is maintained indefinitely, the inflow of specie in each period causes the LM curve to drift to the right, i.e. there is downward pressure on interest rates and a consequent movement along the IS curve down to the right (Figure 5.1). As long as the new level of real income (y′) is below full-employment level, qualitative results will be unaffected by the upward pressure on prices (hence the stress on the relationship between money and output holding prices (and velocity) constant).

For the classical economists, the implicit acceptance of Say's Law meant that the economy was always at full employment, so that all nominal variables in the system would increase in proportion commensurate with the increase in the money stock on top of the demand-induced inflationary effects. Thus, the impact of both the exogenous increase in aggregate demand and the induced increase in the money supply would be to raise both the price level and nominal interest rates, with the (full-employment) level of income remaining constant throughout and the balance of trade falling to zero as domestic prices rise.

Thus, Keynes rejects Say's Law and looks for support in the literature of a period before it was propagated. This analysis is flawed, however.

As we have pointed out, the problem in the 1930s, as Keynes saw it, was too large a capital–labour ratio, moreover, 'there has been a chronic tendency throughout human history for the propensity to save to be stronger than the inducement to invest' (Keynes, 1936), so that the flow of investment would be too little to mop up the flow of savings that would be forthcoming at a full-employment level of income. In the era of the mercantilist writers, by way of

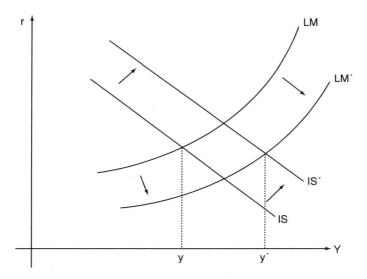

Figure 5.1 The Keynes–Hicks interpretation of mercantilism

contrast, the problem was a paucity of fixed capital relative to labour – a low technical and organic composition of capital; the problem was that there was too little thrift, not too much. In such a case it seems probable that an increase in the money supply would lead to an increase in prices rather than economic activity, as the classicals maintained. As Heckscher notes:

> So far from being a 'general' theory, Keynes' theory is appropriate to a situation which could scarcely exist in the absence of fixed capital investment on a large scale.
>
> (Hecksher, 1955, II, p. 356).

Nevertheless, despite Keynes's rather cavalier treatment of the history of economic thought and penchant to generalize problems of his own time throughout history, his insight into the 'element of truth in mercantilist doctrine' is perhaps not totally misguided. Insofar as the inflow of specie introduced extra liquidity into the economy, entrepreneurship would obviously be facilitated. As we have noted, the classical economists sought to refute this by pointing to price increases. But the mercantilists themselves were not totally ignorant of the effect on prices, and for some this was an important element of the stimulus to trade – see, for example, Law, 1705; Venderlint, 1734; and George Berkeley, 1737. Moreover, for Marx's interpretation of the school, price increases formed an essential part of the doctrine, along with the emphasis on labour-intensive exports and low wages:

> The basis of their theory was the idea that labour is only productive in those branches of production whose products, when sent abroad, bring back more money than they have cost (or than had to be exported in exchange for them); which therefore enabled a country to participate to a greater degree in the products of newly-opened gold and silver mines. They saw that in these countries there was rapid growth of wealth and of the middle class. What in fact was this source of influence exerted by gold? Wages did not rise in proportion to the prices of commodities; that is, wages fell, and because of this relative surplus labour increased and the rate of profit rose – not because the labourer had become more productive but because the absolute wage (that is to say, the quantity of means of existence which the labourer received) was forced down – in a word because the position of the workers grew worse.
>
> (Marx, 1963, p. 154)

In other words surplus value is expanded by cheapening the real cost of labour-power and so the rate of exploitation is raised,

> and it was this, though they were only dimly aware of it, which led the mercantilists to declare that labour employed in such branches of production was alone productive.
>
> (Ibid.)

The real source of Marx's discontent with mercantilism was, however, due to its corollary that value can be created in (international) exchange.

Whilst many economists would disagree with Marx's interpretation, his basic insight into mercantilist ideology is not totally unfounded. Mercantilism was a general social *Weltanschauung* as well as economic doctrine. It advocated the supremacy of the State over its individual constituents, it championed the role of State regulation and institutions such as the various merchant societies and the East India Company. The mercantilist view of a static economic order had its corollary in the idea of international trade as a zero-sum game (of which view Colbert was the notable exponent) which paved the way for the commercial wars of the seventeenth and eighteenth centuries and left the British navigation system and the colonial system as its legacy. In brief, the view was of the mutual political (and hence economic) antagonism of states and of the desire for power; and it was the ratio of power rather than the terms of the ratio which mattered.

All this, of course, was morally repugnant to the children of the Enlightenment, the classical economists; and it was really an ideological shift rather than the discovery of new facts which led to the rise of *laissez-faire*.

It is sometimes asserted that Hume's essay 'On the Balance of Trade' (1752), with its clear exposition of the specie-flow mechanism, rang the death knell of mercantilism; but the doctrine was in its decadence well before this time. It is true that the specie-flow mechanism constituted a refutation of mercantilist doctrine, but like many intellectual revolutions the shift was gradual (see Kuhn, 1970).

The idea of a specie-flow mechanism may be seen as a logically consistent integration of three basic elements:

(i)   The recognition that trade deficits/surpluses are paid in specie.
(ii) The idea of a causal connection between the money supply and the level of prices.
(iii) The idea that exports and imports are both functions of, *inter alia*, relative international prices.

Now (i) was itself an important element of mercantilism, of course, and we have already pointed out that various mercantilists (e.g. Locke) held a quantity theory of money (i.e. proposition (ii)) in varying degrees. It only therefore required the addition of (iii) and the integration of all three elements to point up the logical inconsistency in mercantilism.

Locke (1691) comes very close to the idea of an international distribution of specie and even performs the Humean experiment of imagining the overnight disappearance of half of the English money stock. This, however, is really nothing more than a crude quantity theory; step (iii) is still missing and Locke remains a mercantilist.

Again, North (1691) approaches the formulation of an autonomous and self-regulating mechanism which provides the economy with the 'determinate sum of specific money' required for carrying on the trade of the nation, but stops short of relating this to an international price mechanism and speaks instead of money being minted or melted down.

In 1720 Gervaise advanced the proposition that 'the grand real measure or denominator of the real value of all things' (i.e. gold) tends to be distributed internationally according to population, since only labour (-power) can attract specie:

> When a nation has attracted a greater proportion of the grand denominator of the world than its proper share, and the cause of that attraction ceases, that nation cannot retain the overplus of its proper proportion of the grand denominato.
>
> (Gervaise, 1720, p. 5)

Other works could be cited, but it has been demonstrated that the basic elements of the specie-flow mechanism had been discussed with varying degrees of clarity, before Hume. It was, however, Hume's genius to rationalize all these elements together in a consistent theory.

The road to *laissez-faire*: Hobbes to Smith

The twin pillars of mercantilism, then, were the balance of trade doctrine and the idea of the zero-sum nature of economic relations. To the classical economists, who discovered in particular the specie-flow mechanism and the law of comparative costs, and in general the overall harmony of apparently conflicting economic interests, this seemed like error compounded upon error. If the mercantilist era was marked by the idea of State supremacy, the rise of *laissez-faire* saw the apotheosis of the individual, at least in an atomistic sense. Again, however, this ideological shift was the end process of a barely perceptible flux rather than a sudden break, and an attempt here is made to chart only the landmarks of this development.

Smith's importance in the development of modern economic ideas springs essentially from his moral philosophy as expounded in *The Theory of Moral Sentiments* (1759) and applied in the *Wealth of Nations* (1776). Nevertheless, his ideas can be seen as the last stages in a more general eighteenth-century reaction to Hobbes's selfish system. Hobbes (1651) expressed the basically malevolent nature of man's character and pointed to it as a potential source of conflict between all men ('*bellum omnium contra omnes*'). So for him, selfishness was the basis of all human activity and the corollary was that society is impossible without coercive State intervention; each man must enter into a social contract with every other man to give up his individual rights in order to obtain security from the State. Thus the 'great Leviathan' or 'common-wealth' is formed. Hence, political organization is not simply concerned with the organization of a society that has emerged from the natural and spontaneous tendency of man to build up a web of stable reciprocal relationships; it is rather the means that men, driven by fear, must employ to counteract the natural tendency towards dispersion; it is in fact the prerequisite or *sine qua non* of social, and hence economic, life.

Locke (1690) was among the first to react to Hobbes's pessimistic world-view by asserting man's essential goodness. For Locke, societal conflicts arise not because of man's intrinsic malevolence but from the natural scarcity of economic resources: since not everyone can acquire property as the fruits of their labour, some will attempt to expropriate the property of others. Hence, although society is based upon the naturally social and cooperative nature of men, it is constantly threatened by pressures arising from the parsimony of Nature. Thus, for Locke, the State is not the prerequisite of society, but a guarantor of its permanence as an organ that, *inter alia*, protects property by force of law. State authority does not, as Hobbes thought, imply an alienation of individual liberty, but is rather the instrument through which liberty can be fully defined and protected from any attack or emergence of disorder.

However, the argument for the original rise of society in Locke is given to rationality, a law of reason: against the irrationalism of Hobbes's natural state of strife and discord Locke puts forward the concept of a rational law which at times he traces back to the Deity. But when, according to Locke's empiricist method, the origin of cognition is in sensible experience, this kind of approach is inadmissible. There is thus a dichotomy in Locke's work between a rationalistic approach, and an empirical approach that comes to dominate the development of his ideas, but which is nevertheless contradictory to his original premise.

Hume's (1751) attempt to solve this problem was tantamount to embracing the 'moral sense theory' of Hutcheson (Smith's teacher), according to which there naturally exists in man's psyche a 'sentiment' that, as opposed to selfishness, is associated with a desire to do good, in the sense of affording utility to others and being conducive to social harmony. In fact, Hume did not so much solve the problem as dissolve it into psychology; the development of Hume's system is still impossible unless one goes outside his empiricism, primarily because a methodological framework based on psychological sense impression is inadequate for an analysis of fundamental moral concepts – as Kant was to point out (Kant, 1790).

All this set the stage for Smith. For him, the dual nature of man, the coexistence of self-interest and fellow feeling, was not a stumbling block but in fact the Archimedean point upon which to base his whole system. Smith crystallizes the dichotomy in British psychological ethics and at the same time in a sense resolves it, by separating human activity into two spheres: a moral sphere in which societal utility is derived from the exercise of 'sympathy' and an economic sphere in which utility is consequent upon individual self-interest. This makes it possible to avoid the conflict between selfishness and humanity. The main point of Smith's thesis is that selfishness need not be a disruptive element in society but can instead be conducive to order and development, so long as certain prerequisites are satisfied. Sufficient (and perhaps necessary) conditions are that one man's pursuit of gain does not hinder another's; hence the call for *laissez-faire* and the sweeping away of institutional impediments.

This shift in moral philosophy had a profound influence on economists' perceptions of the functioning of society and hence the economy. From the selfish and internecine world of Hobbes and the mercantilists, analysis gradually turned to the naturally harmonious systems of the classical economists.

The specie-flow mechanism

Despite Smith's trenchant attack on the 'mercantile system', he does not mention the specie-flow mechanism in the *Wealth of Nations*, although there is evidence to suggest that he referred to it in his *Glasgow Lectures* (1896). As we have noted, it was Hume (1752) who published the first clear, systematic account of the mechanism, although Cantillon (1755) also discussed something similar. Hume's exposition is admirably clear. The assumption of Say's Law of markets and the impossibility of a general glut is grafted on to the inherited notions of the quantity theory to forge a definite causal connection between the money supply and the level of prices. Little more than an intuitive notion of the laws of supply and demand are then needed to derive the 'Automatic Mechanism': a trade imbalance (e.g. surplus) leads to a change in the money supply (inflow of specie) and hence in relative prices (home/ export prices rise absolutely, foreign/import prices decline relatively) which automatically leads to a correction of the imbalance – the system exhibits homeostasis. As an intellectual experiment, Hume imagines four-fifths of the English money stock to be wiped out overnight. Implicitly accepting Say's Law, he posits that all nominal variables decline in the same proportion:

> What nation could then dispute with us in any foreign market, or pretend to navigate or to sell manufactures at the same price, which to us would afford sufficient profit? In how little time, therefore, must this bring back the money which we had lost, and raise us to the level of all the neighbouring nations? Where, after we have arrived, we immediately lose the advantage of the cheapness of labour and commodities; and farther flowing in of money is stopped.
>
> (Hume, 1752)

Further, money is attracted in proportion to the 'degree of industry' in the economy, so that countries with, for example, a more productive labour force will be able to sustain a higher level of money stock. An analogy is drawn between an international economic system and a system of hydraulics, where the capaciousness of any particular vessel represents the 'degree of industry' of an economy:

> All water, wherever it communicates, remains always at a level. Ask naturalists the reason; they tell you, that, were it to be raised in any place, the

superior gravity of that part not being balanced, must depress it, till it meet a counterpoise.

(Ibid.)

Similarly, 'it is impossible to heap up money, more than any fluid, beyond its proper level' (ibid.).

Thus, there exists a 'natural distribution of specie' among nations. This idea is not to be confused with the mercantilist doctrine that industry, especially export industry, is only necessary where there does not already exist a natural supply of precious metals; an increase in the money supply from whatever source will be illusory unless it is coupled with increased industry. Hume cites the Great Inflation:

Can one imagine, that it had ever been possible, by any laws, or even by any art or industry, to have kept all the money in Spain, which the galleons have brought from the Indies? Or that all commodities could be sold in France for a tenth of the price which they would yield on the other side of the Pyrenees, without finding their way thither, and draining from that immense treasure?

(Ibid.)

In Hume's account, then, changes in price levels play the predominant role in bringing about the necessary adjustment of trade balances, and the additional correcting factor of exchange rate movements is held to be of minor importance. This was a major achievement in international monetary economics which was to hold the centre stage in that field until at least the first quarter of the present century, and which has seen a recrudescence in various forms in various quarters more recently.

Nevertheless, although the Humean foundations remained intact for a century and a half, substantial additions were made to the edifice. Thornton (1802) applied the Humean framework to the disturbance entailed by a crop failure bringing about increased imports of grain. Wheatley (1807), anticipating the Keynesian concept of effective demand, argued that the fall in output would lead to a fall in general demand, thus compensating for the increased grain imports by allowing more to be exported. Ricardo (1810) also argued against Thornton but with much less cogent reasoning. His argument was that Hume's analysis could not be applied to disturbances of a non-monetary nature; not because of their tendency to be temporary. Assuming next year's crop does not fail, any adjustment of specie levels and relative prices will have to be reversed later, so why bother? Ricardo gives no real reason as to why seasonal movements of specie should be precluded.

Ricardo's most significant contribution in this area was to synthesize the law of comparative costs and the idea of a natural distribution of specie (Ricardo, 1821) with consequent implications for relative wages and prices, leaving the details to be worked out by Nassau Senior 10 years later (Senior, 1830). John Stuart Mill (1848) further elaborated this Seniorian doctrine by adding the complication of transport costs into the analysis. Moreover, although Mill accepts Hume's thesis, complete with its emphasis on movements in the terms of trade, he makes two important extensions. Firstly, and most importantly, he shows that an inflow of specie causes interest rates to decline, thus causing an outflow of capital and an exchange rate adjustment – hence grafting the foreign exchange market and the capital account on to the analysis. Mill was also one of the earliest economists to recommend the use of Bank Rate as a method of protecting reserves and exchange rates, although this idea is often credited to Gossen (1854).

In essence, then, Hume's was the balance of payments theory that economists were still working with in the 1920s and 1930s, and perhaps even up to the outbreak of the Second World War. The Marginalist revolution associated with the names of Menger, Jevons, Walras and Marshall left the thesis virtually intact. If anything, the theory was strengthened. Pigou (1932), for example, applies marginal utility functions to what is essentially a Humean analysis of the effect of war reparations on the terms of trade.

Viner, in 1937, could write:

> The 'classical' theory of the mechanism of international trade, as developed from Hume to J.S. Mill, is still, in its general lines, the predominant theory. No strikingly different mechanism, moreover, has yet been convincingly suggested, although there has been gain in precision of analysis, and some correction of undoubted error.
>
> (Viner, 1937, p. 291)

Short-run marginalism: the elasticities approach

The conventional wisdom in the first quarter of this century, then, was still along distinctly Humean lines, albeit with modifications made to allow for, *inter alia*, the effects of interest rates on capital movements; a fractional reserve banking system (this was the major upshot of the so-called Bullionist controversy, see for example, Ricardo, 1810, Viner, 1937, chs III and IV); and an explicit recognition of the similarity between gold movements and changes in foreign balances. We have noted how this body of theory was left unscathed by the Marginalist revolution. Nevertheless, a (largely complementary) body of balance of payments theory did grow out of marginalism. This was essentially a short-run orientated body of analysis which became known as the 'elasticities approach' and which still survives in one form or another to the present day. The crux of this approach is embodied in a single formula.

Consider a two-country, two-good world. Let supply and demand elasticities be e_i and η_i respectively. Then it can be shown that the effect of a devaluation on country 1's balance of trade is positive if:

$$K = \frac{\eta_1 \, \eta_2 \, (1 + e_1 + e_2) + e_1 \, e_2 \, (\eta_1 + \eta_2 - 1)}{(\eta_1 + e_2) \, (\eta_2 + e_1)} > 0 \tag{1}$$

(see, for example, Haberler, 1949). K is often called the 'elasticity of the balance of payments' (Metzler, 1948).

In particular, from (1) we have:

$$\lim_{\substack{e_1 \to \infty \\ e_2 \to \infty}} (\text{sgn } K) = \lim_{\substack{e_1 \to \infty \\ e_2 \to \infty}} (\text{sgn } (\eta_1 + \eta_2 - 1)) \tag{2}$$

From (2) we can see that, for a devaluation to improve 1's trade balance in a Keynesian model, we require:

$$(\eta_1 + \eta_2) > 1 \tag{3}$$

which is normally referred to as the Marshall–Lerner condition. Expression (1) is usually referred to as the Robinson–Metzler equation or 'four elasticities formula'.

The elasticities approach can be seen as a way of looking for sufficient conditions for there to be a balance of payments (and hence foreign exchange market) equilibrium. The Marshall–Lerner condition is in fact a sufficient condition (assuming perfectly elastic supplies) for each country's offer curve to be monotonically decreasing (equivalent to gross substitutability), which entails that any foreign exchange market equilibrium is both unique and stable. Equivalently, it implies that the supply and demand schedules for foreign exchange do not have pathological slopes (Haberler, 1949).

The elasticities approach seems to have been discovered independently by three economists. The first exposition is by Bickerdike (1920), who makes the point that short-run demand elasticities are likely to be small and so modest balance of payments imbalances may lead to an extremely volatile foreign exchange market. Metzler (1948), following Robinson (1937), argues that Bickerdike does not take adequate account of the likelihood of the stabilizing influence of the inelasticity of short-run export supply. Joan Robinson in her celebrated essay on 'The Foreign Exchanges' (1937), derives essentially similar results to Bickerdike, although she places more emphasis on inelasticity of supply. Brown (1942) presents a broadly similar analysis, although he introduces raw materials and is generally more optimistic concerning the elasticity of export demand.

These, then, are the tools that the international monetary economist had at hand in the interwar years: the (modified) specie-flow mechanism as a long-run automatic adjustment process, and the elasticities approach springing from short-run microeconomic analysis and dealing with tiny increments of economic change. The transition to a broadly Keynesian approach was, as we shall see, the outcome of a number of empirical and theoretical anomalies in international monetary economics and in economics in general. Like all scientific revolutions, the change was gradual and was attributable to more than one writer.

We have already noted anticipations of Keynes in Wheatley and J.S. Mill; contemporary pressure for change can be seen in the work of the Swedish School and particularly in that of Bertil Ohlin (e.g. Ohlin, 1928) and the exchange between Keynes and Ohlin on the 'reparations problem' in the *Economic Journal*, 1929; see also Viner, 1937, ch. 6.

KEYNES AND AFTER

The interwar period: anomalies and revolutions

We have seen that the specie-flow mechanism was based upon a quantity theory of money and therefore implicitly accepted Say's Law of markets. This was the conventional wisdom. The large-scale chronic unemployment of the 1930s generated insuperable anomalies in the orthodoxy, culminating in the Keynesian revolution of which Keynes's *General Theory* (1936) is the central landmark. This revolution fundamentally attacked Say's Law, and hence the specie-flow mechanism. But there were other, more direct, anomalies raised in the field of international monetary economics itself which also created pressure for a fundamental shift in economists' perceptions of the balancing process.

At the instigation of Taussig, a number of empirical studies were made of the international balancing process under regimes of both fixed and floating exchange rates (Williams, 1920; Viner, 1924; White, 1933; Taussig, 1928). These investigations appeared to confirm the classical adjustment theory only too well. Taussig notes:

> The actual merchandise movements seem to have been adjusted to the shifting balance of payments with surprising exactness and speed. The process which our theory contemplates – the initial flow of specie when there is a burst of loans; the fall in prices in the lending country; the eventual increased movement of merchandise out of one and into the other – all this can hardly be expected to take place smoothly and quickly. Yet no signs of disturbance are to be observed such as the theoretic analysis previses.
>
> (Taussig, 1928, p. 239)

During the same period, a prolific number of studies were made of demand elasticities (e.g. Schultz, 1937) which yielded surprisingly low estimates. Later studies enhanced these results for demand elasticities as a whole. Hinshaw (1945), for example, produced an estimate of 0.5 for US import demand elasticity and Chang (1946) presented an estimate of 0.64 for the UK. This created a mood of 'elasticity pessimism'. Metzler observed:

> Not only did the trade balances move with surprising rapidity, but they moved in the expected direction despite the fact that the physical volume of imports is normally responsive only in a slight degree to changes in

relative prices. In order to attribute the observed adjustments to changes in relative prices, it would be necessary to assume that demand elasticities are much higher than those which have actually been measured.

(Metzler, 1948, p. 215)

Thus, overemphasis on the role played by relative price changes was seen as a major defect in the classical analysis. In the words of Taussig: 'It must be confessed that here we have a phenomenon not fully understood. In part our information is insufficient; in part our understanding of other connected topics is also inadequate' (Taussig, 1928, p. 239).

After the publication of the *General Theory* the missing link seemed clear: that part of the adjustment process not achieved through relative price changes would be achieved through shifts in income and employment and hence in effective demand. The mechanism is, of course, well known and need not be spelt out here. Differences between Keynesian and classical explanations of balance of payments adjustment may be brought into relief via the following schema. Assume that there is, in a bilateral world, a trade imbalance in favour of country B against country A:

Keynesian Mechanism	*Classical Mechanism*
There is an injection into the circular flow of income in B (and a withdrawal from A)	There is an outflow of specie from A (and an inflow into B)
↓	↓
This leads to increased (decreased) effective demand in B (A)	This leads to a fall (increase) in prices in A (B)
↓	↓
Import demand rises (falls) in B (A) due to income effects	Import demand rises (falls) in B (A) due to substitution (and income) effects
↓	↓
Imbalance is corrected, perhaps with dampened cycles	Imbalance is corrected, perhaps with dampened cycles

In the Keynesian system, injections and withdrawals and changes in effective demand play the parts played respectively by specie flows and price changes in the classical mechanism. The advantage of the Keynesian analysis is that the world does not have to run on perfectly smooth lines as suggested by the classical mechanism: changes in effective demand can be transmitted even with rigid prices.

Multipliers and elasticities: some attempts at synthesis

As the situation stood in the 1950s, then, there were two distinct approaches to balance of payments theory: the elasticities approach and the Keynesian or international multipliers approach. Some attempts were therefore made to synthesize the two approaches as well as to remedy what were seen as the inadequacies of the elasticities approach – primarily its partial equilibrium nature. Formulators of the elasticities approach had implicitly assumed that income and prices remain constant after a devaluation, which is clearly unrealistic. Sohmen (1957), *inter alios*, had attempted to redefine the relevant elasticities as 'total'.

> as if all adjustments caused by devaluation had been permitted to have their ultimate influence on the price–quantity relationship for the internationally traded goods.
>
> (Clement *et al.*, 1967, p. 287)

Whilst this line of approach may have been theoretically expedient, it was useless for practical policy prescription as the computation of such 'total' elasticities was clearly out of the question.

More specific attempts to synthesize the Keynesian and elasticities approaches were witnessed by the publication of a series of papers in the 1950s (see, *inter alia*, Harberger, 1950; Johnson, 1956; Laursen and Matzler, 1950). These models essentially allowed the initial effects to be determined by the elasticities formula and then introduced secondary income and price effects. Clement *et al.* write:

> this reformulation of the traditional elasticities approach, incorporating as it did either income elasticities or marginal or average propensities to import, gave rise to even more complex stability condition formulas ... Nevertheless, a major advantage of this approach, in comparison with both the '*ceteris paribus*' and 'total' elasticities formulations, was that in explicitly recognizing that devaluation has significant effects beyond merely altering the exchange rate, and hence relative export and import prices, attention is directed to the roles of income effects in the devaluation mechanism.
>
> (Ibid.)

The major criticism levelled against these models, which Clement *et al.* dubbed the 'revised traditional variant', was their complexity. Both theoretically and empirically these models were just too messy.

At this point, mention must be made of Meade's considerable contribution to this literature. Volume I of his *Theory of International Trade* (Meade, 1952), together with its mathematical appendix, may be seen as an attempt to integrate post-Keynesian income theory with general equilibrium theory. Meade's main achievement was to draw analysis in the direction of an explicitly macroeconomic approach by recognition of the aggregate identities and relationships that hold within and between economies. In this, he was evidently much influenced by the targets-instruments analysis of Tinbergen (Tinbergen, 1952). It can be argued that Meade subsequently influenced Alexander by applying an explicitly macro approach (Alexander, 1952). Alexander essentially develops the Keynesian Aggregate Monetary Demand Identity:

$$Y \equiv C + I + G + (X - M) \tag{4}$$
(standard notation, real terms).

Write the balance of trade as B:

$$B \equiv X - M \tag{5}$$

and define (domestic) absorption A:

$$A \equiv C + I + G \tag{6}$$

then:

$$B \equiv Y - A \tag{7}$$

Alexander's analysis is based entirely on identity (7), which emphasizes the fundamental point that trade imbalance can only arise from a difference between domestic output and expenditure.

Taking first differences:

$$\Delta B = \Delta Y - \Delta A \tag{8}$$

Now decomposing the effect of a devaluation into direct (ΔD) and indirect (via ΔY, $c\Delta Y$) effects on absorption:

$$\Delta A = c\Delta Y + \Delta D \tag{9}$$

Thus, from (8) and (9):

$$\Delta B = (1 - c)\,\Delta Y - \Delta D \tag{10}$$

Equation (10) directs our attention to three fundamental factors concerning the outcome of a devaluation: how the devaluation affects real income; how the propensity to absorb (c) affects the outcome; and finally how direct effects are important.

Machlup (1955, 1956) strongly criticized the absorption approach, arguing that it is nothing more than tautological reasoning based on an identity. In Chapter 3 [of Taylor's book], we give an analysis of the use of identities in macro modelling and show how they can be misleading; it suffices to say here that we are basically in agreement with Machlup on this point, and see the utility of the absorption approach primarily in terms of its use as a taxonomic device. As Johnson notes:

> More important and interesting is the light which this approach sheds on the policy problem of correcting a deficit, by relating the balance of payments to the overall operation of the economy rather than treating it as one sector of the economy to be analysed by itself.
>
> (Johnson, 1958, p. 158)

Machlup further criticized Alexander for neglecting relative price effects. Apparently in response to Machlup's criticisms, Alexander produced a second, more rigorous, paper in which he introduced the concept of a reversal factor as the effects of a change in income brought about by the initial elasticities effect on the trade balance (Alexander, 1959). These are thus second-round effects additional to the initial impact effects. If h and m be the marginal propensities to hoard and import respectively, an asterisk denotes a foreign variable, and v denotes the ratio m/h, then Alexander's final synthesis formula may be expressed:

$$\frac{\partial B}{\partial f} = \frac{E}{1 + v + v^*} \tag{11}$$

where E is a four-elasticities formula similar to (1).

Other attempts at synthesis include Brems (1957) and Michaely (1960). Brems works with a highly disaggregated model (38 equations), specific (Leontief) technology and other technical specificities (e.g. Cobb–Douglas demand curves). His main conclusion seems to be that a devaluation will be successful, under his assumptions, if the income effects of a price change are large relative to the substitution effects, and unsuccessful otherwise. Michaely's far less technical analysis concludes that the key to synthesis lies in the real balance effect: the devaluation leads to a change in relative prices and hence real balances and hence absorption. Michaely's stress on monetary factors as the upshot of an attempt at synthesis was symptomatic of a more general trend and foreshadowed Tsiang's paper (Tsiang, 1961) which essentially reverts to the analysis of Meade (1952) and formulates an 11-equation model of a monetary open economy. This realization of the importance of monetary factors, together with attempts to place balance of payments theory in a general equilibrium framework (e.g. Hahn, 1959) and the development of portfolio theory was to lead to the development of the so-called monetary approach to the balance of payments.

[. . .]

General equilibrium models

By the early 1960s, following the work of, *inter alios*, Meade, Harberger and Laursen and Metzler, the standard analysis was one of comparative statics within an explicitly macroeconomic framework, with income demand-determined and with the exchange rate setting relative prices. Since, by way of contrast, the analysis in the pure theory of the international trade had been almost exclusively in terms of general equilibrium models, it is not surprising that attempts were made to introduce money into these models and analyse the balance of payments within this kind of general equilibrium framework.

An early contribution in this vein is Hahn (1959). In this paper, Hahn inserts two fiat currencies into a standard two-country model. His basic result is as follows:

> Assuming the goods market to be in equilibrium both before and after a change in the rate of exchange, the balance of payments of country (1) will change in the same direction as the price of currency (2) in terms of currency (1) changes provided all goods and currencies are gross substitutes.
>
> (Hahn, 1959, p. 117)

Similar results were later obtained by Kemp (1962). Negishi (1968) showed that the Robinson–Metzler four-elasticities formula can be derived within a general equilibrium framework if it is assumed that all cross-price effects are zero.

The most striking result of these analyses, as in the attempts to synthesize the elasticity and Keynesian approaches, was the rediscovery of the importance of monetary factors. Another major impetus in this direction was the development of portfolio theory.

Portfolio balance and international capital movements

In these analyses, the approach is focused primarily on the capital account of the balance of payments. As we have pointed out, attempts at synthesis of the Keynesian and elasticity approaches pointed up important differences arising from the explicit consideration of money. This, together with a dissatisfaction with the limitations of the analysis to the trade account, led to the application of portfolio theory in this context.

This literature is basically an elaboration of early work done by McKinnon (1969) and McKinnon and Oates (1966) and is an extension of more general portfolio theory developed by Markowitz (1959) and Tobin (1965). Other studies which attempt to incorporate portfolio theory into general equilibrium models include Branson, 1968; Lee, 1969; Bryant and Hendershott, 1970; Branson and Hill, 1971; Hodjera, 1971; and Allen, 1973.

In these models the basic point of departure from a more traditional approach is the distinction made between stock and flow equilibria for assets.

Steady-state stock equilibrium prevails when the constellation of asset prices is such that desired and actual asset holdings coincide. In this set-up, international capital flows are only temporary phenomena which bring about stock equilibrium, although flow disequilibrium can be longer lived in a growing economy with capital flows reflecting the equilibrium rate of accumulation of various assets in individual portfolios. In a Mundellian model, for example, a balance of payments deficit could be taken care of by raising domestic interest rates and attracting capital inflows – thus ensuring a flow equilibrium. Clearly, however, there will come a point where foreign investors do not wish to invest any more in the domestic economy – they will have achieved a stock equilibrium.

Although Meade, Johnson and Mundell seemed to be aware of the stock-flow distinction and commented upon it, McKinnon and Oates, 1966; McKinnon, 1969; Oates, 1966; and Ott and Ott, 1965, are the earliest analyses in which portfolio equilibrium is introduced directly by imposing a stock equilibrium constraint (for example, by requiring that the overall balance of payments on the current and capital accounts individually should be equal to zero in full equilibrium – thereby attempting to analyse the full stationary equilibrium. Later papers such as Branson, 1968; Willet, 1967; Willet and Forte, 1969; and Kouri and Porter, 1974, built on a more Tobinesque theory of portfolio choice to analyse capital movements either as a stock adjustment, which would be once-and-for-all, or as a result of differential growth rates of elements of the whole portfolio, in which case it could be continuous.

Most of this literature is concerned with analysing short-term capital movements independently of the current account of the balance of payments. The monetary approach to the balance of payments, in explicitly attempting to capture the essential behavioural features of the whole external account by an appropriate application of the stock equilibrium approach, is in many ways an offshoot of the international portfolio balance literature, although we shall outline important differences.

The monetary approach to the balance of payments

The monetary approach to the balance of payments under fixed exchange rates (MABP) arguably finds its most succinct and articulate exposition in the collection of papers edited by Frenkel and Johnson (1976) – for an extension to the floating rate case see Frenkel and Johnson, 1978. Its line of development, however, can be traced as far back as Polak, 1957 and Johnson, 1958 and even, some authors have maintained, to the Dutch School during the interwar period (de Jong, 1973). Moreover, advocates of the monetary approach have sought to trace their intellectual lineage at least as far back as Hume (1752) (see for example, Frenkel and Johnson, 1976a; Frenkel, 1976). It is indeed true that monetary flows form the core of both the specie-flow mechanism and the MABP, and that each regards the balancing process as essentially self-regulating. In the specie-flow mechanism, however, the variables bringing about the equilibrium are relative commodity prices (this is why the theory is sometimes termed the price-specie-flow mechanism). In the MABP, the important variable is the desired level of real balances as reflected in a stable demand for money function.

The monetary approach was developed in the 1960s and early 1970s primarily by Mundell (1968, 1971) and Johnson (1972) (see also Komiya, 1969). More recent contributors are numerous and include Laidler (1972), Swoboda (1973), Dornbusch (1972), Mussa (1974), Borts and Hansen (1977), Blejer (1979) and Johannes (1981). The approach has been applied as an explanation of world-wide inflationary processes (Johnson, 1972; Whitman, 1975), to the analysis of devaluation in developing countries (Connolly and Taylor, 1976) and as a simplified theoretical basis for policy proposals by groups such as the IMF (Rhomberg and Heller, 1977). The most comprehensive survey is perhaps Kreinin and Officer, 1978.

The MABP goes much further than previous monetary analyses in that instead of just adding money into the model, monetary aspects are regarded as the very core of the analysis. As Frenkel and Johnson write, somewhat tautologically:

> The main characteristics of the monetary approach to the balance of payments can be summarised in the proposition that the balance of payments is essentially a monetary phenomenon.
>
> (Frenkel and Johnson, 1976, p. 21)

The definition of the balance of payments is the starting point of any theory concerned with the external account. MABP theorists implicitly define this term to mean the set of accommodating transactions 'below the line' in the accounts. They thus take this to be a summary of all the other accounts put together. They are therefore able to draw the inference: 'the monetary approach should in principle give an answer no different from that provided by a correct analysis in terms of the other accounts.' (Frenkel and Johnson, 1976a, p. 22).

Basically, the MABP is a supply and demand analysis of the money market in an open economy; any excess stock demand for or supply of money is exactly reflected in flows through the balance of payments. The supply of money can be seen as a multiple of the monetary base which is composed of an international reserve component and a domestic component. Only the latter is directly under the control of the monetary authorities under a fixed-rate regime. If, for example, the stock demand for money is greater than the actual money stock and the authorities do not allow the domestic component of the monetary base to rise accordingly, money will be sucked in through the external account as individuals attempt to increase their real money balances and a balance of payments surplus ensues.

Note that this account implicitly assumes a long-run, 'natural' level of output and, presumably, rapidly adjusting prices and wages, so that the hypothesized real balance effects do not affect the domestic level of economic activity. Further, most expositions assume a small open economy and perfect spatial arbitrage so that interest rates and prices are in fact determined on world markets. Naturally, the approach assumes a stable demand for money as a function of relatively few variables, often of the following form:

$$M_\alpha = L(p, y, r) \tag{15}$$

If m be the money multiplier (assumed exogenously determined or constant) and R and D be the international and domestic components respectively of the monetary base, then we can write the money supply:

$$M_s = m(R + D) \tag{16}$$

so that in equilibrium ($M_s = M_\alpha$);

$$L(p, y, r) = m(R + D) \tag{17}$$

Differentiating logarithmically and rearranging:

$$\frac{dR}{R + D} = \eta_1 \hat{p} + \eta_2 \hat{y} + \eta_3 \hat{r} - \hat{m} - \frac{dD}{R + D} \tag{18}$$

where a circumflex denotes a growth rate and the η_is denote the appropriate elasticities of demand for money (see Johnson, 1972). In the literature, (16) is referred to as the monetary base identity and (18) as the standard reserve flow equation. (18) implies (together with standard neo-classical theory) a number of comparative static effects on the balance of payments which are summarized and contrasted with standard Keynesian results in Table 5.1.

The basic message of the MABP is that, insofar as the domestic credit level is not high enough to satiate the demand for the domestic money stock, the overall balance of payments will be in disequilibrium as reflected by the trend of international reserve acquisition or loss. A corollary is that the authorities can influence the composition, but not the level, of the domestic money stock under a regime of fixed exchange rates.

A number of other implications of the approach under fixed rates should be noted. The first is that, since reserve flows will only persist until there is stock equilibrium in the money market, balance of payments problems are essentially temporary. Secondly, they are inherently self-correcting and although government intervention may speed up the adjustment process, it is likely to be counter-stabilizing. For example, when the economy is running a

Table 5.1 Effect on balance of payments of a rise in (cet. par.)

	y	p	r	D	m	f
Monetary	+	+	−	−	−	0
Keynesian	−	−	+	0	0	+

balance of payments surplus, the authorities might attempt to sterilize the effect of the reserve inflow on the domestic money supply by attempting to reduce the level of domestic credit. Insofar as this preserves the stock disequilibrium in the money market (of which the surplus is only a symptom), imbalance will be prolonged. Other conditions under which imbalance may be prolonged are those of continued growth or stagnation. In such cases, the demand for liquidity might be expected to fall below or outstrip changes in domestic credit; this sort of analysis is often advanced as an explanation of the continuous surpluses of Germany and Japan in recent years.

The policy implications of the MABP are clear – strict *laissez-faire* in international relations will always provide an optimal, albeit long-run, solution. The only effect devaluation or commercial policy can have on the balance of payments is through altering stock equilibria in the money market (see Johnson, 1972; Dornbusch, 1973; Mussa, 1974). For example, a devaluation may raise domestic prices and hence lead to a surplus, or less of a deficit (one might also wish to outline expenditure-switching effects if a distinction is made between tradeables and non-tradeables – see Johnson, 1958). But this effect will only be transitory – once stock equilibrium is attained once more, the effects disappear. In short, the mechanism is self-equilibrating and while adroit government policy may speed up the adjustment process, the outcome will not be significantly altered.

Currie (1976) criticizes the MABP for not taking explicit account of the government budget constraint. This observation is correct and forms at least one distinction between the MABP and the related earlier literature on portfolio balance and international capital flows (e.g. McKinnon, 1969). Where the MABP literature does consider government financing constraints it is indirectly through the examination of open market operations (Frenkel and Rodriguez, 1975). Currie draws the implication that where the government runs a budget deficit, this may be fully equivalent to sterilization of a balance of payments surplus (depending on the method of finance) and so is compatible with long-run imbalance on the external account, as outlined above. In essence, the budget surplus or deficit bypasses the domestic economy and is financed through the external account. Formally he derives his results by noting that in long-run stock equilibrium capital flows must be zero, although balance of trade disequilibrium may be offset by a budget deficit or surplus. With this in mind, the long-run budget constraint is:

$$-\Delta R + T(Y') - g = 0 \qquad (19)$$

where Y' is the long-run level of income, $T(.)$ is the tax function and g is government expenditure (actually, Currie's budget constraint is slightly more complicated to allow for tariff revenue, but this makes no difference to the main thrust of the argument). The external constraint is:

$$\Delta R - X(Y', f) + fM(Y', f, v) = 0 \qquad (20)$$

where X(.) is an export function, M(.) is an import function and v an expenditure-switching parameter. Adding (19) and (20) we obtain:

$$T(Y') + fM(Y', f, v) - g - X(Y', f) = 0 \qquad (21)$$

Differentiating (21) with respect to the various policy parameters then yields Currie's results – that in such a scenario traditional instruments of balance of payments correction will have long-run effects. Nobay and Johnson (1977) argue that this analysis only applies if the authorities are willing and able to withstand continual depletion of reserves in the long run, or conversely, are willing to accumulate reserves indefinitely. If not, then the budget must be balanced in the long run so that $(T(Y') - g)$ is zero. From (19) this implies that ΔR must also be zero in the long run, so that the aggregate constraint (21) cannot be derived in that form. The value of Currie's analysis, however, lies in bringing out the analogy between the budget constraint and the external constraint, instead of ignoring the government sector completely or else treating it only sketchily or implicitly.

As we have pointed out, the MABP is in many ways an offshoot of the literature on portfolio balance and international capital flows; in some ways, however, the MABP is more restrictive than the earlier literature. For example, most expositions focus on the stock of real balances as the major asset. One reason for this is the assumption of perfect bond arbitrage; this is equivalent to assuming foreign and domestic bonds are perfect substitutes in private portfolios, which implies that the markets for foreign and for domestic bonds can be considered as a single market. Explicit considerations of this market can then be avoided by an appeal to Walras's law. Since, *ex hypothesi*, the goods and labour markets are assumed to clear continuously (at least in the long run), and since under fixed exchange rates the authorities must enter the foreign exchange market to clear it at the official parity, we need only consider equilibrium conditions for the money market. This is essentially what the MABP does. Further evidence for the implicit assumption that foreign and domestic bonds are assumed to be perfect substitutes in domestic portfolios is that

> The new approach assumes – in some cases, asserts – that these monetary inflows or outflows associated with surpluses of deficits are not sterilised – or cannot be, within a period relevant to policy analysis – but instead influence the domestic money supply.
>
> (Johnson, 1972)

One condition under which sterilization is impossible is precisely this perfect substitution assumption (see, for example, Obstfeld, 1982). In Chapter 4 [of Taylor's book] we develop a more general portfolio balance model of the balance of payments which, whilst retaining the basic stock-flow distinction, relaxes the perfect substitutability assumption and in fact allows it to be empirically tested and in some sense measured and tracked over time using varying parameter regression methods.

Empirically, the MABP has enjoyed a reasonable amount of success. In Chapter 3 [of our book], however, we give a critical appraisal of some of the empirical methods by which the theory has generally been tested.

Monetarists and Keynesians: some attempts at synthesis

Frenkel *et al.* (1980) have attempted a synthesis of Keynesian and monetary approaches to the balance of payments, and Gylfason and Helliwell (1983) have extended the analysis to incorporate more general portfolio effects and allow for flexible exchange rates. The main thrust of the 1980 paper is that each of the approaches is essentially partial in nature. We might in fact paraphrase the paper by saying that the MABP concentrates on the monetary or 'LM side' of the economy whilst the Keynesian approach concentrates on the real or 'IS side', with neither approach determining prices, interest rates or equilibrium income. It would seem that the logical step is to integrate the two approaches to determine the demand side and to close the model by introducing a supply side. This is what Frenkel *et al.* attempt to do. Formally, their analysis is as follows:

$$\Delta R = p.BT(y, f/p) = K(r) \atop {\scriptstyle -\ +\qquad\quad +} \tag{22}$$

$$M_s = m(R + D) \tag{23}$$

$$M_d = L(p, y, r) \atop {\scriptstyle +\ +\ -} \tag{24}$$

$$M_s = M_d = M \tag{25}$$

$$y = A(y, r) + g + BT\,(y, f/p) \atop {\scriptstyle +\ -\qquad\quad -\ +} \tag{26}$$

$$y = y(p) \atop {\scriptstyle +} \tag{27}$$

where:

R	= level of international reserves;
p	= domestic price level;
y	= real income;
f	= exchange rate (units of domestic currency per unit of foreign currency);
BT(.)	= trade balance relation;
r	= domestic interest rate;
K(.)	= capital inflow relation;
M_s (M_d)	= money supply (demand);
m	= money multiplier;
D	= domestic backing of the monetary base;
g	= government expenditure.

Expression (22) is the Keynesian balance of payments equation, (23) is the monetary base identity and (24) is the money demand function, whilst (25) is the condition for (stock) equilibrium in the money market. Relations (23), (24) and (25) together constitute a set of relationships for equilibrium in the money market, and so can be used to derive the LM equation from (23), (24) and (25):

$$\Delta R = \Delta(1/m)L(p, y, r) - \Delta D \tag{28}$$

which is the MABP reserve flow equation. Equation (26) is the curve and (27) 'is a standard supply function which can be derived from equilibrium conditions in the labour market for a given state of expectations' (Frenkel *et al.*, 1980, p. 588). Solving for p in (27), substituting into (26) and solving for r we obtain:

$$r = r(y, g, f) \tag{29}$$
$$\quad\; - + +$$

Substituting (29) into (22) and (28), we obtain respectively:

$$R = k_1\, y + k_2 g + k_3 f + R_{-1} = Kn(g, f, R_{-1}) \tag{30}$$
$$\quad + \qquad\qquad\qquad\quad\; + + +$$
$$R = m_1\, y + m_2\, g + m_3\, f - D = M(g, f, D) \tag{31}$$
$$\quad + \quad\;\; - \qquad - \qquad\quad\; - - -$$

which Frenkel *et al.* dub the K-schedule and M-schedule respectively. Plotting these in R-y space we obtain Figure 5.2, from which we can deduce a number of comparative static results, summarized in Table 5.2.

On the surface, this analysis appears to be a logically consistent and elegant synthesis. It is, however, open to the criticism that it conflates several issues, most notably the distinction between stock and flow equilibria. The ΔR in equation (22) and the ΔR in equation (28) cannot in fact be the same variable. In (22), for example, ΔR depends on the capital inflow relation $K(r)$, which is a flow relation and in no way depends on the equilibrium stock of assets. In (28), however, ΔR represents a flow necessary to bring about stock equilibrium in the money market. More fundamentally, the MABP assumes that the real side of the economy clears at levels ground out at the Walrasian

Table 5.2 Effect of changes in g, e and D on y, R, r, p and M

	dg	de	dD
dy	+	+	+
dR	?	+	−
dr	+	?	−
dp	+	+	+
dM	?	+	+

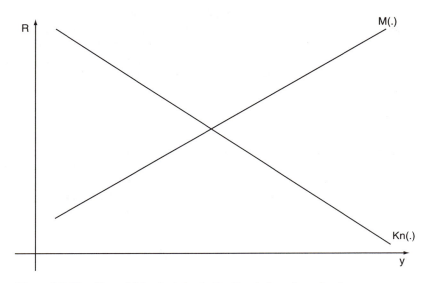

Figure 5.2 The K- and M-schedules in the Frenkel *et al.* synthesis

equilibrium (perhaps with friction) whilst Keynesian theory assumes, for example, that there may be involuntary unemployment and that income is demand-determined. It therefore seems logically incorrect to take a set of equations from each type of model and arbitrarily mix them together.

CONCLUSION

This chapter has sketched the development of over three centuries of thought on the balance of payments. Over this period, there have been three major shifts in emphasis and approach.

Taking as our starting point the mercantilist literature, we showed how the shift to the more harmonious world-view of the classical economists mirrored a shift in moral philosophy. We characterized this shift as going from the selfish system of Hobbes to the dual sphere reconciliation of public and private interest in Smith. Apart from a more optimistic social outlook, the classicals also brought higher standards of analysis to bear on economic problems and so the specie-flow mechanism must be thought of as the first modern balance of payments theory.

The Marginalist revolution left the specie-flow mechanism virtually unscathed, although open economy analysis was supplemented by the elasticities approach. We saw, however, that the quantification afforded by the elasticities approach, coupled with the results of early demand studies, led to a mood of 'elasticity pessimism'. Other empirical work on payments imbalances suggested that the 'automatic mechanism' was working rather too well and that there may be other forces at work – rather in the way that astronomers may infer the presence of a new planet by looking at the gravitational pull on other bodies. These anomalies in the orthodoxy paved the way for revolution in international monetary economics at the same time as the existence of large-scale chronic unemployment led to a reconsideration of macroeconomics in general. The publication of Keynes's *General Theory* thus marks a watershed in international monetary economics as well as in general macroeconomics.

The post-war period has seen the third major shift in ideas in this area – from a broadly Keynesian analysis towards emphasis on the monetary aspects of payments imbalance. To some extent, this shift reflects the general prosperity of the post-war years and consequent increase in the degree of confidence that economists hold in markets. In part also the rise of the monetary approach seems to have been the outcome of a search for greater generality and consistency in the area – either through attempts to synthesize the Keynesian and elasticity approaches, through the application of general equilibrium models, or through a desire to model capital flows through the external account by the use of portfolio theory.

We noted how the pure monetary approach rested on a number of assumptions which one might in principle wish to question. Firstly, there is the assumption that the real side of the economy clears to a first approximation. This, in fact, can be seen as a major difference between Keynesian and monetary approaches to balance of payments determination and any attempt at synthesis must take account of this. Secondly, we saw how the monetary approach implicitly assumes perfect capital mobility – or equivalently that there is a single bond market which can then be eliminated from explicit analysis by application of Walras's law.

REFERENCES

Alexander, S.S. (1952), 'Effects of a Devaluation on the Trade Balance', *International Monetary Fund Staff Papers*, 2, pp. 263–78.

Alexander, S.S. (1959), 'Effects of a Devaluation: A Simplified Synthesis of Elasticities and Absorption Approaches', *American Economic Review*, 49, pp. 23–42.

Allen, P.R. (1973), 'A Portfolio Approach to International Capital Flows', *Journal of International Economics*, 3, pp. 135–60.

Berkeley, G. (1737), *Querist*, London.

Bickerdike, C.F. (1920), 'The Instability of Foreign Exchange', *Economic Journal*, 30, pp. 118–22.

Blejer, M.I. (1979), 'On Causality and the Monetary Approach to the Balance of Payments', *European Economic Review*, 12, pp. 289–96.

Borts, G.H. and Hansen, J.A. (1977), *The Monetary Approach to the Balance of Payments*, mimeo, Brown University, RI.

Branson, W.H. (1968), *Financial Capital Flows in the US Balance of Payments*, Amsterdam: North Holland.

Branson, W.H. and Hill, R.D. (1971), 'Capital Movements Among Some Major OECD Countries: Some Preliminary Results', *The Journal of Finance*, 26, pp. 269–86.

Brems, H. (1957), 'Devaluation, a Marriage of the Elasticity and Absorption Approaches', *Economic Journal*, 67, pp. 49–64.

Brown, A.J. (1942), 'Trade Balances and Exchange Stability', *Oxford Economic Papers*, 6, pp. 57–76.

Bryant, R.C. and Hendershott, P.H. (1970), *Financial Capital Flows in the Balance of Payments of the United States: An Exploratory Empirical Study*, Princeton Studies in International Finance, No. 25, Princeton, NJ: Princeton University International Finance Section.

Cantillon, R. (1755), *Essai sur la Nature du Commerce en Général*, Paris.

Chang, T.-C. (1946), 'The British Demand for Imports in the Inter-War Period', *Economic Journal*, 56, pp. 188–207.

Clement, M.O., Pfister, R.L. and Rothwell, K.J. (1967), *Theoretical Issues in International Economics*, Boston.

Connolly, M. and Taylor, D. (1976), 'Testing the Monetary Approach to Devaluation in Developing Countries', *Journal of Political Economy*, 84, pp. 849–59.

Currie, D.A. (1976), 'Some Criticisms of the Monetary Analysis of Balance of Payments Correction', *Economic Journal*, 87, pp. 771–3.

Dornbusch, R. (1973), 'Devaluation, Money and Non-Traded Goods', *American Economic Review*, 63, pp. 871–83.

Frenkel, J.A. (1976), 'Adjustment Mechanisms and the Monetary Approach to the Balance of Payments: A Doctrinal Perspective', in *Recent Issues in International Monetary Economics*, Claasen, E.-M. and Salin, P. (eds), Amsterdam: North Holland.

Frenkel, J.A. and Johnson, H.G. (eds) (1976), *The Monetary Approach to the Balance of Payments*, London: George Allen and Unwin.

Frenkel, J.A. and Johnson, H.G. (1976a), 'The Monetary Approach to the Balance of Payments: Essential Concepts and Historical Origins', in Frenkel and Johnson (1976).

Frenkel, J.A. and Johnson, H.G. (eds) (1978), *The Economics of Exchange Rates: Selected Studies*, London: Addison-Wesley.

Frenkel, J.A. and Rodriguez, C. (1975), 'Portfolio Equilibrium and the Balance of Payments: A Monetary Approach', *American Economic Review*, 65, pp. 674–88.

Frenkel, J.A., Gylfason, T. and Helliwell, J.F. (1980), 'A Synthesis of Monetary and Keynesian Approaches to Short-Run Balance-of-payments Theory', *Economic Journal*, 90, pp. 582–92.

Gervaise, I. (1720), *The System or Theory of the Trade of the World*, London.

Gossen, H.H. (1854), *Entwickelung der Gesetze des Menslichen Verkehrs, und der Daraus Fliessenden Regeln für Mensliches handeln*, Brunswick.

Gylfason, T. and Helliwell, J.F. (1983), 'A Synthesis of Keynesian, Monetary, and Portfolio Approaches to Flexible Exchange Rates', *Economic Journal*, 93, pp. 820–31.

Haberler, G. (1949), 'The Market for Foreign Exchange and the Stability of the Balance of Payments: A Theoretical Analysis', *Kyklos*, 3, pp. 193–218.

Hahn, F. (1959), 'The Balance of Payments in a Monetary Economy', *Review of Economic Studies*, 26, pp. 110–25.

Harberger, A.C. (1950), 'Currency Depreciation, Income and the Balance of Trade', *Journal of Political Economy*, 58, pp. 47–60.

Heckscher, E.F. (1931), *Mercantilism*, London: Macmillan (second edition 1955).

Hicks, J.R. (1937), 'Mr. Keynes and the Classics: A Suggested Interpretation', *Econometrica*, 5, pp. 147–59.

Hinshaw, R. (1945), 'American Prosperity and the British Balance of Payments Problem', *Review of Economics and Statistics*, 27, p. 4.

Hobbes, T. (1651), *Leviathan or the Matter, Form and Power of a Commonwealth, Ecclesiastical and Civil*, London.

Hodjera, Z. (1971), 'Short-Term Capital Movements of the United Kingdom, 1963–1967', *Journal of Political Economy*, 79, pp. 739–75.

Hume, D. (1751), *An Enquiry Concerning the Principles of Morals*, London.

Hume, D. (1752), 'Of the Balance of Trade', in *Essays, Moral, Political and Literary* (ed. D. Rotwein), London.

Johannes, J.M. (1981), 'Testing the Exogeneity Specification Underlying the Monetary Approach to the Balance of Payments', *Review of Economics and Statistics*, 63, pp. 29–34.

Johnson, H.G. (1956), 'The Transfer Problem and Exchange Stability', *Journal of Political Economy*, 54, pp. 212–25.

Johnson, H.G. (1958), 'Towards a General Theory of the Balance of Payments', in Johnson, H.G., *International Trade and Economic Growth*, London: George Allen and Unwin.

Johnson, H.G. (1972), 'The Monetary Approach to Balance of Payments Theory', *Journal of Financial and Quantitative Analysis*, 7, pp. 220–74.

Jong, F.J. de (1973), *Developments of Monetary Theory in the Netherlands*, Rotterdam: Rotterdam University Press.

Kaldor, N. (1983), *The Economic Consequences of Mrs Thatcher*, Fabian Tract No. 486, London: Fabian Society.

Kant, I. (1790), *Kritik der Urtheilskraft*, Berlin: S.N.

Kemp, M.C. (1962), 'The Rate of Exchange, the Terms of Trade and the Balance of Payments in Fully Employed Economics', *International Economic Review*, 3, pp. 314–27.

Keynes, J.M. (1936), *The General Theory of Employment, Interest and Money*, London: Macmillan.

Komiya, R. (1969), 'Economic Growth and the Balance of Payments: A Monetary Approach', *Journal of Political Economy*, 77, pp. 35–48.

Kouri, P.J.K. and Porter, M.G. (1974), 'International Capital Flows and Portfolio Equilibrium', *Journal of Political Economy*, 82, pp. 443–67.

Kreinin, M.E. and Officer, L.H. (1978), *The Monetary Approach to the Balance of Payments: A Survey*, Princeton Studies in International Finance, No. 43, Princeton, N.J.: Princeton University International Finance Section.

Krueger, A.V. (1969), 'Balance of Payments Theory', *Journal of Economic Literature*, 1, pp. 1–26.

Kuhn, T.S. (1970), *The Structure of Scientific Revolutions*, Chicago: University of Chicago Press.

Laidler, D.E.W. (1972), *Price and Output Fluctuations in an Open Economy*, University of Manchester Discussion Paper No. 7301.

Laursen, S. and Metzler, L. (1950), 'Flexible Exchange Rates and the Theory of Employment', *Review of Economics and Statistics*, 32, pp. 281–99.

Law, J. (1705), *Money and Trade Considered*, Edinburgh.

Lee, C.H. (1969), 'A Stock-Adjustment Analysis of Capital Movements', *Kyklos*, 23, pp. 65–74.

Locke, J. (1690), *Two Treaties of Civil Government*, London.

Locke, J. (1691), 'Some Considerations of the Consequences of the Lowering of Interest, and Raising the Value of Money', in Locke, J., *Several Papers Relating to Money, Interest and Trade*, London.

McCloskey, D.M. (1983), 'The Rhetoric of Economics', *Journal of Economic Literature*, 21, pp. 481–517.

McKinnon, R.I. (1969), 'Portfolio Balance and International Payments Adjustment', in Mundell, R.A. and Swoboda, A.K. (eds), *Monetary Problems of the International Economy*, Chicago: Chicago University Press.

McKinnon, R.I. and Oates, W.E. (1966), *The Implications of International Economic Integration for Monetary, Fiscal and Exchange Rate Policy*, Princeton Studies in International Finance, No. 16, Princeton, N.J.: Princeton University International Finance Section.

Machlup, F. (1955), 'Relative Prices and Aggregate Spending in the Analysis of Devaluation', *American Economic Review*, 45, pp. 225–78.

Machlup, F. (1956), 'The Terms-of-Trade Effects of Devaluation upon Real Income and the Balance of Trade', *Kyklos*, 3, pp. 417–50.

Markowitz, H.M. (1959), *Portfolio Selection: Efficient Diversification of Investments*, New York: Wiley.

Marx, K. (1963), *Theories of Surplus Value*, London: Lawrence and Wishart.

Meade, J.E. (1952), *The Theory of International Economic Policy, Volume I: The Balance of Payments*, Oxford: Oxford University Press.

Metzler, L.A. (1948), 'The Theory of International Trade', in Ellis, H.S. (ed.), *A Survey of Contemporary Economics*, Homewood, Ill.: Irwin.

Michaely, M. (1960), 'Relative-Prices and Income-Absorption Approaches to Devaluation: A Partial Reconciliation', *American Economic Review*, 9, pp. 218–27.

Mill, J.S. (1848), *Principles of Political Economy*, London (references to *Collected Works of John Stuart Mill*, Robson, J.M. (ed.), (1965), London).

Mun, T. (1664), *England's Treasure by Forraign Trade, or the Ballance of our Forraign Trade is the Rule of Our Treasure*, London.

Mundell, R.A. (1968), *International Economics*, New York: Macmillan.

Mundell, R.A. (1971), *Monetary Theory*, California: Goodyear.

Mundlak, Y. (1963), 'Estimation of Production and Behavioural Functions from a Combination of Cross-Section and Time Series Data', in Christ, C.F. (ed.), *Measurement in Economics*, Stanford: Stanford University Press.

Mussa, M. (1974), 'A Monetary Approach to Balance of Payments Analysis', *Journal of Money, Credit and Banking*, 6, pp. 333–51.

Negishi, T. (1968), 'Approaches to the Analysis of Devaluation', *International Economic Review*, 9, pp. 218–27.

Nobay, A.R. and Johnson, H.G. (1977), 'Comment on D. Currie: Some Criticisms of the Monetary Analysis of Balance of Payments Correction', *Economic Journal*, 87, pp. 769–70.

North, D. (1691), *Discourses upon Trade*, London.

Oates, W.E. (1966), 'Budget Balance and Equilibrium Income: A Comment on the Efficacy of Fiscal and Monetary Policy in an Open Economy', *Journal of Finance*, 21, pp. 489–98.

Obstfeld, M. (1982), 'Can We Sterilize? Theory and Evidence', *American Economic Association Papers and Proceedings*, May, pp. 45–55.

Ohlin, B. (1928), 'The Reparations Problem', *Index*.

Ott, D.J. and Ott, A.F. (1965), 'Budget Balance and Equilibrium Income', *Journal of Finance*, 20, pp. 71–7.

Petty, W. (1662), *A Treatise of Taxes and Contributions*, London.

Pigou, A.C. (1932), 'The Effect of Reparations on the Ratio of International Exchange', *Economic Journal*, 42, pp. 532–43.

Polak, J.J. (1957), 'Monetary Analysis of Income Formation and Payments Problems', *International Monetary Fund Staff Papers*, 6, pp. 1–50.

Rhomberg, R.R. and Heller, R.H. (1977), 'Introductory Survey', in *The Monetary*

Approach to the Balance of Payments, International Monetary Fund, Washington, D.C.

Ricardo, D. (1810), *The High Price of Bullion: A Proof of the Depreciation of Bank Notes*, London.

Ricardo, D. (1821), *On the Principles of Political Economy and Taxation*, London.

Robinson, J. (1937), 'The Foreign Exchanges', in Robinson, J., *Essays in the Theory of Employment*, Cambridge.

Schultz, H. (1937), *The Theory and Measurement of Demand*, Chicago: Chicago University Press.

Schumpeter, J.A. (1954), *History of Economic Analysis*, London: George Allen and Unwin.

Seligman, E.R.A. (1930), 'Bullionists', in Seligman, E.R.A. (ed.), *Encyclopaedia of the Social Sciences*, New York: Macmillan.

Senior, N. (1830), *Three Lectures on the Cost of Obtaining Money*, Oxford.

Smith, A. (1759), *The Theory of Moral Sentiments*, London. (References to edition of E. Cannan, 1904, Oxford.)

Smith, A. (1776), *An Inquiry into the Nature and Causes of the Wealth of Nations*, London. (References to edition of E. Cannan, 1904, Oxford.)

Smith, A. (1896), *Lectures on Justice, Police, Revenue and Arms, Delivered in the University of Glasgow by Adam Smith, Reported by a Student in 1763*, (ed. E. Cannan), Oxford.

Sohmen, E. (1957), 'Demand Elasticities and the Foreign Exchange Market', *Journal of Political Economy*, 65, pp. 431–6.

Swoboda, A.K. (1973), 'Monetary Policy under Fixed Exchange Rates: Effectiveness, the Speed of Adjustment, and Proper Use', *Economica*, 41, pp. 136–54.

Taussig, F.W. (1928), *International Trade*, New York: Macmillan.

Thornton, H. (1802), *Paper Credit of Great Britain*, London.

Tinbergen, J. (1952), *On the Theory of Economic Policy*, Amsterdam: North Holland.

Tobin, J.E. (1965), 'The Theory of Portfolio Selection', in Hahn, F.H. and Brechling, F.P.R. (eds), *The Theory of Interest Rates: Proceedings of a Conference Held by the International Economic Association*, London.

Tsiang, S.C. (1961), 'The Role of Money in Trade-Balance Stability: Synthesis of the Elasticity and Absorption Approaches', *American Economic Review*, 51, pp. 912–36.

Venderlint, J. (1734), *Money Answers All Things*, London.

Viner, J. (1924), *Canada's Balance of International Indebtedness, 1900–1913*, Cambridge, Mass.: Harvard University Press.

Viner, J. (1937), *Studies in the Theory of International Trade*, New York: Harper.

Viner, J. (1968), 'Economic Thought: Mercantilist Thought', in Sills, D.L. (ed.), *International Encyclopaedia of the Social Sciences*, New York: Macmillan.

Wheatley, J. (1807), *An Essay on the Theory of Money*, London.

White, H.D. (1933), *The French International Accounts, 1880–1913*, Cambridge, Mass.

Whitman, M.v.N. (1974), 'The Current and Future Role of the Dollar: How Much Symmetry?', *Brookings Papers on Economic Activity*, 3, pp. 539–83.

Willett, T.D. (1967), *A Portfolio Theory of International Short-Term Capital Movements: with a Critique of Recent United States Empirical Studies*, doctoral thesis, University of Virginia.

Willett, T.D. and Forte, F. (1969), 'Interest Rate Policy and External Balance', *Quarterly Journal of Economics*, 83, pp. 242–62.

Williams, J.H. (1920), *Argentine International Trade Under Inconvertible Paper Money, 1880–1900*, Cambridge, Mass.

6   The current account

John Williamson and Chris Milner
The World Economy: A Textbook in International Economics,
Harvester-Wheatsheaf (1991), pp. 185–202, 207–18

Our analysis of balance of payments theory begins by making two simplifying assumptions: that there are no capital movements, and that the exchange
rate is fixed by the action of the central bank. The chapter is organized around
a series of different models, or approaches, that have been developed over the
years. These are introduced in the order in which they emerged historically,
with a sketch of the circumstances that prompted their evolution. Several of
these approaches were presented by their creators as representing a conflict
with the preceding approaches, which have indeed been derided by some as
erroneous orthodoxy. Our view is that such exclusiveness is unmerited: that
any adequate understanding of the macroeconomics of an open economy
demands an integration of all the various approaches within the context of a
general equilibrium model. Accordingly, the final section of the chapter
shows how the various approaches can all be incorporated within the simplest
general equilibrium model available: namely, the IS/LM model.

1 HUME'S PRICE-SPECIE-FLOW MECHANISM

The mercantilist preoccupation with achieving a surplus on the balance of
payments was faulted by Adam Smith for neglecting the basic source of the
gains from trade: the increase in consumption in both countries that is possible by exploitation of their absolute or, more generally, comparative advantage on the basis of balanced trade. But even before Adam Smith's writing,
his fellow Scot David Hume (1711–76) had discredited the *macroeconomic*
basis of the mercantilist position. In 1752 he showed that a permanent payments surplus was not feasible and therefore made no sense as a policy objective, while a deficit would cure itself, so that it was not necessary to worry
about a country losing all its money supply and being reduced to barter in
consequence. The basic claim was that the gold standard contained an
automatic adjustment mechanism, the so-called price-specie-flow mechanism.

In order to understand this mechanism it is necessary to know what a gold
standard is. The essential features are that the countries on the gold standard
fix the values of their currencies in terms of gold, that they settle their balance of payments surpluses and deficits by transferring gold and that they do
not sterilize the effects of those gold flows on their money supplies. These

conditions were satisfied in mid-eighteenth-century Europe for those countries, like Britain, that had a monetary unit equal to a defined weight of gold. Clearly each such currency had a value fixed in terms of gold (and therefore their values were also fixed in terms of one another). Gold could be, and was, shipped from one country to another to settle payments deficits; if British importers could not get enough francs from British exporters to France, they sent some gold sovereigns which were melted down and turned into francs. Finally, except occasionally in times of war, governments did not seek to maintain the money supply by printing paper money when gold flowed out: that is, they did not sterilize a payments deficit.

The basic idea of the gold standard adjustment mechanism was that a payments deficit caused a loss of reserves, which reduced the money supply, which lowered the price level, which made the home country's goods more competitive, which stimulated exports and reduced imports, which improved the balance of payments. This process continued until the deficit was eliminated. The converse process operated when a country had a surplus: gold flowed in, the money supply and prices rose, competitiveness declined and in consequence exports fell and imports expanded so that the payments surplus tended to be eliminated. In either case, therefore, a payments imbalance was self-eliminating so long as the automatic mechanisms inherent in the gold standard were allowed to play themselves out. To look at the matter in a slightly different way, a country had a 'natural' quantity of money corresponding to its productive capacity: it could not sustain more than this quantity (any excess would generate a deficit and leak out), and any shortfall would be made up anyway, so the mercantilist preoccupation with the balance of payments was silly.

The steps in the chain of reasoning described verbally above may be summarized schematically as follows:

Payments deficit → Gold outflow → Fall in money supply → Price decline → Greater competitiveness → More exports, fewer imports → Reduction in payments deficit

It is important to understand exactly what assumptions are necessary to justify each step in this causal chain.

1 An incipient payments deficit can be realized and lead to a loss of reserves (like gold) only if the country has a *fixed exchange rate*. With a flexible exchange rate, the monetary authority is not willing to supply internationally acceptable assets to absorb an excess supply of the currency it issues, so the consequence of such excess supply is a depreciation of the currency rather than a loss of reserves.

2 A reserve loss will lead to a fall in the money supply if the country follows a policy of non-sterilization: that is, does not compensate for the decline in reserves by increasing domestic credit. This became known as following the

'rules of the game'. It seems that central banks did not in fact follow this rule literally even at the apogee of the gold standard in the late nineteenth century. What they typically did was to sterilize partially. With a fractional reserve banking system (which was not a factor in Hume's day, but became important during the nineteenth century), it is possible for a central bank partially to sterilize a reserve loss but for the money supply to fall by more than the loss in reserves.[1] The essential condition for the second step to operate is therefore the *avoidance of complete sterilization*.

3 The assumption that a fall in the money supply would lead to a price decline was based on the *quantity theory of money*, which held that in the 'equation of exchange':

$$MV = PT$$

V (velocity) and T (volume of transactions) are essentially constants, with the former determined by the technology of exchange and the latter by the condition that full employment prevail, while the money supply M is the independent variable, and the price level P is the dependent variable. The validity of this interpretation of the equation of exchange has always been the chief issue underlying disputes between Keynesians and monetarists (though many on both sides of the disputes have been reluctant to acknowledge this). Hume was in this sense a monetarist. He wrote:

> Suppose that four-fifths of all the money in Great Britain [were] to be annihilated in one night, and the nation reduced to the same condition, with regard to specie, as in the reigns of the Harrys and Edwards, what would be the consequence? Must not the price of all labour and commodities sink in proportion, and everything be sold as cheap as they were in those ages?
>
> (Hume 1752, in Cooper 1969, p. 25)

4 A fall in domestic prices will increase international competitiveness provided that it increases the 'real exchange rate', which is defined as ep^*/p. This is, of course, simply the nominal exchange rate e corrected for changes in the general level of prices abroad p^* and at home p. Since we have already assumed e to be constant, a fall in p will certainly increase competitiveness provided that *foreign prices remain constant or rise*. When a small country has a deficit one expects foreign prices to remain constant, while when a large country has a deficit its loss of gold will be sufficient to have a perceptible impact in raising money supplies and hence prices elsewhere.

5 The balance of trade will respond positively to variations in competitiveness provided there is sufficient elasticity in the demand and supply schedules. In the subsequent discussion of the elasticities approach, we shall derive something called the Marshall–Lerner condition, which is a condition on the

elasticities that has to be satisfied if an improvement in competitiveness is to improve the balance of trade. Hume assumed (without knowing it) that the *Marshall–Lerner condition is satisfied.*

6 An improvement in the balance of trade must improve the overall balance of payments if trade is the only component of the balance of payments, as we are assuming. In particular, there must be *no capital mobility* to assure this result.

The italicized phrases in the six preceding paragraphs are the assumptions that are needed to ensure that the price-specie-flow mechanism works as described by Hume. There are in fact strong reasons for believing that the gold standard did *not* work like that. One reason is that capital mobility was very important by the late nineteenth century: assumption 6 was not satisfied. A loss of reserves led a central bank to raise its interest rates to attract a capital inflow and stem the fall in the money supply. In a Keynesian version of what happened next, the high interest rates led to a decline in aggregate demand, recession and a fall in imports: the balance of payments on current account indeed improved, but at the cost of a loss of output, since assumption 3 was not satisfied. The Belgian economist Robert Triffin (b. 1911) argued that a rise in the British interest rate forced stock liquidation by the capital-importing peripheral countries which improved the British terms of trade and thus balance of trade: assumptions 4 and 5 failed. There is also a monetarist alternative interpretation in which prices are determined in each country by arbitrage from the world market (contrary to assumption 3), income is determined at the full-employment level by the natural equilibrating forces of the market and the balance of payments is determined by the condition that the demand for money be equal to the supply.

While the reasons that the gold standard worked differ from one interpretation to another, all of them suggest that there *is* an inherent monetary equilibrating mechanism, albeit one that worked at the cost of output deflation (in the case of the Keynesian interpretation) or crises in the peripheral countries (in Triffin's interpretation). And it is a historical fact that the gold standard did work for the period prior to the First World War, especially the preceding forty-odd years – although interspersed with crises, often sharp but usually fairly short. Then came the war, which brought widespread abandonment of the gold standard and fixed exchange rates.

An attempt was made to restore the gold standard after the war, but in the 1920s there was no evidence of that automatic equilibration that had previously been the essence of the system. Two reasons were advanced to explain this. First, it was said that central banks no longer played by the rules of the game: the newly established Federal Reserve System in the United States, in particular, sterilized the gold inflow so as to avoid fanning inflation. Second, prices did not fall in the deficit countries (notably Britain) in response to tight monetary policies; instead, these suffered deflation and unemployment even amidst the brief spell of world prosperity in the late 1920s. When that prosperity gave way to the Great Depression, the tensions mounted. Britain left the gold standard in the midst of a financial panic in September 1931. From then on it was not sensible to treat Hume's analysis as the centrepiece of payments theory. It was necessary to develop models whose basic hypotheses were in greater accord with the realities of the time.

2 MULTIPLIER ANALYSIS IN AN OPEN ECONOMY

The major professional response to the Great Depression was, of course, by the famous British economist John Maynard Keynes (1883–1946) in his *General Theory of Employment, Interest and Money*, published in 1936. In this work, he developed a macroeconomic theory of how the levels of income and employment are determined when prices do *not* adjust to clear markets as had traditionally been posited by economists. Although the *General Theory* assumed a closed economy virtually throughout, the basic ideas of Keynesian multiplier analysis were soon applied to balance of payments theory by the British economist Roy Harrod (later Sir Roy Harrod, 1900–78) and the Austrian-born economist Fritz Machlup (1902–83).[2]

The basic assumptions of multiplier analysis are that prices (including the exchange rate) are fixed, that the economy is operating below full employment so that output can respond to variations in demand, and that the money supply adjusts passively to variations in the demand for money (due, for example, to the central bank maintaining the interest rate constant). The starting point of the analysis is the income identity:

$$Y = C + I + G + X - M \tag{1}$$

Consumption can be taken as determined by a conventional consumption function $C = C(Y)$, or in linear form:

$$C = c_0 + cY \tag{2}$$

where c is the marginal propensity to consume. Investment (I) and government expenditure (G) are taken as exogenous.

Exports (X) may also be treated as exogenous.[3] Two alternative justifications for this assumption exist. The first is that the country is a small supplier of homogeneous primary products whose price is determined on world markets. It could sell more exports at the going price, but export sales are limited from the *supply* side to the level that is profitable at current prices. The second justification is that the country is selling manufactured goods produced at constant cost; it would like to sell more at current prices, but sales are limited from the *demand* side (given whatever fixprice the suppliers choose to quote).

Imports (M), on the other hand, are endogenous: more domestic income brings in more imports, which the country can buy at a fixed price, given that it is small in the markets for its import goods. An obvious specification for the import function is $M = M(Y)$ or, in linear form:

$$M = m_0 + mY \tag{3}$$

where m is the marginal propensity to import. While it seems rather obvious, this specification in fact implies quite a strong assumption about the nature of the goods being imported. Since prices are constant, Y (income) represents output: hence equation (3) implies that more *production* requires more imports, as is indeed appropriate when imports consist of intermediate goods. But if imports consist of final goods, then one would expect them to be related to expenditure A rather than to income Y. For example, a fall in autonomous consumption exactly matched by a rise in exports would leave output, and therefore imports, unchanged if imports consisted of intermediate goods (petroleum, for example), while imports would fall (and therefore income would rise) if they consisted of consumer goods. In the real world, of course, imports consist of both intermediate and final goods. It is very important to recognize this when constructing econometric models for forecasting or planning purposes, since the import component of different types of expenditure is in fact very different: typically inventory accumulation has the highest import component, followed by fixed investment, followed by consumption or exports, with government expenditure normally least import intensive. However, alternative specifications of the import function make no difference to the qualitative theorems we shall derive below,[4] and so we shall use the simple form (3). Note that m_0 might be negative – domestic production of petroleum, say – without violating accounting conventions so long as $Y > |m_0/m|$.

The basic multiplier formula is derived by substituting (2) and (3) into (1) and manipulating:

$$Y = (c_0 + cY) + I + G + X - (m_0 + mY)$$

$$(1 - c + m)Y = c_0 + I + G + X - m_0$$

$$Y = \frac{1}{s + m}(c_0 + I + G + X - m_0) \tag{4}$$

where $s = 1 - c$ is the marginal propensity to save. The term in front of the parenthesis is the multiplier, while that in the parentheses is the multiplicand. As compared to a closed economy, the effect of introducing foreign trade is to *reduce* the value of the multiplier (since m increases the *denominator* of the multiplier formula), and to *increase* the value of the multiplicand by exports less autonomous imports. The intuitive reason that the multiplier declines is that imports, like saving, constitute a leakage from the income stream, which means that a given level of income generates less (domestic) expenditure than it would in a closed economy. This does not imply that the level of equilibrium income is lower in an open economy, because the stimulating effect of exports in increasing the multiplicand also needs to be taken into account. In fact it is easy to see that the foreign sector has a net stimulating effect whenever there is a trade surplus ($X > M$), and leads to a net reduction in the level of income whenever there is a trade deficit.

The formula for the trade balance, TB, is:

$$TB = X - M = X - m_0 - \frac{m}{s+m}(c_0 + I + G + X - m_0) \tag{5}$$

We are now in a position to derive the basic multiplier theorems for an open economy. These relate to the effects of changes in the exogenous variables I, G and X on the level of income Y and on the trade balance TB. Since I and G (not to mention the autonomous component of consumption, c_0) enter both (4) and (5) in an identical form, it suffices to treat one of them, say G. The comparative statics effects of changes in government spending are deduced by differentiating (4) and (5) with respect to G:

$$dY/dG = I/(s+m) > 0 \tag{6}$$

$$d(TB)/dG = -m/(s+m) < 0 \tag{7}$$

Thus an increase in government spending, or any other form of exogenous domestic spending, increases income by a multiplier effect, while it reduces the trade balance by a fraction of the exogenous increase in spending.

It is clear by inspection of (4) that an increase in exports would have exactly the same multiplier effect on *income* as an increase in domestic expenditures, but its effect on the balance of trade would differ:

$$d(TB)/dX = 1 - m/(s+m) = s/(s+m) > 0 \tag{8}$$

The effect of the initial increase in exports in improving the trade balance is partially but not wholly offset by the increase in imports induced by the rise in income resulting from the higher exports.[5]

It is possible to develop the preceding analysis in diagrammatic form, using a modified version of the elementary Keynesian savings-investment diagram. Figure 6.1(a) shows the savings and investment schedules. One may either suppose that one is treating a simple model where there is no government, or

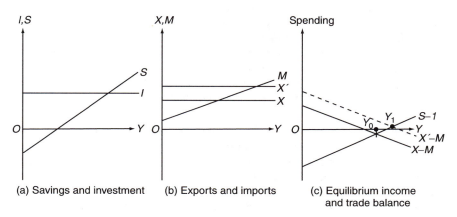

Figure 6.1 Savings, investment and the trade balance

else interpret the *l*-schedule to include G and the *S*-schedule to include T. Figure 6.1(b) shows the export and import schedules. Figure 6.1(c) shows the $(S–I)$ schedule, which is derived from Figure 6.1(a), and the $(X–M)$ schedule, which is derived from Figure 6.1(b). We know that a condition for equilibrium income is that total domestic saving must be equal to the balance of trade: this condition is satisfied *ex ante* in Figure 6.1(c) at the income level Y_0 where the two schedules intersect. It happens that the trade balance is negative at that point.

The comparative statics results already established algebraically can now be confirmed in terms of Figure 6.1. The case shown is that of an exogenous increase in exports, which establishes a schedule $(X'–M)$. It can be seen that income rises (to Y_1) and that the trade balance increases (a deficit is replaced by a surplus), as indicated by equations (6) and (8). However, the increase in the trade balance is less than the increase in exports (which is measured by vertical upward shift in $X–M$), because the $(S–I)$ schedule is positively sloped.

There are two major implications of the foreign trade multiplier analysis. The first is that Keynesian income effects are one of the key elements that have to be incorporated into any model seeking to explain the current account of the balance of payments as a part of the macroeconomic equilibrium of an open economy. The second is that it is possible to explain the international transmission of those economic disturbances known as the business cycle. Exports are exogenous to our country, but they are endogenous with respect to the level of income in our trading partners. Thus a boom there raises their imports and hence our exports, which produces an expansion here as well. In consequence the business cycle is effectively a world rather than a national phenomenon.

3 THE ELASTICITIES APPROACH

The economists who developed the foreign trade multiplier analysis were not under the impression that income effects were the only determinants of trade flows. In fact, one of them, Fritz Machlup, also played a leading role in developing the elasticities approach, which sought to analyze the impact on the trade accounts of the changes in relative prices induced by a devaluation. Analysis of this type was first developed by the great English economist Alfred Marshall (1842–1924) in the heyday of the gold standard, but it became an important part of payments theory only after the Keynesian revolution with the work of Abba Lerner, Joan Robinson, Fritz Machlup, and Gottfried Haberler.

The foreign trade multiplier asks what happens when income changes, with prices constant; the elasticities approach asks what happens when prices change, with income constant. It is simplest to start the analysis if we retain the Keynesian assumption that the general level of internal prices (in both countries) is constant and that changes in relative prices are the result of changes in the nominal exchange rate e. This makes it natural to construct an analysis showing how the demand for and supply of foreign exchange vary

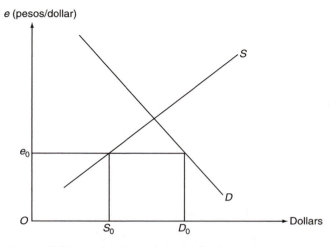

Figure 6.2 Demand and supply in the foreign exchange market

with the exchange rate. (However, the exchange rate is still assumed to be determined by an administrative decision rather than by market forces.)

The demand and supply curves are shown, with orthodox shapes, in Figure 6.2. The horizontal axis shows the quantity of country W's currency, the dollar, that is demanded or offered in exchange for country U's currency, the peso. The dollar here represents foreign exchange in general – as it actually does in the foreign exchange markets of most countries, which are almost all conducted overwhelmingly or exclusively in terms of the United States dollar. If an importer in U wishes to pay a British exporter, his or her bank sells pesos to buy dollars and then sells the dollars on the sterling–dollar market to buy the pounds that the British exporter wishes to receive. Thus there is little abstraction from reality in assuming that all U's external payments involve exchanges of pesos for dollars. The vertical axis shows the exchange rate: that is, the price of a dollar in terms of the peso. A higher value of e represents more pesos per dollar: that is, a devaluation of the peso. (This convention varies. Some countries, especially Anglo-Saxon ones, interpret 'a higher exchange rate' to mean a *stronger* domestic currency.)

The demand for dollars is determined by the need of U's importers to make payments to foreigners, who naturally wish to receive dollars rather than pesos. In reality the demand is supplemented by other sources as well as payment for imports: payments for service imports, making loans to other countries, amortizing loans received from abroad, or any other debit item in the balance of payments. The present treatment is limited to visible trade, for simplicity of presentation, so that we shall analyze what lies behind the demand curve for dollars purely in terms of imports.

The volume of imports is determined by demand and supply. The demand curve for imports shows how the volume of imports will increase as the *peso* price p_m of imports falls, as in Figure 6.3(a). The supply curve of imports

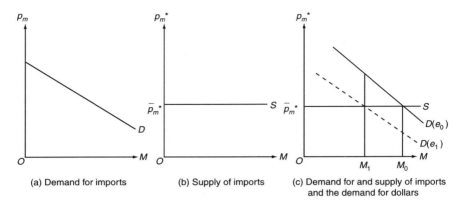

Figure 6.3 Imports and the demand for dollars

shows that country U can buy as many imports as it wants at the fixed world *dollar* price, p_m^* (the assumption that country U is small), as shown in Figure 6.3(b).

In order to find the demand for dollars, it is necessary to translate the demand at a given *peso* price shown in Figure 6.3(a) into the demand at a given *dollar* price. Since $p_m = ep_m^*$, this can be done for any given exchange rate. The curve $D(e_0)$ in Figure 6.3(c) represents the curve D of Figure 6.3(a) at some exchange rate e_0. The demand for dollars at e_0 is the dollar price of imports p_m^* multiplied by the quantity of imports M_0, say D_0 (which is, of course, the area of the rectangle below the supply curve up to the point M_0 in Figure 6.3(c)). The values e_0 and D_0 represent one point on the demand curve for dollars in Figure 6.2.

Now consider the effect of a devaluation of the peso to some higher exchange rate e_1. This leaves the demand and supply curves of Figures 6.3(a) and 6.3(b) unaffected, since they are both specified in terms of the currency that is relevant to those involved (the peso for buyers, the dollar for sellers). The supply curve in Figure 6.3(c) is similarly unaffected. However, the translation of the peso demand curve of Figure 6.3(a) into the dollar demand curve of Figure 6.3(c) was done at the exchange rate e_0 and has to be revised now that the exchange rate has increased to e_1. The quantity M_0, for example, will now only be bought at a lower dollar price, such that ep_m^*, the peso price, is the same as it was before. At the price $p_m = e_1p_m^*$, less than M_0 will be bought, say M_1. In other words, the demand curve in Figure 6.3(c) moves down to $D(e_1)$. The new demand for dollars is p_m^*. M_1, less than before. Hence at the higher exchange rate e_1 the demand for dollars is less: the demand curve of Figure 6.2 slopes down. Incidentally, the elasticity of the demand curve for dollars in Figure 6.2 depends on the elasticity of the demand for imports in Figure 6.3(a): you can confirm this by considering a very inelastic demand for imports, which implies a very inelastic demand for dollars.

The analogous procedure for determining the supply of dollars is shown in Figure 6.4. The small country is assumed to be able to sell all it wants on the

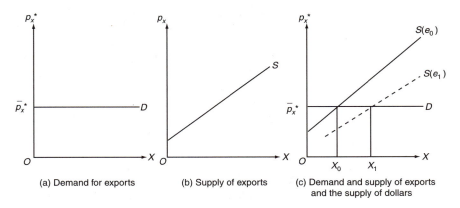

Figure 6.4 Exports and the supply of dollars

world market at the fixed dollar price $\bar{p}_x^*$ (Figure 6.4(a), carried over directly to Figure 6.4(c)). There is an upward-sloping supply curve of exports as a function of the peso price (see Figure 6.4(b)), which can be translated into a supply curve as a function of the dollar price for any defined exchange rate (see Figure 6.4(c)). The intersection of the demand and supply curves (given e_0) determines the quantity of exports X_0 and the supply S_0 of dollars $p_x^*X_0$, which can be associated with e_0 to determine a point on the supply curve of dollars in Figure 6.2. The effect of increasing the exchange rate to e_1 is to increase the peso price $p_x = ep_x^*$ corresponding to any dollar price p_x^*, and thus to increase the supply of exports for any p_x^*: in other words, the supply curve in Figure 6.4(c) shifts to the right as shown. The effect is to increase the quantity of exports to X_1 and the value of exports, or supply of dollars, to $\bar{p}_x^* \cdot X_1$. The supply curve in Figure 6.2 is therefore upward sloping.

We have now shown that, for a small country which neutralizes any impact of an exchange-rate change on the level of income, the demand curve for foreign exchange slopes down and the supply curve up. It follows that there is an equilibrium exchange rate e at which demand equals supply. At a lower exchange rate there is an excess demand for dollars, and at a higher exchange rate there is an excess supply. If the country adopts a policy of devaluing when there is excess demand for dollars and revaluing[6] when there is excess supply, it will approach the equilibrium e. In reality, however, implementing this advice is far from being as simple as it may look in Figure 6.2, partly because no real-world equilibrium remains constant over time and even more because trade flows respond to exchange-rate changes with extended lags rather than instantaneously. We shall return to this point subsequently, but it is important to understand that the analysis of demand and supply applies to a specific time period, sufficiently long to allow volumes to respond to price changes.

The conclusion that a devaluation will always improve the trade balance is, as it happens, critically dependent upon the assumption that the country can sell as many exports as it chooses at the going world price. This is, however, a particularly strong assumption. Many countries that would certainly be described as small by any other economic criterion supply a sufficiently large part of the world market with one or two major export products so as not to face an infinitely elastic demand curve: Tanzania is not a small supplier to the world sisal market, nor is Thailand to the world rice or tapioca market.

It is therefore important to examine how the analysis needs to be modified when a country faces a downward-sloping demand curve for its exports. Figure 6.4(c) is transformed to the form shown in Figure 6.5(a). Now it is no longer true that the rightward shift of the supply curve resulting from a devaluation will necessarily increase the country's dollar receipts from exports. In fact, the behaviour of the dollar value of export receipts as *e* increases depends upon a very simple condition: whether or not the demand curve for exports is elastic. If demand is elastic (that is, if the elasticity of demand exceeds one), export receipts will necessarily increase, and the supply curve of dollars will slope upwards as in Figure 6.2. But if demand is inelastic, the value of export receipts will fall when the exchange rate increases, and hence the supply curve of dollars will bend back as in Figures 6.5(b) and 6.5(c). This may not change the conclusion that devaluation will reduce the excess demand for dollars, as in Figure 6.5(b), where the decline in the demand for dollars induced by devaluation exceeds the decline in supply. But if the demand for imports happens to be very inelastic, it is possible that the demand for dollars declines less than the supply, as at the higher equilibrium exchange rate in Figure 6.5(c). Devaluation then worsens the trade balance because the elasticities are perverse – that is, low.

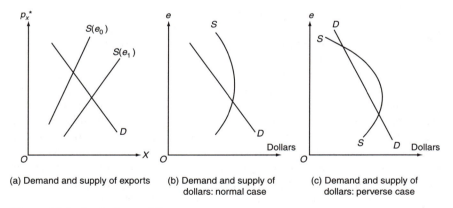

(a) Demand and supply of exports   (b) Demand and supply of dollars: normal case   (c) Demand and supply of dollars: perverse case

Figure 6.5 Inelastic demand for exports

Whether the perverse case shown in Figure 6.5(c) occurs or not depends on the (price) elasticities of demand and supply for both exports and imports. There is a famous algebraic condition, known as the *Marshall–Lerner condition* (named after the two economists who first derived it), which must be satisfied if a devaluation is to improve the trade balance (under the assumptions listed earlier). On the assumption that trade is initially ballanced,[7] the necessary and sufficient condition for devaluation to improve the balance of trade is that:[8]

$$\frac{\varepsilon_x(\eta_x - 1)}{\varepsilon_x + \eta_x} + \frac{\eta_m(1 + \varepsilon_m)}{\varepsilon_m + \eta_m} > 0 \tag{9}$$

where ε_x = price elasticity of supply of exports = $\hat{X}/\hat{p}_x$
η_x = price elasticity of demand for exports = $-\hat{X}/\hat{p}_x{}^*$
ε_m = price elasticity of supply of imports = $\hat{M}/\hat{p}_m{}^*$
η_m = price elasticity of demand for imports = $-\hat{M}/\hat{p}_m$

Since the elasticities of demand (as well as of supply) have been defined to be positive, it is immediately evident from (9) that the perverse case where the Marshall–Lerner condition is not satisfied and devaluation worsens the trade balance can arise only if the demand for exports is inelastic.

There are two special cases of the Marshall–Lerner condition. The first is that of the small country which faces infinitely elastic foreign demand for its exports as well as supply of imports, $\eta_x = \varepsilon_m = \infty$. Our previous finding in this case can be confirmed by taking the limit of (9) as those two elasticities go to infinity:

$$\lim_{\eta_x, \varepsilon_m \to \infty} \left\{ \frac{\varepsilon_x(\eta_x - \cancel{1})}{\cancel{\varepsilon_x} + \eta_x} + \frac{\eta_m(\cancel{1} + \varepsilon_m)}{\varepsilon_m + \cancel{\eta_m}} \right\} = \varepsilon_x + \eta_m > 0$$

(The parameters with a line through them become negligibly small compared to η_x and ε_m, which can then be cancelled.) Thus the balance of payments necessarily improves in the small-country case.

The second special case is the one that has traditionally received a lot of attention, and is indeed sometimes referred to as *the* Marshall–Lerner condition. It is a case that is supposed to be relevant for an industrialized country whose exports consist of manufactures, but most of whose manufactured output is placed on the home market. An addition to export demand will in this case call forth increased output at a constant price: the supply of exports, as well as the supply of imports, is infinitely elastic. Then:

$$\lim_{\varepsilon_x \varepsilon_m \to \infty} \left\{ \frac{\varepsilon_x(\eta_x - 1)}{\varepsilon_x + \eta_x} + \frac{\eta_m(1 + \varepsilon_m)}{\varepsilon_m + \eta_m} \right\} = \eta_x + \eta_m - 1 > 0 \\ \text{or } \eta_x + \eta_m > 1 \tag{10}$$

Thus devaluation will improve the balance of payments if and only if the sum of the demand elasticities exceeds one.

In fact, with one slight change (10) is the condition that is relevant for a small country exporting manufactures, but the model justifying it needs modification. Instead of imaging that cars and television sets are auctioned off in international markets like coffee and tea, and that Ford and Toyota have supply curves with determinate elasticities saying how much they will supply at each price in the London car market, it is more sensible to recognize that the typical manufactured good is sold in a fixprice market. The manufacturer sets the price and is pleased to sell everything that is demanded at that price. This price is typically fixed on a cost-plus basis, with the mark-up coefficient being selected not so much in the light of the level of sales as with a view to the prices being charged by competitors. When competitors' prices rise relative to the firm's own costs, the firm takes the chance of widening its profit margin; when its costs rise relative to competitors' prices, it accepts a squeeze on its profits in order to limit its loss of market share. Devaluation is exactly the sort of shock that increases foreign competitors' prices relative to own costs. Firms typically react by passing through some proportion θ of the exchange-rate change – by adjusting their quoted foreign prices down (up) less than proportionately in response to a devaluation (revaluation). When U devalues, its exporters cut their quoted dollar prices (while allowing their peso profit margins to increase). W's exporters to U raise their quoted peso prices proportionately, given that U is a small country. In the case of initially balanced trade, U's trade balance improves provided that $\theta(\eta_x - 1) + \eta_m > 0.$[9]

When in the 1940s econometricians began estimating elasticities, the estimates of η_x and η_m proved distinctly low. Serious doubt was cast on whether (10) was in fact satisfied. Those who held that the condition was likely to fail were dubbed 'elasticity pessimists' – although it is not clear why, since if the condition really failed it would be extremely lucky for the country in question, which would be able to improve its trade balance *and* its terms of trade (not to mention cutting inflation) by *revaluing* its currency. The fact that countries that allowed their real exchange rates to become overvalued have repeatedly encountered payments crises rather than ever-increasing surpluses is one of the factors that eroded the popularity of elasticity pessimism. Another is the realization that the 'small-country assumption' implies that the trade balance *cannot* deteriorate as a result of devaluation.

But perhaps the dominant factor was a revision of what the econometric evidence seemed to be saying: the typical estimates edged up to perhaps 1.5 for η_x and 0.5 to 1 for η_m.[10] In part this may be because the world changed: the early estimates were based on data for the 1930s and 1940s, when widespread controls did tend to make it difficult for trade flows to respond to price changes, while later estimates were based on data for the more liberal period of the 1950s and beyond. In part it is also attributable to the development of econometric technique. In particular, while early estimates regressed *current* trade on current income and prices (or, at best, allowed a single year's lag), it is now routine to allow for the possibility of lengthy lags in response. The evidence is that, while trade responds quickly (within months) to changes in income, responses to price changes are distinctly slow: reasonably complete adjustment may take three or four years. Presumably this is because much trade is conducted with a customary supplier, and changing the source of supply is something that is done only after due consideration and when the benefits promise to continue long enough to make the switch worthwhile. Many econometric estimates made in the 1980s suggested that elasticities have declined again. The most plausible explanation is that the great variability of exchange rates has undermined business confidence that today's exchange rate is a good guide to future exchange rates, leading to a reluctance to change future plans in the light of exchange-rate changes.

The slow adjustment of trade volumes to the price changes induced by devaluation gives rise to the phenomenon known as the 'J-curve' (see Figure 6.6). Suppose that devaluation occurs at some date t_0. Because trade contracts are signed some time before delivery occurs and the transaction enters the trade statistics, there is no immediate effect on the *volume* of trade. But if, as is typically true among industrial countries, exports are predominantly invoiced in the country's own currency while imports are mainly invoiced in the trading partner's currency, the initial effect is to *worsen* the trade balance: the dollar value of exports falls, while the dollar value of imports remains unchanged. If all trade contracts lasted the same time until delivery, this worsening would persist until some date t_1. From that point on, the contracts entering the trade figures would be those signed after t_0, and would thus reflect the higher *peso* prices charged by exporters to take advantage of the devaluation. The trade deficit would thus shrink, though not back to its predevaluation level, until trade *volumes* adjusted in response to the price changes. If we suppose that happens simultaneously in all industries, at time t_2, we would get a path for the trade balance shown by the histograms: the final portion is positive provided the Marshall–Lerner condition is satisfied. But since not all trade contracts have the same time profile, in reality these three phases get muddled up, and the path of the trade balance is shown instead by something like the thick smooth curve. With a good dose of imagination it is possible to turn that into a J shape, hence the name J-curve. (Non-industrial countries denominate their exports in dollars and are less prone to quote prices in their domestic currency, so their J-curves are weaker, if they exist at all.)

The analysis has up to now been conducted on the assumption that the price level in both countries is constant. However, we live in a world where

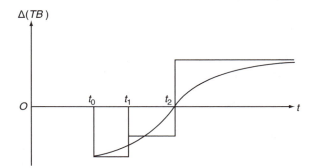

Figure 6.6 J-curve

many countries suffer from perennial inflation, and no analysis that cannot be generalized to recognize this fact is much use. In the present instance, we need to generalize in two directions. First, we need to recognize that what determines the degree of competitiveness of U's products on W's market (and vice versa) is not the nominal exchange rate e, but the real exchange rate ep^*/p.[11] One expects a devaluation to stimulate exports and promote import substitutes at the expense of imports only if ep^*/p is increased: a devaluation that leaves that ratio unchanged, because p has increased relative to p^*, will simply prevent the trade balance worsening. Such a devaluation may be said to have the effect of neutralizing excess domestic inflation.[12]

The second generalization that is needed is to recognize that devaluation is liable to increase the domestic price level. There are a variety of channels through which this can occur. Most directly, import prices rise: this pushes up prices of imported final goods and increases the costs of production and thus the prices of domestic goods that use imported materials and intermediates. The prices of exports and import substitutes are likely to rise, either because they are homogeneous goods with prices determined on world markets or because the devaluation lessens competitive pressure and permits the mark-up to be increased. Because workers face increased prices, trade unions are likely to demand higher wages; and because competitive pressures have been eased, employers are likely to concede them. Thus there are ample theoretical reasons for expecting devaluation to produce a spurt of inflation, and there is ample evidence that this does happen in practice. The fear that most or all of a devaluation will be neutralized by induced inflation is the most persuasive reason for questioning the efficacy of devaluation.

4 THE ABSORPTION APPROACH

In 1952 Sidney Alexander (b. 1916), then employed by the IMF, argued that the elasticities approach tended to give an overfacile view of the ease of correcting a deficit by devaluation – not because the elasticities were low or because any devaluation would be neutralized by inflation, but because devaluation cannot be relied on to increase the excess of income over expenditure. From the national income identity, we know that:

$$TB = Y - A, \qquad \text{or} \qquad \Delta(TB) = \Delta Y - \Delta A$$

It follows that, for devaluation to improve the trade balance, it must either increase real income Y or cut real expenditure (absorption) A. The question is why it should be expected to do either of those things.

The change in expenditure can be broken down into two components: that part which comes about as a result of any change in Y, through customary Keynesian 'induced expenditure' effects, and that part which occurs for any other reason. The former component may be written $c\Delta Y$, where c is the marginal propensity to consume, or, more generally, the marginal propensity to absorb. Alexander argued that, since increases in investment, as well as consumption, might be induced by higher output, c could exceed unity, but few economists have subsequently taken this possibility seriously. The second component we shall denote by A_d: Alexander called it the 'direct effect' on absorption, where it is 'direct' in the sense that it includes all effects that are *not* the result of changes in income. Since $\Delta A = c\Delta Y + A_d$:

$$\Delta(TB) = (1 - c)\Delta Y - A_d \qquad (11)$$

Equation (11) says that in order to examine the effect of devaluation on the trade balance it is necessary to examine both its effect on income and its *direct* effect on absorption.

The obvious effect on income arises if the increased demand for exports and import substitutes (whose magnitude is determined by the elasticities) brings forth an increased supply. However, one of Alexander's central points was that this 'idle resources effect' can operate only if the economy has idle capacity that can be brought into operation by an increase in demand. At the time when Alexander was writing, the world economy was in a virtually continuous boom and there was a general presumption that a country in deficit would not have a margin of spare capacity.

A second effect on income to which Alexander drew attention arises from a change in the terms of trade. It is generally assumed that a devaluation tends to worsen the terms of trade, except in the strict small-country case where they are independent of domestic policy. This is not necessarily true: it is possible for a devaluation to improve the terms of trade. There is in fact a very simple algebraic condition that determines whether the terms of trade worsen in the elasticities model of the previous section,[13] namely:

$$\varepsilon_x\varepsilon_m > \eta_x\eta_m$$

that is, that the product of the supply elasticities exceeds the product of the demand elasticities. This condition is satisfied for the simple industrial-country case. More relevant, the fixprice model also discussed in the previous section implies that the terms of trade will deteriorate if exporters cut their dollar prices by more than foreign suppliers cut the dollar prices at which they supply imports; given that the cut in domestic costs is important to exporters while U's market is a drop in the ocean to W's exporters, there is an overwhelming presumption that this condition is satisfied. Thus the general presumption – shared by Alexander – that devaluation would worsen the terms of trade (if it has any effect at all) is well grounded. This means that devaluation tends to *reduce* real income, which for constant real absorption implies a *bigger* trade deficit.[14]

In subsequent debate, Fritz Machlup added a third channel through which devaluation might influence real income, the resource allocation effect. He argued that a devaluation permitted a relaxation of controls and restrictions, which typically produce microeconomic distortions. A programme of simultaneously abolishing such restrictions and devaluing to maintain the same average incentive to export (or produce import substitutes) could be expected to improve allocative efficiency and thus increase real income. Packages of this character have frequently figured in IMF lending programmes – an example of supply-side economics in action long before the term became faddish.

It is next necessary to examine why and how devaluation might be expected to affect absorption directly: that is, other than as a result of changes induced by changes in real income. The basic argument is that this can be expected, at least in certain circumstances and to some degree, as a result of the inflation that is induced by devaluation. For reasons that were discussed at the end of the previous section, prices rise after a devaluation. This *reduces* the competitive gains that persist, but on the other hand it tends to cut absorption. There are two broad channels through which this can occur, monetary and distributional. Assuming that the devaluation-induced inflation is not accompanied by an equivalent rise in the money supply (as, however, may easily happen in countries with 'passive' monetary policies dedicated to maintaining interest rates constant), the real value of the money supply H/P falls. In consequence interest rates rise and choke off investment (according to the traditional Keynesian analysis), while the negative real balance effect also causes consumers to seek to rebuild their liquid assets and thus curtail consumption (according to the wider perspective popularized by the Israeli economist Don Patinkin (b. 1922) and the leading monetarist and 1976 Nobel laureate Milton Friedman (b. 1912)).

The distributional channels through which devaluation may affect absorption involve government versus public and profits versus wages. A country with a progressive tax system tends to reap an increase in tax revenue more than proportional to the increase in the price level when a one-shot inflation occurs, as a result of taxpayers moving into higher tax brackets. If expenditure remains constant in real terms, and thus increases proportionately in nominal terms, it follows that the real budget surplus increases as a result of inflation (a phenomenon known as 'fiscal drag'). In other words, income is redistributed from the private sector to the public sector; since the latter is normally assumed to determine its spending independently of its short-run revenue, it has a marginal propensity to save of unity, and the income redistribution cuts absorption.

While that tends to happen in response to a single surge of inflation resulting from a one-shot devaluation, it should be noted that the *opposite* is more likely to happen when devaluation becomes a habit and inflation accelerates, as the Argentinian economist Julio Olivera (b. 1929) and the Italian-born economist Vito Tanzi (b. 1935) noted. According to the Olivera–Tanzi effect, an acceleration of inflation reduces the real value of tax collections because of the lag in the payment of taxes. Similarly, government expenditures may increase more than proportionately in response to higher inflation: for example, as a result of subsidized credit to favoured sectors being made available at fixed *nominal* interest rates. Income is thus redistributed from the public sector to the private sector. If the government chooses to finance its increased deficit by resort to the printing press, the stage is set for a vicious circle of accelerating inflation.

Another possible, though unreliable, distribution effect involves profits versus wages. Since many prices (especially of traded goods) are pulled up rather directly by devaluation while any impact on wages is indirect and lagged, income may be redistributed from wages to profits. The Marxist savings function, which says that capitalists save a higher proportion of their income than do workers, implies that this redistribution will also cut absorption.

Looking back at equation (11) we can now see why Alexander was sceptical as to the potency of devaluation to affect the balance of payments. Even if we rule out the possibility $c > 1$, there is no guarantee that $\Delta(TB)$ will be positive, especially if the country is initially at full employment so that Y cannot increase in response to higher external demand. What remains are the negative terms-of-trade effect and the positive resource-allocation effect on income, whose net effect is ambiguous, and the direct effects on absorption. Alexander argued that these would normally be rather weak. As noted in the preceding paragraph, the redistributive effects – especially that involving the government – can easily be perverse. Even if the monetary effect is dependable, the net result may be rather small or even perverse.

The policy conclusion implied is simple. When undertaken from an initial situation of full employment, devaluation must be accompanied by discretionary policy to reduce demand in order to make room for an improvement in the balance of payments. IMF stabilization programmes designed to deal with a payments deficit typically involve deflationary fiscal and monetary measures, as well as devaluation, with this end in view.

[. . .]

6 THE MONETARY APPROACH

The 'orthodox' theory that developed from Keynesian ideas and that was presented in the preceding sections does not preclude the operation of monetary factors. The money supply is recognized as one of the determinants of aggregate demand. By treating the money supply as a policy variable, it is implicitly assumed that the monetary consequences of payments imbalances are sterilized. It is recognized that a rise in the price level induced by devaluation will reduce real money balances and thus real demand. Money is therefore a part of the picture, but it is not placed at the centre of the stage as it was in Hume's analysis of the gold standard. The monetary approach to the balance of payments was developed by those who believe that giving money anything other than pride of place is misleading.

The monetary approach was developed by two distinct schools. The first was based at the IMF and initiated by the work of the Dutch economist J.J. Polak (b. 1914), the former research director of the Fund. This school was rather undogmatic, the main justification offered for the new approach being to develop models that would be usable to monitor macroeconomic management when only the most rudimentary statistical information – which typically centres on monetary statistics – was available. The second school developed at the University of Chicago in the 1960s under the intellectual leadership of the Canadians Robert Mundell (b. 1932) and Harry Johnson. Many of the writings of this school had a polemical edge, involving some perceived clash with Keynesian orthodoxy.

The consolidated balance sheet of a simplified banking system reveals the identity:

$$\text{Reserves} + \text{Domestic credit} = \text{Money supply}$$
$$\text{or} \quad R + D = H \tag{12}$$

Since a deficit in the balance of payments implies a loss of reserves, it follows from equation (12) that there must be a counterpart to a deficit in the form of either credit creation (sterilization) or dishoarding (a fall in H). Since dishoarding is a temporary or disequilibrium phenomenon, a payments deficit can persist only if it is accompanied by credit creation. To put the matter another way, any additional credit creation will ultimately leak out abroad. This is the central theorem of the monetary approach to the balance of payments.

The monetary approach claims to offer a theory of the balance of payments rather than of the current account. We restrict our attention to those topics where the monetary approach has offered contributions specifically relevant to analysis of the current account. The first is a model of payments adjustment with a fixed exchange rate that was developed by Polak and that became the basis for the stabilization programmes sponsored by the IMF. The second concerns the hypothesis that prices are determined by arbitrage, which was used by the German-born economist Rudiger Dornbusch (b. 1942) to analyze devaluation.

Polak model

The Polak model adopts a number of simplifying assumptions in order to highlight the essence of the monetary adjustment mechanism. In addition to assuming capital immobility and a fixed exchange rate, Polak took exports to be exogenous and domestic credit expansion to be a policy variable and therefore also exogenous. There are two substantive assumptions. The first is that the velocity of circulation is constant, as assumed in the old-fashioned quantity theory. That enables one to normalize velocity to unity, with no loss of generality, and to write:

$$Y_t = H_t \tag{13}$$

The second substantive assumption is that imports are always some fixed proportion m of the value of the previous period's nominal income:

$$M_t = mY_{t-1} \tag{14}$$

This implies that the propensity to import is independent of whether a given nominal income is the result of a high price level and low output, or *vice versa*. There is no reason why this should be exactly true, but the approximation simplifies model building enormously. The model is completed by the money supply and balance of payments identities:

$$\Delta H_t = \Delta R_t + \Delta D_t \tag{15}$$

$$\Delta R_t = X_t - M_t \tag{16}$$

Substitution of (14) and (15) into (13) yields:

$$Y_t = H_t = H_{t-1} + \Delta H_t = Y_{t-1} + \Delta R_t + \Delta D_t \tag{17}$$

This gives us the basic monetary theorem already deduced from (12). Since $Y_t = Y_{t-1}$ in equilibrium (by definition), a payments deficit ($\Delta R < 0$) can persist only when domestic credit creation (ΔD) is positive.

It is also possible to use the model to tell a story about the time path of imports and income following an exogenous shock: for example, an increase in domestic credit expansion. Suppose that initially, at $t = 0$, the economy is in equilibrium so $\Delta D = 0$ and $M = M_0$, and that this equilibrium is disturbed at $t = 1$ by an expansion of domestic credit of 1, which is maintained each period thereafter. Table 6.1 traces the expansion of imports and income that this would produce. Column (2) calculates [equation] (14), while column (3) cumulates the difference between current imports and initial imports from column (2). The final column calculates the equation for ΔY derived by substituting (16) into (17) and recognizing that $X_t = X_0 = M_0$:

$$\Delta Y_t = \Delta D_t + \Delta R_t = \Delta D_t + X_t - M_t = \Delta D_t - (M_t - M_0)$$

The final row shows the limit as $t \to \infty$. Imports and income approach new stationary levels with $\Delta M = \Delta Y = 0$, where imports have increased to match the increase in credit creation, while income has increased by $1 + (1 - m) + (1 - m)^2 \ldots = 1/[1 - (1 - m)] = 1/m$, a multiple of the credit expansion determined by the import propensity. In this new 'equilibrium' reserves are falling by the amount of credit creation – the whole of the

Table 6.1 Dynamic adjustment in the Polak model

Time (1)	$\Delta M_t = m \Delta Y_{t-1}$ (2)	$M_t - M_n$ (3)	$\Delta Y_t = \Delta D_t - (M_t - M_0)$ (4)
0	0	0	0
1	0	0	1
2	m	m	$1 - m$
3	$m(1 - m)$	$m[1 + (1 - m)]$	$1 - m(1 + 1 - m) = (1 - m)^2$
4	$m(1 - m)^2$	$m[1 + (1 - m) + (1 - m)^2]$	$(1 - m)^3$
∞	0	1	0

additional credit is leaking out through the balance of payments. Insofar as that cannot persist indefinitely, because ultimately reserves would be exhausted, one cannot consider that to be a long-run equilibrium.

It is also possible to study the impact of a change in exports. The reader should confirm that the long-run impact of a rise in exports will be to increase Y, H and R by $\Delta X/m$ according to the multiplier formula, while imports will gradually rise to match the increase in exports.

The model is a simple one, but its conclusions are quite robust. It suffices to explain the prominent place that the IMF has traditionally given to limiting domestic credit expansion as an element of programmes of balance of payments adjustment. Critics of the Fund claim that it has sometimes paid too little attention to the costs of the decline in income that the model shows will result from credit contraction, tending to assume too readily that falls in nominal income will reflect lower prices rather than lower output.

Arbitrage

The second topic of this section is the role of arbitrage in determining national price levels. The orthodox theory tended to regard price levels as largely fixed by forces internal to each country, whether as constant, being pushed up exogenously by costs, as determined by a Phillips curve, or, in orthodox monetarism, as determined by the quantity of money. In contrast, the global monetarism of the monetary approach argues that price levels are determined by arbitrage from the world market, according to the familiar formula:

$$p = ep^* \qquad (18)$$

This assumption permits some elegant model building. An interesting example is Dornbusch's analysis of devaluation. Consider a small country whose price level is determined by equation (18) – Dornbusch actually assumed a one-good two-money model, to emphasize that devaluation need not necessarily involve relative price changes. Assume away capital flows and credit markets. Suppose that the public has an orthodox demand for money function expressed in real terms so that $H_d = ap$, but that it seeks to adjust any discrepancy between actual and desired money holdings only gradually, at the rate β. Then the rate of hoarding ΔH will be given by:

$$\Delta H = \beta(ap - H) \qquad (19)$$

which implies that hoarding can be shown as a function of the real value of the money supply as in Figure 6.7. Add the assumption of no credit creation, and the vertical axis also shows the payments surplus or deficit.

Suppose that the economy is in equilibrium at point Z_0, and that the exchange rate is then increased by a sudden devaluation. By equation (18), the price level rises proportionately, which implies that H/p falls, for example,

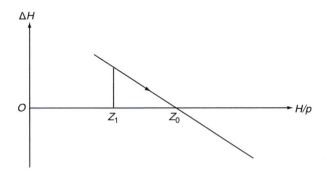

Figure 6.7 Dornbusch model of devaluation

to Z_1. The public now finds itself short of real money balances, so it cuts back on buying goods, which leads to a trade surplus. Real balances climb back slowly towards their equilibrium at Z_0, as shown by the arrow. When they reach Z_0, the payments surplus disappears and the only variables that differ from the initial situation are the price level and the level of reserves. A conclusion much stressed by monetarists is that, while devaluation does indeed cause a surplus, that surplus is temporary.

The mechanism involved here is merely an extreme version of the one responsible for the direct effects on absorption in the absorption approach. From a Meadean perspective, the Dornbusch model implies that devaluation has only expenditure-changing and no expenditure-switching effects. There is very strong empirical evidence that this extreme assumption is not warranted: even traded goods are typically differentiated products, whose prices can differ as between different sources for similar goods, and prices of non-traded goods are even less subject to the influence of arbitrage. The dependent economy model is quite an illuminating way of analyzing the implications of the fact that while arbitrage does have a powerful influence on the prices of traded goods, it nevertheless does not equalize price levels between countries. But one should always remember that in the real world even the assumptions of that model, that the prices of traded goods are equalized by arbitrage, is satisfied only for homogeneous commodities, which do not constitute the bulk of trade.

7 GENERAL EQUILIBRIUM: IS/LM/BP

The balance of payments is determined simultaneously with all other macroeconomic variables. The way that economists recognize such interdependence is by constructing general equilibrium models. The simplest general equilibrium model that is reasonably adequate for integrating the analyses presented in preceding sections is the IS/LM model, extended by the addition of a curve representing balance of payments equilibrium. But even this model suffers from three important limitations, which will be noted subsequently.

The analysis is shown in Figure 6.8. The horizontal axis shows real income,

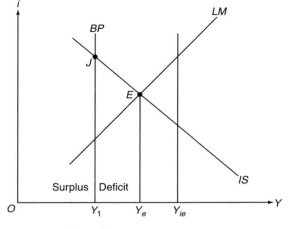

Figure 6.8 IS/LM/BP

and the vertical axis shows the nominal (and real, since we assume away inflationary expectations) interest rate. The *IS* curve represents the locus of points of (flow) equilibrium in the goods market, which are characterized by the condition that $I = S$ *ex ante*.[16] It slopes down because a lower interest rate stimulates investment, which requires a higher income level to generate a corresponding increase in saving. The *LM* curve represents the locus of points of (stock) equilibrium in the asset markets: with a model with only two assets, money and bonds, it matters not whether one describes that as equilibrium in the money market or the bond market. It slopes up because an increase in income raises the transactions demand for money and thus requires an increase in the interest rate to induce a corresponding reduction in speculative demand (to use the Keynesian terminology). In the short run (though a short run sufficiently long for the multiplier process to work itself out), the economy goes to an equilibrium at the intersection of the *IS* and *LM* curves.

The balance of payments can be introduced into this familiar diagram by recalling that the current account balance is lower the higher the level of income (from the multiplier analysis) is. The rate of interest, however, has no direct effect on the balance of payments: it is true that a higher interest rate might improve the current account, but it would do so by cutting income (that is, by inducing a movement along the *IS* curve) rather than directly. Hence the curve representing balance of payments equilibrium is a vertical line, labelled *BP*, at some value Y_1. There is a payments deficit to the right of *BP* and a surplus to the left. In the case shown in Figure 6.8, with income at Y_e, the balance of payments would be in deficit.

The essential ideas of the various approaches analyzed in the preceding sections of this chapter are reflected in this model. First, there is the monetary mechanism of automatic adjustment of Hume and Polak. At the short-run equilibrium shown in Figure 6.8, there is a current account deficit and hence, with no capital mobility, the country is losing reserves. As it does so, with no sterilization, the money supply falls and hence the *LM* curve shifts leftward. The process continues until the *LM* curve intersects the point *J* where *IS* crosses *BP*. At that point the balance of payments is also in equilibrium and so, with downward price rigidity, the economy is in long-run equilibrium. However, the postulated adjustment mechanism involves neither the exclusive price decline of Hume nor even the possibility of a decline in prices as part of the fall in nominal income as in Polak's model, but rather a reduction in real income as in Ohlin's analysis.

Second, consider the multiplier analysis. It has already been pointed out that the position of the *BP* curve reflects this factor. In addition, one needs to consider how the various comparative statics theorems are reflected in this model. An increase in investment pushes *IS* to the right and leaves *BP* unaffected. Since the multiplier analysis presupposes a constant interest rate, the central bank is assumed to accommodate the increase in the demand for money by expansionary open-market operations that push *LM* to the right just far enough to match the shift of *IS*. As the gap between Y_e and Y_1 increases, the balance of payment deteriorates. An increase in exports has the same effect on *IS* and *LM* but also pushes *BP* to the right (by more, though this is not obvious from the diagram), so that income still increases but the balance of payments improves.

Third, consider the elasticities approach. Since prices are not shown in Figure 6.8, the effects of price changes have to be represented by shifts in the curves. A real devaluation definitely pushes *IS* to the right, though the assumption of the algebra is that this effect is neutralized by a contractionary fiscal policy (or by a contractionary monetary policy that pushes *LM* up by enough to maintain *Y* constant). It also pushes *BP* to the right provided the Marshall–Lerner condition is satisfied. However, a nominal devaluation has these effects only to the extent that it leads to a real devaluation rather than being neutralized by price changes. These effects may take several years to work themselves out, and in the interim the balance of payments may deteriorate even if income is held constant rather than being allowed to expand (the J-curve).

Fourth, recall that the absorption approach taught us that a rightward shift of *BP* may not be sufficient to improve the balance of payments. We need to recognize that Figure 6.8 has another important curve, the full-employment benchmark represented by the vertical line above Y_{fe}. If Y_e initially coincides with Y_{fe}, output cannot expand to match an increase in demand, and hence any improvement in the balance of payments is conditional on a cut in absorption. This may come about automatically either because income redistribution has a leftward impact on *IS*, or because the inflation induced by devaluation reduces the real money supply and so pushes *LM* leftward. To the extent that these forces are insufficient to eliminate the inflationary gap, the government needs to take restrictive fiscal-monetary measures to push either *IS* or *LM* (or both) to the left.

Fifth, Meade's analysis is about the combination of policies needed to secure an intersection of all four curves (*IS, LM, BP* and Y_{fe}) at the same point. Internal balance is represented by *E* being on Y_{fe}, and external balance by *E* being on *BP*. To make *E* lie on both simultaneously we need to be able to shift *BP* and at least one of the two curves *IS* and *LM*. Shifting *BP* requires an expenditure-switching policy, while shifting *IS* or *LM* requires an expenditure-changing policy. If devaluation is used as the expenditure-switching policy, it will also shift *IS* right and *LM* left. Remember that it has been argued that in some economies with limited substitution possibilities the leftward shift of *LM* may exceed the righward shift of *IS* so that it might be appropriate to accompany devaluation by expansionary fiscal or monetary policy even if the economy is initially at full capacity.

Finally, the monetary approach has stressed the impact of devaluation on *LM*, and even argued that this may be its *only* effect, as well as reviving the idea of the automatic monetary adjustment mechanism. Monetarists tend not to be overconcerned with the possibility that this will provide insufficient instruments to achieve internal and external balance simultaneously, because they assume that price flexibility can be relied on to secure internal balance without any help from government.

The IS/LM/BP model thus provides a simple general equilibrium framework that suffices to show that the various approaches to payments theory are complementary rather than competitive. The main difference in policy conclusions between monetarists and mainstream economists, which is whether or not one needs to worry about internal balance, does not stem from any inability of orthodox theory to incorporate the behavioural relations stressed in the monetary approach, but from their differing degree of faith in the ability of price flexibility to clear markets.

Useful as the IS/LM/BP model is, however, it must be recognized that it suffers from three important limitations. First, it assumes a given price level and does not incorporate a theory of inflation. Second, it assumes static expectations – of a constant future price level, for example, so that it is unnecessary to distinguish the nominal from the real rate of interest. Third, it assumes given stocks of the various assets – money, bonds and physical capital.

These assumptions can, of course, be relaxed. Indeed, we have already noted the effects of varying the stock of money in shifting *LM*. It is particularly interesting to consider extending the model to include a theory of inflation. Suppose, therefore, that the wage level, instead of being constant, were determined by a Phillips curve (with or without adaptive expectations). It is easy to see that, with this addition, the IS/LM/BP model will generate all the monetarist conclusions as between two positions of long-run equilibrium (with $\hat{w} = 0$). For example, the monetary mechanism of adjustment no longer implies that income would remain at the less than full-employment level Y_1 produced by *LM*'s migration to intersect *BP* and *IS* at *J*. The reason is that at *J* the unemployment would imply declining wages, which would improve competitiveness and so push both *IS* and *BP* right: equilibrium could occur only with full employment (specifically, with unemployment equal to the natural rate). Or, suppose one were to devalue from a position of long-run equilibrium. Unless the direct effects on absorption outweighed the substitution effects induced by the gain in competitiveness, income would increase and unemployment would fall below the natural rate, generating inflation, which would erode the competitive gain from devaluation. Thus the IS/LM/BP model extended by addition of a Phillips curve has long-run comparative statics properties that are essentially monetarist, while its short-run behaviour is eminently Keynesian. This suggests that the relationship between monetarism and Keynesianism is one of the time span judged relevant for policy formation, with monetarists tending to dismiss the short-run and Keynesians to disregard the long-run consequences of policy.

8 SUMMARY

The orthodox theory of the current account, incorporating the income effects of the multiplier analysis and the price effects of the elasticities approach as synthesized by Meade, can be summarized in the equation:

$$TB = TB(\overset{-}{Y}, \overset{+}{ep*/p})\tag{20}$$

The signs over the arguments of the function TB (...) represent the direction of the effects of those variables on the trade balance (that is, the signs of the partial derivatives). The negative sign over Y comes from section 2, while the positive impact of competitiveness assumes that the Marshall–Lerner condition is satisfied. Thus equation (20) should be interpreted in a medium-run rather than short-run sense. This equation is robust to the choice of model and may be used to summarize the results of the present chapter.

Even though they do not imply any modification to the current account equation (20), the absorption approach and the monetary approach also contribute important perspectives. The absorption approach shows that it will normally be necessary to accompany an expenditure-switching policy like devaluation by an expenditure-reducing policy if devaluation is to improve the balance of payments and the economy is initially at full employment. With capital immobility, the monetary approach shows how monetary factors would dominate the adjustment process in the long run even though the behavioural relations and therefore the short-run properties are impeccably Keynesian.

9 ADDENDUM: THE LARGE ECONOMY

The implication for the price-specie-flow mechanism of assuming the domestic economy to be large was noted in the text. With a large economy, the gold outflow will have a non-negligible effect in expanding foreign reserves, and thus the foreign money supply and price level. This *reinforces* the change in competitiveness and spreads the burden of adjustment.

The changes in domestic income analyzed in the multiplier approach will produce a *foreign repercussion* if the economy is large. For example, an increase in domestic investment raises income and increases imports, which are other countries' exports. Foreign income therefore rises by a non-negligible amount, which raises their imports and, thus, our exports and income. The multiplier is therefore larger.

The large country need not face an infinitely elastic foreign supply of imports, just as it will almost certainly not face an infinitely elastic demand for exports. The implications of assuming a finite elasticity of demand for exports were explored in the text, where it was found that this raised the possibility that a devaluation might worsen the balance of payments, if the Marshall–Lerner condition were not satisfied. A finite elasticity of supply of imports has no such significance, as can be seen by inserting an upward-sloping supply curve in Figure 6.3(c) or looking at the second term in equation (9). Another implication is the possibility that a devaluation by one country might provoke devaluation by some others.

The remaining approaches do not require any modifications other than those consequential on the points noted above (for example, a leftward rather than rightward shift of *BP* being induced by devaluation if the Marshall–Lerner condition were to fail), except for the Dornbusch model of devaluation. This was originally presented in a two-country model where prices were continuously equated by arbitrage (but might alter during the adjustment process), while money supplies were slowly redistributed between countries until full equilibrium was achieved.

10 A BIBLIOGRAPHICAL NOTE

The price-specie-flow mechanism was first analyzed by David Hume (1752). The most systematic development of the foreign trade multiplier analysis. Machlup (1943), is now mainly of historical interest. The same might be said of the original writings on the elasticities approach: Machlup (1939), Robinson (1937) and Haberler (1949). The absorption approach was introduced in Alexander (1952); the two most famous contributions to the ensuing controversy were Machlup (1955) and Tsiang (1961). Empirical estimates of income and price elasticities are surveyed by Goldstein and Khan in Chapter 20 of Jones and Kenen (1985, vol. II).

The Polak model was presented in Polak (1957), and reprinted in Heller and Rhomberg (1977), a volume that also contains the other basic papers from the IMF version of the monetary approach. The Dornbusch model of devaluation is in Dornbusch (1973); the gist of that paper, together with an elegant exposition of the theory of the current account (in more mathematical terms than those used above), can be found in Chapters 3–9 of Dornbusch (1980). Most of the principal papers of the Chicago version of the monetary approach are to be found in Frenkel and Johnson (1976). The balance of payments was first incorporated into the IS/LM analysis by Wrightsman (1970).

NOTES

1 The monetary base $B = R + D_1$ and $H = (1/\phi)B$. Define the 'sterilization coefficient' a as that proportion of a change in reserves that is offset by a change in (central bank) domestic credit D_1, so that $\Delta D_1 = - a\Delta R$. A value of a equal to unity signifies total sterilization, while a value of zero signifies zero sterilization. Differencing the first two equations, and substituting, shows that:

$$\Delta H = (1/\phi) (\Delta R + \Delta D_1) = (1/\phi) (1 - a)\Delta R$$

from which it follows that the money supply will fall as long as sterilization is less than complete ($a < 1$), and will fall by more than R when $(1 - a)/\phi > 1$.

2 It is an often-remarked irony of the intellectual history of the period that Keynes had previously (in a debate in the *Economic Journal* in 1929) combated the efforts of Ohlin to apply what later became regarded as the Keynesian analysis of income effects to analysis of the transfer problem posed by German reparations.

3 It is sometimes argued that exports are diverted to the home market by a high level of demand, so that $X = X(Y)$, $dX/dY < 0$, and there is empirical evidence supporting this hypothesis from some countries. The student should check that, if such an effect exists, it will reinforce the conclusions of the analysis of this section.

4 It is worth checking this out by working through with the alternative import function $M = m_1 + m_2A$.

5 Another worthwhile exercise is to analyze the effects on Y and TB of an increase in the domestic production of petroleum.

6 The term 'revalue' is being used, according to current usage, as the opposite of 'devalue', rather than in the old-fashioned (though less ambiguous) way to signify any change in the exchange rate, whether devaluation or 'upvaluation'.

7 This assumption is easily generalized: the first part of the expression in (9) must be weighted by the proportion of exports in total trade, and the second part by the proportion that imports constitute. See Note 8.

8 Proof. From the definitions of ε_x and η_x and the identity $\hat{p}_x = \hat{e} + \hat{p}_x{}^*$, derive $\hat{p}_x{}^* = - \hat{X}/\eta_x = - \varepsilon_x\hat{p}_x/\eta_x = - (\varepsilon_x/\eta_x)(\hat{e} + \hat{p}_x{}^*)$, which solves to yield $\hat{p}_x{}^* = - [\varepsilon_x/(\varepsilon_x + \eta_x)]\hat{e}$ and $\hat{p}_x = [\eta_x/(\varepsilon_x + \eta_x)]\hat{e}$. Similarly, the expressions for ε_m and η_m and the equivalent identity can be solved to give $\hat{p}_m{}^* = - [\eta_m/(\varepsilon_m + \eta_m)]\hat{e}$ and $\hat{p}_m = [\varepsilon_m/(\varepsilon_m + \eta_m)]\hat{e}$. Since the trade balance in dollars is defined as $TB = p_x{}^*X - p_m{}^*M$, one can take the total differential and substitute:

$$
\begin{aligned}
d(TB) &= Xdp_x{}^* + p_x{}^*dX - Mdp_m{}^* - p_m{}^*dM \\
&= Xp_x{}^*\hat{p}_x{}^* + p_x{}^*\varepsilon_x X\hat{p}_x - Mp_m{}^*\hat{p}_m{}^* + p_m{}^*\eta_m M\hat{p}_m \\
&= Xp_x{}^*\frac{[- \varepsilon_x + \varepsilon_x\eta_x]}{\varepsilon_x + \eta_x}\hat{e} + Mp_m{}^*\frac{[\eta_m + \eta_m\varepsilon_m]}{\varepsilon_m + \eta_m}\hat{e} \\
&= Xp_x{}^*\frac{\varepsilon_x(\eta_x - 1)}{\varepsilon_x + \eta_x}\hat{e} + Mp_m{}^*\frac{\eta_m(1 + \varepsilon_m)}{\varepsilon_m + \eta_m}\hat{e}
\end{aligned}
$$

When $Xp_x{}^* = Mp_m{}^*$, it can be seen that devaluation ($\hat{e} > 0$) will improve the trade balance TB if and only if the condition (9) regarding the elasticities is satisfied.

9 Proof. The pass-through coefficient θ is defined as $- \hat{p}_x{}^*/\hat{e}$, which implies that $\hat{p}_x = [1 - \theta)\hat{e}$ given that $\hat{p}_x = \hat{e} + \hat{p}_x{}^*$. One again uses the formulae for the definition of η_x and η_m. Substitution in the total differential of the formula for TB gives:

$$d(TB) = Xdp_x^* + p_x^*dX - Mdp_m^* - p_m^*dM$$
$$= Xp_x^*(-\theta\hat{e}) + p_x^*X\eta_x\theta\hat{e} + p_mM\eta_m\hat{e}$$
$$= Xp_x^*(\eta_x - 1)\theta\hat{e} + Mp_m^*\eta_m\hat{e}$$

10 Note that there is no contradiction involved in every country facing a higher elasticity of demand for its exports than its own elasticity of demand for imports, since exports can substitute for the exports of other countries as well as for import substitutes.

11 Note that recognition of the possibility of foreign inflation would require a reinterpretation of the horizontal axis of Figure 6.2 to refer to 'real dollars' ($/$p^*$), as well as of the vertical axis to refer to the real exchange rate ep^*/p.

12 An alternative definition of the real exchange rate has been adopted by a number of writers in recent years: p_m/p_n, the relative price of traded goods in terms of non-traded goods. Those using this definition usually assume that the price of traded goods is determined by arbitrage from abroad, so that $p_m = ep^*$. If these traded goods include goods produced for export, and the domestic price level p is a weighted average of the prices of traded and non-traded goods so that $p = p_m^a p_n^{(1-a)}$, then the standard definition $ep^*/p = p_m/p_m^a p_n^{1-a} = (p_m/p_n)^{1-a}$ is a monotonic transformation of the alternative definition. In practice most measures of the real exchange rate are based on the definition in the text, but the alternative definition is the more relevant measure of the supply-side incentive to produce export goods in a small economy.

13 Proof. Substitute the expressions for $\hat{p}_x$ and $\hat{p}_m$ in n.8 into the formula for the change in the terms of trade:

$$\hat{p}_x - \hat{p}_m = \frac{\eta_x}{\varepsilon_x + \eta_x}\hat{e} - \frac{\varepsilon_m}{\varepsilon_m + \eta_m}\hat{e}$$
$$= \frac{\eta_x\varepsilon_m + \eta_x\eta_m - \varepsilon_m\varepsilon_x - \varepsilon_m\eta_x}{(\varepsilon_x + \eta_x)(\varepsilon_m + \eta_m)}\hat{e}$$
$$= \frac{(\eta_x\eta_m - \varepsilon_m\varepsilon_x)}{(\varepsilon_x + \eta_x)(\varepsilon_m + \eta_m)}\hat{e}$$

which is negative so long as $\varepsilon_m\varepsilon_x > \eta_x\eta_m$.

14 Almost every time a country devalues, its newspapers make an analytical error which grossly exaggerates the loss to real income from the terms-of-trade deterioration. They claim that the price for which exports are sold falls, while the price the country has to pay for its imports rises. Of course, there is a sense in which both statements are true: the *dollar* price of exports falls, while the *peso* price of imports rises. But to *compare* those two movements is erroneous: the terms of trade must be measured in a common currency. In dollars, the price of *both* exports and imports fall (if the latter changes at all), while in terms of pesos, they *both* rise. [. . .]

16 In the extended model of an open economy with fiscal policy, the condition is, of course, $(I - S) + (G - T) + (X - M) = 0$.

REFERENCES

Alexander, S.S. (1952) 'Effects of a devaluation on a trade balance', *IMF Staff Papers*, April; reprinted in Caves and Johnson (1968).

Caves, R.E. and Johnson, H.G. (eds) (1968) *Readings in International Economics*, Homewood, ILL: Irwin.

Cooper, R.N. (ed.) (1969) *International Finance: Selected readings* London: Penguin.

Dornbusch, R. (1973) 'Devaluation, money and non-traded goods', *American Economic Review*, 63, 871–80.

Dornbusch, R. (1980) *Open Economy Macroeconomics*. New York: Basic Books.

Ellis, H.S. and Metzler, L.A. (eds) (1949) *Readings in the Theory of International Trade*, Philadelphia: Blakiston.

Frenkel, J.A. and Johnson, H.G. (eds) (1976) *The Monetary Approach to the Balance of Payments*, London: Allen & Unwin.

Haberler, G. (1949) 'The market for foreign exchange and the stability of the balance of payments', *Kyklos*, 3, 193–218; reprinted in Cooper (1969).

Heller, H.R. and Rhomberg, R.R. (eds) (1977) *The Monetary Approach to the Balance of Payments*, Washington: International Monetary Fund.

Hume, D. (1752) 'Of the balance of trade', in *Essays, Moral, Political and Literary*, vol. 1. London: Longmans Green, 1898; reprinted in Cooper (1969).

Jones, R.W. and Kenen, P.B. (eds) (1985) *Handbook of International Economics*, vol. 2, Amsterdam: North Holland.

Machlup, F. (1939) 'The theory of foreign exchanges', *Economica*, 6, 375–97; reprinted in Ellis and Metzler (1949).

Machlup, F. (1943) *International Trade and the National Income Multiplier*, Philadelphia: Blakiston.

Machlup, F. (1955) 'Relative prices and aggregate spending in the analysis of devaluation', *American Economic Review*, 65, 255–78.

Polak, J.J. (1957) 'Monetary analysis of income formation', *IMF Staff Papers*, 4, 1–50.

Robinson, J. (1937) 'The foreign exchanges', in J. Robinson, *Essays in the Theory of Employment*, Oxford: Blackwell; reprinted in Ellis and Metzler (1949).

Tsiang, S.C. (1961) 'The role of money in trade-balance stability: synthesis of the elasticity and absorption approaches', *American Economic Review*, 51, 912–36; reprinted in Caves and Johnson (1968) and Cooper (1969).

Wrightsman, D. (1970) 'IS, LM and external equilibrium', *American Economic Review*, 60, 203–8.

Questions

1 Balance of payments theories are all about the alternative mechanisms (or policy instruments) that can be used to equalise receipts with payments. Discuss.
2 'The actual movements of goods seem to have been adjusted to balance of payments disequilibria with surprising exactness and speed.' Do you agree?
3 What are the strengths and weaknesses of the classical (specie-flow) approach to balance of payments adjustment as a process of change in relative prices?
4 What are the strengths and weaknesses of the elasticities approach to balance of payments adjustment as a process of change in relative prices?
5 'The absorption approach is right in its focus on general equilibrium, but it fails where the partial equilibrium elasticities approach seems to have succeeded.' Discuss.
6 'The global monetarist approach is right in its emphasis on the monetary aspects of the balance of payments adjustment, but it fails where the expenditure-based approaches seem to have succeeded.' Discuss.
7 'The global monetarist approach is right in its argument that devaluation will have only a temporary effect on the balance of payments. However, that is because devaluation cannot provide a quick fix to the competitiveness problem and not because balance of payments adjustment is essentially a monetary phenomenon.' Discuss.

Further reading and references

FURTHER READING

For an intermediate-level review of the approaches to balance of payments adjustment, consult Thirlwall (1992), chs 3–5, and Dernburg (1989), chs 8–10. For early contributions to the elasticity debate, see Robinson (1937), pp. 188–202 and Metzler (1948). For the formalisation of the absorption approach, see Alexander (1952). On the origins and basic concepts of the monetarist approach, see Frenkel and Johnson (1976). For a critique of the monetarist approach, see Currie (1976). For attempts at a synthesis in the debate, see Frenkel *et al.* (1980) and Tsiang (1961).

REFERENCES

Alexander, S. (1952) 'Effects of a devaluation on the trade balance', *IMF Staff Papers* 2, 263–78.

Currie, D. (1976) 'Some criticisms of the monetary analysis of balance of payments correction', *The Economic Journal* 86, 508–22.

Dernburg, T.F. (1989) *Global Macroeconomics*, New York: Harper & Row.

Frenkel, J.A. and H.G. Johnson (1976), *The Monetary Approach to the Balance of Payments: Essential Concepts and Origins*, London: George Allen & Unwin.

Frenkel, J.A., T. Gylfason and J.F. Helliwell (1980) 'A synthesis of monetary and Keynesian approaches to short-run balance of payments theory', *The Economic Journal* 90, 582–92.

Metzler, L.A. (1948) 'The theory of international trade', in H.S. Ellis (ed.), *A Survey of Contemporary Economics*, Homewood, ILL: Irwin.

Robinson, J. (1937) *Essays in the Theory of Employment*, London: Macmillan.

Thirlwall, A.P. (1992) *Balance of Payments Theory and the United Kingdom Experience*, 4th edn, Basingstoke: Macmillan.

Tsiang, S.C. (1961) 'The role of money in trade-balance stability: synthesis of the elasticity and absorption approaches', *American Economic Review* 51, 912–36.

Part III

Achieving the internal and external balance simultaneously

Targets and instruments

Introduction

Part III consists of articles examining the assignment of policy instruments to macroeconomic targets. This is the 'activist' approach to macroeconomic policy design. In this approach, the policy instruments (interest rates, government expenditures, the exchange rate, etc.) are assigned to the achievement of macroeconomic targets (e.g. level of output, employment and the balance of payments). We know that this 'activist' approach to macroeconomic policy is only a subset of the wider debate. Therefore, it would be appropriate to start by drawing the reader's attention to what is excluded.

First of all, the debate on 'rules rather than discretion' is not represented here. As is well known, the monetarist and new classical traditions are in favour of rules in policy design. Their preference for rules is justified by various arguments: the inadequacy of the information concerning the structure of the economy, bureaucratic inefficiency, time lags, and the inverse relationship between discretion and policy credibility. All of these arguments, however, are closely related to the overriding assumptions about income determination and market flexibility. Because markets are assumed to be flexible and income is assumed to be determined by supply-side factors, there is little or no scope for active use of stabilisation policy. Nonetheless, this is not the reason for not including the representatives of this debate here. One reason is that the 'rules rather than discretion' debate is generally focused on the closed economy. The other reason is that those contributions focusing on the open economy are too advanced to be included in this intermediate-level reader. Having said that, however, there is no reason why the insights provided by the 'rules rather than discretion' debate should be ignored when evaluating the strengths and weaknesses of the assignment approach to policy design. In fact, this is done in Chapter 10, where we examine the implications of rational expectations for the assignment rule.

Second, the feedback approach to policy design is not included either. There are two variants of this approach: the *ad hoc* and *optimisation-oriented* feedback rules. In the *ad hoc* feedback rule, the policy instrument may be set in relation to a particular target but it must also take account of all other relevant target variables on which the instrument may be effective. For example, interest rates may be assigned to achieve a low level of inflation but it must also be set in relation to asset prices, the balance of payments, the state of the economy, etc. This approach has become popular in the 1990s in the policy design of the Anglo-Saxon countries. For the optimisation-oriented feedback approach, the aim is to mix the targets and instruments with a view to optimising the macroeconomic performance. This view was first put forward by Theil (1961), who rightly argued that there may be diminishing returns in the use of a certain instrument and/or constraints on the extent to which the instrument can be deployed. Again, the exclusion of this strand of the debate does not necessarily imply irrelevance. It merely reflects the constraint imposed by space limitations. The only consolation we can rely on is the fact that the article by Meade (Chapter 9) provides excellent insights into the difficulties faced by the target-instrument design of economic policy.

Having explained the rationale for the organisation of this part, we can now provide a summary of what it includes. Chapter 7 by Mundell is one of the earliest contributions that applied Tinbergen's rule to open-economy macroeconomics. Tinbergen (1952) demonstrated that the government could achieve the desired economic targets only if it has as many independently effective policy instruments as the number of targets sought. What Mundell's article does is to build on this principle and derive two important results. First, in a small open economy with fixed exchange rates and prices and where capital flows are a function of interest rate differential, monetary and fiscal policies are independently effective on the desired targets of internal balance and external balance. Second, it is possible to identify which instrument is relatively more effective on which target – the so-called effective market classification principle. Having derived these results, Mundell demonstrates that it is possible to achieve internal and external balance simultaneously.

In Chapter 8, Williamson and Milner provide a rigorous yet accessible account of Meade's synthesis – which differs from Mundell's approach mainly because of its assumption about a fixed but adjustable exchange rate. In Meade's approach, the assignment problem is resolved by establishing that the exchange is more effective on external balance whereas the instruments acting on the absorption are more effective on the internal balance. Williamson and Milner take a further step and demonstrate that Meade's synthesis may not be sufficient for achieving internal and external balance simultaneously if real wages are rigid. With real wage rigidity, devaluation cannot lead to an improvement in competitiveness. Also, an increase in absorption may not lead to an increase in output or employment if nominal wages increase in response to a reflationary policy. Therefore, the instruments cease to be effective on the targets.

The article by Meade (Chapter 9) is an excellent reply to the concerns raised by Williamson and Milner. Having pointed out the historical context in which his synthesis was developed, Meade focuses on how the internal balance should be (re)defined. The internal balance should refer not only to full employment but also to price stability. Obviously, price stability is closely related to the behaviour of wage setters. In that sense, Meade agrees with

Williamson and Milner's concerns about real wage rigidity. The problem can be resolved by setting up labour market institutions that would induce the wage setters to set wages in line with the demand for and supply of labour. Although one can argue that institutional design is a matter of social engineering, which constitutes an uncharted territory for economists, Meade's diagnosis passes the time test. First of all, it predates the resurgence of interest in this issue in the late 1980s and early 1990s. Second, it highlights the risks associated with current policy, where the emphasis on labour market flexibility has led to increased income inequality.

A further elaboration on the assignment debate is provided in Chapter 10. Here, we take Mundell's assignment rule and Meade's synthesis as given and examine the way in which the simultaneous attainment of internal and external balance may be frustrated when expectations are formed rationally. To do this, we specify the price level and the nominal exchange rate as functions of expected values and other relevant variables. Once this is done, we can see that a policy action aimed at hitting the internal or external balance will overshoot or undershoot the target. In addition, the position of the internal and external balance schedules may change, leading to shifts in their intersection points. Therefore, activist assignment may lead not only to target missing, but also to destabilisation. This is yet another example of how a change in behavioural assumptions can lead to different results.

REFERENCES

Theil, H.C. (1961) *Economic Forecasts and Policy*, 2nd edn, Amsterdam: North-Holland.

Tinbergen, J. (1952) *On the Theory of Economic Policy*, Amsterdam: North-Holland.

7 The appropriate use of monetary and fiscal policy for internal and external stability

*Robert A. Mundell**

IMF Staff Papers, vol. 9, no. 1 (1962), pp. 70–7

This paper deals with the problem of achieving internal stability and balance of payments equilibrium in a country which considers it inadvisable to alter the exchange rate or to impose trade controls. It is assumed that monetary and fiscal policy can be used as independent instruments to attain the two objectives if capital flows are responsive to interest rate differentials, but it is concluded that it is a matter of extreme importance how the policies are paired with the objectives. Specifically, it is argued that monetary policy ought to be aimed at external objectives and fiscal policy at internal objectives, and that failure to follow this prescription can make the disequilibrium situation worse than before the policy changes were introduced.

The practical implication of the theory, when stabilization measures are limited to monetary policy and fiscal policy, is that a surplus country experiencing inflationary pressure should ease monetary conditions and raise taxes (or reduce government spending), and that a deficit country suffering from unemployment should tighten interest rates and lower taxes (or increase government spending).[1]

THE CONDITIONS OF EQUILIBRIUM

Internal balance requires that aggregate demand for domestic output be equal to aggregate supply of domestic output at full employment. If this condition is not fulfilled, there will be inflationary pressure or recessionary potential according to whether aggregate demand exceeds or falls short of, respectively, full employment output. It will be assumed here that, during

---

* Mr. Mundell, economist in the Special Studies Division, received his economics training at the University of British Columbia, the University of Washington, Massachusetts Institute of Technology, and the London School of Economics, and was a postdoctoral fellow at the University of Chicago. He was economist for the Royal Commission on Price Spreads of Food Products, and has taught at Boston University, the University of British Columbia, Stanford University, and the Bologna Center for The Johns Hopkins School of Advanced International Studies. He is the author of numerous articles on international trade and economic theory.

transitory periods of disequilibrium, inventories are running down, or accumulating, in excess of desired changes, according to whether the disequilibrium reflects a state of inflationary or recessionary potential.

External balance implies that the balance of trade equals (net) capital exports at the fixed exchange parity. If the balance of trade exceeds capital exports, there will be a balance of payments surplus and a tendency for the exchange rate to appreciate, which the central bank restrains by accumulating stocks of foreign exchange. And likewise, if the balance of trade falls short of capital exports, there will be a balance of payments deficit and a tendency for the exchange rate to depreciate, which the central bank prevents by dispensing with stocks of foreign exchange.

In what follows it is assumed that all foreign policies and export demand are given, that the balance of trade worsens as the level of domestic expenditure increases, and that capital flows are responsive to interest rate differentials. Then domestic expenditure can be assumed to depend only on fiscal policy (the budget surplus) and monetary policy (the interest rate) at the full employment level of output. The complete system can thus be given a geometric interpretation in the two policy variables, the interest rate and the budget surplus[2] (Figure 7.1).

In the diagram, the *FF* line, which will be referred to as the "foreign-balance schedule," traces the locus of pairs of interest rates and budget surpluses (at the level of income compatible with full employment) along which the balance of payments is in equilibrium. This schedule has a negative slope because an increase in the interest rate, by reducing capital exports and lowering domestic expenditure and hence imports, improves the balance of payments; while a decrease in the budget surplus, by raising domestic expenditure and hence imports, worsens the balance of payments. Thus, from any point on the schedule an increase in the rate of interest would cause an external surplus, which would have to be compensated by a reduction in the budget surplus in order to restore equilibrium. Points above and to the right of the foreign-balance schedule refer to balance of payments surpluses, while points below and to the left of the schedule represent balance of payments deficits.

A similar construction can be applied to the conditions representing internal balance. The *XX* line, or "internal-balance schedule," is the locus of pairs of interest rates and budget surpluses which permits continuing full employment equilibrium in the market for goods and services. Along this schedule, full employment output is equal to aggregate demand for output, or, what amounts to the same condition, home demand for domestic goods is equal to full employment output less exports. There is, therefore, only one level of home demand for domestic goods consistent with full employment and the given level of exports, and this implies that expenditure must be constant along *XX*. The internal-balance line must therefore have a negative slope, since increases in the interest rate are associated with decreases in the budget surplus, in order to maintain domestic expenditure constant.

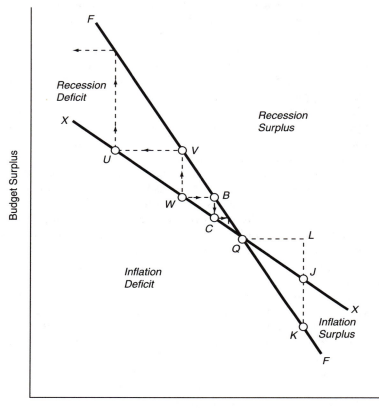

Rate of Interest

Figure 7.1

Both the internal-balance and the foreign-balance schedules thus have negative slopes. But it is necessary also to compare the steepness of the slopes. Which of the schedules is steeper?

It can be demonstrated that *FF* must be steeper than *XX* if capital is even slightly mobile, and by an amount which depends both on the responsiveness of international capital flows to the rate of interest and on the marginal propensity to import. The absolute slope of the internal-balance schedule *XX* is the ratio between the responsiveness of domestic expenditure to the rate of interest and the responsiveness of domestic expenditure to the budget surplus. Now, if it is assumed for a moment that capital exports are constant, the balance of payments depends only on expenditure, since exports are assumed constant and imports depend only on expenditure. In other words, if capital exports are constant, the slope of *FF* also is the ratio between the responsiveness of domestic expenditure to the rate of interest and the responsiveness of such expenditure to the budget surplus. Therefore, apart from the effects of changes in capital exports, the two slopes are the same. It is then possible to see that the responsiveness of capital exports to the rate of interest makes the slope of *FF* greater in absolute value than the slope of *XX*.[3]

Consider, for example, what happens to an initial situation of overall equilibrium at *Q* as this equilibrium is disturbed by an increase in the rate of interest equal to *QL*. Because of the higher rate of interest, there would be deflationary pressure and a balance of payments surplus at the point *L*. If the budget surplus is now lowered, the deflationary pressure can be eliminated at a point like *J* on the internal-balance schedule. But at *J*, expenditure is the same as it was at *Q*, and this means that imports, and hence the balance of *trade*, must be the same as at *Q*. The balance of *payments* is therefore in surplus at *J* because of capital imports attracted by the higher rate of interest; this makes necessary a further reduction in the budget surplus in order to bring the balance of payments again into equilibrium. It follows, then, that the point *K* on the foreign-balance schedule is below the point *J* on the internal-balance schedule, and that *FF* is steeper than *XX*. It can then also be concluded that the absolute difference in slopes is greater, the more mobile is capital (because this causes a larger external surplus at *J*) and the lower is the marginal propensity to import (because this necessitates a larger budget deficit to correct any given external surplus).[4]

In Figure 7.1, the two schedules separate four quadrants, distinguished from one another by the conditions of internal imbalance and external disequilibrium. Only at the point where the schedules intersect are the policy variables in equilibrium.

TWO SYSTEMS OF POLICY RESPONSE

Consider now two possible policy systems determining the behavior of fiscal policy and monetary policy when internal and external balance have not been simultaneously achieved. The government can adjust monetary policy to the requirements of internal stability, and fiscal policy to the needs of external balance, or it can use fiscal policy for purposes of internal stability and monetary policy for purposes of external balance.

It will be demonstrated first that the policy system in which the interest rate is used for internal stability, and fiscal policy is used for external equilibrium, is an unstable system. Consider, for example, a situation of full employment combined with a balance of payments deficit, represented by the point *W*. To correct the deficit by fiscal policy, the budget surplus must be raised from that indicated by *W* to that given by *V*. At *V* there will be equilibrium in the balance of payments, but the increased budget surplus will have caused recessionary pressure. If now the threatening unemployment is to be prevented by monetary policy, the rate of interest must be lowered from that indicated by *V* to that described by *U*. But at *U* there is again a balance of payments deficit, which in turn necessitates a further increase in the budget surplus. The process continues with the interest rate and the budget surplus moving ever further from equilibrium.[5]

To show formally that the system is unstable, it is sufficient to note that the payments deficit at U, after the first round of policy changes, exceeds the deficit at W. This is evident since it is known that the balance of *trade* at U and W is the same but, because of the lower rate of interest, the balance of *payments* at U is worse. It follows that this type of policy reaction is unstable.

On the other hand, the opposite type of policy response is stable. Suppose that the authorities adjust the interest rate to correspond to the needs of external equilibrium and adjust fiscal policy to maintain internal stability. Then from the same disequilibrium point W, the rate of interest would be raised to B, thereby correcting the external deficit. But the tendency toward unemployment generated by the restrictive credit policy must now be corrected by a reduction in the budget surplus or increase in the budget deficit. At C there is again internal balance and a balance of payments deficit, as at W. But it is now possible to see that the deficit at C is *less* than the deficit at W. This follows, as before, because the balance of *trade* at C is identical with that at W but, since the rate of interest is higher at C, the balance of *payments* deficit must be less. The system is therefore stable.

The diagrammatic argument can be absorbed at once when it is realized that at W—or anywhere in the quadrant representing a deficit and recession—the interest rate is lower, and the budget surplus is higher, than is appropriate to the overall equilibrium at Q. The use of fiscal policy for external balance, and monetary policy for internal balance, drives the interest rate and budget surplus further away from equilibrium, while the alternative system moves the instruments closer to equilibrium.

The same argument applies to an initial disequilibrium in the opposite quadrant, representing inflationary pressure and external surplus. To restore equilibrium, the interest rate must be reduced, and fiscal policy must be made more restrictive. Only if monetary policy is used for the external purpose, and fiscal policy for the internal purpose, will correction of the disequilibrium automatically ensue.[6]

In the other two quadrants, monetary and fiscal policies will be moving in the same direction under either system of policy response, because both tighter monetary policy and an increased budget surplus correct inflationary pressure and external deficit, and both easier monetary policy and a reduced budget surplus tend to alleviate recession and external surplus. The distinction between the two policy systems appears less important in these phases of the international trade cycle; it nevertheless remains, since inaccurate information about the exact location of the point Q could propel the situation into one of the quadrants involving either recession and deficit or inflation and surplus.[7]

CONCLUSIONS

It has been demonstrated that, in countries where employment and balance of payments policies are restricted to monetary and fiscal instruments, monetary policy should be reserved for attaining the desired level of the balance of payments, and fiscal policy for preserving internal stability under the conditions assumed here. The opposite system would lead to a progressively worsening unemployment and balance of payments situation.

The explanation can be related to what I have elsewhere called the Principle of Effective Market Classification: policies should be paired with the object-ives on which they have the most influence.[8] If this principle is not followed, there will develop a tendency either for a cyclical approach to equilibrium or for instability.

The use of fiscal policy for external purposes and monetary policy for internal stability violates the principle of effective market classification, because the ratio of the effect of the rate of interest on internal stability to its effect on the balance of payments is less than the ratio of the effect of fiscal policy on internal stability to its effect on the balance of payments. And for precisely this reason the opposite set of policy responses is consistent with the principle.

On a still more general level, we have the principle that Tinbergen has made famous: that to attain a given number of independent targets there must be at least an equal number of instruments.[9] Tinbergen's Principle is concerned with the *existence* and location of a solution to the system. It does not assert that any given set of policy responses will in fact lead to that solution. To assert this, it is necessary to investigate the stability properties of a dynamic system. In this respect, the Principle of Effective Market Classification is a necessary companion to Tinbergen's Principle.

NOTES

1 This possibility has been suggested, and to a limited extent implemented, elsewhere. See, for example, De Nederlandsche Bank N.V., *Report for the Year 1960* (Amsterdam, 1961).
2 The assumptions could be made less restrictive without detracting from the general-ity of the conclusions. Thus, an assumption that capital imports directly affect domestic expenditure, as in theoretical transfer analysis, would tend to reinforce the conclusions. Even the (plausible) assumption that, in addition to capital flows, capital indebtedness is responsive to the rate of interest (to take account of the "stock" nature of much of international floating capital) would not change the conclusions, although it may affect the quantitative extent of the policy changes required.
  Notice, however, that I have implicitly assumed away strong "Pigou" effects, speculation on international markets that is related to the size of the (positive or negative) budget surplus, forward rate movements that more than offset interest-rate-differential changes (an unlikely occurrence), and concern about the precise composition of the balance of payments; the last assumption may mean that the method of achieving equilibrium suggested below is desirable only in the short run.
3 Both the absolute and relative values of the slopes depend on the particular fiscal policy in question. The discussion in the text applies to income tax reductions because that instrument tends to be neutral as between home and foreign spending. The conclusions would be strengthened or weakened, respectively, as the particular fiscal policy was biased toward or against home goods; the more the change in the budget surplus results from a change in spending on home goods, the greater is the difference between the slopes of *XX* and *FF*.
4 The assumption that imports depend only on expenditure, while the latter depends

partly on the rate of interest, means that imports are affected by the rate of interest, although the *share* of imports in expenditure is not. This assumption could be relaxed without fundamentally altering the results, although an exception—remote in practice but possible in theory—does arise, if import goods are highly responsive to the rate of interest while home goods are not, capital flows are only slightly responsive to the rate of interest, and the marginal propensity to buy imports is high relative to the marginal propensity to buy home goods. Under these conditions, it is possible that XX may be steeper than FF. More formally, then, it is necessary to limit the present conclusions to countries in which the ratio of the effect of budget policy on the balance of payments to its effect on domestic excess demand is less than the ratio of the effect of the interest rate on the balance of payments to its effect on excess demand.

5 It need hardly be mentioned that the demonstration of instability in this instance (or of stability in the subsequent analysis) is not dependent upon the particular assumption that the government corrects imbalance first in one sector and then in the other, an assumption which is made only for expositional convenience. The conclusions follow, for example, even if the authorities simultaneously adjust fiscal and monetary policies.

6 Even if the authorities do not wish to pair instruments and targets, they can use the information provided by the analysis to determine the relation between *actual* policies and *equilibrium* policies. Thus, situations of deficit and recession imply that the budget surplus is too high and the interest rate is too low, while situations of surplus and inflation imply the opposite. In this manner, appropriate policies can be determined by observable situations of target disequilibria.

7 The system can be generalized for a two-country world by assuming that the other country adjusts fiscal policy to maintain internal stability. The only difference in the conclusion is that the conditions of dynamic stability of the adjustment process are slightly more restrictive, requiring that the marginal propensities to import be, *on the average*, no greater than one half; this is the usual assumption necessary to rule out any "reverse transfer" that is due to policies affecting expenditure.

8 "The Monetary Dynamics of International Adjustment under Fixed and Flexible Exchange Rates," *Quarterly Journal of Economics*, Vol. LXXIV (1960), pp. 249–50.

9 J. Tinbergen, *On the Theory of Economic Policy* (Amsterdam, 1952).

8 Meade's synthesis
Internal and external balance

John Williamson and Chris Milner
The World Economy: A Textbook in International Economics,
Harvester-Wheatsheaf (1991), pp. 203–7

. . . The central focus of Meade's[1] analysis was on the conditions that had to
be satisfied if a country was to succeed in achieving simultaneously internal
balance and external balance. The major conclusion was that this requires the
use of *two* policy instruments, with differentiated effects on income and the
balance of payments. The general idea that achievement of *n* targets requires
the use of *n* independent instruments was developed simultaneously by one
of the first (1969) winners of the Nobel prize for economics, the Dutch
economist Jan Tinbergen (b. 1903), and is known as 'the theory of economic
policy'.

The concept of *internal balance* refers to the achievement of as high a level
of demand and employment as is consistent with avoidance of the stimula-
tion of unacceptable inflationary pressure. Once upon a time it was customary to refer to this as the achievement of non-inflationary full employment.
Then in 1958 came the idea of the Phillips curve, named after the New
Zealand economist W.A. Phillips (1912–67), which suggested that there was a
continuous trade-off between unemployment and inflation rather than a
sharp cut-off; this led to a reformulation of the concept of internal balance to
refer to the optimal point on the Phillips curve, where society found that the
marginal benefit of any further diminution in unemployment would be outweighed by the marginal cost of the resulting increase in inflation. A decade
later came the natural rate hypothesis of Edmund Phelps (b. 1933) and
Milton Friedman, which held that there was only one rate of unemployment
(the natural rate)[2] that could be sustained in the long run because any lower
rate would stimulate more inflation than people were initially expecting,
which would shift the Phillips curve up as everyone wrote contracts designed
to safeguard their real income against the expected inflation. Similarly,
unemployment higher than the natural rate was conceived to initiate a cumulative deceleration of inflation. The implication was that one had to learn to
live with the facts of life, however much one might dislike them, and accept
an unemployment target high enough to avoid accelerating inflation (or even
to reduce inflation, where inherited inflationary expectations are high).
Internal balance thus becomes more or less synonymous with the natural rate
of unemployment. But whatever one's theory of inflation, internal balance

may be defined as the highest level of demand consistent with a prudent control of inflation.

The concept of external balance gives no difficulties in the present context, where there is no capital mobility. It clearly refers to a situation where the balance of payments is in equilibrium, and there is no need to choose whether this refers to equilibrium overall or on current account, since the two amount to the same thing.

In order to study how policies need to be chosen to permit a country to achieve internal and external balance simultaneously, we shall utilize a diagram (see Figure 8.1) developed independently by the Australian economists W.E.G. Salter and Trevor Swan (b. 1918). On the horizontal axis is shown the level of domestic spending, or absorption. On the vertical axis is shown the international competitiveness of our goods, which can *ceteris paribus* be identified with the real exchange rate, ep^*/p.

The main property of the internal balance schedule can be established by the following argument. Suppose we have some combination of A and ep^*/p which produces just that pressure of demand that corresponds to our concept of internal balance. Consider the effect of adopting a policy (for example, cutting taxes) that stimulates absorption. This would tend to push the economy into a state of excess demand. To counter that and preserve internal balance one could appreciate the currency, so as to divert a part of demand away from domestic producers. Thus the locus of points of internal balance (*IB*) slopes down, as shown, with points of excess demand to the right and of wastefully high unemployment to the left.

A similar argument can be used to establish the slope of the external balance schedule. Suppose absorption increases because of a policy change. We know from the multiplier analysis that that will push the balance of payments into deficit. To preserve external balance, that must be compensated by changing the composition of spending in favour of domestically produced goods, by a real devaluation, as analyzed in the elasticities approach. Thus the external balance (*EB*) schedule slopes up, with a deficit to the right and a surplus to the left.

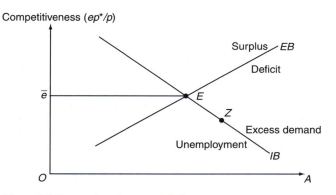

Figure 8.1 Internal and external balance

The basic theme of Meade's analysis was that in order to achieve internal and external balance simultaneously it is necessary to have one policy to influence the level of expenditure and one to influence its composition. This is clear from Figure 8.1: for example, a country that controlled policy instruments able to influence only A could reach the point E of simultaneous internal and external balance only if competitiveness happened to be $\bar{e}$. If competitiveness were less, the currency would be overvalued and in consequence the country would have to choose between unemployment and a payments deficit (or some of each). Harry Johnson later called policies that influenced the level of expenditure 'expenditure-reducing policies', and those that influenced its composition 'expenditure-switching policies.'

Expenditure-reducing policies – expenditure-changing would be a better term since sometimes the need is to increase rather than reduce absorption – are simple to identify. They consist mainly of the demand management policies identified by Keynesian theory: namely, fiscal and monetary policy.

Expenditure-switching policies are those able to influence international competitiveness. Exchange-rate changes are the leading example – though they will succeed in switching expenditure only to the extent that they lead to changes in the *real* exchange rate rather than being neutralized by induced inflation. However, there are many other policies that may be able to switch expenditure as well: for example, tariffs, export subsidies, quantitative import restrictions, other forms of protection, measures to improve the quality of domestically produced goods, export credit facilities . . . the list is virtually endless. These are the policies held constant in the *ceteris paribus* qualification that was inserted when the concept of competitiveness was equated to the real exchange rate. The argument for assigning pride of place to the real exchange rate is not that these other policies are necessarily unimportant, but that microeconomic efficiency rather than the needs of macroeconomic management should be the criterion that determines what is done in those respects. Macro-economic management should be prosecuted with a *general* policy, so as to avoid producing microeconomic distortions.

Suppose that the economy were initially at a point such as Z in Figure 8.1, in internal balance but with a payments deficit. It can be seen that reestablishment of payments balance might be accomplished simply by reducing A – by deflating – until one hit the EB schedule. However, the cost would be unemployment. To avoid that cost one must switch expenditure towards domestic goods: for example, by devaluing. But to devalue without deflating would push the economy to a point vertically above Z where the competitive gain from devaluation would soon be eroded by the inflation resulting from excess demand. In other words, a successful devaluation from a point of full employment must be accompanied by a policy of expenditure reduction – the same policy conclusion as emerged from the absorption approach.

This conclusion, and especially the IMF policies based upon it, has been challenged by economists such as Richard Cooper (b. 1934), Paul Krugman and Lance Taylor (b. 1940). They have recalled that devaluation has not just expenditure-switching effects but also direct effects on absorption: that is, expenditure-reducing effects. A rise in e may reduce A as well as increase ep^*/p, with the relative importance of each dependent on the extent to which devaluation provokes inflation. Hence devaluation may push the economy diagonally upward and to the left from Z, not vertically up. It is possible that the economy will be pushed to a point *below IB* even without the reinforcing deflationary measures called for by IMF orthodoxy, in which case application of those orthodox measures will create wasteful unemployment.

One can make some conjectures as to the type of economy in which this is likely to happen. First, if devaluation provokes an offsetting rise in domestic prices – for example, because of the presence of real-wage resistance – then devaluation will not have much effect in improving competitiveness to counter its absorption-reducing effect. Second, where there are few opportunities for substitution between domestically produced and foreign-produced goods, the *IB* curve will be very steep. The second factor suggests that countries like the Persian Gulf oil exporters or plantation-dominated economies are likely to fit the unorthodox case, while any economy suffering a high degree of real-wage resistance may do so as well because of the first factor. Countries with low elasticities will experience an additional deflationary impact if they initially have a trade deficit, since the domestic-currency value of the trade deficit (which constitutes a leakage from the income stream) will increase.

The reason *why* an economy fits the unorthodox case is important in drawing policy implications. For countries with little elasticity in the production structure, the main alternative to a reduction in absorption has to be foreign borrowing, until such time as new investment can come on stream in the export or import-substituting industries. For countries suffering from real-wage resistance, the opportunities may be somewhat broader. When orthodox fiscal–monetary–exchange-rate policies are inadequate to restore simultaneous internal and external balance, the reason is that real-income claims constrain the economy to points on or to the right of the curve WR (wage resistance) in Figure 8.2. This curve WR might be vertical or it might have a positive slope insofar as workers can be intimidated into accepting lower real wages (requiring lower absorption) by an uncompetitive exchange rate with its threat of bankruptcies. Devaluation from a point like Z would produce a neutralizing inflation that would at best leave ep^*/p unchanged and restore the economy to point Z. The only ways to restore simultaneous internal and external balance are to operate on the supply side, to the extent that may be feasible, or to develop an incomes policy capable of reconciling the labour force to the harsh facts of life, and thus push the curve WR left. Failure to do either guarantees repeated economic crises.

The model underlying the elasticities approach, which together with the multiplier analysis formed the basis for Figure 8.1, is essentially a three-good model with exportables, importables and a large non-traded goods sector. It

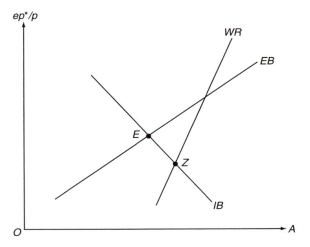

Figure 8.2 Implications of real-wage resistance

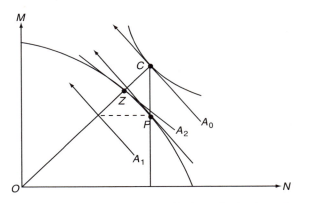

Figure 8.3 Internal and external balance in the dependent economy model

is worth checking that the conclusions of Meade's synthesis are robust, which can be done by examining the dependent economy model. Consider Figure 8.3. Suppose that the price of the non-traded good N is fixed in domestic currency (or at least sticky), while that of the traded good M is determined by arbitrage from the world market at the level $p_m = ep_m^*$. Suppose that the resulting relative price is represented by budget curves with slope equal to that of A_0. If expenditure is initially in excess of income, at the level represented by the budget line A_0, then consumption will occur at the point C and production at the point P. There is internal balance because the production of home goods is equal to consumption, but an external deficit because the consumption of traded goods M exceeds their production. To achieve external balance by deflation alone would require cutting the value of absorption to A_1, but this would create an excess supply of home goods and thus unemployment. To achieve internal and external balance simultaneously requires a devaluation to raise the relative price of traded goods and thus induce substitution by consumers away from traded goods and by producers towards traded goods, combined with an expenditure-reducing policy to cut absorption to A_2. The combination can achieve the point of internal and external balance at Z.

A BIBLIOGRAPHICAL NOTE

The initial conceptualization of internal and external balance is in *A Tract on Monetary Reform* (Keynes 1923). Meade's synthesis was developed in his careful taxonomic masterpiece (Meade 1951). Its popularization in diagrams like Figure 8.1 was due to the Australians: Swan (1960), first written in 1955; Salter (1959); and Corden (1960). The generalization to expenditure-reducing versus expenditure-switching effects was due to Johnson (1961, ch. 6), reprinted in Caves and Johnson (1968) and Cooper (1969). For the argument that devaluation may be contractionary, see Cooper (1971) and Krugman and Taylor (1978). Gylfason and Risegar (1984) investigate empirically the circumstances under which devaluation will improve the balance of payments (virtually always) and be contractionary (sometimes).

NOTES

1 James E. Meade is the winner of the 1972 Nobel prize in economics. His synthesis of the income and price effects of devaluation provides the most authoritative statement of the orthodox balance of payments theory.
2 Also known as the 'non-accelerating inflation rate of unemployment' or 'NAIRU'.

REFERENCES

Caves, R.E. and Johnson, H.G. (eds.) (1968) *Readings in International Economics.* Homewood, Ill: Irwin.
Cooper, R.N. (ed.) (1969) *International Finance: Selected readings*, London: Penguin.
Cooper, R.N. (1971) *Currency Devaluation in Developing Countries.* Princeton Essays in International Finance, no. 86.
Corden, W.M. (1960) 'The geometric representation of policies to attain internal and external balance', *Review of Economic Studies*, October; reprinted in Cooper (1969).
Gylfasen, T. and Risegar, O. (1984) 'Does devaluation improve the current account?', European Economic Review, 51, 129–39.
Johnson, E. and Moggridge, D. (various years) *The Collected Writings of John Maynard Keynes*, 30 vols., London: Macmillan.
Keynes, J.M. (1923) *A Tract on Monetary Reform*, London: Macmillan: reprinted as vol. IV in Johnson and Moggridge (various years).
Krugman, P. and Taylor, L. (1978) 'Contractionary effects of devaluation', *Journal of International Economics*, 9, 445–56.
Meade, J. E. (1951) *The Theory of International Economic Policy, Vol. I: The balance of payments*, London: Oxford University Press.

Salter, W.E.G. (1959) 'Internal and external balance: the rate of price and expenditure effects, *Economic Record*, 35, 226–38.

Swan, T. (1960) 'Economic control in a dependent economy' *Economic Record*, March.

9   The meaning of 'internal balance'

*James E. Meade**

American Economic Review, vol 83, no. 6 (December 1993), pp. 3–9

I

It is a special privilege for me on this occasion to have my name associated with that of Professor Bertil Ohlin. By the younger generation of economists we are no doubt both regarded as what in my country are now known as 'senior citizens'; but I am just that much younger than Professor Ohlin to have regarded him as one of the already established figures when I was first trying to understand international economics. His great work on *International and Interregional Trade* opened up new insights into the complex of relationships between factor supplies, costs of movement of products and factors, price relationships, and the actual international trade in products, migration of persons, and flows of capital. Of the two volumes which I later wrote on International Economic Policy—namely, *The Balance of Payments* and *Trade and Welfare*—it is in the latter that the influence of this work by Professor Ohlin is most clearly marked.

But Professor Ohlin also made an important contribution to what now might be called the macro-economic aspects of a country's balance of payments. In 1929 in *The Economic Journal* he engaged in a famous controversy with Keynes on the problem of transferring payments from one country to another across the foreign exchanges. In this he laid stress upon the income-expenditure effects of the reduced spending power in the paying country and of the increased spending power in the recipient country. In doing so he made use of the usual distinction between a country's imports and exports; but in addition he emphasised the importance of the less usual distinction between a country's domestic non-tradeable goods and services and its tradeable, exportable and importable, goods. I made some use of this latter distinction in my *Balance of Payments*; but looking back I regret that I did not let it play a much more central role in that book.

II

Indeed I realise now, looking back with the advantage of hindsight, that my two books were deficient in many respects. From this rich field of deficiencies

* Nobel Memorial Lecture, December 8, 1977. Meade (Cambridge, England) received the 1977 Nobel Memorial Prize in Economic Science. Copyright © THE NOBEL FOUNDATION 1977.

I have selected one as the subject for today's lecture, because it raises an issue which in my opinion is at the present time perhaps the most pressing of all for the maintenance of a decent international economic order.

The basic analysis in *The Balance of Payments* was conducted in terms of static equilibrium models rather than in terms of dynamic growing or disequilibrium models. The use of this method of comparative statics was a result of Keynes's work.

Keynes in *The General Theory* applied Marshall's short-period analysis to the whole macro-economic system instead of to one single firm or industry. In this model additions to capital stocks are taking place; but we deal with a period of time over which the addition to the stock bears a negligible ratio to the total existing stock. Variable factors, and in particular labour, are applied to this stock with a rising marginal cost until marginal cost is equal to selling price—an assumption which can be modified to accommodate microeconomic theories about determinants of output and prices in conditions of imperfect competition. The rest of the Keynesian analysis with its consumption function, liquidity preference, and investment function can be used to determine the short-period, static, stable equilibrium levels of total national income, output, employment, interest, and so on, in terms of such parameters as the money wage rate, the supply of money, entrepreneurs' expectations, rates of tax, levels of government expenditure, and the foreign demand for the country's exports. The model can then be used to show how changes in these parameters would affect the short-period equilibrium levels of the various macro-economic variables. Keynes was not, I think, interested in the process of change from one short-period equilibrium to another, though he was very interested in the way in which expectations in a milieu of uncertainty would affect the short-period equilibrium, in particular through their effect upon investment. If my interpretation is correct, he judged intuitively that the short-period mechanisms of adjustment were in fact such that at any one time the macro-elements of the system would not be far different from their short-period equilibrium values; and he may well have been correct in this judgement in the 1930's.

The Balance of Payments was essentially based on macro-economic models of this kind. What I tried to elaborate was the international interplay between a number of national economies of this Keynesian type. For this purpose I discussed the different combinations of policy variables which would serve to reconcile what I called 'external balance' with what I called 'internal balance'. By 'external balance' was meant a balance in the country's international payments; and although this idea presents, and indeed at the time was realised to present, considerable conceptual difficulties, nevertheless I still instinctively feel that it is not a foolish one. But can the same be said of the idea of 'internal balance'? Does it mean full employment or does it mean price stability?

I don't believe that I was quite so stupid as not to realise that full employment and price stability are two quite different things. But one treated them under the same single umbrella of 'internal balance' because of a belief or an assumption that if one maintained a level of effective demand which preserved full employment one would also find that the money price level was reasonably stable. The reason for making this tacit or open assumption was, of course, due to a tacit or open assumption that the money wage rate was normally either constant or at least very sluggish in its movements. In this case with the Keynesian model the absolute level of money prices would be rather higher or lower according as the level of effective demand moved the economy to a higher or lower point on the upward-sloping short-period marginal cost curve. But there would be no reason to expect a rapidly rising or falling general level of money prices in any given short period equilibrium position.

This may have been a very sensible assumption to make in the 1930's. It is more doubtful whether it was a sensible assumption to make in the immediate postwar years when *The Balance of Payments* was being written. In any case if I were now rewriting that book I would do the underlying analysis not in terms of the reconciliation of the two objectives of external balance and internal balance, but in terms of the reconciliation of the three objectives of equilibrium in the balance of payments, full employment, and price stability.

Why did I not proceed in this way in the first place?

I was certainly aware of the danger that trade union and other wage-fixing institutions might not permit the maintenance of full employment without a money cost-price inflation. But I suppose that writing immediately after the war I adopted the basic model which was so useful before the war and simply hoped that somehow or another it would be possible to avoid full employment leading to a wage-price inflation. Having done so I found that there remained quite enough important international relationships to examine even on that simplifying assumption. That is not perhaps a very strong defence of my position, but I suspect that it is the truth of the matter.

I am well aware that I could now adopt a more sophisticated line of defence of my past behaviour. It is quite possible to define as the natural level of employment, that level which—given the existing relevant institutions affecting wage-fixing arrangements—would lead to a demand for real wage rates rising at a rate equal to the rate of increase of labour productivity. One has only to add to this the assumption that one starts from a position in which there is no general expectation of future inflation or deflation of money prices to reach the position in which the maintenance of this natural level of employment is compatible with price stability. If this natural level of employment is treated as 'full employment', one has succeeded in defining a situation of 'internal balance' in which 'full employment' and 'price stability' can be simultaneously achieved.

One could then go on to discuss the many institutions which affect this so-called full employment level. Decent support of the living standards of those who are out of work may mean that unemployed persons are legitimately rather more choosey about taking the first alternative job which is offered to them, quite apart from the existence of a limited number of confirmed 'sturdy beggars' who prefer living on social benefits to an honest day's work.

The obligation to make compulsory severance or redundancy payments when employees are dismissed may make some employers less willing to expand their labour force in conditions in which future developments are uncertain. Monopolistic trade union action may put an extra upward pressure on money wage demands which means that unemployment must be maintained at a higher level in order to exert an equivalent countervailing downward pressure. Some statutory wage-fixing bodies in particular occupations may exert a similar influence.

It is not very helpful to squabble about definitions. There is, however, a very real difference of substance between those who do, and those who do not, consider these wage-fixing institutional arrangements to cause very real difficulties. Is it necessary to achieve some radical reform of these institutions in order to make reasonable price stability compatible with reasonably low levels of unemployment? Or is it a fact that, if affairs could for a time be so conducted as to remove the expectation of any marked future inflation of the money cost of living, we would find that even with present institutions the natural level of unemployment would not be at all excessive? I myself would expect that in many countries including the United Kingdom the recasting of wage-fixing arrangements would still be found to be of crucial importance.

As far as the less important question of definition is concerned, I prefer to think of 'full employment' and 'price stability' as being two separate and often conflicting objectives of macro-economic policies. Anyone who has this preference can, of course, be legitimately challenged to define what is meant by full employment. Perhaps I would be driven to the extreme of defining full employment as that level of employment at which the supply-demand conditions would not lead to attempts to push up the real wage rate more rapidly than the rate of increase in labour productivity if there were perfect competition in the labour market—no monopsonistic employers, no monopolistic trade unions, no social benefits to the unemployed, no obligations on employers to make compulsory severance or redundancy payments to dismissed workers, and so on— though I am not at all sure whether this extreme form of definition has much meaning. However, in so far as full employment could be defined somewhere along these lines, one would end up with price stability and full employment as separate macro-economic objectives in any real world situation with wage-fixing arrangements as one of the instruments of policy. This is the way in which I like to think of macro-economic problems.

If one adopted this approach, how should *The Balance of Payments* be recast? In the basic model we would have the three targets of external balance, full employment, and price stability. If one continued to think in terms of matching to each 'target' a relevant policy 'weapon', one could divide the weapons into three main armouries: the first containing the weapons which directly affect the level of money demands (e.g. monetary and budgetary policies); the second containing the weapons which directly affect the fixing of money wage rates; and the third containing the weapons which directly affect the foreign exchanges, such as the fixing of rates of exchange, measures of exchange control, and commercial policy measures designed directly to affect the total value of imports and exports.

My subsequent education in the rudiments of the theory of control of dynamic systems suggested to me that this was not the best way to have proceeded. One should not pair each particular weapon off with a particular target as its partner, using weapon A to hit target A, weapon B to hit target B, and so on. Rather one should seek to discover what pattern of combination of simultaneous use of all available weapons would produce the most preferred pattern of combination of simultaneous hits on all the desirable targets. With this way of looking at things no particular weapon is concentrated on any particular target; it is the joint effect of all the weapons on all the targets which is relevant.

There is no doubt that this is the way in which a control engineer will look at the problem and that in a technical sense it is the correct way to find the most preferred pattern of hits on a number of targets simultaneously. For a considerable period between the writing of *The Balance of Payments* and the present time I was fully enamoured of this method.

But I am in the process of having second thoughts and of asking myself whether the idea of trying to hit each particular target by use of a particular weapon or clearly defined single armoury of weapons is really to be ruled out. This onset of second childhood is due to a consideration of the political conditions in which economic policies must be operated. It is most desirable in a modern democratic community that the ordinary man or woman in the street should as far as possible realise what is going on, with responsibilities for success or failure in the different fields of endeavour being dispersed but clearly defined and allocated. To treat the whole of macro-economic control as a single subject for the mysterious art of the control engineer is likely to appear at the best magical and at the worst totally arbitrary and unacceptable to the ordinary citizen. To put each clearly defined weapon or armoury of weapons in the charge of one particular authority or set of decision makers with the responsibility of hitting as nearly as possible one well defined target is a much more intelligible arrangement.

Of course there are obvious disadvantages in any such proposal. Thus the best way for authority A to use weapon A to achieve objective A will undoubtedly be affected by what authorities B and C are doing with weapons B and C. It depends upon the structure of relationships within the economic system how far these repercussions are of major importance. Perhaps a mysterious dynamic model operated inconspicuously in some back room by control experts for silent information of the authorities concerned might be useful; and in any case in the real world it would be desirable for the different authorities at least to communicate their plans to each other so that, by what one hopes would be a convergent process of mutual accommodation, some account could be taken of their interaction. But in the modern community there is, I think, merit in arrangements in which each authority or set of decision makers has a clear ultimate responsibility for success or failure in the attainment of a clearly defined objective.

III

There are six ways in which each of three weapons can be separately aimed at each of three targets. Some of these patterns make more sense than others. In this lecture I can do no more than give a brief account of that particular pattern which, as it seems to me at present, would make the best sense if one takes into account both economic effectiveness and also comprehensibility of responsibilities in a free democratic society. With this pattern

1 the instruments of demand management, fiscal and monetary, would be used so to control total money expenditures as to prevent excessive inflations or deflations of total money incomes;
2 wage-fixing institutions would be modelled so as to restrain upward movements of money wage rates in those particular sectors where there were no shortages of manpower and to allow upward movements where these were needed to attract or retain labour to meet actual or expected manpower shortages, thus preserving full employment with some moderate average rise in money wage rates in conditions in which demand management policies were ensuring a steadily growing money demand for labour as a whole; and
3 foreign exchange policies would be used to keep the balance of payments in equilibrium.

This pattern implies the use of the weapons of demand management to restrain *monetary* inflation and of wage-fixing to influence the *real* level of employment and output. Many of my friends and colleagues who share my admiration for Keynes will at this point part company from me. 'Surely', they will say, 'you have got it the wrong way round. Did not Keynes suggest that the control of demand should be used to influence the total amount of real output and employment which it was profitable to maintain, while the money wage rate was left simply to determine the absolute level of money prices and costs at which this level of real activity would take place?' I agree that this is in fact the way in which Keynes looked at things in the late 1930's when it could be assumed that the money wage rate was in any case rather constant or sluggish in its movements. What he would be saying today is anybody's guess; and I do not propose to take part in that guessing game except to say that he would be appalled at the current rates of price inflation. It is a complete misrepresentation of the views of a great and wise man to suggest that in present conditions he would have been concerned only with the maintenance of full employment and not at all with the avoidance of money price and wage inflation.

But, whatever Keynes' policy recommendations would be in present circumstances, I would maintain that the way in which I have distributed the weapons among the targets is in no way incompatible with Keynes' analysis. In the 1930's Keynes argued, rightly or wrongly, that cutting money wage rates would have little effect in expanding employment because its main effect would be simply to reduce the absolute level of the relevant money prices, money costs, money incomes, and money expenditures, leaving the levels of real output and employment much unchanged. It is a totally different matter, wholly consistent with that Keynesian analysis, to suggest that the money wage rate might be used to influence the level of employment in conditions in which the money demand was being successfully managed in such a way as to prevent changes in wage rates from causing any offsetting rise or fall in total money incomes and expenditures. If one is going to aim particular weapons at particular targets in the interests of democratic understanding and responsibility, it is, in my opinion, most appropriate that the Central Bank which creates money and the Treasury which pours it out should be responsible for preventing monetary inflations and deflations, while those who fix the wage rates in various sectors of the economy should take responsibility for the effect of their action on the resulting levels of employment.

Earlier I spoke of 'price stability' as being one of the components of 'internal balance'. Yet in the outline which I have just given of a possible distribution of responsibilities no one is directly responsible for price stability. To make price stability itself the objective of demand management would be very dangerous. If there were an upward pressure on prices because the prices of imports had risen or because indirect taxes had been raised, the maintenance of price stability would require an offsetting absolute reduction in domestic money wage costs; and who knows what levels of depression and unemployment it might be necessary consciously to engineer in order to achieve such a result? This particular danger might be avoided by choice of a price index for stabilisation which excluded both indirect taxes and the price of imports; but even so, the stabilisation of such a price index would be very dangerous. If any remodelled wage-fixing arrangements were not working perfectly—and it would be foolhardy to assume a perfect performance—a very moderate excessive upward pressure on money wage rates and so on costs might cause a very great reduction in output and employment if there were no rise in selling prices so that the whole of the impact of the increased money costs was taken on profit margins. If, however, it was total money incomes which were stabilized, a much more moderate decline in employment combined with a moderate rise in prices would serve to maintain the uninflated total of money incomes.

The effectiveness of the pattern of responsibilities which I have outlined rests upon the assumption that there is a reasonably high elasticity of demand for labour in terms of the real wage rate, since success is to be achieved by setting a money wage rate relatively to money demand prices which gives a full employment demand for labour by employers. I have no doubt myself that in the longer-run the elasticity of demand is great enough. But what of the short-run? What if in every industry there is a stock of fixed capital in a form which sets an absolute limit to the amount of labour which can be usefully employed, while for some reason or another of past history there is more labour seeking work than can be usefully employed? There will be unemployment in every industry; and any resulting reduction in money wage rates combined with the maintenance of total money incomes would merely redistribute income from wages to profits.

I have explained the danger in its most exaggerated form; but it would remain a real one even in a much moderated form. There should, of course, never be any question of the wholesale immediate slashing of wage rates in every sector in which there was any unemployment. Any such arrangement would, for the reasons which I have outlined, be economically most undesirable even if it were politically possible. What one has in mind is simply that in a milieu in which total money incomes are steadily rising at a moderate rate, money wage rates should be rising rather more rapidly in some sectors and less rapidly or not at all in other sectors according to the supplies of available labour and the prospects of future demands for labour in those sectors. There would be no requirement that any money wage rates must be actually reduced.

But putting more emphasis on supply-demand conditions in the settlement of particular wage claims could only work if there were general acceptance of the idea by the ordinary citizen; and such acceptance would depend *inter alia* upon a marked change of emphasis about policies for influencing the redistribution of the national income. I have long believed that it is only if, somehow or another, the ordinary citizen can be persuaded to put less emphasis on wage bargaining and more emphasis on fiscal policies of taxation and social security for influencing the personal distribution of income and wealth that we have any hope of building the sort of free, efficient, and humanely just society in which I would like to live. But that raises a host of issues which I cannot discuss today.

There is, however, one feature of this connection between the supply-demand criterion for fixing wage rates and the attitude of the wage earner to his real standard of living on which I do wish to comment. Suppose, for example, because of a rise in the world price of oil or of other imported foodstuffs or raw materials, that the international terms of trade turn against an industrialised country. This is equivalent to a reduction in the productivity of labour and of other factors employed in the country in question. If money wage rates are pushed up as the prices of imported goods go up in order to preserve the real purchasing power of wage incomes, money wage costs are raised for the domestic producer without any automatic rise in the selling price of the domestic components of their outputs. Profit margins are squeezed. The demand for labour will fall unless and until profit margins are restored by a corresponding rise in the selling prices of domestic products. But such a rise would in turn cause a further rise in the cost of living, followed perhaps be a further offsetting rise in money wage rates, with a further round of pressure on profit margins. In fact workers are attempting to establish a real wage rate which, because of the adverse effect of the terms of international trade, is no longer compatible with full employment. The resulting rounds of pressure on profit margins, rises in domestic selling prices, further rises in money wage rates, further pressure on profit margins, and so on, may result in stagflation—a level of employment below full employment with a continuing inflation of money prices.

This story may in fact help to explain what has happened recently in some industrialised countries. But my purpose in telling it is merely to give a vivid illustration of the fact that an effective combination of full employment with the avoidance of inflation necessarily requires that wage-fixing should take as its main criterion the supply demand conditions in the labour market without undue insistence on the attainment and defence of any particular real wage income. The latter must be the combined result of domestic productivity, the terms of international trade, and tax and other measures taken to affect the distribution of income between net-of-tax spendable wages and other net-of-tax incomes.

IV

So much for the specification of targets and for the distribution of weapons among targets. What about the detailed specification of the weapons themselves?

If the velocity of circulation of money were constant, a steady rate of growth in the total money demand for goods and services could be achieved by a steady rate of growth in the supply of money, and this in turn could be the task of an independent Central Bank with the express responsibility for ensuring a steady rate of growth of the money supply of, say, 5 per cent per annum. It is a most attractive and straightforward solution; but, alas, I am still not persuaded to be an out-and-out monetarist of this kind. It is difficult to define precisely what is to be treated as money in a modern economy. At the borderline of the definition substitutes for money can and do readily increase and decrease in amount and within the borders of the definition velocities of circulation can and do change substantially. Can we not use monetary policy more directly for the attainment of the objective of a steady rate of growth of, say, 5 per cent per annum in total money incomes, and supplement this monetary policy with some form of fiscal regulator in order to achieve a more prompt and effective response? For this purpose one would, of course, be well advised to call in aid the skills of the control engineer in order to cope with the dynamic problem of keeping the total national money income on its target path. Am I to be regarded as a member of the lunatic fringe or as an unconscious ally of authoritarian tyranny if I express this remaining degree of belief in the possibilities of rational social engineering?

I find very attractive the idea that this monetary control should be the responsibility of some body which was not directly dependent upon the government for its day-to-day decisions but which was charged by its constitution independently to achieve this stable but moderate growth of money incomes. But there is real difficulty in endowing any such independent body with powers to use fiscal policy as well as monetary policy to achieve its objective.

Let me take an example. Suppose that overseas producers of oil raise abruptly the price charged to an importing country; and, to isolate the point which I want to make, suppose further that the oil producers invest in the importing country any excess funds which they receive from the sale of an unchanged supply of oil, so that there is no immediate need to cut imports or to expand exports in order to protect the foreign exchanges. The abrupt price change will, however, tend to cause a deflation of money incomes in the importing country whose citizens will, out of any given income, spend less on home produced goods in order to spend more on imported oil, the receipts from which are saved by the oil producers. With the scheme of responsibilities which I have outlined it is now the duty of the demand managers to reflate the demand for goods and services in the importing country in order to prevent a fall in money incomes in that country.

But there are at least two alternative strategies for such reflation.

In the first place, the taxation of the citizens of the importing country might be reduced so that, while they have to spend more on imported oil, they have just so much more spendable income to maintain their demands for their own products. In this case the government directly or indirectly borrows funds saved by the oil producers to finance the larger budget deficit due to the reduced tax payments by the domestic consumers. No one's standard of living is immediately affected.

But if this solution is adopted, the importing country faces an ever-growing debt to the foreign oil producers with no corresponding growth of domestic or foreign capital to set against it. If this is considered undesirable, the private citizens must not be relieved of tax; their current consumption standards must be allowed to fall as a result of the rise in the price of oil; and the reflation of domestic incomes must be brought about by measures which stimulate expenditure on extra real capital development at home, the finance of which will mop up the savings of the oil producers. Such action will depend upon monetary policies rather than, or at least as well as, upon fiscal action.

I have told this particular story simply to make the point that the choice between fiscal action and monetary action must often depend upon basic policy issues which should certainly be the responsibility of the government rather than of any independent monetary authority. Perhaps the best compromise is an independent monetary authority charged so to manage the money supply and the market rate of interest as to maintain the growth of total money income on its 5-per-cent-per-annum target path, after taking into account whatever fiscal policies the government may adopt. One would hope, of course, that there would be a suitable discussion of their plans and policies between the government and the monetary authority; but the latter would be given an ultimately independent duty and independent choice of monetary policy for keeping total money incomes on their target path.

The difficulties involved in the specification of the weapons of demand management are real enough; but they fade into insignificance when they are compared with the problems of remodelling wage-fixing arrangements in such a way as to ensure a greater emphasis on supply-demand conditions in each sector of the labour market.

I can think of five broad lines of approach.

First, one can conceive of wage fixing in each sector of the labour market by the edict of some government authority. An efficient use of this method would be extremely difficult in a modern economy with its innumerable different forms and skills of labour in so many different and diverse regions, occupations, and industries. It would, I think, in any case ultimately involve a degree of governmental authoritarian control which I personally would find very distasteful.

Second, there is the corporate state solution in which a monopoly of employer monopolies agrees with a monopoly of labour monopolies on a central bargain for the distribution between wages and profits in the various sectors of the economy of the total national money income which the demand managers are going to provide. I suspect that, in the United Kingdom at any rate, any such bargain would be very difficult to attain without leaving some important, but relatively powerless, sectors out in the cold of unemployment or of very low wages. In any case I ought to reveal my prejudice against being ruled by a monopoly of uncontrolled private monopolists.

Third, the restoration of competitive conditions in the labour market would in theory do the trick, since the competitive search for jobs would restrain the wage rate in any sector in which there was unemployed labour and the competitive search for hands by competitive employers would raise the wage rate in any sector in which manpower was scarce. There is little doubt that in some cases trade unions have attained an excessively privileged position and some reduction of their monopoly powers might help towards a solution. But I do not believe that any full solution is to be found along this competitive road. On the employers' side it may be impossible to ensure effective competition where economies of large scale severely restrict the number of employers. On the employees' side the whole of history suggests the powerful psychological need for workers with common concerns to get together in the formation of associations to represent their common interests. Moreover, reliance on individual competition might well involve the reduction, if not elimination, of support for workers who were unemployed and of compulsory severance or redundancy payments to workers whose jobs disappeared. But what one wants to find is some effective, but compassionate and humane, method which applies supply-demand criteria for the fixing of wage rates for those in employment without inflicting needless hardship and anxiety on those particular individuals who are inevitably adversely affected by economic change.

Fourth, there are those who see the solution in the labour-managed economy in which workers hire capital rather than capital hiring workers. In such circumstances there would be no wage rate to fix. Workers would share among themselves whatever income they could earn in their concerns after payment of whatever fixed interest or rent was necessary to hire their instruments of production. These ideas are very attractive; but, alas, there is, I think, good reason to believe that satisfactory outcome on these lines is possible only in those sectors of the economy where small-scale enterprises are appropriate and where conditions make it fairly easy to set up new competing co-operative concerns.

Finally, there remains the possibility of the replacement in wage bargaining of the untamed use of monopolistic power through the threat of strikes, lockouts, and similar industrial action by the acceptance of arbitral awards made by trusted and impartial outside tribunals—awards which would, however, have to be heavily weighted by considerations of the supply-demand conditions of each particular case, if they were to achieve what I have suggested should be the basic objective of wage-fixing arrangements.

This is the civilised approach; but I am under no illusion that it is an easy one. It relies upon a widespread acceptance of the idea that some such approach is necessary for everyone's ultimate welfare and, in particular, as I have already indicated, upon the belief that there are alternative fiscal and similar policies to ensure social justice in the ultimate distribution of income and wealth. But even if in the course of time such a general acceptance could be achieved, some form of sanction for its application in some particular cases would almost certainly be needed. The punishment of individuals as criminals for taking monopolistic action to disturb a wage award does not hold out much hope of success. But is it pure dreaming to conceive ultimately of a state of affairs in which (1) in the case of any dispute about wages either party to the dispute or the government itself could apply for an award of the kind which I have indicated and (2) certain financial privileges and legal immunities otherwise enjoyed by the parties to a trade dispute would not be available in the case of industrial action taken in defiance of such an award?

Perhaps this is merely an optimist's utopian fantasy; but I can think of nothing better.

V

So much for the attainment of price stability and full employment through the instrumentalities of demand management and wage-fixing. What about the attainment of external balance through foreign exchange policies?

In my view the appropriate division of powers and obligations between national governments and international institutions is that the national governments should be responsible for national monetary, fiscal, and wage policies which combine full employment with price stability and that external balance should be maintained by foreign exchange policies under the supervision of international institutions.

Variations in the rate of exchange between the national currencies combined with freedom of trade and payments should in my view be the normal instrument of such foreign exchange policies. But this is not to say that there will never be occasion for the use of other instruments of foreign exchange policy. Special control arrangements may be appropriate where the removal of an international imbalance requires wholesale industrial development or structural change, or where abrupt changes in the international flow of capital funds require special offsetting measures, or where differences in national tax regimes would distort international transactions in the absence of offsetting measures. But where such exceptions to the free movement of goods and funds arise, these should be under the rules and supervision of appropriate international institutions.

After the war we managed to lay the foundations of an international system of this kind with the pivotal institutions of the International Monetary Fund, the International Bank for Reconstruction and Development, and the General Agreement on Tariffs and Trade, a system which for a quarter of a century resulted in a most remarkable expansion of international trade. In my opinion there was one important original flaw in this system, namely the insistence on the International Monetary Fund's very sticky adjustable peg mechanism for the correction of inappropriate exchange rates. But even this flaw has now gone as the International Monetary Fund seeks to find the most appropriate rules for running a system of international flexible exchange rates.

And yet we seem now to be faced with the possibility of a gigantic tragedy, with this initial success being fated unnecessarily to end in calamity. Why is this so? In my view the answer is obvious; it is simply because so many of the national governments of the developed industrialised countries have failed to find appropriate national institutional ways of combining full employment with price stability.

If they could do so, not only would the domestic tragic waste and social discontent of heavy unemployment in such countries be removed, but the international scene would be transformed. The case for the use by developed countries of massive import restrictions rather than of gradual and moderate changes in exchange rates to look after their balances of payments would, I suspect, evaporate. It is the spectacle of imports competing with the products of domestic industries in which there is already serious unemployment which is the greatest threat to the freedom of imports into the developed countries. With full employment and price stability at home the balance of payments could with much more confidence be left to the mechanism of flexible foreign exchange rates. The developed countries would then have less difficulty in giving financial aid to the third world; and, what in my opinion is even more important, they could much more readily accept the inflow from the third world of their labour-intensive products.

In this lecture I have marked an occasion which is concerned with international economics with a lecture on internal balance. But I suggest that in present conditions this is not anomalous. I do not, I think, exaggerate wildly when I conclude by saying that one—though, of course, only one—of the really important factors on which the health of the world now depends is the recasting of wage-fixing arrangements in a limited number of developed countries.

10 The internal and external balance when policy choice is endogenous

Mehmet Ugur

Both Mundell and Meade assume that the government can be modelled as a 'social planner' whose objective is to steer the economy towards simultaneous achievement of internal balance (IB) and external balance (EB). The internal balance can be defined as full employment and the external balance can be taken to represent balance of payments equilibrium. They also assume that expectations are static, in the sense that economic agents do not revise their expectations of the relevant variables (e.g. prices, exchange rates, etc.) in response to announced government policy. Finally, prices and wages are assumed constant in the short run.

Under these assumptions, macroeconomic policy-making boils down to the solution of two problems: (i) identifying the desired macroeconomic targets and the policy instruments available; and (ii) assigning the instruments to the targets sought. The solution to these problems can be followed in Chapters 7 and 8 above. In this chapter, we will pursue two aims. First, we will revisit the solution provided by Mundell and Meade with a view to generalising the assignment rule. Then, we will introduce expectations into the models and assess the effectiveness of the proposed policy design.

Assume that the government is interested in achieving two targets (IB and EB) by using two instruments (I_1 and I_2). The two targets can be written as functions of two instruments as follows:

$$\text{IB} = \alpha_{11}I_1 + \alpha_{12}I_2 \tag{1}$$
$$\text{EB} = \alpha_{21}I_1 + \alpha_{22}I_2 \tag{2}$$

where α_{ij} (where $i = 1, 2$ and $j = 1, 2$) are parameters to be estimated from the structural model of the economy.

Differentiating and setting equal to zero, we can write:

$$\text{dIB} = \alpha_{11}\text{d}I_1 + \alpha_{12}\text{d}I_2 = 0 \tag{3}$$
$$\text{dEB} = \alpha_{21}\text{d}I_1 + \alpha_{22}\text{d}I_2 = 0 \tag{4}$$

In matrix form, (3) and (4) can be written as follows:

$$\begin{bmatrix} \alpha_{11} & \alpha_{12} \\ \alpha_{21} & \alpha_{22} \end{bmatrix} \begin{bmatrix} I_1 \\ I_2 \end{bmatrix} = \begin{bmatrix} 0 \\ 0 \end{bmatrix} \tag{5}$$

A solution to this set of equations exists if the determinant of the coefficient matrix is different from zero. This implies that $\alpha_{11}\alpha_{22} - \alpha_{21}\alpha_{12} \neq 0$, or $\alpha_{11}\alpha_{22} \neq \alpha_{21}\alpha_{12}$. There is a close relationship between this condition and the rates of substitution between I_1 and I_2 along IB and EB. The rates of substitution along IB and EB can be derived from (3) and (4) as follows:

$$[dI_1/dI_2]_{IB} = -\alpha_{11}/\alpha_{12} \tag{3'}$$

$$[dI_1/dI_2]_{EB} = -\alpha_{21}/\alpha_{22} \tag{4'}$$

Geometrically, equations (3') and (4') represent also the slopes of IB and EB. If the slopes were equal, we could write $\alpha_{11}/\alpha_{12} = \alpha_{21}/\alpha_{22}$ which would also imply that $\alpha_{11}\alpha_{22} = \alpha_{21}\alpha_{12}$. Once this is the case, there is no unique solution to the set of equations (5). Therefore, the solution to (5) requires that the slopes of IB and EB (hence the rates of substitution between I_1 and I_2) be different. If this condition is satisfied, the two schedules will intersect at some point, which will be the desired equilibrium where both IB and EB are achieved.

Thus far, we have established the condition that must be satisfied so that the policy-maker can use I_1 and I_2 to achieve IB and EB simultaneously. The next step is to establish which instrument should be assigned to which target. This problem can be resolved by taking the ratio of (3') and (4'). Denoting this ratio by R, we can write:

$$R = (\alpha_{11}/\alpha_{12})/(\alpha_{21}/\alpha_{22}) \tag{6}$$

which can be re-written as:

$$R = (\alpha_{11}/\alpha_{21})/(\alpha_{12}/\alpha_{22}) \tag{6'}$$

If $R > 1$, then $(\alpha_{11}/\alpha_{21}) > (\alpha_{12}/\alpha_{22})$. This implies that $\alpha_{11} > \alpha_{21}$ and $\alpha_{12} < \alpha_{22}$. In economic terms, $\alpha_{11} > \alpha_{21}$ means that a given change in instrument I_1 will have a greater effect on IB compared to EB. Similarly, $\alpha_{12} < \alpha_{22}$ implies that a given change in instrument I_2 will have a greater effect on EB compared to the effect on IB. Then, efficiency requires that I_1 be assigned to IB and I_2 be assigned to EB. If, however, the ratio (R) is less than one, the assignment must be reversed: I_2 must be assigned to IB and I_1 must be assigned to EB

THE SOLUTION TO THE ASSIGNMENT PROBLEM BY MUNDELL AND MEADE

Mundell assumes that the exchange rate is fixed. Therefore, the policy instruments available to the policy-maker are fiscal policy and monetary policy. If we denote fiscal policy by I_1 and monetary policy by I_2, the problem for Mundell is to establish whether the ratio in (6′) above is greater or smaller than one. Mundell, rightly, argues that the ratio is greater than one. Then, I_1 (fiscal policy) should be assigned to IB and I_2 (monetary policy) should be assigned to EB. To see why, suppose that the economy is faced with recession and deficit, and fiscal policy (I_1) is the only available option. Then the government will undertake a fiscal expansion to achieve internal balance. The effect on IB is direct and will be determined by the open-economy multiplier, which can be written as $[1/(1 - ct + m)]$, where c is marginal propensity to consume, t is marginal tax rate and m is marginal propensity to import. On the other hand, the balance of payments deficit will require fiscal tightening, which will improve the current account in line with the marginal propensity to import. However, the fall in interest rates caused by fiscal tightening will lead to capital outflow and deterioration in the capital account. Therefore, the effect of fiscal policy on EB is uncertain. Given this information, effective use of policy instruments requires that fiscal policy (I_1) be assigned to IB, on which it is relatively more effective and its effect is certain. Then, by default, monetary policy (I_2) should be assigned to EB.

Meade assumes that the exchange rate is fixed, but adjustable in the face of balance of payments disequilibria. Then the policy instruments available to the policy-makers are absorption-regulating instruments (i.e. monetary and fiscal policy) (I_1) and the exchange rate (I_2). Given this specification, what can be said about the ratio in (6′)? Meade too demonstrates that the ratio is greater than one. As above, suppose that the economy is faced with unemployment. This requires reflationary policies – i.e. an increase in absorption. As absorption increases, income will increase in line with the open-economy multiplier. Now suppose that the economy is faced with a balance of payments deficit. This would require absorption-reducing policies. The effect of reduced absorption on the balance of payments will be felt only through falling demand for imports. However, devaluing the domestic currency has a stronger effect on the balance of payments by causing a fall in the demand for imports and an increase in the demand for exports. Therefore, it would be more efficient to target the EB via the exchange rate (I_2). By default, it would be more efficient to assign absorption (I_1) to IB.

Having examined the way in which Mundell and Meade resolve the assignment problem, we can now demonstrate how the correct assignment could enable the policy-maker to steer the economy towards internal and external balance. The targets–instruments equations used by Mundell are the same as (1) and (2) above – with I_1 representing government expenditures and I_2 standing for money supply. Then, we can work backward from the ratio in (6′) above and establish the relative slopes of IB and EB. Given that the ratio is greater than one, we can demonstrate that the absolute value of IB's slope $(-\alpha_{11}/\alpha_{12})$ is greater than that of EB $(-\alpha_{21}/\alpha_{22})$. Therefore, in Figure 10.1 below, IB is drawn steeper than EB. The slope of IB is negative because $\alpha_{11} > 0$ and $\alpha_{12} > 0$. The slope of EB is also negative because $\alpha_{21} < 0$ and $\alpha_{22} < 0$.

The point at which IB and EB intersect is the equilibrium point where both internal and external balance are achieved. At all other points, the economy will be faced with internal and external disequilibria. To see why this is the case, suppose the economy is at a point to the right of the IB schedule. At such a point, government expenditures (I_1) or money supply (I_2) or both are too high to be compatible with IB. Given that $\alpha_{11} > 0$ and $\alpha_{12} > 0$, the economy will be in an inflationary zone. By implication, at any point to the left of IB the economy will be in recession. At any point to the right of the EB schedule, government expenditures or money supply will be too high to be compatible with balance of payments balance. Given that $\alpha_{21} < 0$ and $\alpha_{22} < 0$, the balance of payments will be in deficit. Then, at any point to the left of EB, the balance of payments will be in surplus.

Given this information, the various combinations of internal and external disequilibria will be located in one of the four zones depicted in Figure 10.1. Then, the economy may be faced with one of the following types of disequilibria: recession/surplus (zone I); inflation/surplus (zone II); inflation/deficit (zone III); and recession/deficit (zone IV). In zones I and III, there is no conflict between fiscal policy (I_1) and monetary policy (I_2). If the economy is in zone I (recession/surplus), the policy prescription is expansionary monetary and fiscal policies. If this policy prescription is implemented, the economy will move towards the equilibrium point (a), where both IB and EB are achieved. If the economy is in zone III, the policy prescription will be just the opposite.

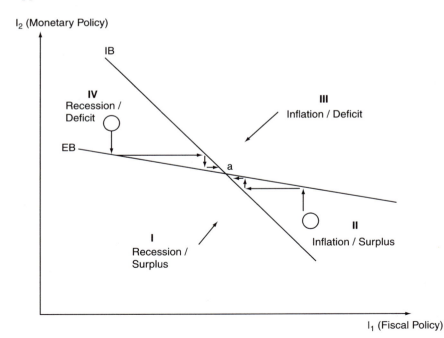

Figure 10.1 Achieving internal and external balance *à la* Mundell

In zones II and IV, however, there is a conflict between the policy instruments. For example in zone II, the inflation requires fiscal tightening whereas the balance of payments surplus requires monetary expansion. This is where the assignment rule is crucial. Provided that fiscal policy (I_1) is assigned to IB and monetary policy (I_2) to EB, successive rounds of fiscal tightening and monetary expansion will eventually take the economy to point (a). When the economy is in IV, the assignment is the same, but the policy stance is just the opposite: fiscal expansion must be combined with monetary tightening to reach point (a).

The instruments suggested by Meade are absorption-regulating policies (I_1) and the exchange rate (I_2). Then, we can follow the same procedure as above. The targets–instruments equations will be the same as in (1) and (2) above – except that the signs of the coefficients will be different. In Meade, the coefficients in the IB equation are both positive – i.e. $\alpha_{11} > 0$ and $\alpha_{12} > 0$. This means that an increase in absorption or an increase in the exchange rate (devaluation) will lead to an increase in output. Then, to remain on EB, an increase in absorption must be combined with a fall in the exchange rate (i.e. appreciation of the domestic currency). This means that the IB schedule will be sloping downward. The coefficients in the EB equation, however, have opposite signs: $\alpha_{21} < 0$ and $\alpha_{22} > 0$. This means that an increase in absorption must be combined with an increase in the exchange rate (a depreciation of the domestic currency) to remain on EB. Then, the EB schedule must be sloping upward. Given that the ratio in (6') is greater than one, the absolute value of IB's slope will be greater than that of EB. The intersection point between the

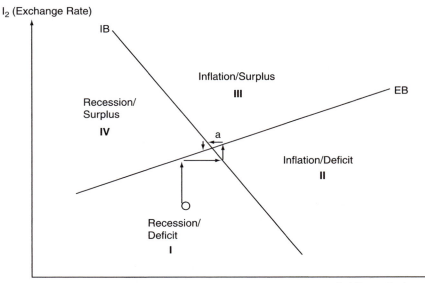

Figure 10.2 Achieving internal and external balance *à la* Meade

two (point a in Figure 10.2) will be the equilibrium point where both IB and EB are achieved.

Given this specification, Figure 10.2 can be divided into four zones representing the combinations of disequilibrium in the economy: recession/deficit (zone I); inflation/deficit (zone II); inflation/surplus (zone III); and recession/surplus (zone IV). A close look at Figure 10.2 will reveal that Meade's assignment rule has to tackle two tasks. First, the correct instrument must be assigned to the correct target. As indicated above, this requires that the exchange rate should be assigned to EB and absorption-regulating policies should be assigned to IB. Second, we must decide which policy instrument should be given a leadership role. For example, in zone I where the economy is faced with recession and deficit, the leadership must be given to the exchange rate. As the exchange rate is increased (the currency is devalued) to eliminate the balance of payments deficit, the resulting improvement in the current account helps reduce the recession. If, however, the leadership were given to absorption-increasing policies, the current account would deteriorate and the required rate of devaluation would be higher. Provided that the assignment is correct and the leadership problem is resolved, the economy can be steered towards point (a), where both IB and EB are achieved.

RATIONAL EXPECTATIONS AND THE ASSIGNMENT RULE

The concept of rational expectations was introduced into macroeconomic modelling in the 1970s by the new classical school. It is true that Keynes was aware of the significance of expectation formation. His theory of investment acknowledges this explicitly. In his specification of the present value, he assumes that the stream of future incomes from investment (i.e. the numerator of the present-value formula) is based on a given state of expectations. If the economic agents expect a positive economic climate, the stream of future incomes will be expected to be higher. Then, with a given discount rate, the desired level of investment will be higher. However, Keynes also assumes that expectations can be treated as an exogenous variable that is not likely to change in the short run. Obviously, the treatment of expectations formation as an exogenous variable is less than satisfactory. What is more problematic, however, is to ignore the impact of a change in expectations when economic agents eventually revise their expectations.

What the new classical school did in the 1970s was to address this problem by incorporating expectations formation into macroeconomic models endogenously. Their specification of expectations is based on the concept of rationality, which, in turn, is based on two axioms. First, economic agents make use of all available information, including past and current information. Second, economic agents make informed decisions, which conform to the results to be derived from theory. Applied to macroeconomic policy, these axioms imply the following: (i) economic agents will revise their expectations about relevant variables (e.g. prices, exchange rates, interest rates) when government policy changes (i.e. when new information becomes available); (ii) they will predict the impact of the policy change on the relevant variables and their predictions will be compatible with what economic theory predicts. Of course, these predictions may not be correct all the time, but the distribution of the error will be random with a mean of zero.

To the extent that this is the case, the policy activism proposed by Mundell and Meade is bound to run into serious difficulties. First of all, any change in government policy will induce the economic agents to revise their expectations of the future accordingly. They will also take actions compatible with the revised expectations so that the policy change does not affect their welfare negatively. Second, the economic agents will predict correctly the implication of the policy change. For example, they will predict that an expansionary monetary policy aimed at increasing output or employment will eventually lead to an increase in prices, a fall in interest rates and a fall in the value of the domestic currency. Then, the result is highly predictable: employees will revise their wage claims to ensure that their real wages do not fall, investors will adjust their portfolios and foreign exchange market operators will begin to sell domestic currency to avoid a capital loss. By engaging in such actions, economic agents will frustrate the government's action and/or ensure that the change in relevant nominal variables occurs sooner rather than later. Therefore, monetary expansion will have no effect on real variables such as employment or output unless the policy is introduced as a surprise. If, however, the economic agents know that the government subscribes to Mundell's or Meade's policy design, the surprise element will disappear. Then, a pre-announced assignment of policy instruments to desired targets will imply that the policy instruments are ineffective. In fact, active use of policy instruments to achieve internal and external balance will only destabilise the economy – as depicted in Figures 10.3 and 10.4 below.

To appreciate the implications of rational expectations formation for Mundell's and Meade's targets – instrument models, we need to formalise the new classical arguments summarised above. We will write down three equations specifying price determination, interest rates and the expected rate of devaluation. These are fairly common specifications used in rational expectation models.

$$p_{t+1} = {}_tp^e_{t+1} + \beta(y_{t+1} - y^*) \tag{7}$$

$$r = r^* + \hat{e} \tag{8}$$

$$\hat{e} = \lambda(\bar{e} - e) \tag{9}$$

All the variables above are expressed as logarithms, with the exception of interest rate – which is measured as unity plus the rate of interest as a fraction. For example, a 5 per cent interest rate will be written as 1.05. The variables refer to the following:

p_{t+1} = price level in period $(t + 1)$

p^e_{t+1} = price expected to prevail in period $(t+1)$ on the basis of
     information available in period (t)
y_{t+1} = the level of output in period $(t+1)$
y^* = the level of output compatible with internal balance
$0 < \beta < 1$
$0 < \lambda < 1$
$\hat{e}$ = expected rate of depreciation
$\bar{e}$ = equilibrium exchange rate
e = prevailing exchange rate
r = domestic interest rate
r^* = foreign interest rate.

Equation (7) states that the price level in period $(t+1)$ will depend on the expected price and the output gap. If expectations are revised upwards, the price prevailing in period $(t+1)$ will increase. This increase in p_{t+1} will be augmented as the output gap is reduced. Equation (8) is the expression for uncovered interest rate parity. For a given foreign interest rate, domestic interest rates will increase as the expected rate of depreciation increases. Finally, equation (9) states that economic agents will expect the currency to appreciate (depreciate) if the prevailing exchange rate is higher (lower) than the equilibrium exchange rate.

Given these formal statements, let us now examine the extent to which a correct assignment can enable the government to achieve IB and EB simultaneously. Figure 10.3 shows the same situation as Figure 10.1. The economy is faced with recession and balance of payments deficit at point (a). Following

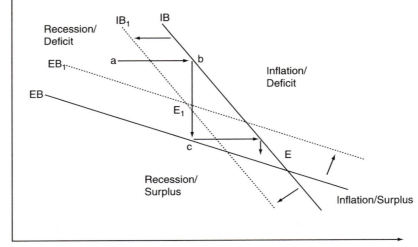

Figure 10.3 Mundell's assignment rule under rational expectations

Mundell's assignment rule, the government attempts to achieve internal balance by increasing public expenditures. From the structural model of the economy, it can be estimated that the amount of increase in public expenditure must be equal to (ab). Rational economic agents will anticipate that the fiscal expansion will eventually lead to an increase in prices. Therefore the expected price will increase. This will immediately lead to an increase in price level. Also, as the economy moves towards IB (as y_{t+1} approaches y^*), the downward effect of the recession on prices will diminish. As a result of both dynamics, the price level in period $(t + 1)$ will be higher than the current period (see equation 7). Predicting this result, wage setters will revise their expectations accordingly. As wage claims are revised upwards, the economy will land in an inflationary zone. In other words, by the time fiscal expansion works its way through, the IB schedule will have shifted to the left. The expectations-augmented IB schedule will now be at IB_1.

Given that the government is committed to Mundell's policy recommendation, it will not anticipate this shift in the IB schedule. Knowing that the economy is in a recession/deficit zone at point (a), it will now introduce a tight monetary policy in order to eliminate the balance of payments deficit. This implies a rise in interest rates, which will attract foreign capital and help rectify the balance of payments deficit. The rise in interest rates, however, must be accompanied by an increase in the expected rate of depreciation (see equation 8). This, however, also implies that the prevailing exchange rate is higher than the equilibrium exchange rate (see equation 9). In other words, the domestic currency must be undervalued. This piece of information will induce the foreign exchange market to expect revaluation in the future. Then the agents in the foreign exchange market will purchase domestic currency and sell foreign currency. This will lead to an increase in reserves beyond the increase caused by foreign capital inflow. Consequently, the monetary tightening from (b) to (c) will be more than what is required to eliminate the balance of payments deficit – i.e. it will push the balance of payments into surplus. This means that the EB schedule must be to the right of point (c) – as indicated by EB_1.

It is obvious from the analysis above that the government will miss its targets if expectations are rational. In addition, the equilibrium where internal and external balance can be achieved simultaneously will move. After the first round of fiscal expansion and monetary tightening, the equilibrium will be at point E_1 rather than E. This change in equilibrium implies further bad news for the targets–instruments activism. On the one hand, the economy is destabilised. On the other hand, the government – as long as it continues to ignore the implication of rational expectation formation – will be chasing the wrong equilibrium at E. This will only exacerbate the destabilising effect of the activist policy. Overall, Mundell's assignment rule cannot enable the government to achieve IB and EB if expectation formation is rational.

A similar result can be obtained when expectation formation is incorporated into Meade's synthesis too. Figure 10.4 demonstrates why this is the

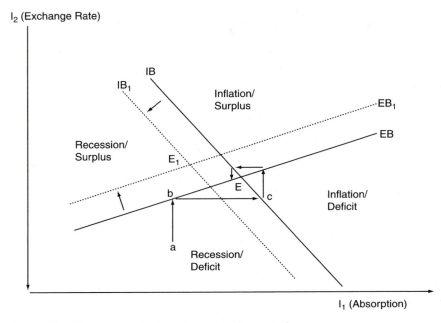

Figure 10.4 Meade's synthesis under rational expectations

case. Observing that the economy is in a recession/deficit zone at point (a), the government attempts to achieve IB and EB by using absorption-regulating and exchange rate policies. At point (a), the leadership role should be given to the exchange rate because devaluation will help eliminate the balance of payments deficit and ameliorate the recession. Using estimates from the structural model of the economy, the government devalues the currency from (a) to (b). In a world of static expectations, EB will be achieved at point (b). In a world of rational expectations, however, this is not the whole story. Devaluation will increase the prevailing exchange rate relative to the equilibrium rate and cause a fall in the expected rate of depreciation (see equation 9). The fall in the expected rate of depreciation will lead to a fall in domestic interest rates (see equation 8). Therefore, investors will start selling domestic assets and purchase foreign assets to avoid an income loss in the future. As a result, the capital account will deteriorate and the improvement in the current account caused by the devaluation may not be sufficient to achieve balance of payments equilibrium. In other words, the economy may still be faced with balance of payments deficit even if the currency is devalued from (a) to (b). Geometrically, this means that the EB schedule will have shifted upwards to EB_1.

According to Meade's synthesis, the next step that government must take is to increase absorption in order to eliminate the recession. The government increases absorption from (b) to (c). Rational economic agents will anticipate that this expansionary policy will eventually lead to an increase in prices.

Therefore the expected price will increase. This will immediately lead to an increase in price level. Also, as the economy moves towards IB (as y_{t+1} approaches y^*), the downward effect of the recession on prices will diminish. As a result of both dynamics, the price level in period $(t + 1)$ will be higher than in the current period (see equation 7). Predicting this result, wage setters will revise their wage claims accordingly. As wages claims are revised upwards, the economy will end up in an inflationary zone. In other words, by the time the expansionary policy works its way through, the IB schedule will have shifted to the left to IB_1.

Just as was the case under Mundell's assignment rule, the equilibrium is no longer at E. The expectations-augmented IB_1 and EB_2 now intersect at point E_1. This change in equilibrium means that the economy is destabilised. Also the government will be chasing the wrong equilibrium in its attempt to achieve EB and IB at E. Then, under rational expectations, Meade's synthesis cannot enable the government to achieve IB and EB simultaneously.

CONCLUSION

Starting from the targets–instruments models used by Mundell and Meade, the paragraphs above have demonstrated that the government would not be able to achieve IB and EB simultaneously if expectations formation were rational. The significance of this result lies not so much in its novelty as in its integrative spirit. What we did was to take Mundell's and Meade's specifications as given and inject into their models some behavioural assumptions based on rational expectations formation. This is nothing but conducting a comparative-static analysis to establish the impact of expectations on policy outcomes in a Keynesian targets–instruments framework. Obviously, this exercise is very simplistic when compared to sophisticated rational expectations modelling. However, its simplicity may be justified for two reasons: (i) it questions the Mundell–Meade type of policy design from within; and (ii) it enables us to compare and contrast the conflicting results that one can derive from a single analytical framework by changing certain assumptions.

The shortcoming in Mundell's assignment rule and Meade's synthesis is that both fail to take Keynes's exogenous expectations formation to its logical conclusions. Even if they are treated exogenously, expectations can change after a policy action (e.g. a fiscal expansion or devaluation) has been announced. Then, it will no longer be appropriate to ignore the impact of this expectation change on the policy outcome. It is necessary to treat the change in expectations as a shift variable that would affect the position of IB and EB. When this is done (i.e. the exogenous approach to expectations is taken to its logical conclusion), we would be faced with essentially new-classical results: the attempt to achieve a certain target by active use of the appropriate policy instrument will remain unsuccessful and the economy will be destabilised. Therefore, the policy recommendation would be to refrain from active use of policy instruments to achieve some desired targets. Instead, the policy design should be based on rules that would tie the hands of the government.

Questions

1 What is the assignment problem? How is it resolved by Mundell and Meade?
2 Mundell's assignment rule implies that there is no conflict between policy instruments when the economy is faced with inflation and external deficit: monetary and fiscal policies must be tightened. Can you detect any deficiency in this policy design?
3 Suppose that the economy is faced with a recession and balance of payments deficit. Mundell's assignment rule dictates monetary tightening combined fiscal expansion. What are the weaknesses of this policy recommendation?
4 Suppose that the economy is faced with recession and inflation. Meade's policy recommendation is absorption-reducing policies and devaluation. What potential problems can this recommendation lead to if this economy is oil-importing and its demand elasticity for exports and imports is very low?
5 Suppose that the internal balance is defined as full employment combined with price stability. What are the implications for:
   (a) Mundell's assignment rule?
   (b) Meade's synthesis?
6 Suppose that expectations formation is rational. We know that asset markets tend to respond to 'news' faster than goods markets. Explain the implications of this asymmetry for Meade's synthesis.
7 We know that the IB and EB schedules derived by Mundell and Meade will not be stable if expectations formation is rational. Given this information, can the government estimate the magnitude of change in policy instruments required to correct disequilibrium?

Further reading and references

FURTHER READING

The pairing of instruments with targets is the central theme of Tinbergen (1952). Mundell (1968) and Meade (1951) provide extensive analysis of the issues concerning policy design in open economies. Dernburg (1989), ch. 12, provides a good overview of the targets – instruments framework, with fixed prices and static expectations. Argy (1994), chs 34 and 35, provides a wider perspective on the range of possible targets and draws attention to the controversy in policy design. On rational expectations, consult Attfield *et al.* (1985). For a review of the empirical evidence on rational expectations hypotheses, consult Clinton and Chouraqui (1987).

REFERENCES

Argy, V. (1994) *International Macroeconomics: Theory and Policy*, London: Routledge.
Attfield, C.L., D. Demery and N.W. Duck (1985) *Rational Expectations in Macroeconomics: An Introduction to Theory and Evidence*, Oxford: Basil Blackwell.
Clinton, K. and J.C. Chouraqui (1987) 'Monetary policy in the second half of the 1980s: how much room for manoeuvre?', *OECD Economics and Statistics Working Papers* 19, Paris: OECD.
Dernburg, T.F. (1989) *Global Macroeconomics*, New York: Harper & Row.
Meade, J.E. (1951) *The Balance of Payments: The Theory of International Economic Policy I*, Oxford: Oxford University Press.
Mundell, R.A. (1968) *International Macroeconomics*, London: Macmillan.
Tinbergen, J. (1952) *On the Theory of Economic Policy*, Amsterdam: North-Holland.

Part IV

Interdependence and macroeconomic policy co-ordination

Introduction

Part III was devoted to the resolution of the assignment problem within a single country. Yet we know that national macroeconomic policies cannot be designed in total isolation from the rest of the world. Therefore the analysis in Part III is a necessary but not a sufficient basis for understanding macroeconomic policy in open economies. Part IV aims to address this gap by presenting the case for and against international policy co-ordination. As will be seen in Chapters 11 and 12, the government's choice of instruments can lead to suboptimal outcomes even if the assignment problem is resolved correctly and the assumptions of Mundell and Meade are taken as given. This is due to the fact that interdependence between countries could either slow down the process of achieving the desired targets or induce national governments to engage in retaliatory policy actions, which make all countries worse off.

Given this state of affairs, Hamada's contribution in Chapter 11 fits into the structure of this book perfectly for two reasons. First, it is organically linked to the targets–instruments debate examined in Part III. In fact, Hamada's starting point is Mundell's assignment rule and Meade's synthesis in the context of a two-country model. Second, it is a rigorous yet accessible piece of work that would engage the reader and provide her or him with the analytical framework necessary to follow the wider debate on policy co-ordination.

Hamada first provides a brief assessment of the assignment rule under interdependence. He identifies two weaknesses in the assignment approach. One is already mentioned in the introduction to Part III: if there are trade-offs between policy instruments and if the targets are not independent of each other, we need to adopt an optimising approach to ensure that the policy mix maximises the objective function of the policy-maker. This is the problem identified by Theil (1961) and Niehans (1968). The other limitation is due to the implicit assumption that a particular assignment is necessarily incentive-compatible. In other words, the assignment approach does not tackle the question as to whether there are sufficient incentives for national authorities to stick to their duties as implied by the internationally agreed division of labour.

Because of these limitations, argues Hamada, it is necessary to adopt a 'strategic' approach to the assignment problem in open and interdependent economies. This approach is based on the argument that each country's policy choice would depend not only on whether the policy is the right one for the desired target, but also on what the country in question expects other countries to do. Take, for example, the case of fiscal policy in a fixed exchange rate regime. Mundell's assignment rule implies that fiscal policy should be assigned to internal balance. Therefore, a country faced with recession should introduce a fiscal expansion. However, the policy-makers are aware of the fact that fiscal expansion is conducive to current account deficits in the initiating country and, by default, to current account surpluses in its trading partners. Given this knowledge, should we not expect the policy-makers in the recession-hit country to be reluctant in their resort to fiscal activism? In other words, would they not prefer other countries to take the initial step? To the extent this is the case, is it not obvious that fiscal expansion is not necessarily an incentive-compatible policy recommendation?

The rest of Hamada's article is devoted to the demonstration of how strategic considerations of this nature could lead to suboptimal outcomes and whether such outcomes can be avoided. He begins with a Keynesian two-country model where the exchange rate is fixed, prices are constant, but output (and hence employment) is variable in the short run. He then derives a country's indifference curves, which are drawn against the level of income and change in reserves (i.e. monetary policy). Given his interest in monetary policy under interdependence, he then transposes these indifference curves into a plane delineated by monetary policies of two countries – with country 1's monetary policy depicted along the horizontal axis and country 2's along the vertical axis. This exercise enables him to derive two essential tools: (i) each country's reaction curve, and (ii) the joint contract curve for the two countries. While the former traces the points of tangency between a country's indifference curves and the horizontal or vertical lines that represent the partner's policy choice, the latter passes through the points of tangency between the two countries' indifference curves. This strategic interaction model yields a non-cooperative equilibrium that is Pareto-inefficient.

The explanation is as follows: country 1 knows that expansionary monetary policy under fixed exchange rates is conducive to balance of payments deficit at home, but balance of payments surplus in country 2. To the extent that country 1 is concerned about external deficit, it will refrain from monetary expansion. In fact, it may choose to tighten monetary policy in order to achieve a balance of payments surplus, which is deemed desirable. Obviously, country 2 will be induced to follow suit, for otherwise it will be faced with a balance of payments deficit. The result is excessive tightening in both countries, which is likely to cause global recession. Then, the Pareto-efficient policy choices require both countries to co-ordinate their policies so that recession can be avoided.

In the case of a flexible exchange rate regime, each country's monetary policy becomes independent. That is because both countries can choose the monetary policy compatible with full employment at home and let the exchange rate adjust to ensure balance of payments equilibrium. In this scenario, the co-operative and non-cooperative equilibria are the same and they are both Pareto-efficient.

However, this is a deceptively simple view of the flexible exchange rate environment. Consider a monetary expansion in country 1 aimed at increasing the national income. Monetary expansion in country 1 leads to depreciation and current account improvement at home. The mirror image of these effects is appreciation and current account deterioration in country 2. Therefore, monetary expansion in country 1 may be no more than an export of the recession abroad. The natural reaction of country 2 is to engage in monetary expansion of its own. Then, no country will gain and the global inflation level will increase. The problem here is not so much policy independence *per se*, but the beggar-my-neighbour consequences of policy independence. Therefore, there is still scope and need for policy co-ordination.

The problem with policy co-ordination, however, is twofold. First, the contract curve reflecting the range of co-ordinated (hence Pareto-efficient) equilibria presents a large number of possible solutions. The particular solution to be picked up would depend on negotiations between the countries. Second, even if the two countries agree on a particular solution, there are always incentives to renege on the agreement. The solution to this problem requires an independent authority that would facilitate negotiations and enforce the agreement without trembling hands.

The article by Mooslechner and Schuerz in Chapter 12 complements Hamada's contribution in two ways. First, it enables the reader to place Hamada's contribution within the wider debate on policy co-ordination. Being a review of the literature in this area, it also provides the reader with an extensive list of references reflecting the most significant and up-to-date contributions. Second, it cautions the reader about the possibility that policy co-ordination may in fact be counter-productive. In other words, it elaborates on issues about which Hamada's article is either silent or too optimistic. In addition to this complementary nature, Chapter 12 also links the policy co-ordination debate with a pending issue in Europe: policy co-ordination in the European Monetary Union (EMU).

Mooslechner and Schuerz press the reader to pay attention not only to what is meant by policy co-ordination, but also to recent developments in the literature. For example, is there a universally accepted definition of policy co-ordination? What is the link between policy co-ordination and institutions? Are the latter the consequence of or facilitators for co-ordination? Can policy co-ordination be disguised collusion between governments at the expense of the private sector? Can co-ordinated policy choices increase or reduce the credibility of the announced policy commitments?

As can be seen from the summary above, Part IV aims to achieve two objectives. On the one hand, it seeks to ensure progress by providing additional pieces for the jigsaw puzzle called macroeconomic policy in open economies. On the other hand, it tries to stretch the reader's imagination by raising new issues and posing new questions. We hope that this combination will enable the reader to make an informed intervention into the debate on macroeconomic policy and induce them to consolidate their knowledge of the theory underpinning it.

REFERENCES

Niehans, J. (1968) 'Monetary and fiscal policies in open economies under fixed and flexible exchange rates; an optimising approach', *Journal of Political Economy* 76, July–August, 893–943.

Theil, H.C. (1961) *Economic Forecasts and Policy*, 2nd edn, Amsterdam: North-Holland.

11 International monetary interdependence in a Keynesian model

*Koichi Hamada**
The Political Economy of International Monetary Interdependence,
The MIT Press (1985), pp. 45–65

We will examine the interplay of economic policies among countries when a particular monetary regime has been adopted as the outcome of the first stage of the game. Judging from the recent succession of international financial crises, it seems that the choice the world faces is not among several variants of the fixed exchange rate system, such as the gold standard or the adjustable peg, but among the fixed exchange rate system, the floating exchange rate system, and an appropriate combination of the two. We therefore focus on the interdependence of monetary policies under a system of fixed exchange rates and one of floating exchange rates. To prepare for the discussion, let us look at the literature concerning the coordination and conflicts of economic policies among national economies and see what problems remain.

SURVEY OF STUDIES OF POLICY INTERDEPENDENCE

As early as the 1950s one can find, at least implicitly, substantial discussion about the consistency of national economic policies in a two-country model (Meade 1951, ch. 10). However, Meade is not so much concerned with international policy conflicts between two countries as with policy conflicts within each country. It is Cooper (1968) who puts forth the necessity of international cooperation directly and most persuasively. Taking as an example the Atlantic Community, which was under a fixed exchange rate regime, he points out that increasing interdependence complicates the successful pursuit of national objectives by way of three mechanisms.

First, increasing interdependence increases the number and magnitude of disturbances to which each country's balance of payments is subjected, and this directs national policy instruments toward the restoration of external balance. Second, increasing interdependence slows down the process by which policy authorities are able to attain domestic objectives. Finally, greater integration may lead a community of nations to engage in retaliatory actions, which leave all countries worse off than they need be. Therefore, Cooper

* I am indebted to Akihiro Amano, Richard N. Cooper, Jurg Niehans, and Eisuke Sakakibara for helpful criticisms and suggestions concerning this chapter.

argues, it is necessary for the Atlantic Community to engage at least partly in the joint determination of economic objectives and policies.

Thus the central problem of international economic cooperation is defined to be "how to keep the manifold benefits of extensive international intercourse free of crippling restrictions, while at the same time preserving a maximum degree of freedom for each nation to pursue its legitimate economic objectives" (Cooper 1968, p. 15). According to Cooper, as with marriage, the benefits of close international relations can be enjoyed only at the expense of giving up a certain amount of independence or autonomy. Here the main theme in the analysis of economic cooperation is clearly presented. In particular, the third factor mentioned above, that the independent pursuit of individual national policies may not lead to a desirable situation for the community as a whole, is the crucial reason for the need for cooperation in a highly integrated world economy.

Cooper also suggests that both the static and dynamic aspects of international cooperation should be considered. Even when all national objectives are consistent and there are a sufficient number of policy instruments with which to attain them, growing interdependence greatly slows down the process by which independently acting national authorities attain their economic objectives (the second factor above). Cooper distinguishes between policy coordination, where the gains are achieved from better mutual timing, and policy harmonization, which is based on static efficiency grounds. This dynamic aspect of coordination is developed further in Cooper 1969. By using a two-country Keynesian model with monetary and fiscal policies, Cooper calculates the values of the characteristic roots of the dynamic system of adjustment equations, assuming different degrees of interdependence. He finds that increasing interdependence reduces the absolute value of the dominant (negative) characteristic root and hence slows down the speed of adjustment of the system. The lack of coordination among policymakers delays the achievement of national objectives, such as full employment and target rates of growth, and, under fixed exchange rates, increases the need for international reserves. Most significantly, these delays in attaining targets and the need for reserves increase with the degree of economic interdependence among nations.

Given the problem of coordination as it is proposed here, one needs an analytical framework in order to analyze policy interactions among national economies. A series of illuminating models for this purpose has been developed by Mundell (1962, 1963, 1968). One of the common features of this variety of models is that they are general equilibrium models incorporating such monetary aspects as the stock of money and bonds. For the analysis of policy interdependence, two-country versions of these models are utilized.

There are several alternative approaches, which are not necessarily competing but often complementary, for analyzing policy interactions, coordination, and conflicts. The first and most natural approach is to advocate direct cooperation or joint actions among national policy authorities. Cooper's works are examples of what one might call the direct coordination approach.

Later, when we examine economic cooperation under floating exchange rates, the proposal by McKinnon (1974) to create a tripartite agreement among the major countries of the world will be taken as one of the pleas for direct consultation and cooperation among national monetary authorities.

The second approach is the celebrated policy assignment approach, skillfully applied to international economics by Mundell. This approach, which is based on the general theory of economic policy of Tinbergen (1952), seeks to find the optimal assignment of targets to instruments of economic policy. Mundell advises that the achievement of desirable ends requires that each instrument be assigned to the market where it is relatively effective. Thus, this approach is also known as the principle of effective market classification.

In a generalized version of the two-country model, Swoboda and Dornbusch (1973) study the problem of global policy assignment and, in particular, that of reconciling national income targets in an interdependent world economy. They show that gearing monetary policies to the desired reserve distribution and fiscal policies to income targets constitutes a stable assignment of instruments to targets, while the reverse pairing leads to instability.

In fact, it is in the case of two (or more) countries in an integrated world economy that the principle of effective market classification really comes into its own (Niehans 1968), because in a national economy it is rather hard to find reasons why decentralized decision making among various branches of the government is needed, except perhaps for the sake of conserving on information flows between branches in the short run.

An international system is characterized by decentralized decision making almost by definition. The instruments of each country are assigned to its own targets. Since each country's policies usually have a comparative advantage with respect to its own targets, this assignment usually satisfies the requirement of effective market classification.

However, there are cases in which the international division of policy assignments does not necessarily coincide with the above "natural" assignments. As an example of the division of international policy assignments, Mundell (1971) advocates the following assignment of policies under the dollar standard: The United States adjusts its money supply to peg the price level for the world economy, and Europe (or the rest of the world) adjusts its money supply to maintain balance of payments equilibrium.

In Figure 11.1, the rate of monetary expansion in country 1 (say, the United States) is measured along the horizontal axis and that of country 2 (Europe) along the vertical axis. The downward-sloping line AA indicates the rates of money growth in the two countries that would keep the international price level stable. The upward-sloping line OB shows the rates of money growth that would keep the balance of payments in each country in equilibrium. The downward slope of AA reflects the proposition that the world price level depends on the weighted average of the rate of monetary expansion in each country, while the positive slope of the OB schedule follows from the approximate dependence of the balance of payments on the difference between the money growth rates in the two countries.

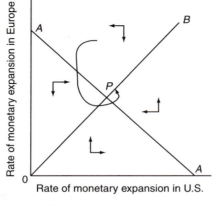

Figure 11.1

Above line *AA* the world suffers from inflationary pressures; below it, from deflationary pressures. On the right side of line *OB* the balance of payments of the United States is in deficit; on the left it is in surplus. The policy assignment defined above (the assignment of the monetary policy of the United States to the price level target and that of Europe to the balance of payments target) will yield a stable result as indicated by the arrows; the reverse assignment will lead to instability.

A corollary of this assignment approach is what is called the "redundancy" problem (Mundell 1968, appendix to chapter 13). For the world as a whole, the sum of each country's balance of payments is equal to zero or, more generally, to the increase in the amount of outside money in the international system (gold or SDRs). This is a direct consequence of the first element of interdependence. If there are *n* countries, only (*n*–1) of them can succeed in reaching their independent balance of payments targets; at least one of them must accept the position of acting as an international residual. In other words, interdependence necessarily imposes another constraint on national targets in order to render them consistent. Mundell argues that if each country has a distinct instrument with which to control its balance of payments, there is an additional degree of freedom. This redundant degree of freedom should be used to control the international price level according to Mundell (see also Cooper 1968 and Niehans 1968).

The strength of the assignment approach lies in its simplicity. One need be concerned only with the one-to-one correspondence between instruments and targets. The economy of information that results when this prescription is followed by policymakers is its advantage.

However, there are limitations to this approach that require it to be supplemented by alternative approaches. First, if one looks at the process of achieving economic targets, it is clear that a one-to-one pairing of instruments and targets is not sufficient because an optimal mix of economic policies of varying strengths is needed in order to achieve an efficient realization of conflicting goals. As a result, there is a need for another approach—the optimizing approach developed by Niehans (1968). The first element is a social welfare function providing a ranking of the relevant bundles of target values. The second element is an efficient target frontier that specifies the maximum value of an objective that can be obtained for given values of the other objectives. The optimal combination of policy instruments is the one that maximizes the social welfare function within the feasible region of target combinations. Normally this point occurs at the point of tangency between the efficient target frontier and a social indifference curve.

The second limitation of the assignment approach, in particular when it is applied to the division of burdens in the international economy, is that it does not take into account the problem of whether there are sufficient incentives for national policy authorities to pursue the economic objective that should be assigned to them in order to achieve the best division of labor. In order for an international policy assignment to be sustainable by policy authorities, it is necessary that the policy assignment be "incentive compatible" in the sense that each country has an incentive to take the necessary actions if others are taking the necessary actions as well.

In Mundell's example of the dollar standard, incentives exist for Europe (or the rest of the world other than the United States) to adopt contraction-ary policies when its balance of payments is in deficit. But it is not always true that Europe has an incentive to adopt expansionary policies when its balance of payments is in surplus. Moreover, the United States does not necessarily have an incentive to play the role of benevolent world leader by adjusting its monetary or fiscal policies to keep the world price level constant.

Probably part of the reason why the Bretton Woods regime collapsed is that the rest of the world did not play the game symmetrically and the United States had to be concerned with domestic policy objectives other than world price stability (see also Niehans 1968, n. 22).

This second limitation leads to the necessity of adopting a strategic approach—that is, an approach based on the joint reactions and counter-reactions of each participating country. This approach is most effectively implemented when one applies the theory of duopoly or oligopoly and some simple concepts of game theory to the problem.

As a matter of fact, further application of the optimizing approach to a two-country situation leads naturally to the strategic approach. As shown by Niehans (1968), once the optimizing approach is applied to a two-country model, each country's behavior depends on what it expects concerning the other's behavior. The remaining chapters represent an attempt to apply a strategic approach directly to the problem of international monetary interdependence.

The application of a strategic approach to international economics is not completely new. If we broaden our perspective to an area outside the scope of monetary or macroeconomic conflicts, we find that works by Scitovsky (1941), Johnson (1953), and Gorman (1958) on tariffs and retaliation are pioneering analyses of the interdependence and strategic nature of trade conflicts. The mutual taxation of foreign investment incomes can also be formulated as a game in which an agreement to avoid double taxation helps to achieve a contract curve situation (Hamada 1966). In the field of monetary relations only recently have the political or strategic aspects of confrontations concerning monetary policy and institution making begun to be treated explicitly in a theoretical framework.

It is just as hard, if not harder, to conduct a positive empirical analysis of policy interdependence as it is to test a hypothesis in duopoly or oligopoly theory incorporating conjectural variations on the behavior of others. In fact, the existing empirical literature is at most a verification of some of the theoretical propositions using two-country simulation models that are either constructed as hypothetical numerical examples or estimated with actual data.

In his analysis of the speed of adjustment in an interdependent economy, Cooper (1969) calculates the dominant characteristic roots corresponding to numerical models with varying degrees of interdependence. He also shows by way of simulations how income and reserve requirements vary with and without cooperation.

Using the linked American and Canadian econometric models, Helliwell and McRae (1977) study the effect of mutual responses of monetary policies on an initial fiscal disturbance in one country. The results of their simulation, which assumes that the same type of monetary policy is used in both countries, suggest that the effect of Canadian policies on the United States is larger and more cyclical if both countries follow the monetary policy of pegging interest rates than if they peg the money supply. In general, it is found that the nature of the transmission of economic disturbances takes different forms depending on the modus operandi of monetary policies adopted in the two countries.

A series of interesting studies on the role of sterilization policies has been conducted by De Grauwe (1975, 1977). By estimating the balance of payments equations for European countries and then experimenting with this system of equations, he finds that the systematic use of sterilization policies by two or more countries in an attempt to offset the monetary effects of balance of payments disequilibria is most likely to lead to explosive reserve flows and therefore to the breakdown of the system. Even when those policies do not lead to unstable reserve flows, their effectiveness is extremely limited. According to De Grauwe, because of the increased interdependence in the 1960s as compared to the 1950s, the use of sterilization policies should have created more acute policy conflicts during the second period.

Finally, Parkin (1977), in his study of the impact of monetary policy on world inflation and the balance of payments, shows that the main conclusion of the monetary approach to analyzing the balance of payments is approximately valid, and that the influence of productivity increase is also important. It is also noteworthy that a formula is derived for the rate of monetary expansion that is required for the attainment of price stability in the world economy (or in a monetary union).

One cannot deny that empirical analyses of macroeconomic coordination are still sparse, especially concerning policy reaction behavior. The importance of the studies mentioned here, however, should not be undervalued because, to the extent that they clarify the nature of interdependence in the current world economy, they are the steps required to provide a solid foundation for the empirical analysis of strategic policy interplay. Moreover, some of them (for example, the studies by De Grauwe and by Parkin) provide the rationale for the new type of monetary cooperation under the post-Smithsonian regime suggested by McKinnon.

STRATEGIC ANALYSIS OF POLICY INTERACTIONS IN THE FIXED PRICE MODEL

A variety of models may be used to analyze the interdependence of monetary policies under alternative monetary systems; however, to avoid complicating the analysis, I will base the discussion on the simplest macro-economic models. The first model to be considered in this book is the textbook version of the Keynesian model that assumes fixed price levels but allows income and employment to adjust (Mundell 1968, chapters 16, 18; Niehans 1968). Recently, however, this model has been subjected to the criticism that it fails to capture the essence of Keynes's original idea.[1] Moreover, although this model may have some relevance to the case of fixed exchange rates, it may not be applicable to the case of flexible exchange rates, as daily fluctuations in the exchange rate may alter the relative price level between two countries.

At the other extreme is the so-called monetarist or quantity theory model that assumes fixed employment levels but flexible prices. In this model, real economic variables are determined by relative prices and the rational choice of economic agents. Monetary policy affects only financial variables such as the price level and the balance of payments and has no effect on income and employment. Whereas the former approach is concerned mainly with fluctuations in effective demand, the latter deals with long-run price trends and their relationship to the balance of payments.

The choice between these two extreme models depends primarily on one's interpretation of macroeconomic relations—namely, on whether one believes in the Phillips curve or in the natural rate of unemployment and on whether one views unemployment as frictional or structural. It is perhaps fair to say that the simple Keynesian model provides a good approximation of reality during periods of secular recession and that the monetarist model is useful for analyzing periods of chronic inflation. However, neither the Keynesian model nor the monetarist model alone seems to provide an adequate framework for analyzing the current state of the world economy in which unemployment and inflation coexist.

Recently the monetary approach has been introduced into analyses of the balance of payments with considerable success. This approach views the balance of payments as a relationship between a country's credits and debits on international account and the exchange rate as the relative price of two currencies and advocates that changes in these two variables be explained in terms of changes in the demand for, and the supply of, money. However, the monetary approach to the balance of payments should be distinguished from monetarism. The monetary approach is not so much an extension of the quantity theory to an open economy as an attempt to understand the balance of payments problem in a general equilibrium framework that takes Walras's Law into account (Komiya 1969). Thus, using the monetary approach does not necessarily entail adopting monetarist assumptions concerning the domestic economy. Indeed, I use the monetary approach to analyze a situation with unemployment.

[. . .] In the latter half of this chapter, the game of the interplay of monetary policies will be analyzed in a model that assumes fixed price levels. [. . .] Policy makers in each nation react to each other on the basis of some knowledge of the interdependence of their various policies. The strategic analysis here will appeal to the optimizing approach developed by Niehans rather than the fixed-target approach. Rather than counting the number of targets and policy instruments and assigning instruments to targets, we consider the tradeoff between targets along social indifference curves, as well as along the feasibility locus. Under the assumption that national economies try to use their monetary policies to optimize the combination of their objectives, we discuss what kind of overall outcome is most likely to occur as the result of the interdependence of monetary policies under alternative exchange-rate systems.

In some sense this analysis may be regarded as a generalization of Niehans's short-run analysis of two dependent economies under fixed exchange rates to the long-run growth process as well as to economies operating under flexible exchange rates. However, my treatment of the balance of payments is different. A surplus in the balance of payments is not always desirable. One of the recent findings from the analysis of seigniorage gains using the monetary approach is that a deficit in the balance of payments is desirable, at least from the consumers' standpoint, as long as a country can afford to continue the deficit. This is because a deficit in the balance of payments implies that the amount the country consumes and invests for future consumption, domestically or abroad, exceeds the amount it currently produces.

Of course, many central bankers prefer surpluses to deficit if the surpluses are not excessive, and this attitude is more likely to be reflected in actual economic policy. The outcome for the world economy depends crucially on the attitudes of the participating countries toward the balance of payments.

MONETARY INTERDEPENDENCE UNDER FIXED EXCHANGE RATES

Let us think of the world economy as consisting of two economies linked by international trade and capital movements. We assume that the world capital market is competitive and that the same interest rate prevails in both countries.

In the simplest Keynesian model, the price level of each country is fixed and the income of each country is variable. We are interested chiefly in short-run fluctuations in national income and employment. The formal model used in the analysis is a variant of the two-country model developed by Mundell (1968).

The following notation will be used:

Y = real income
I = investment
S = saving
B = balance of trade
M = money supply
D = demand for money
R = international reserves
r = real rate of interest
q = foreign exchange rate (price of the home currency in terms of the foreign currency)
p = price level
W = world reserves.

Variables with no superscript refer to the home country; those with an asterisk refer to the other country.

The commodity market is in equilibrium if the trade balance offsets the gap between saving and investment.[2]

$$I(r) + \bar{I} - S(Y) + B\left(Y, Y^*, \frac{qp}{p^*}\right) = 0 \tag{1}$$

where $\bar{I}$ indicates exogenous (government) spending. For the other country,

$$I^*(r^*) + \bar{I}^* - S^*(Y^*) - qB\left(Y, Y^*, \frac{qp}{P^*}\right) = 0 \tag{2}$$

The money market is in equilibrium if

$$\frac{M}{P} = L(r, Y) \tag{3}$$

and for the other country

$$\frac{M^*}{P^*} = L^*(r^*, Y^*) \tag{4}$$

The money supply is the sum of international reserves and the liabilities of the banking system:

$$M = D + R \tag{5}$$

$$M^* = D^* + qR^* \tag{6}$$

International reserves are assumed constant in the short run:

$$R + R^* = \overline{W} \tag{7}$$

Moreover, in a Keynesian framework in which the price levels are fixed, nominal interest rates are equal to real interest rates, and by the assumption of perfect capital mobility, we have

$$r = r^* \tag{8}$$

Also, by a suitable choice of units, we can put $p = p^* = 1$, and $q = 1$ under a system of fixed exchange rates. The equilibrium condition in the bond market is suppressed here because, by virtue of Walras's law, equilibrium in both money and commodity markets implies equilibrium in the bond market. Once a change in D or D^* occurs, capital moves to equate the rates of interest. But at the new equilibrium, net capital flows offset the trade balance, so that the amount of reserves remains constant.

Monetary policy in this system is viewed as an increase in the liabilities of the banking system, that is, an increase in D and D^*. It has been shown by Mundell that

$$\frac{\partial Y}{\partial D} > 0, \frac{\partial Y^*}{\partial D} > 0, \frac{\partial Y}{\partial D^*} > 0, \frac{\partial Y^*}{\partial D^*} > 0 \tag{9}$$

Also, it is easy to see that

$$\frac{\partial R}{\partial D} < 0, \frac{\partial R^*}{\partial D} > 0, \frac{\partial R}{\partial D^*} > 0, \frac{\partial R^*}{\partial D^*} < 0 \tag{10}$$

The choice open to the country under a system of fixed exchange rates is to adopt a suitable mix of monetary and fiscal policies to achieve the most desirable combination of targets—national income and the balance of payments, in the present example. Since we are primarily interested in the interaction of monetary policies, we assume that government spending is constant.

The country is assumed to have a preference ordering over various combinations of income levels and increases in reserves, following Niehans. Niehans assumes that a temporary surplus in the balance of payments is always desirable; however, for those countries that do not have a severe need for international reserves, and especially for those that can create international reserves by issuing debt to foreigners, the opposite may be true, as suggested in the discussion of seigniorage gains. A current account deficit implies that a country is consuming and investing in physical assets more than it currently produces. A deficit in the overall balance of payments implies that a country consumes and invests for future consumption, abroad as well as domestically, more than it currently produces.

We adopt the simplifying assumption here that the welfare of a country depends on its overall balance of payments at that moment. Thus, for any country, there must be a certain level of increase in international reserves beyond which any further increase implies a deterioration rather than an improvement in national welfare. Similarly, there must be a certain level of income beyond which further increases are not desirable because of inflation, although temporary increases in income may be possible.

There are problems with analyzing the risk of inflation in a model with fixed price levels, however, we will allow ourselves to assume that a temporary increase in national income above a certain level is not desirable for the country in question in order to illustrate the interdependence of monetary policies. We are justified in doing so because the interdependence of monetary policies continues to hold qualitatively even if the extreme assumption of fixed prices is not made. The indifference curves are not drawn above the levels at which even temporary increases in real income are not possible. Thus the indifference curves do not look like the ordinary price theory textbook versions but rather have a saturation point or center.

Figure 11.2 depicts the government's indifference curves with respect to the level of national income and the international balance of payments. The center of these curves, that is, the saturation point or the optimal combination of income and increase in reserves, differs for various countries depending in part on their initial reserves. This point also depends on the eagerness of the country to attain full employment at the risk of inflation, on its position in the international financial system, and on the strength of restraints against losing international reserves. For a reserve currency country like the United States, the optimal increase in reserves may be negative because of its

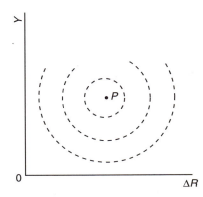

Figure 11.2 Y = real income; ΔR = increase in international reserves; P = optimal combination of Y and ΔR

ability to increase the consumption level of its citizens by issuing its debt to other countries.[3]

Even within a country, judgments will differ on the best combination of income levels and increases in reserves. Thus, economists educated by Mundell, for example, will prefer a deficit, and the center of the circles will be near the vertical axis. Traditional bankers, on the other hand, will prefer a payments surplus, and the center will be relatively further to the right of the vertical axis. For those who prefer expansion, the center will be further above the horizontal axis, and for those who prefer economic stability, it will be nearer this axis.

Our main concern is the preference ordering of the monetary authority that has the power to determine monetary policy. This preference ordering is not absolutely fixed; its structure may change with economic education and past balance of payment experiences. Moreover, one country may find it profitable to teach or persuade another country to change its preference ordering concerning the balance of payments.

If we assume that each country has a preference ordering and that there are only two countries, we can superimpose the Stackelberg diagram on the plane ordinated by the monetary policies of the two countries (Figure 11.3). The abscissa indicates the money supply of the home country expressed in terms of the liabilities of the banking system D, and the ordinate indicates the money supply of the other country in terms of D^*.

Note that Figures 11.2 and 11.3 have been drawn with different combinations of variables on the axes. As can be seen from equation 10, the balance of payments of country 1 deteriorates as D increases and improves as D^*

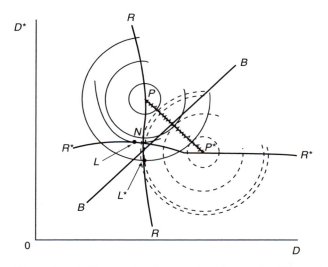

Figure 11.3 PP^* is contract curve; RR is country 1's reaction curve; R^*R^* is country 2's reaction curve; N is Nash equilibrium; L is leadership solution with country 1 as leader; L^* is leadership solution with country 2 as leader

increases. Furthermore, we can analyze mathematically the monetary approach to the balance of payments to show that, as long as we ignore differences in the elasticities of money demand with respect to income and the interest rate, the balance of payments of the two countries to a large extent is determined by differences in their rates of monetary expansion. Therefore, the combinations of D and D^* that equilibrate the international balance of payments (of both countries) can be represented by the upward sloping BB curve in Figure 11.3. The region to the right (left) of BB indicates a balance of payments surplus (deficit) for country 2 and a balance of payments deficit (surplus) for country 1. And from equation 9 we note that an increase in D in one country raises incomes in both countries. In Figure 11.3 the indifference curves of the first country are drawn with solid lines and those of the second country with dotted lines. Since from equation 10 the region to the lower right of BB indicates a temporary deficit in the balance of payments for the first country, the indifference map of the first country is approximately an oblique mirror image of the indifference map shown in Figure 11.2, while that of the second country is an oblique transposition.

Depending on the relative positions of the centers of the indifference curves—the relative positions that each country likes best—the policy inter-action between the two countries will take different forms. Figure 11.3 depicts the case where neither country is satisfied with the initial level of reserves and both desire to accumulate more.

We proceed to analyze the strategic situation using Figure 11.3. If we plot the locus of tangency between these two families of indifference curves, we obtain the contract curve PP^*—that is, the locus of Pareto-efficient points. A country situated on this contract curve cannot improve its satisfaction level without causing a deterioration in the satisfaction level of the other country. Thus, the cooperative solution of this interplay of monetary pol-icies, or of this two-person game, will be some point on this contract curve. Needless to say, the first country prefers a situation close to P and the second a situation close to P^*. The relative bargaining strengths of the two countries will determine to which point on the contract curve cooperative action leads.

Reaction curves RR and R^*R^* are drawn in such a way that RR is the locus of the points where the indifference curves of the first country are tangent to a horizontal line and R^*R^* is the locus of the points where the indifference curves of the latter country are tangent to a vertical line. They indicate the optimal monetary policy of one country if it believes that the other country will keep its monetary policy constant. Thus the intersection of these reaction curves N is the point at which each country has no incentive to move away provided the other keeps its policy unchanged. Using game theory termin-ology, this is the Nash equilibrium. As Niehans pointed out, this intersection is generally not on the contract curve; the non-cooperative solution is inferior to the cooperative solution.

The leadership solution is the best point on the opponent's reaction curve. If country 1 knows that country 2 will remain on its reaction curve, R^*R^*, country 1 will choose the money supply that will achieve L, the best point from country 1's standpoint on R^*R^*. Similarly we can find the leadership solution of country 2 as L^*.

In Figure 11.3 where each country is assumed to prefer a temporary surplus in its balance of payments, which is the case analyzed by Niehans, the non-cooperative solution will have a bias toward recession.[4] However, this conclusion depends on the relative positions of the centers of the two countries' indifference curves and may not always be valid. Several typical cases are depicted in Figure 11.4. In the situation represented by Figure 11.4a, each country desires a deficit in its balance of payments. It is easy to see that the non-cooperative solution N has an expansionary bias. In Figure 11.4b, country 1 desires a deficit and country 2 desires a surplus but one smaller than the deficit preferred by country 1. This situation also leads to a non-cooperative solution with an expansionary bias. Figure 11.4c represents the case in which both countries desire balance of payments equilibrium but each has a different preference concerning the level of income. In this case, the non-cooperative solution will lie in the region where the more expansion-minded country ends up with a deficit in its balance of payments. The situation that prevailed immediately prior to President Nixon's adoption of the New Economic Policy in the summer of 1971 (the growing balance of payments surpluses of Japan and West Germany) may be interpreted in terms of case 11.4b. Here the U.S. corresponds to country 1, and Japan and West Germany correspond to country 2. [. . .]

The textbook version of the Keynesian model that assumes fixed price levels is inadequate for the analysis of the transmission of inflation and stagflation across countries.

The economic significance of the above analysis can be summarized as follows. If two countries cooperate, they will reach a point on the contract curve whose position depends on their relative bargaining strengths. If they do not cooperate but passively respond to each other, they will reach the non-cooperative (Nash) equilibrium, which is not on the Pareto-efficient contract curve. Moreover, if one country takes advantage of the fact that the other will remain on its reaction curve, the leadership solution will emerge which is favorable to the leader and unfavorable to the follower. Whether non-cooperative solutions lie on the inflationary or deflationary side of the contract curve depends on the attitudes of the two countries toward their balance of payments.

This situation is quite similar to the prisoner's dilemma. If both parties cooperate, high payoffs to both result; if neither cooperates, low payoffs occur. But if one cooperates and the other does not, the payoff to the cooperating party is very low while that to the non-cooperating party is very high.

This analysis of the fixed exchange rate system reveals the public-good character of monetary assets. If each country desires a surplus in its balance of payments, monetary expansion is a "public good" because each country prefers a higher rate of expansion of the total money supply but wants to expand its own money supply at a slower rate than that of other countries. On the other hand, if each country desires a deficit in its balance of payments,

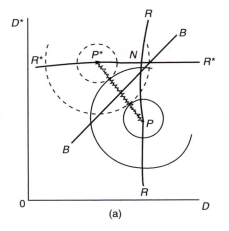

(a)

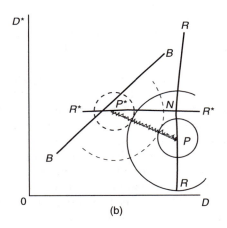

(b)

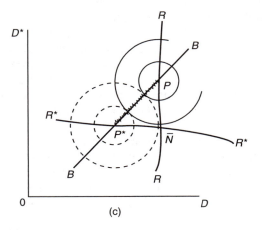

(c)

Figure 11.4

then monetary expansion becomes a "public bad" because each country wants to expand its own money supply at a higher rate than that of other countries but at the same time does not want the total money supply to expand too rapidly. In either case, the non-cooperative solution is likely to result in an unfavorable situation with a scarcity of public goods or with a glut of public bads.

Thus far we have assumed two participating countries. If the number of countries increases, what modifications will be required? The formal structure is not hard to generalize. In the monetary model, for example, movements in the world price level will depend on the weighted average of rates of monetary expansion of all countries, while the balance of payments of a particular country will depend essentially on the difference between this average and its own rate of monetary expansion.

The analysis of strategic situations is more difficult. Small countries are more likely to behave passively, that is, to remain on their reaction curves. Thus, it might be easier for a large country to act as a leader. Another difference is that the contract curve solution may become more difficult to maintain because international agreement requires multilateral as well as bilateral agreement, and there is always the temptation for a country to become an outsider (Cooper 1968, pp. 172–3).

Various modifications to this argument are necessary if it is to be applied to more realistic situations. For example, the adjustable peg system differs from the fixed exchange rate system in allowing abrupt changes in parities. In the former system, the excessive accumulation of international reserves is undesirable not only because it implies the current sacrifice of consumption and investment but also because it involves the risk that the currency held as reserves might be devalued. Therefore, the shape of the indifference map becomes more sensitive to the cost of the accumulation of foreign currencies.

In the typical example of the prisoner's dilemma the two parties are unable to communicate with one other, but in the case of the interaction of monetary policies countries can communicate with one another by various means. One may therefore argue that the Cournot solution and the Stackelberg solution are irrelevant and that one should concentrate on the structure of cooperative solutions instead. However, even if one takes the optimistic view that negotiations will lead to outcomes close to a cooperative solution, an understanding of non-cooperative solutions is still necessary inasmuch as there usually exist multiple cooperative solutions and the non-cooperative solutions provide benchmarks for comparing the gains of these alternative cooperative solutions.

Moreover, the attainment of a cooperative solution becomes more and more difficult as the number of participants increases. The situation is further complicated by the fact that it is sometimes profitable for a country to conceal its preferences and to signal false information. The medium and speed of communication, as well as the level of mutual trust, will affect the performance of the world economy.

The creation of an international reserve asset such as SDRs can be utilized to move the non-cooperative solution closer to the contract curve. If every country always desires to acquire more reserves, deflationary pressures will emerge in the world economy. The creation of an international asset will lead to the easing of deflationary pressures because a country can now obtain its desired reserves without running a balance of payments surplus. In terms of Figure 11.3, the indifference maps of the two countries will move toward the central ray *BB*. Thus the creation of international reserves by an international organization is meaningful, although there remains the problem of how to distribute such reserves.

MONETARY INDEPENDENCE UNDER FLEXIBLE EXCHANGE RATES

Policy interactions under a system of floating exchange rates are now examined. Let us first consider the short-run problem of fluctuations in employment and effective demand, again using the Keynesian model. Monetary policy works differently under floating rates than under fixed exchange rates. Monetary expansion by one country increases its own income, but with capital mobility the income of the other country decreases rather than increasing. This result occurs because the monetary expansion and the decline in the interest rate induce an outflow of capital, as a result of which the exchange rate depreciates, causing recessionary effects on the other country. However, the other country can increase its own money supply to stimulate effective demand.

Formally, in the system of equations 1–8, R, R^*, and W can be equated to zero, meaning that the money supply of a country is equal to the liabilities of the banking system.

Letting q be variable it can be shown that (Mundell 1968)

$$\frac{\partial Y}{\partial D} > 0, \quad \frac{\partial Y^*}{\partial D} < 0, \quad \frac{\partial Y}{\partial D^*} < 0, \quad \frac{\partial Y^*}{\partial D^*} > 0 \tag{11}$$

Also it is easy to see that

$$\frac{\partial r}{\partial D} < 0, \quad \frac{\partial r}{\partial D^*} < 0 \tag{12}$$

In this system there is no room for international transfers of purchasing power through payments deficits or surpluses. Such transfers could be effected through the acquisition of foreign currencies by private economic units for transactions or speculative purposes, but we cannot deal with that possibility here. Thus, the only major concern of each country is the level of income. Accordingly, the Stackelberg diagram becomes degenerate, as shown in Figure 11.5. The upward-sloping curves are indifference curves, and the thick curve shows the optimal level of income. The upward slope of both

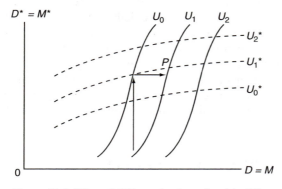

Figure 11.5 (U_1 and U_1^* are both optimal indifference curves and, at the same time, reaction curves)

families of curves reflects the fact that one country's monetary expansion depresses the other country's income level and necessitates monetary expansion in the other country in order to maintain the same income level.

In the absence of capital mobility, each country will determine its income level without reference to the monetary policy of the other country. In this special case, the indifference curves become straight lines: country 1's indifference curves are vertical while country 2's are horizontal. Therefore no strategic conflict arises.

Even if both families of curves are upward-sloping in a world with capital mobility, the reaction curves will coincide with the highest indifference curves provided that both countries are concerned solely with their income levels. In this general case, no serious strategic problem exists as far as the equilibrium solution is concerned. The intersection of reaction curves, namely the Nash equilibrium, coincides with the unique Pareto-optimal point. Thus, a system of floating exchange rates allows each country to pursue an independent monetary policy.

However, we should note the following interdependent aspects of monetary policies in the competitive world capital market. First, let us look at the adjustment process to the Nash equilibrium solution, which takes the form indicated by the arrows in Figure 11.5. The time span during which this short-run analysis is applicable might be shorter than the time span during which the adjustment process takes place. That being so, a country's monetary expansion may cause a temporary reduction in the income level of the other country. Thus, with capital mobility, monetary expansion in one country may in the short run have a beggar-thy-neighbor effect on the rest of the world.

Second, a country cannot decide the interest rate by itself. From equation 12, the iso-interest curves could be superimposed as downward-sloping curves in Figure 11.5. And if each country has a preference ordering concerning the combinations of interest rates and income levels, the situation shown in Figures 11.3 and 11.4 can still occur under floating exchange rates. This aspect of interdependence is more sophisticated than that discussed under fixed exchange rates because there the rate of interest was not taken into account in the preference ordering. By relaxing the balance of payments constraint, the floating exchange rate system provides a country with more freedom to pursue other policy objectives.

CONCLUSIONS

A system of fixed exchange rates is more likely to bring about a confrontation of economic policies analogous to the prisoner's dilemma; the outcome of this conflicting situation depends on the degree of cooperation among countries. On the other hand, we have found that a system of floating exchange rates offers more independence and more room for monetary policies even though some conflict with respect to the real rate of interest may still exist. This suggests that even in the first stage of the game—that of agreeing on a particular system—the degree of mutual trust among countries affects the prospective payoffs. The two stages are linked by the degree of trust. If faith in the other country's economic policies is not strong enough, the system of floating exchange rates offers a safe (if not the best) strategy for guaranteeing a certain degree of independence. Thus, for a nation to adopt a flexible exchange rate by itself is something very close to the maximin strategy.

NOTES

1 See, for example, Leijonhufvud 1968, Negishi 1979, and Uzawa 1978–1979. The analysis of international interdependence in an explicit disequilibrium framework constitutes a major topic for further research.
2 More precisely, S should denote saving plus net interest income on international lendings, but for simplicity, the latter is ignored here.
3 That is, R or R^* can even become negative as a result of an expansion in D or D^*.
4 In order to understand more fully the character of the Cournot and Stackelberg solutions, we need to know whether the outcomes generated by the process of policy interplays would converge ultimately to these solutions along a stable time path. We also need to know the speed of this process relative to the speed of adjustment assumed in the Keynesian model.

REFERENCES

Aliber, R.Z., (ed.) (1977) *The Political Economy of Monetary Reform*. London: Macmillan.

Cooper, R.N. (1968) *The Economics of Interdependence*. New York: McGraw-Hill.

Cooper, R.N. (1969) "Macroeconomic Policy Adjustment in Interdependent Economies." *Quarterly Journal of Economics* 83 (February).

De Grauwe, P. (1975) "The Interaction of Monetary Policies in a Group of European Countries." *Journal of International Economics* 5.

De Grauwe, P. (1977) "Monetary Interdependence among Major European Countries," in Aliber 1977.

Gorman, W.M. (1958) "Tariffs, Retaliation and the Elasticity of Demand for Imports." *Review of Economic Studies* 25 (June).

Hamada, K. (1966) "Strategic Aspects of the Taxation of Foreign Investment Income," *Quarterly Journal of Economics* 80 (August): 361–75.

Helliwell, J., and R. McRae. (1977) "The Interdependence of Monetary, Debt and Fiscal Policies in an International Setting," in Aliber 1977.

Johnson, H.G. (1953). "Optimum Tariffs and Retaliation," *Review of Economic Studies* 21.

Komiya, R. (1969) "Economic Growth and the Balance of Payments: A Monetary Approach," *Journal of Political Economy* 77.

Leijonhufvud, A. (1968) *On Keynesian Economics and the Economics of Keynes*, New York: Oxford University Press.

McKinnon, R.I. (1974) "A Tripartite Agreement or a Limping Dollar Standard?" *Essays in International Finance*, no. 106, Princeton University Press.

Meade, J.E. (1951) *The Theory of International Economic Policy*. Vol. 1: *The Balance of Payments*, London: Oxford University Press.

Mundell, R.A. (1962) "The Appropriate Use of Monetary and Fiscal Policy under Fixed Exchange Rates," *IMF Staff Papers* 9 (March).

Mundell, R.A. (1963) "Capital Mobility and Stabilisation Policy under Fixed and Flexible Exchange Rates," *Canadian Journal of Economics and Political Science* 29 (November): 475–85.

Mundell, R.A. (1968) *International Economics*, New York: Macmillan.

Mundell, R.A. (1971) *Monetary Theory: Inflation, Interest, Growth in the World Economy*, Pacific Palisades, Calif.: Goodyear.

Negishi, T. (1979) *Microeconomic Foundations of Keynesian Macroeconomics*, Amsterdam: North-Holland.

Niehans, J. (1968) "Monetary and Fiscal Policies in Open Economies under Fixed Exchange Rates: An Optimizing Approach," *Journal of Political Economy* 76 (July–August): 893–943.

Parkin, N. (1977) "World Inflation, International Relative Price and Monetary Equilibrium under Fixed Exchange Rates," in Aliber 1977.

Scitovsky, T. (1941) "A Reconsideration of the Theory of Tariffs," *Review of Economic Studies* 9 (Summer).

Swoboda, A.K. and R. Dornbusch. (1973) "Adjustment, Policy, and Monetary Equilibrium in a Two-Country Model," in M.B. Connolly and A.K. Swoboda (eds), *International Trade and Money*, London: George Allen & Unwin.

Tinbergen, J. (1952) *On the Theory of Economic Policy*, Amsterdam: North-Holland.

Uzawa, H. (1978–79) "Fukinkō Dōgaku Josetsu" (An introduction to disequilibrium dynamics), I–IV," *Kikan Gendai Keizai*.

12 International macroeconomic policy coordination: any lessons for EMU?

A selective survey of the literature

Peter Mooslechner and Martin Schuerz*
Empirica: Journal of Applied Economics and Economic Policy, vol. 26,
no. 3 (1999), pp. 171–99

I INTRODUCTION

International economic policy coordination is not merely an economic issue, it is and has also to be treated as a political topic. Consequently, this article aims to provide a selective survey not only of relevant economic literature, but also of political economy literature on international macroeconomic coordination.[1] Particular emphasis will be placed on surveying the literature both on an analytical level, with a focus on divergent methodologies, and on a level of substance, where the coordination topic's key questions are touched upon.[2]

In the section on methodologies three analytical approaches for dealing with economic policy coordination are distinguished: (i) policy optimization analysis, (ii) regime analysis and (iii) international relations approaches. These three analytical perspectives do not necessarily exclude each other but, rather, overlap and demonstrate a difference in the scope of analytical interest. While some empirical approaches cannot be easily subsumed under this typology or simply do not fit this scheme, this differentiation, nevertheless, proves to be helpful to understand analytical differences between the approaches.[3]

In the section on the substance of the coordination literature the coordination literature will be surveyed along the lines of their particular relevance for understanding the policy process and its conflicts. The treatment of the coordination literature will also be related to a number of relevant coordination questions emerging within the context of European Monetary Union.

The survey is organized as follows. After a short introduction Section II starts by reviewing the variety of definitions of coordination. Subsequently Section III considers the rationale for coordination on the one hand or non-coordination on the other. Section IV deals with coordination from the perspective of three different analytical approaches, whereas the likely empirical gains of coordination are evaluated in Section V. The following two sections in particular discuss the role of shocks and other difficulties encountered in

* *Oesterreichische Nationalbank, Economic Analysis and Research, P.O. Box 61, A-1011 Vienna, Austria.* © 1999 *Kluwer Academic Publishers.*

coordination, as for example uncertainty. Finally some analytical questions relevant for the topic of coordination in EMU are outlined. An extensive bibliography is attached.

II DEFINITION OF ECONOMIC POLICY COORDINATION

Unfortunately the term coordination has been used in a confusing variety of ways. Wallich (1984, p. 85) provides the classical definition of coordination as "a significant modification of national policies in recognition of international economic interdependence". This definition is quoted extensively in the economic literature. However, it does not distinguish independent policy-making that considers international factors from internationally negotiated adjustments to national policies. It rather assumes that policymakers will first formalize policies without recognizing actions by others and then modify these policies.

The definition of coordination by Webb (1995, p. 11) – "negotiated mutual adjustment that causes states to pursue different policies than they would have chosen had policy-making been unilateral" – which resembles Keohane's definition of cooperation in *After hegemony* (1984, pp. 51–52) and also the understanding of Kenen (1990, p. 66) that "Coordination is the most rigorous form of economic cooperation, because it involves mutually agreed modifications in the participants' national policies. In the macroeconomic domain, it involves an exchange of explicit, operational commitments about the conduct of monetary and fiscal policies", is for analytical purposes therefore preferable. Coordination in a strong sense will involve jointly designed mutual adjustments of national policies – commitments about the time paths of policy instruments and not merely aspirations about the time paths for ultimate-target variables.

Less ambitious forms of interaction are often called economic co-operation. Rather confusing is that in game theory, however, "*co-operation*" involves the existence of a binding agreement (that has to be enforced by an outside authority).[4]

Following Currie, Holtham and Hughes Hallett (1989, p. 24) we may distinguish different levels of cooperation. The spectrum of policy cooperation might comprise:

1   In the simplest case, cooperation might consist only of the exchange of information. Policymakers may exchange information about policy targets and priorities, but they will take their decisions in an autonomous way.
2   Coordination in the form of crisis management will have an ad hoc character and will be limited to reactions on episodes of particular difficulties.
3   Policymakers may agree on targets such as the exchange rate or intermediate monetary targeting. A variable might be used as a kind of surrogate for coordination.
4   Partial coordination would involve agreeing on policy assignments.

5   In the form of full coordination, policymakers aim at a bargain across all targets and policy instruments.

III THE RATIONALE FOR COORDINATION AND FOR NON-COORDINATION

> Coordination of macroeconomic policies is certainly not easy; maybe it is impossible. But in its absence, I suspect nationalistic solutions will be sought – trade barriers, capital controls and dual exchange-rate systems. Wars among nations with these weapons are likely to be mutually destructive. Eventually, they, too, would evoke agitations for international coordination.
>
> (James Tobin 1987, p. 68)

There is broad concurrence in the economic literature on the rationale for coordination. Almost every economic textbook explains that international macroeconomic coordination in an interdependent world economy[5] is desirable when externalities and public goods are important (e.g., Buiter and Marston, 1985). The presence of international linkages implies that policy actions in one country will have spill-over effects into other countries. Spill-over effects may arise from changes in fiscal or monetary policy, taxation, trade or industrial policy.

From a policy perspective the concern is that non-coordination might lead to sub-optimal results. For example a tightening of monetary policy to fight inflation in one country might lead to an appreciation of the currency and to inflationary pressures in other countries whose currencies depreciate. When all countries tighten monetary policy under worldwide inflationary pressures, the result may be an overtightening of monetary policy worldwide (see Oudiz and Sachs, 1984; Miller and Salmon, 1985). A mismatch between fiscal and monetary policy will be characterized by high fiscal deficits and a tight monetary policy. This combination would result in a tendency toward appreciation in the exchange rate and an unbalanced policy mix. The other negative alternative would be an easening of monetary policy combined with loose budgetary policies. The policy mix would be growth supportive in the short run but damaging in the long run.

Some economists have argued that international economic policy coordination will have undesirable effects. Vaubel (1983) concluded that policy coordination is harmful because it reduces competition among governments. Coordination could raise the cost of policy errors if the wrong approach is followed collectively. And Fischer (1988, p. 12) underlined:

> It would in general be far better if the major industrial countries concentrated on the pursuit of sound domestic economic policies and reserved the pursuit of international cooperation for those subjects like international trade and national security in which cooperation is truly essential.

Their main argument is that coordination might deflect the attention of national governments from domestic policy issues – which should have a higher priority. However, it is hard to see the exclusiveness of alternatives, i.e., either the pursuit of sound domestic economic policies or the search for coordinated solutions.

Another argument by Rogoff (1985) against coordination has been considered extensively in the literature. Rogoff constructed a two-country model based on a complete rational-expectations framework that includes a role for interest rates. Explicit coordination might be counterproductive if a subgroup of players cooperate in the absence of relevant third parties (in Rogoff's theoretical model it is the private sector which is excluded).[6] The theoretical consideration of the Rogoff paper of likely negative effects of coordination has not been supported by empirical studies (see Section V). Carraro and Giavazzi (1991) provide a counter-example in which with three players – government, firms and trade unions – cooperation is welfare enhancing. They rightly point out that a comparison of the outcome of a game in which central banks cooperate and wage setters expect them to cooperate with a game in which monetary authorities do not cooperate and are not expected to cooperate is misleading, as the case where central banks cooperate is not an equilibrium of the sequential game.

The academic economic literature on international policy coordination started already with the work of Meade (1951) stressing the importance of the problem of policy conflicts. In the studies of Cooper (1968) strategic monetary interdependence was analyzed under a fixed exchange rate system. Cooper argued that a lack of economic policy coordination becomes costly because increasingly interdependent economies complicate the achievement of national policy goals.

International coordination of macroeconomic policies attracted much attention in the academic literature in the 1970s after the regime shift from a system of fixed exchange rates to a system of flexible exchange rates. The techniques of game theory have provided useful tools for analyzing the strategic aspects of policy conflicts and coordination. Much of the analysis took place within a regime of fixed exchange rates.[7] Starting with the contributions of Hamada (1974, 1976, 1979) rigorous game-theoretical techniques have been applied to questions of policy coordination. Hamada's studies were limited to simple symmetrical two-country models without dynamics – interdependence was analyzed in terms of a single-shot game – and implicitly assumed backward-looking expectations of the private sector. In a static game non-coordinated economic policy is typically inefficient because of a prisoner's dilemma in policy choices.

The results of coordination analysis change by moving from a static to a dynamic analysis. In the case of repeated games the variety of outcomes will increase. If strategic interactions are repeated then analysis has to focus on the path and not on the single move. Important are models with structural time dependence where the welfare loss in any period depends on actions in the past as well as present actions.

The question of time consistency of policies gained importance in the

1980s.[8] The interest in such studies was linked to a general revival of political interest in policy coordination. From 1985 onwards the focus of policy interest was mainly on monetary policy and foreign exchange interventions. Research on international economic coordination since then has been mainly developed along two lines, firstly, by analyzing in simplified models the theoretical aspects of strategic behavior and, secondly, by exploring in empirical structural models the interaction of economies.

The focus is on expectational interactions among national policymakers and between governments and the private sector. Special emphasis is given to time consistency and the possibility that policymakers may renege on implicit agreements with the private sector. Information or signals get a crucial role in dynamic games (see Currie and Levine, 1985). Conditional for these models is a high degree of information; the correct model is assumed to be known to all actors participating in the strategic game, and there is the assumption of perfect knowledge about the type of economic disturbances.[9] Dynamic games come up with two kinds of solutions: an open-loop solution and a closed-loop solution. The former considers cases where policymakers set the complete time path of strategies as a function of time. In dynamic games with closed-loop solutions the strategy of the policymaker does depend on time and on state variables.

IV DIVERGING ANALYTICAL PERSPECTIVES ON POLICY COORDINATION

There are a number of differences in the analytical perspective between policy optimization and regime analysis and, consequently, rather diverging policy conclusion will result. Both approaches tend from a policy perspective to be rather normative, as they concentrate on likely advantages of coordination achieved either by international optimization or by agreed rules of the game. International relation approaches remain in comparison more descriptive ("*story-telling*") and are more concerned with the political process itself that leads to a coordinated outcome, focusing on power, norms and institutional issues. None of the three approaches consistently has a leading position in explaining coordination but each of them catches important elements of political economy.

1 Policy-optimization analysis

The economic literature on macroeconomic policy cooperation is dominated by policy-optimization analysis. Policy optimization concentrates on explicit coordination. What is the economic outcome when policymakers set economic policy in a coordinated way?

The notion of policy interdependence has been operationalized in the framework of a policy-optimizing approach. In such an analysis the agents are national governments, which have well-defined, exogenously given preferences (loss functions). The interactions among national economies (the way in which policies and shocks originating in one country affect other countries) and the alternative strategies available to national governments are exogenous to the analysis. The decisions of national governments are treated as cooperative or non-cooperative games.[10] Each national government is a unitary decision-making agent who acts in a strategic way according to its interests which are biased towards domestic welfare.

In a non-cooperative game structure, policymakers try to maximize their own country's welfare, taking the policies of other national governments as given. Unilateral national behavior is often modeled as Nash or Stackelberg non-cooperative behavior.[11] A *Nash equilibrium* is deemed to be the optimal non-cooperative decision, it is the result of a strategic game in which each party maximizes its objectives by taking the action of the other party or parties as given. In a Nash equilibrium all parties are on their reaction curve and are acting in a credible way.

Stackelberg behavior results when one nation takes a leadership position vis-à-vis others. Such a leader–follower solution to two-country models provides a kind of halfway point between the Nash and cooperative equilibria. This behavior will be contrasted with cooperative approaches and the incentives to deviate from cooperative outcomes are studied. In a cooperative game structure the national governments will jointly maximize a weighted average of their individual welfare (a joint welfare function).[12] Cooperative games will generate Pareto-optimal outcomes.

The policy-optimizing approaches rest on rational choice assumptions and on the hypothesis of an unitary-actor.[13] One of the problems of economic arguments relating to the international macroeconomic coordination is the assumption that policy-making is a technical exercise in welfare maximization. According to this approach nations have well-defined loss functions and act to optimize their decisions accordingly. This suggestion is far from convincing. Macroeconomic policy-making might rather be understood as government actions to achieve a variety of conflicting aims. Many of these goals might have more to do with domestic policy than with policy optimization.

Apparently, the typical assumption of policy optimization that each government can be treated analytically as a unitary actor does not represent the political and institutional facts of life. A multiplicity of domestic players with different interests should make analysis a lot more difficult. In reality it will be difficult to define a uniform national interest. There will rather be conflicting interests between influential groups such as producers and consumers, trade unions and employers' organisations or exporters and importers. And in any case, coordination does not necessarily reflect national interests. It rather reflects each government's perception of its own interest, which may differ from what independent experts define as national interests.

2 Regime analysis

Regime analysis studies policy coordination from a different standpoint, namely assuming that policy coordination is needed in order to produce certain public goods, such as stability. However, the contrast between policy optimization and regime analysis is not a sharp one. If policy optimization concentrates on explicit coordination then regime analysis might be said to concentrate on international economic coordination through presumptive rules. It should be noted that we do not understand the term regime as a substitute for the hegemon's role but rather as an alternative to explicit coordination.[14]

The general mode of cooperation in a regime is mutual recognition by participants of the rules, which are at least to some degree subject to multilateral surveillance. Rules are expected to have a number of advantages: It is often argued that policymakers prefer to follow well-designed rules that are easily monitored and that will be appreciated by the public. The expected advantages of reputation and credibility might be viewed by policymakers as favorable even if policy rules will exert discipline on the policy-making process. In addition rules are expected to protect the small players against the large ones.

The questions posed by regime analysis are: What kind of rules of the game help to achieve the most efficient economic outcome? In practice policymakers (and the literature) have focused almost exclusively on the exchange rate.[15]

The performance of alternative international regimes which are confronted with various shocks in relation to a certain goal is evaluated by structural multi-country models.[16]

Policy coordination in practice may be directed mainly to regime preservation and not to policy optimization. Exchange rate cooperation in the 1980s would in this terminology be called regime preservation, and we will argue that coordination under EMU would also fall in this category.

There is the famous Williamson–Miller (1987) extended target zone approach proposing that fiscal policy should be used to aim at internal nominal demand growth, while monetary policy focuses at the external balance by holding exchange rates within wide bands around an *equilibrium exchange rate level*. Currie and Wren-Lewis (1989a, 1989b, 1990) found that the extended target scheme could have improved the economic performance over the period 1975–1986.[17]

Taylor (1989) examined a number of monetary rules under different exchange rate regimes.[18] In the comparison of a fixed exchange rate system with a flexible exchange rate system in which monetary policies have different aims – such as stabilizing the price level or nominal income or both price and output with different elasticities – the conclusion of the study is that a *mixed price–real output rule* is likely to have better stabilization properties in the case of exogenous shocks to the economy than a *pure rule based on either prices or nominal GNP*.

In conflict with these results is the outcome of a study by Hughes Hallett, Holtham and Hutson (1989), which, based on the MCM model of the Federal Reserve Board, analyzed the advantages of a combination of exchange rate targeting and pursuing at the same time independent policies. Their conclusion is that there are prospects for improving policy coordination by exchange-rate management.

Levine *et al.* (1989) conclude by using a reduced two-bloc version of the OECD Interlink model that policy coordination can be effective when the rules are kept simple and that there is scope to use simple rules as a surrogate for stronger versions of coordination. In the study of Bryant *et al.* (1993) it was tried to rank regimes according to their performance.[19] One of the robust generalizations emerging was the relatively poor performance of exchange rate targeting relative to the other international regimes studied.[20] In general the performance of simple policy rules depended on the nature of shocks facing the economies.

To a certain degree regimes work as a kind of substitute for coordination. In the gold standard system the adjustment mechanism – the famous price specie flow variant – worked in an automatic way.[21] The rules of the game – an asymmetric fixed exchange rate system – were explicitly defined. Policy-makers of non-reserve currency countries had to intervene in order to keep exchange rates fixed, while the policymaker of the reserve country could follow an independent monetary policy. The rules of the game were therefore clear and the interplay of policies was determined by these rules of the game.

3 International relations approaches

The term international relations approaches is rather broad as it comprises realist, neorealist and liberal institutionalist approaches in international relations theory.[22] International relations approaches have tended to focus on the systemic level of analysis, on the sources of and constraints on cooperative behavior among states as a function of the international system. Much of this literature has also used game theory and interpreted the prisoners' dilemma as the key element of international politics. Reference to the social context will be of help for an adequate understanding of the process of economic policy coordination.[23]

In political economy literature the issue of power is underlined for strategic problems (Webb 1995, ch. 2) and leadership becomes a key element for successful coordination. Power – following the definition by Krasner (1983, p. 342) "the ability to determine who plays the game, or to define the rules, or to change the values within the payoff matrix" – shapes the distribution of burden of adjustment to international macroeconomic imbalances, and international bargaining power is crucial for understanding why policy coordination has happened and why not, and also for the question why the burden of adjustment is distributed as it is among countries.

Webb argued (1995, p. 46ff) that "the record of international macro-economic coordination . . . suggests that the key issue in international negotiations has been determining how burdens of adjustment . . . will be distributed among countries, not overcoming obstacles to cooperation posed by the fear of cheating in an anarchic world". In the case of the Bonn summit 1978 the outcome helped influential groups in each country to achieve domestic aims.

Krasner (1991) pointed out that in the case of pure coordination games, distributional conflicts over Pareto-optimal outcomes are likely to be resolved through the exercise of power. International bargaining power is considered to be of greater importance for governments than concerns about maximizing welfare (which motivates the discussions of international policy coordination in the framework of policy-optimizing approaches as we have seen in section 2.1).[24] However, political scientists themselves often follow rather abstract approaches such as improving the state's international power position. And very similar to the policy optimization approach in realism, states are treated as unitary and rational actors engaged in the pursuit of national self-interest.

As there is not one theory of cooperation in international relations literature, we have to concentrate on the hypotheses with which the divergent approaches came up: Hegemony is often understood as the key for understanding the extent of policy coordination. The leadership of a hegemon may facilitate a desirable outcome (see Kindleberger, 1973; Gilpin, 1975; and Keohane, 1984).[25] If stability can be understood as a public good, all countries benefit from it irrespective of whether they contribute to its production or not.[26]

Two propositions have to hold simultaneously: First, the presence of a dominant actor should lead to the provision of greater stability in the international environment, and second this greater stability has to benefit all states in the system. In the *benevolent strand of hegemony theory* literature (Snidal, 1985) the hegemon is willing to pay an undue part of the short-run costs of the public good either because he expects to gain in the long run and/or because he expects gains in other fields (Kindleberger, 1986, p. 8).[27] The *coercive strand of hegemony theory* describes the idea how a hegemon might use its power to create an international economic system. Rather than providing the public good unilaterally by adjusting its policy, the hegemon could offer rewards and threat with punishment to persuade other countries to adjust their policies.

Realism takes a rather pessimistic view of state behavior. The realist assumption is that states are egoistic and that policymakers will act rational on the basis of what they perceive as their self-interest. The realist approach has important limitations for a general understanding of the sources of defection from cooperation. The overemphasis on the state has explanatory disadvantages. Keohane urges to reformulate realism "because it fails to take into account that states' conceptions of their interests, and of how their objectives should be pursued, depend not merely on national interests, and the distribution of world power, but on the quantity, quality, and distribution of information" (Keohane, 1984, p. 245).

In concentrating on the state as an actor, the ways in which other actors might use institutions is neglected and the way in which the state interest is changed by actions of institutions is not considered. State interest can be shaped by epistemic communities or by institutional structures: *Institutionalism* refers to the regimes set up by hegemons. The regimes consist of principles, norms and rules and decision-making procedures on which the expectations of actors converge. The importance of institutions – a set of practices and expectations – is underlined because they help policymakers to pursue their own interest through cooperation. Regimes might reduce uncertainty and make cooperation easier as they provide transparency and information to relieve likely fears that arise in a multipolar world (e.g., the fear that countries will act unilaterally). Regimes create the expectation that all participating parties will interact indefinitely and that a defection of one party will be punished by another party's non-cooperation in the future. Regime members calculate reputational gains from coordination. This would imply that regimes shape preferences of the members and encourage cooperation (Moravcsik, 1993).

An *epistemic community* might be viewed as a prerequisite for cooperation. It means "a professional group that believes in the same cause-and-effect relationships, truth tests to accept them and shares common values; its members share a common understanding of a problem and its solution" (Haas, 1992, p. 55). When uncertainty is high, decision-makers might be more willing to permit scientific elites access to the policy process with the chance that their views get institutionalized in the policy process, and might change national preferences. It remains an open issue why and when an epistemic community will have an impact on the domestic policy system.

One strand of the literature focuses on the issue whether the source of state preferences is *international* or *domestic*. The use of game theory with its assumption of unitary and rational actors has influenced the decision in literature to neglect domestic politics. Unlike the state-centric theories, a two-level approach considers domestic conflicts as inevitable. Policymakers will have to reconcile domestic and international imperatives (Putnam, 1988). In *"two level game theory"*[28] policymakers act at two levels – a domestic one and an international one. Milner (1992) suggested that domestic political situations often leave states unable to implement internationally cooperative policies. The key obstacles to strengthening policy coordination were interpreted to be domestic, not international (Webb, 1995). Monetary and especially fiscal policies were traditionally considered as policies designed to internal goals.[29]

A further hypothesis is that "the prospects for cooperation diminish as the number of players increases" (Oye, 1986, p. 18). This view is shared in economic literature by Taylor (1987), who believes that difficulties of monitoring compliance tend to increase with the number of participants, but has been challenged by others. The point that a large number of states creates collective action problems, because the probability of defection will increase and the feasibility to sanction the defector will be reduced, has explanatory weaknesses. A large number of players provides more opportunities for exchanges and side payments (Grieco, 1988).

The international relations literature on coordination remains to a large part game-theoretic. It has been guided by a systemic focus and by observations of problems that compel coordination among governments. Even if the simplifying assumption of policy-optimizing approaches were left and analysis was located in the social context that is almost excluded in economic analysis, the international relations approaches have a number of drawbacks. Their hypothetical character makes them vulnerable to empirical counter-examples. As strategic processes are often described in a metaphorical way the concepts lack explanatory power. It is remarkable that to a large extent international relations literature neglects domestic politics. Similar to economic literature on coordination, international relations approaches rely heavily on unexamined assumptions about the determination of the payoff structures of states, the likely strategies to alter systemic conditions and the capacity of states to ratify and implement cooperative arrangements.[30]

V GAINS FROM ECONOMIC POLICY COORDINATION?

In empirical studies (Oudiz and Sachs, 1984; McKibbin and Sachs, 1989; Taylor, 1985) the results of a welfare function, where each country maximizes its welfare (weights are assigned to various economic objectives in each country), are compared with the values when countries maximize a joint welfare function. The difference between the two calculations is taken as a measure of the gains to coordination.

In their pioneering study, Oudiz and Sachs (1984) investigated the quantitative gains to international policy coordination by treating policy formulation as a static game.[31] They estimated that the gains from cooperation among the G3 countries in the mid-1970s would be about 0.5% of GDP to each country compared with the best Cournot–Nash non-cooperative outcome. In a more general analysis Hughes Hallett (1986) estimated the gains to be between 0.5% and 1.5% of GNP for USA, EEC and Japan.

Gains of this size are not much bigger than the forecast standard of errors of the target variables. But the question whether the gains from coordination are sizable is in fact not well defined. The standards of comparison for this judgement are unclear and the results are sensitive to the choice of weights. It is impossible to distinguish welfare improvement resulting from economic policy coordination from improvement attributable to less ambitious forms of cooperation (e.g., consultation). The counterfactual outcome – optimization by policymakers in the Nash non-cooperative equilibrium – is not necessarily convincing. A comparison between optimal coordinated policies and optimal non-coordinated policies is not realistic as it should be more relevant to compare sub-optimal coordinated policies with sub-optimal non-coordinated policies.

In addition, measurement of gains can be sensitive to the range of policies considered. The magnitude of gains might increase if not only macro- and microeconomic factors but also non-economic issues are considered. A wide domain of policies considered will change the results on coordination gains.

Small demonstration models (Currie and Levine, 1985; Miller and Salmon, 1985; Oudiz and Sachs, 1985; Levine and Currie, 1987) where each economy is represented by a few simplified equations suggested that the gains from coordination are likely to be small but significant. However, the equations restrict the framework to a world of two identically symmetric economies with either no dynamics or steady state dynamics. The policy responses are known with certainty and there are no information innovations. The results are similar in simple but estimated models of Carlozzi and Taylor (1985), Sachs and McKibbin (1985) and Taylor (1985).[32]

A great advance in the 1980s has been the increasing flow of empirically based results that would make the theoretical research more relevant for policymakers. There are a huge number of studies based on large-scale empirical multi-country models (see e.g., Canzoneri and Minford, 1988; Currie, Levine and Vidalis, 1987; Currie and Wren-Lewis, 1990; Frankel, 1990b; Frenkel, Goldstein and Masson, 1989; Hughes Hallett, Holtham and Hutson, 1989; McKibbin and Sachs, 1989, 1991; and Taylor, 1985, 1989).

Studies agree on the conclusion that the gains from coordination are not evenly distributed. Oudiz and Sachs 1984 came up with the result that gains are distributed approximately 2:1 in favor of Germany relative to the USA in two different models. Hughes Hallett (1986) found, by using a range of bargaining models, gains to be distributed 2:1 in favour of the EEC relative to the USA. This result is somewhat sensitive to alternative types of exogenous shocks (Hughes Hallett, 1987). Cooperation in the form of an agreement on the exchange rate path might lead to an asymmetrical distribution of gains among the G-5 countries (Hughes Hallett, 1989).

Policy optimization and international relation approaches converge in stressing the argument that significant gains may result merely from information exchange between policymakers and from strategic rather than myopic actions (Keohane, 1984; Bryant, 1987; Currie, Holtham and Hughes Hallett, 1989). Canzoneri and Edison (1989) concentrate on the selection of a "*good*" non-cooperative solution from a set of Nash equilibria. The differences in Nash solutions may result from information sharing and surveillance, the choice of policy instruments and the adoption of reputational strategies. They conclude that coordination in terms of information and surveillance is far more important than coordination of instruments. Even limited cooperation such as information exchanges should bring gains in terms of more efficient noncooperative policies – outcomes reached without proper coordination. Information exchanges about the initial conditions of economies and about expected shocks may help to reduce uncertainty, they "appear to be a key part of the coordination process, irrespective of the model or the time period" (Currie and Levine, 1991, p. 402). Also the institutionalist literature underlines the importance of mere consultations and information exchange (see Keohane, 1984). Information exchange and regular consultations about policy intention will yield benefits in any case but will be of particular help when serious crises emerge.

A number of factors caution against drawing policy conclusions from the studies on gains of coordination. Firm evidence on the signs and sizes of the spillover effects among countries is not available. The results may be sensitive to specific features of the chosen model.

A number of gains of policy coordination – to be expected because of issue-linkages and package deals in other policy areas – will not be caught by the policy-optimizing approaches because of its narrow focus.

VI THE SPECIFIC ROLE OF SHOCKS IN POLICY COORDINATION

The role of shocks has drawn attention in a number of studies. Canzoneri and Minford (1988), Currie *et al.* (1987) found relatively small gains in the absence of major shocks, based on calculations from versions of the Liverpool and OECD models for the USA and the EEC or OECD respectively. The mix of shocks (the size and nature of exogenous shocks) can affect the gains form coordination. Persistent shocks and the existence of *"reputation"* increase the importance of coordination (Currie *et al.*, 1987).

McKibbin and Sachs (1991) have shown that the benefits from monetary policy coordination are quite limited, because of the importance of supply-side spillover effects arising from fiscal policy. If policy is more constrained, then the benefits from coordination will fall.

Currie *et al.* (1987) found in a dynamic analysis – a reduced version of the OECD model – the gains of coordination to be small in the face of temporary disturbances. But benefits will increase as the persistence of the disturbance rises and the existence of "reputation" increases the importance of coordination. However, it is not clear why a non-coordinated outcome should not also be affected by exogenous shocks.

Canzoneri and Henderson (1991) make a difference between symmetric and asymmetric shocks. They showed that the Cournot–Nash equilibrium is overcontractionary for symmetric shocks. In the case of asymmetric shocks it can be overcontractionary for one country and overexpansionary for the other country. Fratianni and von Hagen (1992) conclude that the desirability of the European Monetary System (EMS) critically depended on the relative size of asymmetric and symmetric shocks and on the correlation pattern between them.

A further contribution by Canzoneri and Henderson (1991) was the development of an analytical framework in which policymakers are confronted with periodic supply shocks. When monetary authorities in the case of a negative supply shock are only concerned with the inflationary impact and not with the consequence for the foreign country – a real depreciation of its currency – then the worldwide monetary expansion would turn out to be too low.

VII DIFFICULTIES FOR MACROECONOMIC POLICY COORDINATION

In the case of models which assume perfect knowledge about the type of economic disturbances and of the policymakers' reaction function, the analysis had to concentrate on the problem of inefficient equilibria. However, the results from studies assuming perfect foresight by policymakers may be biased against finding large gains of coordination.

1 Unsustainability

A point made by several authors is that coordination without reputation might be counterproductive (see Miller and Salmon (1985); for a standard illustrative model incorporating the key international spillover effects see Levine and Currie (1987) and Currie, Levine and Vidalis (1987); and for a static model Canzoneri and Henderson (1988), Currie and Levine (1991)).[33] Without government reputation *vis-à-vis* the private sector cooperation between policymakers may not pay, and when it does the benefits would be minimal.[34]

A coordination solution will be unsustainable when policymakers do not stick to their commitment and cheat by deviating in their future policies from the agreed policy stance. Analytically this issue is treated by considering forms of reneging. With the passage of time a country or more countries might come to a point where there is an incentive to renege on the cooperative outcome. Such cooperative agreement will lack credibility, and rational policymakers will not enter into such an agreement. The *folk theorem of repeated games* stresses the point that even if players have an incentive to renege (to deviate from the coordinated outcome) they will not do so because they fear to lose payoffs when other players can punish them in the subsequent periods.

The traditional method to restore sustainability is to devise an incentive mechanism through sanctions against reneging. If there are supranational institutions which can legally enforce the coordinated solution then policy will be credible. The institution will prevent that policymakers renege on each other or on the private sector. This implies a *"loss of sovereignty"* as Canzoneri and Henderson (1988) contrast it with a sovereign policy-making process whereby countries coordinate on an agreed outcome and employ trigger mechanism to enforce that outcome.

As Cooper already pointed out in 1985, the term *"time inconsistency"* may be inappropriate for reference to the policy process as it refers only to a particular analytical framework for choosing optimal policy over a finite period of time. Cooper concluded that the problem of forward-looking expectations has been exaggerated within that framework. What in his view is more important is a lack of trust. But as there is no empirical evidence on this issue a definitive judgement results difficult. Following Kenen (1990) and Bryant (1995) the issue of reneging and cheating (Hughes Hallett, 1986b) stressed in literature has to be considered as exaggerated by looking to historical experiences. What seems to be far more important is the question of uncertainty.

2 Uncertainty

> uncertainties about the effects of one country's policies on the economies of other countries make it impossible to be confident that coordinated policy shifts would actually be beneficial.
>
> (Feldstein, 1988)

The literature on coordination, which in the 1970s mainly focused on the choice of policies and policy bargains, moved on to analyze also the implications of the choice of models and model bargains. Model uncertainty – which means the technical reference to uncertainty about the *true* model – was explicitly introduced in the theoretical analysis by Ghosh and Masson (1987, 1991, 1994), Masson (1992), Frankel (1988, 1990), and Frankel and Rockett (1988).

Frankel and Rockett (1988) were pessimistic about the gains from coordination under conditions of uncertainty. They provided a static framework for evaluating a specific type of policy uncertainty – namely uncertainty about the true model of the economy. Their analysis is based on ten large multi-country models (USA and Europe), with the assumptions that each country uses its own model to measure the gains of a coordination solution and that governments do not exchange information but that they agree to coordinate when their own calculation of welfare effects shows that it will be beneficial for them. In other words: each government believes in its own model and knows the other models. They showed that misperceptions about economic behaviour can lead to welfare-worsening policy bargains.

Some caution about these results seems to be necessary as the assumption that policymakers do not consider the possibility that the models used by their counter-parties might be correct is not convincing. The results – that the gains to one country that unilaterally discovered the correct model and adjusted its policies accordingly are much greater than the potential gains from coordination – are of little help for policymakers as we may doubt that they will ever find the *true* model.[35]

In addition, a number of studies have reversed these results. The presence of model uncertainty may provide an additional incentive to coordinate policies, provided that policymakers recognize that they cannot know the true model. In particular Ghosh and Masson (1991) showed that, by allowing for the possibility of learning that the model used by others may be correct, coordination dominates uncoordinated regimes.[36] Under the assumption of Bayesian learning the ex post gains from coordination turn out to be positive in their simulation exercises.

In the case of uncertainty not only the interaction among policymakers is of relevance but also epistemic communities, i.e., "networks of professionals with recognized expertise and competence in a particular domain and an authoritative claim to policy-relevant knowledge" (Haas 1992, p. 3), might get an important role as a source of information that will contribute to overcome uncertainty about policy coordination.[37] In economic literature the term used is not epistemic communities, but consensus on ideas is also underlined (Frankel, 1988; Cooper *et al.*, 1989; Eichengreen, 1997).

Coordination literature has concentrated on game-theoretic dilemmas of collective actions and on uncertainty. In reality there are multiple obstacles to successful coordination, such as differences in policy objectives between policymakers, the lack of a coherent common understanding how macro-economy works and how it should work, heterogenous national institutions, and contingent political and social factors. If there are differences in fundamental matters such as the role of the state or in the degree of necessary liberalization then coordination will result extremely difficult. In reality coordination will be complicated by political, bureaucratic and legal constraints on jurisdictional divisions within governments. Looking back in monetary history we may conclude that coordination has been successful in cases where it was systematically institutionalized and where the political consensus was broad.

VIII FUTURE POLICY-ORIENTED RESEARCH AREAS: COORDINATION WITHIN EMU?

Without doubt, the formation of a Monetary Union in Europa has raised a large number of new and important questions concerning policy coordination and, in fact, led to new and increasing interest in the topic. A large number of future policy-oriented research areas in this field can be identified which deserve our interest.[38]

First of all, the EMU regime might be interpreted as a surrogate for far-reaching forms of policy coordination. More ambitious forms of coordination aiming at explicit coordination so as to optimize the policy mix in EMU are confronted in any case with coordination constraints imposed by the EMU-regime, such as the independence provision of the ESCB and the supreme monetary policy goal of maintaining price stability.

The central argument is that the EMU game is mainly about regime preserving, i.e., about preserving monetary dominance. For example, the tight fiscal rules of the Stability and Growth Pact should increase further the credibility of the single monetary policy and should ensure compliance with the independence requirement of the ESCB.

The basic characteristic of playing according to the rules of the EMU game is that policies have to be compatible with the operation of the regime. If policies become incompatible the rules of the game will point to the need for adjustment. International cooperation understood as a two-level process (Bryant, 1995)[39] means that in exceptional periods negotiations take place at the top level (e.g., Treaty on the European Union, Stability and Growth Pact). The ongoing policy decision at the lower level will then be influenced by the rules of the game agreed at the higher level. Now that the EMU regime – a kind of monetary dominance regime – has actually been put in place the participants have moved on to the subgame of how to play in EMU.

Three areas of particular interest can be selected on which policy-oriented research in the field of coordination in EMU might focus. All approaches will have to assign importance to all kinds of uncertainty.

Exceptional crises/shocks (asymmetric or symmetric): The *rules of the EMU game* – as perhaps the rules of all games we can think about – can never cover all contingencies. A threat that therefore has to be considered in any regime – but in EMU in particular because of its multi-level structure – is that under a given set of rules defects might emerge which cannot be resolved through calls for discipline by the leader. Historical experience has taught that international regimes are threatened by crises (in EMU, e.g., the risk of a pan-European crisis) and that the issue of coordination might be reformulated as a question for the adequate form of crisis management.

Social context of EMU: Rule-based regimes cannot by themselves create credibility. They "depend for their effectiveness on adherence to the spirit as well as to the letter of the agreed rules" (Cooper, 1985, p. 1229) and as Frankel (1990, p. 110) pointed out "if a cooperative regime is to be successful, it must be built on an accumulation of trust". Trust may be particular fragile in EMU, which is after all no political Union and not founded in a world of surrendered sovereignty, rather the contrary.

In this respect the importance of scientific research on the question of social context was underlined in the literature survey. The advantages of a rules-based regime can be realized if it is not only strongly backed by macro-economics and structural policies but also by the political will. This means on the one hand that the rules of the EMU game will have to be based on a consensus relating to the economic policy paradigm among policymakers, epistemic communities, institutions and the monetary authority. Paradigms have changed – e.g., with the demise of the Keynesian consensus in the 1970s and early 1980s – and might change again. But on the other hand, the political will itself has to be based on a social consensus. A lack of credibility, which signifies in a broad sense political sustainability, might emerge if the policy mix of the EMU regime turns out unfavorable.

Further political science research is needed on the question whether a technical institution such as the ECB might get into trouble by playing a strategic role in the European policy process. Viewed from a normative democratic-oriented approach, a monetary dominance regime lacks legitimacy. As the principal cannot transfer its legitimacy to the agent, the legitimacy of the latter depends on the outcome and remains fragile.

As an issue such as democratic accountability in EMU cannot be limited to the question of transparency it will not be sufficient for the ESCB to be, first, transparent about its policy intentions in monetary policy, second, to demonstrate technical competence in monetary policy and, third, to leave no doubt about monetary leadership in the regime.

Preferences in society about the interplay of monetary policy with other policies, the solution of trade-offs between policy objectives and the institutional possibilities in the case of crises may diverge. This fact is bound to complicate, in every scenario, the coordination process. A strategy of clear division of responsibilities among monetary and fiscal authorities seems to be more feasible in a national context where technical solutions aiming at efficiency are based on a consensus. It is an open issue whether a game of monetary leadership is socially sustainable in the long run.

Structure of incentives/strategic interactions: An analysis of the EMU regime has to take account of a changed incentive structure of players in EMU. The monetary authorities are involved in a game with private-sector wage- and price-setters and fiscal authorities. For the outcome of this game, it will be decisive whether the design of the EMU regime is robust vis-à-vis non-coordination, this means if policymakers and social partners undertake exactly those policies that are required to sustain the regime. Even from the point of efficiency, a threat strategy of the Eurosystem – to announce countervailing action in the case of loose fiscal policy or excessive wage policies – might be dangerous as it concentrates on misbehavior and does not extend adequately on the policy reaction in the case of sound macroeconomic behavior.

The independent ECB might opt on the basis of its strategic leadership role for a less or more cooperative policy equilibrium. In any case it will be decisive whether EU governments and social partners are willing to take the role of Stackelberg followers of the Eurosystem that has the possibility of disciplining other policy areas in order to achieve the aims of the Maastricht Treaty. To establish credibility of its price stability target by neglecting the costs for the policy mix will be suboptimal.

As a rule-based regime can by no means be a substitute for far-reaching coordination it is preferable to regard the three analytical approaches presented in the survey as rather complementary. The key weakness of the EMU regime is that it was never conceptually coherent but marks rather a further step in an open integration process of the EU, which has to be kept in mind in each policy-oriented analysis of coordination in EMU.

IX CONCLUDING REMARKS

The theoretical case for international coordination was well established, and presumed settled, in the 1970s. In the mid-1980s, the focus of research shifted to intertemporal aspects of economic interdependence. In the early 1990s, the subject no longer generated as much interest among economists as it might have deserved from an economic policy perspective. With EMU, the topic of coordination has once again found its way onto the political and scientific agenda.

The standard approach followed in coordination literature is policy optimization. The contribution of this strand of literature is rather methodological and the models it employs point to a number of possible explanations and patterns of interaction.

As the assessment of potential gains is at best tentative, assessment results do not allow for straightforward policy conclusions. The strength of policy optimization literature on coordination lies in its axiomatic structure, which permits analytical rigor and specificity. However, this explanatory vigor can also be seen as the source of the policy optimization approach's main weaknesses.

Economists' and political scientists' studies on coordination will not be suited to serve as blueprints of policy coordination for policymakers to follow at summit meetings. As a matter of fact, the practical information value to be gained from theoretical analysis and empirical models can only be described as limited. However, the research helps to clarify policymakers' incentive structures in the face of different kinds of policy conflicts. Coordination literature, overall, provides useful analytical insights in the structure of coordination. And an improved analytical understanding of macroeconomic interaction is a prerequisite for more successful efforts at policy coordination.

Even if the key question, how much relevance the abundant literature on coordination may hold for the "real world", could not be answered definitely, at least the survey may be seen as an attempt to *deconstructing the rhetoric of coordination*.

NOTES

1　See further literature surveys on coordination in chronological order by Cooper (1985), Artis and Ostry (1986), Kenen (1987), Currie and Levine (1991), Bryant (1995a) and Hamada and Kawai (1997).

2　For a review of historical perspectives on international economic policy coordination see Putnam and Bayne (1987), Dobson (1991), the appendix in Ghosh and Masson (1994) and Eichengreen (1985).

3　Bryant (1995a) suggests a similar categorization in his literature survey on coordination.

4　In this survey the term coordination will be used despite its strict meaning in a rather vague and broad sense as it has been used in the literature rather arbitrarily.

5　Macroeconomic interdependence will not only increase the number of disturbances but will also alter the magnitude of disturbances.

6　Other welfare-decreasing outcomes of cooperative solutions are considered by Miller and Salmon (1985), who focus on time-consistent solutions in a two-country model with forward-looking expectations, Levine and Currie (1987), for an empirical two-bloc model where the gains from cooperation without reputation can be negative, and for issues of fiscal coordination Kehohe (1987, 1991).

7　In a symmetric fixed exchange rate system each country has to share the adjustment burden of international reserves in a symmetric way with the aim to keep exchange rates fixed.

8　See many of the papers in Buiter and Marston (eds.) 1985 which provide thorough analyses of problems emerging in dynamic games, Bryant and Portes (eds.) 1987, Currie and Levine 1993.

9　The importance of the time-consistency problem might have been exaggerated in theory. We follow the conclusion of Kenen (1987, p. 34) that "policy changes do not necessarily call into question a government's credibility or damage its reputation, except in the theorist world, where everyone knows enough to identify each new disturbance immediately and thus to decide whether the government is exploiting a time inconsistency in its current policy plan or revising that plan appropriately to deal with a new disturbance."

10　A game consists of a set of players, a set of strategies and a payoff function for each player.

11　For a reference to this analytical perspective see e.g., Canzoneri and Henderson (1991).

12　Usually an arithmetic or geometric average of the welfare functions of the national states.

13 Putnam and Henning (1989, p. 106): "The right question is not whether the unitary-actor assumption is unrealistic, but whether it is misleading. Unfortunately we believe that it is the latter."

14 There is an ambiguous use of the term regime in coordination literature: Hamada and Kawai (1997) use the term regime choice approach, Kenen (1990) distinguishes regime choice from regime preserving; Bryant (1995b) labels the term regime environment. In any case the economic terminology has the disadvantage that the term regime is used in the international relation literature quite differently and in rather broad terms, comprising principles, norms and rules and decision-making procedures on which the expectations of actors converge. Currie, Holtham and Hughes Hallett (1989) distinguish between relative and absolute coordination.

15 For a proposal for presumptive rules see Williamson and Miller (1987) and Frankel (1990b).

16 A well studied example of a regime is the Bretton Woods System where countries aimed to maintain fixed exchange rates and domestic policies were constrained by the balance of payment and their reserve positions, or the EMS where policy cooperation to a large extent became endogenous.

17 It was not tested how robust the scheme would be under alternative models (e.g., models involving forward looking expectations). For targeting regimes being an impefect substitute for full coordination as a general proposition see Hughes Hallett (1994).

18 Assumptions of the models are sticky nominal wages and potential output and fiscal policy are exogenous.

19 Bryant *et al.* (1993) includes analyses with simplified theoretical models, deterministic simulations and stochastic simulations.

20 As Bryant (1995) mentioned, the project focused only on simple rules for domestic monetary policies and not on the combined functioning of monetary policy and fiscal policy operating regime (Bryant 1995, p. 417).

21 Eichengreen (1985, p. 171) quotes "a story which illustrates central bankers' attitudes toward policy coordination and consultation. It seems to have been the tradition at the Netherlands Bank for the President and the Directors to personally count the bank notes withdrawn from circulation at a meeting held directly after lunch. One day in 1912 or 1913 two Directors of the Reichsbank paid a visit to Amsterdam, and the President of the Bank had the novel idea of taking them to lunch. The conversation was 'highly interesting', and the President arrived at the bank note meeting fifteen minutes late with what he thought was an adequate excuse. The oldest of the Directors was unappeased and commented, 'Your work is here, not in coffeehouses'."

22 For a realist analysis see Gilpin (1975), Krasner (1976). For a critique and a liberal institutionalist approach see Kindleberger (1986), Keohane (1984), Grieco (1988).

23 "[T]he main comparative advantage of political science has been not so much theoretical formalization as sensitivity to institutions and contexts – in short story-telling" (Putnam and Henning, 1989, p. 13).

24 However also in economic literature the importance of the issue of *dominant players* is recognized (see Hamada and Kawai, 1997).

25 Kindleberger (1981) argued that American hegemony worked as a substitute for coordination. For Kindleberger a hegemon must be lender of last resort and play the role of providing countercyclical financing, discounting in times of crises and ensure an open market.

26 We understand stability as an outcome that is likely to maintain itself over time; it can be measured in terms of the persistence of the rules and procedures that characterize a particular international regime. Webb rightly concludes that analysts may be mistaking stability for policy coordination.

27 Keohane (1984) maintained that hegemony uniquely facilitates cooperation and that cooperation was therefore most extensive when the USA was at the peak of

power in the 1950s and 1960s. Eichengreen (1989) offered two examples of hegemons: the UK in the classical gold standard and the USA in the Bretton Woods System. He concluded that a system predicated on the existence of a hegemon may be dynamically unstable.

28 However, the term *"theory"* is misleading as it is rather a metaphor. Its power to describe reality has to be demonstrated empirically case by case. In the case of the Bonn summit 1978 the provocative conclusion of Putnam and Henning (1989) is that the agreement was possible only because each of the major governments was internally divided.

29 For a chronological analysis of negotiated mutual adjustment of monetary and fiscal policies since the late 1970s see Webb (1995, chapter 5).

30 For an evaluation of strengths and weaknesses of international theories of cooperation see Milner (1992).

31 Oudiz and Sachs use policy multipliers from a number of large-scale models of the world economy.

32 Currie and Levine (1985), Miller and Salmon (1985), Oudiz and Sachs (1985) and Taylor (1985) extended the static game approach and considered identically symmetric economies and dynamic decisions; Canzoneri and Gray (1985) explored on static decisions and allowed asymmetric spillovers.

33 Kehohe (1991) showed in the context of capital taxation how a lack of credibility can make policy coordination counterproductive.

34 Non-reputational policies might be considered as non-cooperation between the public and the private sector.

35 Bryant (1988) criticized in his comment the analysis of Frankel and Rockett (1988) as "too much of a mechanical bean counting exercise. It classifies outcomes as welfare increasing or reducing merely by looking at the signs of the effects; it gives very small gains or losses the same weight as large gains and losses".

36 Ghosh and Masson (1987) chose a single two-region macro-econometric model and introduced parameter uncertainty at the structural level of the model. Ghosh and Masson (1991) adopted a general, two-country Mundell–Fleming model with sticky prices and rational exchange rate expectations. Estimations were done on the basis of the IMF's MULTIMOD model.

37 For example, central bankers that formed part of the Delors committee at the end of the 1980s can be considered as an epistemic community.

38 Many of the ideas and suggestions raised in this section are based on the intensive debate of the subject at the OeNB Workshop, where a preliminary version of the paper was presented.

39 This two-level game characteristics are quite similar to the two-level metaphor (domestic and international) from Putnam and Henning (1989).

REFERENCES

Allsopp, C. and Vines, D. (1998) 'The Assessment: Macroeconomic Policy after EMU,' *Oxford Review of Economic Policy* 14(3), 1–24.

Artis, M. and Ostry, S. (1986) *International Economic Policy Coordination*, Chatham House Papers 30, London: The Royal Institute of International Affairs.

Artis, M. and Winkler, B. (1997) 'The Stability Pact: Safeguarding the Credibility of the European Central Bank,' *National Institute Economic Review*.

Axelrod, R. (1984) *The Evolution of Cooperation*, New York: Basic Books.

Barrell, R. and Whitley, J. (eds) (1992) *Macroeconomic Policy Coordination in Europe. The ERM and Monetary Union*, Newbury and London: Sage Publications. National Institute of Economic and Social Research.

Barro, R.J. and Gordon, D. (1983) 'Rules, Discretion and Reputation in a Model of Monetary Policy,' *Journal of Monetary Policy* 12, 10–121.

Blackburn, K. (1993) 'Monetary Policy and Reputation,' in Fratinanni, M. and Salvatore, D. (eds) *Monetary Policy in Developed Economies. Studies in Comparative Economic Policies Volume 3*, Amsterdam: North-Holland, pp. 125–64.

Blackburn, K. and Overgaard Ravn, M. (1995) 'Growth, Human Capital Spillovers and International Policy Coordination,' *Scandinavian Journal of Economics* 95(4), 495–515.

Blommestein, H.J. (ed.) (1991) *The Reality of International Economic Policy Coordination. Contributions to Economic Analysis*, Amsterdam: North-Holland.

Branson, W.H., Frenkel, J.A. and Goldstein, M. (eds) (1990) *International Policy Coordination and Exchange Rate Fluctuations*. A National Bureau of Economic Research Conference Report, Chicago: University of Chicago Press.

Bryant, R.C. (1987) 'Intergovernmental Coordination of Economic Policies: An Interim Stocktaking in International Monetary Cooperation: Essays in Honor of Henry C. Wallich,' *Essays in International Finance No. 169*, Princeton University Press.

Bryant, R.C. (1995a) *International Coordination of National Stabilization Policies*, Washington, DC: The Brookings Institution.

Bryant, R.C. (1995b) 'International Cooperation in the Making of National Macro-economic Policies: Where Do We Stand?', in Kenen, P.B. (ed.), *Understanding Interdependence. The Macroeconomics of the Open Economy*, Princeton, NJ: Princeton University Press.

Bryant, R.C. and Hodgkinson, E. (1989) 'Problems of International Cooperation,' in Cooper, R.N. *et al.* (eds), *Can Nations Agree? Issues in International Economic Cooperation*, Washington, DC: The Brookings Institution, pp. 1–12.

Bryant, R.C. and Portes, R. (eds) (1987) *Global Macroeconomics. Policy Conflict and Cooperation*, CEPR, Macmillan Press.

Bryant, R.C., Currie, D.A., Frenkel, J.A., Masson, P.R. and Portes, R. (eds) (1989) *Macroeconomic Policies in an Interdependent World*, The Brookings Institution/ CEPR/IMF.

Bryant, R.C. *et al.* (1993) *Evaluating Policy Regimes: New Research in Empirical Macroeconomics*, Washington, DC: The Brookings Institution.

Buiter, W.H. and Marston, R.C. (eds) (1985) *International Economic Policy Coordination*, Cambridge: Cambridge University Press.

Canzoneri, M.B. and Diba, B. (1996) *Fiscal Constraints on Central Bank Independence and Price Stability*, CEPR Discussion Paper No. 1463.

Canzoneri, M.B. and Edison, H.J. (1989) *A New Interpretation of the Coordination Problem and its Empirical Significance*. International Finance Discussion Paper No. 340. Board of Governors of the Federal Reserve System, Washington DC.

Canzoneri, M.B. and Gray, J. (1985) 'Monetary Policy Games and the Consequences of Non-cooperative Behavior,' *International Economic Review* 26(3), 547–64.

Canzoneri, M.B. and Henderson, D.W. (1988) 'Is Sovereign Policy Making Bad?', in Carnegie-Rochester Conference Series on Public Policy 28 (spring), pp. 93–140.

Canzoneri, M.B. and Henderson, D.W. (1991) *Monetary Policy in Interdependent Economies: A Game-theoretic Approach*, Cambridge, MA/London: The MIT Press.

Canzoneri, M.B. and Minford, P. (1988) 'When International Policy Coordination Matters: An Empirical Analysis,' *Applied Economics*, 20, 1137–54.

Caporale, G.M. (1996) *International Economic Policy Coordination: A Brief Survey of the Literature*. Discussion Paper No. 22–96, Center for Economic Forecasting/ London Business School.

Carlozzi, N. and Taylor, J. (1985) 'International Capital Mobility and the Coordination of Monetary Rules,' in Bhandari, J. (ed.), *Exchange Rate Management under Uncertainty*, Cambridge, MA: MIT Press, pp. 186–211.

Carraro, C. and Giavazzi, F. (1991) 'Can International Policy Co-ordination Really be Counterproductive?', in Carraro, C., Laussel, D., Salmon, M. and Soubeyran, A. (eds) *International Economic Policy Coordination*, Oxford/Cambridge, MA: Blackwell, pp. 184–98.

Carraro, C., Laussel, D., Salmon, M. and Soubeyran, A. (eds) (1991) *International Economic Policy Co-ordination*, Oxford/Cambridge, MA: Blackwell.

Castrén, O. (1998) *Fiscal-Monetary Policy Coordination and Central Bank Independence*, Bank of Finland Studies E:12.

Chang, R. (1997) 'Financial Integration with and without International Policy Coordination,' *International Economic Review* 38(3), 547–64.

Christodoulakis, N., Garrat, A. and Currie, D. (1996) 'Target Zones and Alternative Proposals for G3 Policy Coordination: An Empirical Evaluation Using GEM,' *Journal of Macroeconomics*, Winter 18(1), 49–68.

Cohen, D. (1997) *How Will the Euro Behave? Seminar on EMU and the International Monetary System*, IMF Washington, DC.

Cooper, R. (1968) *The Economics of Interdependence*, New York: McGraw-Hill.

Cooper, R. (1969) 'Macroeconomic Adjustment in Interdependent Economies,' *Quarterly Journal of Economics* 98, November, 1–24.

Cooper, R.N. (1985) 'Economic Interdependence and Coordination of Economic Policies', in *Jones/Kenen Handbook of International Economics Vol. II*, Amsterdam: North-Holland, pp. 1195–235.

Cooper, R.N., Eichengreen, B., Henning, C.R., Holtham, G. and Putnam, R.D. (eds) (1989) *Can Nations Agree? Issues in International Economic Cooperation*, Washington, DC: The Brookings Institution.

Crockett, A. (1989) 'The Role of International Institutions in Surveillance and Policy Coordination,' in Bryant, R.C., Currie, D.A., Frenkel, J.A., Masson, P.R., Portes, R. (eds), *Macroeconomic Policies in an Interdependent World*, The Brookings Institution/CEPR/IMF, pp. 343–64.

Currie, D.A. (1993) 'International Cooperation in Monetary Policy: Has it a Future?' *The Economic Journal* 103(416), 178–88.

Currie, D.A. and Levine, P. (1985) 'Macroeconomic Policy Design in an Interdependent World,' in Buiter, W.H. *et al.* (eds), *International Economic Policy Coordination*, Cambridge: Cambridge University Press, pp. 228–71.

Currie, D.A. and Levine, P. (1991) 'The International Co-ordination of Monetary Policy: A Survey,' in Green, C.J. and Llewellyn, D.T. (eds), *Survey in Monetary Economics, Volume 1: Monetary Theory and Policy*, Cambridge, MA/Oxford: Blackwell, pp. 379–417.

Currie, D.A. and Levine, P. (1993) *Rules, Reputation and Macroeconomic Policy Coordination*, Cambridge: Cambridge University Press.

Currie, D.A. and Wren-Lewis, S. (1989a) 'An Appraisal of Alternative Blueprints for International Policy Coordination,' *European Economic Review* 33, 1769–1785.

Currie, D.A. and Wren-Lewis, S. (1989b) 'Evaluating Blueprints for the Conduct of International Macro Policy,' *American Economic Review Papers and Proceedings* 79(2), 264–69.

Currie, D. and Wren-Lewis, S. (1990) 'Evaluating the Extended Target Zone Proposal for the G3,' *The Economic Journal 100* (March 1990), pp. 105–23.

Currie, D.A., Levine, P. and Vidalis, N. (1987) 'International Cooperation and

Reputation in an Empirical Two-Bloc Model,' in Bryant, R.C. and Portes, R. (eds), *Global Macroeconomics. Policy Conflict and Cooperation*, CEPR, Macmillan Press, pp. 75–121.

Currie, D.A., Holtham, G. and Hallett, A.H. (1989) 'The Theory and Practice of International Policy Coordination: Does Coordination Pay?', in Byrant, R.C. *et al.*, *Macroeconomic Policies in an Interdependent World*, The Brookings Institution/CEPR/IMF, pp. 14–47.

Demertzis, M., Hughes Hallett, A.H. and Viegi, N. (1998) *Independently Blue? Accountability and Independence in the New European Central Bank*, CEPR Discussion Paper No. 1842.

Demertzis, M., Hughes-Hallett, A.H. and Viegi, N. (1999) *Can the ECB Be Truly Independent? Should it Be?* Paper for the VOWA workshop 1999-01-21.

Devereux, M.B. and Mansoorian, A. (1992) 'International Fiscal Policy Coordination and Economic Growth,' *International Economic Review* 33(2), 249–68.

Dobson, W. (1991) *Economic Policy Coordination: Requiem or Prologue?* Washington DC: Institute for International Economics.

Dornbusch, R. and Frenkel, J.A. (eds) (1979) *International Economic Policy. Theory and Evidence*, Baltimore and London: The Johns Hopkins University Press.

Eichengreen, B. (1985) 'International Policy Coordination in Historical Perspective: A View from the Interwar Years,' in Buiter, W.H. *et al.*, *International Economic Policy Coordination*, Cambridge: Cambridge University Press, pp. 139–84.

Eichengreen, B. (1989) 'Hegemonic Stability Theories of the International Monetary System,' in Cooper, R.N. *et al.*, *Can Nations Agree?. Issues in International Economic Cooperation*. Washington, DC: The Brookings Institution, pp. 255–99.

Eichengreen, B. (1996) *Globalizing Capital: A History of the International Monetary System*, Princeton, NJ: Princeton University Press.

Eichengreen, B. (1997) *European Monetary Unification and International Monetary Cooperation*, Working Paper No. C97-091, Center for International and Development Economics Research, Berkeley.

Fearon, J.D. (1998) 'Bargaining, Enforcement and International Cooperation,' *International Organization*, 52(2), 269–307.

Feldstein, M.S. (1988) 'Distinguished Lecture on Economics in Government: Thinking about International Economic Coordination,' *Journal of Economic Perspectives* 2(2), 3–13.

Fischer, S. (1988) 'Macroeconomic Policy,' in Feldstein, M. (ed.), *International Economic Cooperation*, Chicago: University of Chicago Press.

Frankel, J.A. (1987) *Obstacles to International Macroeconomic Policy Coordination*, IMF Working Paper No. 87/28.

Frankel, J.A. (1988) 'Obstacles to International Macroeconomic Policy Coordination,' in *Princeton Studies in International Finance No. 64*, Princeton.

Frankel, J.A. (1990a) 'International Nominal Targeting (INT): A Proposal for Monetary Policy Coordination in the 1990s,' *The World Economy* 13(2), 263–73.

Frankel, J.A. (1990b) 'Obstacles to Coordination, and a Consideration of Two Proposals to Overcome Them: International Nominal Targeting and the Hosomi Fund', in Branson *et al.* (eds), *International Policy Coordination and Exchange Rate Fluctuations*. A National Bureau of Economic Research Conference Report, Chicago: University of Chicago Press, pp. 109–45.

Frankel, J.A. and Rockett, K.E. (1988) 'International Macroeconomic Policy Coordination when Policymakers Do Not Agree on the True Model,' *The American Economic Review* 78(3), 318–40.

Fratianni, M. and von Hagen, J. (1992) *The European Monetary System and European Monetary Union*, Boulder, San Francisco, Oxford: Westview Press.

Fratianni, M.U. and Salvatore, D. (eds) (1993) *Monetary Policy in Developed Economies. Studies in Comparative Economic Policies*, Amsterdam: North-Holland.

Frenkel, J.A., Goldstein, M. and Masson, P. (1988) *International Coordination of Economic Policies: Scope, Methods and Effects*, International Monetary Fund Working Paper WP/88/53.

Frenkel, J.A., Goldstein, M. and Masson, P.R. (1989) 'Simulating the Effects of Some Simple Co-ordinated Versus uncoordinated Policy Rules', in Byrant, R.C. *et al.*, *Macroeconomic Policies in an Interdependent World*, The Brookings Institution/ CEPR/IMF, pp. 203–40.

Frenkel, J.A., Goldstein, M. and Masson P.R. (1990) 'The Rationale for, and Effects of International Economic Policy Coordination', in Branson *et al.* (eds), *International Policy Coordination and Exchange Rate Fluctuations*, A National Bureau of Economic Research Conference Report, Chicago: University of Chicago Press, pp. 9–63.

Friedman, J.W. (ed.) (1994) 'Problems of Coordination', in *Economic Activity. Recent Economic Thought Series*, London.

Fudenberg, D. and Tirole, J. (1996) *Game Theory*, Cambridge, MA and London: The MIT Press.

Ghosh, A.R. and Ghosh, S.R. (1991) 'Does Model Uncertainty Really Preclude International Policy Coordination?', *Journal of International Economics* 31(3/4), 325–40.

Ghosh, A.R. and Masson, P.R. (1987) *International Policy Coordination in a World with Model Uncertainty*. International Monetary Fund Working Paper WP/87/81.

Ghosh, A.R. and Masson, P.R. (1991) 'Model Uncertainty, Learning, and the Gains from Coordination', *The American Economic Review*, 465–79.

Ghosh, A.R. and Masson, P.R. (1994) *Economic Cooperation in an Uncertain World*, Cambridge, MA/Oxford: Blackwell.

Gilpin, R. (1975) *U.S. Power and the Multinational Corporations*, New York: Basic Books.

Goldstein, M. (1984) *The Exchange Rate System: Lessons of the Past and Options for the Future*. IMF Occasional Paper No. 30. Washington DC.

Goldstein, M. (1994) 'Improving Economic Policy Coordination: Evaluating Some New and Some Not-So-New Proposals', in Kenen, P.B. and Papadia, F. and Saccomanni (eds), *The International Monetary System. Proceedings of a Conference Organized by the Banca d'Italia*, Cambridge: Cambridge University Press, pp. 298–324.

Gourevitch, P.A. (1996) 'Squaring the Circle: The Domestic Sources of International Cooperation', *International Organization* 50(2), 349–73.

Green, C.J. and Llewellyn, D.T. (eds) (1991) 'Survey in Monetary Economics', Vol. 1, *Monetary Theory and Policy*, Cambridge, MA/Oxford: Blackwell.

Grieco, J.M. (1988) 'Anarchy and the Limits of Cooperation: A Realist Critique of the Newest Liberal Institutionalism,' *International Organization* 42(3), 485–507.

Guth (Moderator) (1988) *Economic Policy Coordination. Proceedings of an International Seminar held in Hamburg*, IMF/HWWA.

Haas, P. (1990) *Saving the Mediterranean: The Politics of International Environmental Cooperation*, New York: Columbia University Press.

Haas, P. (1992) 'Knowledge, Power and International Policy Coordination', *Special Issue of International Organization* 46(1).

Hamada, K. (1974) 'Alternative Exchange Rate Systems and the Interdependence of Monetary Policies', in Aliber, R.Z. (ed.), *National Monetary Policies and the International Financial System*, Chicago: University of Chicago Press.

Hamada, K. (1976) 'A Strategic Analysis of Monetary Interdependence', *Journal of Political Economy* 84(4), 677–701.

Hamada, K. (1979) 'Macroeconomic Strategy and Coordination under Alternative Exchange Rates', in Dornbusch, R. and Frenkel, J.A. (eds), *International Economic Policy. Theory and Evidence*, Baltimore and London: The Johns Hopkins University Press, pp. 292–324.

Hamada, K. (1985) *The Political Economy of International Monetary Interdependence*, Cambridge, MA and London: The MIT Press.

Hamada, K. and Kawai, M. (1997) 'International Economic Policy Coordination: Theory and Policy Implications', in Fratianni, M.U., Salvatore, D. and Hagen, J. (eds), *Macroeconomic Policy in Open Economies*, Westport, Conn.: Greenwood Press.

Hamada, K. and Sakurai, M. (1978) 'International Transmission of Stagnation under Fixed and Flexible Exchange Rates', *Journal of Political Economy* 86(5), 877–897.

Holtham, G. and Hughes Hallett, A. (1987) 'International Policy Coordination and Model Uncertainty', in Bryant, R. and Portes, R. (eds), *Global Macroeconomics: Policy Conflict and Cooperation*, London: Macmillan, pp. 128–84.

Holtham, G. and Hughes Hallett, A. (1992) 'International Macroeconomic Policy Coordination when Policymakers Do Not Agree on the True Model: Comment', in *American Economic Review* 82, 1043–51.

Horne, J. and Masson, P.R. (1988) *Scope and Limits of International Economic Cooperation and Policy Coordination*, IMF Staff Papers 35 (June), 259–96.

Hughes Hallett, A.J. (1986a) 'Autonomy and the Choice of Policy in Asymmetrically Dependent Economies. An Investigation from International Policy Co-ordination', *Oxford Economic Papers* 38, 516–44.

Hughes Hallett, A.J. (1986b) 'International Policy Design and the Sustainability of Policy Bargains', *Journal of Economic Dynamics and Control* 10, 467–94.

Hughes Hallett, A.J. (1989) 'What are the Risks in Co-ordinating Economic Policies Internationally?', in MacDonald, R. and Taylor, M.P. (eds), *Exchange Rates and Open Economy Macroeconomics*, Cambridge: Basil Blackwell, pp. 307–58.

Hughes Hallett, A.J. (1992a) 'Policy Collaboration and Information Exchanges with Risk Averse Policymakers: The Case for Making Strategic Model Choices', in Barrell, R. and Whitley, J. (eds), *Macroeconomic Policy Coordination in Europe*, London and Newbury, CA: Sage, pp. 152–71.

Hughes Hallett, A.J. (1992b) 'Target Zones and International Policy Coordination. The Contrast between the Necessary and Sufficient Conditions for Success', *European Economic Review* 36, 893–914.

Hughes Hallett, A.J. (1994) 'On the Imperfect Substitutability of Policy Regimes: Exchange Rate Targeting vs Policy Coordination', *Economics Letters* 44(1–2), 159–64.

Hughes Hallett, A.J. and Vines, D. (1993) 'On the Possible Costs of European Monetary Union', *The Manchester School* LXI(1), 35–64.

Hughes Hallett, A.J. and Yue Ma (1995) *Economic Cooperation within Europe: Lessons from the Monetary Arrangements in the 1990s*.

Hughes Hallett, A.J., Holtham, G. and Hutson, G. (1989) 'Exchange-rate Targetting as Surrogate International Cooperation', in Miller, M. *et al.*, *Blueprints for Exchange-rate Management*, Berkeley/New York/Centre for Economic Policy Research: Academic Press, pp. 239–78.

Johansen, L. (1982) 'A Note on the Possibility of an International Equilibrium with Low Levels of Activity', *Journal of International Economics* 13, 257–65.

Jones, R.W. and Kenen, P.B. (eds.) (1985) *Handbook of International Economics*, Vol. II, *International Monetary Economics and Finance*, Amsterdam: North-Holland.

Kehohe, P.J. (1987) 'Coordination of Fiscal Policies in a World Economy', *Journal of Monetary Economics* 19, 349–76.

Kehohe, P.J. (1991) 'Policy Co-operation among Benevolent Governments May Be Undesirable: An Extension', in Carraro, C. *et al.* (eds), *International Economic Policy Co-ordination*, Oxford/Cambridge, MA: Blackwell, pp. 166–83.

Kenen, P.B. (1987) *Exchange Rates and Policy Coordination*, Brookings Discussion Papers on International Economics, No. 61, Washington DC.

Kenen, P.B. (1990) 'The Coordination of Macroeconomic Policies', in Branson, W.H., Frenkel, J.A. and Goldstein, M. (eds), *International Policy Coordination and Exchange Rate Fluctuations. A National Bureau of Economic Research Conference Report*, Chicago: University of Chicago Press, pp. 63–102.

Kenen, P.B. (ed.) (1995) *Understanding Interdependence. The Macroeconomics of the Open Economy*, Princeton, NJ: Princeton University Press.

Kenen, P.B., Papadia, F. and Saccomanni, F. (eds.) (1994) *The International Monetary System. Proceedings of a Conference Organized by the Banca d'Italia*. Cambridge: Cambridge University Press.

Keohane, R.O. (1984) *After Hegemony. Cooperation and Discord in the World Political Economy*, Princeton, NJ: Princeton University Press.

Kindleberger, C. (1973) *The World in Depression 1929–39*, Berkeley: University of California Press.

Kindleberger, C. (1986) 'International Public Goods without International Government', *The American Economic Review* 76(1), 1–13.

Krasner, S.D. (1976) 'State Power and the Structure of International Trade', *World Politics* 28(3), 317–47.

Krasner, S.D. (1983) *International Regimes*, Ithaca, NY: Cornell University Press.

Krasner, S.D. (1991) 'Global Communications and National Power: Life on the Pareto Frontier', *World Politics* 43, 336–66.

Krichel, T., Levine P. and Pearlman, J. (1996) 'Fiscal and Monetary Policy in a Monetary Union: Credible Inflation Targets or Monetized Debt?', *Weltwirtschaftliches Archiv* 132(1), 28–53.

Kydland, F.E. and Prescot, E.C. (1977) 'Rules rather than Discretion: The Inconsistency of Optimal Plans', *Journal of Political Economy* 85, 473–91.

Levine, P. and Currie, D. (1987) 'Does International Macroeconomic Policy Coordination Pay and Is It Sustainable: A Two Country Analysis', *Oxford Economic Papers* 39, 38–74.

Levine, P., Currie, D.A. and Gaines, J. (1989) 'The Use of Simple Rules for International Policy Agreements', in Miller *et al.* (eds), *Blueprints for Exchange Rate Management*, New York/Berkeley: CEPR. Academic Press.

McCallum, B.T. (1997) *Issues in the Design of Monetary Policy Rules*, NBER Working Paper No. 6016.

MacDonald, R. and Taylor, M.P. (eds.) (1989) *Exchange Rates and Open Economy Macroeconomics*, Cambridge MA/Oxford: Basil Blackwell.

Machlup, F., Fels, G. and Müller-Groeling, H. (eds) (1981) *Reflections on a Troubled World Economy: Essays in Honour of Herbert Giersch*, London: Trade Policy Research Centre, Macmillan Press.

McKibbin, W.J. and Sachs, J.D. (1989) 'Implications of Policy Rules for the

World Economy', in Byrant, R.C., Currie, D.A., Frenkel, J.A., Masson, P.R. and Portes, R. (eds), *Macroeconomic Policies in an Interdependent World*, The Brookings Institution/CEPR/IMF, pp. 151–94.

McKibbin, W.J. and Sachs, J.D. (1991) *Global Linkages. Macroeconomic Interdependence and Cooperation in the World Economy*, Washington, DC: The Brookings Institution.

Martinez Oliva, J.C. (1991) 'One Remark on Spillover Effects and the Gains from Coordination', *Oxford Economic Papers* 43, 172–76.

Masson, P.R. (1992) *Portfolio Preference Uncertainty and Gains from Policy Coordination*, International Monetary Fund Staff Papers 39 (March), pp. 101–20.

Meade, J.E. (1951) *The Theory of International Economic Policy*, Vol. 1, *The Balance of Payments*, London: Oxford University Press.

Miller, M. and Salmon, M. (1985) 'Policy Coordination and Dynamic Games' in Buiter, W.H. *et al.* (eds), *International Economic Policy Coordination*, Cambridge: Cambridge University Press, pp. 184–220.

Miller, M., Eichengreen, B. and Portes, R. (eds) (1989) *Blueprints for Exchange-rate Management*, New York/Berkeley: Centre for Economic Policy Research, Academic Press.

Milner, H. (1992) 'International Theories of Cooperation among Nations: Strengths and Weaknesses', *World Politics* 44(3), 466–96.

Morales, A.J. and Padilla, A.J. (1995) *Designing Institutions for International Monetary Policy Coordination*. Center for Economic Policy Research Discussion Paper No. 1180 May.

Moravcsik, A. (1993) 'Introduction: Integrating International and Domestic Theories of International Bargaining', in Evans, P.B., Jacobson, H.K. and Putnam, R.D. (eds), *Double-edged Diplomacy: International Bargaining and Domestic Politics*, Berkeley: University of California Press.

Motamen-Scobie, H. and Starck, C. (1992) *Economic Policy Coordination in an Integrating Europe*, Bank of Finland.

Niou, E.M.S. and Ordeshook, P.C. (1994) 'Less Filling, Tastes Great: The Realist – Neoliberal Debate', *World Politics* 46(2), 209–35.

Nolan, C. and Schaling, E. (1996) 'International Monetary Policy Co-ordination: Some Lessons from the Literature', *Bank of England Quarterly Bulletin*, November, 412–17.

Nordhaus, W.D. (1994) 'Policy Games: Coordination and Independence in Monetary and Fiscal Policies', *Brookings Papers on Economic Activity* 2, 139–216.

Oudiz, G. (1985) 'European Policy Coordination: An Evaluation', *Recherches Economiques de Louvain* 51, 301–9.

Oudiz, G. and Sachs, J.D. (1984) 'Macroeconomic Policy Coordination among the Industrial Economies', *Brookings Papers on Economic Activity* 1, 1–76.

Oudiz, G. and Sachs, J.D. (1985) 'International Policy Coordination in Dynamic Macroeconomic Models', in Buiter, W.H. and Marston, R.C. (eds), *International Economic Policy Coordination*, Cambridge: Cambridge University Press, pp. 274–318.

Oye, K.A. (1986) *Cooperation under Anarchy*, Princeton, NJ: Princeton University Press.

Persson, T. and Tabellini, G. (1995) *Double-edged Incentives: Institutions and Policy Coordination*, Centre for Economic Policy Research Discussion Paper No. 1141.

Persson, T. and Tabellini, G. (1996) *Monetary Cohabitation in Europe*, Centre for Economic Policy Research Discussion Paper No. 1380, May.

Polak, J.J. (1991) 'International Policy Coordination and the Functioning of the International Monetary System – A Search for Realism', in Blommestein, H.J. (ed.), *The Reality of International Economic Policy Coordination. Contributions to Economic Analysis*, Amsterdam: North-Holland, pp. 151–72.

Power, S. and Rowe, N. (1998) 'Independent Central Banks: Coordination Problems and Budget Deficits', *Economic Issues* 3(1), 69–75.

Putnam, R.D. (1988) 'Diplomacy and Domestic Politics: The Logic of Two-level Games', *International Organization* 42, 427–60.

Putnam, R.D. and Bayne, N. (1987) *Hanging Together: Cooperation and Conflict in the Seven-Power Summits*, Cambridge, MA: Harvard University Press.

Putnam, R.D. and Henning, C.R. (1989) 'The Bonn Summit of 1979: A Case Study in Coordination', in Cooper, R.N. *et al.* (eds), *Can Nations Agree?* Washington, DC, pp. 12–140.

Rogoff, K. (1985) 'Can International Monetary Policy Cooperation be Counterproductive?', *Journal of International Economics* 18, 199–217.

Sachs, J. and McKibbin, W. (1985) *Macroeconomic Policies in the OECD and LDC External Adjustment*, NBER Working Paper No. 1534.

Salvatore, D. (1995) 'The Operation and Future of the International Monetary System', *Journal of Policy Modeling* 17(5), 513–30.

Scharpf, F.W. (1994) 'Games Real Actors Could Play. Positive and Negative Coordination in Embedded Negotiations', *Journal of Theoretical Politics* 6(1), 27–53.

Snidal, D. (1985) 'The Limits of Hegemonic Stability Theory', *International Organization* 394, 579–614.

Solomon, R. (1991) 'Background Paper', in *Partners in Prosperity: The Report of the Twentieth Century Fund Task Force on the International Coordination of National Economic Policies*, New York: Priority Press Publications.

Tanzi, V. (1988) *International Coordination of Fiscal Policies: A Review of Some Major Issues*. International Monetary Fund Working Paper WP/88/70.

Taylor, J.B. (1985) 'International Coordination in the Design of Macroeconomic Policy Rules', *European Economic Review* 28, 53–81.

Taylor, J.B. (1989) *Policy Analysis with a Multicountry Model*, in Byrant *et al.* (eds), *Macroeconomic Policies in an Interdependent World*, The Brookings Institution, Centre for Economic Policy Research and International Monetary Fund, pp. 122–42.

Taylor, M. (1987) *The Possibility of Cooperation*, Cambridge: Cambridge University Press.

Tobin, J. (1987) 'Agenda for International Coordination of Macroeconomic Policies', in *International Monetary Cooperation: Essays in Honor of Henry C. Wallich, Essays International Finance*, No. 169, Princeton, NJ: Princeton University Press, pp. 61–9.

Turnovsky, S.J. and D'Orey, V. (1986) 'Monetary Policies in Interdependent Economies with Stochastic Disturbances: A Strategic Approach', *The Economic Journal* 96, 696–721.

Turnovsky, S.J., Basar, T. and D'Orey, V. (1988) 'Dynamic Strategic Monetary Policies and Coordination in Interdependent Economies', *The American Economic Review* (June), 341–61.

Van der Ploeg, F. (1988) 'International Policy Coordination in Interdependent Monetary Economies', *Journal of International Economics* 25, 1–23.

Van Lennep, E. (1991) 'Institutional Aspects of International Economic Policy

Cooperation and Coordination', in Blommestein, H.J. (ed.), *The Reality of International Economic Policy Coordination. Contributions to Economic Analysis*, Amsterdam: North-Holland, pp. 61–74.

Vaubel, R. (1983) 'Coordination or Competition among National Macro-economic Policies', in Machlup, F. *et al.* (eds), *Reflections on a Troubled World Economy. Essays in Honour of Herbert Giersch*, London: Trade Policy Research, pp. 3–28.

Wallich, H.C. (1984) 'Institutional Cooperation in the World Economy', in Frenkel, J.A. and M.L. Mussa (eds), *The World Economic System: Performance and Prospects*, Dover, MA: Auburn House.

Webb, M.C. (1994) 'Understanding Patterns of Macroeconomic Policy Co-ordination in the Post-War Period', in Stubbs, R. and Underhill, G.R.D. (eds), *Political Economy and the Changing Global Order*, Basingstoke: Macmillan, pp. 176–89.

Webb, M.C. (1995) *The Political Economy of Policy Coordination. International Adjustment since 1945*, Ithaca, NY and London: Cornell University Press.

Williamson, J. and Miller, M.H. (1987) *Targets and Indicators: A Blueprint for International Coordination of Economic Policy. Policy Analyses in International Economics 22*, Washington, DC: Institute for International Economics.

Questions

1 Suppose two countries are linked through a flexible exchange rate regime and follow the same assignment rule: fiscal policy for the achievement of internal balance and monetary policy for the achievement of external balance. What bias would you expect to prevail in: (a) fiscal policy, (b) monetary policy?

2 'International macroeconomic policy co-ordination is necessary to avoid excessive recessions when two countries pursue a fixed exchange rate policy.' Discuss.

3 'International policy co-ordination is necessary but not sufficient to ensure Pareto-efficient policy choices.' Discuss.

4 'International policy co-ordination does a great deal of harm, never does any good, and there ought to be none of it.' Do you agree?

5 'International policy co-ordination is necessary because competition leads to under-provision of public goods but over-supply of public "bads"'. Discuss with reference to monetary or fiscal policy in an interdependent world.

6 'A co-ordinated solution will be unsustainable because the players will have incentives to defect from co-operation.' Do you agree? How would you revise your conclusions if the co-ordination game between these players were repeated over time?

7 Suppose two countries are linked via trade flows and pursue a fixed exchange rate policy. Suppose also that these countries experience an asymmetric demand shock whereby the demand for country 1's exports increases whereas that of country 2 decreases. (a) What would be the outcome of un-coordinated response? (b) On what policy instrument can they agree to co-ordinate?

8 'The European Central Bank can be seen as collusion between European central bankers. Therefore, it can be expected to have an anti-employment bias.' Do you agree?

Further reading and references

FURTHER READING

For a good collection of articles on the twin issues of interdependence and policy co-ordination, see Kennen (1995). For a quantitative estimate of gains from policy co-ordination, see Oudiz and Sachs (1984). For an overall assessment of the theory of policy co-ordination, see Currie *et al.* (1989) and Bryant (1995). For a critique of policy co-ordination, see Rogoff (1985).

REFERENCES

Bryant, R.C. (1995) 'International cooperation in the making of national macro-economic policies: where do we stand?', in P.B. Kennen (ed.) *Understanding Interdependence: The Macroeconomics of the Open Economy*, Princeton, NJ: Princeton University Press.

Currie, D.A., G. Holtham and A.H. Hallett (1989) 'The theory and practice of international policy coordination: does coordination pay?', in R.C. Bryant *et al.* (eds), *Macroeconomic Policies in an Interdependent World*, Washington, DC: Brookings/CEPR/IMF.

Kennen, P.B. (ed.) (1995) *Understanding Interdependence: The Macroeconomics of the Open Economy*, Princeton, NJ: Princeton University Press.

Oudiz, G. and J.D. Sachs (1984) 'Macroeconomic policy coordination among the industrialised economies', *Brookings Papers on Economic Activity*, 1, 1–76.

Rogoff, K. (1985) 'Can international monetary policy coordination be counter-productive?', *Journal of International Economics*, 18, 199–217.

Part V

The international monetary system and monetary policy

Design and institutions

Introduction

Part IV was concerned with the policy implications of the strategic interaction between governments. The reader will recall that interdependence between countries can lead to suboptimal policy outcomes even if the assignment problem is resolved correctly within each country. Part V takes this debate further by focusing on the strategic interaction between government and the private sector. Because of this focus, it may be considered as a digression from the open economy context. This, however, would be a hasty conclusion because strategic interactions between government and the private sector cannot be appreciated fully unless the international context is taken into account. In addition, the subject matter itself – i.e. the international monetary environment and monetary policy – makes the international dimension both necessary and inevitable.

There are three articles in Part V. Chapter 13 by Braasch and Hesse provides a well-informed analytical account of the effects of changes in the international monetary environment on the design and conduct of monetary policy. Its main concern is about how increased capital mobility influences the government–private-sector interaction and, thereby, the conduct of monetary policy. Chapter 14 by Goodhart overlaps with the previous article in its elaboration on the difficulties involved in controlling the base money. Then it takes the debate further by going into the details of what the central banks can and should do to ensure that monetary policy is conducive to the achievement of a selected inflation target. Finally, the article by Cukierman in Chapter 15 looks at the institutional aspects of monetary policy design – mainly the significance of central bank independence and its effect on policy outcomes. A common theme to all these articles can be stated as follows: what are the optimal rules and/or institutions for achieving a low inflation target – given that the choice of instrument is made largely endogenous by the strategic interaction between the government and the private sector?

Braasch and Hesse start with a brief summary of the dramatic changes in the international financial markets witnessed over the last two decades. They emphasise the significance of the rise of institutional investors, the liberalisation of capital movements, and the disciplining effect that these developments have had on national governments. As the weight of international market forces has increased, the choice of monetary policy has become increasingly endogenous in the sense that the government must pick the policy stance that would satisfy the market forces. Otherwise, it will bear the cost of speculative movements and/or miss its target. This conclusion is derived from various observations pointing to increased ability of institutional investors to frustrate 'irresponsible' monetary policy and high levels of fluctuations in the asset-induced demand for money. Braasch and Hesse are inclined to favour the use of interest rates rather than monetary aggregates as instruments for achieving price stability.

In Chapter 14 Goodhart complements the previous chapter by providing a different explanation as to why the central bank should use interest rates and why central bank independence is necessary to achieve the desired target of low inflation. The central bank should use interest rates rather than the monetary base because daily change in the public's demand for cash will have to be accommodated by the central bank. Any such accommodation will cause the residual available to the commercial banks to be either excessive or deficient, leading to excessively lower or excessively higher interest rates. Goodhart's second argument is that monetary policy should aim to achieve a single target rather than a multiplicity of targets. This is in line with the assignment rule, but it is based on a different rationale. The multiplicity of targets will imply trade-offs and choice between targets – hence greater political oversight. This, however, will undermine the credibility of the monetary policy and the independence of the agent implementing it – i.e. the central bank. Once monetary policy credibility is lost, the government will be unable to achieve the desired targets. Then, the central bank should be assigned one target – price stability – and be granted independence to achieve it. Goodhart provides evidence from the experience of Canada, New Zealand and the United Kingdom to substantiate his arguments.

In Chapter 15 Cukierman expands on why central bank independence is crucial for the assignment rule to work. The thrust of Cukierman's article is that central bank independence can act as a commitment device that would enable the government to resist the temptation to introduce monetary surprises, which may be beneficial in the short run but detrimental in the long run. In other words, central bank independence is essential to avoid the 'prisoner's dilemma' that would result from government–private-sector interaction when the government has discretion over monetary policy. Cukierman refers to a large number of studies that establish a negative relationship between central bank independence and inflation. In addition, these studies tend to show that the level of output is not affected by central bank independence. Therefore, central bank independence is an efficient policy design as it reduces inflation at no cost in terms of lost output or employment.

The reader will quickly realise that Part V is actually nothing but a variation on the theme of targets and instruments examined in Parts III and IV. What it does is focus on a particular assignment problem (i.e. the assignment of monetary policy to price stability) and demonstrate that even a correct assignment may not produce the desired result unless further conditions are satisfied. One condition is that the instrument must be specified correctly. The balance of the argument in the three chapters above suggests that the central bank should use interest rates rather than monetary aggregates to control inflation. The other condition is that the institutional framework must be conducive to reducing (if not eliminating) the scope for switching targets (i.e. changing horses in mid-stream) once the assignment has been decided. We hope that the issues raised in this part will help the reader consolidate his or her understanding of macroeconomic policy design in open economies; and the extensive list of bibliography provided by the authors will prompt further reading.

13 Global capital movements, exchange rates and monetary policy

*Bernd Braasch and Helmut Hesse**

Karl-Josef Koch and Klang Jaeger (eds), *Trade, Growth and Economic Policy in Open Economies: Essays in Honour of Hans-Jürgen Vosgerau*, Berlin: Springer-Verlag (1998), pp. 249–68

1 THE CHANGE IN THE MONETARY ENVIRONMENT

Today's central banks are operating in an environment which differs fundamentally from that which was characteristic of the 1970s and 1980s. The international financial markets have undergone both a qualitatively and quantitatively rapid development, which has made decisions regarding financial and monetary policy distinctly more difficult.

The deregulation and liberalization of capital movements, as well as technical advances in communications and data processing, have made it possible today to transfer large amounts of capital across national borders in seconds. In increasing numbers, individual investors have transferred the management of their savings to institutional investors, such as pension funds, mutual funds, and insurance companies, who monitor and follow the relevant market trends worldwide.[1] The fund managers, acting globally, make decisions on the investment of asset amounts, which in recent years have risen rapidly, amounting e.g. in 1993 to 165% and 126% of GDP the United Kingdom and in the United States respectively (cf. IMF, 1995, p. 165).

In order to be able to survive the tough international competition, the funds are forced to exploit even the smallest differences in capital yields and to transfer capital to other currency markets for that purpose. Therein lies a fundamental reason for the quantum leap in the expansion of turnover on world financial markets. The average daily turnover in the global exchange market in April 1995 amounted to about 1¼ trillion U.S. dollars net. Only 1½% to 2½% of this sum was not accounted for by the financing of international trade in goods and services. Correspondingly, in 1994 cross-border security trading reached a value of about 30,000 trillion dollars (Mitchell, 1994) and grew much faster than GDP in many countries (cf. BIS, 1995a, p. 11).

The financial superstructure of the industrial countries increasingly appears to be detaching itself from the real economy. Interest and exchange

* Landeszentralbank in Bremen, Niedersachsen and Sachsen-Anhalt, Hannover, Germany.

rates in highly integrated financial markets have come under the dominant influence of capital movements, with the portfolio investments of globally acting fund managers providing the actual momentum in these capital movements, whereas transactions (motivated by real economic principles) for the financing of trade in goods and services hardly affect the movements of interest and exchange rates.[2] Accordingly, the increasing volatility on the international financial markets can hardly be accounted for fundamental data.[3]

International market forces have gained considerable weight in relation to institutions of national economic policy. While, during the time of Bretton Woods, the international monetary system was a "government-led system" "combined with an embryonic market component", today the opposite is the case. The international monetary system has developed into a "market-led system" (Padoa-Schioppa/Saccomanni, 1994, p. 240). National financial markets (as well as merchandise markets) are becoming integral components of unified world markets. National borders play a negligible role in movements of money and capital. The process of global economic integration thereby creates a fundamental problem of the current international order. "What's at issue is one of the great conflicts of our time: the collision between sovereign states and stateless economic forces. No one can say how this economic and political drama will end, but the theme is clear" (Samuelson, 1987, p. 39).

The "electronic army of currency and bond traders" worldwide keeps a close eye on every state and its economic policies. Should threats to stability arise, fund managers very quickly withdraw their capital and steer it into the safer havens of states which, in their judgement, are pursuing a more credible stabilization policy. With this "flight to quality", markets sanction unwelcome political developments and increasingly take on the role of global trade police. This international judge and jury incorruptibly "rate" the national stability policies, reporting the movements of interest and exchange rates like seismographs. Exchange rates therefore mirror the complex judgement of global markets on the entire policy of a state, including its financial and economic policy (Tietmeyer, 1995, p. 2).

Market developments can over- and understate and thereby cause considerable difficulties especially for internationally operating companies. Nevertheless, it is neither desirable nor possible once again to lace the financial markets into a corset of administrative restrictions or of national protectionism. Despite possible "misalignments" and uncertainty resulting from volatility, the conclusion cannot be drawn that markets fundamentally and permanently overlook or falsely value the "fundamentals" of economic policy. "On the whole, most of the policy changes that have been forced by international capital markets seem to us to have been in the right direction." (Mussa/Goldstein, 1993, p. 300). Experience shows: "In the long term, the markets are right more often than many policy-makers, who often argue in short-run and primarily nationalist terms" (Tietmeyer, 1995a, p. 2). Therefore, it is necessary to strengthen the disciplining power of markets through high levels of transparency and clarification of economic policy in order to prevent unwelcome developments.[4]

It is not to be expected that the outlined development of the international financial markets and border-crossing capital movements will correct themselves in the future. The monetary politicy makers, like all other economic policy makers, must see the new conditions and must stand up to the increasing competition in quality. This demands especially that central banks repeatedly review their monetary policy strategies to determine whether they are still appropriate and promising in the changing monetary policy environment.

2 DIFFICULTIES FOR NATIONAL MONETARY POLICY

The introduction of floating exchange rates after the collapse of the Bretton Woods system was commonly associated with the hope that the previously vulnerable external flank of monetary policy would be virtually closed, and that central banks would again receive sufficient playing room to more successfully gear their policy independent of disturbing external influences to maintaining the economic stability of their national currencies. As the conditions for a more monetarist policy of monetary targeting appeared to be favorable at that time, many central banks adopted a strategy of preannounced monetary targets of anticipating money supply objectives. However, in view of the qualitative and quantitative leaps in world financial markets in recent years, it needs to be clarified whether, in the "international economy" (Koehler, 1990) of today, the conditions for an efficient national monetary management strategy are still adequately met. What particularly comes to be the focus of attention is whether and how the stability of the correlation between interest rates, money supply and prices becomes disturbed by the changes in the international financial markets, and whether the development of the national money supply thereby loses its ability to guide monetary policy.

2.1 Impairment of the indicator and intermediate target functions

For various reasons, growing monetary aggregates are associated with the strong growth in financial assets and explosive increases in turnover in the financial markets. Considerations of risk make it seem advisable to hold some assets in the form of money (compare Hesse/Braasch, 1994). The proclivity to engage in speculative commitments, for which one must be armed with liquidity, has increased. If sustained price increases are expected on the securities markets, the purchase of securities will be financed in many cases by taking up credit. Asset induced money demand increases even if international investors, expecting an appreciation of the German mark or rising rates on the national capital markets, purchase German bonds from domestic non-banks. The national money stock rises without any involvement by the central bank at the moment when the non-banks sell the foreign claims back for national currency. Owing to the globalization of the financial markets and the more influential role of institutional investors, as well as German public bonds in the portfolio of internationally operating investors, this transmission channel has attained increasing importance.

It is important to recognize that a price increase on the asset markets causes a higher demand for money.[5] Because financial assets and turnover in securities trading in Germany, as well as in other countries, have recently grown considerably faster than the national product, financial assets, in comparison with the national product, have become a more significant determinant of money demand.

The resultant problems for any monetary management strategy are numerous, and can be presented here only as examples of the following problem areas, which to some extent overlap.

(1) With the increasing significance of the asset-induced demand for money, it becomes more difficult for the central bank to estimate the future inflationary potential in the real sector of the economy when the monetary target is overshot. This is because the connection between money stock and domestic price levels may thereby be disrupted or loosened: As the intermediate goal of the monetary policy, the money supply – in Germany the money stock M3 – should signal an early warning to the central bank regarding the stability of the general price level. This demands that the development of the money supply adequately and reliably reflect the future demand for goods and services, which in turn determines the inflation rate measured in the real sector of the economy. Thus, the money supply must chiefly include such liquidity as, with a time lag, such liquidity affects expenditures with the power to increase prices.

The stability of the connection between the money supply and prices is all the more assured as long as the demand for money primarily mirrors the transaction requirements for real economic purposes. One cannot always automatically assume that in the current and future sphere of monetary policy. For example, if an institutional investor in the United States decides to increase the significance of German securities in his/her portfolio because s/he expects a more secure and higher yield on an investment in Germany than on one in other countries, these influxes of capital could push the growth of the money supply above the annual target. This target is meant to signal to the public which expansion of the money stock the Bundesbank considers appropriate for non-inflationary growth. However, one cannot reliably predict the extent to which overshooting the target corridor nationally, as a result of asset transactions, leads to an increase in the demand for goods and services with the potential to raise prices. This applies all the more as international economic influences on the money supply show varying longevity. Stateless financial market forces can lead to an erosion of the fundamental relations of a promising domestically oriented monetary management strategy. With the progressive worldwide integration of the financial markets and the increasing size and mobility of movements of capital across national borders, the growth of the national money supply might be influenced increasingly by restructuring the portfolios of the "global players".

(2) Difficulties arise for monetary policy not only as a result of the growth in asset-induced money demand, but also as a result of the fact that demand is subject to much sharper fluctuations than the money demand for real economic transactions. Transfers of financial assets are carried out at the least sign of lower interest rates or price changes. The pronounced oscillations of price on the financial markets are therefore reflected in stronger fluctuations in the development of the money supply. This is the case, especially in periods of increased interest rate uncertainty, which tampers monetary capital formation. Liquid assets, which primarily serve the formation of long-term savings capital, are temporarily "lodged" in short-term interest-bearing time deposits, which are a component of the money supply, because of the uncertain expectations regarding further interest rate movements on the capital market. Hence the boundary between those financial assets which are counted towards the money supply or to monetary capital is more blurred than was the case in the 1970s and 1980s. The share of deposits bearing interest at market-related rates in the money supply M3 is tending to increase; the relations of substitution between the interest-bearing components of M3 and competing forms of investment have become significantly closer.

(3) This process is being further strengthened by the professionalization of investment behavior. Fund managers observe and analyze the movements of the market much more intensively than individual investors would be able to do. They are virtually forced by the intense competition to respond quickly to changes in the pattern of interest rates on national financial and capital markets, and to regroup between long-term and short-term investments. The growing orientation towards yields and the flexibility of savings behavior likewise contribute to the fact that the border between money and monetary capital today cannot be drawn so clearly any more. This is especially the case in view of the fact that the weight of the money supply M3 in the total financial assets of the domestic non-banks has decreased over the years. Hence, asset transfers affected monetary developments much more than they used to. This can temporarily distort the monetary development, for if the central bank raises interest rates to stem the growth of the money supply, then an incentive arises for transfers out of money capital into time deposits. This is because the interest rates for time deposits react more quickly than capital market rates to increases in central bank rates. In this instance, the movement of the money supply falsely mirrors the course of the monetary policy.

(4) With sharper fluctuations in the demand for money it is to be expected, on account of the stronger growth of financial derivatives, that the volatility of interest rates and prices on the financial markets will increase. The 1990s are already being characterized as the decade of the derivative. At the end of 1995, the Bank of International Settlements (BIS) published the preliminary results of the first worldwide statistical investigation of derivatives in the areas of foreign exchange, interest rates, shares, and goods. At the end of

March 1995, after the exclusion of all double-counting, the contract amounts of off-the-floor derivatives came to a nominal US$ 41 trillion. Added to these are positions in derivatives in on-the-floor trading amounting to a nominal US$ 17 trillion plus daily purchases and sales totalling US$ 1.1 trillion.[6]

Furthermore, if the implications of the increasing use of derivatives for financial policy are not finally clarified, monetary policy will have to adapt to greater price volatility in monetary markets as an unavoidable side effect of this process (Deutsche Bundesbank, 1994; Issing 1995). In a more volatile environment, however, a stabilization of expectations is more unlikely to be achieved.

(5) Until now, the prevailing fundamental relations between the money supply and the national price level have been weakened by the increasing use of the German mark as a parallel currency in other countries. At the moment, approximately 30 to 40 percent of the total German mark currency in circulation is abroad (Seitz, 1995). This portion is not used in the short to medium term for the financing of national transactions. In general, because of growing foreign demand, the money definition for purposes of monetary policy in terms of the degree of liquidity or the function of payment medium is being impeded, but monetary policy in Germany is not being seriously disrupted because of the relatively small share of (just over 10%) aggregate currency in circulation in the money stock M3. In addition, international demand for currency is not developing rapidly.

Nevertheless, monetary policy must adjust to the fact that, with the global integration of financial markets, the growing significance of asset transactions and the changing behavior of investors, the informative value of the money supply M3 as an indicator and intermediate target for monetary policy is being weakened. This is because stronger fluctuations in the demand for money around this trend may occur. Recently in Germany, failures to achieve the money supply target have mostly been caused by the asset management of economic agents. Developments in the money supply, which increasingly follow the oscillations of the financial system and vary around the goal path with larger amplitudes, compromise the certainty of planning and expectations in the economy, and no longer constitute a reliable compass for the central bank according to which it can set the course of its monetary policy.

2.2 Difficulties for the management of the money supply

The qualitative and quantitative leap in national and international financial markets places new demands not only on "correct" diagnoses, but also on monetary management. Central banks must consider whether the change in financial and monetary environment also leads to a change in their mode of implementation, and whether, in the light of the increasing market forces, they and their instruments still have enough impact to steer the money supply in line with the target and to assert their dominant influence over the conditions on the domestic money market. In this regard, it is instructive to refer to three impediments to monetary policy.

(1) Inside a system of fixed exchange rates (e.g. within the framework of the European monetary union), central banks are nowadays barely able effectively to contribute through interventions to the stabilization of unsettled foreign exchange markets and of the expectations of capital investors. This is, not least, one of the lessons learned from the crises in the European Monetary System in 1992 and 1993. With the increasing concentration of assets in the hands of globally operating funds, with the high mobility of international capital, and with the advance of financial innovations involving great leverage, the potential for being put under pressure has risen considerably. Within the framework of the European Monetary System, in the seven months from June to December 1992, 284 billion German marks were sold by European central banks; of these, 188 billion German marks served to support the central rates of the currencies. Nevertheless, the central banks were not able to accomplish anything against the mass of speculative capital movements. There is also the fact that, under a system of fixed rates of exchange, countries that are confronted with considerable inflows of capital are subject to strong inflationary surges due to intervention. This is because central banks are able only in limited measure, through the deployment of countervailing to sterilize the liquidity effects of interventions in the foreign exchange markets on the domestic banking system and also are thereby able to maintain control over the domestic monetary base in periods of monetary crisis.

In September 1992 alone, the purchases made by the Bundesbank to support the EMS currencies, as well as the sales of German marks financed by the Bundesbank through EMS partner central banks, amounted to over 92 billion marks. This "implied a liquidization of the domestic banking system, which amounted to several times more than the central bank money requirements for the entire year" (Deutsche Bundesbank (1993), p. 23). The Bundesbank can flexibly offset these influxes of liquid assets due to interventions within the framework of its repo operations and other short-term sterilization measures. But the then outstanding volume of repurchase agreements, amounting to 147 billion German marks, shows how quickly this sterilization potential is exhausted. If the central rates had been further protected through interventions, in a relatively short time the Bundesbank could have lost control over the domestic money market.

(2) Monetary management is also made more difficult by the international interest links at the long end of the market, which have become much close in recent years with the globalization of the financial markets. In fact, differences in interest rates still remain between the individual countries; these differences reflect the divergent performance of financial and monetary policies. It is more important to note that the movements of interest in industrial countries indicate an ever stronger synchronization.[7] Thus, German capital market yields are increasingly dependent on developments in the US bond market. In integrated financial markets, the level of and change in capital

market rates are no longer national phenomena, but rather are determined increasingly by supply and demand on the "global capital market."

The closer international interest rate links signify at the same time that the dependence of the German capital market on developments of the domestic money market has relaxed, and that the transmission mechanism of monetary policy impulses on capital market yields has changed correspondingly. A fundamental cause is that the structure of purchasers on the German bond market changed significantly with the globalization of the financial markets and the ever-greater influence of globally operating funds. As long as German banks are the dominant purchasers on the domestic bond market, in fixed-interest securities, monetary policy has an impact on the capital market, too, through the banking system, effect on the banking system as well as on the financial market, because purchases of bonds by credit institutions depend above all on the state of their liquidity – and thus, on central bank policy – and on the domestic demand for credit. As all measures of the central bank initially affect the banking system, nearly immediate implementation of central bank policy results over the whole spectrum of bank activity – i.e. also over the supply and demand generated by credit institutions on the bond market (cf. Häuser, 1982, p. 312) via the banking system.

In the last few years, however, the proportion of foreign investors on the German bond market has risen noticeably. In the first half of the 1980s, foreign buyers acquired only 6.5% of the fixed-interest securities that were sold in Germany. In the first half of the 1990s, the proportion rose to almost one third; occasionally to more than 50%. Worldwide operating funds differ from domestic banks in the sense that they are not subject to direct control by German monetary policy. They are guided by an entire spectrum of international financial data when making investment decisions, and transfer their capital to those currency markets which promise them the highest returns after taking due account of the expected development of the rate of price increases, of the exchange rate, and of interest rates. Thus monetary policy is increasingly exerting an influence on the domestic capital market via interest and exchange rate expectations.

International market forces are thus gaining growing influence over a key variable in the transmission mechanism of national monetary policy because capital market yields constitute an important determinant of the formation of monetary capital and of lending, which in Germany is primarily at long term. Traditional patterns of the transmission process are disappearing; expectations are playing an ever greater role in the level of interest rates at the long end of the market.

(3) As a result of deregulation, and also as a result of the increasing securitization of credit relations, banks are facing new competitors in deposit and lending business. With the advance of investment funds that in the short run offer securitized deposit substitutes, such as fungible money market certificates, banks are experiencing increased pressure to offer higher-yielding forms of deposits which count towards the money stock. In order to ward off the outflow of resources to the money market funds, German credit

institutions have increasingly created what are known as money market accounts, which make possible the payment of interest money market terms. Within the money supply M3, the significance of components with fairly market-related yield is therefore rising. With the increasingly autonomous interest-bearing character of the monetary aggregates, the interest elasticity of the demand for money is decreasing because the opportunity costs of holding liquid funds is declining. This impairs the controllability of the broadly defined monetary aggregate; monetary policy makers must intensify their interest rate measures in order to have the same impact on monetary developments.[8]

3   MONETARY POLICY AND "ASSET PRICE INFLATION"

As financial assets, in comparison with the national product, are becoming an ever more significant determinant of the demand for money, a money supply policy geared to continuity and certainty of future expectations may in future often find itself in the dilemma that events in the financial sector call for a different monetary policy stance from developments in the real economy. This problem arises, for example, when the asset-induced demand for money develops anticyclically relative to the real economic sector (Hesse, 1994, p. 15). On the stock market, market players, in anticipation of a future economic upswing, push up share prices and turnover by their purchase at a time when the real sector of the economy is still in a recession. In so far as these purchases are financed by credit or carried out by international investors, the demand for money rises, which can lead the money supply target being overshot. In such a situation, the central bank faces the dilemma of whether to allow the overshooting of the target and thereby risking an "asset price inflation", or whether to formulate its policy more restrictively and deepen the recession in the real economy.

That these considerations are not merely theoretical is shown by the fact that the price explosion in many asset stock markets at the end of the 1980s and the beginning of the 1990s – which was especially pronounced in Japan, the United Kingdom, Australia, New Zealand, and in several Scandinavian countries – was accompanied by a very strong credit expansion, and often by excessive monetary growth. In Japan, for instance, the Nikkei-Index rose by 200% from the end of 1985 to the end of 1989 to the all-time high of 39,915. At that time, the market value of the outstanding shares, at 630 trillion yen, corresponded to 1.6 times the nominal gross national product. The value of land in Japan rose from 1 trillion yen at the end of 1985 to 2.4 trillion yen at the end of 1990. Thus, at the end of 1990, Japanese land was four times as valuable as all the land in the United States.

Despite the policy of easy money, a considerable reason for the emergence of the Japanese "bubble economy," the rate of price increases in the second half of the 1980s, at barely 2%, ran at the lowest level since 1970, measured by the deflator of the gross domestic product. The quiet price climate in the real sector of the economy afforded little cause for Japan to sharpen its monetary political course. With strong monetary and credit expansion, share prices and real estate prices could ratchet-up without any reciprocal increase in real income. A monetary policy which measures its success in combating inflation solely, or primarily, by the development of conventional "factor prices", such as consumer prices or the deflator of the gross domestic product, runs the risk of not fully capturing inflationary pressures which can develop in the asset stock markets.

Historically, the best protection against excessive growths was a tight, long-term, anti-inflationary orientation of the monetary policy. However, this alone is not sufficient. "The varying sensitivity of the prices for asset values and the sensitivity of the general price level to the conditions of credit can indicate a serious conflict of goals for the monetary authorities who have to weigh the risk of not being able to stem speculative conduct against the danger resulting from undesired effects of contractions in the real economy" (BIS, 1993, p. 199).

In this changed environment, monetary policy must devote greater attention than previously to price movements on asset stock markets.[9] This is especially the case in periods during which asset prices rise while consumer prices develop in a relatively stable fashion and may not reliably mirror inflationary pressures in the economy. Moreover, in the long run asset stock markets cannot absorb an expansive monetary policy. Recent developments show – especially in the case of Japan – that the accumulation of private debt to finance share and real estate purchases maintains momentum during periods of strong price increases but, after the bursting of the speculative bubble in many sectors of the economy, demands sharp and expensive adjustment measures which curb growth and employment in the long run. Households endeavor to compensate for the shrinking of the inflationary swollen asset values by stepping up their savings, and accordingly reduce their demand for consumer goods. In the banking sector, the value of credit collateral decreases following the collapse of real estate prices. The "asset quality" of the banks dramatically declines; many loans must be deemed irrevocable or in default. With this development, not only is the stability of the financial system threatened, but in addition the compulsion to consolidate bank balance sheets leaves credit institutions little room for granting new loans to the private sector. In this phase of the "credit crunch", it is hardly possible for central banks to stimulate lending by lowering interest rates. In Japan, not even the reduction of the discount rate to the historically low level of 0.5% and the institution of economic support programs have been able to prevent a slide into recession – exacerbated by the appreciation of the yen.

The trade-off between monetary policy and price movements in asset stock markets is not a new problem. In the wake of the stock market crash at the end of the 1920s, whether and to what extent monetary policy should strive to avoid speculative bubbles was discussed (cf. Kindleberger 1995). In addition, the monetarist theory of relative prices suggests that monetary shocks first affect stock and real estate markets before they affect price movements in the real sector of the economy. Against the current background of the deregulation, liberalization, and innovation process, however, Kindleberger (1995) correctly points out that current research largely focuses on the price formation of individual assets and the efficiency of capital markets. "The field does not deal with what asset prices and changes in them may mean for inflation. The field is relatively new" (p. 19).

In the case of Japan, initial empirical studies support the hypothesis that the effects of monetary policy, as a result of deregulating the financial markets, are concentrated more than before on asset stock markets. Hoffmaister and Schinasi (1994) come to the conclusion "that while monetary expansion typically led to consumer price inflation before the mid-1980s, it has since tended to manifest itself in asset price inflation because of structural changes. In sum, the empirical results suggest that financial deregulation, which took place in the late 1970s and throughout the 1980s, had an important influence in redirecting the influence of monetary factors toward asset markets" (pp. 19). During the period of extensive financial regulation in Japan (1970–1983), monetary factors (overnight rate and lending to private individuals) explained no more than 35% of the fluctuations in land prices; this increased to 75% under the "liberalized system" (1984–1993). The analysis of Samiei and Schinasi (1994) likewise substantiated this outcome for the United States and Japan. From 1983 to 1992, a period of rapid financial innovations and deregulations, the influence of monetary policy on land prices – and in Japan[10] on the stock markets – rose considerably.

There is every reason to believe that structural changes in financial markets as well as advances in financial innovations have led to a situation in which surplus liquid assets flow more strongly to the large funds. Therein lies a fundamental reason why today a strong monetary and credit expansion leads to excess demand on the asset markets rather than on the markets for goods and services. Savers have turned in increasing numbers to "trust and pension funds" as well as to insurance companies. In this phenomenon, and in the development of new financial instruments, Hargraves, Schinasi and Weisbrod (1993) see a fundamental reason for "asset price inflation" in the United States, the United Kingdom, and in Japan.

The recognition that, in the changed monetary politicy environment, monetary policy must more carefully monitor and analyze developments in the stock and real estate markets does not imply that cut and dried solutions are available for how central banks should react to movements in asset prices. These are significantly more volatile than other price indexes. A cardinal problem consists in recognizing early the emergence of speculative overheating and distinguishing that from mere restructurings of asset values within existing portfolios, as well as from fundamentally legitimate adjustments of relative prices. However, it must be rated a serious warning signal when a rise in stock prices and in real estate prices is accompanied by a considerable accumulation of private debt.

There are no simple answers to the question of how a monetary policy that is geared primarily to national and real economic target variables should respond to movements in asset prices. "Many, perhaps most, economists believe in rules; and especially in rules to be laid down in macroeconomic policy. Ignore asset markets is one such." However, in the conflict between price movements in highly integrated financial markets and the needs of the real economy, "monetary authorities confront a dilemma calling for judgement, not cookbook rules of the game. Such a conclusion may be uncomfortable. It is, I believe, realistic" (Kindleberger, 1995, p. 35).

4 REQUIREMENTS OF MONETARY POLICY

The increasing significance of financial assets as determinants of money demand touches the very foundations of the German monetary policy. In particular, the question arises whether the monetary targeting strategy practiced by the Bundesbank sufficiently takes into account the growing influence of the financial sector on important variables in the transmission mechanism of monetary policy, and whether the current derivation formula used for the past two decades to calculate the annual monetary target is still appropriate in the changed environment.

4.1 Estimation of the asset-induced demand for money when deriving the monetary target

For a monetary management regulation whose target variable is the rate of price increases arising in the real economic sector, it is necessary, when deriving the annual monetary target, first of all to determine the level of those transaction holdings which are needed in the course of the formation and expenditure of the national product. In the medium run, the money stock and the volume of real economic transactions should increase to the same extent; in this manner inflationary tensions are avoided. Therefore, it is evident how to estimate such money supply growth as is the rise in real production potential and to a normative rate of price increases.

When deriving the monetary target, the asset-induced demand for money is not explicitly included. It occurs only implicitly by taking due account of the trend in the velocity of the circulation of money. This is tending to decline, since the money stock M3 has been growing faster than DNP for years past in the Federal Republic of Germany. The monetary target is set correspondingly more broadly. If the reduction in the trend in the velocity of money were not taken into consideration in the forecast of the money stock, a central bank would run the risk of cutting the monetary coat too tightly. In its derivation of the annual monetary target, the Bundesbank includes changes in the trend of relations between money supply and nominal production potential. Recently it made an allowance of 0.5% for the falling trend in the velocity of circulation of M3, and a surcharge of 1% since 1994. Simple though this method is, it is not convincing. The clear-cut theoretical substantiation of the falling trend is missing. One cannot decide whether the trend can be simply extrapolated or not owing to a lack of verified theories.

The velocity of circulation is a "catch-all variable": It concentrates the effects of various factors and in no way mirrors the growth of asset-induced cash holdings. These factors are to be attributed partly to the asset sector and partly to the real economic sector. In part, they are to be assigned to neither of these two sectors exclusively; one should consider the organizational advances in cash holdings and the execution of payment transactions, which counteract a drop in the velocity of circulation. Some of these factors are of a cyclical nature, others solely influence the trend in the velocity. All of this means: The extent to which the falling trend in the velocity of money is determined by the growth of asset-induced money demand cannot be said with certainty. Therefore it is highly uncertain whether one can record the additional money demand induced by assets by ascertaining and extrapolating the trend in the velocity of money.[11]

Specifically, one cannot assess in advance whether a trend calculated with the help of past data will persist unchanged, or whether a structural break will emerge. That this problem arises particularly at the current trend becomes clear in the light of developments on worldwide financial markets, which Lamfalussy (1994, p. 4) has characterized as an "acceleration of history" and a "genuinely new environment." Especially with regard to Germany, Lamfalussy argues (1994, p. 5): "Only time will tell us whether the acceleration of financial innovation which is now under way in Germany will lead to the kind of unpredictable behaviour in the demand-for-money function which occurs elsewhere in the developed world."

The conclusion to be drawn from these considerations is obvious. Central banks are in danger of miscalculating the asset-induced money demand and then orienting themselves completely toward a target money stock which does not precisely reflect the growth of the financial requirements of the economy consistent with stability. The consequences of that would be diverse and grave.

If the central bank were to set the trend component too low, overshootings of the monetary target would be programmed which might be caused by the asset-induced demand for money being stronger than had been foreseen. The central bank would be under pressure to counteract the excessive monetary expansion by restrictive measures, regardless of the economic situation and regardless of whether the price increases in the real economic sector decelerated or accelerated. Although the cause of the overshooting of the monetary target lies in the field of asset-induced money demand, in this case the real sector would be encumbered with a heavy adaptation burden even if the demand for money there were weak owing to a recession. If, out of consideration for the real economic sector, central banks were to allow the target to be overshot in order to counteract a rise in interest rates, they would risk the creation and consolidation of inflation expectations, for in the long-standing practice of monetary targets, market participants have learned that instances of exceeding the target result in higher rates of price increases after a time-lag of 1½ to 2 years.

If the opposite were the case, and the trend components were set too high in the calculation of the monetary target, inflationary tendencies in the real economic sector possibly would not be recognized early and counteracted. The statutory mandate to safeguard the value of the currency would not be fulfilled under those circumstances.

Not only establishing the trend of the velocity of money has become problematic through the increasing significance of financial assets; additionally – as explained above – fluctuations in the long-term trend also increase with the asset-induced money demand.[12]

Moreover, these fluctuations will become more pronounced in the future. As the relations of substitution between interest-bearing components of M3 and competing forms of investment have become much closer, "the quantitative analysis of the measured development in terms of trend components and components which deviate from the trend is made difficult" (Reither, 1994, p. 290).

In the derivation of the monetary target, capturing the growing asset-induced demand for money only indirectly by means of "collective surcharge" for the falling trend in the velocity of money, no longer does justice to the changed environment of monetary policy. The danger is too great, on the one hand, of gauging the monetary framework too narrowly and thereby encumbering the real economic sector with an adjustment burden that it can hardly carry; or, on the other hand, of setting the monetary framework too widely and thereby, through a price increase in the capital markets, triggering an inflationary development in the real economy.

Therefore, it appears necessary to examine more closely and to explicitly capture the causes and the level of the asset-induced demand for money as part of the derivation of the money supply target. For this it is necessary to replace the unreflected extrapolation of the trend by an analysis of its causes, which certainly is not easy and demands great efforts on the part of the monetary theorists.

4.2 Transparency and certainty of expectations

In the complex contemporary financial world, central banks must create certainty of expectations through a clear and credible strategy in which the stability of the national price level has priority. If one criticizes the unstable conditions on the international financial markets, one must not overlook the fact that fluctuations in exchange rates and interest rates often are only the symptoms, and that the actual causes lie in the discretionary monetary and fiscal policies.[13]

Central banks must ensure the participants in the international financial markets a high degree of transparency regarding their monetary policy stance. In this manner, the perception is taken into account that the evolution of markets cannot be turned back, but rather that their disciplining power must be reinforced as well through the credible and consistent explanation of monetary policy. Otherwise, central banks could contribute to exacerbating mis-developments and fluctuations on the financial markets, because "the lower transaction cost in derivatives make it cheaper to incorporate news into prices" (Crockett, 1994, p. 16).[14] "The central bank must therefore be sensitive to the market's perception of its margin for manoeuvre and communicate accordingly" (Raymond, 1994, p. 24). This is especially the case during periods in which the development of the money supply deviates from the target corridor and for the public the orientation power of the money supply objective is weakened.

In the future, with the growing significance of asset-induced money demand and the resultant impairment of the indicator quality of the money supply (especially in periods of uncertainty), this aspect may increase in importance.

Players on the national and international financial markets can scarcely arrive at reliable expectations without clear signals. Central banks, which must increasingly consider the potential effects on world financial markets when taking their national interest rate decisions, therefore, require signaling instruments with which they can indicate changes in the underlying course of their monetary policy. Changes in central rates make the international coordination of monetary policy easier within the framework of coordinated interest rate measures, especially in critical phases, for in view of the overwhelming volume of transactions on financial markets, central banks could do little to counteract massive capital movements. In Germany until now, the discount rate and the Lombard rate have proved to be superior signaling instruments, since the general public does not connect short-term repo rate changes with clear statements of policy by central banks, but rather with fluctuations in the bidding behavior of credit institutions.

At times of increasing volatility, national central banks must avoid becoming elements in a globally oscillating financial system and thereby losing some of their executive power and no longer being able to provide security of expectations for the economy (cf. Hesse, 1995). Therefore, it appears all the more important for monetary policy to be anchored in the real economy, while the central bank keeps a permanent financing window open, through which only securitized claims of commercial banks on their borrowers can be submitted, claims which have arisen in direct, close connection with real economic transactions (cf. Hesse and Braasch, 1994). The rates for recourse to this facility would be changed only sporadically, and primarily when an excessive demand for goods and services leads to risks for price stability in the real sector of the economy.

5 FINAL CONCLUSIONS

The qualitative and quantitative leap in the financial sphere of the economy has led to a monetary policy environment which forces the central banks of the world into a competition of monetary stability. Thereby, almost unavoidably, the Bundesbank is forced to credibly stay on a strict course of stability. National money supply management in a volatile global economy is bound to tend to adjust to a destabilization of previously valid fundamental monetary relations. In particular, more pronounced asset-induced fluctuations in money demand are to be expected, which will conflict with the strategy of an annual monetary target. Therefore, unlike the German Bundesbank, many central banks have turned away from the monetary targeting strategy. In Germany, the long-term relations between money supply and prices are still stable. Temporary disturbances brought about by particular influences have not (yet) altered that. A fundamental reason for this is that, in Germany, capital movements and the financial markets were liberalized and deregulated much earlier, and, therefore, financial market structures changed gradually. Nevertheless, even the Bundesbank, with the increasing volatility of financial markets, must repeatedly subject the structure of its monetary strategy to a critical test. This is the case especially in the light of the fact "that through turning to a set of monetary instruments geared to market requirements and through the emergence of financial innovations, the effects of the monetary policy on nominal developments have become more uncertain and probably are not directly perceptible" (Duisenberg, 1994, p. 18).

NOTES

1 "The institutionalization of financial investment management has resulted in a concentration of market activity in the hands of comparatively few financial institutions (banks, securities houses, mutual funds, hedge funds etc.), all operating simultaneously in foreign-exchange, money, and bond markets, often with highly leveraged positions and using broadly similar "technical analyses" and conventions of behavior" (Padoa-Schioppa and Saccomanni, 1994, p. 246).

2 "[T]he movements of the exchange rate are unrelated to movements of the underlying fundamental variables . . . It looks as if exchange rate movements have a life of their own. This feature comes from the speculative dynamics in which some speculators use forward looking rules, and others backward looking rules." (De Grauwe, 1994, p. 5).

3 Thus, Borio and McCauley (1995), in an analysis of the turmoil on the international bond markets in 1994, reach the conclusion "that market's own dynamics seem to provide a stronger explanation than variations in market participants' apprehensions about economic fundamentals" (p. 3).

4 "In this increasingly uncertain environment, one thing is sure: plenty more clashes between global markets and national governments lie ahead. The danger is that some governments will be tempted to respond to market excesses by trying to force the global capital market back into a straitjacket. But they would be bound to fail. Governments would do better to rethink the way they conduct policy to avoid destabilising market expectations, and ensure that markets are better informed so they can become stricter disciplinarians" (Woodall, 1995, p. 7).

5 "[T]here are several reasons why asset prices might be expected to be relevant to the demand for money. Higher aggregate asset prices are typically associated with a higher value of transactions in financial and real asset; higher money balances may be needed to carry out these transactions. More importantly, a rise in asset prices leads to a revaluation of the stock of wealth, which should have a positive influence on the demand for money, especially in the case of broad aggregates" (Borio, Kennedy and Prowse, 1994, p. 48). – Upon valuation of the demand for money in Germany, Kole and Meade (1995, pp. 927) come to the conclusion: "inclusion of real net wealth substantially reduced the estimated responsiveness of money demand to real income, producing a more plausible result (most earlier studies reported an income elasticity well in excess of unity, a finding that does not accord with economic theory)."

6 Unadjusted for double-counting.
7 "Between 65% and 85% of the time, monthly total rates of return for the broad market indexes of the G-7 countries, expressed in local currencies, have moved in the same direction. In other words, if an investment in US bond market turns in a positive performance in any particular month, the odds are extremely high that an investment in the Canadian, the German, the British, or the Japanese bond market will also be positive" (Kaufman, 1995, p. 3).
8 However, it is to be taken into account that, with increasing securitization, the transmission of monetary impulses via the interest rates is strengthened because the monetary measures are acting on a growing block of current assets valued according to the market (Deutsche Bundesbank, 1995).
9 "In my judgement, monetary policy will need to take into account to a far greater extent than it does at present the impact of financial market developments on changes in the value of financial assets and the impact of those changes on the net worth of the private sector" (Kaufman, 1995, p. 17).
10 In the USA, Bianconi (1995), for the connection between monetary policy and share prices, finds "that the monetary effects are transitory, indicating that there is no long-run relationship between money and stock prices" (p. 496).
11 "An alternative interpretation of the gap between excess money growth and actual inflation – one that is particularly relevant for the 1980s – is that it is a residual that represents potential inflationary pressures in markets, pressures that are not captured by national income account measures of output and prices" (Hargraves and Schinasi, 1993, p. 83).
12 Borio, Kennedy and Prowse (1994, p. 50) come to the conclusion that in Japan and the United Kingdom, "at least 70% of the variance in velocity is accounted for by real asset price movements. For Australia it is well in excess of 50%."
13 "Excess volatility of exchange rates, misalignments and speculative capital flows are basically the result of an instable monetary and an undisciplined fiscal policy. Therefore, the key for stabilizing the exchange rates is a non-inflationary financial policy in the corresponding countries" (Willms, 1990, p. 348).
14 "It is that as these innovations develop, and as markets learn to respond more rapidly to information, we may see greater fluctuations in the financial markets than we've seen before" (Fischer, 1993, p. 381).

REFERENCES

Bank for International Settlements (1993), 63. Annual Report, Basel.

Bank for International Settlement (1995), *Grenzüberschreitende Abwicklung von Wertpapiergeschäften*. Bericht des Ausschusses für Zahlungs- und Abrechnungssysteme der Länder der Zehnergruppe, Basel.

Bianconi, Marcelo (1995), "Inflation and the real price of equities: Theories with some empirical evidence", *Journal of Macroeconomics*, 17(3), 495–514.

Borio, C.E.V., Kennedy, N. and Prowse, S.D. (1994), *Exploring Aggregate Asset Price Fluctuations across Countries. Measurement, Determinants and Monetary Policy Implications*. Bank for International Settlements, Economic Papers, No. 40.

Borio, Claudio E.V. and McCauley, Robert N. (1995), *The Anatomy of the Bond Market Turbulence of 1994*. Bank for International Settlements. Working Paper No. 32.

Crockett, Andrew (1994), "Financial Innovation: Macro-Economic and Macro-Prudential Consequences". A paper presented to the 25th Konstanz Seminar on Monetary Theory and Monetary Policy, 26 May (Manuscript).

Deutsche Bundesbank (1993), "Zum Einfluß von Auslandstransaktionen auf Bankenliquidität, Geldmenge und Bankkredite", *Monatsbericht*, 45(1), 19–34.

Deutsche Bundesbank (1994), "Geldpolitische Implikationen der zunehmenden Verwendung derivativer Finanzinstrumente", *Monatsbericht*, 46(11), 41–57.

Deutsche Bundesbank (1995), "Verbriefungstendenzen im deutschen Finanzsystem und ihre geldpolitische Bedeutung", *Monatsbericht*, 47(4), 19–33.

Duisenberg, Wim F. (1994), "Die Rolle der Zentralbanken in einer sich wandelnden Finanzwelt", *Mitteilungen und Berichte*. Institute für Bankwirtschaft und Bankrecht an der Universität zu Köln, 25(70), 7–22.

Fischer, Stanley (1993), Overview, in: *Changing Capital Markets: Implications for Monetary Policy*. A symposium sponsored by the Federal Reserve Bank of Kansas City, Jackson Hole, Wyoming, August 19–21, pp. 379–87.

Grauwe, Paul De (1994), *Exchange Rates in Search of Fundamental Variables*, Centre for Economic Policy Research, Discussion Paper No. 1073.

Hargraves, Monica, Schinasi, Garry J., and Weisbrod, Steven R. (1993), *Asset Price Inflation in the 1980s: A Flow of Funds Perspective*, IMF Working Paper, (October), No. 77.

Hargraves, Monica and Schinasi, Garry J. (1993), "Monetary Policy, Financial Liberalization, and Asset Price Inflation", *International Monetary Fund, World Economic Outlook*, May, pp. 81–95.

Häuser, Karl (1982), "Die Geldmarktabhängigkeit des deutschen Kapitalmarketes", in: Ehrlicher, W. und Simmert, D.B. (eds), *Geld- und Währungspolitik in der Bundesrepublik Deutschland*, Beihefte zu Kredit und Kapital, vol. 7, pp. 309–318.

Hesse, Helmut (1994), "Als Wissenschaftler in der Politik?" in: Deutsche Bundesbank (ed.), *Auszüge aus Presseartikeln*, 47, 6–15.

Hesse, Helmut (1995), "Zu den Aufgaben der Bundesbank 1995", in: Deutsche Bundesbank (ed.), *Auszüge aus Presseartikeln*, 4, 5–10.

Hesse, Helmut und Braasch, Bernd (1994), "Zum 'optimalen' Instrumentarium der Europäischen Zentralbank", in: Gahlen, Bernhard *et al.* (eds), *Europäische Integrationsprobleme aus wirtschaftswissenschaftlicher Sicht*. Schriftenreihe des Wirtschaftswissenschaftlichen Seminars Ottobeuren, Bd. 23, Tübingen, pp. 161–83.

Hoffmaister, Alexander W. and Schinasi, Garry J. (1994), *Asset Prices, Financial Liberalization and the Process of Inflation in Japan*, IMF Working Paper, No. 153.

International Monetary Fund (1995), "Increasing Importance of Institutional Investors", in: *World Economic and Financial Surveys. International Capital Markets*, Washington D.C., August, pp. 165–74.

Issing, Otmar (1995), Derivate und Geldpolitik, Beitrag zur Tagung des Ausschusses für Geldtheorie und Geldpolitik im Verein für Socialpolitik am 24/25 Februar (Manuscript).

Kaufman, Henry (1995), The "Burgeoning Global Bond Markets: Issues and Implications". A talk before the Euromoney International Bond Congress, London, 14 September (Manuscript).

Kindleberger, Charles P. (1995), "Asset Inflation and Monetary Policy", *Quarterly Review*, Banca Nazionale del Lavoro, Rome, No. 192, pp. 17–37.

Köhler, Claus (1990), *Internationalökonomie. Ein System offener Volkswirtschaften*. Berlin.

Kole, Linda S. and Meade, Ellen E. (1995), "German Monetary Targeting: A Retrospective View", *Federal Reserve Bulletin*, 81(10), 917–31.

Lamfalussy, Alexandre (1994), "Central Banking in Transition", Deutsche Bundesbank (ed.), *Auszüge aus Presseartikeln*, 43, 4–8.

Mitchell, Edson V. (1994), "Die Globalisierung ist zur Realität geworden", in: *Börsen-Zeitung*, 169(2) Sept., 16.

Mussa, Michael and Goldstein, Morris (1993), "The Integration of World Capital Markets", in: *Changing Capital Markets: Implications for Monetary Policy*. A Symposium Sponsored by the Federal Reserve Bank of Kansas City, Jackson Hole, Wyoming, August 19–21, pp. 245–313.

Padoa-Schioppa, Tommaso and Saccomanni, Fabrizio (1994), "Managing a Market-Led Global Financial System", in: Kenen, Peter B. (ed.), *Managing the World Economy. Fifty Years after Bretton Woods*, Institute for International Economics, Washington D.C., pp. 235–268.

Raymond, Robert (1993), "Currency Crises and Central Banks", *Central Banking*, 4(2) (Autumn), 23–31.

Reither, Franco (1994), "Das Ende für M3?", *Wirtschaftsdienst*, 6, 289–290.

Samiei, Hossein and Schinasi, Garry J. (1994), *Real Estate Price Inflation, Monetary Policy, and Expectations in the United States and Japan*, IMF Working Paper, No. 12.

Samuelson, R.J. (1987), "The United States Can't Solve the Crisis by Itself", *Newsweek*, 9 November, p. 38.

Seitz, Franz (1995), "Der DM-Umlauf im Ausland", Discussions paper (May), no. 1, Volkswirtschaftliche Forschungsgruppe der Deutschen Bundesbank.

Tietmeyer, Hans (1995), "Die Wirtschafts- und Währungsunion als Stabilitätsgemeinschaft", in: Deutsche Bundesbank (ed.), *Auszüge aus Presseartikeln*, 79, 1–4.

Tietmeyer, Hans (1995a), "Globale Finanzmärkte und Währungspolitik", Deutsche Bundesbank (ed.), *Auszüge aus Presseartikeln*, 65, 1–5.

Willms, M. (1990), "Concepts and Implications of International Monetary Coordination", *Außenwirtschaft*, 45(3), 329–352.

Woodall, Pam (1995), "Who's in the Driving Seat?", *Economist*, October 7, pp. 5–7.

14 What should central banks do?

What should be their macroeconomic objectives and operations?

Charles A.E. Goodhart*

The Economic Journal, vol. 104 (November 1994), pp. 1424–36

I WHAT CAN CENTRAL BANKS DO?

Before turning to the normative question of what Central Banks (hereafter CBs) *should* do, we need to deal with the contentious issue of what CBs actually *can* do in the field of monetary control. One might think that this should be a relatively straightforward matter of fact. Instead, there is a yawning chasm of mutual misunderstanding, which has persisted for decades, between economists and those working in CBs, which has bedevilled the subject.

Virtually every monetary economist believes that the CB *can* control the monetary base (hereafter Mo), and, subject to errors in predicting the monetary multiplier, the broader monetary aggregates as well. After all, Mo (apart from some relatively unimportant qualifications about coins from the Mint), represents the liabilities of the CB, and the CB should be able to control its own liabilities by open market operations. Hence the normal assumption is that Mo is controllable within a narrow margin. If the Central Bank should fail to do so, it must be because it has chosen some alternative operational guide for its open market operations, e.g. holding interest rates constant at some level, which operational rule is frequently decried as sub-optimal. Assuming that CBs can, almost perfectly, control Mo, economists have constructed several simulated schemes of how an optimal rule for so doing might be set up; McCallum (1993a, b) provides good recent examples.

Almost all those who have worked in a CB believe that this view is totally mistaken; in particular it ignores the implications of several of the crucial institutional features of a modern commercial banking system, notably the need for unchallengeable convertibility, at par, between currency and deposits, and secondly that commercial bank reserves at the CB receive a zero, or below-market, rate of interest. The first means that fluctuations in the public's demand for cash, which are both strongly seasonal and somewhat unpredictable, must be accommodated. The second means that commercial banks will not willingly hold free reserves at the end of each day (assuming

* © Royal Economic Society 1994. I am grateful to Norbert Schandt and Dirk Schoenmaker for helpful suggestions.

for this purpose that a stated reserve ratio has to be held on each day, rather than averaged over, say, a couple of weeks) beyond that needed to meet late fluctuations in the demand for cash after the money market has closed, or become thin. Only if interest rates fall to the very low levels of the 1930s, and/ or risks of interest rate variability or late-in-the-day cash runs increase, would commercial banks increase their desired free reserves. Thus, given the unpredictable fluctuations in cash flows, including late-in-the-day payments or receipts by government, any attempt by the CB on any day to achieve either some particular level, or rate of change, in Mo is bound to cause the residual available to commercial banks for their free reserves either to be excessive, or deficient.

With no interest being paid on reserves at the CB, any alternative over-night yield is better than none at all. Hence whenever a Mo target led to excess bank reserves, overnight rates would be driven down approximately to zero. Per contra, a deficiency of reserves, given the low demand for free reserves, would force commercial banks below their (legal) requirements. Such a deficiency, at the end of any day, would drive interest rates up either to the (penal) rate at which the CB is prepared to fill the shortage, or the rate which makes the commercial banks willing to face such penalties as are imposed on *ex post* reserve deficiencies, whichever is less.

Allowing reserve requirements to be averaged over some period, as in Germany, does reduce interest rate fluctuations consequent on a random cash flow on any day. But as the reserve calculation period nears its close, the CB still finds that surplus reserves would drive interest rates to zero, while deficient reserves *have* to be restored at an interest rate chosen by the CB, unless the commercial banks are to transgress their legal requirements. So reserve averaging allows the authorities to reduce the frequency of open market operations, (consistent with a desired level of interest rate volatility), but does not provide the means for tight control over Mo (Schnadt, 1994).

If the CB tried to run a system of monetary base control, it would fail. Much, perhaps most, of the time it would still be *accommodating* the day-to-day demand of the banking system for reserves at a penal interest rate of its own choice, whenever its Mo target was below the system's demand for reserves. Otherwise when its target was *above* the system's demand, overnight rates would fall to near zero. Some economists might prefer such a staccato pattern of interest rates, but it would not seem sensible to practitioners.

There is, of course, nothing to stop CBs using the path of Mo as an *information* variable, as a possible important input in the decision of whether, and how much, to vary interest rates. This could even be done by some rule, e.g. of the form

$$di = f(Mo_{t-1} - Mo^*_{t-1}),$$

where the term in brackets is the deviation of the actual from the desired path of Mo. The operation of the non-borrowed reserve base system in the USA between October 1979 and Summer 1982 worked in much this way.

But using the path of Mo as a guide to interest rate adjustments is *not* the same as monetary base control (though if such adjustments are required by rule to be large it may approximate to such control), and also immediately raises the question of why one should tie interest rates to movements in Mo rather than a (larger) set of information variables.

One factor preventing CBs from being able to undertake monetary base control is the zero, or below market, interest rate on (free) reserves, since then desired *free*, close-of-day, reserves are low. While the payment of interest rates on (required) reserves would reduce the distortionary tax on banking, the payment of a (near) market rate of interest on free reserves would not eliminate the problems of trying to run a Mo control system. While such a payment might encourage the banks voluntarily to hold a larger *average* volume of reserves, the demand for reserves would then fluctuate depending on interest differentials, between that paid on reserves and in the money market, which the authorities cannot closely control. So the reserve/deposit ratio would become much more volatile than now, and greater control over the monetary base would not translate to a similarly improved control over the broader monetary aggregates. Moreover, the choice of the level, and changes in, the interest rate on reserves would become another important (and discretionary?) interest rate choice for the CB.[1]

Consequently those in charge of CBs generally regard monetary base control as a non-starter. The instrument which they can, and do, control is the short-term money market rate. They are as fully aware as their critics among monetary economists that holding nominal interest rates *constant* indefinitely would be a recipe for instability. Instead, they ask what should be their optimal reaction function, i.e. in response to what economic developments, how much, and how fast, should they adjust short-term interest rates, their main instrument.

Critics, especially among Monetarists, often state that no-one, including those in CBs, has the information necessary to devise a satisfactory (forecasting) method for (discretionary) setting of interest rates (Brunner and Meltzer, 1993). Instead, they reiterate their preference for some monetary rule. CBs respond that such a rule is operationally infeasible; the most that can be done, as in Germany, is to use some monetary aggregate(s) as an information variable in the process of deciding on interest rate adjustments. The two groups confront each other, each believing that the other has misguidedly failed to grasp a few simple issues. A nice example of this is given by McCallum (1993b) and the rejoinder by Okina (1993).

Moreover, the relationship between interest rate changes, and the various monetary aggregates is uncertain, and subject to quite long and variable lags; as is also, of course, the relationship between the monetary aggregates and nominal incomes and inflation. This makes the use of monetary aggregates as intermediate targets more problematic.

Nevertheless, amidst all this uncertainty *there is a temptation* to err on the side of financial laxity. Raising interest rates is (politically) unpopular, and lowering them is popular. Even without political subservience, there will usually be a case for deferring interest rate increases, until more information on current developments becomes available. Politicians do *not* generally see themselves as springing surprise inflation on the electorate. Instead, they suggest that an electorally inconvenient interest rate increase should be deferred, or a cut 'safely' accelerated. But it amounts to the same thing in the end.

This political manipulation of interest rates, and hence of the monetary aggregates (but indirectly, rather than directly), leads to a loss of credibility, and cynicism about whether the politician's contra-inflation rhetoric should be believed. The disadvantages of time-inconsistent behaviour have become well-understood, including among politicians. This has provided much of the impetus for granting CBs more autonomy ('independence') to vary interest rates as they, the independent CBs, think right, but for the attainment of an objective, i.e. price stability, which has been imposed by government. What Fischer (1994) describes as *operational* independence, but without *goal* independence. We turn to this next, and show how, in the process, it may help to finesse the disagreements between the Monetarists and CBs.

II WHAT MACRO VARIABLE SHOULD THE CENTRAL BANK SEEK TO CONTROL?

It is easier for a principal to appoint an agent, if she can instruct her agent to achieve a single, quantifiable, easily recognised, measured and understood outcome. This facilitates monitoring and accountability. When the principal has multiple objectives for her agent, and when these objectives potentially conflict (e.g. there are trade-offs), then the principal will be disinclined to delegate the choice among such objectives to the agent. The agent will need much closer control and supervision. Thus, with utilities the government wants limitations on prices to consumers, an efficient provision of present and future services, and a rate of return sufficient to reward investors for providing funds, hence Ofwat, Ofgas.

When an exploitable trade-off was perceived between inflation and unemployment, along the Phillips curve, the choice of the optimal point was inherently, and rightly, a political decision. So, when monetary policy aims at several objectives *simultaneously*,[2] with the need for choice, and balance, between them, policy will be subject to greater political oversight and the CB will be subservient. Greater autonomy is more likely when CBs are asked to achieve a *single* macro outcome, such as the maintenance of the Gold Standard up till 1914, or price stability now.

Thus current enthusiasm for independent CBs rests importantly on general acceptance of the vertical longer-term Phillips curve; that there is no medium, or longer term trade-off to exploit; that the best sustainable outcome that the authorities can achieve through monetary policy is price stability.

Those who do not accept this analysis, or who place great emphasis on the short-term, in which there remains a downward sloping Phillips curve, will find such argumentation unappealing. For those who *do* accept the analysis, a shift to CB 'independence', in circumstances where there is a single, quantifiable objective which the CB is mandated to achieve, makes the CB much more, rather than less, democratically accountable (Roll Report, 1993). Both its objective, and success in achieving that target, can be made crystal clear.

In those countries like Canada, New Zealand and the United Kingdom where the objective of price stability has been quantified, the target has been defined as a band for the rate of increase of the Retail (or Consumer) Price Index, e.g. 0–2% in New Zealand, to be achieved between two and four years hence. There are many questions about the best way to quantify this general objective. One major issue is whether the objective should be price inflation alone, or for nominal incomes. There are several reasons for advocating a nominal income, rather than a price inflation target (Meade, 1994). The former gives some weight to deviations of output from its 'equilibrium'. Also, policy makers should not react to an adverse supply shock (e.g. the oil shocks of 1973 and 1979) by further deflating the economy. In practice, the latter point is largely met in the small print, or qualifications, to the inflation targets, whereby indirect tax increases, severe terms of trade shocks, energy and food price increases, and the own effects of interest rate increases on the RPI may be disregarded for the purpose of such targetry. Among the problems of using nominal GDP as a target are the delays in getting the data, and the errors and revisions in the series. Moreover, estimation of trend real output is difficult and contentious. Finally, the relatively long horizon for the RPI/CPI target provides some leeway for adjusting to cyclical fluctuations in the shorter term, while sticking to a single medium-term price inflation target. Consequently those countries adopting quantified final objectives have chosen a measure of inflation alone, *not* nominal incomes.

The next question is whether that target should be set in terms of a desired price *level*, or a desired *rate of change* of prices. *Ex ante*, there is no real difference; a proposed future target level can be equivalently described in terms of a desired rate of change, and vice versa. The difference occurs *ex post*, when a miss in period $t - 1$ in achieving a *level* has to be rectified in period t, whereas for targets expressed in terms of rates of change, bygones are bygones, thereby causing the price level in the latter case to trace out a random walk. Consequently, the variance and uncertainty about future price levels are much less under a levels target. Moreover, when the regime has become credible, a target expressed in levels should be more self-stabilising; unexpected deflation (inflation) should lead to an expectation of future price inflation (deflation) to restore the desired level; this will drive *ex ante* real interest rates in an equilibrating direction. The theoretical advantages of a target expressed in terms of levels have been thoroughly rehearsed by Scarth (1994), by Fillion and Tetlow (1994), and by Duguay (1994).

Nevertheless all quantified targets so far adopted have been in terms of the rate of increase of the RPI/CPI. Moreover, descriptions given by senior CB officials, in countries where no quantified target has been set, of their definition of price stability are often in terms of a rate of increase low enough not to enter into people's consciousness and calculations (Greenspan, 1988). One reason may be that the desired optimal *ex ante* rate of price change is not zero, but a (very) low positive number, perhaps because of concern about an upwards bias, e.g. relating to quality changes, in the RPI, though this has been calculated as only about 0.5% (Crawford, 1993, also see Fischer, 1994). There is also fear of downwards nominal wage rigidity and some residual feeling that a little inflation may serve as a lubricant to the economic system, though there is little hard evidence of that (see Crawford and Dupasquier, 1994). Even so, this would not of itself necessarily settle the issue of levels *vs* rates of change, because the *ex ante* target could still be set in terms of a slowly rising *level*. Perhaps, stating that the price *level* in three years' time, (starting from 100), should be 106.1, within a band of 105 to 107, sounds less impressive than that inflation should be held between 1 and 3% throughout the period.

Of course, a levels target is more demanding, since misses then have to be rectified. Given that this whole approach is in its initial phase; that quantified price objectives and 'independent' CBs are only now being introduced; that sustained low inflation, let alone zero inflation, has yet to be achieved; that political and public support for this regime has in many instances yet to become solid; for all these transitional reasons there is a need not to over-egg the pudding in the transitional phase. If this new regime is shown to have worked, and sustained (very) low or zero inflation is achieved, we may, perhaps, then switch to the theoretically preferable basis of a target defined in levels.

The next question is which index should be chosen. We have already considered some reasons why the RPI or CPI is preferred to the GDP deflator. The latter is only provided quarterly, with considerable delay; often subject to considerable revision; the public do not find it easy to understand. The RPI (or CPI), however, only measures changes in present goods and services prices, and excludes current changes in the prices of future goods, i.e. omitting adjustments in asset prices, houses, land, equity, etc. Some economists have argued that such asset price changes should, in theory, be included in the cost of living index (Alchian and Klein, 1973, Goodhart, 1993). But the theoretical basis for including asset prices in a price index remains contentious, and asset prices are erratic, subject to fads and fashions. The question is posed, 'If there was a (speculative) boom in the equity market, would you want, just for that reason, to deflate the economy?' Per contra, asset prices, flexibly set in efficient markets, may often reflect the thrust of monetary policy before stickier current goods and service flow prices react. So, the present consensus is that asset prices are among the set of useful information variables, but should not be included in the index measuring inflation itself.

Perhaps the most important asset price, at least for smaller, open economies, is the exchange rate. The exchange rate represents the most commonly used *intermediate* target. Many smaller countries have seen advantages in pegging their currency to that of a large neighbour, especially one with a good counter-inflation reputation, notably within the ERM; but there are many other examples. This paper, however, is not the place to discuss exchange rate regimes. The point here is that both final and intermediate targets are frequently used *in tandem*, but one of them dominates as the one quantified target, the *main* information variable to help determine interest rate changes. Thus countries within the ERM saw this as their best strategy for ultimately achieving price stability; but this latter was not quantified, whereas the ERM bands were, and were the main influence on interest rate adjustments. Per contra, in New Zealand the RPI target is the dominant quantified objective, but in working practice the RBNZ has established unofficial intermediate bands for the exchange rate, which, if broken, may trigger an interest rate response. Thus the exchange rate acts as an information variable about likely future progress to the final objective.

Such an intermediate exchange rate target, e.g. via a Currency Board mechanism, as in Argentina, Hong Kong and Estonia, or by an (adjustable) peg, as in the ERM, leaves the ultimate decision of how to set targets to achieve price stability to the hegemonic, central country. The main choice for the latter lies between a final objective for the rate of change of the RPI and an intermediate target for some monetary aggregate, as in Germany.

Opinion, I believe, is moving in favour of making the final objective predominant as the quantified target. Given that both objectives (final and intermediate) can be clearly and precisely quantified, there is, other things being equal, a natural advantage in going straight to the final objective. It is, by definition, what people care about; it is, therefore, likely to be better understood; restrictive policies may be more easily accepted if they are imposed to control inflation, rather than to control a monetary aggregate. At the best of times the links between the intermediate target and the final objective may appear complex and uncertain to the layman. With the disturbances to, perhaps break-down of, the stability of demand-for-money, and velocity, functions, uncertainty about their use has spread to experts as well. Persson and Tabellini (1994: 14–15),

> it is clear that the inflation contract is more direct and simpler to enforce . . . Hence, a contract based on an intermediate monetary target is much more demanding on the principal's information compared to an inflation target . . . Generally, the principal finds it easier to monitor the outcome rather than the policy instrument, because the optimal instrument choice depends on detailed information which may not be available to the principal.

But, *ceteris paribus* does not hold. The key argument for an intermediate target is that this may be quicker and easier to achieve. Thus Persson and Tabellini ask (p. 15):

> Why do we see exchange rate targets or monetary targets often imposed (or self imposed) on central bankers, but rarely see central bankers accountable for the rate of inflation? One reason may have to do with the

commitment technology available to the principal. The effect of policy actions on asset prices or the money supply is readily [*sic*] observable.[3] The effect on prices is observable only with substantial delay. It may thus be harder for society to commit to "punishing" a central bank for actions undertaken six months or a year ago. If the central bank deviates from a financial target the penalty is more immediately related to the policy actions. It may therefore be easier to sustain such penalties than in the case of inflation targets.

In contrast to their optimism about the ease and speed of achieving intermediate monetary targets, monetarists emphasise the difficulty of forecasting inflation (on a policy unchanged basis), and hence of knowing how to set interest rates to achieve a given rate of inflation. Indeed Brunner and Meltzer (1993) reckon that this is so difficult that trying to set interest rates in order to achieve price stability directly is more likely than not to be destabilising.

No doubt such forecasting is difficult and subject to considerable error. The role of chief forecaster in a CB committed to an inflation target is both difficult and exposed. Yet most officials, practitioners and even economists who have worked inside CBs would, I believe, *not* put the difficulty or speed of achieving final RPI objectives as much worse than the task of attaining intermediate monetary targets. During the period of the Medium Term Financial Strategy the intended downwards path for inflation was almost exactly achieved (1980–5), but the monetary aggregate targets were not. So far the targets for inflation in Canada and New Zealand have either been met or exceeded (i.e. inflation *below* the lower band). This has also been true for the United Kingdom since Autumn 1992, but it remains to be seen how much autonomy the Bank of England may have to vary interest rates if the desired inflation bands (1–4%) look like being broken.

Indeed, in some respects experience with final inflation targets, at least in New Zealand, have been too good in that success so far in holding inflation within a band-width of 2% may lead the public to believe that this standard can regularly be met, whereas unforeseen shocks may cause misses quite often when the bands are so narrow. The question of optimal band-width involves issues of credibility, as well as of the size of shocks and ability to forecast.

With CB officials themselves often happier to go for final price objectives than for intermediate monetary targets, why not let them try? Monetarists may predict failure, but as long as the cost of failure is internalised in CBs by an appropriate incentive structure, there would not seem a disadvantage for society in this strategy. Perhaps the recent relative success with hitting inflation targets in Canada and New Zealand has been due to the greater incentives on CB officials so to do.

This introduces the final question here, of the appropriate incentive structure for CBs in order to give society the best chance of price stability under this regime. At present, the main incentive is that the Governor may not be reappointed if the target is missed. The unwillingness of the incoming Liberal government in Canada to reappoint John Crow may have been due to their concern about the prior undershoot, and the extent of deflation in keeping near to, or below, the bottom band. When the target is expressed as an inflation rate in some terminal year, CB governors with a strong incentive to deliver will want to get inflation to, or below, the required rate a year or so in advance, to give themselves the best chance of hitting the final target.

Nevertheless, the idea that the incentive of reappointment may already be too potent would seem fanciful to many. As an external adviser to the RBNZ before the 1989 Act, I advocated relating bonus payments to senior officials to the outcome, relative to the target. Although many thought that such a scheme had been introduced, it was actually rejected on the presentational argument that it would evoke headlines such as 'Governor makes $500,000 by taking action to throw 500,000 out of work'.

Anyhow, CB officials are (curiously) reluctant to have their salaries tied to their own success in achieving their targets, even though this should considerably raise their expected average salaries. Perhaps they find payment by results demeaning; perhaps, as Persson and Tabellini (1994) suggest, they are very risk averse. One fallacious argument is that the outcome will be affected by unforeseeable shocks. So, of course, are business profits, but few would argue that businessmen's remuneration should not be partially profit related. It still strikes me as sensible to relate the remuneration of senior CB officials to their success.

I ended Section I by suggesting that the adoption of price stability targets for CBs might reduce the intensity of dispute between Monetarists and CB officials over operational techniques. If CBs are mandated to achieve price stability, and the incentive structure properly rewards them for success (penalises failure), then CB officials have every incentive to find the best way to achieve that objective. If they continue to believe that this can only, or best, be done by interest rate adjustments, that is their responsibility, and it is they who would suffer if they got it wrong.

III WHY USE CENTRAL BANKS TO TRY TO ACHIEVE PRICE STABILITY?

CB officials have expressed their determination to defeat inflation for decades. Yet, for a variety of reasons, inflation accelerated into the 1970s, and though now more subdued, is hardly eliminated. The public can easily imagine political and economic events that could reignite inflation. In this context the institutional innovation of giving the CB a formal, legal mandate to achieve price stability, and both the autonomy and incentives to do so, should help to improve on the past record, and may succeed in delivering the desired objective.

Nevertheless it remains to be seen whether this institutional reform succeeds. If the CB cannot develop and maintain a supportive constituency among both the general public and the main political parties, the regime may not prove sustainable, irrespective of the CB's technical expertise.

Some monetary economists, mostly, but not only, of the Free Banking

School (for a definition see Laidler (1992), Schuler and White (1992), and White (1984)), argue that this route, via Central Bank 'independence', is not the only way to achieve price stability, and may not be the best way. Rather than start with a fiat currency, which then has to be stabilised by (discretionary) CB operations, why not have the government *define* the unit of currency, the numeraire, in terms of a basket of commodities and then leave it to private commercial banks to maintain convertibility between their deposits *and* their bank notes, which they could freely and competitively issue, and that basket. Achieve price stability by defining the currency base so that it is stable; do away with the CB altogether; and allow commercial banks to compete freely in the provision of both bank note and deposit liabilities. Such a switch to a revised basket-commodity-based monetary system could be undertaken, while still keeping the CB: but advocates of the policy change would fear that governments would be once again tempted, so long as subservient CBs existed, to revert to an increasing fiduciary issue, and thence to fiat money. So the Free Banking set of institutional changes, involving a new basis for the currency, abolition of the CB and 'free banking', is usually presented as a package.

In their view the main problem with the Gold Standard was that the currency base was defined in terms of convertibility into a single commodity, so that world monetary conditions were subject to idiosyncratic shocks affecting it. Broaden the base to a representative basket of goods (and services), and the desired stable price level may be achieved, so it is claimed, almost by definition. There are, of course, different views about what the components of the basket should be, or whether the standard should be defined in terms of (a basket of) goods and services, or over labour (Thompson, 1986), but these are second order.[4]

The first serious problem is how convertibility in such a system would be enforced. Someone doubting the solvency of one particular bank, or perhaps of banks overall, can hardly go into a bank and withdraw a basket of goods, let alone services, or labour time. One suggestion (Greenfield and Yeager, 1989) is that convertibility be maintained *indirectly*, by having the banks hold reserves in gold and paying out as much gold as necessary to allow the creditor to exchange her notes/deposits so as always to buy the guaranteed amount of basket goods/services/labour.

Obviously the amount of gold needed to pay the given sum to be withdrawn would vary as gold prices shifted relative to the basket. This idea is close to Irving Fisher's compensated dollar. A problem, however, is that it would seem to involve a bank, in the process of meeting its convertibility guarantee, often having to set a price of gold in terms of the basket different from that set in the market. This might lead to massive arbitrage flows, and hence to great instability in banks' gold reserves, and in interest rates (Schnadt and Whittaker, 1993). Should Central Bank 'independence' fail to deliver price stability, this issue (currently, perhaps, regarded as arcane and academic), might suddenly become policy relevant.

Assuming that a resolution is found, and indirect convertibility becomes possible, what then are the comparative advantages and disadvantages of such a system; but compared with what? If Central Bank 'independence' should deliver (acceptable) price stability, the case for a massive jump to a new, and therefore uncertain, institutional framework would not attract much following. The case for switching to a completely different monetary system is conditional on how current institutional reforms work, and we do not yet know this.

To continue the discussion, assume that CBs fail to deliver the desired outcome. What are the remaining pros and cons? There are some minor issues. The resource costs of each bank holding its own reserves of gold would be greater. There might be some greater informational problems, and resource costs, with each (major) bank issuing its own notes. Against this, competition in note issue might lead to an improved product, possibly cracking the problem of an effective means of paying interest on currency.

Somewhat more important, governments would lose command over seigniorage. In countries without high reserve requirements and with low inflation, seigniorage represents a small proportion of government revenue (Rovelli, 1994), but every little helps. This source of government revenue is relatively painless, provides a tax on the black economy (large cash users), and helps to reduce other distorting taxes. Although the purpose of this exercise is to eliminate the inflation tax, that is the final source of revenue to a government in desperation when tax collection breaks down and the bond market dries up. Countries in the throes of war, revolution or collapsing civil order will, inevitably, turn to the printing press. Glasner (1989) argues that this is why the creation of money has been so closely tied with sovereignty.

The main issue is, however, whether a free banking system, without a CB, would suffer banking crises and panics, or would be inherently stable. This micro-level question is the chief bone of contention between those in favour of free banking, and those against.

Bank runs rarely arise from a stochastic cumulation of ordinary, personal depositors seeking early withdrawal of deposits into cash (Diamond and Dybvig, 1983). Instead they arise, in the context of informational asymmetries, when large commercial and interbank depositors fear, but do not exactly know, that the bank involved has made serious losses on its asset portfolio (Jacklin and Bhattacharya, 1988). If bank assets had an immediately calculable market value (not necessarily constant), this main source of runs should be halted, either by increasing restrictions on the bank's actions, ultimately closure, as its capital became impaired [FDICIA goes in this direction], or by moving towards mutual fund banking, in which the value of bank liabilities varies with that of bank assets. Such mutual fund banking is growing rapidly in the United States.

With an improved payment system, mutual fund banking, and mark-to-market valuation of bank assets, it *is* possible to envisage a *future* in which the CB's role in ensuring systemic stability, as Lender of Last Resort, supervisor, etc., could be phased out. But that time has *not* yet come, and there are good grounds for believing that banking crises and panics can still occur. Even thereafter, parts of the wider financial system might still be subject to (liquidity) crises, and a need for a LOLR may well remain.

The sizeable number of bank failures in several countries, e.g. Scandinavia and New England, and weakness elsewhere (e.g. Japan and Victoria in Australia), recently is evidence that systemic instability can still occur. Some free banking advocates claim that such problems are largely caused by the moral hazard associated with (improperly priced) CB insurance. If the CB was not there to protect them, banks would, they suggest, hold larger reserves and capital, so systemic instability would naturally decline.

There is evidence of a downwards trend in bank capital ratios, prior to the Basle Capital Adequacy Requirements in 1988, which trend may possibly be ascribed to the protection felt to be given to the system by CBs. Otherwise I have seen little persuasive evidence that the presence of CBs (as contrasted with complete, 100% deposit insurance, e.g. as provided by FDIC and FSLIC, which *did* play a large role in the S & L debacle), was responsible for the banking crises of recent decades, e.g. the UK fringe bank crisis of 1973 [those banks had *not* been under the wing of the Bank of England], the LDC crisis in 1982, and the property-related crises in 1990–2.

Moreover there were plenty of banking crises and panics prior to the formation of CBs (Sprague, 1910; the 1893 crisis in Australia; Dowd, 1992). Indeed, to lessen the intensity and incidence of such banking crises was one of the main reasons for the establishment of CBs. In some cases, as in the United States in 1929–33, the CB's own policies may well have aggravated the disaster. But so long as panics and crises continue to be possible, and feared, the public, and politicians, will want to maintain some institutional mechanism for intervening in order to prevent such systemic instability, and that mechanism is, and will remain, the Central Bank.

NOTES

1 Moreover, the institutional arrangements which shape commercial banks' demand for reserves are in the process of rapid change. These include the form of the payments system; the opening and closing hours of the money market and the times and conditions of potential access to CB assistance; the fact that the shortest period for which money can now be lent or borrowed is overnight; and that the only time at which bank reserve positions are *officially* calculated and reviewed is at the close of business. All these institutional data are now likely to change, e.g. under the influence of modifications to the (international) payments systems.
2 The European Central Bank (ECB) and the Bundesbank have as their overriding, primary objective the achievement of price stability. Both have a secondary objective, to assist the general policy of the Government, but this is conditional on this latter not being inconsistent with the attainment of price stability, i.e. a lexicographic ordering.
3 Like many other monetary economists, Persson and Tabellini exaggerate the speed and ease of achieving monetary targets. As already explained, CB officials see no practicable and/or sensible alternative to the use of short term interest rates as their main instrument. The effect of such interest rate adjustments on the monetary aggregates is neither 'readily observable', nor necessarily quick acting, nor of well understood and predictable magnitude.

4 Hayek has advocated allowing banks to compete by offering convertibility into whichever objects of value they individually choose. Network economies of scale, however, make it efficient for a government to define the monetary standard in its own area.

REFERENCES

Alchian, A.A. and Klein, B. (1973). 'On a correct measure of inflation.' *Journal of Money, Credit and Banking*, vol. 5, pp. 183–191.

Brunner, K. and Meltzer, A.H. (1993). *Money and the Economy: Issues in Monetary Analysis*. Cambridge: Cambridge University Press.

Crawford, A. (1993). 'Measurement biases in the Canadian CPI.' Bank of Canada, Technical Report No. 64.

Crawford, A. and Dupasquier, C. (1994). 'Can inflation serve as a lubricant for market equilibrium?' In *Economic Behaviour and Policy Choice under Price Stability*, pp. 49–80. Ottawa: Bank of Canada.

Diamond, D.W. and Dybvig, P.H. (1983). 'Bank runs, deposit insurance and liquidity.' *Journal of Political Economy*, vol. 91, pp. 401–419.

Dowd, K. (ed.) (1992). *The Experience of Free Banking*. London and New York: Routledge.

Duguay, P. (1994). 'Some thoughts on price stability versus zero inflation.' Paper presented at 'Paolo Baffi' Centre for Monetary and Financial Economics, Conference, 4 March, on *Central Bank Independence and Accountability*. Milan: Università Commerciale Luigi Bocconi.

Fillion, J.-F. and Tetlow, R. (1994). 'Zero inflation or price stability'. In *Economic Behaviour and Policy Choice under Price Stability*, pp. 129–166. Ottawa: Bank of Canada.

Fischer, S. (1994). 'Modern central banking.' Paper prepared for the tercentenary of the Bank of England Central Banking Symposium, 9 June. London: Bank of England.

Glasner, D. (1989). *Free Banking and Monetary Reform*. Cambridge: Cambridge University Press.

Goodhart, C.A.E. (1993). 'Price stability and financial fragility.' Paper presented at Bank of Japan Conference, Tokyo. 28/29 October, on *Financial Stability in a Changing Environment*. London: Macmillan.

Greenfield, R.L. and Yeager, L.B. (1989). 'Can monetary disequilibrium be eliminated?' *Cato Journal*, vol. 9, pp. 405–21.

Jacklin, C.J. and Bhattacharya, S. (1988). 'Distinguishing panics and information-based bank runs: Welfare and policy implications.' *Journal of Political Economy*, vol. 96, pp. 568–592.

Laidler, D.E.W. (1992). 'Free banking theory.' In *The New Palgrave Dictionary of Money and Finance* (ed. P. Newman, M. Milgate and J. Eatwell), vol. 2, pp. 196–197. London: Macmillan.

McCallum, B.T. (1993a). 'Specification and analysis of a monetary policy rule for Japan.' *Bank of Japan Monetary and Economic Studies*, vol. 11, pp. 1–45.

McCallum, B.T. (1993b). 'Monetary policy rules and financial stability.' Paper presented at Bank of Japan Conference, Tokyo, 28/29 October, on *Financial Stability in a Changing Environment*. London: Macmillan.

Meade, J.E. (1994). *Full Employment without Inflation*. London: Social Market Foundation.

Okina, K. (1993). 'Comments on "Specification and analysis of monetary policy rule for Japan": a central banker's view.' *Bank of Japan Monetary and Economic Studies*, vol. 11, pp. 47–54.

Persson, T. and Tabellini, G. (1994). 'Credibility and accountability in monetary policy.' Paper presented at 'Poalo Baffi' Centre for Monetary and Financial Economics, Conference, 4 March, on *Central Bank Independence and Accountability*. Milan: Università Commerciale Luigi Bocconi.

Roll Report, a report of an independent panel chaired by Eric Roll. (1993). *Independent and Accountable: A New Mandate for the Bank of England*. London: The Centre for Economic Policy Research.

Rovelli, R. (1994). 'Central banking, seignorage and the financing of the government.' Paper presented at the 'Paolo Baffi' Centre for Monetary and Financial Economics, Conference, 4 March, on *Central Bank Independence and Accountability*. Milan: Università Commerciale Luigi Bocconi.

Scarth, W. (1994). 'Zero inflation vs. price stability.' In *Economic Behaviour and Policy Choice under Price Stability*, pp. 89–119. Ottawa: Bank of Canada.

Schnadt, N. (1994). *The Domestic Money Markets of the UK, France, Germany and the US*. Subject Report VII, Paper 1, City Research Project. London: London Business School.

Schnadt, N. and Whittaker, J. (1993). 'Inflation-proof currency? The feasibility of variable commodity standards.' *Journal of Money Credit and Banking*, vol. 25, pp. 214–221.

Schuler, K. and White, L.H. (1992). 'Free banking history.' In *The New Palgrave Dictionary of Money and Finance* (ed. P. Newman, M. Milgate and J. Eatwell), vol. 2, pp. 198–199. London: Macmillan.

Sprague, O.M.W. (1977 [1910]). *History of Crises under the National Banking System*. Fairfield, NJ: Augustus M. Kelley. Original edn., US National Monetary Commission (61st Congress, 2nd session, Senate doc. no. 538), Washington, DC: Government Printing Office.

Thompson, E.A. (1986). 'A perfect monetary system.' Paper presented at the Liberty Fund/Manhattan Institute Conference on Competitive Monetary Regimes, New York.

White, L.H. (1984). *Free Banking in Britain: Theory, Experience and Debate (1800–1845)*. Cambridge: Cambridge University Press.

15 Central bank independence and monetary control

*Alex Cukierman**
The Economic Journal, vol. 104 (November 1994), pp. 1437–48

I INTRODUCTION

The last few years have witnessed a veritable wave of changes in central bank (CB) legislation that are designed to increase the legal independence of the bank. Since the end of the 1980s, countries such as New Zealand, Chile, Mexico, Argentina, Spain, France and the United Kingdom, as well as many former socialist states, have, or are, considering changes in legislation that would make the CB more autonomous from government. The changes in legislation usually give more authority to the CB and also direct it to focus mainly on the objective of price stability even at the cost of disregarding other objectives such as high employment, growth, low interest rates or the financing of budget deficits. The success of the highly independent Bundesbank and Swiss National Banks in maintaining comparatively low rates of inflation for prolonged periods of time as well as the recent liberalisation of capital flows in Europe and elsewhere has no doubt contributed to this tendency.

Effective monetary control is a means rather than a final objective. This essay takes the position that the main final objective to be achieved by monetary policy is price stability. It is well accepted, from the quantity of money, that inflation cannot persist without sustained increases in the money supply. It follows that the achievement of price stability (which I will take to mean also a low rate of inflation) requires the imposition of effective constraints on monetary expansion. A subsidiary objective, whose interaction with the primary objective is discussed towards the end of the essay, is stability of the financial system.

The intellectual case for central bank independence (CBI) rests on two pillars. One is theoretical and the other empirical. The theoretical argument is based on the view that policy-makers are subject to an inflationary bias. Monetary policy enables them quickly, but temporarily to achieve various real objectives such as high employment, financing of the budget deficit and low interest rates. In the process, high-powered money is increased fueling inflation and inflationary expectations and creating an inflationary bias

* The Eitan Berglas School of Economics, Tel-Aviv University and Center for Economic Research, Tilburg University.

that persists long after the desirable effects of monetary expansion have disappeared.

Although the inflationary bias normally arises because of several objectives, the best-known example is the one associated with the employment objective for monetary expansion. Due to the existence of nominal wage contracts inflation stimulates employment by reducing the cost of labour to employers. This tempts policy-makers to reduce the real wage by means of inflation. However, since they are aware of this temptation at contracting time, unions demand a premium to offset this bias upfront. As a consequence, in equilibrium, there is no effect on employment, but inflation is excessive.[1]

The inflationary policy bias can be eliminated by precommitting policy prior to contracting time to price stability or to a low rate of inflation. One way of implementing this commitment in practice is to give sufficient independence to the CB and to direct it by law and/or other means to focus on price stability even if that implies a relative neglect of other objectives.

The empirical case for CBI rests on the observation that there is, cross-sectionally, a negative correlation between various proxies for CBI and inflation. In particular several studies find that, within the group of industrial countries, there is a negative relationship between legal independence and inflation.[2] Some of these studies also find that there is no connection between growth and legal independence. Based on this evidence they reach the conclusion that, for industrialised economies, CBI offers a free lunch. It brings about lower inflation without interfering with the process of growth.

Legal independence is a reasonable proxy for actual independence provided there is sufficient respect for the rule of law in the country under consideration. There is reason to believe that, at least as far as CB legislation is concerned, the law is a poorer indicator of actual practice in less developed countries (LDCs) than in industrial economies.[3] More behaviourally oriented proxies of CBI are therefore preferable in LDCs. Such indices are based on the actual turnover of the CB governor and on the likelihood that he will be removed from office following a political transition. The evidence indicates that in LDCs there is a negative relationship between CBI as proxied by the inverses of each of these indicators and inflation.[4] The general conclusion is that, provided the appropriate indices of independence are used in each group of countries, inflation is negatively related to CBI in both industrial as well as in developing nations.

The space limitations of this essay do not make it possible to survey systematically the non-negligible amount of empirical work that has recently been done on CBI and the performance of the economy.[5] Instead, after a brief description of some of the findings, I will try to draw (sometimes partial and tentative) conclusions for current policy questions such as:

- How effective is CBI as a commitment device in comparison to other commitment devices in building up credibility?
- Can legal independence alone function as an effective barrier against expansionary temptations?

- How effective are CBI and the announcement of targets in achieving price stability and credibility?
- Should pre-announcements refer to some monetary aggregate or to the price level?
- What are the tradeoffs, if any, between the achievement of price stability and of financial stability?
- What are the tradeoffs between CBI and the accountability of its management to the nation's elected officials?
- What are the implications of the discussion for the design of future policy-making institutions such as a potential European Monetary Union (EMU) and CB reform in former socialist countries?

II CENTRAL BANK INDEPENDENCE AND THE PERFORMANCE OF THE ECONOMY

There exist currently four types of indices of CBI: legal indices derived from the charters of central banks, questionnaire-based indices, the actual turnover of CB governors and the political vulnerability of the bank. The last measure is defined as the fraction of political transitions that are followed within six months by a replacement of the CB governor. The first group of indices reflects, in the first place, the level of independence that legislators meant to confer on the CB.

Legal proxies for independence have two problems. First the law is highly incomplete in that there are many contingencies under which it does not specify the limits of authority between the CB and the political authorities. Second there are, particularly in developing countries, substantial deviations between actual practice and the letter of the law. The questionnaire-based indices, which are based on the responses of experts in various central banks, are useful for identifying informal practices and other dimensions of independence that are not captured by the legal indices. The remaining two indices have the advantage of being based on actual behaviour. They appear to be particularly appropriate measures of dependence in LDCs.[6] The correlation between the legal indices and the remaining proxies is insignificant, suggesting that they capture different dimensions of independence.

Some of the findings concerning the relationships between CBI and the performance of the economy are summarised in the following conclusions.[7]

- Within industrial economies inflation is negatively related to legal independence and unrelated to CB governors' turnover.
- Within LDCs there is no relation between inflation and legal independence. However, there is a strong positive association between inflation and CB governors' turnover.
- Inflation and its variability are positively related to the political vulnerability of the CB. This finding persists even after allowance is made for the effect of political instability on inflation.

- Other things being the same, countries whose monetary authorities have made monetary announcements enjoy lower rates of inflation.
- Average real growth is unrelated to (legal) CBI within industrial economies.
- After controlling for other determinants of growth (such as initial GDP and terms-of-trade shocks) CBI is found to have a positive effect on growth in LDCs.
- The variability over time of growth within a given country is negatively related to its level of development and unrelated to the independence of its CB as proxied by turnover.
- Less CBI as proxied by a higher governor's turnover or by more political vulnerability of the CB is associated with a negative effect on the share of private investment within LDCs.

Abstracting from details, these conclusions imply that inflation is lower the higher is CBI and that, given independence, countries that pre-announce monetary policy have even lower rates of inflation. Furthermore, there is no evidence that CBI retards growth or investment. As a matter of fact, for LDCs, the evidence points in the opposite direction. Low independence is associated with lower growth and investment.

Some economists feel that excessive independence may interfere with the potential stabilisatory function of monetary policy. Since fluctuations in the growth rate of the economy are found to be unrelated to CBI, this does not appear to be the case.

III COMMITMENT VIA CENTRAL BANK INDEPENDENCE AND CREDIBILITY

Precommitment of monetary policy to a pre-announced course is a device for reducing inflationary expectations and through them the rate of increase in wages and prices. Delegation of authority to a semi-independent institution like the CB, together with an unequivocal mandate to focus on price stability, is one institutional device for committing monetary policy. Another device is the maintenance of a fixed parity with the currency of a country that puts high priority on stable prices. Obviously this requires that the rate of monetary expansion be chosen so as to maintain the fixed parity.

Which of these two devices is more effective in building up credibility? This is largely an open question. However, past experience suggests that it is not the choice of monetary anchor that is the prime determinant of credibility, but rather the record of policy-makers in sticking to their commitments whether this is achieved through a fixed exchange rate or by making the CB sufficiently independent. Whatever the institutional device, credibility is built up gradually by demonstrating to the public that the commitment is taken seriously. But there are reasons to believe that commitment via CBI is more appropriate for large and relatively closed economies while commitment by means of a fixed exchange rate is more suitable for small open economies.

Neither of the two is necessary for nominal stability. As a matter of fact in some isolated cases, price stability has been achieved even with a dependent CB and a flexible exchange rate. This is the case of Japan where credibility-enhancing policies were conducted by the relatively powerful treasury. Nonetheless, the weight of the evidence is that the tendency to accommodate inflation is weaker the higher the degree of CB independence and, within industrial economies, it is lower (given the level of independence) in countries with fixed exchange rates.

CBI appears to be efficient mostly as a safeguard against the onset of high inflation rather than as a remedial device. The experience of high-inflation countries has demonstrated that the stabilisation of high inflation, once it has been allowed to develop, cannot be achieved only by delegation of authority to the CB. It requires the active and full involvement of the entire political establishment. But once inflation has been conquered and sufficient credibility established, delegation of authority to the CB can function as an effective preventive device against the repetition of such episodes. The recent enhancements in the legal independence of the central banks of Chile, Mexico and Argentina can be understood in these terms.

The recent tendency of political authorities to delegate more authority to the CB by legal means is also spreading to industrial economies like New Zealand, France, Spain and the United Kingdom.[8] This raises a question about the effectiveness of legal stipulations in assuring the actual independence of the CB. Legal independence appears to be a necessary but not sufficient condition for actual independence. In the absence of legal defences with respect to matters such as job security of the bank high officials, clear rules for the resolution of conflicts between the bank and the political establishment and limitations on borrowing by government from the bank, the latter cannot be independent. But this does not mean that legal independence alone is *always* sufficient for assuring actual independence. Many developing countries have copied various features of the CB laws of industrial nations, but have failed to apply them with an equal amount of determination. A striking example is Argentina between 1950 and 1989. During this period the legal term in office of the CB governor was four years, but the *actual* average term in office was about one year only. It therefore appears that the effectiveness of legal independence in providing actual CBI depends on the general respect for the rule of law.

Since compliance with the law is generally better within industrialised countries than in LDCs and in democracies than in non-democratic regimes,[9] my expectation is that ongoing legal reforms of CB charters will be more effective in assuring higher independence for industrial democracies than in the remaining group of countries. A corollary is that recent central bank reforms in former socialist countries are unlikely to be successful in the absence of sufficient respect for the rule of law.

IV THE ROLE OF MONETARY AND OF
INFLATION TARGETS

Monetary targets, official forecasts, or statements of intention are (or have been) made in Germany, the United States, Japan, Britain, France, Canada, Switzerland, Australia and New Zealand. These are imperfect, but not meaningless, indicators of planned policy actions and of future inflation. Their precision varies across countries. Thus, until 1989, the pre-announcements of the Bundesbank and of the Bank of Japan proved to be more reliable than those of the Federal Reserve Bank and of the Bank of England. Evidence from approximately twenty countries suggests that the rate of inflation is lower in countries that make announcements and even lower in those whose announcements turn out to be more precise.[10]

The collapse of the ERM and the quest for an alternative nominal anchor have recently revived the interest in monetary or in inflation targets among policy-makers. In spite of the evidence cited above, the usefulness of pre-announcements and of monetary stock targets in particular has not gained universal acceptance. One objection is based on the observation that due to financial innovations the monetary stock targets are not as meaningful as they were when the structure of the financial system was more stable.[11]

Even if one accepts, as I do, that pre-announcement of *some* target is a good idea, it is not obvious whether it should refer to an intermediate target or to a final objective and, in the first case, which intermediate stock should be targeted. As a normative matter two opposing considerations should affect the choice of target-controllability versus transparency. Two extreme possibilities can be used to illustrate the tradeoffs involved. At one extreme the CB could commit to targeting of the monetary base, and at the other to an inflation target. In the first case the precision of control is high since the base is part of the bank's liabilities over which control is perfect. However, due to the relatively tenuous connection between the base and the level of prices such a commitment is not very transparent, and particularly so for individuals who do not operate routinely in financial markets. At the other end, an inflation or a price level target is highly transparent since it is directly focused on the final objective, but the CB controls it imperfectly.

In between those two extremes there is a whole range of possible intermediate targets such as M_1, M_2, M_3, etc. which yield different combinations of transparency and of control precision. As one moves away from the base towards wider aggregates and finally to an inflation target, it is likely that transparency increases, but also that precision decreases. As a matter of principle the ultimate choice of target should take into consideration the impact of each of those elements on the formation of inflationary expectations and on credibility.[12]

A related issue concerns the identity of the institution that is empowered to decide the type and the quantitative magnitude of the target. This question is connected to the issue of CB accountability which is discussed in the following section.

V CENTRAL BANK INDEPENDENCE
AND ACCOUNTABILITY

Delegation of authority to an independent CB is sometimes criticised as being undemocratic on the grounds that it entrusts economic policy to technocrats who have not been elected by voters. Since the inflationary bias of policy arises precisely because of the way politicians operate, this argument raises a dilemma. CBI reduces the inflationary bias of policy at the cost of placing policy in the hands of unelected officials. This dilemma becomes more important in times of particularly large unexpected shocks. One way of dealing with it and still to reap the benefits of delegation during tranquil times is to grant independence, but also to introduce escape clauses into the CB law. Both the 1989 CB of New Zealand law, as well as the recent Roll (1993) proposal for reforming the Bank of England charter allow the political principals to override the decisions of the CB. However, this has to be done overtly and tabled in parliament. This contrasts with the subtle and often covert political pressures that are exerted by the political establishment on the U.S. Federal Reserve.

A related, but not identical, objection is that independence without accountability may induce central bankers to behave in an opportunistic manner that will not lead to the achievement of society's policy objectives in various areas including, in particular, price stability. On this view the CB is a bureaucratic agent with its own private agenda which is not necessarily identical to that of society. This problem can be handled by devising an optimal contract between the political principals and the CB who is viewed as an agent. The basic idea is to create a structure of incentives that will induce the officials of the CB to act in a way that maximises social welfare.[13] The new CB law in New Zealand possesses such an element. It requires the governor to pre-announce an inflation target and makes his tenure dependent on being sufficiently close to the target.[14]

An attractive feature of the recent New Zealand legislation is that it gives the bank reasonable authority, but also holds the chief executive officer of the bank accountable for achieving the pre-announced inflation target. In addition, since they can always override the governor, the political principals retain final authority over monetary policy. However, since they must use this authority overtly they cannot do that and simultaneously hold the bank responsible for not attaining the inflation target. One virtue of this arrangement is that it deters the political principals from using their override option frivolously because once they exercise it the blame for not attaining the inflation target becomes theirs.

From the point of view of the optimal contract framework the New Zealand law, although original and novel, is not without loopholes. One loophole is that it lets the agent (in this case the governor) choose the inflation target. This can create a moral hazard problem, since the governor may be tempted to choose a target that is more easy to achieve than that which is feasible. New Zealand probably has in places less formal mechanisms that reduce the likelihood of such an event. The point is only that future CB law framers will have to pay attention to this factor.

One practical difficulty with the application of the optimal contract framework to the question of CBI is that it is based on the presumption that the political principals devise the contract as if they were a benevolent social planner. However, in the presence of ideological differences and re-election concerns, the political principals may choose to frame a CB law that deviates from the one that would have been chosen by a social planner.[15]

VI PRICE STABILITY VERSUS FINANCIAL STABILITY

One of the traditional functions of central banks is to contain runs on deposits and financial panics by acting as a lender of last resort. A related activity is prudential regulation and supervision of financial institutions. The latter is meant to contain various moral hazard problems of banks and other financial institutions. The institutional location of prudential regulation, supervision and deposit insurance varies widely across countries. In some countries it is performed by the CB and in others by separate regulatory bodies.[16]

The recent reorientation of central bank objectives towards more emphasis on price stability requires a fresh look at the tradeoffs between price stability and the lender of last resort functions of the CB as well as at the location of various regulatory functions between the CB and other institutions. Is there a tradeoff between price stability and financial stability? Baltensperger (1993) argues persuasively that, at least in the long run, the pursuit of price stability actually strengthens financial stability. Financial disruptions and crises are frequently linked to instability of inflation and interest rates. Sharp fluctuations in interest rates induce large changes in the asset values of banks and make it more likely that financial crises will occur. The pursuit of price stability prevents this sequence of events from occurring in the first place.

However, even against the background of reasonably stable prices, there may be a short-run tradeoff between financial stability and price stability. Since they lend for longer periods of time than the periods for which they borrow, banks' profits and liquidity are adversely affected by increases in the level of interest rates that were unanticipated when they committed funds to (fixed rate) loan contracts. The reason is that, when this occurs, each individual bank must raise the rate on deposits in order to prevent a drain of funds. In such circumstances marginal banks experience liquidity problems that force the CB to raise the money supply in order to inject liquidity into the system. Thus, short-run liquidity problems force the CB to de-emphasise the price stability objective, at least temporarily in order to perform its lender of last resort function.[17]

However, to the extent that interest rates fluctuate randomly around some long-run value, this tradeoff is only temporary. This reason is that when interest rates unexpectedly go down, raising the liquidity of banks, the CB can mop up the previously created liquidity without endangering the stability of the financial system. The upshot is that the CB can, within some range, perform the lender of last resort function without abandonment of price stability as its primary objective. Institutionally this combined objective can be attained by directing the CB to maintain on average a low rate of growth of liquidity, but to raise it above the average in periods of liquidity squeezes and to reduce it below the average in the remaining periods. This argument is obviously predicated on the presumption that effective safeguards against base drift can be found. In the absence of such safeguards the excess liquidity injected during liquidity crises will not necessarily be mopped out in the remaining periods.

What is conventional wisdom with respect to the optimal allocation of regulation, deposit insurance and the lender of last resort function between the CB and other institutions? Some of the arguments for and against separation of those functions from general monetary policy (to be aimed at price stability) are presented in the recent Roll (1993) report for reforming the Bank of England (pp. 43–5). Those arguments are not reproduced here. Instead I raise an additional factor for consideration.

When deposit insurance and other prudential functions are allocated to the CB, large-scale bank failures risk being monetised more easily than when those functions are performed outside the CB. In the first case bad debts are likely to be automatically monetised without much budgetary legislation. By contrast when these functions are institutionally separate from the CB it is more likely that the budgetary implications of rescue operations will be more visible to the public eye. This should help restrain both monetisation as well as overly generous rescue operations. A possible drawback, however, is that financial crises will not be handled as swiftly as when the CB has direct responsibility. This suggests that the basic tradeoff here is between the risk of fiscal permissiveness coupled with excess monetisation on the one hand and the risk of an insufficiently quick response to financial crises on the other.

VII CONCLUDING REMARKS AND A LOOK AHEAD

The recent dramatic acceleration in delegation of legal authority to central banks raises an interesting positive question. Why did the movement towards more delegation happen only recently rather than in previous periods? There are, I believe, several reasons. First is the fact that highly independent banks such as the Bundesbank and the Swiss National Bank produced a very good record in achieving price stability. Second, the inflationary experiences of the 1970s increased the quest of the public and its elected officials in developed economies for price stability. The conjunction of these two elements raised the respectability of monetarists' prescriptions, and at least partly, triggered the Volcker and Thatcher deflations in the early 1980s. Although these deflations were achieved without formal enhancements in the independence of the Fed and of the Bank of England, they did raise their prestige and created a sympathetic attitude towards the idea of CBI.

During the mid- and the second part of the 1980s the quest for price stability spread to high-inflation countries in Latin America and elsewhere. After stabilising inflation, countries such as Chile, Mexico and Argentina started to look for devices that would prevent the recurrence of high inflation. Under these conditions delegation of more authority to the CB was a natural course of action.

The demonstration effect of the success of CBI in assuring price stability was particularly strong in the EMS countries whose members managed to get, for a while, some of the credibility of the Bundesbank by maintaining fixed parities with the mark. The prospect of a European Monetary Union, the Maastricht Treaty and the breakdown of the ERM all reinforced the search for alternative nominal anchors. The record of the Bundesbank and the insistence of Germany on structuring a future European CB on the Bundesbank model supplied further impetus for achieving nominal stability by granting more independence to the CB.

The breakdown of the Soviet Union and the attempt of former socialist states to create institutions that would quickly transform them into market economies is another strong current source of demand for CBI.[18] Lurking behind the recent wave of delegation of authority to the CB is the removal of barriers on international capital movements. This broadens opportunities for raising capital abroad and induces politicians to compete more strenuously to attract finance and investment from abroad and to prevent capital flights. Ceding new authority to the CB helps them attract and/or reassure actual or potential investors and creditors.[19]

Looking ahead into the future, two big unanswered questions are: First, if a European Monetary Union is created what should be the internal structure of its governing body? Second, what are the prospects for actual CBI for economies in transition? With respect to the first question preliminary work by Cukierman (1991) and by Von Hagen and Suppel (1994) indicates that the commitment to price stability is likely to be stronger under a centralised than under a decentralised structure for the European CB. However, much more additional work remains to be done.

In spite of recent legal reforms in the charters of some of the economies in transition, the attainment of true independence is not likely to occur quickly for several reasons. The narrowness of domestic capital markets makes it likely that in spite of legal limitations on lending to government, the main source of financing of budget deficits will be seigniorage. Evidence on compliance with legal limitation on lending from the rest of the world indicates that it is generally poor (Cukierman (1992) pp. 441–3). In addition, the existence of financial arrears and the lack of developed capital markets for private investment may force central banks of economies in transition to function as investment banks at the cost of price stability. Finally, legal independence can assure actual independence provided there is enough tradition and respect for the rule of law. If the experience of LDCs is any guide, legal independence alone may not suffice to deliver actual CBI in some of the economies in transition.

NOTES

1 A detailed analysis of this mechanism appears in chapter 3 of Cukierman (1992). Other motives for monetary expansion and the emergence of inflationary biases are analysed in other chapters in part 1 of the same book. Decentralisation of monetary policy decisions across different policy-makers with differing budgetary objectives also leads to an inflationary bias that rises with the number of policy-makers involved. This type of bias is due to the fact that each policy-maker gives a higher weight to the financing of his preferred expenditures than to inflation prevention since the inflationary consequences of raising his expenditures are of second nature in comparison to the benefits of raising his preferred expenditures. An analysis of this mechanism appears in Aizenman (1992).
2 Alesina (1988), Grilli, Masciandaro and Tabellini (1991), Cukierman (1992), Cukierman, Webb and Neyapti (1992).
3 Details appear in Pal (1993).
4 Information on CB governors' turnover and on its relation with inflation appears in chapters 19 and 20 of Cukierman (1992) and in Cukierman, Webb and Neyapti (1992). Information on the vulnerability of the governor to political change and on the relation of this variable with inflation appears in Cukierman and Webb (1994). Interestingly, the evidence shows no relation between legal independence and inflation in LDCs. This finding is consistent with the view that legal independence is a poor proxy for actual independence in this group of countries.
5 Such a survey can be found in Cukierman (1993).
6 Details on the construction of the first three indices appear in chapter 19 of Cukierman (1992) and in Cukierman, Webb and Neyapti (1992). Data on the political vulnerability of the CB governor is presented in Cukierman and Webb (1994). A general discussion of the relative merits and limitations of the various indices appears in Cukierman (1993).
7 The first four conclusions draw on work presented in the references that appear in the previous footnote. The remaining conclusions draw on Cukierman, Kalaitzidakis, Summers and Webb (1993) and on Alesina and Summers (1993).
8 A positive analysis of some of the factors that induce politicians to delegate authority to the CB appears in Cukierman (1994). De Haan and Van't Hag (1993) present some evidence.
9 More information on these issues appears in Pal (1993) and in Cukierman and Webb (1994).
10 Details appear in table 20.4 of Cukierman (1992).
11 A discussion of this issue and of the recent Canadian experience with inflation targeting appears in Friedman (1994) and in Freedman (1994).
12 The effect of transparency on credibility in the context of alternative exchange rate regimes is discussed in Cukierman, Kiguel and Leiderman (1996).
13 Persson and Tabellini (1994) cast this problem into an optimal contract framework.
14 A description and evaluation of the recent New Zealand CB law can be found in Wood (1994).
15 A positive analysis of the incentives of politicians when they decide how much authority to delegate to the CB appears in Cukierman (1994).
16 A detailed description and analysis of these institutional arrangements in various countries appears in Goodhart and Shoenmaker (1993).
17 A detailed verbal and analytical discussion of this mechanism appears in chapter 7 of Cukierman (1992). The introduction of variable rate loans obviously mitigates its impact. But as long as rates on some loans are more sticky than on deposits, there is some tradeoff between financial stability and price stability.
18 A discussion of CB reform in economies in transition appears in Hochreiter (1994).
19 This point of view is developed by Maxfield (1993).

REFERENCES

Aizenman, J. (1992). 'Competitive externalities and the optimal seigniorage.' *Journal of Money, Credit and Banking*, vol. 24, pp. 61–71.

Alesina, A. (1988). 'Macroeconomics and politics.' In *NBER Macroeconomics Annual* (ed. Stanley Fischer). Cambridge, MA: MIT Press.

Baltensperger, E. (1993). 'Central bank policy and lending of last resort.' In *Prudential Regulation, Supervision and Monetary Policy*, Proceedings of a conference organized by the 'Paolo Baffi' Center at Bocconi University, Milan, February 1993 (ed. F. Bruni).

Cukierman, A. (1991). 'Policy outcomes in stage two and in the EMS versus outcomes in a union.' Presented at the joint *CEPR*/'Paolo Baffi' conference on Monetary Policy in Stage Two of EMU, Milan, September 1991.

Cukierman, A. (1992). *Central Bank Strategy, Credibility and Independence: Theory and Evidence*. Cambridge, MA: MIT Press.

Cukierman, A. (1993). 'Central bank independence, political influence and macroeconomic performance: a survey of recent developments.' *Cuadernos de Economía*, vol. 30, pp. 271–92.

Cukierman, A. (1994). 'Commitment through delegation, political influence and central bank independence.' In *A Framework for Monetary Stability*, Financial and Monetary Studies (ed. J.O. de Beaufort Wijnholds, S.C.W. Eijffinger and L.H. Hoogduin). Dordrecht: Kluwer Academic Publishers.

Cukierman, A., Webb, S.B. and Neyapti, B. (1992). 'Measuring the independence of central banks and its effect on policy outcomes.' *World Bank Economic Review*, vol. 6, pp. 353–98.

Cukierman, A., Kalaitzidakis, P., Summers, L.H. and Webb, S.B. (1993). 'Central bank independence, growth, investment and real rates.' *Carnegie–Rochester Conference Series on Public Policy*, vol. 39, Autumn.

Cukierman, A. and Webb, S.B. (1994). 'Political influence on the central bank – international evidence.' Manuscript, Tel-Aviv University, January.

Cukierman, A., Kiguel, M. and Leiderman, L. (1996). 'Transparency and the evolution of exchange rate flexibility in the aftermath of disinflation.' In *Financial Factors in Economic Stabilization and Growth* (ed. Mario I. Blejer, Z. Eckstein, Z. Hercowitz and L. Leiderman). Cambridge: Cambridge University Press.

de Haan, J. and Van't Hag, G.J. (1993). 'Determinants of central bank independence: some provisional empirical evidence.' Manuscript, University of Groningen, December.

Freedman, C. (1994). 'Formal targets for inflation reduction: the Canadian experience.' In *A Framework for Monetary Stability*, Financial and Monetary Studies (ed. J.O. de Beaufort Wijnholds, S.C.W. Eijffinger and L.H. Hoogduin). Dordrecht: Kluwer Academic Publishers.

Friedman, B.M. (1994). 'Intermediate targets versus information variables as operating guides for monetary policy.' In *A Framework for Monetary Stability*, Financial and Monetary Studies (ed. J.O. de Beaufort Wijnholds, S.C.W. Eijffinger and L.H. Hoogduin). Dordrecht: Kluwer Academic Publishers.

Goodhart, C. and Shoenmaker, D. (1993). 'Institutional separation between supervisory and monetary agencies.' In *Prudential Regulation, Supervision and Monetary Policy*, Proceedings of a conference organized by the 'Paolo Baffi' Center at Bocconi University, Milan, February 1993 (ed. F. Bruni).

Grilli, V., Masciandaro, D. and Tabellini, G. (1991). 'Political and monetary institutions and public financial policies in the industrial countries.' *Economic Policy*, vol. 13, pp. 341–92.

Hochreiter, E. (1994). 'Central banking in economies in transition: institutional and exchange rate issues.' Paper presented at the 'Paolo Baffi' conference on Central Bank Independence and Accountability, March 1994, Milan, Italy.

Maxfield, S. (1993). 'International sources of central bank convergence in the 1990s.' Manuscript, Political Science Department, Yale University, October.

Noga, P. (1993). 'The effect of statutory laws on turnover at the central bank.' Graduate Term Paper, Department of Economics, Tel-Aviv University.

Persson, T. and Tabellini, G. (1994). 'Credibility and accountability in monetary policy.' Paper presented at the 'Paolo Baffi' conference on Central Bank Independence and Accountability, March 1994, Milan, Italy.

Roll, E. (1993). *Independent and Accountable: A New Mandate for the Bank of England* – A CEPR Sponsored Report of an Independent Panel chaired by Eric Roll, October.

Von Hagen, J. and Suppel, R. (1994). 'Central bank constitutions for federal monetary unions.' Paper presented at the 'Paolo Baffi' conference on Central Bank Independence and Accountability, March 1994, Milan, Italy.

Wood, G.E. (1994). 'Central bank independence in New Zealand: analytical, empirical and institutional aspects.' Paper presented at the 'Paolo Baffi' conference on Central Bank Independence and Accountability, March 1994, Milan, Italy.

Questions

1 'The international monetary system has developed into a market-led system.' Discuss the implications of this statement for monetary policy design at the national level.
2 Suppose that the asset-induced demand for money develops anti-cyclically relative to transactions-demand for money. Explain why this may be the case and comment on the implications for assigning monetary policy to a low inflation target.
3 'Central bank independence may resolve the credibility problem, but it leads to a problem of accountability.' Discuss with reference to the UK experience.
4 'The current enthusiasm for central bank independence rests on the acceptance that there is no medium- or long-term employment–inflation trade-off to be exploited.' Discuss.
5 'Central bank independence offers a free lunch. It brings about lower inflation without interfering with the process of growth.' Discuss.
6 'Central bank independence is not necessarily a more effective commitment device compared to a fixed exchange rate commitment.' Discuss.

Further reading and references

FURTHER READING

For issues raised by the change in the international monetary system, consult Kenen (1994) and BIS (1993). For arguments in favour of nominal GDP rather than inflation targeting, see Meade (1994). On the case for and against central bank independence and the issue of accountability in the UK context, see the Roll Report (1993). For a comprehensive review of the issues surrounding central bank independence, see Cukierman (1992). On the issue of commitment via delegation, see Cukierman (1994). For a critique of the central bank independence argument, see Posen (1993).

REFERENCES

BIS (1993), *Annual Report*, Basle: Bank for International Settlements.

Cukierman, A. (1992), *Central Bank Strategy, Credibility and Independence: Theory and Evidence*, Cambridge, Mass.: MIT Press.

Cukierman, A. (1994), 'Commitment through delegation, political influence and central bank independence', in J.O. de Beaufort Wijnholds, S.C.W. Eijffinger and L.H. Hoogduin (eds), *A Framework for Monetary Stability*, Dordrecht: Kluwer Academic Publishers.

Kenen, P.B. (ed.) (1994) *Managing the World Economy: Fifty Years after Bretton Woods*, Washington DC: Institute for International Economics.

Meade, J.E. (1994), *Full Employment without Inflation*, London: Social Market Foundation.

Posen, A. (1993), 'Why central bank independence does not cause low inflation: there is no institutional fix for politics', in *The Amex Bank Review, Finance and International Economy*, Oxford: Oxford University Press.

Roll Report (1993), *Independent and Accountable: A New Mandate for the Bank of England* (A report of an independent panel chaired by Eric Roll), London: The Centre for Economic Policy Research.

Part VI

Exchange rate determination and policy

Introduction

In the preceding chapters, the choice of exchange rate regime has been treated more or less as a 'non-problem'. The approach has been that a country would choose between a fixed or a floating exchange rate regime, and the policy implications would be analysed accordingly. This assumption, however, begs two important questions: what do we know about the behaviour of the exchange rate and which exchange rate regime is more appropriate? The articles in Part VI address these questions.

MacDonald and Taylor (Chapter 16) tackle the first question. The article introduces the two major theories of exchange rate determination and reviews the empirical work testing their relevance. MacDonald and Taylor begin with an overview of the early contributions to exchange rate economics. They give credit to pioneering work by Meade, Friedman, Mundell and Fleming. Then they introduce the monetary approach to exchange rate determination – in its flexi-price and sticky-price varieties. The common thread in these versions is that the determinants of the exchange rate are the relative stocks of and demand for domestic and foreign currency. This is quite intuitive because the exchange rate is nothing but the price of foreign currency in terms of domestic currency. Then, assuming that the demand for money is given and stable, the exchange rate will increase (the domestic currency will depreciate) if the domestic money supply grows faster than the foreign money supply.

Where the flexi-price and sticky-price approaches differ is the speed at which purchasing power parity (PPP) is restored. As we know, purchasing power parity is ensured by arbitrage and implies that domestic and foreign goods would be sold at the same price when the price is defined in a common unit. The flexi-price monetary approach assumes that PPP holds continuously; whereas the sticky-price approach envisages that goods prices would adjust sluggishly compared to asset prices – of which the exchange rate is one. Despite this difference, both varieties of the monetary approach predict the following:

1   The domestic currency will depreciate if the domestic money supply increases relative to foreign money supply.
2   The domestic currency will appreciate if domestic income increases faster

than foreign income (as the increase in domestic income increases the demand for domestic currency).

3   The domestic currency will depreciate if domestic interest rates are higher than foreign interest rates (as higher domestic interest rates reduce the demand for domestic currency).

As indicated by MacDonald and Taylor, however, empirical support for these predictions has been in short supply. The behaviour of the exchange rate, especially in the short run, has proved more erratic than what the monetary approach would predict. To address this problem, the sticky-price approach provided an elegant explanation as to why short-run exchange rate movements might over- or under-shoot the long-run equilibrium. The explanation was based on the different speeds at which the exchange rate and goods prices would adjust. As the former adjusts more quickly because of the faster arbitrage in the foreign exchange market, it will depreciate (appreciate) more than necessary in response to a monetary expansion (contraction). Then, to return to the long-run PPP value, the exchange rate will have to appreciate (depreciate) – thus leading to excessive volatility in the short run.

The portfolio-balance approach develops a different explanation for the short-run volatility of the exchange rate. On the one hand, this explanation concurs with the sticky-price monetary approach as it also considers the goods prices to be constant in the short run. On the other hand, however, it differs in a significant way as it considers the effect of monetary policy change not only on the demand for money but also the demand for other assets, including domestic and foreign bonds. In other words, it takes into account the interaction between the exchange rate and the level of wealth. For example, a monetary expansion will cause depreciation not only because it increases the domestic money supply relative to foreign money supply, but also because it will increase the level of wealth which, in turn, increases the demand for foreign bonds. In addition, the impact of monetary expansion on the exchange rate will differ depending on whether the expansion is intro-duced by open market operations in domestic currency or foreign exchange market operations.

MacDonald and Taylor then provide a comprehensive review of the empirical research on exchange rate determination. Their findings can be summarised as follows: (i) the exchange rate behaviour in the period soon after the move to floating tends to be compatible with the predictions of the flexi-price monetary models; (ii) the flexi-price monetary models begin to fail to explain the exchange rate behaviour from late 1970s onwards; (iii) the empirical support for the sticky-price monetary models as well as portfolio-balance models is mixed. Given these findings, it can be argued that one is left with more rather than less mystery about exchange rate behaviour. Although such pessimism is justified to some extent, the positive contributions of the monetary and portfolio-balance approaches to exchange rate determination and the sophisticated methods developed for testing their relevance should not be ignored.

First of all, the research effort has enabled the students of open-economy macroeconomics to extend the knowledge frontier. Second, it highlighted the probability that flexible exchange rates, at least in the short run, would tend to be more volatile than changes in economic fundamentals would justify. Third, it prompted a new line of research focusing on micro-level factors that may generate excessive exchange rate volatility.

Both monetary and portfolio-balance approaches try to explain such volatility without questioning the efficiency of the foreign exchange market – i.e. without questioning the extent to which market operators act on the basis of the information they have about economic fundamentals. The new line of research distances itself from this assumption and explores the possibility that, at least in the short run, foreign exchange market operators may be engaged in extrapolative behaviour. The most common type of such behaviour is to use recurring patterns in past exchange rate data as a basis for predictions involving a short time-span. Another reason for foreign exchange market inefficiency could be due to speculative bubbles. In this case, the foreign exchange market operators are acting rationally, but creating a bandwagon effect by relying too heavily on the most recent information available to them.

The article by Frankel in Chapter 17 constitutes a perfect complement to MacDonald and Taylor for two reasons. First, it reviews the most important contributions to the literature on extrapolative behaviour and speculative bubbles. Second, it takes a further step to discuss the ways in which exchange rate volatility can be stabilised. Frankel agrees with the findings of the research pointing to foreign exchange market inefficiency, but he has serious doubts as to whether governments can manage the exchange rate. First, he is aware of the argument that fixed exchange rates can be an anchor for disinflation. But he criticises the fixed exchange rate option because such arrangements are generally conducive to foreign exchange crises. These could be either speculative crises as in the case of the Exchange Rate Mechanism (ERM) in 1992–3 or crises justified by economic fundamentals. Second, he agrees that a tax on foreign exchange transactions can help in reducing exchange rate volatility, but he is suspicious of the extent to which such a measure can be implemented internationally. Finally, he considers the relevance of target zones, supported by international co-operation. Frankel argues that such arrangements tend to suffer from a trade-off between credibility and policy independence. Therefore, he concludes that the recommendations for exchange rate policy must be necessarily eclectic in the sense that they must reflect a country's preference for policy independence and its need for credible disinflationary policies.

The last article in this part, by Edwards, squares the circle by presenting the findings of an empirical test concerning the determinants of the exchange rate policy choices. Edwards identifies a number of political economy factors that may affect a country's exchange rate policy choice. These are: political instability, inflationary temptations and the history of inflation. He reports that a country is more likely to choose a floating exchange rate regime the higher is the level of political instability, the higher is the inflationary temptation, and the longer is the history of inflation.

These findings enable us to make a detour and qualify Frankel's pessimism about the extent to which the exchange rate can be managed. It is true that fixed or managed exchange rates can be conducive to foreign exchange crises and international co-operation may be difficult to secure. These problems, however, must be set against the problem identified by Edwards – namely the attractiveness of the floating regime for countries that are either less concerned with or unable to pursue credible macroeconomic policies. In addition, foreign exchange regimes may be prone to speculative foreign exchange crises but these may also be due to lax macroeconomic policies that undermine the credibility of the fixed rate. Then, an inevitable question follows: will the case for a fixed exchange regime not be strengthened if foreign exchange crises are due to credibility problems and if the floating regime constitutes an escape route for countries unwilling or unable to commit themselves to sound macroeconomic policies? We hope that the articles in this part and the extensive list of references they contain will prompt further reading and elaboration on this question.

16 Exchange rate economics

A survey

Ronald MacDonald and Mark P. Taylor*
IMF Staff Papers, vol. 39, no. 1 (1992), pp. 1–27

The past two decades have seen an enormous growth in the literature on exchange rate economics. Given the importance attached to the exchange rate in the success or failure of an open economy, it is not surprising that exchange rate economics is one of the most heavily researched areas of the discipline. The period since the advent of generalized floating exchange rates in 1973 has generated a wealth of data on exchange rates and on the factors that supposedly determine them, giving econometricians and applied economists an unprecedented opportunity to test a number of propositions relating to foreign exchange markets. Despite this extensive research, a large number of unresolved issues remain, and exchange rate economics continues to be an extremely challenging area.

This paper surveys the vast literature that this intense research activity has generated. In particular, we examine the two main views of exchange rate determination that have evolved since the early 1970s: the monetary approach (in flexible-price, sticky-price, and real interest differential formulations) and the portfolio balance approach. We then examine the empirical evidence on these models and conclude by speculating how the future research strategy is likely to develop. We also discuss the literature on foreign exchange market efficiency, exchange rates and "news," and international parity conditions.

This contribution may be viewed as an extension and update of earlier surveys of empirical work on exchange rates by, among others, Kohlhagen (1978), Levich (1979, 1985), and Isard (1988), and as a simplification and synthesis of surveys of exchange rate theory by Mussa (1984), Frenkel and Mussa (1985), and Obstfeld and Stockman (1985).

*   © 1992 International Monetary Fund. Mark P. Taylor, an Economist in the External Adjustment Division of the Research Department, holds master's degrees from the Universities of Oxford and London and a doctorate from London University. He was previously Morgan Grenfell Professor of Financial Markets at the City University Business School, London.

Ronald MacDonald is Robert Fleming Professor of Finance and Investment at Dundee University and holds a bachelor's degree from Heriot Watt University and master's and doctoral degrees from Manchester University. This paper was largely written while he was a Visiting Scholar in the Research Department.

The authors are grateful to a number of IMF colleagues for comments on a previous draft.

I THEORIES OF EXCHANGE RATE DETERMINATION

Early contributions to the postwar literature on exchange rate economics include Nurkse (1945) and Friedman (1953). Both of these contributions are to a large extent concerned with the role of speculation in foreign exchange markets. Nurkse warns against the dangers of "bandwagon effects," which may generate market instability.[1] Friedman's classic apologia for floating exchange rates (Friedman, 1953) is remarkable in its anticipation of much of the literature of the following two decades and is still cited as the seminal article on stabilizing speculation.

Meade (1951a, Part III) laid the foundations for simultaneous analysis of internal and external balance in an open economy, which were built upon a decade later in the pathbreaking contributions of Mundell (1961, 1962, 1963, 1968) and Fleming (1962). In the verbal exposition of his capital account theory, Meade worked through the stock equilibrium implications of a movement in international interest rate differentials, but did not faithfully represent this feature in his mathematical exposition (Meade, 1951b, p. 103). Mundell (1961, 1962, 1963, 1968) and Fleming (1962) followed Meade's mathematical representation and thus abstracted from the stock-flow implications of interest rate differential changes. Therefore, although the integration of asset markets and capital mobility into open economy macro-economics was an important contribution of the Mundell–Fleming model, the model was largely rejected on a priori grounds as a serious contender for the explanation of exchange rate movements at the beginning of the recent float. This was because it was judged to contain a fundamental flaw—it is cast almost entirely in flow terms. In particular, the model allows current account imbalances to be offset by flows across the capital account, without any requirement of eventual stock equilibrium in the holding of net foreign assets.

Other papers dating from the 1950s—Polak (1957) and Johnson (1958)—had stressed the distinction between stock and flow equilibria in the open economy context, and this was to become a hallmark of the monetary approach to balance of payments analysis (see, for example, Frenkel and Johnson (1976), and subsequently, the monetary approach to the exchange rate (see, for example, Frenkel and Johnson, 1978). More generally, work done in the late 1960s by Oates (1966), McKinnon and Oates (1966), McKinnon (1969), and Ott and Ott (1965) began to integrate analyses of open economy macroeconomics and financial portfolio balance by imposing stock equilibrium constraints. Later work by Branson (1968), Willet and Forte (1969), and Kouri and Porter (1974) built on this work by incorporating more general features of financial portfolio choice (Tobin, 1965).[2]

Flexible-price monetary model

Since an exchange rate is, by definition, the price of one country's money in terms of that of another, it makes sense to analyze the determinants of that price in terms of the outstanding stocks of and demand for the two monies. This is the basic rationale of the monetary approach to the exchange rate (Frenkel (1976), Kouri (1976), and Mussa (1976, 1979)).

The early, flexible-price monetary model relies on the twin assumptions of (continuous) purchasing power parity (PPP) and the existence of stable money demand functions for the domestic and foreign economies. The (logarithm of the) demand for money may be assumed to depend on (the logarithm of) real income, y, the (logarithm of the) price level, p, and the level of the interest rate, r (foreign variables are denoted by an asterisk). Monetary equilibria in the domestic and foreign country, respectively, are given by

$$m_t^s = p_t + \phi y_t - \lambda r_t \tag{1}$$

and

$$m_t^{s*} = p_t^* + \phi^* y_t^* - \lambda^* r_t^* \tag{2}$$

Equilibrium in the traded goods market ensues when there are no further profitable incentives for trade flows to occur—that is, when prices in a common currency are equalized and PPP holds. The PPP condition is

$$s_t = p_t - p_t^* \tag{3}$$

where s_t is the logarithm of the nominal exchange rate (domestic price of foreign currency). Thus, if PPP holds continuously, the logarithm of the real exchange rate, q_t, say ($q_t \equiv s_t - p_t + p_t^*$), is a constant. The world price, p_t^*, is exogenous to the domestic economy, being determined by the world money supply. The domestic money supply determines the domestic price level, and hence, the exchange rate is determined by relative money supplies. Algebraically, substituting equations (1) and (2) into (3) yields, after rearranging

$$s_t = (m^s - m^{s*})_t - \phi y_t + \phi^* y_t^* + \lambda r_t - \lambda^* r_t^* \tag{4}$$

which is the basic flexible-price monetary model equation. Equation (4) says that an increase in the domestic money supply, relative to the foreign money stock, will lead to a rise in s_t—that is, a fall in the value of the domestic currency in terms of the foreign currency. This seems intuitive enough. An increase in domestic output, as opposed to the domestic money supply, *appreciates* the domestic currency (s_t falls). Similarly, a rise in domestic interest rates depreciates the domestic currency (in the Mundell–Fleming model; this would lead to capital inflows and, hence, an *appreciation*).

In order to resolve these apparent paradoxes, one has to remember the fundamental role of relative money demand in the flexible-price model. A relative rise in domestic real income creates an excess demand for the domestic money stock. As agents try to increase their (real) money balances, they reduce expenditure and prices fall until money market equilibrium is achieved. As prices fall, PPP ensures an appreciation of the domestic currency in terms of the foreign currency. An exactly converse analysis explains the response of the exchange rate to the interest rate—an increase in interest rates reduces the demand for money and so leads to a depreciation.

It is instructive to write the equation for the flexible-price monetary model in two alternative but equivalent formulations. Assuming that the domestic and foreign money demand coefficients are equal ($\phi = \phi^*$, $\lambda = \lambda^*$), equation (4) reduces to

$$s_t = (m - m^*)_t - \phi(y - y^*)_t + \lambda(r - r^*)_t \tag{5}$$

A further assumption underlying the flexible-price model is that uncovered interest parity holds continuously—that is, the domestic–foreign interest differential is just equal to the expected rate of depreciation of the domestic currency. Thus, using a superscript e to denote agents' expectations formed at time t, we may substitute Δs^e_{t+1} for $(r - r)^*_t$ in equation (5) to get

$$s_t = (m - m^*)_t - \phi(y - y^*)_t + \lambda \Delta s^e_t t_{+1} \tag{6}$$

Thus, the expected change in the exchange rate and the expected change in the interest differential, both of which reflect inflationary expectations, are interchangeable in this model. Some researchers relax the constraint that the income and interest rate elasticities are equal:

$$s_t = (m - m^*)_t - \phi y_t + \phi^* y^*_t + \lambda \Delta s^e_{t+1} \tag{7}$$

Note also that equation (7) can be expressed as

$$s_t = (1 + \lambda)^{-1}(m - m^*)_t - (1 + \lambda)^{-1}\phi y_t + (1 + \lambda)^{-1}\phi y^*_t + \\ \lambda(1 + \lambda)^{-1}s^e_{t+1} \tag{8}$$

If expectations are assumed to be rational,[3] then by iterating forward, it is easy to show that equation (7) can be expressed in the "forward solution" form:

$$s_t = (1 + \lambda)^{-1}\sum_{i=0}^{\infty}\left[\frac{\lambda}{1+\lambda}\right]^i [(m - m^*)^e_{t+i} + \phi y^e_{t+i} + \phi^* y^{*e}_{t+i}] \tag{9}$$

where it is understood that expectations are conditioned on information at time t. Equation (9) makes clear that the monetary model, with rational expectations, involves solving for the expected future path of the "forcing variables"—that is, relative money and income. As is common in rational expectations models, the presence of the discount, factor, $\lambda/(1 + \lambda) < 1$, in equation (9) implies that expectations of the forcing variables need not, in general, be formed into the *infinite* future—so long as the forcing variables are expected to grow at a rate less than $(1/\lambda)$.

Sticky-price and real interest differential monetary models

A problem with the early, flexible-price variant of the monetary approach, however, is that it assumes *continuous* PPP—equation (3). Under continuous PPP, the real exchange rate—that is, the exchange rate adjusted for differences in national price levels—cannot vary, by definition. Yet, a major character-istic of the recent experience with floating has been the wide gyrations in the real rates of exchange between many of the major currencies, bringing with them the very real consequences of shifts in international competitiveness (see, for example, Dornbusch (1987)). Clearly, therefore, the simple, flexible-price monetary approach does not fit the observable facts. An attempt to rehabilitate the monetary model led to the development of a second generation of monetary models, beginning with Dornbusch (1976). The sticky-price monetary model allows for substantial overshooting of both the nominal and the real price-adjusted exchange rates beyond their long-run equilibrium (PPP) levels, because the jump variables in the system—exchange rates and interest rates—compensate for sluggishness in other variables—notably goods prices.[4]

The intuition behind the overshooting result in the sticky-price monetary model is relatively straightforward. Imagine the effects of a cut in the nominal U.K. money supply. Sticky prices in the short run imply an initial fall in the real money supply and a consequent rise in interest rates in order to clear the money market. The rise in domestic interest rates then leads to a capital inflow and an appreciation of the nominal exchange rate (that is, a rise in the value of the domestic currency in terms of the foreign currency), which, given sticky prices, also implies an appreciation of the real exchange rate.

Foreign investors are aware that they are artificially forcing up the exchange rate and that they may therefore suffer a foreign exchange loss when the proceeds of their investment are reconverted into their local currency.[5] However, so long as the *expected* foreign exchange loss (expected rate of depreciation) is less than the *known* capital market gain (that is, the interest differential), risk-neutral investors will continue to buy sterling assets. A short-run equilibrium is achieved when the expected rate of depreciation is just equal to the interest differential (uncovered interest parity holds). Since the expected rate of depreciation must then be nonzero for a nonzero interest differential, the exchange rate must have overshot its long-run equilibrium (PPP) level. In the medium run, however, domestic prices begin to fall in response to the fall in money supply. This alleviates pressure in the money market (the real money supply rises), and domestic interest rates begin to decline. The exchange rate then depreciates slowly in order to converge at the long-run PPP level. This model thus explains the paradox that countries with relatively high interest rates tend to have currencies whose exchange rate is expected to depreciate. The *initial* rise in interest rates leads to a step appre-ciation of the exchange rate, after which a slow depreciation is expected in order to satisfy uncovered interest parity.

The Dornbusch overshooting model was further developed by Buiter and

Miller (1981), who allowed for a nonzero rate of core inflation and considered the impact of natural resource discoveries on output and the exchange rate.

Frankel (1979) argued that a shortcoming of the Dornbusch (1976) formulation of the sticky-price monetary model was that it did not allow a role for differences in secular rates of inflation. His model was an attempt to allow for this defect, and the upshot was an exchange rate equation that included the real interest rate differential as an explanatory variable.

The sticky-price monetary model is clearly an advance over the simple (continuous PPP) monetary model, in that it more accurately explains the observable facts. It is, however, fundamentally monetary, in that attention is focused on equilibrium conditions in the money market. Monetary models of the open economy are able to maintain this focus by assuming perfect substitutability of domestic and foreign nonmoney assets (but *non*substitutability of monies—see Calvo and Rodriguez (1977) and Girton and Roper (1981), for a relaxation of this assumption). The markets for domestic and foreign nonmoney assets can then be aggregated into a single extra market ("bonds") and excluded from explicit analysis by application of Walras' law. This "perfect substitutability" assumption is relaxed in the portfolio balance model of exchange rate determination. In addition, the portfolio balance model is stock-flow consistent, in that it allows for current account imbalances to have a feedback effect on wealth and, hence, on long-run equilibrium.

Portfolio balance model

In common with the flexible-price and sticky-price monetary models, the level of the exchange rate in the portfolio balance model is determined, at least in the short run, by supply and demand in the markets for financial assets. The exchange rate, however, is a principal determinant of the current account of the balance of payments. Now, a surplus (deficit) on the current account represents a rise (fall) in net domestic holdings of foreign assets, which in turn affects the level of wealth, which in turn affects the level of asset demand, which again affects the exchange rate. Thus, the portfolio balance model is an inherently dynamic model of exchange rate adjustment, which includes in its terms of reference asset markets, the current account, the price level, and the rate of asset accumulation. Although, as we noted above, a number of researchers had, in the late 1960s, discussed the implications of open economy portfolio balance in an open economy in the context of a fixed exchange rate, the seminal contributions to the literature on the portfolio balance approach to exchange rate determination were Kouri (1976), Allen and Kenen (1980), Branson (1977, 1983, 1984), Dornbusch and Fischer (1980), and Isard (1983).

The portfolio balance model, like the sticky-price model, allows one to distinguish between short-run equilibrium (supply and demand equated in asset markets) and the dynamic adjustment to long-run equilibrium (a static level of wealth and no tendency of the system to move over time). Unlike the sticky-price model, it also allows for the full interaction between the exchange rate, the balance of payments, the level of wealth, and stock equilibrium.

In the short run (on a day-to-day basis), with the portfolio balance model the exchange rate is determined solely by the interaction of supply and demand in asset markets. During this period, the level of financial wealth (and the individual components of that level) can be treated as fixed. In its simplest form, the portfolio balance model divides net financial wealth of the private sector (W) into three components: money (M), domestically issued bonds (B), and foreign bonds denominated in foreign currency (F); B can be thought of as government debt held by the domestic private sector, and F is the level of net claims on foreigners held by the private sector. Since, under a free float, a current account surplus on the balance of payments must be exactly matched by a capital account deficit (that is, capital outflow and, hence, an increase in net foreign indebtedness to the domestic economy), the current account must give the rate of accumulation of F over time.

With domestic and foreign interest rates given by r and r^* as before, we can write down our definition of wealth and the simple domestic demand functions for its components as follows:[6]

$$W = M + B + SF \tag{10}$$

$$M = M(r, r^*)W \quad M_r < 0, M_r^* < 0 \tag{11}$$

$$B = B(r, r^*)W \quad B_r > 0, B_r^* < 0 \tag{12}$$

$$SF = F(r, r^*)W \quad F_r < 0, F_r^* > 0 \tag{13}$$

Relation (10) is an identity defining wealth. Two noteworthy characteristics of equations (11)–(13) are that, as is standard in most expositions of the portfolio balance model, the scale variable is the level of wealth, W, and the demand functions are homogeneous in wealth; they can thus be written in nominal terms (assuming homogeneity in prices and real wealth, prices cancel out) (see Tobin (1969)).

The model thus provides a simple framework for analyzing the effect of, for example, monetary and fiscal policy on the exchange rate. Thus, a contractionary monetary policy (a fall in M) reduces nominal financial wealth (through equation (10)), and so reduces the demand for both domestic and foreign bonds (through equations (12) and (13)). As foreign bonds are sold, the exchange rate appreciates (the foreign price of domestic currency rises). The effects of fiscal policy (operating through changes in B) on the exchange rate are more ambiguous, depending on the degree of substitution between domestic and foreign bonds.

Masson (1981), Branson (1983, 1984), and Dooley and Isard (1982) have also extended this model to incorporate rational expectations. Branson (1984), for example, demonstrates that under rational expectations, real disturbances will generate monotonic adjustment of the exchange rate in the portfolio balance model, while monetary disturbances will generate exchange rate overshooting. Masson (1981) and Buiter (1984) also consider the stability of the portfolio balance model when net domestic holdings of foreign assets are negative.

II EMPIRICAL EVIDENCE ON EXCHANGE RATE MODELS.

In this section the empirical evidence on exchange rate models is looked at from three perspectives: the monetary exchange rate models using interwar data and data from the recent float before 1978; monetary models including more recent data from the current float; and the portfolio balance model.

First-period tests of monetary models

The empirical evidence on the three formulations of the monetary exchange rate model—the flexible-price, sticky-price, and real interest differential specifications—can be divided into two periods. The first-period evidence relates to studies of the interwar period and of the recent float up until about 1978 and is largely supportive of the monetary model. The second-period evidence, which covers the period of the recent float extending beyond the late 1970s, is not so supportive of the monetary model.

One of the first tests of equation (7) was conducted by Frenkel (1976) for the deutsche mark–U.S. dollar exchange rate over the period 1920–23. Since this period corresponds to the German hyperinflation, Frenkel argued that domestic monetary impulses will overwhelmingly dominate equation (7), and, thus, the domestic income and foreign variables can be dropped, and attention focused simply on the effects of German money and the expected inflation (operating through expected depreciation). Frenkel reported results supportive of the flexible-price model during this peric l.

A number of researchers have estimated flexible-price model equations for the more recent experience with floating exchange rates. For example, Bilson (1978) tested for the deutsche mark–pound sterling exchange rate (with the forward premium, fp_t, substituted for Δs_{t+i}^e, and without any restrictions on the coefficients on domestic and foreign money) over the period January 1972 through April 1976. Bilson incorporated dynamics into the equation and used a Bayesian estimation procedure; his results were in broad accordance with the monetary approach. Hodrick's (1978) tests of the flexible-price model for the U.S. dollar–deutsche mark and pound sterling–U.S. dollar over the period July 1972 to June 1975 were also highly supportive. Putnam and Woodbury (1979) estimated equation (5) for the sterling–dollar exchange rate over the period 1972–74, and reported that most of the estimated coefficients were significantly different from zero at the 5 percent significance level, and all were correctly signed according to the flexible-price model. However, the money supply term was significantly different from unity.

Dornbusch (1979) reported results broadly supportive of the flexible-price model for the mark–dollar exchange rate over the period March 1973 to May 1978, in a specification incorporating the *long-term* interest rate differential.

Although Dornbusch introduced this differential as an econometric expedient, an interpretation may be placed on this term that is consistent with Frankel's real interest differential equation, which we discussed above. Thus, Frankel (1979), in his implementation of the real interest differential model for the mark–dollar exchange rate over the period July 1974–February 1978, used a long bond interest differential as an instrument for the expected inflation term, on the assumption that long-term real rates of interest are equalized. Frankel argued that since the coefficients on the interest rate and expected inflation terms were both significant, both the flexible-and sticky-price models were rejected in favor of the real interest differential model.

Second-period tests of the monetary models

Although the monetary approach appears reasonably well supported for the period up to 1978, the picture alters dramatically once the sample period is extended. For example, estimates of the real interest differential model reported by Dornbusch (1980), Haynes and Stone (1981), Frankel (1984), and Backus (1984) cast serious doubt on its ability to track the exchange rate in-sample: few coefficients were correctly signed (many were wrongly signed); the equations had poor explanatory power as measured by the coefficient of determination; and residual autocorrelation was a problem. In particular, estimates of monetary exchange rate equations for the deutsche mark–U.S. dollar for the post-1978 period often report coefficients that suggest that a relative increase in the domestic money supply leads to a rise in the foreign currency value of the domestic currency (exchange rate appreciation). Frankel (1982a) called this phenomenon—the price of the mark rising as its supply is increased—the "mystery of the multiplying marks."

How can one explain this poor performance of the monetary approach equations for the second half of the floating sample? Rasulo and Wilford (1980) and Haynes and Stone (1981) have suggested that the root of the problem may be traced to the constraints imposed on relative monies, incomes, and interest rates. The imposition of such constraints may be justified on the grounds that if multicollinearity is present, constraining the variables will increase the efficiency of the coefficient estimates. However, Haynes and Stone showed that the subtractive constraints used in monetary approach equations were particularly dangerous because they could lead to biased estimates and sign reversals.

Frankel (1982a) provided an alternative explanation for the poor performance. He attempted to explain the mystery of the multiplying marks by introducing wealth into the money demand equations. Germany, he argued, was running a current account surplus in the late 1970s, which was redistributing wealth from U.S. residents to German residents, thus increasing the demand for marks and reducing the demand for dollars independently of the other arguments in the money demand functions. By including home and foreign wealth (defined as the sum of government debt and cumulated current account surpluses) in his empirical equation, and by not insisting on the constraint that the domestic and foreign income, wealth, and inflation terms had to have equal and opposite signs, Frankel came up with a monetary approach equation that fit the data well and in which all variables, apart from the income terms, were correctly signed and most were statistically significant.

As noted by Boughton (1988a), a further explanation for the failure of the monetary approach equations may be traced to the relative instability of the underlying money demand functions and the simplistic functional forms that are normally implicitly assumed for money demand. Indeed, a number of single-country money demand studies strongly indicate that there have been shifts in velocity for the measure of money used by the above researchers (see Artis and Lewis (1981) for a discussion). In Frankel (1984), shifts in money demand functions were incorporated into the empirical equation by the introduction of a relative velocity shift term, $(v - v^*)$, which was modeled by a distributed lag of $[(p + y - m) - (p^* + y^* - m^*)]$. Including the $(v - v^*)$ term in the estimating equation for five exchange rates led to most of the monetary variable coefficients becoming statistically significant and with the correct signs. However, significant first-order residual autocorrelation remained a problem in all of the reported equations.

Driskill and Sheffrin (1981) argued that the poor performance of the monetary model could be traced to a failure to account for the simultaneity bias introduced by having the expected change in the exchange rate (implicitly) on the right-hand side of the monetary equations. One potential method of circumventing such simultaneity is offered by the rational expectations solution of the monetary model, which effectively yields an equation purged of the interest differential-forward exchange rate effect. A number of researchers have begun to test this version of the model, with some success. For example, Hoffman and Schlagenhauf (1983) implemented a version of the "forward solution" flexible-price model formulation (equation (9)) by specifying a time-series model for the stochastic evolution of the fundamentals. The equation is estimated jointly with time-series models for relative money and income for the franc, the deutsche mark, and the pound sterling against the U.S. dollar. Hoffman and Schlagenhauf computed likelihood ratio tests for the validity of the rational expectations hypothesis and the validity of this hypothesis plus the coefficient restrictions implied by the flexible-price model (such as the unit coefficient on relative money supplies). Although the expectations restrictions are not rejected for any of the countries, the coefficient restrictions are rejected for Germany. Kearney and MacDonald (1990) carried out a similar procedure for the Australian dollar–U.S. dollar and could not reject the restrictions implied by the rational expectations hypothesis.

MacDonald and Taylor (1991), using multivariate cointegration techniques (see Engle and Granger, 1987 and Johansen, 1988), tested the validity of the monetary model as a long-run equilibrium relationship for the U.S. dollar–deutsche mark, U.S. dollar–pound sterling, and U.S. dollar–yen exchange rates over the period January 1976 through December 1990. They found that an unrestricted version of equation (4) could not be rejected as a long-run equilibrium for these exchange rates and that, for the U.S. dollar–deutsche mark rate, none of the coefficient restrictions implicit in equation (5) could be rejected. Note that, since all of the monetary models collapse to an equilibrium condition of the form equation (4) or (5) in the long run, these tests have no power to discriminate between them. They do suggest, however, that while short-run exchange rate behavior may be difficult to model, economic fundamentals should not be rejected out of hand as a description of long-run exchange rate behavior.

The rational expectations solution to the flexible-price model has spawned further empirical work that tests for the presence of speculative bubbles. It is well known from the rational expectations literature that equation (9) is only one solution to equation (7) from a potentially infinite sequence (see, for example, Blanchard and Watson, 1982). If we denote the exchange rate given by equation (9) as $\hat{s}_t$, then it is straightforward to demonstrate (see MacDonald and Taylor, 1989b) that equation (7) has multiple rational expectations solutions, each of which may be written in the form

$$s_t = \hat{s} + b_t \tag{14}$$

where b_t—the "rational bubble" term—satisfies

$$b^e_{t+i} = \lambda^{-1}(1 + \lambda)b_t.$$

Meese (1986) tested for bubbles by applying a version of the Hausman (1978) specification test suggested by West (1986) for present value models. The test involves estimating a version of equation (7) (which produces consistent coefficient estimates regardless of the presence or otherwise of rational bubbles) and a closed-form version of equation (9) (which produces consistent coefficient estimates only in the absence of bubbles). Hausman's specification test is used to determine if the two sets of coefficient estimates are significantly different. Such a difference would suggest the existence of a speculative bubble. For the dollar–yen, dollar–mark, and dollar–sterling exchange rates (monthly data over the period October 1973 to November 1982), Meese in fact found that the two sets of coefficient estimates were significantly different and therefore rejected the hypothesis of no bubbles. Kearney and MacDonald (1986) applied a version of this methodology to the Australian dollar–U.S. dollar exchange rate and could not reject the hypothesis.

An alternative way of testing for bubbles is to adopt the variance-bounds test methodology originally proposed by Shiller (1979) in the context of interest rates. This may be illustrated in the following way. If we define the ex post rational or perfect foresight exchange rate as what results from replacing expected future values of money and income in equation (9) with their actual values:

$$s_t^* = (1 + \lambda)^{-1} \sum_{i=1}^{\infty} \left[\frac{\lambda}{1 + \lambda} \right]^i [(m - m^*)_{t+i} - \phi y_{t+1} + \phi^* y_{t+i}]$$

then s_t^* will differ from $\hat{s}_t$ given by (9) by a rational forecast error, u_t (that is, $s_t^* = \hat{s}_t + u_t$). Given that u_t is a rational expectations forecast error, $\hat{s}_t$ and u_t must be orthogonal to one another; thus, we have

$$\text{var}(s_t^*) = \text{var}(\hat{s}_t) + \text{var}(u_t) \tag{15}$$

which implies

$$\text{var}(s_t^*) \geq \text{var}(\hat{s}_t) \tag{16}$$

In the absence of bubbles, the inequality given by equation (16) should hold. However, in the presence of bubbles, (16) is likely to be violated since, on using equation (14), we have $s_t^* = s_t - b_t + u_t$, and the relationship corresponding to (15) is

$$\text{var}(s_t^*) = \text{var}(s_t) + \text{var}(b_t) + \text{var}(u_t) - 2 \, \text{cov}(s_t, b_t) \tag{17}$$

Since, in the presence of bubbles, s_t and b_t may be positively correlated, we cannot derive equation (16) from equation (17). Thus, violation of (16) (excess volatility) could be taken as evidence of the presence of rational bubbles.

Huang (1981) tested versions of equation (16) for the dollar–mark, dollar–sterling, and sterling–mark exchange rates for the period March 1973 to March 1979. His results were supportive of excess volatility and, by inference, he rejected the no-bubbles hypothesis. Kearney and MacDonald (1986) implemented tests of equation (16) for the Australian dollar–U.S. dollar over the period January 1984–December 1986 and generally found in favor of the no-bubbles hypothesis.

There are, however, a number of problems with this kind of approach. First, it is conditional on an assumed model of the exchange rate: violation could be due to an inappropriate choice or specification of model. Second, and perhaps more important, there may be other possible explanations for the presence of bubbles, such as measurement error in computing the perfect foresight exchange rate, inappropriate stationary-inducing transformations, or small-sample bias.

Evans (1986) tested for bubbles in the U.S. dollar–pound sterling exchange rate over the period 1981–84 by testing for a nonzero median in excess returns from forward market speculation (the forward rate forecasting error adjusted for risk). Evans designed and applied nonparametric tests for a nonzero median in returns that are similar to runs tests. He decisively rejected the zero-median hypothesis and inferred that this result provided evidence of speculative bubbles. Note, however, that Evans may have been detecting peso problems;[7] moreover, there is no guarantee that his method of risk adjusting the excess returns (based on real interest differentials) is correct.

We now turn to the empirical evidence on the reduced form of the sticky-price model. Driskill (1981) presented an estimate of an equation representative of the Dornbusch (1976) overshooting model for the Swiss franc–U.S. dollar rate for the period 1973–77 (quarterly data) and reported results largely favorable to the sticky-price model. Other tests have been conducted by Backus (1984), Hacche and Townend (1981), and Wallace (1979). Wallace reported results supportive of the model for the float of the Canadian dollar against the U.S. dollar during the 1950s. However, Backus, who tested the model for the float between the two currencies during the recent floating experience (from the first quarter of 1971 to the fourth quarter of 1980), reported different estimation results. Unlike Wallace, he found few statistically significant coefficients.

Estimates of a more dynamic version of the sticky-price model, provided by Hacche and Townend (1981) for the effective exchange rate of the pound sterling from May 1972 to February 1980, do suggest exchange rate overshooting. But in other respects the estimated equation is unsatisfactory: many coefficients are insignificant and wrongly signed, and the equation does not exhibit sensible long-run properties.

Papell (1988) argued that the price and exchange rate dynamics underlying the Dornbusch sticky-price model cannot be captured by single-equation estimation methods. To capture such dynamics, he argued, it is necessary to use a systems method of estimation that incorporates the cross-equation constraints derived from the structural equations and the assumption of rational expectations. His procedure allows domestic income and interest rates to be modeled endogenously, but not the money supply. Effectively, Papell reduced the structural model to a reduced-form, vector-autoregressive, moving-average model with nonlinear parameter constraints. He estimated this jointly with equations for income and the interest rate, for the effective exchange rates of Germany, Japan, the United Kingdom, and the United States for the period 1973:1 to 1984:4. Papell found that most of the estimated structural coefficients had the expected sign, were of reasonable magnitude, and were statistically significant. He thus concluded that his results supported Dornbusch's model.

Barr (1989) and Smith and Wickens (1988, 1990) empirically implemented a version of the sticky-price model formulated by Buiter and Miller (1981) for the pound sterling exchange rate. All reported favorable in-sample estimates of the model. The results reported in these papers are likely to be fairly robust since both sets of authors took care in specifying the model dynamics; also, Smith and Wickens estimated the model structurally. In simulating their model, Smith and Wickens (1988) found that the exchange rate overshoots by 21 percent in response to a 5 percent change in the money supply.

Wadhwani (1984) used the sticky-price model to generate s^* and to test for excess volatility; he found that the inequality (16) is violated for the U.S. dollar–pound sterling rate over the period 1973:1 to 1982:3. His results are therefore supportive of those generated by Huang (1981) using the flexible-price model.

Empirical evidence on the portfolio balance model

Compared to the monetary approach to the exchange rate, less empirical work has been conducted on the portfolio balance model, perhaps due to the limited availability of good disaggregated data on nonmonetary assets. The research that has been done may be broadly divided into two types of tests. The first concentrates on solving the short-run portfolio model as a reduced form (assuming expectations are static), in order to determine its explanatory power. The second, indirect test exploits the fact that the portfolio balance model rests on the assumption of imperfect substitutability between domestic and foreign assets. An alternative way of expressing this assumption is to view the return on domestic and foreign assets as being separated by a risk premium. Thus, an indirect test of the portfolio balance model is to test for the significance of such risk premia. In addition, Branson (1984) examined the time-series behavior of a number of financial variables for several countries to see if they were consistent with the predictions of the model.

The reduced-form exchange rate equation derived from a system such as equations (10)–(13) may be written as (see Branson, Halttunen, and Masson (1977); the assumed short-run nature of the relationship allows income and prices to be assumed exogenous and constant):

$$S_t = g(M_t, M_t^*, B_t, B_t^*, fB_t, fB_t^*) \tag{18}$$

where fB and fB^* denote foreign holdings of domestic and foreign bonds, respectively. Branson, Halttunen, and Masson (1977) estimated a log-linear version of an equation similar to this for the deutsche mark–U.S. dollar exchange rate over the period August 1971–December 1976. However, they dropped the terms relating to domestic and foreign bond holdings because of their ambiguous effect on the exchange rate, depending on the degree of substitutability between traded and nontraded bonds. But as Bisignano and Hoover (1982) pointed out, this rather arbitrary exclusion will generally result in biased regression coefficients.

Although the estimates reported by Branson, Halttunen, and Masson (1977) were supportive of the portfolio balance model, once account is taken of acute first-order residual autocorrelation, only one coefficient, that on the U.S. money supply, is statistically significant. After specifying a simple reaction function that is purported to capture the simultaneity between the exchange rate and the money supply, Branson, Halttunen, and Masson re-estimated their equation using two-stage least squares and reported more satisfactory estimates of the portfolio balance empirical model; however, residual autocorrelation remained a problem (the estimated first-order autocorrelation coefficient was 0.87, which suggests that unexplained shocks have persistent effects on the exchange rate and, hence, that this version of the portfolio balance model does not fully explain the mark–dollar exchange rate).

In Branson, Halttunen, and Masson (1979), a log-linear exchange rate equation was estimated for the longer period August 1971–December 1978, for the mark–dollar, but the results did not differ significantly from the earlier ones; again, persistent autocorrelation was a problem. In another paper, Branson and Halttunen (1979) estimated the equation for five currencies (the yen, the French franc, the lira, the Swiss franc, and the pound sterling) against the deutsche mark for a variety of different sample periods over the 1970s. Although their results seemed supportive of the portfolio balance model, in terms of statistically significant and correctly signed coefficients, a note of caution must again be sounded, since the residuals in their ordinary-least-square equations were all highly autocorrelated.

One problem with the Branson, Halttunen, and Masson (1977, 1979) implementation of the portfolio balance model lies in their use of cumulated current accounts for the stock of foreign assets. Such an approximation will, of course, include *third-country* items that are not strictly relevant to the determination of the *bilateral* exchange rate in question. Bisignano and Hoover (1982) picked up on this point, arguing that the portfolio balance approach should be implemented using only bilateral data for foreign assets, and, to be consistent, domestic and foreign bond holdings should be included in the reduced form of the model (see above). Incorporating such modifications in their estimates of the portfolio balance equation for the Canadian dollar–U.S. dollar over the period March 1973 to December 1978, Bisignano and Hoover reported moderately successful econometric results; in particular, they showed that it is wrong to neglect domestic and foreign nonmonetary asset stocks in exchange rate reduced forms.

Dooley and Isard (1982) were the first to attempt to construct data on domestic and foreign bond holding without assuming that the current account deficit is financed entirely in one of the two currencies under consideration. For example, in an analysis of the U.S. dollar–deutsche mark exchange rate, the U.S. demand for U.S. bonds is viewed as one component of the total demand (the other demand components being attributed to private German wealth holders, private and official OPEC[8] residents, and private and official residents of the rest of the world). The total demand is then assumed equal to the supply of outside dollar-denominated bonds, viewed as equal to the cumulative U.S. budget deficit, less the stock of bonds removed from private circulation through Federal Reserve open market operations, and less cumulative U.S. and foreign official intervention purchases of dollar-denominated bonds. Dooley and Isard estimated their model for the dollar–mark exchange rate over the period May 1973 through June 1977, using an iterative estimation procedure to impose model-consistent (that is, broadly speaking, rational) expectations, and compared the predictions of the model to naive forecasts using the forward rate and the lagged spot rate. They summarized the performance of the model as follows:

The model is better than the forward rate as a predictor of the change in the exchange rate . . . [H]owever . . . the model fails to explain the major portion of observed changes in exchange rates: the coefficient of correlation between predicted and observed changes is 0.4, and the model incorrectly predicts the direction of one out of every three changes.

(Dooley and Isard 1982, p. 273)

Dooley and Isard pointed out that the ability of the model to outperform the forward rate as a spot rate predictor challenged the view that exchange risk premia were nonexistent. However, the empirical shortcomings of the model suggest either that their simplifications of the theoretical model were too severe or that observed exchange rate movements were predominantly unexpected.

Boughton (1988b) introduced term-structure effects into an empirical portfolio balance model and estimated jointly a "semireduced form" consisting of a real exchange rate portfolio balance equation that includes long- and short-term interest rates, an equation for the short-term rate (essentially an inverted *LM* curve), and a forecasting equation for the long- and short-term interest rate spread. He used data on the real effective exchange rates for the U.S. dollar and on real bilateral dollar–yen and dollar–mark exchange rates for the period May 1973 through December 1985. His estimation results were broadly satisfactory in terms of the sign and statistical significance of the estimated coefficients. Boughton then used these results in a number of counterfactual simulations to analyze the strong appreciation of the dollar over the 1980–85 period. He concluded that a major contributory factor to the rise of the dollar over the period, according to his model, was a failure of the "rest of the world" (Germany, Japan, the United Kingdom, and France) to tighten monetary policy sufficiently, as measured by the significance of the short-term interest rate differential in explaining the swings in the dollar: in December 1980 the weighted average, short-term rate for the four countries outside the United States would have had to have risen from 11.2 percent to 21.3 percent in order to have prevented the subsequent appreciation of the dollar.

In an attempt to improve on the estimates of monetary approach and portfolio balance equations and, in particular, to overcome the model misspecification suggested by the typically high value of the first-order residual autocorrelation coefficient in such equations, a number of researchers have attempted to combine features of both the monetary and portfolio balance approaches into a reduced-form exchange rate equation. Thus, if risk is important the reduced-form monetary approach will be misspecified to the extent that it ignores the imperfect substitutability of nonmoney assets. In the portfolio balance model with rational expectations, agents would be expected to revise their estimates of the expected real exchange rate as new information about the future path of the current account reached the market: the spot exchange rate in a reduced-form portfolio balance should include news about the current account as an explanatory variable.

We now turn to some empirical attempts to synthesize the portfolio and monetary approaches, with emphasis on the modeling of the risk premium and news about the current account. Versions of hybrid models with characteristics such as these have been estimated by a number of researchers (Hooper and Morton (1982), Frankel (1983, 1984), Isard (1983), and Hacche and Townend (1981)). In Hooper and Morton's implementation, the risk premium was assumed to be a function of the cumulated current account surplus net of the cumulation of foreign exchange market intervention. Their equation was estimated for the U.S. dollar effective exchange rate 1973:2 to 1978:4, using an instrumental variables estimator. Hooper and Morton reported mixed results, with only some of the coefficients (mainly those relating to the monetary approach variables) significant and of the correct sign.

Using Hooper and Morton's specification, Hacche and Townend (1981) tested the portfolio balance model with an additional term to allow for the impact of oil prices on the sterling effective exchange rate over the period June 1972 to December 1981. The results were largely disappointing: few coefficients were significant and of those that were, the estimated risk premium coefficient was wrongly signed and the point estimate of the oil price coefficient was correctly signed.

In his implementation of the hybrid reduced-form model, Frankel (1984) did not consider the current account news term, and he derived the risk premium as the solution to the portfolio balance model. He estimated a hybrid equation for five currencies against the dollar for the period 1974–81 (monthly data, with the exact beginning and end points currency specific). In general, Frankel found that the estimated coefficients of the monetary approach variables were statistically insignificant, and some wrongly signed.

As noted earlier, an alternative, indirect method of testing the portfolio balance model is to model the exchange risk premium—the deviation from uncovered interest rate parity—as a function of the relative stocks of domestic and foreign debt outstanding. The Dooley and Isard (1982) study discussed above can be interpreted as a test of this kind. Direct attempts to model deviations from uncovered interest parity as a function of relative international debt outstanding have been made by Frankel (1982b, 1983) for the deutsche mark–U.S. dollar rate, and by Rogoff (1984) for the Canadian dollar–U.S. dollar exchange rate. In each case, however, statistically insignificant relationships were reported. Fisher and others (1990) formulated an exchange rate equation, in which the deviation from uncovered interest rate parity (for the pound sterling effective rate, with both the exchange rate and interest rate expressed in real terms) was modeled as a function of the ratio of the current account balance to gross domestic product; this formulation outperformed other exchange rate equations used in major econometric models of the U.K. economy, beating a random walk in out-of-sample forecast tests.[9]

Out-of-sample forecasting performance of exchange rate models

So far, we have considered only the *in-sample* properties of the asset approach reduced forms. A stronger test of the models' validity would be to determine how well they perform *out-of-sample*, compared to an alternative. Meese and Rogoff (1983) conducted such a study for the dollar–pound sterling, dollar–mark, dollar–yen, and trade-weighted dollar exchange rates using data running from March 1973 through June 1981. The exchange rate models they tested correspond to the flexible-price, the real interest differential, and the portfolio-monetary synthesis of Hooper and Morton (1982). Meese and Rogoff compared the out-of-sample performance of these equations to the forecasting performance of the random walk model, the forward exchange rate, a univariate autoregression of the spot rate, and a vector autoregression. They computed their forecasts as follows. First, the equations were estimated using data from the beginning of the sample to November 1976, and four forecasts were made for 1, 3, 6, and 12 months ahead. The data for December 1976 were then added to the original data set, the equations were re-estimated, and a further set of forecasts were made for the four time horizons. This "rolling regression" process was then repeated continually. The statistics used to gauge the out-of-sample properties of the models are the mean error (ME), mean absolute error (MAE), and the root mean-square error (RMSE). A sample of Meese and Rogoff's RMSE results (for the six-month forecast and excluding the forward rate, univariate, and vector autoregression forecasts) are reported in Table 16.1, where the reduced forms derived from structural models have been estimated using the Fair (1970) procedure.

The conclusion that emerges from the Meese–Rogoff study is that none of the exchange rate models using the asset approach outperforms the simple random walk model—a result that was seen as devastating for research on these models. Moreover, this result is all the more striking when it is remembered that the reduced-form forecasts were computed using *actual* values of the various independent variables.

In an attempt to improve on the poor performance of the asset models, Meese and Rogoff attempted a number of alternate approaches: estimating the models in first differences; allowing home and foreign magnitudes to enter

Table 16.1 Root mean-square forecast errors for selected exchange rate equations

Exchange rate	Random walk	Flexible-price model	Real interest differential	Monetary/ portfolio synthesis
US$/DM	8.71	9.64	12.03	9.95
US$/yen	11.58	13.38	13.94	11.94
US$/£ stg.	6.45	8.90	8.88	9.08
Trade-weighted U.S. dollar	6.09	7.07	6.49	7.11

Source: Meese and Rogoff (1983).
Notes: The forecast horizon is six months.

unconstrained; including price levels as additional explanatory variables; using different definitions of the money supply; and replacing long-term interest rates with other proxies for inflationary expectations. But all to no avail: the modified reduced-form equations still failed to outperform the simple random walk.

In a later paper, Meese and Rogoff (1984) considered possible explanations for the failure of the reduced-form asset models to beat the random walk model out-of-sample. In particular, they showed—using the vector auto-regressive methodology—that the instruments used in simultaneous estimates of reduced-form asset models may not be truly exogenous, and thus the estimated parameter estimates may be extremely imprecise. To overcome this problem, Meese and Rogoff imposed coefficient constraints, culled from the empirical literature on money demand equations, and re-estimated the RMSEs for the same period, as in their 1983 paper. They found that although the coefficient-constrained reduced forms still failed to outperform the random walk model for most horizons up to a year, in forecasting beyond a year (which had not been possible with the unconstrained estimates in Meese and Rogoff (1983) because of problems with degrees of freedom), the asset reduced forms did outperform the random walk model in terms of RMSE. As Salemi (1984) pointed out, this finding suggests that the exchange rate acts like a pure asset price in the short term (that is, approximately a random walk—see, for example, Samuelson, 1965), but that in the longer term its equilibrium is systematically related to other economic variables.

A large segment of the literature has been devoted to determining whether Meese and Rogoff's specification of the asset reduced-form equations, their estimation strategy, or the models themselves are at fault. Woo (1985) and Finn (1986) estimated versions of the rational expectations form of the flexible-price model (equation (9)), with the addition of a partial adjustment term in money demand, and performed a Meese–Rogoff forecasting exercise. Finn reported that this model forecast as well as the random walk model (but failed to *outperform* it); while Woo's formulation outperformed the random walk model, in terms of both the MAE and RMSE, for the deutsche mark–U.S. dollar exchange rate. Somanath (1986) also used a partial adjustment term in his formulation of various asset reduced-form equations for the mark–dollar exchange rate. Interestingly, for the period studied by Meese and Rogoff, he found that the structural exchange rate models outperformed the random walk model in terms of the standard criteria, and that for a sample period extending beyond that of Meese and Rogoff, the basic (that is, without any additional dynamics) flexible-price, real interest differential, and hybrid equations outperformed the random walk.[10]

Wolff (1987) and Schinasi and Swamy (1989) used a time-varying parameter model as the preferred estimation technique for econometric implementation of the real interest differential and flexible-price equations. Both Wolff and Schinasi and Swamy argued that the poor forecasting performance noted by Meese and Rogoff may have been due to their failure to account for parameter instabilities. There are, in fact, a number of reasons why the parameters in empirical exchange rate equations are unlikely to be constant for the recent floating experience. For example, instabilities in the underlying structural equations (money demand and PPP equations), changes in policy regime (see Lucas (1976)), and heterogeneous beliefs by agents (leading to a diversity of responses to macroeconomic developments over time) could all impart parameter instabilities.

Using the Kalman filter methodology, Wolff (1987) reworked Meese and Rogoff's results (same currencies and time period), for the reduced forms of the flexible-price and real interest differential models, assuming that the parameters followed a random walk process. However, the two models won out over the random walk only in the case of the U.S. dollar–deutsche mark exchange rate (for both the dollar–yen and the dollar–pound sterling exchange rates the random walk performed better across all forecast horizons; and, indeed, if one takes the *average* across all currencies and forecast horizons, the random walk model dominates).

Schinasi and Swamy (1989) used a less restrictive time-varying model than Wolff, and their model resulted in consistently better forecasts (than a random walk) for the flexible-price, real interest differential, and hybrid equations (for the mark–, yen–, and pound–dollar bilateral exchange rates). However, it is not entirely clear if the improved performance of the structural models was due to the use of time-varying parameters or simply to the fact that Schinasi and Swamy used a multistep random walk forecast, rather than the one-step forecast used by Meese and Rogoff. In a further experiment, Schinasi and Swamy added a lagged dependent variable to the various reduced forms of the monetary equations and compared their forecasting performance to a one-step-ahead random walk. For all cases the time-varying parameter version was always superior to the fixed coefficients version and, furthermore, it outperformed the random walk in almost all cases.

Finally, Boughton (1984b) tested the out-of-sample forecasting performance of a preferred habitat version of the portfolio balance model (using fixed coefficient methods) for a variety of currencies against a random walk model. In every case, this model outperformed the random walk model. However, this result most likely reflects Boughton's use of quarterly data (all the other studies use monthly data), since his estimates of the hybrid equation also generally outperformed the random walk model.

Empirical exchange rate models: new directions

The broad conclusion that emerges from our survey is that the asset-approach models have performed well for some time periods, such as the interwar period, and, to some extent, for the first part of the recent floating experience (that is, 1973–78); but they have provided largely inadequate explanations for the behavior of the major exchange rates during the latter part of the float.

The failure of simple asset-approach equations may be due to misspecification. This misspecification may be of an econometric nature, insofar as the dynamic properties of the asset equations have (in relation to the Hendry, Pagan, and Sargan (1984) dynamic modeling methodology) been very poorly specified (the persistent indication of first-order auto-correlation is supportive of this view). Simple asset-approach equations may also be misspecified from an economic point of view. Thus, the "breakdown" in the performance of the monetary model could be a consequence of the omission of important variables such as the current account, wealth, and risk factors. However, even when these additions are made to the simple asset models, little improvement in equation performance is reported.

Some authors (for example, Papell, 1988 and Isard, 1988) have argued that a useful way of ensuring that exchange rate models are correctly specified is to estimate the models structurally, and this seems to be a useful avenue for future research.[11] Examples of existing studies that have applied this approach to modeling the exchange rate—with some degree of success— include Kearney and MacDonald (1985), Blundell-Wignall and Masson (1985), Masson (1988), Papell (1988), and Smith and Wickens (1988, 1990). Note, however, that the systems approach raises a further set of issues concerning the assumed structure of the whole economy (see, for example, Fisher and others (1990) on the econometric evaluation of the exchange rate in large-scale models of the U.K. economy).

In attempting to explain the poor empirical performance of the asset approach, some authors have suggested that foreign exchange rates may have consistently deviated from their underlying "fundamental" levels (that is, as predicted by economic theory), due to the presence of rational bubbles, as discussed above (see, for example, Flood and Hodrick (1989)). Other researchers have concentrated on the influence of foreign exchange analysts who base their predictions not on economic theory but on the identification of supposedly recurring patterns in graphs of exchange rate movements— that is, "technical" or "chart" analysts. Frankel and Froot (1986, 1990), for example, suggested a model of the foreign exchange market in which traders based their expectations partly on the advice of fundamentalists (that is, economists) and partly on the advice of nonfundamentalists (that is, chartists). They argued that such a model could explain the heavy overvaluation of the U.S. dollar during the mid-1980s.

Some support for the view that nonfundamentalist advice may be an important influence in foreign exchange markets is provided by Taylor and Allen (1992), who conducted a survey of chief foreign exchange dealers in the London foreign exchange market; they found that a high proportion of these dealers used some form of chart analysis in forming their trading decisions, particularly at the shorter horizons. At the shortest horizons (intraday to one week), Taylor and Allen found that over 90 percent of their survey respondents reported using some form of chart analysis, and about 60 percent judged charts to be at least as important as fundamentals at this horizon. As the time horizon was lengthened, however, the weight given by dealers to fundamental analysis increased. At the longest forecast horizons considered (one year or longer), nearly 30 percent of chief dealers reported relying on pure fundamental analysis and 85 percent judged fundamentals to be more important than chart analysis at this horizon.

In addition, Allen and Taylor (1990) analyzed the accuracy of a number of individual chart analysts' one-week and four-week ahead forecasts of the U.S. dollar–pound sterling, U.S. dollar–deutsche mark, and U.S. dollar–yen exchange rates and found that some of them consistently outperformed a whole range of alternative forecasting procedures, including the random walk model, vector autoregressions, and univariate autoregressive moving average time-series models.

Given this evidence, it is hardly surprising that empirical models based on pure, fundamental economic theory fail to provide an adequate explanation of short-term movements in exchange rates. However, the revelation that foreign exchange participants focus more on fundamentals at longer horizons suggests that more attention might fruitfully be paid to modeling the fundamental determinants of *long-term* exchange rates. This is consistent with evidence in favor of the monetary model as a long-run equilibrium condition reported by MacDonald and Taylor (1991).

Masson and Knight (1986, 1990) and Frenkel and Razin (1987) emphasized the role of shifts in fiscal policy stance among the major Organization for Economic Cooperation and Development (OECD) countries as important determinants of exchange rate behavior (see also Dornbusch (1987)). These authors have argued that the large autonomous changes in national saving and investment balances—in particular, those influenced by shifts in public sector fiscal positions in the largest industrial countries—must exert a very strong influence on current account positions, real interest rates, and, hence, exchange rates.

Dooley and Isard (1991) focused their attention on factors affecting the choice of where to locate tangible assets and other "taxable" forms of wealth. In support of this view, Dooley and Isard pointed to the experience of a number of debt-burdened developing countries during the 1980s that experienced substantial depreciations of their real exchange rate around the time of the outbreak of the international debt crisis in 1982. Dooley and Isard (1991) argued that these depreciations could be attributed primarily to a set of events that considerably reduced the attractiveness of owning assets located in the debt-burdened countries, thus giving rise to a "'transfer problem' in which real depreciation played an important role in the adjustment to substantially smaller net capital inflows and current account deficits" (p. 163). Dooley, Isard, and Taylor (1991) suggested that changes in relative country preferences should be systematically reflected in the price of gold, which can be viewed as "an asset without a country." Hence, if the effects of monetary shocks on gold prices can be isolated, evidence that residual changes in the price of gold are capable of explaining or predicting residual changes in exchange rates might be regarded as indirect evidence that exchange rate behavior largely reflects changes in country preferences. Dooley, Isard, and Taylor, in fact, provided econometric evidence that is largely supportive of this view for a number of major exchange rates. They also demonstrated that the price of gold is a crucial factor in beating a random walk in post-sample prediction tests.

Dornbusch (1987) stressed the importance of analyzing a country's industrial structure in any attempt to explain the behavior of its exchange rate. For example, the effect of an exchange rate change on a firm's pricing decisions (and, hence, on further changes in the exchange rate) will depend on whether the industry faces competition from imports that are close substitutes for its goods and whether the market is characterized by, for example, oligopoly or imperfect competition; another important determinant is the functional form of the specific market demand curve. Although conceding the absence of clear-cut results, Dornbusch nevertheless found this approach promising as an avenue for further research.

Which of these directions is likely to lead us toward a better understanding of exchange rate behavior? In our view, the rational bubbles explanation is perhaps the least attractive, not least because a growing amount of empirical research now suggests that asset market participants may not be endowed with fully rational expectations (Frankel and Froot, 1987 and Taylor, 1988).

The Taylor and Allen (1992) evidence on the prevalence of nonfundamentalist analysis in foreign exchange markets suggests that, as a guide to the *short-run* behavior of exchange rates, the fundamentals versus nonfundamentals approach seems promising. Unfortunately, this road may be rocky because of the difficulties involved in developing reliable models of exchange rate behavior from this approach. For example, Allen and Taylor (1990), after analyzing survey data on chartists' exchange rate forecasts, reported a significant degree of heterogeneity among chartist forecasts—not all chartists see the same patterns (or draw the same conclusions from them) at the same points in time. They argued, moreover, that the degree of consensus is likely to shift significantly over time in a fashion that may be hard to model empirically. Thus, while this approach may help us to rationalize the *past* behavior of exchange rates (for example, Frankel and Froot, 1990), it may prove rather more difficult to apply it to predicting *future* short-term exchange rate behavior.

Given the Taylor–Allen evidence that foreign exchange market participants rely more on fundamental economic analysis at longer horizons, it would seem that more attention ought to be focused on modeling the *long-run equilibrium* exchange rate. It is perhaps in this area that the new approaches that take into account fiscal policy stance, locational decisions, and industrial organization might be most fruitfully applied. In addition, the development of econometric techniques that aid in the identification of long-run relationships using short-run data (see, for example, Engle and Granger (1987)) is likely to provide a further impetus in this direction (see MacDonald and Taylor, 1991).

[. . .]

NOTES

1 See Bilson (1981), Frankel and Froot (1987), and Allen and Taylor (1990) for recent discussions of bandwagon effects in foreign exchange markets.
2 Taylor (1990) analyzes in detail the evolution of thinking on open economy macroeconomics.
3 The application of rational expectations to exchange rates was first considered by Black (1973).
4 In fact, the main features of the sticky-price model would be captured in a framework in which the domestic currency prices of domestic goods are sticky but domestic currency prices of foreign goods can move with the exchange rate.
5 Even if investors effect forward cover—that is, sell the proceeds of their investment against their local currency in the forward market—the cost of this cover will be close to the expected rate of depreciation of the domestic currency (and exactly equal if the forward market is efficient and agents are risk neutral; see below).
6 We use the notation, $X_j = \partial X/\partial j$.
7 The peso problem (Krasker (1980)) refers to the situation where agents attach a small probability to a large change in the economic fundamentals, which does not occur in-sample. This will tend to produce a skew in the distribution of forecast errors even when agents are rational, and thus may generate evidence of nonzero excess returns from forward speculation. See MacDonald and Taylor (1989b) for further analysis of the peso problem.
8 That is, oil producing and exporting countries.
9 See the next section. Note that this study used quarterly data, as does Boughton (1984b).
10 The forecasting performance of these equations is even better for the extended sample period when money market dynamics are allowed for.
11 Thus, Isard (1988, p. 197) writes: "Strong support exists for the view that simultaneous-equation frameworks are preferable to single-equation semi-reduced-form models for capturing the associations between exchange rates, interest differentials, and actual or expected inflation differentials in response to different types of exogenous shocks."

REFERENCES

Allen, H.L. and M.P. Taylor, "Charts, Noise and Fundamentals in the Foreign Exchange Market," *Economic Journal*, Vol. 100, Supplement (1990), pp. 49–59.

Allen, Polly Reynolds, and Peter B. Kenen, *Asset Markets, Exchange Rates, and Economic Integration: A Synthesis* (Cambridge; New York: Cambridge University Press, 1980).

Artis, Michael J., and Mervyn K. Lewis, *Monetary Control in the United Kingdom* (Oxford: Philip Allan, 1981).

Backus, David, "Empirical Models of the Exchange Rate: Separating the Wheat from the Chaff," *Canadian Journal of Economics*, Vol. 17 (November 1984), pp. 824–46.

Barr, David G., "Exchange Rate Dynamics: An Empirical Analysis," in *Exchange Rates and Open Economy Macroeconomics*, ed. by Ronald MacDonald and Mark P. Taylor (New York: B. Blackwell, 1989).

Bilson, John F.O., "Rational Expectations and the Exchange Rate," in *The Economics of Exchange Rates: Selected Studies*, ed. by Jacob A. Frenkel and Harry G. Johnson (Reading, MA: Addison-Wesley, 1978).

——, "The 'Speculative Efficiency' Hypothesis," *Journal of Business*, Vol. 54 (October 1981), pp. 435–51.

Bisignano, J., and K. Hoover, "Some Suggested Improvements to a Simple Portfolio Balance Model of Exchange Rate Determination with Special Reference to the U.S. Dollar/Canadian Dollar Rate", *Weltwirtschaftliches Archiv*, Vol. 118, No. 1 (1982), pp. 19–38.

Black, Stanley W., *International Money Markets and Flexible Exchange Rates*, Princeton Studies in International Finance No. 32 (Princeton, NJ: Princeton University Press, 1973).

Blanchard, Olivier J., and Mark W. Watson, "Bubbles, Rational Expectations, and Financial Markets," in *Crises in the Economic and Financial Structure*, ed. by Paul Wachtel (Lexington, MA: Lexington Books, 1982).

Blundell-Wignall, Andrew, and Paul R. Masson, "Exchange Rate Dynamics and Intervention Rules," *Staff Papers*, International Monetary Fund, Vol. 32 (March 1985), pp. 132–59.

Boughton, James M., "Exchange Rate Movements and Adjustment in Financial Markets: Quarterly Estimates for Major Currencies," *IMF Staff Papers*, Vol. 31 (September, 1984a), pp. 445–68.

——, "Tests of the Performance of Reduced-Form Exchange Rate Models," *Journal of International Economics*, Vol. 31 (September 1984b), pp. 41–56.

——, *The Monetary Approach to Exchange Rates: What Now Remains?* Princeton Essays in International Finance, No. 171 (Princeton, NJ: Princeton University Press, 1988a).

——, "Exchange Rates and the Term Structure of Interest Rates," *Staff Papers*, International Monetary Fund, Vol. 35 (March 1988b), pp. 36–62.

Branson, William H., *Financial Capital Flows in the U.S. Balance of Payments* (Amsterdam: North-Holland, 1968).

——, *Asset Markets and Relative Prices in Exchange Rate Determination*, Reprints in International Finance, No. 20 (Princeton, NJ: Princeton University Press, June 1980); reprinted from *Sozialwissenschaftliche Annalen*, Band 1 (1977).

——, "Macroeconomic Determinants of Real Exchange Risk," in *Managing Foreign Exchange Risk*, ed. by Richard J. Herring (Cambridge; New York: Cambridge University Press, 1983).

——, "Exchange Rate Policy After a Decade of 'Floating,'" in *Exchange Rate Theory and Practice*, ed. by John F.O. Bilson and Richard C. Marston (Chicago: University of Chicago Press, 1984).

Branson, William H., and Hannu Halttunen, "Asset-Market Determination of Exchange Rates: Initial Empirical and Policy Results," in *Trade and Payments Adjustments under Flexible Exchange Rates*, ed. by John P. Martin and Alasdair Smith (London: Macmillan, 1979).

Branson, William H., Hannu Halttunen, and Paul Masson, "Exchange Rates in the Short Run: The Dollar–Deutschemark Rate," *European Economic Review*, Vol. 10 (December 1977), pp. 303–24.

——, "Exchange Rates in the Short Run: Some Further Results," *European Economic Review*, Vol. 12 (October 1979), pp. 395–402.

Buiter, Willem H., "Comment on Branson," in *Exchange Rate Theory and Practice*, ed. by John F.O. Bilson and Richard C. Marston (Chicago: University of Chicago Press, 1984).

—— and Marcus H. Miller, "Monetary Policy and International Competitiveness: The Problem of Adjustment," in *The Money Supply and the Exchange Rate*, ed. by W.A. Eltis and P.J.N. Sinclair (New York: Oxford University Press, 1981).

Calvo, Guillermo A., and Carlos A. Rodriguez, "A Model of Exchange Rate

Determination under Currency Substitution and Rational Expectations," *Journal of Political Economy*, Vol. 85 (June 1977), pp. 617–25.

Dooley, Michael P., and Peter Isard, "Capital Controls, Political Risk, and Deviations from Interest-Rate Parity," *Journal of Political Economy*, Vol. 88 (April 1980), pp. 370–84.

——, "A Portfolio-Balance Rational-Expectations Model of the Dollar–Mark Exchange Rate," *Journal of International Economics*, Vol. 12 (May 1982), pp. 257–76.

——, "A Note on Fiscal Policy, Investment Location Decisions, and Exchange Rates," *Journal of International Money and Finance*, Vol. 10 (March 1991), pp. 161–88.

Dooley, Michael P., Peter Isard, and M.P. Taylor, "Exchange Rates, Country Preferences, and Gold" (unpublished; Washington: International Monetary Fund, January 1991).

Dornbusch, Rudiger, "Expectations and Exchange Rate Dynamics," *Journal of Political Economy*, Vol. 84 (December 1976), pp. 1161–76.

——, "Monetary Policy under Exchange Rate Flexibility," in *Managed Exchange-Rate Flexibility: The Recent Experience*, Federal Reserve Bank of Boston Conference Series No. 20 (Boston: Federal Reserve Bank of Boston, 1979).

——, "Exchange Rate Economics: Where Do We Stand?" *Brookings Papers on Economic Activity: 1* (Washington: The Brookings Institution, 1980), pp. 143–85.

——, "Exchange Rate Economics," *Economic Journal*, Vol. 97 (March 1987), pp. 1–8.

Dornbusch, Rudiger, and Stanley Fischer, "Exchange Rates and the Current Account," *American Economic Review*, Vol. 70 (December 1980), pp. 960–71.

Driskill, Robert A., "Exchange-Rate Dynamics: An Empirical Investigation," *Journal of Political Economy*, Vol. 89 (April 1981), pp. 357–71.

Driskill, Robert A., and Steven M. Sheffrin, "On the Mark: Comment," *American Economic Review*, Vol. 71 (December 1981), pp. 1068–74.

Engle, Robert F., and C.W.J. Granger, "Cointegration and Error Correction: Representation, Estimation, and Testing," *Econometrica*, Vol. 55 (March 1987), pp. 251–76.

Evans, George W., "A Test for Speculative Bubbles in the Sterling–Dollar Exchange Rate: 1981–84," *American Economic Review*, Vol. 76 (September 1986), pp. 621–36.

Fair, Ray C., "The Estimation of Simultaneous Equation Models with Lagged Endogenous Variables and First Order Serially Correlated Errors," *Econometrica*, Vol. 38 (May 1970), pp. 507–16.

Finn, Marry G., "Forecasting the Exchange Rate: A Monetary or Random Walk Phenomenon?", *Journal of International Money and Finance*, Vol. 5 (June 1986), pp. 181–93.

Fisher, P.G., S.K. Tanna, D.S. Turner, K.F. Wallis, and J.D. Whitley, "Econometric Evaluation of the Exchange Rate in Models of the U.K. Economy," *Economic Journal*, Vol. 100 (December 1990), pp. 1230–44.

Fleming, Marcus, "Domestic Financial Policies under Fixed and Floating Exchange Rates," *IMF Staff Papers*, Vol. 9 (November 1962), pp. 369–80.

Flood, Robert P., and Robert J. Hodrick, "Testable Implications of Indeterminacies in Models with Rational Expectations," NBER Working Paper No. 2903 (Cambridge, MA: National Bureau of Economic Research, March 1989).

Frankel, Jeffrey A., "On the Mark: A Theory of Floating Exchange Rates Based on

Real Interest Differentials," *American Economic Review*, Vol. 69 (September 1979), pp. 610–22.

——, "The Mystery of the Multiplying Marks: A Modification of the Monetary Model," *Review of Economics and Statistics*, Vol. 64 (August 1982a), pp. 515–19.

——, "In Search of the Exchange Risk Premium: A Six-Currency Test Assuming Mean-Variance Optimization," *Journal of International Money and Finance*, Vol. 1 (December 1982b), pp. 255–74.

——, "Monetary and Portfolio-Balance Models of Exchange Rate Determination," in *Economic Interdependence and Flexible Exchange Rates*, ed. by Jagdeep S. Bhandari, Bluford H. Putnam, and Jay H. Levin (Cambridge, MA: MIT Press, 1983).

——, "Tests of Monetary and Portfolio Balance Models of Exchange Rate Determination," in *Exchange Rate Theory and Practice*, ed. by John F.O. Bilson and Richard C. Marston (Chicago: University of Chicago Press, 1984).

Frankel, Jeffery A., and Kenneth A. Froot, "Understanding the Dollar in the Eighties: The Expectations of Chartists and Fundamentalists," *Economic Record*. Supplement (1986), pp. 24–38.

——, "Using Survey Data to Test Standard Propositions Regarding Exchange Rate Expectations," *American Economic Review*, Vol. 77 (March 1987), pp. 133–53.

——, "Chartists, Fundamentalists, and the Demand for Dollars," in *Private Behavior and Government Policy in Interdependent Economies*, ed. by Anthony S. Courakis and Mark P. Taylor (Oxford: Clarendon Press, 1990).

Frenkel, Jacob A., "A Monetary Approach to the Exchange Rate: Doctrinal Aspects and Empirical Evidence," *Scandinavian Journal of Economics*, Vol. 78, No. 2 (1976), pp. 200–24.

Frenkel, Jacob A., and Harry G. Johnson, eds., *The Monetary Approach to the Balance of Payments* (London: Allen and Unwin, 1976).

——, *The Economics of Exchange Rates: Selected Studies* (Reading, MA: Addison-Wesley, 1978).

Frenkel, Jacob A., and Michael M. Mussa, "Asset Markets, Exchange Rates, and the Balance of Payments," in *Handbook of International Economics*, Vol. 2, ed. by Ronald B. Jones and Peter B. Kenen (New York; Amsterdam: North-Holland, 1985).

Frenkel, Jacob A., and Assaf Razin, *Fiscal Policies and the World Economy: An Intertemporal Approach* (Cambridge, MA: MIT Press, 1987).

Friedman, Milton, "The Case for Flexible Exchange Rates," in *Essays in Positive Economics* (Chicago: University of Chicago Press, 1953).

Girton, Lance, and Don Roper, "Theory and Implications of Currency Substitution," *Journal of Money, Credit and Banking*, Vol. 12 (February 1981), pp. 12–30.

Hache, Graham, and John Townend, "Exchange Rates and Monetary Policy: Modeling Sterling's Effective Exchange Rate, 1972–80," in *The Money Supply and the Exchange Rate*, ed. by W.A. Eltis and P.J.N. Sinclair (New York: Clarendon Press, 1981).

Hausman, Jerry A., "Specification Tests in Econometrics," *Econometrica*. Vol. 46 (November 1978), pp. 1251–71.

Haynes, Stephen E., and Joe A. Stone, "On the Mark: Comment," *American Economic Review*, Vol. 71 (December 1981), pp. 1060–67.

Hendry, David F., Adrian R. Pagan, and Denis Sargan, "A Dynamic Specification," in *Handbook of Econometrics*, Vol. II, ed. by Zvi Griliches and Michael D. Intriligator (New York; Amsterdam: North-Holland, 1984).

Hodrick, Robert J., "An Empirical Analysis of the Monetary Approach to the Determination of the Exchange Rate," in *The Economics of Exchange Rates*, ed. by Jacob A. Frenkel and Harry G. Johnson (Reading, MA: Addison-Wesley, 1978).

Hoffman, Dennis, and Don E. Schlagenhauf, "Rational Expectations and Monetary Models of Exchange Rate Determination: An Empirical Examination," *Journal of Monetary Economics*, Vol. 11 (March 1983), pp. 247–60.

Hooper, Peter, and John Morton, "Fluctuations in the Dollar: A Model of Nominal and Real Exchange Rate Determination," *Journal of International Money and Finance*, Vol. 1 (April 1982), pp. 39–56.

Huang, Roger D., "The Monetary Approach to Exchange Rates in an Efficient Foreign Exchange Market: Tests Based on Volatility," *The Journal of Finance*, Vol. 36 (March 1981), pp. 31–41.

Isard, Peter, *Expected and Unexpected Changes in Exchange Rates: The Roles of Relative Price Levels. Balance of Payments Factors, Interest Rates, and Risk*, International Finance Discussion Papers, No. 156 (Washington: Board of Governors of the Federal Reserve System, 1983).

——, "Exchange Rate Modeling: An Assessment of Alternate Approaches," in *Empirical Macroeconomics for Interdependent Economies*, ed. by Ralph C. Bryant, Dale W. Henderson, Gerald Holtham. Peter Hooper, and Steven A. Symansky (Washington: The Brookings Institution, 1988).

Johansen, Søren, "Statistical Analysis of Cointegration Vectors," *Journal of Economic Dynamics and Control*, Vol. 12 (June/September 1988).

Johnson, Harry Gordon, "Towards a General Theory of the Balance of Payments," in *International Trade and Economic Growth*, ed. by Harry Gordon Johnson (London: Allen and Unwin, 1958).

Kearney, Colm, and Ronald MacDonald, "Asset Markets and the Exchange Rate: A Structural Model of the Sterling–Dollar Exchange Rate, 1972–1982," *Journal of Economic Studies*, Vol. 12, No. 3 (1985), pp. 3–20.

——, "Intervention and Sterilisation under Floating Exchange Rates: The UK, 1973–1983," *European Economic Review*, Vol. 30 (April 1986), pp. 345–64.

——, "Exchange Rate Volatility, News and Bubbles," *Australian Economic Papers*, Vol. 70 (June 1990), pp. 1–20.

Kohlhagen, Steven W., *The Behavior of Foreign Exchange Markets—A Critical Survey of the Empirical Literature*, Monograph Series in Finance and Economics, 1978–3 (New York: New York University, Graduate School of Business Administration, 1978).

Kouri, Pentti J.K., "The Exchange Rate and the Balance of Payments in the Short Run and in the Long Run: A Monetary Approach," *Scandinavian Journal of Economics*, Vol. 78, No. 2 (1976), pp. 280–304.

Kouri, Pentti, J.K. and Michael G. Porter, "International Capital Flows and Portfolio Equilibrium," *Journal of Political Economy*, Vol. 82 (May/June 1974), pp. 443–67.

Krasker, William S., "'The Peso Problem' in Testing the Efficiency of Forward Exchange Markets," *Journal of Monetary Economics*, Vol. 6 (April 1980), pp. 269–76.

Levich, Richard M., "On the Efficiency of Markets for Foreign Exchange," in *International Economic Policy: of Theory and Evidence*, ed. by Rudiger Dornbusch and Jacob A. Frenkel (Baltimore: Johns Hopkins University Press, 1979).

——, "Empirical Studies of Exchange Rates: Price Behavior, Rate Determination, and Market Efficiency," in *Handbook of International Economics*, Vol. II, ed. by

Ronald W. Jones and Peter B. Kenen (New York; Amsterdam: North-Holland, 1985).

Lucas, Robert E., "Econometric Policy Evaluation: a Critique," in *The Phillips Curve and Labor Markets*, ed. by Karl Brunner and Allan H. Meltzer, Carnegie-Rochester Conference Series, Vol. 1 (New York; Amsterdam: North-Holland, 1976).

Macdonald, Ronald, and Mark P. Taylor (1989a), "Foreign Exchange Market Efficiency and Cointegration: Some Evidence from the Recent Float," *Economics Letters*, Vol. 29, No. 1, pp. 63–68.

—— (1989b), eds., *Exchange Rates and Open Economy Macroeconomics* (Oxford; New York: Basil Blackwell).

——, "The Monetary Approach to the Exchange Rate: Long-Run Relationships and Coefficient Restrictions" (unpublished; Washington: International Monetary Fund 1991).

Masson, Paul R., "Dynamic Stability of Portfolio Balance Models of the Exchange Rate," *Journal of International Economics*, Vol. 11 (November 1981), pp. 467–77.

——, "Strategies for Modeling Exchange Rates and Capital Flows in Multi-country Models," *Journal of Policy Modeling*, Vol. 10 (Summer 1988), pp. 209–28.

Masson, Paul R., and Malcolm Knight, "International Transmission of Fiscal Policies in Major Industrial Countries," *IMF Staff Papers*, Vol. 33 (September 1986), pp. 387–438.

——, "Economic Interactions and the Fiscal Policies of Major Industrial Countries: 1980–1988," in *Private Behavior and Government Policy in Interdependent Economies*, ed. by Anthony S. Courakis and Mark P. Taylor (Oxford: Oxford University Press, 1990).

McKinnon, Ronald T., "Portfolio Balance and International Payments Adjustment," in *Monetary Problems of the International Economy*, ed. by Alexander K. Swoboda and Robert A. Mundell (Chicago: University of Chicago Press, 1969).

McKinnon, Ronald T., and Wallace E. Oates, *The Implications of International Economic Integration for Monetary, Fiscal, and Exchange-Rate Policy*, Princeton Studies in International Finance, No. 16 (Princeton, NJ: Princeton University Press, 1966).

Meade, James E., *The Balance of Payments*, Vol. 1 in *The Theory of International Economic Policy* (London; New York: Oxford University Press; 1951a reprinted 1965).

——, *The Balance of Payments* (supplement), Vol. 1 in *The Theory of International Economic Policy* (London; New York: Oxford University Press; 1951b reprinted 1965).

Meese, Richard A., "Testing for Bubbles in Exchange Markets: A Case of Sparkling Rates?" *Journal of Political Economy*, Vol. 94 (April 1986), pp. 345–73.

Messe, Richard A., and Kenneth Rogoff, "Empirical Exchange Rate Models of the Seventies: Do They Fit Out of Sample?" *Journal of International Economics*, Vol. 14 (February 1983), pp. 3–24.

——, "The Out-of-Sample Failure of Empirical Exchange Rate Models: Sampling Error or Misspecification?" in *Exchange Rates and International Macroeconomics*, ed. by Jacob A. Frenkel (Chicago: University of Chicago Press, 1984).

Mundell, Robert A., "Flexible Exchange Rates and Employment Policy," *Canadian Journal of Economics and Political Science*, Vol. 27 (November 1961), pp. 509–17.

320   *Ronald MacDonald and Mark P. Taylor*

——, "The Appropriate Use of Monetary and Fiscal Policy for Internal and External Stability," *Staff Papers*, International Monetary Fund, Vol. 9 (March 1962), pp. 70–79.

——, "Capital Mobility and Stabilization Policy under Fixed and Flexible Exchange Rates," *Canadian Journal of Economics and Political Science*, Vol. 29 (November 1963), pp. 475–85.

——, *International Economics* (New York: MacMillan, 1968).

Mussa, Michael L., "The Exchange Rate, the Balance of Payments, and Monetary and Fiscal Policy under a Regime of Controlled Floating," *Scandinavian Journal of Economics*, Vol. 78, No. 2 (1976), pp. 229–48.

——, "Empirical Regularities in the Behavior of Exchange Rates and Theories of the Foreign Exchange Market," in *Policies for Employment, Prices, and Exchange Rates*, ed. by Karl Brunner and Allan H. Meltzer, Carnegie–Rochester Conference Series on Public Policy, Vol. 11 (New York; Amsterdam: North-Holland, 1979).

——, "The Theory of Exchange Rate Determination," in *Exchange Rate Theory and Practice*, ed. by John F.O. Bilson and Richard C. Marston (Chicago: University of Chicago Press, 1984).

Nurkse, Ragnar, *International Currency Experience: Lessons of the Interwar Period* (Geneva: League of Nations, 1945).

Oates, Wallace E., "Budget Balance and Equilibrium Income: A Comment on the Efficacy of Fiscal and Monetary Policy in an Open Economy." *Journal of Finance*, Vol. 21 (September 1966), pp. 489–98.

Obstfeld, Maurice, and Alan C. Stockman, "Exchange Rate Dynamics," in *Handbook of International Economics*, Vol. 2, ed. by Ronald W. Jones and Peter B. Kenen (Amsterdam; New York: North-Holland, 1985).

Ott, David J., and Attiat F. Ott, "Budget Balance and Equilibrium Income," *Journal of Finance*, Vol. 20 (March 1965), pp. 71–77.

Papell, David H., "Expectations and Exchange Rate Dynamics after a Decade of Floating," *Journal of International Economics*, Vol. 25 (November 1988), pp. 303–17.

Polak, J.J., "Monetary Analysis of Income Formation and Payments Problems," *IMF Staff Papers*, Vol. 6 (November 1957), pp. 1–50.

Putnam, B.H., and J.R. Woodbury, "Exchange Rate Stability and Monetary Policy," *Review of Business and Economic Research*, Vol. 15, No. 2 (1979), pp. 1–10.

Rasulo, James A., and D. Sykes Wilford, "Estimating Monetary Models of the Balance of Payments and Exchange Rates: A Bias," *Southern Economic Journal*, Vol. 47 (July 1980), pp. 136–46.

Rogoff, Kenneth, "On the Effects of Sterilized Intervention: An Analysis of Weekly Data," *Journal of Monetary Economics*, Vol. 14 (September 1984), pp. 133–50.

Salemi, Michael K., "Comment on Meese and Rogoff," in *Exchange Rates and International Macroeconomics*, ed. by Jacob A. Frenkel (Chicago: University of Chicago Press, 1984).

Samuelson, P.A., "Proof that Properly Anticipated Prices Fluctuate Randomly," *Industrial Management Review*, Vol. 6 (Spring 1965), pp. 41–49.

Schinasi, Gary, and P.A.V.B. Swamy, "The Out-of-Sample Forecasting Performance of Exchange Rate Models when Coefficients Are Allowed to Change," *Journal of International Money and Finance*, Vol. 8 (September 1989), pp. 375–90.

Shiller, Robert J., "The Volatility of Long-Term Interest Rates and Expectations Models of the Term Structure," *Journal of Political Economy*, Vol. 87 (December 1979), pp. 1190–1219.

Smith, P., and M. Wickens, "A Stylised Econometric Model of an Open Economy: U.K. 1973–1981" (unpublished; Southampton: University of Southampton, 1988).

——, "Assessing Monetary Shocks and Exchange Rate Variability with a Stylized Econometric Model of the U.K.," in *Private Behavior and Government Policy in Interdependent Economies*, ed. by A.S. Courakis and Mark P. Taylor (Oxford: Oxford University Press, 1990).

Somanath, V.S., "Efficient Exchange Rate Forecasts: Lagged Models Better than the Random Walk," *Journal of International Money and Finance*, Vol. 5 (June 1986), pp. 195–220.

Taylor, Mark P., "What Do Investment Managers Know? An Empirical Study of Practitioners' Predictions," *Economica*, Vol. 55 (May 1988), pp. 185–202.

——, *The Balance of Payments: New Perspectives on Open Economy Macroeconomics* (Aldershot, Hants.: Edward Elgar, 1990).

Taylor, Mark P., and Helen L. Allen, "The Use of Technical Analysis in the Foreign Exchange Market," *Journal of International Money and Finance* (April 1992).

Tobin, James, "The Theory of Portfolio Selection," in *The Theory of Interest Rates*, Proceedings of a Conference Held by the International Economic Association, ed. by F.H. Hahn and F.P.R. Brechling (London: Macmillan, 1965).

——, "A General Equilibrium Approach to Monetary Theory," *Journal of Money, Credit and Banking*, Vol. 1 (February 1969), pp. 15–29.

Wadhwani, Sushil B., "Are Exchange Rates 'Excessively' Volatile?" Centre for Labour Economics Discussion Paper No. 198 (London: London School of Economics and Political Science, July 1984).

Wallace, Miles S., "The Monetary Approach to Flexible Exchange Rates in the Short Run: An Empirical Test," *Review of Business and Economic Research*, Vol. 15 (Spring 1979), pp. 98–102.

West, Kenneth D., "A Specification Test for Speculative Bubbles," NBER Working Paper No. 2067 (Cambridge, MA: National Bureau of Economic Research, November 1986).

Willett, Thomas D., and Francesco Forte, "Interest Rate Policy and External Balance," *Quarterly Journal of Economics*, Vol. 83 (May 1969), pp. 242–62.

Wolff, Christian P., "Forward Foreign Exchange Rates, Expected Spot Rates, and Premia: A Signal-Extraction Approach," *Journal of Finance*, Vol. 42 (June 1987), pp. 395–406.

Woo, Wing T., "The Monetary Approach to Exchange Rate Determination under Rational Expectations," *Journal of International Economics*, Vol. 18 (February 1985), pp. 1–16.

17 Recent exchange-rate experience and proposals for reform

*Jeffrey A. Frankel**

American Economic Review, vol. 86, no. 2 (1996), pp. 153–8

Some have concluded that the foreign-exchange market is not working well. The conclusion is fed by recent developments in international financial markets, on the one hand, and by a number of academic findings on the other. I review the grounds for these concerns and then review various proposals that have been made for improving the system.

I BUBBLES AND CRISES IN THE FOREIGN EXCHANGE MARKET

In the 1970's, the majority view among economists was that floating exchange rates were the right way to avoid misalignments, such as the overvaluation to which the dollar had become increasingly subject in the 1960's. The market knows better than governments what is the true value of the currency. Most economists had become persuaded by the argument of Milton Friedman (1953): that speculators would be stabilizing rather than destabilizing, because any who increased the magnitude of exchange-rate fluctuations could only do so by buying high and selling low, which is a recipe for going out of business pretty quickly.

The pendulum began to swing back in the 1980's. The decade began with Robert Mundell (1992) and a few supply-siders arguing for some version of a return to the gold standard. Concerns about floating rates became much more widespread with the dollar bubble in 1984–1985. The market, it seems, sometimes gets things wrong.

The notion that financial markets might suffer from excessive volatility has been boosted by the theory of rational speculative bubbles. The initial motivation for the theory was purely as a mathematical curiosity. But the theory turned out to be a demonstration that speculators could be destabilizing without losing money. In a rational speculative bubble, the price goes up in each period because traders expect it to go up further the next period. Even though the price becomes increasingly far removed from the value justified by economic fundamentals, each individual trader knows that he would lose money if he tried to buck the trend on his own. These rational speculative

* Department of Economics, University of California, Berkeley, CA 94720–3880.

bubbles are an effective answer to Friedman's point that destabilizing speculators would lose money.

A further reason that the pendulum swung partway from floating to fixed in the 1980's was the emergence of the nominal-anchor argument. This is a prescription to peg exchange rates firmly as a credible precommitment on the part of the monetary authorities not to inflate. It became a popular argument for southern European countries joining the European Monetary System (EMS) and for LDC's using currency pegs to disinflate.

The disenchantment with pure floating has now given way to a renewed disenchantment with fixing. The reason: a number of disruptive crises have occurred where countries had tried to fix their rates. It is true that many of these exchange-rate crises are the result of governments trying to defend parities that are no longer justified by fundamentals. Examples are the crises that hit the pound and lira in 1992, and the Mexican peso in 1994. These crises were largely the fault of the governments, not of the markets.

However, unwarranted speculative attacks can happen under fixed rates or target zones too (e.g., the French franc in 1993). Judged by such macro-economic fundamentals as inflation and interest rates, the franc was not over-valued against the mark. Yet it was forced by speculative attack to abandon its 2.25-percent margins. The appropriate theory has been supplied in so-called "second-generation" models of speculative attacks, featuring multiple equilibria (e.g., Maurice Obstfeld, 1995). These speculative attacks are the fixed-rate analogue of the speculative bubbles that arise under floating rates.

II THE ACADEMIC LITERATURE: WHY IS IT THOUGHT THAT SOMETHING MAY BE WRONG WITH THE FOREIGN-EXCHANGE MARKET?

Everyone describes floating exchange rates as highly volatile. But volatile compared to what? They are more volatile than they were expected to be before the 1973 move to floating rates, more volatile than the prices of goods and services, and more volatile than apparent monetary fundamentals. This is not the same, however, as saying that they are excessively volatile. Even if foreign-exchange markets are functioning properly, fundamental economic determinants, such as monetary policy, should produce a lot of variability in the exchange rate. Dornbusch's famous "over-shooting theory" of exchange-rate determination, for example, predicts that a relatively small increase in the money supply will cause a relatively large increase in the price of foreign exchange. The important questions are whether volatility is higher than necessary and what the harmful effects might be.

The concern about exchange-rate volatility has always involved possible adverse effects on trade and investment. They have been a major motivation behind attempts to link European currencies, via the ERM (European Exchange Rate Mechanism), and now via EMU (Economic and Monetary Union). Most empirical studies have concluded that the effect of short-term volatility on trade is small, if any. More importantly, the observed exchange-rate variability could be inevitable real risk, which would pop up elsewhere if suppressed in the foreign-exchange market. But, on this last point there is relevant evidence.

Econometric research has failed to explain most exchange-rate movements by fundamentals, especially on a short-term basis.[1] Logically, this failure leaves two possible explanations: (i) unobservable fundamentals or (ii) bubbles, defined as exchange-rate movements not based on fundamentals. In the first case, one still has the standard presumption of neoclassical economics that, if volatility were somehow suppressed in the foreign exchange market, it would simply show up elsewhere. Imagine, for example, that the fundamental origin of the appreciation of the dollar in the first half of the 1980's were an increase in worldwide demand for U.S. goods and, therefore, an increase in demand for U.S. currency to buy those goods (a real appreciation). An attempt on the part of the U.S. monetary authorities to suppress the appreciation would consist of purchases of foreign currencies, putting more dollars in the hands of the public. This increase in the U.S. money supply would have been inflationary. The increase in U.S. relative prices (the real appreciation) would have occurred anyway, but it would simply have taken the undesirable form of inflation. Can one judge that exchange-rate movements are due to unobservable fundamentals, rather than bubbles?

Arguing against the unobservable-fundamentals explanation is the pattern whereby nominal and real exchange-rate variability has increased whenever there is a shift from a fixed to a floating regime.[2] Furthermore, there is no reduction in the variability of monetary fundamentals necessary to keep the exchange rate in line, when moving from floating-rate regimes to fixed-rate regimes. This seems to leave speculative bubbles as the remaining explanation for much of the short-term variation in exchange rates. It would likely follow that exchange rates are unnecessarily volatile.

Another concern is the widely documented apparent bias in the forward exchange market. The forward discount actually points the wrong way as a predictor of the exchange rate.[3] The bias is usually interpreted simply as an exchange risk premium, but there is some evidence against this view.[4] It is possible that the bias is evidence of market inefficiency.

There is also apparent evidence in survey data of extrapolation on the part of market participants, in forecasts at short horizons of under three months. If traders act based on such extrapolative expectations, they will create bandwagons: an upward blip will generate expectations of future appreciation, leading to buy orders and thereby contributing to the upward trend. This is evidence of destabilizing speculation. At longer horizons of from three months to one year, however, forecasts seem to fit better the patterns of adaptive, regressive, or distributed lag expectations. All three mechanisms of expectations formation, if acted upon by traders, would lead to stabilizing speculation.

Which horizon dominates actual foreign-currency trading? The horizon at which most trading takes place is actually shorter than one day. Traders at most banks take large positions for a few hours but limit their overnight and weekend positions sharply, or close them out altogether. This does not in itself necessarily mean that the determination of the market price is dominated by short horizons. If traders are fully rational, even though they trade at short horizons, their expectation of how much a currency will be worth one period from now will be tied down by their rational forecast of how much it will be worth one year from now. The question is whether this tying of the short-term to the long-term expectation is in fact operative. The survey data results seem to suggest that short-term expectations are not in fact formed by looking far into the future. Given the high level of volatility, the rationally expected year-long return to fundamentals equilibrium is a very minor factor in the traders' calculation on each one-hour trade.

Finally, effects of exogenous changes in monetary policy are apparently not instantaneous, as they should be in theory, but rather are drawn out over time (Martin Eichenbaum and Charles Evans, 1995). This could be an example of how speculative bubbles get started.

The main problem with the theory of *rational* speculative bubbles is that it has nothing to say about what gets bubbles started. Under the theory, the exchange rate is simply indeterminate. The theory also offers no particular grounds for thinking that such destabilizing speculation would disappear with government action. Episodes such as the 1984–1985 dollar and 1994–1995 yen may be better understood by models with small deviations from rational expectations. Some models have two classes of actors: short-horizon technical analysts or "noise traders," on the one hand, and the traditional fundamentalists (whose expectations would be rational, were it not for the existence of the noise traders) on the other hand. The result can be a speculative bubble developing on the back of a movement that originated in fundamentals. I call this "overshooting the overshooting equilibrium." It is capable of explaining some of the other puzzling findings, such as the tendency for the currency to move up in the future when the forward discount or interest differential actually points down. In the aftermath of an increase in the interest-rate differential, the currency appreciates over the subsequent year, rather than appreciating instantaneously and then depreciating gradually as it should in the efficient-markets overshooting theory.

III PROPOSED CURES FOR THE FOREIGN-EXCHANGE MARKET

Proposals to stabilize exchange rates can be grouped into three categories.

A Fixed exchange rates: "irrevocably fixed" peg or currency board (or gold standard)

Exchange-rate pegs are looking less attractive then they did in the 1980's when many small and medium-sized countries made a return to fixed exchange rates a cornerstone of monetary disinflation programs. It had been claimed that sincere commitment on the part of the monetary authorities was sufficient to end inflation. The 1992–1993 ERM crises and 1994 peso crisis have changed minds. In practice there is no such thing as "irrevocably fixed." Even the French-speaking countries of West and Central Africa devalued against the franc in 1994, for the first time in 35 years of independence.

It has become fashionable in some quarters to say that the solution is a more credible commitment to a fixed exchange rate, such as is offered by a currency board. This might make some sense, for certain countries. These are countries that (i) are very small, open, and well-integrated with the world economy, (ii) crave further rapid integration with major neighbors, or (iii) desperately need to import monetary stability, due to a history of hyper-inflation or absence of stable institutions. To the list of requirements should be added possession of sufficiently large international reserves. Enough reserves for 100-percent backing of central-bank money might not be sufficient; enough to back the entire domestic money supply might be required, to deal with potential banking crises. To acquire such reserves can be a tall order. But in any case, currency boards and fixed exchange rates are not appropriate for most large countries.

B Capital controls

James Tobin (1978) proposed a levy on all foreign-exchange transactions—the Tobin tax. It may not be quite as crazy as most economists think. There are two standard critiques: (i) that there is no reason why the Tobin tax would screen out the undesirable destabilizing speculation without also screening out desirable investment and (ii) that it cannot be enforced. There is an answer to the first critique. The studies based on survey data, mentioned above, suggest that short-horizon speculators tend to extrapolate, and that long-horizon speculators tend to forecast a return to long-run equilibrium. A tax could be small enough to be fairly negligible for importers, exporters, and long-term investors and yet wipe out a lot of short-term speculation. A tax of 0.1 percent, measured in terms of annualized expected rates of return, would come out to a 43-percent penalty on one-day speculation. This would discourage short-term transactions, which are the ones that, on average, seem to be based on extrapolative forecasting and, therefore, destabilizing (see Frankel, 1996).

Thus the Tobin tax might have the effect of reducing unnecessary volatility, provided it could be enforced. (Also, it would raise a lot of revenue. If governments used it to replace, say, tariff or income-tax revenue, it would be hard to argue that, on net, overall allocation of resources was damaged.) But enforcement is a big problem. Certainly if some countries adopted the Tobin tax but others did not, the foreign-exchange trading would simply move to where it was not taxed. For this reason, everyone agrees that it would have to be imposed in virtually all countries, large and small. This would require more widespread support than seems possible politically.

Other varieties of proposals for capital controls raise questions of practicality, for major developed countries. Examples include the *interest-equalization tax* and the *dual exchange rate*, as proposed by Rudiger Dornbusch (1986), or the recent proposal of Barry Eichengreen and Charles Wyplosz (1996) for *deposit requirements on domestic-currency loans* from domestic banks to foreign residents.

C More formal institutions for intervention

Other ideas for institutions to stabilize exchange rates include the following:

1   *Multilateral Intervention Fund.*—Such a fund has been proposed by, for example, Michel Camdessus (1994). It would be administered by the IMF.
2   *Target Zone, à la ERM.*—The developments of 1992–1993 make this option look less attractive. As long as France, Italy, and Spain had capital controls, in the 1980's, the ERM worked. But by 1990, when the German reunification shock hit, such controls had been removed. Intervention postponed the exchange-rate adjustment, but only for two years. The episode proved once again the Impossible Trinity: it is not possible to have exchange-rate stability, financial openness, and monetary independence all at once.
3   *Target zone, à la John Williamson (1987).*—This proposal has the virtue that the central parity is regularly adjusted when fundamentals so dictate (e.g., if inflation is higher in one country than another), so that crises are less likely. But this improvement regarding practicality also seriously vitiates the two standard arguments in favor of the ERM-style target zone: the nominal anchor, and the "honeymoon effect" whereby private speculation supposedly helps drive the currency away from the zone limits if speculators know that there will not be a realignment.

Those calling for radical reform of the international monetary system can be usefully classified in a two-by-two table, distinguishing them, first, by their convictions regarding whether the markets always know better than the governments and, second, by whether their proposals call for international cooperation or, to the contrary, are motivated by a desire to let governments choose monetary policies independently of each other (see Table 17.1).

The list is not complete without a mention of Ronald McKinnon (1988). He is unique in combining elements of each of the other schools. First, he believes that foreign-exchange markets left to themselves are excessively volatile, as does the Tobin–Dornbusch school. Second, he believes that purchasing-price parity (PPP) is a useful guide for setting the exchange rate, as do the monetarists. Third, he believes that devaluation is not a useful instrument for adjusting relative prices or improving the trade balance, as do the supply-siders. And fourth, he believes that the world needs a tripartite monetary agreement (among the United States, Japan, and Germany) to govern world monetary policy, as does the Bergsten-Williamson school (see C. Fred Bergsten and Williamson, 1983).

Table 17.1 Four schools of radical reform

Motivation	Conviction	
	Markets know best	*Need government activism*
Want national independence	Pure free-float works best (Friedman and monetarists)	Anti-speculator controls (Tobin, Dornbusch, *et al.*)
Want an international agreement	Discipline from fixed rates; gold standard (Mundell and supply-siders)	Activist international cooperation (Bergsten, Williamson, *et al.*)

Having looked over the various proposals for radical reform, one is left wondering whether their drawbacks are not greater than those of the present system of (managed) floating, imperfect as it is.

NOTES

1 Frankel and Andrew Rose (1995) survey the empirical literature on exchange-rate determination.
2 The example of Ireland is a particularly convincing demonstration (see Michael Mussa, 1990).
3 Charles Engel (1996) has recently surveyed the subject.
4 Chapters in Frankel (1993) document this point, and the next.

REFERENCES

Bergsten, C. Fred and Williamson, John. "Exchange Rates and Trade Policy," in William Cline, ed., *Trade Policy in the 1980s*. Washington, DC: Institute for International Economics, 1983, pp. 99–120.
Camdessus, Michel. "The IMF at 50—An Evolving Role but a Constant Mission." Speech delivered at Institute for International Economics, excerpted in *IMF Survey*, 13 June 1994, vol. 23.
Dornbusch, Rudiger. "Flexible Exchange Rates and Excess Capital Mobility." *Brookings Papers on Economic Activity*, 1986, (1), pp. 209–26.
Eichenbaum, Martin and Evans, Charles. "Some Empirical Evidence on the Effects of Monetary Policy Shocks on Exchange Rates." *Quarterly Journal of Economics*, November 1995, 110(4), pp. 975–1110.
Eichengreen, Barry and Wyplosz, Charles. "Taxing International Financial Transactions: Issues, Evidence, Alternatives," in Inga Kaul *et al.*, eds, *New and Innovative Sources of Financing Development*. New York: Oxford University Press, 1996.
Engel, Charles. "The Forward Discount Anomaly and the Risk Premium: A Survey of Recent Evidence." *Journal of Empirical Finance*, 1996.
Frankel, Jeffrey. *On Exchange Rates*. Cambridge, MA: MIT Press, 1993.
—— ."How Well Do Foreign Exchange Markets Function: Might a Tobin Tax Help?" in Inga Kaul *et al.*, eds, *New and Innovative Sources of Financing Development*. New York: Oxford University Press, 1996.
Frankel, Jeffrey and Rose, Andrew. "Empirical Research on Nominal Exchange

Rates," in Gene Grossman and Kenneth Rogoff, eds., *Handbook of International Economics*. Amsterdam: North-Holland, 1995, pp. 1689–1729.

Friedman, Milton. "The Case for Flexible Exchange Rates," in Milton Friedman, ed., *Essays in Positive Economics*. Chicago: University of Chicago Press, 1953, pp. 157–203.

McKinnon, Ronald. "Monetary and Exchange Rate Policies for International Financial Stability." *Journal of Economic Perspectives*, Winter 1988, 2(1), pp. 83–103.

Mundell, Robert. "The Global Adjustment System," in M. Baldassarri, J. McCallum, and R. Mundell, eds., *Global Disequilibrium in the World Economy*. New York: St. Martin's Press, 1992, pp. 351–464.

Mussa, Michael. *Exchange Rates in Theory and in Reality*. Princeton Essays in International Finance No. 179. Princeton, NJ: International Finance Section, Princeton University, 1990.

Obstfeld, Maurice. "The Logic of Currency Crises," in B. Eichengreen, J. Frieden, and J. von Hagen, eds., *Monetary and Fiscal Policy in an Integrated Europe*. New York: Springer-Verlag, 1995, pp. 62–90.

Tobin, James. "A Proposal for International Monetary Reform." *Eastern Economic Journal*, July/October 1978, 4(3–4), pp. 153–59.

Williamson, John. "Exchange Rate Management: The Role of Target Zones." *American Economic Review*, May 1987 (*Papers and Proceedings*), 77(2), pp. 200–4.

18 Exchange rates and the political economy of macroeconomic discipline

*Sebastian Edwards**

American Economic Review, vol. 86, no. 2 (1996) pp. 159–63

During the last few years there has been an increasing interest in understanding the relationship between exchange-rate regimes and macroeconomic stability. Some recurrent policy questions are: (a) why do countries still choose fixed, nominal exchange-rate regimes 25 years after the abandonment of the Bretton Woods system? (b) do fixed exchange-rate regimes impose an effective constraint on monetary and fiscal behavior, thus lowering inflation rates over the long run? and (c) are exchange-rate-based stabilization programs superior to money-based programs? This paper deals with the first question—the selection of the exchange-rate regime—from a political-economy perspective. Why certain countries choose a particular type of exchange-rate regime is a highly relevant question. Why does Austria have a fixed exchange rate, for example, while the United Kingdom has a flexible one? Why has Argentina chosen a fixed exchange rate, while Chile has a flexible-cum-bands system? More generally, in December 1992, why did 84 countries (out of the 167 reported in the IMF's *International Financial Statistics*) peg their currencies to a major currency or a currency composite? The theoretical discussion deals with the trade-off between credibility and flexibility, and it emphasizes the role of politics and institutions. In the empirical section I use a large cross-country panel data set to analyze the role of various factors, including political instability, in deciding whether a pegged or a flexible exchange-rate system will be chosen.

I THE POLITICAL ECONOMY OF EXCHANGE-RATE REGIMES

Consider the case of a two-period economy where the authorities' preferences are quadratic and depend on a nominal variable (inflation) and on deviations of a real variable (unemployment) from their target. The authorities choose between a pegged or a flexible exchange-rate system. In making this decision the authorities face an important trade-off: namely, under a

* Anderson Graduate School of Management, UCLA, Los Angeles, CA 90024, and National Bureau of Economic Research. I thank Daniel Lederman and Fernando Losada for their assistance.

pegged exchange rate inflation will be lower, but the deviation from a given unemployment target will be higher than under flexible rates.

The authorities also consider a positive probability (q) of abandoning the parity under a pegged regime. In other words, the authorities fix the exchange rate during the first period, but an "escape clause" can be exercised at the beginning of the second period. When the pegged rate is abandoned, the country adopts a flexible rate, but the authorities incur a political cost (C). This assumption captures the stylized fact, noted by Richard Cooper (1971), that stepwise devaluations are often associated with political upheaval and, in many cases, with the fall of the government. The magnitude of this cost will depend on the political and institutional characteristics of the country, including its degree of political instability. The political ramifications of a major economic disturbance, such as the abandonment of a promised parity, will tend to be more pronounced in countries with a higher degree of structural political instability. This reasoning can explain why the vast majority of stepwise devaluations take place during the early years of an administration, when its degree of political popularity is higher. The degree of political instability will also affect a government's discount factor (β). Leaders in more unstable political systems will tend to be more impatient, discounting the future more heavily. In sum, C and β can be expressed as functions of the degree of political instability (ρ):

$$C = C(\rho) \quad C' > 0 \tag{1}$$

$$\beta = \beta(\rho) \quad \beta' < 0.$$

The exchange-rate system decision rule will be based on an *ex ante* comparison between loss functions:

$$K = E\{L^F - L^P\}. \tag{2}$$

Where L^F and L^P are the loss functions under flexible and pegged regimes. If $K > 0$, then a pegged regime is preferred. It is possible to write K as

$$K = \gamma(\pi^F)^2 + \mu[(\kappa^F)^2 - (\kappa^P)^2] \tag{3}$$

$$+ \beta(1 - q)\, \gamma(\pi^F)^2_{i+1} + \beta(1 - q)$$

$$\times \mu[(\kappa^F)^2_{i+1} - (\kappa^P)^2_{i+1}] - q\beta C$$

where π^F is inflation under the flexible regime ($\pi^P = 0$), $(\kappa^F)^2 = (u^F - u^*)^2$ and $(\kappa^P)^2 = (u^P - u^*)^2$, u^F and u^P are the rates of unemployment under fixed and flexible rates, u^* is the target rate of unemployment, and γ and μ are parameters that measure the relative importance of π and deviations from u^* in the authorities' loss function (see Edwards, 1996). It is easy to show that for both periods $[(\kappa^F)^2 - (\kappa^P)^2] < 0$. From equation (3) it is possible to derive a number of hypotheses regarding the likelihood of a country's choosing a particular regime. A higher π (in either period) will increase the likelihood that a pegged regime will be chosen. In contrast, a higher degree of external volatility will increase the likelihood that a flexible system will be selected, because the volatility of unemployment will increase under fixed rates. A higher C will reduce the *ex ante* probability of selecting a pegged rate, while a higher q will have an ambiguous effect.

A particularly important issue is how political instability affects the choice of regime. In principle there will be two offsetting forces. First, a higher degree of political instability increases the cost of abandoning the peg and thus will reduce the *ex ante* probability that a pegged regime will be chosen. Second, a higher degree of instability increases the authorities' discount rate, reducing the importance of "the future" in their decision-making process. In sum, the net effect of political instability on regime selection is an empirical question. I tackle this issue in the following section. Finally, the analysis sketched above suggests that a more "ambitious" unemployment target (a lower u^*) will result in a temptation to "overinflate." Since the public will be aware of this incentive, the authorities will face a serious credibility problem, and the economy will reach a high-inflation equilibrium. This credibility problem can be solved (partially) by selecting an exchange-rate system that constrains the authorities' ability to generate inflation. Thus, countries with a more ambitious real target, with other things given, will have an incentive to select a pegged regime as a way of reducing their credibility problem.

II DATA

The data set includes 63 countries and covers 1980–1992. Countries were classified according to their exchange-rate regime in a binary fashion. The IMF's *International Financial Statistics* (IFS) was used to classify countries according to their regimes. Thus, a dependent variable (Peg 1) was defined, taking a value of 1 for countries with pegged currencies, and 0 for countries with "limited flexibility" or "more flexible" regimes.[1] Two classes of independent variables were used in the analysis: the first attempts to capture long-term structural characteristics, both political and economic, of these countries, and are assumed to change very slowly through time. They are usually defined as an average for the decade prior to the one included in the analysis. The second class of independent variables tries to capture, for each country, the evolution of some key economic variables through time, and thus their value varies from year to year (for details on the data set see Edwards, 1996).

Political Instability.—Empirical measures of political instability tend to be rather simplistic. Alex Cukierman *et al.* (1992) used the frequency of governmental change as a measure of political turnover and instability. A limitation of this measure is that it treats *every* change in the head of state as an indication of political instability, regardless of whether the new leadership belongs to the same party. In this paper I use a new index of political instability that focuses on instances where there has been a *transfer of power* from a party or group in office to a party or group formerly in the opposition, also between 1972 and 1980. This index (TP) measures the instability *of the political system* by defining a transfer of power as a situation where there is a break in the governing political party's (or dictator's) control of executive power.[2]

External Shocks.—Two alternative indexes were used to measure the extent of external-shock variability: (a) a coefficient of variation of real export growth for 1970–1980, denoted as CVEX, was constructed with raw data obtained from IFS; and (b) a coefficient of variation of real, bilateral exchange-rate changes for 1970–1980, EXVAR, was constructed from data obtained from IFS. The extent of potential endogeneity problems was reduced by using CVEX and EXVAR for periods prior to 1980–1992. It is expected that the coefficients of these variables in the probit regressions will be negative. In addition, an interactive variable (VAR—OPEN) was included in the regressions to analyze how the degree of openness, defined as the trade-to-GDP ratio, affects the extent to which external variability influences the choice of regime.

Inflationary "Temptation."—A cornerstone of the model sketched above is the idea that countries with a very "ambitious" unemployment objective will have an incentive to "tie their own hands," by selecting a pegged-exchange-rate regime to solve their credibility problem. This degree of "ambition" is difficult to measure, particularly when only a handful of countries have data on unemployment. For this reason I used the lagged average real GDP growth in 1970–1980 as a proxy for the countries' incentives to "tie their own hands." I assume that countries with a historically low rate of growth will be more tempted to "overinflate." It is expected, then, that the coefficient of GROWTH will be negative in the probit regressions.

Probability of Abandoning the Peg.—Since it is not possible to observe q directly, three variables that capture the probability of abandoning the parity were considered in the empirical analysis, using IFS data. (a) Countries with a history of rapid inflation will tend to have a greater propensity to devalue. The historical (log) rate of inflation (LOGINF) is defined as the average for 1970–1980. (b) Higher international liquidity, with other things given, reduces the probability of abandoning the peg. The one-year lagged ratio of international reserves to high-powered money (RESMONEY) was used in the analysis. (c) Countries with a higher rate of growth of domestic liquidity will have a lower ability to maintain a peg. This variable (CREGRO) was defined as a five-year moving average.

Since it can be argued that less-advanced countries do not have the institutional capacity to implement flexible-exchange-rate regimes, the log of income per capita (PCGDP), measured in 1989 dollars, was included in the analysis in addition to the variables discussed above. This variable was taken from the World Bank's *World Development Report*.

III EMPIRICAL RESULTS

Table 18.1 contains the main results from the probit analysis. Regressions (i) and (ii) were run on the complete data set, and (iii) was run only for developing countries. Of the 832 observations in (i), in 443 the value of Peg1 was 0, and in 387 it was 1. Overall the results provide broad support for the model presented in the preceding section. The estimates suggest that political instability plays an important role in regime selection: more unstable countries have a lower probability of selecting a pegged-exchange-rate system. The consistently negative coefficient of TP indicates that the direct effect of a higher political cost of devaluing offsets the effect via a higher discount rate.

The coefficients of EXVAR and CVEX are also negative, as expected, and significantly so. The positive coefficients of the interactive VAR—OPEN are rather puzzling. They seem to indicate that the influence of EXVAR on the probability of choosing a pegged rate declines with higher levels of openness.

The estimated coefficients of the variables that capture the ability to maintain the peg have the expected sign and are also significant at conventional

Table 18.1 Probit regression results: Peg 1 as dependent variable

Variable	Regression (i)	(ii)	(iii)
Constant	2.914 (10.744)	3.131 (11.945)	2.677 (9.194)
TP	−1.752 (−4.821)	−1.487 (−4.199)	−1.761 (−3.614)
EXVAR	−0.119 (3.359)	—	−0.256 (−4.581)
CVEX	—	−0.242 (−1.531)	—
VAR–OPEN	—	0.036 (1.933)	0.039 (1.949)
CREGRO	−0.199 (−1.929)	−0.147 (−2.039)	−0.102 (−1.184)
LOGINF	−1.054 (8.347)	−1.223 (−10.803)	−0.919 (−6.795)
RESMONEY	0.577 (5.129)	0.608 (5.694)	0.171 (1.822)
GROWTH	−0.056 (− 2.911)	−0.081 (−3.204)	−0.117 (−3.976)
PCGDP	−0.035 (−4.902)	−0.027 (−3.687)	0.394 (3.851)
N	832	873	566
X^2	278.0	284.6	182.6

levels. The coefficient of lagged inflation is significantly negative, suggesting that countries with a history of inflation will have a lower probability of maintaining the peg and will thus tend to favor the adoption of a more flexible system. Moreover, the coefficients of CREGRO are also negative. The coefficient of RESMONEY is significantly positive in all regressions, indicating that countries with lower holdings of international reserves will have a lower probability of adopting a pegged-exchange-rate regime.

The estimated coefficient of GROWTH is significantly negative, suggesting that countries with a lower growth rate will tend to prefer a more rigid regime. To the extent that historical growth is a good proxy for the "temptation to inflate," this result can be interpreted as providing evidence in favor of the "tying its own hands" hypothesis. Countries with poorer historical performance, as measured by GROWTH, will have a greater incentive to renege on their low-inflation promises and, thus, will benefit from adopting a more rigid exchange-rate system. In order to analyze the robustness of these results I used the yearly difference between the rate of unemployment and its long-term historical average (1970–1990) as an alternative measure of the "temptation to inflate." The number of observations in this case was only 280, and most countries in this reduced sample were high-income nations. For these reasons, the results obtained from these estimates should be interpreted with caution. In the context of the credibility approach, the estimated coefficient of this variable is expected to be positive. In equation (i) of Table 18.1, when the differential in unemployment was substituted for the rate of GDP growth, its coefficient was indeed positive as expected (0.113) and significant (t statistic = 2.65).

Finally, the coefficient of PCGDP is significantly negative in equations (i) and (ii), indicating that, to the extent that the adoption of a flexible regime requires sophisticated institutions, more advanced countries will have a tendency to select more flexible rates. This result, however, is highly influenced by the way in which the industrial countries, and in particular the ERM nations, are classified.

To sum up, these results are encouraging for the political-economy approach. Nonetheless, much more could be learned through future work focusing on three broad areas: (a) on generating better measures of political instability; (b) on improving the indexes of the authorities' temptation to over-inflate; and (c) on analyzing whether exchange-rate regimes affect macroeconomic performance.

NOTES

1 IFS uses a three-way classification of exchange-rate regimes: "pegged," "flexible," and "limited flexibility." See Edwards (1996) for probit regression results with alternative definitions of a pegged currency.
2 The merits of this type of index were first discussed in Edwards and Guido Tabellini (1994).

REFERENCES

Cooper, Richard. *Currency Devaluation in Developing Countries*, Princeton Essays in International Finance. Princeton, NJ: International Finance Section, Princeton University, 1971.

Cukierman, Alex; Edwards, Sebastian and Tabellini, Guido. "Seignorage and Political Instability." *American Economic Review*, June 1992, 82(3), pp. 537–55.

Edwards, Sebastian. "Exchange Rate Regimes and Macroeconomic Stability: A Political Economy Approach." Mimeo, World Bank, Washington, DC, January 1996.

Edwards, Sebastian and Tabellini, Guido. "Political Instability, Political Weakness, and Inflation," in Christopher A. Sims, ed., *Advances in Econometrics*. New York: Cambridge University Press, 1994, pp. 355–76.

Questions

1 Derive the flexi-price monetary model of exchange rate determination and comment on its predictions.
2 Can the sticky-price monetary approach explain the failure of the flexi-price approach to predict short-run volatility in the exchange rate?
3 'Monetary approaches to exchange rate determination can explain long-term exchange rate behaviour whereas the portfolio-balance is more suitable for the short run.' Discuss.
4 Suppose that the budget of this country is expected to be in deficit for two successive years. What is the impact of this information on the exchange rate? Which approach is more appropriate to determine the effect on the exchange rate?
5 How could speculative bubbles emerge and what are their implications for the choice of exchange rate regime?
6 'The shortcomings of the floating regime is obvious enough, but the problems posed by fixed exchange rates are more severe.' Discuss.
7 'The floating exchange rate regime may well be an escape route for countries unable and/or unwilling to make credible policy commitments.' Discuss.

Further reading and references

FURTHER READING

For an intermediate textbook treatment of the exchange rate determination, consult Rivera-Batiz and Rivera-Batiz (1994), ch. 19. For a comparison between the monetary and portfolio-balance approaches to exchange rate determination, see Pilbeam (1998), chs 7–9. On the origins of the monetary approach to exchange rate determination, see Frenkel (1978). Dornbusch (1976) represents the first sticky-price monetary model. The early contributions to the portfolio-balance approach were those of Kouri (1976) and Allen and Kenen (1980). On the issue of non-fundamentalist behaviour in the foreign exchange market, see Taylor and Allen (1992) and Frankel (1993). The latter source can also be consulted on the divergence between the forward discount and the actual exchange rate.

REFERENCES

Allen, P.R. and P.B. Kenen (1980) *Asset Markets, Exchange Rates and Economic Integration: A Synthesis*, Cambridge: Cambridge University Press.

Dornbusch, R. (1976) 'Expectations and exchange rate dynamics', *Journal of Political Economy* 84, December, 1161–76.

Frankel, J. (1993) *On Exchange Rates*, Cambridge, MA: MIT Press.

Frenkel, J. (1978) 'A monetary approach to the exchange rate: doctrinal aspects and empirical evidence' in J. Frenkel and H. Johnson, *The Economics of Exchange Rates: Selected Studies*, Reading, MA: Addison-Wesley.

Kouri, P.J.K. (1976) 'The exchange rate and the balance of payments in the short run and the long run: a monetary approach', *Scandinavian Journal of Economics* 78(2), 280–304.

Pilbeam, K. (1998) *International Finance*, 2nd edn, London: Macmillan.

Rivera-Batiz, F.L. and L.A. Rivera-Batiz (1994) *International Finance and Open Economy Macroeconomics*, (2nd edn) Upper Saddle River, NJ: Prentice Hall.

Taylor, M.P. and H.L. Allen (1992) 'The use of technical analysis in the foreign exchange market', *Journal of International Money and Finance* 10.

Part VII

Monetary unions and the EMU

Introduction

Part VII follows the preceding two parts naturally for two reasons. First, it examines a special case of the exchange rate policy choice examined in Part VI – namely the monetary union as an irrevocably fixed exchange rate arrangement. Second, it revisits the issue of credibility in the conduct of monetary policy, discussed in Part V. An additional factor that makes Part VII even more relevant is the fact that the subject matter it covers – monetary integration – has generated a very large volume of research both in Europe and elsewhere. Therefore, a reader on macroeconomic policy in open economies would remain significantly deficient unless it reflects the contributions of this research effort.

The articles by Mundell and McKinnon are two of the early but seminal contributions on monetary unions. The third article by De Grauwe builds on Mundell's and McKinnon's contributions not only by operationalising some of their findings but also by pointing out the need to qualify the original optimum currency area (OCA) theory. Finally, the article by Eichengreen looks beyond the costs and benefits of OCAs and reviews the most recent contributions analysing a number of policy issues in the European Monetary Union (EMU) such as fiscal policy co-ordination, central bank credibility and external implications of the EMU.

Mundell and McKinnon provide a concise yet highly perceptive analysis of the factors that could make a currency area optimum. Mundell emphasises the significance of convergence between the economic structures of the regions (or countries) within a currency area. Given that a currency area involves relinquishing the exchange rate as an instrument that can be used for correcting external imbalances, an OCA requires structural convergence so that the risk of asymmetric shocks is minimised. McKinnon does not question the relevance of the convergence requirement, but adds another factor to be taken into account: the degree of openness to trade (or the ratio of tradables to non-tradable goods). The higher the degree of openness is, the lower is the cost of establishing a currency area. That is because devaluations in highly open economies would be quickly translated into higher domestic prices and, consequently, would lead to an upward revision in nominal wages. Therefore, devaluations are less likely to be effective in securing improvement in competitiveness and correcting external imbalances.

The convergence and openness criteria (together with factor mobility between OCA members) have constituted the core of the debate in the OCA literature that followed. Yet, there are two further points that Mundell and McKinnon raised. The one raised by Mundell is that currency unions within single countries do not necessarily constitute OCAs. Regional divergence within one country may well expose the regions in that country to asymmetric shocks. Therefore, there is no guarantee that national monetary unions are necessarily optimal. This conclusion suggests that the choice between national and multinational OCAs is essentially a choice between two second-best arrangements rather than between first-best and second-best options. The other point is raised by McKinnon and relates to destabilising effects of the flexible exchange rate regime as the alternative to monetary unions. In small open economies, flexible exchange rates may generate excessive demand for foreign currency as a substitute for domestic currency. This would be the case when the usefulness of domestic currency as a unit of account and/or medium of exchange is impaired by inflationary tendencies. Then, flexible exchange rates can be a source of external imbalance rather than a mechanism ensuring external balance.

De Grauwe introduces new issues that would require some qualification of the traditional OCA criteria. First of all, he questions the relevance of the convergence criterion in the presence of intra-industry trade. Given that trade between EU countries is increasingly of an intra-industry nature, a fall in the demand for certain goods would affect all countries in the same direction. Although intra-industry trade strengthens the case for monetary unions, the impact of the latter on the concentration of production should also be considered. Judging by the US experience, one can expect further concentration of production in the EU after the monetary union. Then, the positive implications of intra-industry trade must be set against the negative implications of further concentration.

Second, the divergence in terms of growth rates could be less important than what the traditional OCA theory would suggest. Traditionally, it is assumed that flexible exchange rates are necessary to ensure trade balance between fast-growing countries that are more likely to experience trade deficits and slow-growing countries that are more likely to experience trade surpluses. If the currency is allowed to depreciate (appreciate) in fast-growing (slow-growing) countries, trade deficits or surpluses will be eliminated without costly corrections through aggregate demand and output. But De Grauwe points out that the case for flexible exchange rates is not as strong as this argument would suggest. On the one hand, the income elasticity of exports of fast-growing countries is higher than the income elasticity of exports of slow-growing countries. On the other hand, the income elasticity of the exports of fast-growing countries is higher than the income elasticity of their imports. To the extent that this is the case, exchange rate changes become less necessary to eliminate deficits in fast-growing countries and surpluses in slow-growing countries.

Third, De Grauwe draws attention to the possibility that the monetary union might reduce the institutional differences between national labour markets. As monetary policies are centralised in a monetary union, there will be less scope for discounting inflation more heavily compared to unemployment. Under this scenario, trade unions in different countries will face a more or less similar government reaction curve. As a result, trade unions in relatively more accommodating countries will have to revise their expectations and moderate their wage claims accordingly.

Last but not least, De Grauwe introduces the issue of policy credibility into the analysis of OCAs. Drawing on the Barro–Gordon model of rules versus discretion, he demonstrates that a monetary union could emerge as a commitment device that would enable the government to resolve the dilemma between optimal and credible policies. The importance of this finding is twofold. On the one hand, it weakens the case for a flexible exchange rate regime as the latter provides the government with incentive to maintain 'wet' policies – which are costly in terms of inflation and ineffective in terms of reducing unemployment below the non-accelerating-inflation rate of unemployment. On the other hand, it strengthens the case for monetary unions, as commitment to a fixed exchange rate regime is not as strong as the commitment implied by a monetary union.

The last article, by Eichengreen, fulfils a different but complementary role. Its complementary role is ensured by its review of the recent literature on two issues that recur frequently in the preceding chapters: the importance of abandoning the exchange rate as a policy instrument in the face of low labour mobility, and the credibility of EMU institutions. With respect to the former, Eichengreen derives two conclusions. First, he points out that devaluations after the 1992/3 ERM crises have contributed to balance of payments improvements but they have not affected overall growth rates. Second, low levels of labour mobility within the euro zone are likely to increase the cost of abandoning the exchange rate, but labour mobility is low not only between but also within European countries. With respect to the credibility issue, he indicates that the proof of the pudding will be in the eating. In other words, we need to wait and see whether the European Central Bank (ECB) will be as credible as the Bundesbank.

The novelty of Eichengreen's article lies in its elaboration on issues that are not touched upon in the preceding articles. Of these, two issues are important so far as the perspective of this book is concerned. One is the issue of fiscal policy co-ordination within the EMU – an issue that has been a subject of extensive research in the 1990s. My reading of Eichengreen's review suggests that the gains from fiscal policy co-ordination may be uncertain but it may still be a better option compared to the Growth and Stability Pact (GSP) and the Excessive Deficit Procedure (EDP) adopted by the EU. That is because the GSP and EDP carry the risk of switching off automatic stabilisers and require a shift towards fiscal federalism – an arrangement unlikely to emerge due to political constraints.

The other issue concerns the external dimension of the EMU. As far as the exchange rate policy of the euro zone is concerned, there is a certain degree of consensus indicating a preference for a flexible euro rate *vis-à-vis* the rest of the world. This is to be expected, given that the EMU is a large bloc that would be less open than its constituent parts. With respect to the extent to which the euro will be a significant reserve currency, the existing research indicates that the emergence of the euro as a reserve currency will be slow and depend on the extent to which the ECB will be involved in day-to-day liquidity management. The Maastricht Treaty provisions suggest that the ECB will not be involved in day-to-day liquidity management. In the absence of another European institution ready to act as a lender of last resort in the face of sudden movements in asset prices, the transaction demand for euros in the securities market will be dampened and the demand for the euro as a reserve currency will be lower than the EMU's size would suggest.

Given the intensity of the current public debate on the EMU, we hope that the articles in this part will enable the reader to identify the issues involved and make an informed intervention. We also hope that they will familiarise the reader with the extensive literature.

19 A theory of optimum currency areas

Robert A. Mundell*
American Economic Review, vol. 51, no. 4 (1961), pp. 657–65

It is patently obvious that periodic balance-of-payments crises will remain an integral feature of the international economic system as long as fixed exchange rates and rigid wage and price levels prevent the terms of trade from fulfilling a natural role in the adjustment process. It is, however, far easier to pose the problem and to criticize the alternatives than it is to offer constructive and feasible suggestions for the elimination of what has become an international disequilibrium system.[1] The present paper, unfortunately, illustrates that proposition by cautioning against the practicability, in certain cases, of the most plausible alternative: a system of national currencies connected by flexible exchange rates.

A system of flexible exchange rates is usually presented, by its proponents,[2] as a device whereby depreciation can take the place of unemployment when the external balance is in deficit, and appreciation can replace inflation when it is in surplus. But the question then arises whether all existing national currencies should be flexible. Should the Ghanian pound be freed to fluctuate against all currencies or ought the present sterling-area currencies remain pegged to the pound sterling? Or, supposing that the Common Market countries proceed with their plans for economic union, should these countries allow each national currency to fluctuate, or would a single currency area be preferable?

The problem can be posed in a general and more revealing way by defining a currency area as a domain within which exchange rates are fixed and asking: What is the appropriate domain of a currency area? It might seem at first that the question is purely academic since it hardly appears within the realm of political feasibility that national currencies would ever be abandoned in favor of any other arrangement. To this, three answers can be given:

1   Certain parts of the world are undergoing processes of economic integration and disintegration, new experiments are being made, and a conception of what constitutes an optimum currency area can clarify the meaning of these experiments.

2   Those countries, like Canada, which have experimented with flexible

*   The author is an economist in the Special Research Section of the International Monetary Fund.

exchange rates are likely to face particular problems which the theory of *optimum* currency areas can elucidate if the national currency area does not coincide with the optimum currency area.

3   The idea can be used to illustrate certain functions of currencies which have been inadequately treated in the economic literature and which are sometimes neglected in the consideration of problems of economic policy.

I CURRENCY AREAS AND COMMON CURRENCIES

A single currency implies a single central bank (with note-issuing powers) and therefore a potentially elastic supply of interregional means of payments. But in a currency area comprising more than one currency the supply of international means of payment is conditional upon the cooperation of many central banks; no central bank can expand its own liabilities much faster than other central banks without losing reserves and impairing convertibility.[2] This means that there will be a major difference between adjustment within a currency area which has a single currency and a currency area involving more than one currency; in other words there will be a difference between inter-regional adjustment and international adjustment even though exchange rates, in the latter case, are fixed.

To illustrate this difference consider a simple model of two entities (regions or countries), initially in full employment and balance-of-payments equilibrium, and see what happens when this equilibrium is disturbed by a shift of demand from the goods of entity B to the goods of entity A. Assume that money wages and prices cannot be reduced in the short run without causing unemployment, and that monetary authorities act to prevent inflation.

Suppose first that the entities are countries with national currencies. The shift of demand from B to A causes unemployment in B and inflationary pressure in A.[4] To the extent that prices are allowed to rise in A, the change in the terms of trade will relieve B of some of the burden of adjustment. But if A tightens credit restrictions to prevent prices from rising, all the burden of adjustment is thrust onto country B; what is needed is a reduction in B's real income and if this cannot be effected by a change in the terms of trade— because B cannot lower, and A will not raise, prices—it must be accomplished by a decline in B's output and employment. The policy of surplus countries in restraining prices therefore imparts a recessive tendency to the world economy on fixed exchange rates or (more generally) to a currency area with many separate currencies.[5]

Contrast this situation with that where the entities are regions within a closed economy lubricated by a common currency; and suppose now that the national government pursues a full-employment policy. The shift of demand from B to A causes unemployment in region B and inflationary pressure in region A, and a surplus in A's balance of payments.[6] To correct the unemployment in B the monetary authorities increase the money supply. The monetary expansion, however, aggravates inflationary pressure in region A: indeed, the principal way in which the monetary policy is effective in correcting full employment in the deficit region is by raising prices in the surplus region, turning the terms of trade against B. Full employment thus imparts an inflationary bias to the multiregional economy or (more generally) to a currency area with common currency.

In a currency area comprising different countries with national currencies, the pace of employment in deficit countries is set by the willingness of surplus countries to inflate. But in a currency area comprising many regions and a single currency, the pace of inflation is set by the willingness of central authorities to allow unemployment in deficit regions.

The two systems could be brought closer together by an institutional change: unemployment could be avoided in the world economy if central banks agreed that the burden of international adjustment should fall on surplus countries, which would then inflate until unemployment in deficit countries is eliminated; or a world central bank could be established with power to create an international means of payment. But a currency area of either type cannot prevent both unemployment and inflation among its members. The fault lies not with the type of currency area, but with the domain of the currency area. The optimum currency area is not the world.

II NATIONAL CURRENCIES AND FLEXIBLE EXCHANGE RATES

The existence of more than one currency area in the world implies (by definition) variable exchange rates. In the international trade example, if demand shifts from the products of country B to the products of country A, a depreciation by country B or an appreciation by country A would correct the external imbalance and also relieve unemployment in country B and restrain inflation in country A. This is the most favorable case for flexible rates based on national currencies.

Other examples, however, might be equally relevant. Suppose that the world consists of two countries, Canada and the United States, each of which has separate currencies. Also assume that the continent is divided into two regions which do not correspond to national boundaries—the East, which produces goods like cars, and the West, which produces goods like lumber products. To test the flexible exchange rate argument in this example assume that the United States dollar fluctuates relative to the Canadian dollar, and that an increase in productivity (say) in the automobile industry causes an excess demand for lumber products and an excess supply of cars.

The immediate impact of the shift in demand is to cause unemployment in the East and inflationary pressure in the West, and a flow of bank reserves from the East to the West because of the former's regional balance-of-payments deficit. To relieve the unemployment in the East, the central banks in both countries would have to expand the national money supplies, or to prevent inflation in the West, contract the national money supplies. (Meanwhile the Canada–United States exchange rate would move to preserve equilibrium in the national balances). Thus, unemployment can be prevented in both countries, but only at the expense of inflation; or, inflation can be restrained in both countries but at the expense of unemployment; or, finally, the burden of adjustment can be shared between East and West with some unemployment in the East and some inflation in the West. But both unemployment and inflation cannot be escaped. The flexible exchange rate system does not serve to correct the balance-of-payments situation between the two regions (which is the essential problem) although it will do so between the two countries; it is therefore not necessarily preferable to a common currency or national currencies connected by fixed exchange rates.

III REGIONAL CURRENCY AREAS AND FLEXIBLE EXCHANGE RATES

The preceding example does not destroy the argument for flexible exchange rates, but it might severely impair the relevance of the argument if it is applied to national currencies. The logic of the argument can in fact be rescued if national currencies are abandoned in favor of regional currencies.

To see this suppose that the "world" reorganizes currencies so that Eastern and Western dollars replace Canadian and United States dollars. Now if the exchange rate between the East and the West were pegged, a dilemma would arise similar to that discussed in the first section. But if the East–West exchange rate were flexible, then an excess demand for lumber products need cause neither inflation nor unemployment in either region. The Western dollar appreciates relative to the Eastern dollar thus assuring balance-of-payments equilibrium, while the Eastern and Western central banks adopt monetary policies to ensure constancy of effective demand in terms of the regional currencies, and therefore stable prices and employment.

The same argument could be approached from another direction. A system of flexible exchange rates was originally propounded as an alternative to the gold-standard mechanism which many economists blamed for the worldwide spread of depression after 1929. But if the arguments against the gold standard were correct, then why should a similar arguments not apply against a common currency system in a multiregional country? Under the gold standard depression in one country would be transmitted, through the foreign-trade multiplier, to foreign countries. Similarly, under a common currency, depression in one region would be transmitted to other regions for precisely the same reasons. If the gold standard imposed a harsh discipline on the national economy and induced the transmission of economic fluctuations, then a common currency would be guilty of the same charges; interregional balance-of-payments problems are invisible, so to speak, precisely because there is no escape from the self-adjusting effects of interregional money flows. (It is true, of course, that interregional liquidity can always be supplied by the national central bank, whereas the gold standard and even the gold-exchange standard were hampered, on occasion, by periodic scarcities of internationally liquid assets; but the basic argument against the gold standard was essentially distinct from the liquidity problem.)

Today, if the case for flexible exchange rates is a strong one, it is, in logic, a case for flexible exchange rates based on *regional* currencies, not on national currencies. The optimum currency area is the region.

IV A PRACTICAL APPLICATION

The theory of international trade was developed on the Ricardian assumption that factors of production are mobile internally but immobile internationally. Williams, Ohlin, Iversen and others, however, protested that this assumption was invalid and showed how its relaxation would affect the real theory of trade. I have tried to show that its relaxation has important consequences also for the monetary theory of trade and especially the theory of flexible exchange rates. The argument for flexible exchange rates based on national currencies is only as valid as the Ricardian assumption about factor mobility. If factor mobility is high internally and low internationally, a system of flexible exchange rates based on national currencies might work effectively enough. But if regions cut across national boundaries or if countries are multiregional, then the argument for flexible exchange rates is only valid if currencies are reorganized on a regional basis.

In the real world, of course, currencies are mainly an expression of national sovereignty, so that actual currency reorganization would be feasible only if it were accompanied by profound political changes. The concept of an optimum currency area therefore has direct practical applicability only in areas where political organization is in a state of flux, such as in ex-colonial areas and in Western Europe.

In Western Europe the creation of the Common Market is regarded by many as an important step toward eventual politial union, and the subject of a common currency for the six countries has been much discussed. One can cite the well-known position of J.E. Meade (1957 pp. 385–86), who argues that the conditions for a common currency in Western Europe do not exist; and that, especially because of the lack of labor mobility, a system of flexible exchange rates would be more effective in promoting balance-of-payments equilibrium and internal stability; and the apparently opposite view of Tibor Scitovsky (1958 Ch. 2)[7] who favors a common currency because he believes that it would induce a greater degree of capital mobility, but further adds that steps must be taken to make labor more mobile and to facilitate supranational employment policies. In terms of the language of this paper, Meade favors national currency areas while Scitovsky gives qualified approval to the idea of a single currency area in Western Europe.

In spite of the apparent contradiction between these two views, the concept of optimum currency areas helps us to see that the conflict reduces to an empirical rather than a theoretical question. In both cases it is implied that an essential ingredient of a common currency, or a single currency area, is a high degree of factor mobility; but Meade believes that the necessary factor mobility does not exist, while Scitovsky argues that labor mobility must be improved and that the creation of a common currency would itself stimulate capital mobility. In other words neither writer disputes that the optimum currency area is the region—defined in terms of internal factor mobility and external factor immobility—but there is an implicit difference in views on the precise degree of factor mobility required to delineate a region. The question thus reduces to whether or not Western Europe can be considered a single region, and this is essentially an empirical problem.

V UPPER LIMITS ON THE NUMBER OF CURRENCIES AND CURRENCY AREAS

A dilemma now arises: Factor mobility (and hence the delineation of regions) is most usefully considered a relative rather than an absolute concept, with both geographical and industrial dimensions, and it is likely to change over time with alterations in political and economic conditions. If, then, the goals of internal stability are to be rigidly pursued, it follows that the greater is the number of separate currency areas in the world, the more successfully will these goals be attained (assuming, as always, that the basic argument for flexible exchange rates per se is valid). But this seems to imply that regions ought to be defined so narrowly as to count every minor pocket of unemployment arising from labor immobility as a separate region, each of which should apparently have a separate currency!

Such an arrangement hardly appeals to common sense. The suggestion reflects the fact that we have, thus far, considered the reasons for keeping currency areas small, not the reasons for maintaining or increasing their size. In other words we have discussed only the stabilization argument, to which end it is preferable to have many currency areas, and not the increasing costs which are likely to be associated with the maintenance of many currency areas.

It will be recalled that the older economists of the nineteenth century were internationalists and generally favored a world currency. Thus, John Stuart Mill wrote:

> So much of barbarism, however, still remains in the transactions of most civilised nations, that almost all independent countries choose to assert their nationality by having, to their own inconvenience and that of their neighbours, a peculiar currency of their own.
>
> (Mill 1894, p. 176)

Mill, like Bagehot and others, was concerned with the costs of valuation and money-changing, not stabilization policy, and it is readily seen that these costs tend to increase with the number of currencies. Any given money qua numeraire or unit of account fulfills this function less adequately if the prices of foreign goods are expressed in terms of foreign currency and must then be translated into domestic currency prices. Similarly, money in its role of medium of exchange is less useful if there are many currencies; although the costs of currency conversion are always present, they loom exceptionally large under inconvertibility or flexible exchange rates. (Indeed, in a hypo-

thetical world in which the number of currencies equaled the number of commodities, the usefulness of money in its roles of unit of account and medium
of exchange would disappear, and trade might just as well be conducted in
terms of pure barter.) Money is a convenience and this restricts the optimum
number of currencies. In terms of this argument alone the optimum currency
area is the world, regardless of the number of regions of which it is composed.

There are two other factors which would inhibit the creation of an arbitrarily large number of currency areas. In the first place markets for foreign
exchange must not be so thin that any single speculator (perhaps excepting
central banks) can affect the market price; otherwise the speculation argument against flexible exchange rates would assume weighty dimensions. The
other argument limiting "Balkanization" concerns the very pillar on which
the flexible exchange-rate argument tests. The thesis of those who favor flexible exchange rates is that the community in question is not willing to accept
variations in its real income through adjustments in its money wage rate or
price level, but that it is willing to accept virtually the same changes in its real
income through variations in the rate of exchange. In other words it is
assumed that unions bargain for a money rather than a real wage, and adjust
their wage demands to changes in the cost of living, if at all, only if the cost-
of-living index excludes imports. Now as the currency area grows smaller and
the proportion of imports in total consumption grows, this assumption
becomes increasingly unlikely. It may not be implausible to suppose that there
is some degree of money illusion in the bargaining process between unions
and management (or frictions and lags having the same effects), but it is
unrealistic to assume the extreme degree of money illusion that would have to
exist in small currency areas. Since the necessary degree of money illusion
becomes greater the smaller are currency areas, it is plausible to conclude that
this also imposes an upper limit on the number of currency areas.

VI CONCLUDING ARGUMENT

The subject of flexible exchange rates can logically be separated into two
distinct questions. The first is whether a system of flexible exchange rates can
work effectively and efficiently in the modern world economy. For this to be
possible it must be demonstrated that:

1   an international price system based on flexible exchange rates is dynamic-
    ally stable after taking speculative demands into account;
2   the exchange rate changes necessary to eliminate normal disturbances to
    dynamic equilibrium are not so large as to cause violent and reversible
    shifts between export- and import-competing industries (this is not ruled
    out by stability);
3   the risks created by variable exchange rates can be covered at reasonable
    costs in the forward markets;
4   central banks will refrain from monopolistic speculation;
5   monetary discipline will be maintained by the unfavourable political

consequences of continuing depreciation, as it is to some extent maintained today by threats to the levels of foreign exchange reserves;
6   reasonable protection of debtors and creditors can be assured to maintain an increasing flow of long-term capital movements; and
7   wages and profits are not tied to a price index in which import goods are heavily weighted.

I have not explicitly discussed these issues in my paper.

The second question concerns how the world should be divided into currency areas. I have argued that the stabilization argument for flexible exchange rates is valid only if it is based on regional currency areas. If the world can be divided into regions within each of which there is factor mobility and between which there is factor immobility, then each of these regions should have a separate currency which fluctuates relative to all other currencies. This carries the argument for flexible exchange rates to its logical conclusion.

But a region is an economic unit while a currency domain is partly an expression of national sovereignty. Except in areas where national sovereignty is being given up, it is not feasible to suggest that currencies should be reorganized; the validity of the argument for flexible exchange rates therefore hinges on the closeness with which nations correspond to regions. The argument works best if each nation (and currency) has internal factor mobility and external factor immobility. But if labor and capital are insufficiently mobile within a country, then flexibility of the external price of the national currency cannot be expected to perform the stabilization function attributed to it, and one could expect varying rates of unemployment or inflation in the different regions. Similarly, if factors are mobile across national boundaries, then a flexible exchange system becomes unnecessary, and may even be positively harmful, as I have suggested elsewhere.[8]

Canada provides the only modern example where an advanced country has experimented with flexible exchange rates. According to my argument the experiment should be largely unsuccessful as far as stabilization is concerned. Because of the factor immobility between regions, an increase in foreign demand for the products of one of the regions would cause an appreciation of the exchange rate and therefore increased unemployment in the remaining regions, a process which could be corrected by a monetary policy which aggravated inflationary pressures in the first region; every change in demand for the products in one region is likely to induce opposite changes in other regions which can not be entirely modified by national stabilization policies. Similarly the high degree of external capital mobility is likely to interfere with stabilization policy for completely different reasons: to achieve internal stability the central bank can alter credit conditions but it is the change in the exchange rate rather than the alteration in the interest rate which produces the stabilizing effect; this indirectness conduces to a cyclical approach to equilibrium. Although an explicit empirical study would be necessary to verify that the Canadian experiment has not fulfilled the claims made for flexible exchange rates, the prima facie evidence indicates that it has not. It must be emphasized, though, that a failure of the Canadian experiment would cast doubt only on the effectiveness of a flexible exchange system in a multi-regional country, not on a flexible exchange system in a unitary country.[9]

NOTES

1 I have analyzed this system in some detail in Mundell (1961).
2 See, for example Friedman 1953, Lutz 1954 and Meade 1955.
3 More exactly, the rates at which central banks can expand monetary liabilities depend on income elasticities of demand and output elasticities of supply.
4 For present purposes inflation is defined as a rise in the prices of home-produced goods.
5 The tendency of surplus countries to control (what is, from a national point of view) inflation can be amply documented from United States and French policy in the 1920's and West Germany policy today. But it is unfortunate that a simple change in world relative prices is interpreted, in the surplus countries, as inflation.
6 Instructive examples of balance-of-payments problems between different regions of the United States can be found in Harris (1957, Ch. 14). For purposes of this paper, regions are defined as areas within which there is factor mobility, but between which there is factor immobility.
7 These statements of course cannot do full justice to the arguments of Meade and Scitovsky.
8 In my paper, "The Monetary Dynamics of International Adjustment Under Fixed and Flexible Exchange Rates," (Mundell 1960) I advanced the argument that stabilization policy would be more difficult under fixed exchange rates if short-term capital were immobile than if it were mobile, and more difficult under flexible exchange rates if capital were mobile than if it were immobile. Although the method of analysis was fundamentally different, the conclusions support the hypothesis of this paper that the fixed exchange-rate system is better within areas where factors are mobile and the flexible exchange-rate system is better for areas between which factors are immobile. The argument of my other paper imposes an additional argument against increasing the number of currencies.
9 Other economists have advanced arguments in favor of Balkanization of multi-regional countries (see for example, A.D. Scott 1950); and the argument for regional currency areas adds to the list; but, as Scott is careful to emphasize, no country can make such decisions on purely economic grounds.

REFERENCES

Friedman, Milton. "The Case for Flexible Exchange Rates," *Essays in Positive Economics*. Chicago 1953.

Harris, S.E. *Interregional and International Economics*. New York 1957.

Lutz, F.L. "The Case for Flexible Exchange Rates," Banca Naz. del Lavoro, Dec. 1954.

Meade, J.E. "The Case for Variable Exchange Rates," *Three Banks Review*, Sept. 1955.

Meade, J.E. "The Balance of Payments Problems of a Free Trade Area," *Economic Journal*, Sept. 1957, 67, 379–96.

Mill, J.S. *Principles of Political Economy*, Vol. II, New York 1894.

Mundell, R.A. "The International Disequilibrium System," *Kyklos*, 1961 (2), 14, 153–72.

Mundell, R.A. "The Monetary Dynamics of International Adjustment under Fixed and Flexible Exchange Rates," *Quart. Jour. Econ.*, May 1960, 74, 227–57.

Scitovsky, Tibor. *Economic Theory and Western European Integration*. Stanford 1958.

Scott, A.D. "A Note on Grants in Federal Countries," *Economica*, Nov. 1950, 17 (N.S.), 416–22.

20 Optimum currency areas

*Ronald McKinnon**

American Economic Review, vol. 53, no. 4 (1963), pp. 718–25

In a recent note, Robert A. Mundell (1961) has suggested that little in the way of a systematic attempt has been made to define the characteristics of an area over which it is optimal to have a single currency regime, or—what is almost the same thing—a fixed exchange-rate system with guaranteed convertibility of currencies. The extensive literature on the relative merits of fixed versus flexible exchange rates has been rendered somewhat sterile by this omission. Existing national boundaries have been implicitly used to define the single currency area to which flexible external exchange rates would or would not be applied. However, when different possibilities for the grouping of nations in single currency areas exist, as in the EEC, or when resource mobility is low within individual countries, Mundell demonstrates that it is necessary to ask what economic characteristics determine the optimum size of the domain of a single currency. I shall develop the idea of optimality further by discussing the influence of the openness of the economy, i.e., the ratio of tradable to non-tradable goods, on the problem of reconciling external and internal balance, emphasizing the need for internal price-level stability.

"Optimum" is used here to describe a single currency area within which monetary-fiscal policy and flexible external exchange rates can be used to give the best resolution of three (sometimes conflicting) objectives: (1) the main-tenance of full employment; (2) the maintenance of balanced international payments; (3) the maintenance of a stable internal average price level. Object-ive (3) assumes that any capitalist economy requires a stable-valued liquid currency to insure efficient resource allocation. Possible conflicts between (1) and (2) have been well discussed in the literature, especially by J.E. Meade (1951), but joint consideration of all three is not usually done. For example, J.L. Stein (1963) explicitly assumes internal price-level stability in his discus-sion of optimal flexibility in the foreign exchange rate. The inclusion of objective (3) makes the problem as much a part of monetary theory as of international trade theory. The idea of optimality, then, is complex and dif-ficult to quantify precisely, so what follows does not presume to be a logically complete model.

"The ratio of tradable to non-tradable goods" is a simplifying concept

* The author is assistant professor of economics at Stanford University.

which assumes all goods can be classified into those that could enter into foreign trade and those that do not because transportation is not feasible for them. A physical description of both tradable and non-tradable goods would correspond to that given by R.F. Harrod (1957, pp. 53–56). This overly sharp distinction between classes of tradable and non-tradable goods is an analytically simple way of taking transportation costs into account. By tradable goods we mean: (1) exportables, which are those goods produced domestically and, in part, exported; (2) importables, which are both produced domestically and imported. The excess of exportables produced over exports will depend directly on the amount of domestic consumption, which is likely to be small when exportable production is heavily specialized in few goods. Similarly, the excess of importables consumed over imports will depend on the specialized nature of imports. Therefore, the value of exportables produced need not be the same as the value of importables consumed, even in the case of balanced trade where the values of imports and exports are equal. However, the total value of tradable goods produced will equal the value of tradable goods consumed under balanced trade. Thus, the expression "the ratio of tradable to non-tradable goods" can apply unambiguously to production or consumption.

I A SIMPLE MODEL

Ideally, one would like to consider a large group of countries jointly and then decide how they should be divided up into optimum currency regions. The analytical framework for such a task does not exist, so it is necessary to consider a much narrower problem and hope it throws light on the general one—besides being of interest in itself. Consider a well-defined single currency area in which we wish to determine whether or not there should be flexible exchange rates with the outside world. The outside world is itself assumed to be a single currency area which is very large.

If the area under consideration is sufficiently small, we may assume that the money prices of the tradable goods in terms of the outside currency are not influenced by domestic exchange rates or domestic currency prices.[1] In actual practice, the domestic money prices of tradable goods will be more closely tied to foreign prices through existing exchange rates than will the domestic money prices of the non-tradable goods. Under this invariance assumption, i.e., fixed foreign-currency prices, the terms of trade will necessarily be immune to domestic economic policy. Some justification is given for this in R. Hinshaw (1951) even for fairly large countries. We now inquire into whether external exchange-rate flexibility or internal fiscal-monetary expansion or contraction is most suitable to maintaining external balance, i.e. shifting production and expenditures between the tradable and non-tradable goods.

Case 1

Suppose exportables X_1 and importables X_2 together make up a large percentage of the goods consumed domestically. Suppose further a flexible exchange-rate system is used to maintain external balance. The price of the non-tradable good, X_3, is kept constant in terms of the domestic currency. Exchange-rate changes will vary the domestic prices of X_1 and X_2 directly by the amount of the change. Thus, if the domestic currency is devalued 10 per cent, the domestic money prices of X_1 and X_2 will rise by 10 per cent and thus rise 10 per cent relative to X_3. The rationale of such a policy is that the production of X_1 and X_2 should increase, and the consumption of X_1 and X_2 should decline, improving the balance of payments. Direct absorption reduction from the price rise in tradable goods may have to be supplemented by deliberate contractionary monetary-fiscal policy, if unemployment is small. Substantial theoretical justification for considering relative price changes between tradable and non-tradable goods to be more important than changes in the terms of trade for external balance is given by I.F. Pearce (1961).

From Case 1, it is clear that external exchange-rate fluctuations, responding to shifts in the demand for imports or exports, are not compatible with internal price-level stability for a highly open economy, objective (3). In addition, such a policy by itself may not succeed in changing relative prices or affecting the trade balance. In a highly open economy operating close to full employment, significant improvement in the trade balance will have to be accomplished via the reduction of domestic absorption, i.e., real expenditures, which is the only possible way of keeping the price of X_3 constant in terms of the domestic currency. Thus, a substantial rise in domestic taxes may be necessary whether or not there is any exchange rate change. In the extreme case where the economy is completely open, i.e., all goods produced and consumed are tradable with prices determined in the outside world, the only way the trade balance can be improved is by lowering domestic expenditures while maintaining output levels. Changes in the exchange rate will necessarily be completely offset by internal price-level repercussions with no improvement in the trade balance.

To restate the core of the argument: if we move across the spectrum from closed to open economies, flexible exchange rates become both less effective as a control device for external balance and more damaging to internal price-level stability. In fact, if one were worried about unwanted speculative movements in a floating exchange rate in Case 1 of an open economy, a policy of completely fixed exchange rates (or common currency ties with the outside world) would be optimal. Blunt monetary and fiscal weapons which evenly reduced expenditures in all sectors could be counted on to improve immediately the trade balance by releasing goods from domestic consumption in the large tradable-goods sector. Exportables previously consumed domestically would be released for export; imports would be directly curtailed, and domestically produced importables made available for substitution with imports. The reduction of expenditures in the relatively small non-tradable-goods sector would initially only cause unemployment which, depending on the degree of inter-industry resource mobility and price flexibility, might eventually be translated into more production in the tradable-goods sectors, and possibly improve the trade balance in the longer run. The smaller this non-tradable-goods sector, the smaller will be the immediate impact of reducing expenditures on employment and total production, and thus the more efficient this policy of expenditure reduction will be as a device for improving external balance (the surplus of production over expenditures).

Any region within a common currency area faced with a loss of demand for its products will be forced to cut its expenditures through a loss of bank reserves and regional income, thus eventually correcting the trade balance. A separate currency region with fixed exchange rates may have to carry out the cutback of expenditures more through deliberate policy if bank reserve losses are effectively sterilized. In either case, the immediate reduction in real income cannot be avoided if the trade balance is to be improved.

Case 2

Suppose the production of non-tradable goods is very large compared to importables and exportables in the given area. Here the optimal currency arrangements may be to peg the domestic currency to the body of non-tradable goods, i.e., to fix the domestic currency price of X_2 and change the domestic price of the tradable goods by altering the exchange rate to improve the trade balance. A currency devaluation of 10 per cent would cause the domestic prices of X_1 and X_2 to rise by 10 per cent, but the effect on the general domestic price index is much less than in Case 1.

The desired effect of the relative price increase in the tradable goods is to stimulate the production of tradable compared to non-tradable goods and thus improve the trade balance. On the other hand, if monetary-fiscal policy is primarily relied on to reduce domestic demand to maintain external balance, unemployment will be much higher. Much of the immediate impact of the reduction of expenditures will be in the extensive non-tradable-goods industries. If there are any rigidities in resource mobility, the trade balance will not improve much in the first instance. Through this policy, it may be actually necessary to achieve a fall in the domestic money prices of X_3, the numerous non-tradable goods, before sufficient expansion in the production of X_1 and X_2 can be obtained. Since a major component of X_3 will be labor services, it may be necessary to lower wage costs *vis-à-vis* the domestic money prices of X_1 and X_2, which are fixed by the inflexible external exchange-rate system. Such a policy would contain all the well-known Keynesian difficulties of getting labor to accept a cut in money wages. In addition, a successful policy of lowering prices of the numerous X_3 goods would have a large impact on the average domestic price level. Effectively, we would have permitted the tail (tradable goods) to wag the dog (non-tradable goods) in pursuing restrictive monetary and fiscal policies, with fixed exchange rates to improve the trade balance, for a small proportion of tradable goods.

Our open economy of Case 1 somewhat resembles what Stein (1963) has called a "conflict" economy. In a conflict economy, export production is sufficiently large to dominate the generation of domestic income, and thus fluctuations in both are positively correlated. Therefore, with a fixed exchange rate, periods having low income will also have unfavorable trade balances, and vice versa. For income stabilization, objective (1), Stein concludes that a floating exchange rate will be optimal for a conflict economy in a Keynesian environment. The foreign exchange rate would then rise at the top of the cycle and fall at the bottom. These exchange rate changes will stimulate domestic production and income at the bottom of the cycle and damp them at the top. But it is precisely in this case of a highly open economy that exchange-rate changes will mean great fluctuations in internal price levels—sufficiently great, that any effects of exchange rate changes on domestic production may be small. However, there may still remain a direct policy conflict between objectives (1) and (3) in the use of a floating exchange rate. Certainly, the liquidity value of the domestic currency will depend directly on the short-run fortunes of the export commodity(ies) for a floating exchange rate.

Qualifications

The sharp distinction between tradable and non-tradable goods makes the above model analytically much easier to work with; but in practice there is a continuum of goods between the tradable and non-tradable extremes. The relaxation of this sharp distinction does not invalidate the basic idea of the openness of the economy affecting optimum economic policies; but the empirical measurement of the ratio of tradable to non-tradable goods becomes more difficult. Some kind of weighting system for determining the total production in each category might be possible. Certainly, knowledge of total imports and exports would give one a good lead in determining total production of exportables and importables. In addition, the idea of openness would have to be modified when the area was large enough to affect external prices.

II MONETARY IMPLICATIONS OF THE MODEL

The above discussion has been concerned with the way by which relative price changes in tradable and non-tradable goods can be brought about, and the conditions under which monetary and fiscal policy can be used efficiently to maintain external balance. Minimizing the real cost of adjustments needed to preserve external balance hinged to a large extent on minimizing necessary fluctuations in the overall domestic price level. Thus the argument is very much concerned with the liquidity properties of money, and it is worthwhile to look at some of the more general monetary implications of the model. Suppose X_1, X_2, and X_3 are classes of goods rather than single goods as in the Pearce model. One of the aims of monetary policy is to set up a stable kind of money whose value in terms of a representative bundle of economic goods remains more stable than any single physical good. Indeed, it is the maintenance of this stable value which gives money its liquidity properties. The process of saving and capital accumulation in a capitalist system is greatly hampered unless a suitable *numéraire* and store of value exists. It may be still more difficult if a more desirable money is available from another source, e.g., from a larger currency area. This latter possibility is discussed below.

If the area under consideration is sufficiently large so that the body of non-tradable goods is large, then pegging the value of the domestic currency to this body of non-tradable goods is sufficient to give money liquidity value in the eyes of the inhabitants of the area in question. It may not be sufficient from the viewpoint of potential investors in the outside world. However, if the area is large, what outside investors think need not be an overriding consideration. Efficient internal capital accumulation and full employment are more important than external capital movements. If, under these circumstances, trade patterns are so unstable that substantial relative price changes in tradable and non-tradable goods are required to maintain external balance and full employment, then flexible external exchange rates may well be optimal. Resulting internal price changes will not destroy the value of the domestic currency as money.

If the area under consideration is small so that the ratio of tradable to non-tradable goods is large and the prices of the former are fairly well fixed in the outside currency, then the monetary implications of pegging the domestic currency to the non-tradable goods are less satisfactory. Such a class of non-tradable goods may not constitute a typical bundle of economic goods. The class of importables may be more representative, and a currency pegged to maintain its value in terms of importables into a small area may have a higher liquidity value than one pegged to the domestically produced non-tradable goods. However, pegging a currency of a small area to maintain its value in terms of a representative bundle of imports from a large outside area is virtually the same thing as pegging it to the outside currency. Alternatively, if we have a number of small areas which trade extensively with each other, and each pegs its currency to a representative bundle of imports, then each currency will be pegged to the others. To maintain the liquidity value of individual currencies for small areas, a fixed exchange-rate system is necessary. In addition, capital movements among small areas are more needed to promote efficient economic specialization and growth than free capital movements among large, economically developed areas. Contractual arrangements for such movements are greatly facilitated by a common currency. These arguments give us some insight into why each of the fifty states in the United States could not efficiently issue its own currency, aside from the inconvenience of money changing.

If we have a small area whose currency is not convincingly pegged in terms of the currency of a larger area, and so on this account its liquidity value is less, then domestic nationals will attempt to accumulate foreign bank balances. This will occur even though the marginal efficiency of investment in the small area is greater than that outside. As long as the functions of savings and investment are specialized, savers will attempt to accumulate cash balances in the more liquid currency. The illiquidity of domestic currency may also reflect monetary mismanagement as well as small size. In either case, we would expect small countries with weak currencies to have a tendency to finance the balance-of-payments deficits of larger countries with more desirable currencies. Thus, we have capital outflows from countries where the need for capital may be rather high and which arise from "monetary" rather than "real" considerations. Authorities in such countries are generally forced to maintain rather strict exchange controls unless the currency can be pegged in a convincing fashion to that of the larger area.

The above argument is relevant to the use of uncontrolled floating exchange rates. This device of maintaining external balance will only work well when the currency in question has liquidity value of the same order as that of the outside world—or the world's major currencies. This condition was approximately satisfied in the case of the Canadian dollar up to 1961. However, a floating exchange rate for the Korean yen may lead to less satisfactory results. If the official rate were made equal to the black-market rate and there were no further exchange restrictions, there would still be a capital flight out of Korea into currencies with superior liquidity value, aside from problems of political stability. A floating exchange rate in itself is not a sufficient control device and does not necessarily eliminate the need for exchange controls.

By contrast, short-term capital flows among currencies of approximately equal liquidity value are less likely with a floating exchange rate because of the exchange risk and the liquidity equivalence. The possibility of carrying out different degrees of easy or tight monetary policy in different countries is greater as capital flows would not be so responsive to interest-rate differentials. Once the world is divided into a number of optimal-sized currency areas permitting efficient internal capital accumulation, the desirability of short-term capital flows among areas well developed economically becomes less great, and it becomes desirable to insulate the monetary policies of the areas from each other in order that monetary policy may be used more freely to support full employment. However, it does not make any sense to advocate a floating exchange-rate system without first defining the optimal domains of individual currencies.

Suppose we look at the problem of a depressed subregion of a common currency area. Consider the case of West Virginia where non-tradable goods are largely labor services. We have an illustration of an excess supply of non-tradable goods and an excess demand for the tradable goods because of internal price rigidities. Thus, in this sense West Virginia has an *ex ante* balance-of-payments deficit even though in an *ex post* accounting sense there is a balance-of-cash flow in and out of the state. Would the adjustment of external balance and internal full employment be facilitated if West Virginia were incorporated as a country with its own currency? To the extent that the ratio of tradable to non-tradable goods was high, such a monetary system would have little chance of success. A devaluation would be associated with a large domestic price-level increase and hence money illusion would not be much help in getting labor to accept a cut in real wages (Mundell 1961, p. 663). Labor unions would still continue to bargain in terms of U.S. dollars. In addition, a West Virginian currency tied to a representative bundle of non-tradable goods would not be an entirely acceptable store of value. There undoubtedly would be attempts by West Virginians to accumulate U.S. bank balances. However, if the depressed area were substantially larger, with a small proportion of production in tradable goods, a separate monetary system might be preferable as a device for maintaining full employment and external balance in the absence of factor mobility.

III A CONCLUDING NOTE ON FACTOR MOBILITY

The idea of factor mobility has two distinct senses: (1) geographic factor mobility among regions; (2) factor mobility among industries. I think it is fair to say that Mundell (1961) had interpretation (1) primarily in mind. His discussion of optimum currency areas in large measure is aimed toward having high geographic factor mobility within each single currency area and using flexible external exchange rates to make up for the lack of factor mobility among areas. Thus, for a given amount of geographic factor mobility in the world, this method of division into currency areas would maximize the possibility of world income and employment, subject to the constraint of maintaining external balance. Of course, the currency arrangements themselves would affect factor mobility, so the extent of factor mobility has to be considered *ex post*. Once we consider problems of factor immobility among industries, it may not be feasible to consider slicing the world into currency areas along industrial groupings rather than geographical groupings. However, from our above discussion, an optimal geographic size still exists even when we are only concerned with inter-industry factor immobility.

Consider the special but perhaps common case of factor immobility between regions, each with its own specialized industries, the case where it is difficult to distinguish geographical and inter-industrial immobility. Suppose there is a rise in the demand for the products of region A and a decline in the demand for goods of region B. The value of the marginal products of the potentially mobile factors of production in region B in B-type industries will fall, and rise in region A in A-type industries. Now if the possibility of developing or extending A-type industries in B is feasible, then need for factor movement between A and B is not great. The existing immobility between regions can be accepted through monetary arrangements giving both regions their own currencies, thus permitting more flexibility in enabling each area to pursue monetary and fiscal policies geared to internal stability. But if B cannot easily develop A-type industries, then factor movements to A may be the only thing that will prevent a large fall in the unit incomes of potentially mobile factors of production in B. So a policy aimed directly at overcoming the immobility of factor movements between A and B may be optimal, and perhaps the two should be joined in a common currency area. This argument becomes stronger when one considers small areas trying to develop industries in which economies of scale or indivisibilities are very great instead of efficiently moving factors elsewhere.

In a world where trade patterns are not perfectly stable, there will always be the problem of changing the world pattern of resource use among various industries to preserve external balance, full employment, and efficient resource use. In the simple model given in Section I above, we considered the optimum extent of a currency area in terms of its size and structure, i.e., the ratio of tradable to non-tradable goods, in promoting shifts in resources among various industries. The model accepted the degree of internal resource immobility among industries as an obstacle to be overcome as smoothly as possible. The arguments given there for applying flexible exchange rates to optimal-sized currency areas to efficiently overcome factor immobility hold in the main, whether the degree of internal mobility among industries is large or small. Such factor immobility among industries is a painful fact of economic life which has to be overcome as efficiently as possible. However, this criterion of size and openness of a single-currency economy in facilitating inter-industry production shifts certainly has to be balanced with purely geographic factor-mobility considerations in determining the optimum extent of a currency area.

NOTE

1 If we apply this assumption to the standard elasticities model, then both the elasticity of foreign demand for home exports η_f and the elasticity of foreign supply of home imports ε_f, are assumed infinite. Thus a devaluation, i.e., a rise in the foreign exchange rate k, would always improve the trade balance, B, by an amount proportional to the sum of the home elasticity of demand for imports and the home elasticity of supply of exports, η_h and ε_h respectively, i.e.,

$$\frac{dB}{dk} = Z(\varepsilon_h + \eta_h)$$

where Z is the value of exports in the case of balanced trade. The trouble with this standard model is that η_h and ε_h depend on the amount of domestic absorption permitted in the course of devaluation as well as the openness of the economy; and it is difficult to make explicit what internal price repercussions may occur since the body of non-tradable goods does not enter explicitly in the model. Assuming both η_f and ε_f to be infinite is different from the usual simplification that both supply elasticities, ε_f and ε_h, are infinite, and in my opinion is more appropriate to the consideration of most small areas.

REFERENCES

Harrod, R.F. *International Economics*, 5th edition. Cambridge, 1957.

Hinshaw, Randall. "Currency Appreciation as an Anti-Inflationary Device," *Quart. Jour. Econ.*, Nov. 1951, 65, 447–62.

Meade, J.E. *The Theory of International Economic Policy*. Vol. I, *The Balance of Payments*. London 1951.

Mundell, Robert A. "A Theory of Optimum Currency Areas," *American Economic Review*, Sept. 1961, 51, 657–64.

Pearce, Ivor F. "The Problem of the Balance of Payments," *International Economic Review*, Jan. 1961.

Stein, Jerome L. "The Optimum Foreign Exchange Market," *American Economic Review*, June 1963, 53, 384–402.

21 The theory of optimum currency areas
A critique

Paul De Grauwe
The Economics of Monetary Integration, Oxford University Press
(1992), pp. 30–60

INTRODUCTION

In the previous chapter [of my book] we analysed the reasons why countries
might find it costly to join a monetary union. Recently, this analysis, which is
known as the theory of optimum currency areas, has come under criticism.[1]
This criticism has been formulated at different levels. First one may question
the view that the differences between countries are important enough to
bother about. Secondly, the exchange rate instrument may not be very effective in correcting for the differences between nations. Thirdly, not only may the
exchange rate be ineffective, it may do more harm than good in the hands of
politicians.

In this chapter we analyse this criticism in greater detail.

1 HOW RELEVANT ARE THE DIFFERENCES
BETWEEN COUNTRIES?

There is no doubt that countries *are* different. The question, however, is
whether these differences are important enough to represent a stumbling-
block for monetary unification.

1.1 Is a demand shock concentrated in one country a likely event?

The classical analysis of Mundell started from the scenario in which a
demand shift occurs away from the products of one country in favour of
another country. Is such a shock likely to occur frequently between the European countries that are planning to form a monetary union? There is a major
argument that leads us to conclude that such differential shocks in demand
may occur less frequently in a future European monetary union.

Trade between the industrial European nations is to a large degree intra-
industry trade. This trade is based on the existence of economies of scale and
imperfect competition (product differentiation). It leads to a structure of
trade in which countries buy and sell to each other the same categories of
products. Thus, France sells cars to and buys cars from Germany. And so

does Germany. This structure of trade leads to a situation where most demand shocks will affect these countries in a similar way. For example, when consumers reduce their demand for cars, they will buy fewer French *and* German cars. Thus, both countries' aggregate demand will be affected in similar ways.

The removal of barriers with the completion of the single market will reinforce these tendencies. As a result, most demand shocks will tend to have similar effects.[2] Instead of being asymmetric, these shocks will tend to be more symmetric.

Does this mean that we can discard Mundell's analysis of asymmetric demand shocks as irrelevant for the process of European monetary integration? Not necessarily. There is another feature of the dynamics of trade with economies of scale that may make Mundell's analysis very relevant. Trade integration which occurs as a result of economies of scale also leads to regional concentration of industrial activities.[3] The basic argument here is that when impediments to trade decline this has two opposing effects on the localization of industries. It makes it possible to produce closer to the final markets, but it also makes it possible to concentrate production so as to profit from economies of scale (both static and dynamic). This explains why trade integration in fact may lead to more concentration of regional activities rather than less.

The fact that trade may lead to regional concentration of industrial activities is illustrated rather dramatically by comparing the regional distribution of the automobile production in the USA and in Europe (see Table 21.1). The most striking feature of this table is that the US production of automobiles is much more regionally concentrated than the EC's. (This feature is found in many other industrial sectors, see Krugman (1991)). There is also no doubt that the US market is more highly integrated than the EC market, i.e. there are fewer impediments to trade in the USA than in the EC. This evidence therefore suggests that when the EC moves forward in the direction of a truly integrated market, it may experience similar kinds of regional concentrations of economic activities as those observed in the USA today. It is therefore not to be excluded that the automobile industry, for example, will tend to be more concentrated in say Germany (although we are not sure it will be Germany, it could also be another country). Sector-specific shocks may then become country-specific shocks. Countries faced with these shocks may then prefer to use the exchange rate as an instrument of economic policy to correct for these disturbances.

Table 21.1 Distribution of auto production

	USA		EC
Midwest	66.3	Germany	38.5
South	25.4	France	31.1
West	5.1	Italy	17.6
North-east	3.2	UK	12.9

Source: Paul Krugman (1991)

We conclude here that further trade integration in Europe has an ambiguous effect on the likelihood that demand shocks will tend to be asymmetric between countries. We should not discard the possibility that in a more integrated Europe, negative demand shocks will be concentrated on one country, because that country has a large concentration of the activities of one industry.

1.2 Institutional differences in labour markets

The differences in the workings of the labour markets in different countries are well documented. These differences, however, have accumulated over the years, partly because European countries have experienced separate policy regimes. The issue is whether monetary integration will not drastically change the behaviour of labour unions, so that the differences we observe today may disappear.[4]

An example may clarify this point. In Fig. 21.1 we present the labour markets of two countries that are candidates for a monetary union. The figure is based on the model of McDonald and Solow (1981).[5] On the vertical axis we have the real wage level, on the horizontal axis the level of employment (N). The convex curves are the indifference curves of the labour union. It is assumed that there is only one labour union in each country. the union maximizes its utility which depends on both the real wage level and the employment of its members. The negatively sloped line is the economy-wide demand-for-labour curve. For the union, which maximizes its utility, the demand-for-labour curve is a constraint: thus, the union will select a point on it which maximizes it utility. This is represented in Fig. 21.1 by the points A and B.

The interesting feature of this model is that the employment line takes into account the reaction of the authorities to what the labour unions are doing. If we assume that the authorities give a higher weight to employment in their utility function than the labour unions, we may have the following situation.

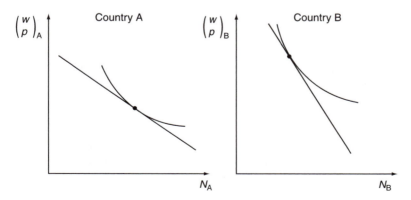

Figure 21.1 The Solow–MacDonald model in two countries

When the labour unions set a wage that reduces the employment level below the level that the authorities find optimal, they will react by changing their policies. For example, they will engage in more expansionary monetary and fiscal policies to absorb the unemployed, they may create public jobs, etc. To the extent that labour unions take this reaction of the authorities into account, the constraint the unions face will change. More specifically, the employment line becomes steeper because an increase in the real wage level reduces private employment and, thus, induces the authorities to intensify their job-creating policies. As a result, an increase in the real wage level has a less pronounced effect on the total level of employment.[6] Thus, the steepness of this employment line also reflects the willingness of the authorities to engage in expansionary employment policies when the wage rate increases.

In Fig. 21.1 we have drawn the employment line of country B steeper than that of country A, assuming that the authorities of country B are more willing to accommodate the union's wage-setting behaviour by expansionary employment policies. Monetary union now will change the possibility for the national governments to follow such accommodating policies. Monetary policies will now be centralized, so that the unions of the two countries face the same reactions of the monetary authorities. This will make the employment lines similar, so that the two unions will tend to select a similar combination of wage rates and employment levels.

The differences, however, are unlikely to disappear completely. National governments have other employment policies at their disposal besides monetary policies. For example, they can create jobs in the government sector, financing these extra expenditures by issuing debt. A monetary union does not necessarily constrain this accommodating government behaviour. Thus, although the differences in the behaviour of the labour unions will be less pronounced, they will certainly not be eliminated completely.

Finally, it should also be stressed that the previous analysis assumes a completely centralized union in both countries. As pointed out earlier, unions are different across countries because of different degrees of centralization. It is not clear how monetary union will change these institutional differences.

We conclude that the institutional differences in the national labour markets will continue to exist for quite some time after the introduction of a common currency. This may lead to divergent wage and employment tendencies, and severe adjustment problems when the exchange rate instrument has disappeared.

1.3 Do differences in growth rates matter?

Fast-growing countries experience fast-growing imports. In order to allow exports to increase at the same rate, these countries will have to make their exports more competitive by real depreciations of their currencies. If they join a monetary union, this will be made more difficult. As a result, these countries will be constrained in their growth. This popular view of the constraint imposed on fast-growing countries that decide to join a monetary union has very little empirical support.

In Fig. 21.2 we present data (as collected by the EC Commission (1990), p. 147) on the growth rates of EC countries during 1973–88 and their real depreciations (or appreciations). The high-growers are above the horizontal line, the low-growers below. We observe that among the fast-growers there are countries that saw their currency appreciate and others depreciate. The same is true for the slow-growers.[7]

This lack of relation between economic growth and real depreciations has been given an elegant interpretation recently by Paul Krugman (1989). Economic growth has relatively little to do with the static view implicit in the story told in the earlier sections. Economic growth implies mostly the development of new products. Fast-growing countries are those that are able to develop new products, or old products with new qualitative features. The result of this growth process is that the income elasticities of the exports of fast-growing countries are typically higher than those of slow-growers. More importantly, these income elasticities of the export goods of the fast-growers will also typically be higher than the income elasticities of their imports. (See Krugman (1989) for empirical evidence.) As a result, these countries can grow faster without incurring trade balance problems. This also implies that the fast-growers can increase their exports at a fast pace without having to resort to real depreciations.

There is a second reason why the fast-growing countries should not worry too much that joining a monetary union will constrain their potential for growth. This has to do with the existence of capital flows. A fast-growing country is usually also a country where the productivity of capital is higher than in slow-growing countries. This difference in the productivity of capital will induce investment flows from the slow-growing countries to the

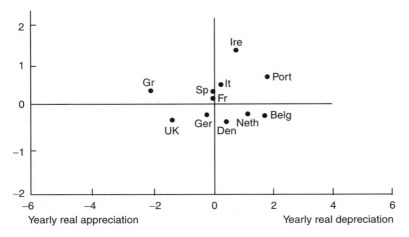

Figure 21.2 Real depreciation and growth, 1973–88

Source: EC Commission (1990: 147).

fast-growing countries. These capital flows then make it possible for the fast-growing country to finance current account deficits without any need to devalue the currency.

There is even an argument to be made here that fast-growing countries that join a monetary union with slow-growing countries will find it easier to attract foreign capital. With no exchange rate uncertainty, investors from the slow-growing area may be more forthcoming in moving their capital to the high-growing country in order to profit from the larger returns.

One can conclude that differences in the growth rates of countries cannot really be considered as an obstacle to monetary integration. In other words, fast-growing countries will, in general, not have to reduce their growth rates by joining a monetary union.

2 NOMINAL AND REAL DEPRECIATIONS OF THE CURRENCY

The cost of relinquishing one's national currency lies in the fact that a country cannot change its exchange rate any more to correct for differential developments in demand, or in costs and prices. The question, however, is whether these exchange rate changes are effective in making such corrections. Put differently, the question that arises is whether *nominal* exchange rate changes can permanently alter the *real* exchange rates of the country.

This is a crucial question. For if the answer is negative, one can conclude that countries, even if they develop important differences between themselves, would not have to meet extra costs when joining a monetary union. The instrument they lose does not really allow them to correct for these differences.

In order to analyse this question of the effectiveness of exchange rate changes we return to two of the asymmetric disturbances analysed in the previous chapter [of my book].

2.1 Devaluations to correct for asymmetric demand shocks

Let us take the case of France. We assume that a shift occurred away from French products in favour of German products. In order to cope with this problem France devalues its currency. We present the situation in Fig. 21.3. As a result of the devaluation aggregate demand in France shifts back upwards and corrects for the initial unfavourable demand shift. The new equilibrium point is *F*.

It is unlikely that this new equilibrium point can be sustained. The reason is that the devaluation raises the price of imported goods. This raises the cost of production directly. It also will increase the nominal wage level in France as workers are likely to be compensated for the loss of purchasing power. All this means that the aggregate supply curve will shift upwards. Thus, prices increase and output declines. These price increases feed back again into the wage-formation process and lead to further upward movements of the

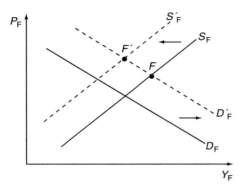

Figure 21.3 Price and cost effects of a devaluation

aggregate supply curve. The final equilibrium will be located at a point like F'. The initial favourable effects of the devaluation tend to disappear over time. It is not possible to say here whether these favourable effects of the devaluation on output will disappear completely. This depends on the openness of the economy, on the degree to which wage-earners will adjust their wage claims to correct for the loss of purchasing power. There is a lot of empirical evidence, however, that for most of the European countries this withering away of the initially favourable effects of a devaluation will be strong.[8]

The conclusion can be phrased as follows. Nominal exchange rate changes have only temporary effects on the competitiveness of countries. Over time the nominal devaluation leads to domestic cost and price increases which tend to restore the initial competitiveness. In other words, nominal devaluations only lead to temporary *real* devaluations. In the long run nominal exchange rate changes do not affect the real exchange rate of a country.

Does this conclusion about the long-run ineffectiveness of exchange rate changes imply that countries do not lose anything by relinquishing this instrument? The answer is negative. We also have to analysis the short-term effects of an exchange rate policy aiming at correcting the initial disturbance, and we have to compare these to alternative policies that will have to be followed in the absence of a devaluation. This is done in Fig. 21.4. We have added here a line (TT) which expresses the trade account equilibrium condition. It is derived as follows. Trade account equilibrium is defined as equality between the value of domestic output and the value of spending by residents (sometimes also called absorption). Thus we have equilibrium in the trade account if and only if:

$$P_d Y = P_a A \tag{1}$$

where P_d is the price of the domestic good, Y the domestic output level, P_a is the average price index of the domestic and the imported good, A is absorption (in real terms). The level of real absorption depends on many factors (e.g. government spending, the real interest rate). If these are fixed, we can

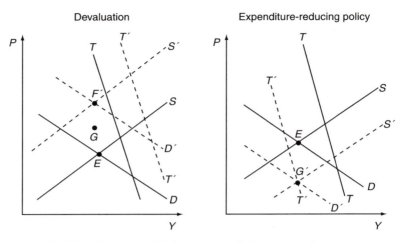

Figure 21.4 Devaluation and deflationary policies compared

derive a negative relation between P_d and Y which maintains the equality (1), in other words which maintains trade account equilibrium. The negative relationship follows from the fact that as P_d increases, P_a (which contains the import price) increases less than proportionately, so that the left-hand side increases relative to the right-hand side of (1). Thus, when P_d increases, the value of output increases relative to the value of absorption, tending to produce a trade account surplus. It follows that domestic output should decline to maintain trade account equilibrium. Put differently an increase in P_d (for a given import price) is equivalent to an improvement in the terms of trade. This allows the country to reduce domestic output and still maintain equilibrium in the trade account.

Points to the left of this TT-line are ones where the country has a trade deficit, i.e. the level of domestic output is too low compared to the level of absorption. Points to the right of the TT-line are those where the country produces more than it spends.

In Fig. 21.4, we assume that the country has been hit by a negative demand shock which has brought the output point to E. As a result, the country has a trade account deficit which will have to be corrected. One way to correct the disequilibrium is to devalue the currency. The dynamics of the adjustment after the devaluation is shown in the left-hand panel of Fig. 21.4. The devaluation shifts the demand and the supply curves upwards, as explained earlier. However, it also shifts the TT-curve to the right (to TT'). This follows from the fact that the devaluation increases the price of imports. Thus, in equation (1), P_a increases. It follows that P_d and/or Y must increase to maintain trade account equilibrium (at least if the real level of absorption A remains unchanged).

The new equilibrium in the goods market is now located at point F'. It can be seen that there is still a trade account deficit because the new output point is located to the left of the TT' line. In order to restore trade account equilibrium, the government will have to follow policies reducing real absorption. These policies have the effect of shifting the TT'-line to the left. The reason is that with a lower level of absorption (due to say lower government spending), the level of output that maintains trade account equilibrium is also reduced. These expenditure-reducing policies also affect the demand curve, however. In general, expenditure-reducing policies reduce domestic demand for the domestic good. It can be shown that there exists a combination of devaluation and expenditure-reducing policy that will bring the economy to a point like G, located vertically above the initial output point.[9] In the end the devaluation is neutral in that it does not affect output permanently.

In the right-hand panel of Fig. 21.4 we present the case where the country chooses *not* to devalue. Since in the initial situation (point E) there is a trade account deficit, the authorities will have to do something to correct this. This will necessarily have to be a policy which reduces absorption. Thus, deflationary monetary and/or fiscal policies will have to be instituted. These shift the trade account equilibrium line TT to the left.

These expenditure-reducing policies, however, also reduce aggregate demand for the domestic goods. Thus, the aggregate demand line also shifts to the left. The economy will go through a deflationary process, which reduces output. With sufficient wage and price flexibility, this will also tend to shift the supply line downwards, because the decline in prices leads to lower nominal wages. If wages and prices are not very flexible, this may require a considerable time. In the long run, the economy will settle at a point like G'. The output level is equal to its initial level, and the trade account is in equilibrium.

We conclude that in *the long run* the two policies (devaluation and expenditure-reducing) lead to the same effect on output and the trade account. Put differently, in the long run the exchange rate will not solve problems that arise from differences between countries that originate in the goods markets. This result is also in the tradition of the classical economists. These stressed that money is a veil. Structural differences should be tackled with structural policies. Manipulating money (its quantity or its price) cannot change these real differences.

The difference between the two policies, a devaluation or an expenditure-reducing policy, is to be found in their *short-term dynamics*. When the country devalues, it avoids the severe deflationary effects on domestic output during the transition. The cost of this policy is that there will be inflation. With the second policy, inflation is avoided. The cost, however, is that output declines during the transition period. In addition, as we have seen, this second policy may take a long time to be successful if the degree of wage and price flexibility is limited.

One can conclude that although a devaluation does not have a permanent effect on competitiveness and output, its dynamics will be quite different from the dynamics engendered by the alternative policy which will necessarily have to be followed if the country has relinquished control over its national money. This loss of a policy instrument will be a cost of the monetary union.

In Box 21.1 we present a case-study of a recent devaluation (Belgium in 1982) that helped this country to restore domestic and trade account equilibrium at a cost that was most probably lower than if it had not used the

---

Box 21.1 The devaluation of the Belgian franc of 1982

In 1982 Belgium devalued its currency by 8.5%. In addition, fiscal and monetary policies were tightened, and an incomes policy, including temporary abolition of the wage-indexing mechanism, was instituted. This decision came after a period of several speculative crises during which the BF was put under severe pressures. These crises were themselves triggered by the increasing loss of competitiveness (in turn due to excessive wage increases) which the Belgian economy experienced during the 1970s. This has led to unsustainable current account deficits.

It can now be said that the devaluation (together with the other policy measures) was a great success. Not only did it lead to a rapid turnaround in the current account of the balance of payments (see Table 21.2 below). It managed to do so without imposing great deflationary pressures on the Belgian economy. As Table 21.3 shows, there was a pronounced recovery in employment after 1983. This recovery in employment proceeded at a pace that was not significantly different from the rest of the Community after that date.

Table 21.2 Current account of Belgium (as a %age of GDP)

1981	−3.8
1982	−3.6
1983	−0.6
1984	−0.4
1985	0.5
1986	2.0

Source: EC Commission (1990).

Table 21.3 Growth rate of employment (Belgium and EC)

	Belgium	*EC*
1981	−2.0	−1.2
1982	−1.3	−0.9
1983	−1.1	−0.7
1984	0.0	0.1
1985	0.8	0.6
1986	1.0	0.8

Source: EC Commission (1990).

exchange rate instrument. There were other noteworthy and successful devaluations during the 1980s. The French devaluations of 1982–3 (coming after a period of major policy errors) stand out as success stories (see Sachs and Wyplosz, 1986). Similarly, the Danish devaluation of 1982 was quite successful in re-establishing external equilibrium without significant costs in terms of unemployment (see De Grauwe and Vanhaverbeke, 1990).

2.2 Devaluations to correct for supply shocks

The preceding analysis can also be applied to the situation where one country experiences cost and price increases as a result of a supply shock. We show the dynamics of the adjustment process in Fig. 21.5. The country is initially at point *A* and is hit by a negative supply shock, say a wage explosion of the type France experienced during the famous 'events of 1968'. This moves the economy to *K*, where we have a current account deficit and a general loss of competitiveness. With a devaluation, the aggregate demand curve shifts upwards and so does the aggregate supply curve. The economy settles at the new equilibrium point *J*. This is no improvement in terms of output compared to point *K*. Thus, the devaluation does not solve the real consequences of the negative supply shock. It does help, however, to improve the current account.

The policy of expenditure reduction has the same long-run consequences on output if prices and wages are flexible as a policy of devaluation. We show this in the right-hand panel of Fig. 21.5. The expenditure-reducing policy shifts the *TT*-line to the left. It also reduces aggregate demand for domestic goods. If, in addition, wages and prices are flexible, the supply curve shifts downwards. The new long-run equilibrium point is at *J'*. During the transition, however, the economy will experience a decline in output.

Here also the conclusion is that a devaluation cannot in the long run undo the supply shock. In this sense money is neutral in the long run. A

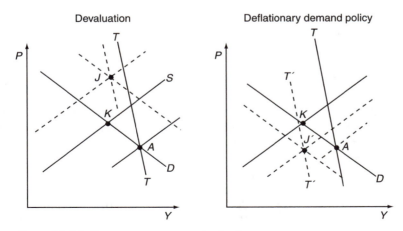

Figure 21.5 Policy responses to supply shock

devaluation can, however, be used to change the dynamics of the adjustment, making the latter less costly in terms of lost output and employment during the transition period towards long-run equilibrium.

3 DEVALUATION, TIME CONSISTENCY, AND CREDIBILITY

The idea that when the government follows particular policies it plays a game with the private sector has conquered macro-economic theory since the publication of the path-breaking articles of Kydland and Prescott (1977) and Barro and Gordon (1983).[10] This literature stresses that economic agents follow optimal strategies in response to the strategies of the authorities, and that these private sector responses have profound influences on the effectiveness of government policies. In particular, the reputation governments acquire in pursuing announced policies has a great impact on how these policies are going to affect the economy.

This literature also has important implications for our discussion of the costs of a monetary union. It leads to a fundamental criticism of the view that the exchange rate is a policy tool that governments have at their disposal to be used in a discretionary way. In order to understand this criticism it will be useful to present first the Barro–Gordon model for a closed economy, and then to apply it to an open economy, and to the choice of countries whether or not to join a monetary union.

3.1 The Barro–Gordon model: a geometric interpretation

Let us start from the standard Phillips curve which takes into account the role of inflationary expectations. We specify this Phillips curve as follows:

$$U = U_{\mathrm{N}} + a(\dot{p}^{\mathrm{e}} - \dot{p}) \tag{2}$$

where U is the unemployment rate, U_{N} is the natural unemployment rate, $\dot{p}$ is the observed rate of inflation, and $\dot{p}^{\mathrm{e}}$ is the expected rate of inflation.

Equation (2) expresses the idea that only unexpected inflation affects the unemployment rate. Thus, when the inflation rate $\dot{p}$ is higher than the expected rate of inflation, the unemployment rate declines below its natural level.

We will also use the rational expectations assumption. This implies that economic agents use all relevant information to forecast the rate of inflation, and that they cannot be systematically wrong in making these forecasts. Thus, *on average $\dot{p} = \dot{p}^{\mathrm{e}}$*, so that *on average $U = U_{\mathrm{N}}$*.

We represent the Phillips curve in Fig. 21.6. The vertical line represents the 'long-term' vertical Phillips curve. It is the collection of all points for which $\dot{p} = \dot{p}^{\mathrm{e}}$. This vertical line defines the natural rate of unemployment U_N which is also called the NAIRU (the non-accelerating-inflation rate of unemployment).

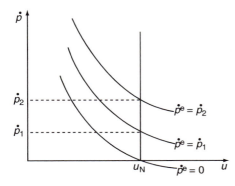

Figure 21.6 The Phillips curve and natural unemployment

The second step in the analysis consists in introducing the preferences of the monetary authorities. The latter are assumed to care about both inflation and unemployment.

We represent these preferences in Fig. 21.7 in the form of a map of indifference curves of the authorities. We have drawn the indifference curves concave, expressing the idea that as the inflation rate declines, the authorities become less willing to let unemployment increase in order to reduce the inflation rate. Put differently, as the inflation rate declines, the authorities tend to attach more weight to unemployment. Note also that the indifference curves closer to the origin represent a lower loss of welfare, and are thus preferred to those farther away from the origin.

The slope of these indifference curves expresses the relative importance the authorities attach to combating inflation or unemployment. In general, authorities who care much about unemployment ('wet' governments) have steep indifference curves, i.e. in order to reduce the rate of unemployment by one percentage point, they are willing to accept a lot of additional inflation.

On the other hand, 'hard-nosed' monetary authorities are willing to let the unemployment rate increase a lot in order to reduce the inflation rate by one percentage point. They have flat indifference curves. At the extreme, authorities who care only about inflation have horizontal indifference curves. We represent a few of these cases in Fig. 21.8.

We can now bring together the preferences of the authorities and the Phillips curves to determine the equilibrium of the model. We do this in Fig. 21.9.

In order to find out where the equilibrium will be located, assume for a moment that the government announces that it will follow a monetary policy rule of keeping the inflation rate equal to zero. Suppose also that the economic agents believe this announcement. They therefore set their expectations for inflation equal to zero. If the government implements this rule we move to point A.

It is now clear that the government can do better than point A. It could cheat and increase the rate of inflation unexpectedly. Thus, suppose that after having announced a zero inflation, the authorities increase the inflation rate

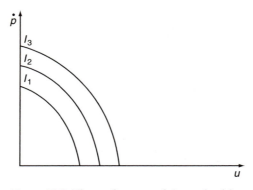

Figure 21.7 The preferences of the authorities

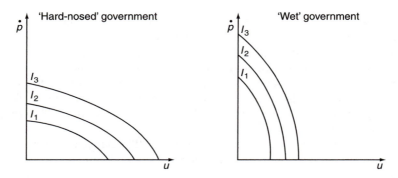

Figure 21.8 The preferences of the authorities

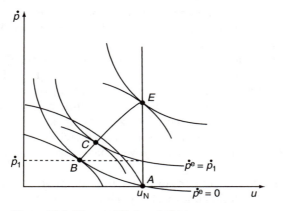

Figure 21.9 The equilibrium inflation rate

unexpectedly. This would bring the economy to point *B*, which is located on a lower indifference curve. One can say that the government has an incentive to renege on its promise to maintain a zero inflation rate.

Will the government succumb to this temptation to engineer a surprise inflation? Not necessarily. The government also knows that economic agents are likely to react by increasing their expectations of inflation. Thus, during the next period, the Phillips curve is likely to shift upwards if the government decides to increase the rate of inflation unexpectedly. The government should therefore evaluate the short-term gain from cheating against the future losses that result from the fact that the Phillips curve shifts upwards.

But suppose now that the government consists of short-sighted politicians who give a low weight to future losses, and that it decides to cheat. We then move to point *B*. This, however, will trigger a shift of the Phillips curve upwards. Given these new expectations, it will be optimal for the authorities to move to point *C*. This will go on until we reach point *E*. This point has the following characteristics. First, it is on the vertical Phillips curve, so that agents' expectations are realized. They have therefore no incentives any more to change their expectations further. Secondly, at *E* the authorities have no incentive any more to surprise economic agents with more inflation. A movement upwards along the Phillips curve going through E would lead to an indifference curve located higher, and therefore to a loss of welfare.

Point *E* can also be interpreted as the equilibrium that will be achieved in a rational expectations world when the authorities follow a *discretionary* policy, i.e. when they set the rate of inflation optimally each period given the prevailing expectations.

It is clear that this equilibrium is not very attractive. It is however the only equilibrium that can be sustained, given that the authorities are sufficiently short-sighted, and that the private sector knows this. The zero inflation rule (or any other constant inflation rule below the level achieved at *E*) has no credibility in a world of rational economic agents. The reason is that these economic agents realize that the authorities have an incentive to cheat. They will therefore adjust their expectations up to the point where the authorities have no incentive to cheat any more. This is achieved at point *E*. A zero inflation rule, although desirable, will not come about automatically.[11]

It should be stressed that this model is a static one. If the policy game is repeated many times, the government will have an incentive to acquire a reputation of low inflation. Such a reputation will make it possible to reach a lower inflation equilibrium. One way the static assumption can be rationalized is by considering that in many countries political institutions favour short-term objectives for politicians. For example, the next election is never far away, leading to uncertainty whether the present rulers will still be in place next period. Thus, what is implicitly assumed in this model is that the political decision process is inefficient, leading politicians to give a strong weight to the short-term gains of inflationary policies. The politicians as individuals are certainly as rational as private agents; the political decision process, however, may force them to give undue weight to the very short-term results of their policies.

Before analysing the question of how a monetary union might help the authorities to move to a more attractive equilibrium, it is helpful to study what factors determine the exact location of the 'discretionary' equilibrium (point *E*).

We distinguish two factors that affect the location of the discretionary equilibrium, and therefore also the equilibrium level of inflation.

(*a*) *The preferences of the authorities.* In Fig. 21.10 we present the cases of the 'wet' (steep indifference curves) and the 'hard-nosed' (flat indifference curves) governments. Assuming that the Phillips curves have the same slopes, Fig. 21.10 shows that in a country with a 'wet' government, the equilibrium inflation will be higher than in the country with a 'hard-nosed' government.

Note also that the only way a zero rate of inflation rule can be credible is when the authorities show no concern whatsoever for unemployment. In that case the indifference curves are horizontal. The authorities will choose the lowest possible horizontal indifference curve in each period. The inflation equilibrium will then be achieved at point *A*.[12]

(*b*) *The level of the natural rate of unemployment.* Suppose the level of the natural unemployment rate increases. It can then easily be shown that if the preferences of the authorities remain unchanged, the new equilibrium inflation rate increases. This is made clear in Fig. 21.11 which shows the case of an increase of the NAIRU. Its effect is to increase the equilibrium rate of inflation from *p* to *p'*.

3.2 The Barro–Gordon model in open economies

In the previous sections we showed how a government, which is known to care about inflation and unemployment, will not credibly be able to announce

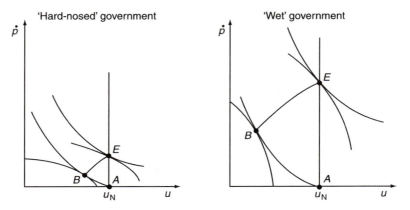

Figure 21.10 Equilibrium with 'hard-nosed' and 'wet' governments

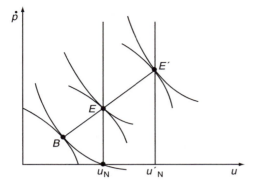

Figure 21.11 Equilibrium and the level of natural unemployment

a zero inflation rate. It is therefore stuck in a suboptimal equilibrium with an inflation rate that is too high.

This analysis can be extended to open economies. Let us now assume that there are two countries. We call the first country Germany, and assume its government is 'hard-nosed'. The second country is called Italy, where the government is 'wet'. We use the purchasing-power parity condition, i.e.

$$\dot{e} = \dot{p}_I - \dot{p}_G$$

We show the inflation outcome in Fig. 21.12. Italy has a higher equilibrium rate of inflation than Germany. Its currency will therefore have to depreciate continuously. The problem of Italy is that it could achieve a much lower inflation equilibrium than point E if its government were able to convince its citizens that, once at point A, it would not try to reach point B.

This Barro–Gordon model for open economies allows us to add important insights into the discussion of the costs of a monetary union.

3.3 Credibility and the cost of a monetary union

Can Italy solve its problem by announcing that it will join a monetary union with Germany? In order to answer this question, suppose, first, that Italy announces that it will fix its exchange rate with the German mark. Given the purchasing-power parity, this fixes the Italian inflation rate at the German level. In Fig. 21.12 we show this by the horizontal line from C. Italy appears now to be able to enjoy a lower inflation rate. The potential welfare gains are large, because in the new equilibrium the economy is on a lower indifference curve.

The question, however, is whether this rule can be credible. We observe that once at the new equilibrium point F, the Italian authorities have an incentive to engineer a surprise devaluation of the lira. This surprise devaluation leads to a surprise increase in inflation and allows the economy to move towards point G. Over time, however, economic agents will adjust their expectations,

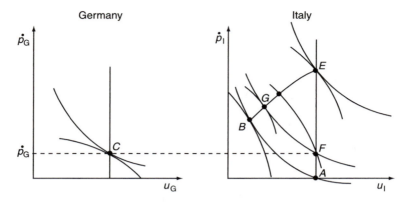

Figure 21.12 Inflation equilibrium in a two-country model

so that the equilibrium inflation rate ends up to be the same as before the exchange rate was fixed. Thus, merely fixing the exchange rate does not solve the problem, because the fixed exchange rate rule is no more credible than a fixed inflation rate rule.[13]

There are, however, other arrangements that can potentially solve the high-inflation problem of Italy. Imagine that Italy decided to abolish its currency and to adopt the currency of Germany. If that arrangement could be made credible, i.e. if the Italian citizens were convinced that once this decision is taken and the mark becomes the national money, the Italian authorities would never rescind this decision, then Italy could achieve the same inflation equilibrium as Germany. In Fig. 21.12 the horizontal line connecting the German inflation equilibrium with Italy defines a credible equilibrium for Italy. The point *F* is now the new Italian inflation equilibrium. Since Italy has no independent monetary policy any more, its monetary authorities (with 'wet' preferences) have ceased to exist and therefore cannot devalue the lira. In the words of Giavazzi and Pagano (1987), Italy has borrowed credibility from Germany, because its government has its monetary hands firmly tied.[14]

This is certainly a very strong result. It leads to the conclusion that there is a large potential gain for Italy in joining a monetary union with Germany. In addition, there is no welfare loss for Germany. Thus, a monetary union only leads to gains. This analysis has become very popular especially in Latin countries where the distrust for one's own authorities runs very deeply.

There are two considerations, however, that tend to soften this conclusion. First, it should be clear from the previous analysis that only a full monetary union establishes the required credibility for Italy. That is, Italy must be willing to eliminate its national currency, very much like East Germany did on 1 July 1990 when it adopted the West German mark. Anything less than full monetary union will face a credibility problem. As was pointed out, when Italy fixes its exchange rate relative to the mark and keeps its own currency, as it does in the EMS, the credibility of this fixed exchange rate arrangement will be in doubt.

Secondly, and more importantly for our present purpose, we have assumed that the central bank of the monetary union is the German central bank. In this arrangement, Italy profits from the reputation of the German central bank to achieve lower inflation. Suppose, however, that the new central bank is a new institution, where both the German and the Italian authorities are represented equally. Would that new central bank have the same reputation as the old German central bank? This is far from clear. If the union central bank is perceived to be less 'hard-nosed' than the German central bank prior to setting up the union, the new inflation equilibrium of the union will be higher than the one which prevailed in Germany before the union. Italy may still gain from such an arrangement. Germany, however, would lose, and would not be very enthusiastic to form such a union.

We conclude from the preceding analysis that problems of credibility are important in evaluating the costs of a monetary union. First, the option to devalue the currency is a two-edged sword for the national authorities. The knowledge that it may be used in the future greatly complicates macro-economic policies. Secondly, the time-consistency literature also teaches us some important lessons concerning the costs of a monetary union: a devaluation cannot be used to correct every disturbance that occurs in an economy. A devaluation is not, as it is in the analysis of Mundell, a flexible instrument that can be used frequently. When used once, it affects its use in the future, because it engenders strong expectational effects. It is a dangerous instrument that can hurt those who use it. Each time the policy-makers use this instrument, they will have to evaluate the advantages obtained today against the cost, i.e. that it will be more difficult to use this instrument effectively in the future.

This has led some economists to conclude that the exchange rate instrument should not be used at all, and that countries would even gain from irrevocably relinquishing its use. This conclusion goes too far. There were many cases, observed in Europe during the 1980s, in which devaluations were used very successfully (see the previous section). The ingredients of this success have typically been that the devaluation was coupled with other drastic policy changes (sometimes with a change of government, e.g. Belgium in 1982 and Denmark in the same year). As a result, the devaluation was perceived as a unique and an extraordinary change in policies that could not easily be repeated in the future. Under those conditions the negative reputation effects could be kept under control. Some countries, in particular Denmark in 1982, even seem to have improved their reputation quickly after the devaluation. Relinquishing the possibility of using this instrument for the indefinite future does imply a cost for a nation.

4 THE COST OF MONETARY UNION AND THE OPENNESS OF COUNTRIES

Although it will remain difficult to evaluate the importance of all the arguments developed in the previous sections, and therefore of the costs of relinquishing one's national currency, we have learned one thing about which there can be relatively little dispute. The cost of relinquishing one's national currency declines with the openness of a country. This relation between the cost of joining a monetary union and the openness of the country was implicit in much of our previous analysis. Let us make it more explicit here.

The ability of a country to affect output and employment by exchange rate changes is certainly a function of its openness. Let us return to Fig. 21.3 where we analysed the effects of a devaluation. We now consider two countries, one that is relatively open, the other that is relatively closed. We represent these two countries in Fig. 21.13.

The major difference between open and relatively closed countries has to do with the supply shifts that follow a devaluation. More than a relatively closed country, a very open economy will quickly be faced with the problem that a devaluation just raises the domestic price level without affecting its output. Thus, for a very open economy the exchange rate is a particularly ineffective instrument. Relinquishing this instrument, therefore, involves little loss.

McKinnon (1963) has stressed this point in his important contribution to the theory of optimum currency areas. When the country is very open, economic agents (workers and employers) may start using the foreign price level when setting contracts. In that case, changing the exchange rate would be completely redundant, because these economic agents would automatically adjust the domestic currency value of all these contracts. The country could take over the foreign currency without any loss.

In addition, for small open economies the alternative instruments needed to bring back equilibrium in the balance of payments are less likely to impose the same kind of large costs as for relatively closed countries. This can be illustrated by considering the following simple Keynesian model of aggregate demand in small and large economies. Let us define a very open country as one with a high marginal propensity to import, and a relatively closed country as one with a low marginal propensity to import. The multiplier of government spending can then be derived for the two countries to be the following:

for the open economy

$$Y = \frac{1}{s+m} G$$

for the relatively closed country

$$Y^* = \frac{1}{s^*+m^*} G^*$$

where G and G^* are the levels of government spending in the two countries, s and s^* are the marginal propensities to save, and m and m^* are the marginal propensities to import in the two countries.

Suppose both countries use government spending as their instrument to

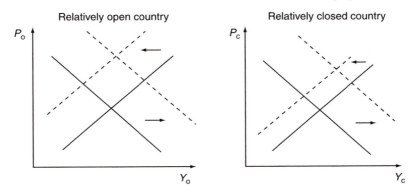

Figure 21.13 Effectiveness of devaluation as a function of openness

reduce the deficit on the trade account. The effect of reducing government spending on the trade account is then described by the following equations:

for the open economy

$$B = \frac{m}{s + m} G$$

for the relatively closed country

$$B^* = \frac{m^*}{s^* + m^*} G^*$$

where B and B^* are the trade accounts of the open and the relatively closed countries.

It can be seen from these expressions that to obtain the same effect on its trade account the more open economy will have to reduce government spending more than the relatively closed country. An example makes this clear. Suppose the marginal propensity to import is 0.5 in the first country and 0.1 in the second one. Let us also assume that the marginal propensities to save are equal to 0.2 in both countries. Then the multipliers of government spending on the trade account are 0.71 and 0.33, respectively. This implies that if the objective is to reduce the trade account by 100, the relatively closed economy will have to reduce government spending by 300 whereas the relatively open economy achieves the same reduction of its trade account by reducing government spending by 140. Thus, reducing the trade account by general fiscal policies will be less costly for the relatively open economy than for the relatively closed one.

We can summarize these ideas about the costs of a monetary union and the openness of the country in Fig. 21.14 (which is borrowed from Krugman, 1990). On the vertical axis the cost of a monetary union is set out (i.e. the cost of relinquishing the exchange rate instrument). This cost is expressed as a per cent of GDP. On the horizontal axis the openness of the country relative to the countries with whom it wants to form a monetary union is set

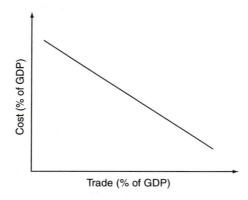

Figure 21.14 The cost of a monetary union and the openness of a country

out. This openness is represented by the trade share in the GDP of the country considered here. We see that as the openness increases the cost of joining a monetary union declines.

5 CONCLUSION

The criticism against the traditional theory of optimal currency areas, as developed by Mundell and McKinnon, has enabled us to add important nuances to this theory. In particular, it has changed our view about the costs of a monetary union. The traditional theory of optimal currency areas tends to be rather pessimistic about the possibility for countries to join a monetary union at a low cost. The criticism we have discussed in this chapter is much less pessimistic about this, i.e. the costs of forming a monetary union appear to be less forbidding. Despite this criticism the hard core of the optimum currency analysis still stands. This can be put as follows:

1 There are important differences between countries that are not going to disappear in a monetary union. This raises the question whether counties should gladly relinquish control over their ability to follow an independent monetary policy, including setting (and changing) the price of their currency.

2 Despite the fact that exchange rate changes usually have no permanent effects on real variables, such as output and employment, variations in the exchange rate remain a powerful instrument to help countries to eliminate important macroeconomic disequilibria, and to make the adjustment process less costly in terms of lost output and employment. The examples of France, Belgium, and Denmark that devalued their currencies during the 1980s (and coupled this devaluation with the right domestic policies) illustrate this point.

3 The argument that exchange rate changes are dangerous instruments in the hands of politicians is important. The experience of many countries illustrates that when devaluations are used systematically, they will lead to more inflation without gains in terms of output and employment. In addition, they

easily lead to macroeconomic instability as economic agents continuously tend to expect future devaluations. Contrary to the old view, devaluations are not instruments that policy-makers can use flexibly and costlessly.

This argument should, however, not be pushed too far. The fact that such an instrument can be misused is not sufficient reason to throw it away, when it can also be put to good use, when countries face extraordinary circumstances. The abandonment of the exchange rate instrument to deal with possible extraordinary disturbances should certainly be considered to be a cost of monetary union.

NOTES

1 See EC Commission (1990) and Gros and Thygesen (1991).
2 Peter Kenen (1969) also stressed the importance of the similarity of the trading structure for making a monetary union less costly.
3 This is an old idea that was developed by Myrdal (1957) and Kaldor (1966). For a survey see Balassa (1961). Krugman gives a more rigorous underpinning of these ideas in some of his recent writing. See Krugman (1991).
4 See Gros and Thygesen (1991), ch. 9.
5 For a discussion of this model see Carlin and Soskice (1990).
6 This employment line must in fact be interpreted as the reaction curve of the government. The union operates as a 'Stackelberg' leader and selects the optimal point on this reaction line.
7 This visual evidence is confirmed by the regression equation that the Commission (1990: 146) computed:

$$\text{GDP} = \underset{(0.30)}{0.36} + \underset{(0.105)}{0.095} * \text{REER} \qquad \text{Corrected } R^2 = -0.02$$

where GDP = growth rate of GDP minus EC growth, and REER = the average growth rate of unit labour costs relative to Community partners. Standard errors are in brackets. It can be seen that the coefficient of REER is not statistically different from zero.
8 See EC commission (1990), ch. 6.
9 See De Grauwe (1983), ch. 9.
10 The Barro–Gordon model has been applied to open economies by Mélitz (1988) and Cohen and Wyplosz (1989) among others.
11 In the jargon of the economic literature it is said that the policy rule of zero inflation is 'time inconsistent', i.e. the authorities face the problem each period that a better short-term outcome is possible. The zero inflation rule is incentive-incompatible.
12 Rogoff (1985) has suggested that the best thing that could happen to a country is that its monetary policy be run by an orthodox central banker.
13 Some economists have argued that fixing the exchange rate can be a rule that inherently has more credibility than announcing a constant inflation rate rule. [See, for example, Giavazzi and Pagano (1988) – editor's note.]
14 See also Giavazzi and Giovannini (1989).

REFERENCES

Balassa, B. (1961) *The Theory of Economic Integration*, London: Allen & Unwin.
Barro, R., and Gordon, D. (1983) 'Rules, Discretion and Reputation in a Model of Monetary Policy', *Journal of Monetary Economics*, 12: 101–21.

Carlin, W., and Soskice, D. (1990) *Macroeconomics and the Wage Bargain*, Oxford: OUP.

Cohen, D., and Wyplosz, C. (1989) 'The European Monetary Union: An Agnostic Evaluation', typescript.

De Grauwe, P. (1983) *Macroeconomic Theory for the Open Economy*, Aldershot, Hants: Gower.

De Grauwe, P., and Vanhaverbeke, W. (1990) 'Exchange Rate Experiences of Small EMS Countries. The Cases of Belgium, Denmark and the Netherlands', in V. Argy and P. De Grauwe (eds.), *Choosing an Exchange Rate Regime*, Washington DC: International Monetary Fund.

EC Commission (1990) 'One Market, One Money', *European Economy*, 44.

Giavazzi, F., and Giovannini, A. (1989) *Limiting Exchange Rate Flexibility: The European Monetary System*, Cambridge, MA.: MIT Press.

Giavazzi F., and Pagano, M. (1988) 'The Advantage of Tying One's Hands: EMS Discipline and Central Bank Credibility', *European Economic Review* 32: 1055–82.

Gros, D., and Thygesen, N. (1991) *European Monetary Integration: From the European Monetary System towards Monetary Union*, London: Longman.

Kaldor, N. (1966) *The Causes of the Slow Growth of the United Kingdom*, Cambridge: CUP.

Kenen, P. (1969) 'The Theory of Optimum Currency Areas: An Eclectic View', in R. Mundell and A. Swoboda (eds.), *Monetary Problems of the International Economy*, Chicago: University of Chicago Press.

Krugman, P. (1989) 'Differences in Income Elasticities and Trends in Real Exchange Rates', *European Economic Review*, 33/5: 1031–47.

—— (1990) 'Policy Problems of a Monetary Union', in P. De Grauwe, P. and L. Papademos (eds.), *The European Monetary System in the 1990s*, London: Longman.

—— (1991) *Geography and Trade*, Cambridge, MA.: MIT Press.

Kydland, F., and Prescott, E. (1977) 'Rules Rather than Discretion: The Inconsistency of Optimal Plans', *Journal of Political Economy*, 85.

McDonald, I., and Solow, R. (1981) 'Wage Bargaining and Employment', *American Economic Review*, 71: 896–908.

McKinnon, R. (1963) 'Optimum Currency Areas', *American Economic Review* 53/4: 717–25.

Mélitz, J. (1988) 'Monetary Discipline, Germany and the European Monetary System: A Synthesis', in F. Giavazzi, S. Micossi, and M. Miller (eds.), *The European Monetary System*, Cambridge: Cambridge University Press.

Myrdal, G. (1957) *Economic Theory and Underdeveloped Regions*, New York: Duckworth.

Rogoff, K. (1985) 'The Optimal Degree of Commitment to an Intermediate Monetary Target', *Quarterly Journal of Economics*, 100: 1169–90.

Sachs, J., and Wyplosz, C. (1986) 'The Economic Consequences of President Mitterand', *Economic Policy*, 2.

22 European monetary unification

A *tour d'horizon*

Barry Eichengreen*

Oxford Review of Economic Policy, vol. 14, no. 3 (1998), pp. 24–40

I INTRODUCTION

For European monetary unification, this is the point of maximum anticipation, as the audience falls silent, the actors hold their breath, and the curtain starts to rise. What is true for officials is true also for academics: they have not fallen silent, to be sure, but they have increasingly turned their attention to this stage. This would seem an opportune time to take stock of the literature and anticipate future directions.

In a number of areas, a reasonable degree of consensus now exists as the result of a decade of scholarship. My own stock-taking concentrates instead on areas where significant questions remain. I start in section II with the implications of surrendering the exchange rate and an independent national monetary policy as instruments of adjustment. The focus here, inevitably, is on labour markets, and on the extent to which wage flexibility and labour mobility can substitute for the forgone instruments. Section III considers the conduct of fiscal policy under the Excessive Deficit Procedure and the Stability Pact, asking how constrained automatic fiscal stabilizers and discretionary counter-cyclical fiscal stabilization will be. In section IV I ask how quickly the European Union (EU) is likely to develop an EU-wide system of fiscal federalism to accompany its monetary union.

Sections V–VII turn from fiscal to monetary issues. Section V asks whether the European Central Bank (ECB) will be as inflation-adverse as the Bundesbank, section VI what exchange-rate policy the ECB will pursue, and section VII whether the euro will be a leading reserve currency. Section VIII raises what may now be the most contentious issue of all, namely, whether Europe's monetary union could collapse after it begins.

To repeat, throughout this paper I concentrate on issues where significant disagreement remains. While it is not possible to offer definitive answers to all the questions raised, posing a series of open questions and offering tentative answers at least has the merit of pointing to an agenda for research.

* University of California, Berkeley. An early draft of this paper was completed while the author was affiliated to the International Monetary Fund, whose views those in this paper naturally do not represent. He thanks Alessandro Prati for helpful comments. © 1998 Oxford University Press and the Oxford Review of Economic Policy Limited.

II SURRENDERING THE EXCHANGE RATE AS AN
INSTRUMENT OF ADJUSTMENT

Monetary unification means abandoning the exchange rate and independent national monetary policies as adjustment mechanisms within the monetary union. Unless other adjustment mechanisms take up the slack, serious economic imbalances and political tensions could arise. The classic Mundellian alternative is greater labour-market flexibility in the form of both wage adjustments and worker mobility. Wage flexibility is hardly a European strength, to put an understated gloss on the point. From this perspective, the fact that labour is less mobile in Europe than in the United States is disturbing. This fact is widely cited by sceptics of the advisability of Europe's monetary union project (see, *inter alia*, Feldstein, 1997a). Migration has a path-dependent character: statutory barriers that have stifled it in the past will also discourage it in the future—and continue to do so even once they have been removed—insofar as they slow the development of expatriate networks and support greater cultural and linguistic diversity than is characteristic of monetary unions such as the United States. Couple this with the fact that wage flexibility is less than in North America, and one is left with only one adjustment mechanism, namely, changes in intra-European exchange rates.

   The idea that Europe needs to rely more on exchange-rate flexibility because it lacks labour mobility rests, of course, on the assumption that exchange-rate flexibility is effective. But if real wages are rigid—that is, money wages respond quickly to the change in the exchange rate—then Europe's low level of labour mobility is not a compelling argument against giving up the exchange-rate instrument. Indeed, the revealed preference of European countries not to use monetary-cum-exchange-rate policy as an instrument of adjustment suggests that they harbour doubts about its efficacy.

   The counter-argument is that policy-makers' reluctance actively to utilize the exchange-rate instrument reflects political rather than economic considerations, and in particular their strategy of using exchange-rate-stabilization agreements as a device for propelling forward the integration process. Europe's revealed preference, by this interpretation, is to avoid causing political disruptions through active use of the exchange rate; it is not an indication that exchange-rate changes are ineffective for adjustment purposes.

   Strikingly, this question, perhaps the most fundamental of all entries on the cost side of the EMU ledger, has yet to be definitively answered. How much stabilization capacity Europe is sacrificing remains uncertain even at this late date. Anecdotal evidence from the 1990s, when Italy and the United Kingdom withdrew from the Exchange Rate Mechanism (ERM), is frequently invoked to suggest that exchange-rate changes retain their power. However, Bergin and Moersch (1997) have cast doubt on this conclusion. While confirming that those countries which depreciated their currencies boosted their exports, they do not find that this relatively rapid export growth translated into faster overall economic growth.

Gordon (1998) offers a solution to this puzzle: that countries which depreciated their currencies after 1992, Italy, Spain, Finland, and Sweden prominent among them, took the opportunity also to cut their budget deficits. Currency depreciation boosted exports and stimulated growth, other things equal, but insofar as governments took advantage of the incipient acceleration of growth to cut their deficits, they further curtailed domestic demand. With little perceptible acceleration in inflation relative to countries with unchanged ERM parities, there was a shift in relative prices toward traded goods in countries which depreciated their currencies and a surge in exports, but no acceleration in growth owing to the compensatory compression of the budget deficit. (The one country that does not fit this schema is the United Kingdom, where no dramatic Italian-style budgetary retrenchment was required, but there the business cycle was out of phase with that of Continental Europe: recovery had begun earlier and decelerated at roughly the same time when the other countries depreciating their currencies felt the export surge.) The implication is that intra-European exchange rates retain some capacity to stabilize the economies of the member states if governments only permit them to operate.

An objection to the sceptics' emphasis on Europe's low level of labour mobility is that mobility is low *within*, not just *between*, European countries. OECD (1990) notes that 3 per cent of Americans change their region of residence annually, but that the same is true of only 0.6 per cent of Italians and 1.1 per cent of Britons and Germans. The same cultural and linguistic diversity that works to discourage cross-national migration would also appear to discourage intra-national migration. But this low level of mobility within European countries has not posed a threat to the viability of their national monetary unions. If mobility is low within France but the French monetary union still functions perfectly adequately, the question then becomes, why should the same not be true of Europe?

The answer, according to the EMU sceptics, is that the low level of mobility within European countries reflects an absence of asymmetric, region-specific shocks. Little migration is observed, not because there are barriers to mobility, but because there is little incentive to move. However, a number of studies have cast doubt on this hypothesis. Viñals and Jimeno (1996) find that two-thirds of the conditional variance of regional unemployment rates within European countries is due to region-specific factors. Forni and Reichlin (1997) attribute less importance to region-specific disturbances but still conclude that the contribution of such shocks—and the incentive to migrate—is as great within European countries as within the United States. Structural models (Eichengreen, 1993) and vector autoregressions (Obstfeld and Peri, 1997) suggest that labour is simply less responsive to wage and unemployment differentials than in the United States.

Alternatively, Europe's low level of mobility may reflect not cultural and linguistic obstacles but an extensive system of inter-regional transfers which limits the incentive to move for residents of Europe's low-productivity, high-unemployment regions. North–South transfers within Italy are the most prominent example, but the phenomenon is general. The same tendency exists within North America: inter-regional redistribution is greater in Canada than in the United States (Bayoumi and Masson, 1995), and inter-regional mobility is correspondingly lower (Obstfeld and Peri, 1998). This is another channel for path dependence: the absence of expatriate networks has helped to sustain local cultures, leading voters to support inter-regional transfers in order to prevent their cultural distinctiveness from being diluted by immigration.

Persistence does not mean stasis. However low mobility may have been in the past, it should be higher in the future. This is obvious to the apostles of the Lucas Critique: once there no longer remains the option of exchange-rate changes to facilitate adjustment, workers and unions will recognize the need to substitute greater labour-market flexibility (Wijkander, 1997). And authors such as Alogoskoufis and Smith (1991), looking across exchange-rate regimes, tend to confirm the existence of greater nominal wage flexibility when exchange rates are fixed than when they are flexible. The need for greater wage flexibility is, of course, prominent in the policy debate, and baby steps have already been taken in this direction. The Schengen agreement to remove border controls and the portability of pensions will encourage mobility, however modestly, and promote the creation of expatriate networks. The homogenizing influence of the media and the spread of English-language skills should loosen the hold of cultural specificity. European economists will be aware of the tendency for their colleagues to respond to the lure of attractive positions in academia or the financial sector in countries other than their own. Such observations suggest that mobility is relatively high among skilled workers, even if union rules, apprenticeship programmes, and training schemes limit it among the unskilled. Mauro and Spilimbergo (1998) confirm this directly: using data on migration between Spanish regions disaggregated by level of education, they find that migration is high for the high-school and college educated but low for the illiterate and primary-school educated, among whom unemployment and declining participation rates take up most of the slack in response to a negative employment shock.

The question is how soon we will observe further increases in labour-market flexibility. Here too, the jury is still out. The authors of a number of country case studies—Hochreiter and Winckler (1995) on Austria, Kremers (1990) for Ireland, Gressani *et al.* (1988) for Italy, and Artus and Salomon (1996) for France, for example—do find some evidence of greater wage and price flexibility with the hardening of the government's exchange-rate commitment. Cross-country econometric analyses are less uniformly supportive of the existence of a significant exchange-rate-wage-flexibility link. Artis and Omerod (1991) estimate wage equations for the leading ERM countries but find only modest evidence of a structural break around the advent of the European Monetary System (EMS). In a follow-up study (Artis and Omerod, 1996) for a longer period, which can distinguish the less credible pre-1988 EMS from the 'New EMS' of the post-1988 years, they find limited evidence of an EMS effect, most notably for Belgium. Anderton and Barrell (1995) report the results of a statistical study of ten European countries, concluding that, with the exception of Italy, there is not much evidence of an EMS-related structural shift in the wage-determination process. It remains to reconcile these findings.

III FISCAL POLICY UNDER THE EXCESSIVE DEFICIT PROCEDURE AND THE STABILITY PACT

Fiscal policy may be the aspect of monetary union on which consensus remains most elusive. On one side are those who argue that a European country which ties its monetary hand behind its back should keep its fiscal hand free. Having abandoned the exchange rate and an independent national monetary policy as instruments of adjustment, it is essential that it retain its fiscal flexibility.

On the other side are those who insist on the need for the close coordination of fiscal policies within the monetary union and, by implication, for restrains on fiscal autonomy. A popular justification for such restraints is as protection for the ECB from pressure to extend an inflationary debt bail-out. If the government gets into fiscal trouble and neighbouring EMU countries experience negative repercussions, this argument goes, the ECB may feel compelled to buy up the bonds of the government in distress, with inflationary consequences monetary-union wide.

What this thesis ignores is that when sub-central governments control their own tax instruments rather than relying for their revenues on transfers from the centre, they possess a third possible response to debt problems (in addition to default and obtaining a central-bank bail-out), namely, raising their own taxes. Given the existence of this alternative, the central authorities should be able to commit themselves to not extending a bail-out. The fact that countries in which subcentral governments collect the bulk of their own revenues typically do not limit the fiscal freedom of the latter is consistent with this view (von Hagen and Eichengreen, 1996). And, absent the development of an EU-wide system of fiscal federalism (see section IV), this is the vertical fiscal structure that will continue to prevail in Europe.

A second popular rationale for fiscal restraints is to neutralize inflationary pressure more generally. The ECB, concerned with the efficiency of the European economy, will in this view seek to balance the deadweight cost of inflation against the deadweight cost of other taxes. If governments participating in the monetary union run large deficits and accumulate large debts, the ECB will have an incentive to run more inflationary policies to minimize the efficiency losses associated with other taxes, undermining its commitment to price stability (De Grauwe, 1996).

At the same time, there are reasons to question that the ECB will simply apply the one-period Ramsey Rule, raising the inflation tax in line with the other taxes. It will be engaged in a multi-period game in which it seeks to convince governments and the markets of its commitment to price stability, even if doing so entails short-term deadweight losses. If it refuses to inflate, governments will find the deadweight cost of taxation to be higher, and they will adapt their behaviour accordingly (Chari and Kehoe, 1997). It is not clear, in other words, that the ECB will play Stackelberg follower to the government's lead in a series of one-shot games.

A third rationale for fiscal restraints is to internalize cross-border interest-rate spill-overs. National policy-makers, in this view, have inadequate incentive to take into account the impact of their borrowing on interest rates in other member states. Excessive borrowing in one country will therefore drive up the level of interest rates monetary-union wide. The problem with this argument is that European countries borrow on world financial markets, not on European financial markets. Italy may be large relative to Europe, but it is small relative to global capital markets. It is hardly plausible that a single medium-sized country can drive up the level of interest rates world-wide. And as the globalization of financial markets proceeds, it will become still less likely that European capital markets will remain significantly segmented and that interest-rate spill-overs will be limited to one continent.

A final rationale for the fiscal restrictions of the Maastricht Treaty is to encourage policy coordination more generally. It is desirable that national fiscal policies be coordinated (for reasons such as those given in the preceding paragraph) and that monetary and fiscal policies be harmonized (to prevent a bad policy mix of loose fiscal and tight monetary policies from leading to a chronically overvalued real exchange rate). But most [. . .] empirical studies of policy coordination suggest that the benefits are slight. Oudiz and Sachs (1984) reach this conclusion for the major industrial countries, Masson and Taylor (1993) for the European Union. Moreover, there is the danger that the Excessive Deficit Procedure and the Stability Pact, by limiting the flexibility of national fiscal policies, may actually impede the coordination of policies. Numerical deficit ceilings are a blunt instrument, in other words, for addressing this problem.

If these are the benefits of fiscal restrictions, the corresponding danger is that they will weaken the operation of automatic fiscal stabilizers and discretionary policy. In assessing the realism of this fear, it is important to be clear on what the Stability Pact entails. It consists of two Council regulations—one on the Excessive Deficit Procedure and one on surveillance—and a European Council resolution which provides guidance to the Council and member states on the application of the pact. The Council regulations clarify the meaning of the Excessive Deficit Procedure, elaborating the clauses referring to exceptional and temporary circumstances under which the 3 per cent reference value for the general government budget deficit can be exceeded without a determination that the deficit is excessive. In addition, they commit participants in the monetary union to the medium-term objective of budgets that are balanced or close to balance.

A country can escape a determination that its deficit is excessive and avoid having to make non-remunerated deposits if its real GDP declines by at least 2 per cent in the year in question. A recession in which GDP declines by less than 2 per cent but more than 0.75 per cent may also qualify with the concurrence of the Council. The Commission will receive definitive data on a country's deficit in year t around March of year $t + 1$. The government will then have to take corrective action to prevent the excess from persisting into year $t + 2$. If no such action is taken by the end of year $t + 1$, non-remunerated deposits will be required. But since it is the deficit in year $t + 2$ that must conform to the requirements of the treaty, 2 successive years of excess can occur without penalty. Moreover, the passage in which it is stated that excessive deficits should be corrected no later than the year following the identification of the excess ends with the qualifying phrase, 'unless there are special circumstances'. Presumably a country such as Finland, which suffered budgetary difficulties in the early 1990s owing to the collapse of the Soviet Union, would be allowed to invoke this clause.

How binding these provisions turn out to be will depend on countries' proximity to the 3 per cent ceiling when a slow-down strikes. If governments have balanced budgets or surpluses, they will have more room for manoeuvre. In the seven deepest recessions experienced in the OECD in the last 30 years, deficits widened by a bit over 6 per cent of GDP for 2 years (Eichengreen and Wyplosz, 1998). Thus, 3 per cent surpluses in normal times would be sufficient to accommodate even the largest recessions, although assuming 3 per cent surpluses involves an element of wishful thinking. In any case, the largest recessions will qualify as exceptional circumstances. This makes it more interesting to consider a deficit that may not so qualify, of, say, 1.75 per cent of GDP. OECD (1996) suggests that if growth declines by 1.75 per cent for 2 years rather than rising by 2.25 per cent per annum (as needed to keep the deficit from growing), the 4 per cent swing will cause an increase in the budget deficit of a bit less than 4 per cent of GDP. Thus, a 1 per cent surplus will still suffice to accommodate this swing, even if exceptional circumstances are not granted. European Commission (1997) makes the same point: it analyses 24 severe recessions, defined as episodes of negative growth of GDP of 0.75 per cent or more, finding that output gaps widened on average by 5.5 percentage points, while actual budget deficits increased by 3.5 percentage points of GDP.

But if countries are already up against the 3 per cent limit when the recession strikes, they will not be able to increase their deficits so freely. How much difference would this make? Bayoumi and Eichengreen (1995) use the IMF's MULTIMOD model to show that automatic stabilizers reduce the first-year effect of a 5 per cent reduction in the marginal propensity to consume on real GDP by as much as half. With automatic stabilizers, output falls by 2.8 per cent; without them it falls by 3.2–4.6 per cent (depending on whether cuts in government consumption or increases in net taxes are used to close the budget gap). This conclusion is supported by Sorensen and Yosha (1997), who consider the impact on consumption rather than output. Although their point estimates of the stabilization effect are more modest, they find that between 40 and 50 per cent of shocks to output are smoothed by EU countries in the sense of not showing up in consumption. Half of this smoothing takes place through changes in government saving and dissaving at the national level. Allsopp *et al.* (1997) also provide similar estimates.

Simulations of a small structural model in Eichengreen and Wyplosz (1993) similarly suggest that less counter-cyclical fiscal action will mean larger output gaps and slower growth. The difference in any given year is small—no more than a fraction of a percentage point of growth on average over the business cycle—but even small growth effects can cumulate into large changes in levels if they persist for decades. Simulations for the period 1974–95 suggest output losses of 5–9 per cent owing to the imposition of Stability-Pact-like ceilings.

IV FISCAL FEDERALISM

The debate over the need for fiscal federalism to accompany the monetary union has swung from one extreme to the other. The early view (as in the MacDougall Report, 1977) was that a smoothly functioning monetary union requires the stabilization provided by a federal fiscal system. Ingram (1959) had already documented the operation of this mechanism in the United States. Sala-i-Martin and Sachs (1992) lent econometric rigour to his case, estimating that changes in taxes and transfers paid to and received from the federal government by the states offset 30–40 per cent of declines in state incomes. The implication was that Europe would find it difficult to operate a monetary union so long as it failed to develop comparable mechanisms of fiscal federalism, especially insofar as other means of adjustment, notably wage flexibility and labour mobility, were absent.

Subsequent authors revised downward Sala-i-Martin and Sachs's estimates. They emphasized that these early results did not distinguish equalization (ongoing transfers from high- to low-income regions) from stabilization (increases in transfers when one region suffers a decline in income relative to another). The first to attempt to do so was von Hagen (1992), who examined year-to-year changes in incomes, taxes, and transfers to get at the stabilization effect, and long-period averages to get at the equalization effect. For the United States he estimated the extent of stabilization to be less than a third of that reported by Sala-i-Martin and Sachs, while his estimated redistribution effect was nearly 50 cents on the dollar. His approach was extended to Canada by Bayoumi and Masson (1995), who found a stabilization effect for the United States of 31 percent, quite similar to Sala-i-Martin and Sachs's original estimate (but different from von Hagen's because these authors analyse personal income rather than gross state product), and a redistribution effect of 22 cents. For Canada, where regional equalization is a constitutional principle, the proportions are reversed: redistribution is 39 per cent, stabilization 17 per cent. Obstfeld and Peri (1998), using a vector autoregression (VAR) methodology, confirm Bayoumi and Masson's estimates of the magnitude of stabilization for Canada, but their estimates for the United States are closer to the more modest figures reported by von Hagen. Thus, the emerging consensus appears to be that the original Sala-i-Martin and Sachs estimates should be regarded as upper bounds.

This suggests that the automatic stabilization conducted by the member states of the European Union offsets roughly the same share of local income shocks as is neutralized by fiscal federalism within the United States. The implication is that there is no need for a European system of fiscal federalism so long as member states' automatic stabilizers are allowed to operate. But if these are disabled, there may arise pressure for fiscal federalism, as national governments plump for a union-wide system to provide the stabilization they are prevented from providing themselves (von Hagen and Eichengreen, 1996).

Which alternative is preferable? Recent authors, emphasizing the advantages of subsidiarity, stress the drawbacks of EU-wide fiscal federalism. Mélitz and Vori (1992) note that shocks to real per-capita GDP are positively correlated across member states, limiting the potential for mutual insurance. Mélitz (1994) argues further that unemployment-based co-insurance would benefit only a small number of European workers. In addition, a programme under which member states with high unemployment are rewarded by budgetary transfers from their EU partners will be a source of moral hazard. These transfers would have to come with strong conditions attached to prevent countries from succumbing to the incentive to pursue risky macroeconomic strategies that maximize growth in certain states of the world but aggravate unemployment in others. If some countries are particularly prone to this form of moral hazard, they may be ongoing recipients of intra-EU transfers. Unlike the Structural Funds, to which countries lose access when their incomes approach the EU average, there would arise the prospect of such transfers continuing indefinitely, which might threaten, rather than bolster, EU solidarity.

V WILL THE ECB BE AS PRICE-STABILITY-ORIENTED AS THE BUNDESBANK?

Popular discussion continues to focus on whether the ECB will take to heart its mandate to pursue price stability. The statute of the European System of Central Banks singles out price stability as the paramount goal of policy. Yet it also makes the ECB responsible for the stability of the payments and financial systems. And the new central bank will surely come under pressure to reduce interest rates when growth slows, even if doing so conflicts with the pursuit of low inflation. The politicization of the selection of the founding president of the central bank and the creation of a Euro-11 committee of finance ministers to serve as a political counterweight to the monetary technocrats of the central bank board are two not-so-subtle reminders of this danger.

The stability orientation of the ECB is not something that can be predicted before the fact. But the outcome will provide evidence on the explanatory power of two views of monetary policy-making. One view is that central

396   Barry Eichengreen

banks are mere political sounding boards. The ECB will come under pressure to represent the interests of the participating countries, and since other countries are less price-stability-oriented than Germany, the ECB will focus less narrowly on this goal than the Bundesbank. The greater the aversion of constituents to instability in output and employment, the greater the pressure they will bring to bear on the central bank, and the less will be the credibility of the latter's commitment to price stability (Alesina and Grilli, 1992, 1994). Hence, the larger the monetary union and the more lax the enforcement of the Excessive Deficit Procedure and the Stability Pact, the more inflationary monetary policy will be. In particular, because other EU countries will enter EMU with heavier debts than Germany and will not inherit the latter's culture of price stability, the ECB is likely to follow more inflationary policies than the Bundesbank.

The other view is that central bank policies are a function of institutional structure. In particular, institutional independence insulates a central bank from pressure to pursue goals other than price stability. Grilli *et al.* (1991) distinguish political and economic independence. Economic independence increases when the central bank is not authorized to provide monetary financing of the budget deficit, when it sets its own discount rate, and when there are no constraints on the composition of its asset portfolio. Political independence increases when new governments are not automatically entitled to appoint new central bank governors or board members, when the latter serve long terms in office, when the government does not participate in or approve monetary policy decisions, and when the central bank statute gives priority to price stability. By the calculations of these authors, the Dutch and German central banks have been the most independent politically, while the Bundesbank is most independent economically. (Some statutory provisions have changed subsequently, since the Maastricht Treaty requires countries preparing for EMU to buttress the independence of their national central banks.) Alesina and Grilli estimate that the ECB will be as independent as the Bundesbank, not surprisingly since its statute is patterned after that of the German central bank.

Two qualifications should be noted. One is that the Euro-11 committee may inject political considerations into monetary policy-making in ways that are yet to be seen. Euro-11 may be nothing but a coffee klatsch of finance ministers, but their ability to pressure the ECB will presumably be greater when they speak with a single voice. Working in the other direction is the fact that calculations of political independence do not take into account the central bank's political accountability (Cooper, 1992). The German Bundesbank may have the independence to choose its monetary tactics, but if these are viewed as fundamentally incompatible with the priorities of its political constituency, the government can threaten to revoke or scale back its independence. The ECB is subject to no analogous threat, since its statute is embedded in an international treaty which can be changed only with the consent of all 15 national signatories. Kenen (1995) attaches rather more importance to the fact that the President of the Council of Ministers and a member of the

Commission will participate (but not vote) in the meetings of the Governing Council of the ECB, and to the fact that the President of the ECB must present an annual report to the parliament, which will then debate it, as well as to the Council.

Thus, Stage III will provide a test of whether the institutional or the pressure-group model has more explanatory power.

VI WHAT EXCHANGE-RATE POLICY FOR THE ECB?

There is some confusion about how the ECB will manage the exchange rate of the euro against other major currencies. Article 109 of the Maastricht Treaty empowers the Council of Ministers, acting by qualified majority, to adopt general orientations for exchange-rate policy *vis-à-vis* non-EU currencies. It does not stipulate how general those orientations must be, however, or how regularly they might be issued. Nor does Article 109 provide a mechanism that would make the Council's orientations binding on the ECB. It only specifies that those orientations must not jeopardize price stability without indicating who will decide whether jeopardy exists.

In contrast, the power to decide whether the euro will be part of a system of pegged exchange rates for the industrial countries, as suggested by Volcker (1995), or a global system of target zones, à la Williamson (1985), resides not with the ECB but with the Council of Ministers. The Council must act unanimously after consulting with the ECB and attempting to reach a consensus on the compatibility of its decision with price stability. In this case the Council's decision will bind the ECB.

What kind of exchange-rate policy will the ECB be inclined to pursue? With the creation of an economic and monetary union, the EU will become more of a large, relatively closed economy, like the United States. The bulk of member-state commercial and financial transactions already take place with other member states. Theories suggesting a further expansion of transactions within the integrated economic zone imply that this will be even more true in the future. Exchange-rate fluctuations *vis-à-vis* the rest of the world will then become less disruptive. According to the theory of optimum currency areas and the associated evidence (Bayoumi and Eichengreen, 1997), such a relatively large, closed economy should be inclined to float its currency.

Moreover, the ECB in its early years will be reluctant to commit itself to concerted foreign-exchange-market intervention, given the need to establish the credibility of its commitment to price stability. Excessive interest in other targets, including the exchange rate, might be seen as calling that commitment into doubt (European Monetary Institute, 1997). This implies that the Governing Board will be inclined toward a stringent interpretation of Article 109, rejecting the Council's general orientations when these seem incompatible with price stability. This point applies with even greater force to schemes for pegged exchange rates or G-3 target zones. While the ECB would be bound by the Council's decision to participate in such a system, the possibility that its Board might object in a way that damaged the Council's reputation for financial probity, not to mention the viability of the exchange-rate agreement itself, would give the ECB at least potential veto power (akin to the Bundesbank's sway over the German Chancellor).

These are the standard arguments why the ECB will be inclined to follow policies of benign neglect toward the euro–dollar and euro–yen exchange rates. What they leave out is the exchange rate as a gauge of monetary policy. At the beginning of Stage III, the value of alternative measures of the stance of policy will not be clear. There will be shifts in the demand for various monetary aggregates, loosening further the already loose link between the growth of the money supply and the rate of inflation (Begg *et al.*, 1997a). Such shifts are part and parcel of the inauguration of a new monetary regime, and what is Stage III but a new regime? Similarly, insofar as monetary unification is accompanied by changes in financial structure (as banks and other intermediaries capitalize on the opportunities afforded by integration), the links between interest rates, inflation, and other variables are likely to shift (Ramaswamy and Sloek, 1997). Uncertainty about these links may force the ECB to attach less weight to intermediate targets and more to indicators of the ultimate objectives of policy.

Insofar as any newly created index of inflation for the euro zone will be subject to more than the usual degree of imprecision, this may mean attaching greater weight to fluctuations in the exchange rate. Market participants as well as members of the ECB's Governing Board could be so inclined. A significant depreciation of the euro could then be seen as casting doubt on the credibility of monetary policy. The argument should not be pushed too far, for the exchange rate will be only one of several useful indicators. But neither is it likely to be disregarded.

The more volatile the exchange rate, the more inclined will the ECB be to intervene in the foreign exchange market. Some have expressed concern that Europe's exchange rates *vis-à-vis* the rest of the world will grow more volatile with the advent of EMU (viz. Benassy-Queré *et al.*, 1997). Prevent European exchange rates from moving, in this view, and the same shocks to global markets will have to be vented through movements in the exchange rates between the euro and other currencies. In the worst-case scenario, the dollar–euro rate will behave as erratically as the yen–dollar rate.

This argument ignores the fact that policy-makers themselves create many of the shocks that disturb foreign exchange markets. The yen exchange rate has been erratic because policy in Japan has been erratic. Japanese policy in the 1980s created an asset-price bubble which, upon bursting, left behind a banking crisis. To cope with the consequences, the Japanese authorities reduced interest rates to zero. It is hardly surprising that this series of policy steps and missteps has resulted in wide fluctuations of the yen–dollar exchange rate.

Thus, how erratically the dollar–euro rate behaves will depend first and foremost on whether the Federal Reserve System and the European Central Bank commit similar policy mistakes. There being no a priori reason for pessimism, there is no reason to anticipate euro exchange rates as volatile as the historical yen–dollar rate.

VII THE EURO AS A RESERVE CURRENCY

When the European Central Bank comes into operation in 1999 and the single currency is issued in 2002, shifts will occur in the reserve portfolios of central banks. While the euro will loom larger in foreign-exchange reserves than what is currently Europe's dominant reserve currency, the Deutschmark, how much more important it will become and how quickly it will become more important remain to be seen. Bergsten (1997), for one, argues that since EMU will create an integrated monetary and financial zone larger than the United States, the euro will quickly rival and perhaps even surpass the dollar as the leading reserve asset in central bank portfolios.

Other arguments suggest more caution regarding the euro's prospects. In particular, history suggests that an incumbent international currency, like an incumbent politician running for re-election, has a built-in advantage (Ilzkovitz, 1996; Eichengreen, 1998). It pays for central banks to hold their foreign exchange reserves in a currency that is widely used for settling international financial transactions; that is, in a currency in which the markets are liquid and stable. It follows that it will pay for them to hold their reserves in the same currencies held by other central banks and international investors. This network externality lends inertia and path dependence to the development of reserve-currency status. The point is illustrated by the continued importance of the pound sterling as a reserve vehicle, and invoicing currency well after Great Britain's dominance of international financial and commodity markets had passed.

If the attractions of the euro as a reserve currency will turn on how widely it is used in international transactions more generally, the latter will depend on whether Europe comes to rival the United States as a financial centre. And this may itself hinge on the scope of the responsibilities assumed by the European Central Bank. It is assumed, in line with Bundesbank practice, that the ECB will engage in relatively limited day-to-day liquidity management (Folkerts-Landau and Garber, 1992). Following the Bundesbank, it will provide refinancing to the private sector perhaps once a week, using reverse transactions (repos). While such periodic transactions are appropriate for bank-based financial systems in which the inter-bank market can be relied on to match financial institutions with excess demands and supplies of liquidity, securitized financial systems are characterized by more generalized excess supplies and demands. The consequent volatility of overnight rates will greatly widen bid–ask spreads and reduce the attractiveness of transacting in the European market (Schnadt, 1994). Preventing such spikes in overnight rates requires continuous liquidity management by the central bank, not just periodic intervention.

In addition, the depth, breadth, and stability of the market will depend on the extent of last-resort lending by the central bank. The Maastricht Treaty does not make provision for last-resort lending and bank supervision by the ECB. It adopts the Continental European model in which the responsibility for bank supervision and support is separated from monetary policy and assigned to an agency under the control of the Ministry of Finance.

To quote Article 25, 'the ECB *may offer advice and be consulted by* the Council, the Commission, and the competent authorities of the EU countries on the scope and implementation of Community legislation relating to the prudential supervision of credit institutions and the stability of the financial system' (emphasis added). But while the ECB will propose, the national authorities will dispose. It is they who will design and implement supervisory and regulatory policies.

In bank-based financial systems, such as those of Continental Europe, there is a logic to separating monetary policy from bank supervision. Doing so insulates the central bank from lobbying by influential financial institutions. And where finance is bank based, there is less need for the central bank to inject liquidity to prevent financial markets from seizing up. To be sure, it may still be necessary to prevent problems in individual banks from setting off system-wide panics, but there exist a variety of instruments for containing the impact of isolated banking problems, notably lifeboat operations by the banks themselves and recapitalization by the fiscal or supervisory authorities.

In countries with highly securitized financial markets, in contrast, the central bank has repeatedly acted as lender of last resort. The implication is that securitized financial systems, to be stable in the face of sudden movements in asset prices, need a governmental authority with the ability to backstop the market. This is the case in both the USA and the UK, where securitized finance is well advanced. But the Maastricht Treaty says little about the ECB's responsibilities in this connection. Admittedly, it gives the ECB responsibility for promoting the 'smooth operation' of the payments system. But how will problems in that system be detected if the ECB lacks supervisory responsibility? Will the ECB be prepared to provide liquidity to financial institutions if it lacks timely information on whether they are facing liquidity or solvency problems and has no basis on which to value the collateral against which banks (including central banks) traditionally lend?

European policy-makers are aware of these issues. The question is whether, once Stage III begins, the ECB will become more responsive to the needs of Europe's capital markets. One answer is yes—that political imperatives to model the ECB's operating procedures on those of the Bundesbank will become less powerful once monetary union is a *fait accompli*. Once German participation in the monetary union is no longer at issue, it may be possible for central banks and officials to make known their preference for a different model.

But another answer is no, that the ECB will not move over time towards more active liquidity management and backstopping operations, because its initial approach to monetary policy and the structure of European financial markets will become locked in. The dominance of bank-based finance will encourage the ECB to cater to the needs of a bank-based financial system, which do not include the liquidity-management and backstopping functions required by securities markets. As a result, bank-based finance will retain a comparative advantage relative to securitized finance, and the consequent persistence of the bank-based system will encourage the ECB to stick to its initial approach, in a classic case of a positive feedback loop. If so, the convergence of the Anglo-American and Continental European financial systems could turn out to be much less dramatic than sometimes supposed.

Given these uncertainties, reserve holders will wait and see. In the words of Joseph Yam of the Hong Kong Monetary Authority (quoted by Reuters on 19 January 1998), 'It will take time for the Euro to become a liquid currency. . . . We need to see whether the market develops in line with our expectations. At that time, it should not be too late for us to decide how we should manage our reserves.'

VIII THE COLLAPSE OF EMU

Until recently, the prospect of creating a European monetary union was sufficiently remote that discussion focused on the prospect of it starting, not that it might collapse once it began. Now that Stage III is a certainty, discussion has turned to the latter question. In fact, there is no shortage of monetary unions which have disintegrated: these include the successor states of the Austro-Hungarian Empire (Dornbusch, 1991), the successor states of the former Soviet Union (Bofinger and Gros, 1992), and the successor states of the former Czechoslovakia.

These are all cases where the decision to file for a political divorce led to the decision to go for a monetary divorce. In each case the successor states of a political union sought to reassert their policy autonomy. Different political and economic objectives from their former partners implied the desire for different monetary policies. And given the destruction of the political institutions that had bound them together, there existed neither mechanisms for reconciling those divergent views nor means for extending compensatory side payments.

Feldstein (1997b) has raised the spectre of similar problems in Stage III. EU member states with very different preferences will be shackled to one another by a single monetary policy. There will be no political union at the outset. National leaders will continue to plump for policies that reflect the preferences of their national constituencies. Inevitably, some will be disappointed. And since Europeans are unlikely to accede to large-scale cross-border transfers prior to the creation of a real political union (Eichengreen, 1996), there will be no way of compensating the losers. Disagreement over the stance of monetary policy could then mean serious dispute.

Technically, it is straightforward to exit a monetary union: a government need only start up the presses and resume printing its national currency. (It would also have to take a number of book-keeping steps, such as authorizing its banks to offer domestic-currency-denominated deposits, requiring the payment of taxes in domestic currency, and so forth. This means that it may be slightly easier to exit during Stage IIIA, when national currencies continue to circulate, domestic-currency-denominated bank deposits continue to exist, and tax returns in at least some countries, such as Germany, are calculated in domestic-currency units.) If a country left the monetary union because it felt that the ECB was following excessively inflationary policies, its 'good' domestic currency would drive out the 'bad' European currency. If that country instead left the monetary union because it felt that the ECB's overly restrictive policies were aggravating unemployment, it would have to declare that the euro would no longer be accepted as legal tender within its borders.

And of course, the markets will anticipate governments' actions. Imagine that Germany is contemplating leaving Stage IIIA out of dissatisfaction with the inflationary policies of the ECB. Imagine further that investors expect all Deutschmarks still circulating in the monetary union to become liabilities of a newly reconstituted Bundesbank and that the Deutschmark will appreciate against the EMU currencies once Germany exits. Investors then have an incentive to hold Deutschmarks rather than, say, French francs. (Note, however, that until 2002 national currencies will retain their legal tender status within the national boundaries of the existing issuers, which may limit the extent of the switch.) As agents sell francs for marks, the ECB will instruct the Bundesbank, its German operating arm, to sell marks for francs at par. While settlement terms have yet to be specified, one presumes that the Bundesbank would request settlement in a certain amount of euros, which the Banque de France would provide in the form of the corresponding number of francs. The Banque de France's balance sheet would shrink, while the Bundesbank's would expand.

So long as both countries remain committed to participation in the monetary union, nothing can disrupt this process, as authors such as Dooley (1997) and Buiter and Sibert (1997) have emphasized. But if Germany is contemplating whether to leave the monetary union, the Bundesbank may be reluctant to accept franc-denominated assets on which it stands to suffer a capital loss (Goldman Sachs, 1998). If it hesitates to exchange francs for marks at par, a premium on the latter could arise. That premium could convince the markets that break-up is imminent, accelerating the movement into marks.

In Stage IIIB, only euros will circulate, but there will still be a distinction between French and German bank deposits and the possibility that bank deposits payable in France will trade at a discount relative to bank deposits payable in Germany when the monetary union breaks apart. The transfer of funds between French and German banks will be facilitated by the TARGET payment system that will come into operation at the beginning of the monetary union. Garber (1997a, 1997b) observes that this will give speculators the opportunity to take very large positions. Imagine that international investors and domestic residents sell euro bank deposits payable in France for euro bank deposits payable in Germany, anticipating that the latter will be redenominated in Deutschmarks which will then appreciate against the euro. The French payment system will deduct euros from the French bank's account at the Banque de France and, using TARGET, pass those euros to the Bundesbank, which will add them to the German bank's account. Critically, the ability of French depositors to transfer funds at par to German banks will not be limited by the French banking system's deposits at the Banque de France. Under TARGET, the Banque de France is entitled to daytime overdraft privileges; if the payments it is asked to make to Germany exceed the euros it has on hand, it receives credit from the Bundesbank limited only by the acceptable collateral (liquid euro securities) of its clients. Given the large volume of such liquid securities, essentially all French bank deposits could be quickly and costlessly converted into German bank deposits.

Once again, if Germany and the Bundesbank stand ready to defend the monetary union, this unlimited extension of credit by the Bundesbank to the Banque de France means that there is no way for EMU to collapse. Effectively, intervention by the Bundesbank on behalf of the Banque de France will permanently fix the relative price of French and German bank deposits. (Insofar as the TARGET's daytime overdraft privileges cause the Deutschmark-denominated money supply to expand even faster than the franc-denominated money supply contracts, this could be sterilized by further intervention by the ECB.) But if there are doubts about the depth of that commitment, this same arrangement means that investors betting on a change in the relative price of French and German deposits can take even larger positions than under a normal fixed-rate system, in which the amount of credit that one central bank will extend to another is limited (as emphasized by Eichengreen and Wyplosz, 1993), and in which the peg will collapse once positions exceed the reserves of the central bank under attack plus the limited credits it receives from its foreign counterparts.

This raises the prospect of a self-fulfilling attack on Stage III. Assume that the likelihood of Germany abandoning its EMU commitment is an increasing function of the capital losses it will suffer on the Bundesbank's holdings of French securities once the monetary union dissolves. Assume further that its capital losses are strictly increasing in the level of Bundesbank holdings of French securities. Then transfers of French bank deposits to Germany in anticipation of this possibility, by increasing the Bundesbank's French security holdings, can precipitate the very event motivating investors.

This assumes, of course, that calculations of marginal costs and benefits could really tip the balance between a country supporting and abandoning the monetary union. The counter-argument is that abandoning the monetary union will violate an international treaty signed by 15 European countries. It will cast into doubt the entire European construction back to the Treaty of Rome. A country abandoning the monetary union would thus incur a high fixed cost, which represents a considerable barrier to exit. This idea that countries will hesitate to abandon EMU because doing so will place at risk the entire European project underlies the belief that the monetary union, once started, is doomed to succeed.

A more plausible scenario for a Stage III crisis is not, then, that participating countries will experience mild disagreements over the stance of their common monetary policy, but that a fully fledged banking and financial crisis in one member state will require a massive bail-out by the others. Imagine a run on the Italian banking system in which depositors rush to withdraw their funds from Italian banks and transfer them over TARGET to German financial institutions. The Bank of Italy will then discount eligible paper on behalf of domestic banks while obtaining daytime overdrafts via TARGET. At some point, other national central banks—the German Bundesbank in the present example—might decide that they do not wish to finance a bail-out of the Italian banking system, because, for example, they do not feel that the Italian authorities are taking the requisite steps to distinguish insolvent from illiquid institutions and to close down the former. (Note that this problem could be aggravated by the fact that the ECB and other national central banks under its umbrella have no direct supervisory authority over commercial banks; even for information, they must rely on national regulatory authorities and governments.) The Bundesbank could then halt the provision of credits to the Bank of Italy via TARGET, and a premium on German deposits relative to Italian deposits would emerge. The Italian authorities might then decide to resume printing their own currency in an effort to reliquefy the banking system.

All this might seem far-fetched. But a precedent from the early years of the Federal Reserve System suggests that it cannot be ruled out (Eichengreen, 1992). The US central bank was established as a federal system (note its name) that assigned considerable independence to the regional reserve banks. Only in 1935 was authority over the discounting and monetary policy operations of the regional reserve banks centralized in the hands of the Board of Governors in Washington, DC. That change was prompted by the problems that arose in handling the 1933 banking crisis. By March 1933, bank runs had spread to virtually every state of the union. The question is why the central bank did not do more to stabilize the system. A simple answer (Wigmore, 1987) is that the Fed was constrained by the gold cover provisions of the Gold Standard Act. Gold losses were borne unevenly by reserve banks, with New York, from whose banks foreign deposit withdrawals were greatest, experiencing the most intense pressure. On 4 March, when US monetary gold reserves were 44 per cent of the note and deposit liabilities of the system, the gold backing of the notes of the New York Fed had fallen to the 40 per cent statutory minimum. In contrast, the Chicago Fed's gold reserve ratio was still 65 per cent. On 1 March, the Chicago Fed lent $105 m to the New York Fed on the collateral of a matching amount of the latter's government securities and acceptances. Two days later, however, Chicago withdrew its cooperation. Policy-makers at the Chicago Fed had several concerns: that a bank bailout would create moral hazard and that their own financial position might be weakened. The New York Fed was forced to curtail its lender-of-last-resort intervention. The New York Stock Exchange and New York banks suspended operations the same day.

This crisis did not result in a premium on Chicago deposits over New York deposits or break-up the US monetary union because President Roosevelt immediately declared a nationwide bank holiday, and because the Federal Reserve Board then compelled Chicago and other reserve banks to resume inter-district rediscounting on behalf of the New York Fed. But given similarities in the structure of the early Fed and the European System of Central Banks, this cautionary tale should not be ignored.

IX CONCLUSION

While there is now wide consensus on a range of EMU-related issues, that consensus remains less than complete. To illustrate this, I allude in closing to three further issues, each of which is currently a subject of active debate.

One active area of research and discussion concerns the instruments of monetary policy (Enoch *et al.*, 1997). As noted in section VII, the presumption is that the ECB, in implementing its monetary policy, will rely on repurchase agreements, but that for fine-tuning and signalling it may also use open-market operations, foreign exchange market intervention, and the collection of fixed-term deposits. But the central bank's relative reliance on these instruments and its choice of counterparties remain to be determined. And it is unclear whether the central bank will also use reserve requirements. If so, it will have to decide how to trade off the additional reporting burden on banks against the excessive window-dressing that occurs in countries relying on, *inter alia*, end-month data (Remsperger, 1997).

A second issue is exchange-rate relations between the 'ins' and 'outs'. European officials foresee an ERM-2 in which the currencies of member states that are not founding members of the monetary union are connected to the euro by bands. This will be a hub-and-spoke system in which each bilateral rate will have its own band, in contrast to the old ERM's multilateral grid. But it remains to be seen how widely subscribed the ERM-2 turns out to be since countries such as the UK and Sweden have already made clear their reluctance to commit to exchange-rate targets. Presumably participation will depend on how anxious the remaining member states are to gain entry to the monetary union, and how quickly the population of such states is augmented by enlargement of the European Union. And, ultimately, how much support the ECB extends to the currencies of the outsiders will determine how stable the system proves.

A final issue concerns the euro's introduction at the beginning of 1999 and strategies for ensuring that the bilateral conversion rates preferred by governments equal the rates actually delivered by the markets at the close of business on 31 December 1998. The Maastricht Treaty requirement ruling out jumps in the external value of the ecu implies that the conversion of national currencies into euro must occur at the bilateral rates prevailing at the end of 1998 (De Grauwe, 1997). Options for steering actual rates towards desired levels include continuous foreign-exchange intervention in the spot and forward markets in the period between the announcement of desired conversion rates and the end of 1998 (Obstfeld, 1997), and massive last-minute intervention (Begg *et al.*, 1997b). One presumes that flexibly minded European central banks will use a combination of these strategies.

REFERENCES

Allsopp, C.J., Davies, G., McKibbin, W. and Vines, D. (1997), 'Monetary and Fiscal Stabilization of Demand Shocks within Europe', in C. Deissenberg, R.F. Owen, and D. Ulph (eds), *European Economic Integration*, Oxford: Blackwell, special supplement to *Review of International Economics*, 5(4), 55–76.

Alesina, A. and Grilli, V. (1992), 'The European Central Bank: Reshaping Monetary Politics in Europe', in M. Canzoneri, V. Grilli and P. Masson (eds), *Establishing a Central Bank: Issues in Europe and Lessons from the US*, Cambridge: Cambridge University Press, 49–70.

—— (1994), 'On the Feasibility of a One-Speed or Multispeed European Monetary Union', in B. Eichengreen and J. Frieden (eds), *The Political Economy of European Monetary Integration*, Boulder, CO: Westview Press, 107–28.

Alogoskoufis, G. and Smith, R. (1991), 'The Phillips Curve, the Persistence of Inflation, and the Lucas Critique: Evidence from Exchange Rate Regimes', *American Economic Review*, 81, 1254–75.

Anderton, R. and Barrell, R. (1995), 'The ERM and Structural Change in European Labor Markets', *Weltwirtschaftliches Archiv*, 131, 47–66.

Artis, M.J. and Omerod, P. (1991), 'Is There an "EMS" Effect in European Labour Markets?', CEPR Discussion Paper No. 598 (December).

—— (1996), 'Another Look at the "EMS Effect" in European Labor Markets', in P. De Grauwe, S. Micossi and G. Tullio (eds), *Inflation and Wage Behaviour in Europe*, Oxford: Clarendon Press, 231–41.

Artus, J. and Salmon, M. (1996), 'The EMS, Credibility and Disinflation: The French Case', in P. DeGrauwe, S. Micossi and G. Tullio (eds), *Inflation and Wage Behavior in Europe*, Oxford: Clarendon Press, 30–58.

Bayoumi, T. and Eichengreen, B. (1995), 'Restraining Yourself: The Implications of Fiscal Rules for Economic Stabilization', *Staff Papers*, 42, 32–48.

—— (1997), 'Optimum Currency Areas and Exchange Rate Variability: Theory and Evidence Compared', in B. Cohen (ed.), *International Trade and Finance: Essays in Honour of Peter Kenen*, Cambridge: Cambridge University Press, 216–46.

—— and Masson, P. (1995), 'Fiscal Flows in the United States and Canada: Lessons for Monetary Union in Europe', *European Economic Review*, 39, 253–75.

Begg, D., Giavazzi, F. and Wyplosz, C. (1997a), 'Options for the Future Exchange Rate Policy of the EMU', CEPR Occasional Paper No. 17.

—— von Hagen, J., and Wyplosz, C. (1997b), 'EMU: Getting the End Game Right', *Monitoring European Integration*, 7, London, Centre for Economic Policy Research.

Benassy-Queré, A., Mojon, B. and Pisani-Ferry, J. (1997), 'The Euro and Exchange Rate Stability', in T. Krueger, P. Masson and B. Turtelboom (eds), *European Monetary Union and the International Monetary System*, Washington, DC: International Monetary Fund, 157–94.

Bergin, P. and Moersch, M. (1997), 'EMU and Outsiders: Fixed Versus Flexible Exchange Rates', in P.J.J. Welfens (ed.), *European Monetary Union: Transition, International Impacts and Policy Options*, Berlin and New York: Springer, 71–122.

Bergsten, C.F. (1997), 'The Impact of the Euro on Exchange Rates and International Policy Cooperation', in P.R. Masson, T.H. Krueger and B.G. Turtelboom (eds),

EMU and the International Monetary System, Washington, DC: International Monetary Fund, 17–48.

Bofinger, P. and Gros, D. (1992), 'A Multilateral Payments Union for the Commonwealth of Independent States, Why and How?', CEPR Discussion Paper No. 654, May.

Buiter, W.H. and Sibert, A. (1997), 'Transition Issues for the European Monetary Union', NBER Working Paper No. 6292, November.

Chari, V.V. and Kehoe, T. (1997), 'Fiscal Constraints in a Monetary Union', unpublished manuscript, Federal Reserve Bank of Minneapolis.

Cooper, R. (1992), 'Whither Europe?', *Yale Review*, 80, 10–17.

De Grauwe, P. (1996), 'Comment', in H. Siebert (ed.), *Monetary Policy in an Integrated World Economy*: Tubingen: J.C.B. Mohr, 232–8.

—— (1997), 'The Indeterminacy of Euro Conversion Rates: Why It Matters and How It Can Be Solved', unpublished manuscript, University of Leuven.

Dooley, M. (1997), 'Speculative Attacks on a Monetary Union?', unpublished manuscript, University of California, Santa Cruz.

Dornbusch, R. (1991), 'Monetary Problems of Post-Communism: Lessons from the End of the Austro-Hungarian Empire', *Weltwirtschaftsliches Archiv*, 128, 391–424.

Eichengreen, B. (1992), 'Designing a Central Bank for Europe: A Cautionary Tale from the Early Years of the Federal Reserve System', in M. Canzoneri, P. Masson, and V. Grilli (eds), *Establishing a Central Bank: Issues in Europe and Lessons from the US*, Cambridge: Cambridge University Press.

—— (1993), 'Labor Markets and European Monetary Unification', in P. Masson and M. Taylor (eds), *Policy Issues in the Operation of Currency Areas*, Cambridge: Cambridge University Press, 130–62.

—— (1996), 'A More Perfect Union: The Logic of Economic Integration', *Princeton Essays in International Finance*, No. 198, Princeton, NJ: International Finance Section, Department of Economics, Princeton University, June.

—— (1997), 'The Euro as a Reserve Currency', *Journal of the Japanese and International Economies*, 12 (4) (December), 483–506.

—— and Wyplosz, C. (1993), 'The Unstable EMS', *Brookings Papers on Economic Activity*, 1, 51–143.

—— (1998), 'The Stability Pact: More than a Minor Nuisance?', *Economic Policy*, 26, 65–114.

Enoch, C., Hilbers, P. and Kovanen, A. (1997), 'Some Issues in the Design of Instruments for the Operation of European Economic and Monetary Union', IMF Working Paper WP/97/178, December.

European Commission (1997), 'Economic Policy in EMU, Part B: Specific Topics', Economic Paper No. 125, Brussels: European Commission, Directorate General II, November.

European Monetary Institute (1997), *The Single Monetary Policy in Stage Three: Elements of the Monetary Policy Strategy of the ESCB*, Frankfurt: European Monetary Institute.

Feldstein, M. (1997a), 'The Political Economy of European Economic and Monetary Union: Political Sources of an Economic Liability', *Journal of Economic Perspectives*, 11, 23–42.

—— (1997b), 'EMU and the International Conflict', *Foreign Affairs*, 76(6), Council on Foreign Relations, Inc., 60–73.

Folkerts-Landau, D. and Garber, P. (1992), 'The European Central Bank: A Bank or a Monetary Policy Rule?', NBER Working Paper No. 4016.

Forni, M. and Reichlin, L. (1997), 'National Forces and Local Economies: Europe and the United States', CEPR Discussion Paper No. 1632, April.

Garber, P. (1997a), 'Is Stage III Attackable?', *Euromoney*, August, 58–9.

—— (1997b), 'Notes on the Role of TARGET in a Stage III Crisis', unpublished manuscript, Brown University.

Gressani, D., Guiso, L. and Visco, I. (1988), 'Disinflation in Italy: An Analysis with the Econometric Model of the Banca d'Italia', *Journal of Policy Modeling*, 8, 163–203.

Goldman Sachs (1998), 'Could Speculation Break EMU Apart?', *European Economics Analyst*, EMU Briefing 98/1 (January).

Gordon, R.J. (1998), 'The Aftermath of the 1992 ERM Breakup: Was There a Macroeconomic Free Lunch?', NBER Currency Crises Conference, 6–7, February.

Grilli, V., Masciandaro, D. and Tabellini, G. (1991), 'Political and Monetary Institutions and Public Finance Policies in the Industrial Democracies', *Economic Policy*, 6, 342–92.

Hochreiter, E. and Winckler, G. (1995), 'The Advantages of Tying Austria's Hands: The Success of the Hard Currency Strategy', *European Journal of Political Economy*, 11, 83–111.

Ilzkovitz, F. (1996), 'Les Perspectives d'Internationalisation de l'Euro', *Revue d'Economie Financière*, 36, 151–69.

Ingram, J. (1959), 'State and Regional Payments Mechanisms', *Quarterly Journal of Economics*, 73, 619–32.

Kenen, P.B. (1995), *Economic and Monetary Union in Europe: Moving Beyond Maastricht*, Cambridge: Cambridge University Press.

Kremers, J.J.M. (1990), 'Gaining Policy Credibility for a Disinflation', *IMF Staff Papers*, 37, 116–45.

MacDougall Report [European Commission] (1977), *Report of the Study Group on the Role of Public Finance in European Integration*, Brussels: European Commission.

Masson, P. and Taylor, M. (1993), 'Fiscal Policy within Common Currency Areas', *Journal of Common Market Studies*, 31, 29–44, March.

Mauro, P. and Spilimbergo, A. (1998), 'Persistent Geographic Unemployment Differences and the Wage Bargaining System', unpublished manuscript, European University Institute and International Monetary Fund.

Mélitz, J. (1994), 'Is There a Need for Community-Wide Insurance Against Cyclical Disparities?', *Economie et Statistique*, Special Issue, 99–106.

—— and Vori, S. (1992), 'National Insurance against Unevenly Distributed Shocks in a European Monetary Union', unpublished manuscript, INSEE and Bank of Italy.

Obstfeld, M. (1997), 'A Strategy for Launching the Euro', *European Economic Review*, 41.

—— and Peri, G. (1998), 'Regional Non-Adjustment and Fiscal Policy', *Economic Policy*, 26(April), 207–59.

OECD (1990), *OECD Employment Outlook*, Paris: Organization for Economic Cooperation and Development, July.

—— (1996), 'Labor Market Performance, Budget Control, and Social Transfers'. *OECD Economic Outlook*, 59(June), 23–38.

Oudiz, G. and Sachs, J. (1984), 'Macroeconomic Policy Coordination among the Industrial Economies', *Brookings Papers on Economic Activity*, 1, 1–64.

Ramaswamy, R. and Sloek, T. (1997), 'The Real Effects of Monetary Policy in the European Union: What Are the Differences?', IMF Working Paper No. 97/160.

Remsperger, H. (1997), 'Which Instruments for the European System of Central Banks?', in S. Collignon (ed.), *European Monetary Policy*, London: Pinter, 315–34.

Sala-i-Martin, X. and Sachs, J. (1992), 'Federal Fiscal Policy and Optimum Currency Areas', in M. Canzoneri, V. Grilli, and P. Masson (eds), *Establishing a Central Bank: Issues in Europe and Lessons from the US*, Cambridge: Cambridge University Press, 195–220.

Schnadt, N. (1994), *The Domestic Money Markets of the UK, France, Germany and the US*, City Research Project, London: London School of Economics.

Sorensen, B. and Yosha, O. (1997), 'International Risk Sharing and European Monetary Unification', unpublished manuscript, Brown University and Tel Aviv University.

Viñals, J. and Jimeno, J.F. (1996), 'Monetary Union and European Unemployment', Working Paper No. 9624, Servicio de Estudios, Bank of Spain.

Volcker, P. (1995), 'The Quest for Exchange Rate Stability: Real or Quixotic?', unpublished manuscript, London School of Economics.

Von Hagen, J. (1992), 'Fiscal Arrangements in a Monetary Union: Evidence from the US', in D.E. Fair and C. de Boissieu (eds), *Fiscal Policy, Taxation, and the Financial System in an Increasingly Integrated Europe*, Dordrecht: Kluwer, 337–60.

—— and Eichengreen, B. (1996), 'Federalism, Fiscal Restraints, and European Monetary Union', *American Economic Review, Papers and Proceedings*, 86, 134–8.

Wigmore, B. (1987), 'Was the 1933 Banking Crisis a Run on the Dollar?', *Journal of Economic History*, 47, 739–56.

Wijkander, H. (1997), 'Wage Policy Implications of EMU', Brussels: European Commission, Directorate-General for Economic and Financial Affairs.

Williamson, J. (1985), 'The Exchange Rate System', *Policy Analyses in International Economics*, no. 5, revised, Washington, DC: Institute of International Economics.

Questions

1 'If the case for flexible exchange rates is a strong one, it is a case for flexible exchange rates between regional (i.e. sub-national) rather than national currencies.' Discuss.
2 'The necessary degree of money illusion becomes greater the smaller are the currency areas. Therefore, there must be an upper limit on the number of currency areas in the world.' Discuss.
3 'As we move across the spectrum from closed to open economies, flexible exchange rates become both less effective as a control device for external balance and more damaging to internal price-level stability.' Discuss.
4 'The loss of the exchange rate as a policy instrument is a cost of the monetary union because the government will have one less instrument to achieve a given number of targets.' Discuss.
5 'The loss of the exchange rate does not involve significant costs because there is no guarantee that the government will use it responsibly.' Discuss.
6 'Institutional differences and labour market rigidity should not be considered as severe obstacles to monetary union because the latter will induce convergence and flexibility in European labour markets.' Discuss.
7 'Given the loss of exchange rate and the centralisation of monetary policy, euro zone governments should have a higher degree of freedom in the conduct of their fiscal policies.' Discuss.
8 'The euro may not emerge as a significant reserve currency.' Do you agree?

Further reading and references

FURTHER READING

The debate on EMU was largely shaped by considerations concerning the costs and benefits of monetary unions, as implied by the optimum currency area theory. For a good summary of the debate on the costs and benefits, see De Grauwe (1992), chs 1 and 3. For an extensive study of costs and benefits of the EMU, see Emerson *et al.* (1990). As indicated in Chapter 21 above, the debate has moved beyond cost–benefit analysis to focus on challenges to macroeconomic policy within monetary unions. One such challenge concerns economic policy co-ordination. For example, see Italianer (1999) for an introduction to economic policy co-ordination within the euro zone.

REFERENCES

De Grauwe, P. (1992) *The Economics of Monetary Integration*, Oxford: Oxford University Press.

Emerson, M., D. Gros, A. Italianer, J. Psiani-Ferry and H. Reichenbach (1990) *One Market, One Money*, Oxford: Oxford University Press.

Italianer, A. (1999) 'The Euro and internal economic policy co-ordination', *Empirica* 26, 201–16.

Van der Ploeg, F. (1991) 'Macroeconomic policy coordination issues during the various phases of economic and monetary integration in Europe', *European Economy*, special edition no. 1.

Part VIII

Tax policy in open economies

Competition versus co-ordination

Introduction

During the 1980s, developed countries went through a period of financial liberalisation. The concomitant effect was an increase in capital mobility. In the face of this development, tax policy reforms acquired a predictable urgency for two reasons. On the one hand, governments came under increased pressure for reducing the statutory tax rates on capital income in order to attract foreign direct investment as well as portfolio capital. On the other hand, governments tried to compensate for the revenue loss by widening the tax base and increasing the rate of statutory tax on less mobile factors of production, especially labour. Widening the tax base can increase efficiency as the incidence of distortion is reduced. Shifting the tax burden from relatively mobile to relatively immobile factors, however, has an adverse effect on efficiency as well as equity.

Given these complications, it was not surprising to observe the emergence of a new policy debate. This time the emphasis was on the adverse effects of harmful tax competition and the need for tax policy co-ordination. The two articles in this part take issue with this debate. Although they have an OECD-wide focus, their primary concern is Western Europe as the latter has gone through a process of deeper financial integration and the size of European countries is relatively small. This combination provides a fertile ground for harmful tax competition as deeper integration leads to higher capital mobility and small size implies relatively higher capital supply elasticity with respect to changes in tax rates.

Chapter 23 presents some extracts from a 1998 report by the OECD's Committee on Fiscal Affairs. Acting in response to a call by OECD ministers in 1996, the Committee has studied the factors that can help identify harmful tax competition and made some recommendations for counteracting the practice. Interestingly enough, the European Union itself also initiated a similar but more comprehensive action in 1996–7. These government-led initiatives suggest clearly that governments are becoming increasingly concerned about the impact of tax competition on their revenue in particular and economic efficiency in general.

The Committee is of the view that bilateral tax agreements, although useful in avoiding double taxation, are not sufficient to tackle harmful tax competition – which is a result of uncoordinated interaction between self-interested governments. Therefore, it recommends that bilateral agreements should be supplemented by a higher degree of international tax policy co-ordination. To facilitate such co-ordination, the Committee performs three tasks. First, it develops a definition of harmful tax competition, which, it is hoped, would provide a starting point acceptable for all OECD members. Second, it delineates the factors that could help identify harmful tax competition, which can take the form of *tax havens* or *harmful preferential tax regimes*. Finally, it develops a number of recommendations for counteracting harmful tax competition through bilateral as well as multilateral arrangements.

The reader will have realised that the Committee's report is nothing but a specific application of the theory of policy co-ordination examined in Part IV. As is well known, policy co-ordination in an interdependent world can cut both ways. On the one hand, it can enable governments to overcome the inefficiency resulting from independent actions that do not take account of the spill-over effects. On the other hand, however, it can create a different type of inefficiency due to collusion between governments or loss of policy credibility. The article by Sørensen addresses these issues in the context of tax policy co-ordination. In other words, it tests the relevance of the OECD's tax policy recommendations and examines the extent to which co-ordinated policy is likely to improve welfare in EU countries.

Sørensen's article is a timely intervention because it fits very well with the ongoing public policy debate. More importantly, however, it makes compelling reading because its general equilibrium model allows for simulations of different scenarios concerning not only symmetry/asymmetry between countries but also distributional consequences for countries as well as groups within countries. The article first provides evidence on the extent to which tax competition has led to a fall in statutory tax rates on capital income since the mid-1980s. The evidence indicates that the statutory rates on retained corporate income fell by 17 percentage points in small countries and 8 percentage points in large countries. The rates on interest income, on the other hand, fell by 16 and 11 percentage points, respectively. This alarming tendency is then compared with effective tax rates – which take into account the widening of the tax base as well as other counterbalancing measures. The result is dramatically different: effective tax rates on capital income have remained more or less constant, but the effective rates on labour income have been consistently higher than the capital income tax rates and recorded a further increase of 3 percentage points in all countries. Therefore Sørensen indicates rightly that tax competition has been intense, especially for attracting portfolio investment and the taxable 'paper profits' of multinational corporations.

The article then moves on to identify the range of spill-over effects generated by tax competition. The elaboration on various types of tax-related externalities indicates that capital income taxes could be either too high or too low under tax competition. Therefore, the argument for or against tax policy co-ordination can be resolved only by quantitative analysis. To tackle this task, Sørensen conducts three types of simulations.

First, he solves the general equilibrium model for the benchmark results under tax competition. The results are in line with the effective tax rates on capital income reported above. They clearly indicate that, under tax competition, capital income tax rates would remain lower than labour income taxes in all European countries except the UK. The latter and the USA would have higher capital income taxes relative not only to labour income taxes but also compared to the capital income taxes in their European counterparts. In a way, this result can be interpreted as confirmation of the theoretical conclusion that taxes on mobile factors (capital) could be either too low or too high under tax competition.

Second, Sørensen simulates the effect of tax policy co-ordination at different levels. When co-ordination takes place at a regional level between European countries and the US policy remains the same, capital income taxes increase by almost 13 percentage points from 33.8 per cent to 46.2 per cent. The tax on labour income falls by 1.5 percentage points from 49.8 per cent to 48.3 per cent. When both Western Europe and the USA co-ordinate their tax policies, European tax rates on capital income increase and those on labour income fall only slightly. When tax policies are co-ordinated globally, the capital income tax in Western Europe increases by another 6 percentage points to 55.2 per cent and labour income tax falls by another percentage point to 47.5 per cent. These results indicate that the current European tax rates on capital income are 14 percentage points lower than what they would be under tax policy co-ordination. Therefore, it is not surprising to see that tax policy co-ordination would increase European welfare. The increase will be about 0.16 per cent of GDP if co-ordination is within Europe and 0.32 per cent of the GDP is co-ordination is global.

Finally, Sørensen examines the distribution of the co-ordination gains between countries as well as between income groups. The evidence on inter-country distribution is varied but highly informative. As asymmetry between countries increases (for example in terms of preference for income redistribution, share of foreign ownership, and total factor productivity) the distribution of co-ordination gains tends to be more unequal. For example, in the presence of asymmetry in terms of preference for redistributive policies, the Nordic and continental European countries tend to gain, whereas the UK tends to lose from tax policy co-ordination. This is compatible with the UK government's reluctance to embrace tax policy co-ordination. It is also interesting in the sense that income inequality (hence the bias in favour of capital income) in the UK is the highest in Europe. Sørensen's study also reveals that the lower-income groups would benefit disproportionately compared to the loss incurred by higher-income groups in Europe. For example, the welfare of the least wealthy group that controls 2 per cent of the national wealth would increase by 2.22 per cent while the welfare of the most wealthy group, controlling 53 per cent of the national wealth, would decline by 0.85 per cent.

Given the results obtained by Sørensen, we can derive the following tentative conclusions. First, the OECD's concerns about harmful tax competition are largely justified. Capital income taxes under tax competition are and will continue to remain lower than would be the case under tax policy co-ordination. Second, because the gains from tax policy co-ordination are small (less than 1 per cent of GDP), the incentive for tax policy co-ordination is small. Then, we are left with the following question: why should the OECD and its member states be concerned about harmful tax competition? A tentative answer would be that they are becoming increasingly more concerned about revenues. Even if this is the case, an argument in favour of tax policy co-ordination can still be made because the increase in capital income taxes that would follow is not welfare-reducing. Also, tax policy co-ordination may be effective in reducing income inequality and inducing governments to compete through 'infrastructure spending' rather than subsidies on capital income – which would be a more 'constructive' competition.

23 Harmful tax competition

An emerging global issue

*OECD Committee on Fiscal Affairs**
OECD, Harmful Tax Competition: An Emerging Global issue, OECD
(1998)

1 INTRODUCTION

[This] report is intended to develop a better understanding of how tax
havens and harmful preferential tax regimes, collectively referred to as harmful tax practices, affect the location of financial and other service activities,
erode the tax base of other countries, distort trade and investment patterns
and undermine the fairness, neutrality and broad social acceptance of tax
systems generally. Such harmful tax competition diminishes global welfare
and undermines taxpayer confidence in the integrity of tax systems. The
report recognises the distinction between acceptable and harmful preferential tax regimes and carefully analyses the features of both residence and
source country tax systems that may lead to the damaging impact of harmful
preferential tax regimes. The report recognises that there are limitations on
unilateral or bilateral responses to a problem that is inherently multilateral
and identifies ways in which governments can best establish a common
framework within which countries could operate individually and collectively
to limit the problems presented by countries and fiscally sovereign territories
engaging in harmful tax practices. By discouraging the spread of tax havens
and harmful preferential tax practices to review their existing measures, the
report will serve to strengthen and improve tax policies internationally.

[. . .]

2 TAX COMPETITION: A GLOBAL PHENOMENON

Historically, tax policies have been developed primarily to address domestic
economic and social concerns. The forms and levels of taxation were established on the basis of the desired level of publicly provided goods and transfers, with regard also taken to the allocative, stabilizing and redistributive
aims thought appropriate for a country. Whilst domestic tax systems of
essentially closed economies also had an international dimension in that they
potentially affected the tax imposed on foreign source income of domestic

---

* Extracts from OECD, *Harmful Tax Competition: An Emerging Global Issue* (Paris: 1998).
 Paragraph numbers in the original text are omitted and stylistic changes are indicated in [ ].

residents and typically included in the tax base the domestic income of non-residents, the interaction of the tax systems was relatively unimportant, given the limited mobility of capital. The decision to have a high rate of tax and a high level of government spending or low taxes and limited public outlays, the mix of direct and indirect taxes, and the use of tax incentives, were all matters which were decided primarily on the basis of domestic concerns and had principally domestic effects. While there were some international spillover effects on other economies, those effects were generally limited.

The accelerating process of globalisation of trade and investment has fundamentally changed the relationship among domestic tax systems.

[. . .]

[T]he removal of non-tax barriers to international commerce and investment and the resulting integration of national economies have greatly increased the potential impact that domestic tax policies can have on other economies. Globalisation has also been one of the driving forces behind tax reforms, which have focused on base broadening and rate reductions, thereby minimizing tax-induced distortions. Globalisation has also encouraged countries to assess continually their tax systems and public expenditures with a view to making adjustments where appropriate to improve the 'fiscal climate' for investment. Globalisation and the increased mobility of capital have also promoted the development of capital and financial markets and have encouraged countries to reduce tax barriers to capital flows and to modernize their tax systems to reflect these developments. Many of these reforms have also addressed the need to adapt tax systems to this new global environment.

The process of globalisation has led to increased competition among businesses in the global marketplace. Multinational enterprises (MNEs) are increasingly developing global strategies and their links with any one country are becoming more tenuous. In addition, technological innovation has affected the way in which MNEs are managed and made the physical location of management and other service activities much less important to the MNE. International financial markets continue to expand, a development that facilitates global welfare-enhancing cross-border capital flows. This process has improved welfare and living standards around the world by creating a more efficient allocation and utilisation of resources.

As indicated [above], globalisation has had a positive effect on the development of tax systems. Globalisation has, however, also had the negative effects of opening up new ways by which companies and individuals can minimise and avoid taxes and in which countries can exploit these new opportunities by developing tax policies aimed primarily at diverting financial and other geographically mobile capital. These actions induce potential distortions in the patterns of trade and investment and reduce global welfare. As discussed below, these schemes can erode national tax bases of other countries and may alter the structure of taxation (by shifting part of the tax burden from mobile to relatively immobile factors and from income to consumption) and may hamper the application of progressive tax rates and the achievement of redistributive goals. Pressure of this sort can result in changes in tax structures in which all countries may be forced by spillover effects to modify their tax bases, even though a more desirable result could have been achieved through intensifying international co-operation. More generally, tax policies in one economy are now more likely to have repercussions on other economies. These new pressures on tax systems apply to both business income in the corporate sector and to personal investment income.

Countries face public spending obligations and constraints because they have to finance outlays on, for example, national defence, education, social security, and other public services. Investors in tax havens, imposing zero or nominal taxation, who are residents of non-haven countries may be able to utilise in various ways those tax haven jurisdictions to reduce their domestic tax liability. Such taxpayers are in effect 'free riders' who benefit from public spending in the home country and yet avoid contributing to its financing.

In a still broader sense, governments and residents of tax havens can be 'free riders' of general public goods created by non-haven country. Thus, on the spending side, as well, there are potential negative spillover effects from increased globalisation and the interaction between tax systems.

[. . .]

Harmful effects may also occur because of unintentional mismatches between existing tax systems, which do not involve a country deliberately exploiting the interaction of tax systems to erode the tax base of another country. Such unintentional mismatches may be exploited by taxpayers to the detriment of either or both countries. The undesirable effects of such mismatches may be dealt with by unilateral or bilateral measures. If, however, an issue cannot be resolved at this level, it may be examined on the basis of the criteria set out in section 3 below.

Unlike the situation of mismatching, where the interaction of tax systems is exploited by the enactment of special tax provisions which principally erode the tax base of other countries, the spillover effects on the other countries is not a mere side effect, incidental to the implementation of a domestic tax policy. Here the effect is for one country to redirect capital and financial flows and the corresponding revenue from the other jurisdictions by bidding aggressively for the tax base of other countries. Some described this effect as 'poaching' as the tax base 'rightly' belongs to the other country. Practices of this sort can appropriately be labelled harmful tax competition as they do not reflect different judgements about the appropriate level of taxes and public outlays or the appropriate mix of taxes in a particular economy, which are aspects of every country's sovereignty in fiscal matters, but are, in effect, tailored to attract investment or savings originating elsewhere or to facilitate the avoidance of other countries' taxes.

Tax havens or harmful preferential tax regimes that drive the effective tax rate levied on income from mobile activities significantly below rates in other countries have the potential to cause harm by:

- distorting financial, and, indirectly, real investment flows;
- undermining the integrity and fairness of tax structures;
- discouraging compliance by all taxpayers;
- re-shaping the desired level and mix of taxes and public spending;
- causing undesired shifts of part of the tax burden to less mobile tax bases, such as labour, property and consumption; and
- increasing the administrative costs and compliance burdens on tax authorities and taxpayers.

[. . .]

The available data do not permit a detailed comparative analysis of the economic and revenue effects involving low tax jurisdictions. It has also proven difficult to obtain data on activities involving preferential tax regimes, given the problems in separating their effects from aggregate data in countries with otherwise normal tax systems, and the fact that such regimes often are non-transparent. However, the available data do suggest that the current use of tax havens is large, and that participation in such schemes is expanding at an exponential rate. For example, foreign direct investment by G7 countries in a number of jurisdictions in the Caribbean and in the South Pacific island states, which are generally considered to be low-tax jurisdictions, increased more that five-fold over the period 1985–94, to more than \$200 billion, a rate of increase well in excess of the growth of total outbound foreign direct investment. The Committee continues to attach importance to collecting additional data on developments in tax havens and in the use of preferential tax regimes.

A regime can be harmful even where it is difficult to quantify the adverse economic impact it imposes. For example, the absence of a requirement to provide annual accounts may preclude access to data required for an analysis of the economic effects of a regime. Yet, despite the inability to measure the economic damage, countries would agree that such regimes are harmful and should be discouraged.

Globalisation and the intensified competition among firms in the global marketplace have had and continue to have many positive effects. However, the fact that tax competition may lead to the proliferation of harmful tax practices and the adverse consequences that result, as discussed here, shows that governments must take measures, including intensifying the international co-operation, to protect their tax bases and to avoid the world-wide reduction in welfare caused by tax-induced distortions in capital financial flows.

3 FACTORS TO IDENTIFY TAX HAVENS AND HARMFUL PREFERENTIAL TAX REGIMES

[This section] discusses the factors to be used in identifying, within the context of this report, tax-haven jurisdictions and harmful preferential tax regimes in non-haven jurisdictions. It focuses on identifying the factors that enable tax havens and harmful preferential tax regimes in OECD Members and non-member countries to attract highly mobile activities such as financial and other service activities. The [section] provides practical guidelines to assist governments in identifying tax havens and in distinguishing between acceptable and harmful preferential tax regimes.

[. . .]

At the outset, a distinction must be made between three broad categories of situations in which the tax levied in one country on income from geographically mobile activities, such as financial and other service activities, is lower than the tax that would be levied on the same income in another country:

1   the first country is a tax haven and, as such, generally imposes no or only nominal tax on income;
2   the first country collects significant revenues from tax imposed on income at the individual or corporate level but its tax system has preferential status that allows the relevant income to be subject to low or no taxation;
3   the first country collects significant revenues from tax imposed on income at the individual or corporate level but the effective tax rate that is generally applicable at that level in that country is lower than that levied in the second country.

All three categories of situations may have undesirable effects from the perspective of the other country. However, as already noted [above], globalisation has had a positive effect on the development of tax systems, being, for instance, the driving force behind tax reforms which have focused on base broadening and rate reductions, thereby minimising tax-induced distortions. Accordingly, and insofar as the other factors referred to in this [section] are not present, the issues arising in the third category are outside the scope of this report. Any spillover effects for the revenue of the other country may be dealt with by a variety of means at the unilateral or bilateral level. It is not intended to explicitly or implicitly suggest that there is some general minimum effective rate of tax to be imposed on income below which a country would be considered to be engaging in harmful tax competition.

The first two categories, which are the focus of this report, are dealt with differently. While the concept of 'tax haven' does not have a precise technical meaning, it is recognised that a useful distinction may be made between, on the one hand, countries that are able to finance their public services with no or minimal income taxes and that offer themselves as places to be used by non-residents to escape tax in their country of residence and, on the other hand, countries which raise significant revenues from their income tax but whose tax system has features constituting harmful tax competition.

In the first case, the country has no interest in trying to curb the 'race to the bottom' with respect to income tax and is actively contributing to the erosion of income tax revenues in other countries. For that reason, these countries are unlikely to co-operate in curbing harmful tax competition. By contrast, in the second case, a country may have a significant amount of revenues, which are at risk from the spread of harmful tax competition, and it is therefore more likely to agree on concerted action.

Because of this difference, this report distinguishes between jurisdictions in the first category, which are referred to as tax havens, and jurisdictions in the second category, which are considered as countries which have potentially harmful preferential tax regimes.

[. . .]

3.1 Tax havens

Many fiscally sovereign territories and countries use tax and non-tax incentives to attract activities in the financial and other services sectors. These territories and countries offer the foreign investor an environment with no or only nominal taxation which is usually coupled with a reduction in regulatory or administrative constraints. The activity is usually not subject to information exchange because, for example, of strict bank secrecy provisions. As indicated [above], these jurisdictions are generally known as tax havens.

Tax havens generally rely on the existing global financial infrastructure and have traditionally facilitated capital flows and improved financial market liquidity. Now that the non-haven countries have liberalised and de-regulated their financial markets, any potential benefits brought about by tax havens in this connection are more than offset by their adverse tax effects. Since tax and non-tax advantages tend to divert financial capital away from other countries, tax havens have a large adverse impact on the revenue bases of other countries. This section describes the factors that can be used to identify tax havens for the purpose of this report.

Because tax havens offer a way to minimise taxes and obtain financial confidentiality, tax havens are appealing to corporate and individual investors. Tax havens serve three main purposes: they provide a location for holding passive investment ('money boxes'); they provide a location where 'paper' profits can be booked; and they enable the affairs of taxpayers, particularly their bank accounts, to be effectively shielded from scrutiny by tax authorities of other countries.

The necessary starting point to identify a tax heaven is to ask (a) whether a jurisdiction imposes no or only minimal taxes (generally or in special circumstances) and offers itself, or is perceived to offer itself, as a place to be used by non-residents to escape tax in their country of residence. Other key factors which can confirm the existence of a tax haven are: (b) laws or administrative practices which can prevent the effective exchange of relevant information with other governments on taxpayers benefiting from the low or no tax jurisdiction; (c) lack of transparency and (d) the absence of requirement that the activity be substantial, since it would suggest that a jurisdiction may be attempting to attract investment or transactions that are purely tax driven. (Transactions may be booked there without the requirement of adding value so that there is little real activity, i.e., these jurisdictions are essentially 'booking centres').

[. . .]

3.2 Harmful preferential tax regimes

Many OECD Member and non-member countries have already established or are considering establishing preferential tax regimes to attract highly mobile financial and other service activities. These regimes generally provide a favourable location for holding passive investments or for booking paper profits. In many cases, the regime may have been designed specifically to act as a conduit for routing capital flows across borders. These regimes may be found in the general tax code or in administrative practices, or they may have been established by special tax and non-tax legislation outside the framework of the general tax system. This section discusses factors that may help identify harmful preferential tax regimes, without targeting specific countries.

Four key factors assist in identifying harmful preferential tax regimes: (a) the regime imposes a low or zero effective tax rate on the relevant income; (b) the regime is 'ring-fenced'; (c) the operation of the regime is non-transparent; (d) the jurisdiction operating the regime does not effectively exchange information with other countries. . . . A harmful preferential tax regime will be characterised by a combination of a low or zero effective tax rate and one or more other factors set out [below].

1   *No or low effective tax rates*: A low or zero effective tax rate on the relevant income is a necessary starting point for an examination of whether a preferential tax regime is harmful. A zero or low effective tax rate may arise because the schedule rate itself is very low or because of the way in which a country defines the tax base to which the rate is applied. [. . .]

2   *'Ring-fencing' of regimes*: There are good reasons for the international community to be concerned where regimes are partially or fully isolated from the domestic economy. Since the regime's 'ring-fencing' effectively protects the sponsoring country from the harmful effects of its own incentive regime, that regime will have an adverse impact only on foreign tax bases. Thus, the country offering the regime may bear little or none of the financial burden of its own preferential tax legislation. Similarly, taxpayers within the regime may benefit from the infrastructure of the country providing the preferential regime without bearing the cost incurred to provide that infrastructure. [. . .]

3   *Lack of transparency*: The lack of transparency in the operation of a regime will make it harder for the home country to take defensive measures. To be deemed transparent in terms of administrative practices, a tax

regime's administration should normally satisfy both of the following conditions: [first], it must set forth clearly the conditions of applicability to taxpayers in such a manner that those conditions may be invoked against the authorities; second, details of the regime, including any applications thereof in the case of a particular taxpayer, must be available to tax authorities of other countries concerned. Regimes which do not meet these criteria are likely to increase harmful tax competition since non-transparent regimes give their beneficiaries latitude for negotiating with the tax authorities and may result in inequality of treatment of taxpayers in similar circumstances. [. . .]

4   *Lack of effective exchange of information*: The ability or willingness of a country to provide information to other countries is a key factor in deciding upon whether the effect of a regime operated by that country has the potential to cause harmful effects. A country may be constrained in exchanging information, for the purpose of the application of a tax treaty as well as for the application of national legislation, because of secrecy laws which prevent the tax authorities from obtaining information for other countries on taxpayers benefiting from the operation of a preferential tax regime. In addition, even where there are no formal secrecy laws, administrative policies or practices may impede the exchange of information. For example, the country may determine as a matter of administrative policy that certain transactions or relations between enterprise and its customers are a business secret which need not be disclosed under Article 26 paragraph 2 (c) of the OECD Model Tax Convention, or the country with the preferential tax regime may simply be uncooperative with other countries in providing information. Such laws, administrative policies, practices or lack of co-operation may suggest that the preferential tax regime constitutes harmful tax competition.

4 COUNTERACTING HARMFUL TAX COMPETITION

A variety of counteracting measures are currently used by countries that wish to protect their tax base against the detrimental actions of other countries that engage in harmful tax competition. The manner in which these measures apply varies widely from country to country.

These measures are typically implemented through unilateral or bilateral action by the countries concerned. A rigorous and consistent application of existing tools can go a long way towards addressing the problem of harmful tax competition. There are limits, however, to such a unilateral or bilateral approach to a problem that is essentially global in nature. First, the jurisdictional limits to the powers of a country's tax authorities restrict the ability of these authorities to counter some forms of harmful tax competition. Second, a country may believe that taxing its residents in a way that neutralises the benefits of certain forms of harmful tax competition will put its taxpayers at a competitive disadvantage if its actions are not followed by other countries. Third, the necessity to monitor all forms of harmful tax competition and to enforce counter-measures effectively imposes significant administrative costs on countries adversely affected by such competition. Fourth, uncoordinated unilateral measures may increase compliance costs on taxpayers.

[. . .]

Although one country's actions can be influential in curbing harmful tax practices, it is difficult for the actions of any single country to eliminate harmful tax practices. In fact, for many reasons, individual countries may not have a strong incentive to take action against harmful tax practices since, by so doing, they can worsen their position relative to where they would have been if they had not acted at all. For example, as a result of some defensive measures an individual country takes to counteract harmful tax practices, the targeted activity may simply move to another location that is not taking measures to combat such practices. Thus, individual actions do not completely solve the problem; they may merely displace it. For this reason, a multilateral approach is required and the OECD is the most appropriate forum to undertake this task.

The present report provides a useful starting point for improving international co-operation to counter harmful tax competition. The effectiveness of many of the recommendations concerning domestic legislation and tax treaties . . . will depend to a large extent on whether the measures concerned can be taken in a co-ordinated fashion. As explained in the introduction to this [section], a co-ordinated response to the problem of harmful tax competition will greatly reinforce the effectiveness of unilateral measures. Such a response will involve a number of elements, the most important of which are:

- the adoption of a set of Guidelines intended to ensure that Member countries refrain from adopting preferential tax regimes constituting harmful tax competition and gradually eliminate those harmful preferential tax regimes that currently exist;
- the creation of a subsidiary body of the Committee [on Fiscal Affairs], the Forum on Harmful Tax Practices, to allow, among other things, for an ongoing discussion of experiences with the problems posed by tax havens and harmful preferential tax regimes and of the effectiveness of measures taken in response to such practices. The Forum will monitor the implementation of Recommendations . . . and . . . the Guidelines;
- the preparation of a list of jurisdictions constituting tax havens; and
- the development and active promotion of principles of Good Tax Administration relevant to counteracting harmful tax practices.

24 The case for international tax co-ordination reconsidered

*Peter Birch Sørensen**

Economic Policy, vol. 31 (October 2000), pp. 431–61, 466–72

1 INTRODUCTION

In open economies linked by trade and capital flows, the tax policy of one country may affect economic activity and public revenue in other countries. This observation has led to numerous calls for international tax co-ordination in the wake of deepening economic integration. In particular, the formation of Economic and Monetary Union in Europe has revitalized the European debate on the need for co-ordination of capital income taxation to ensure realization of the expected gains from further integration of European capital markets.

This paper investigates the scope for co-ordination of capital income taxes within the EU, allowing for the concern of policy makers that higher capital taxes in Europe may cause a flight of capital to the rest of the world. The paper develops a quantitative general equilibrium model describing the allocation and distribution effects of tax competition and tax co-ordination within a unified framework. The analysis highlights the differences between global tax co-ordination and regional co-ordination within a subset of countries. In the case of regional co-ordination, it also illustrates the importance of the policy response from the rest of the world. Fiscal competition will not wipe out capital income taxes, but it will generate an inefficiently low level of capital taxes relative to taxes on labour. Fiscal competition will also cause a significant drop in redistributive public transfers and an increase in productive government spending benefitting mobile capital. The results indicate that the gains from international co-ordination of capital taxes are likely to be unevenly distributed across countries and particularly *within* each country, with the bulk of the gains accruing to the poorer sections of society. This suggests that the case for international tax co-ordination must rest on

* Københavns Universitet, EPRU and CESifo. I wish to thank Philippe Bacchetta, Andreas Haufler, Ben Heijdra, Harry Huizinga, Bruno Jullien, Michael Keen, Christian Keuschnigg, Henrik Kleven, Kai A. Konrad, Jack Mintz, Ulrik Nødgaard, Guttorm Schjelderup. Hans-Werner Sinn, Alfons Weichenrieder, David Wildasin and a referee for comments on an earlier draft of this paper. Lars Eriksen provided invaluable computer assistance and Thomas Worm Andersen helped in collecting data. Any remaining shortcomings are my own responsibility. The activities of the Economic Policy Research Unit are supported by a grant from the Danish National Research Foundation.

fairly egalitarian policy preferences and that co-ordination may be hard to implement politically.

Before substantiating these claims, I will give some background to the current debate on tax co-ordination in Section 2 and offer some evidence of tax competition in Section 3. Section 4 will then present my general equilibrium model designed to analyse the allocation and distribution effects of international tax co-ordination. In Section 5 I will show how this model supports the conclusions mentioned above. Section 6 summarizes my main results.

2 TAX COMPETITION OR TAX CO-ORDINATION?

Early advocates of tax co-ordination like Peggy Musgrave (1969) and Richard Musgrave (1969, Part III) focused on the problem of international double taxation. Double taxation occurs when the taxpayer's country of residence imposes a tax on foreign-source income on top of the tax which has already been paid to the foreign-source country. Guided by the OECD Model Double Taxation Convention (OECD, 1977), policy makers have now established an intricate web of bilateral tax treaties to alleviate international double taxation. Within the EU, the so-called 'Parent-Subsidiary Directive' provides for double tax relief in the field of corporate taxation.

The issue of double taxation has thus become less pressing. Instead there has been a growing concern that income from international activity may be *undertaxed*, as increasing capital mobility reduces the incentive for source countries and the ability of residence countries to tax mobile activities. Residence countries have difficulties monitoring and taxing accrued income from outward foreign investment. At the same time source countries are reluctant to impose high taxes on inward foreign investment for fear of provoking capital flight. Indeed, the attempts of governments to attract mobile capital by offering a favourable tax climate may trigger a process of international *tax competition* in which taxation and public spending is driven below the optimal level – the (in)famous 'race to the bottom'.[1] Concern about such effects of tax competition was already expressed by Oates (1972, p. 143). Later, it was underpinned by Zodrow and Mieszkowski (1986) and Wilson (1986) who showed that reliance on source-based capital income taxes will cause an underprovision of public goods in an environment of tax competition. Gordon (1986) and Razin and Sadka (1991) projected that capital income taxes will vanish altogether in small open economies faced with perfect capital mobility, given that residence countries cannot enforce taxes on foreign-source capital income, and given that they can tax immobile factors. Sinn (1997) argued that tax competition will not cause an underprovision of public goods when governments can tax immobile labour, but it will imply a more unequal income distribution and cause the welfare state to break down altogether if labour mobility is added to capital mobility. Keen and Marchand (1997) pointed out that, just as fiscal competition may induce governments to change their tax structures with undesirable consequences for income distribution, it may also lead to an increase in expenditures bene-fiting mobile capital at the expense of spending on public goods benefiting immobile consumers.

Despite these and many other contributions indicating negative effects of tax competition,[2] the case for international tax co-ordination is by no means universally accepted. In the spirit of Brennan and Buchanan (1980), several writers have argued that fiscal decentralization and the ensuing tax competi-tion helps to constrain the rent-seeking activities of politicians, bureaucrats and special interest groups. For example, in defence of Britain's opposition to a withholding tax on interest paid to EU residents, an editorial in *The Economist* (27/11/99) argued that 'tax competition (tending to lower tax rates) is just what the EU needs'. But even if a fraction of government spending may represent pure 'waste', capital income tax competition will be welfare-improving only if the 'waste' fraction exceeds the elasticity of the tax base with respect to the capital income tax rate – a result demonstrated by Edwards and Keen (1996). This condition seems unlikely to be met in a world of high capital mobility where the capital income tax base is very elastic.

Most of the literature emphasizing welfare losses from tax competition has focused on the effects of capital mobility. Another strand of literature stresses labour mobility, arguing that tax competition in a world with mobile indi-viduals helps local jurisdictions to achieve an efficient level and pattern of public spending, as citizens reveal their preferences for public goods by voting with their feet, moving to the jurisdiction offering their preferred fiscal policy package. This is the famous Tiebout (1956) hypothesis. Unfortunately the conditions necessary for an efficient Tiebout equilibrium are very restrictive. First, the government must be able to collect a 'head tax' from each resident equal to the cost of providing him with the chosen level of public goods and services. Similar lump sum taxes may be necessary to ensure an efficient location of mobile firms (see Richter, 1994; Richter and Wellisch, 1996). Secondly, an efficient decentralized Tiebout equilibrium will not exist if there are economies of scale in the provision of public goods (Bewley, 1981; Sinn, 1997). Moreover, the Tiebout literature focuses entirely on efficiency issues, neglecting the fact that factor mobility weakens the ability of governments to redistribute income from rich to poor. Finally, in an international context with cultural and political barriers to labour mobility, governments compete mainly to attract mobile capital, and the efficiency-enhancing process of citizens voting with their feet cannot be relied upon.

Against this background I will seek to explain and to quantify the losses from international fiscal competition and the potential gains from tax co-ordination. I will focus on fiscal competition for mobile capital, since international labour mobility is still rather limited. Without denying their importance, I will leave aside issues of commodity tax competition, recently surveyed by Keen and Smith (1996) and Lockwood (1999).

3 EVIDENCE OF TAX COMPETITION

Because of monitoring problems, it is difficult for residence countries to enforce taxes on foreign-source capital income. This holds in particular for personal taxes on income from foreign portfolio investment. In the area of corporate income taxation many residence countries explicitly exempt foreign-source income from domestic tax, and most other countries only tax the foreign-source income of their 'resident' multinationals to the extent that this income is repatriated to the parent company, and only in so far as the domestic tax liability exceeds the source tax which has already been paid to the foreign country. As a first approximation, it is therefore fair to say that the source principle prevails in the taxation of capital income.[3]

In the field of portfolio investment where the transaction costs of shifting between domestic and foreign investment are small, the combination of capital mobility and source-based taxation is likely to exert a strong downward pressure on tax rates. Since investment in debt instruments accounts for the bulk of foreign portfolio investment, we would thus expect to observe a significant drop in tax rates on interest income in an era when capital controls are lifted and financial markets are liberalized.

The impact of rising capital mobility on the taxation of direct business investment is more subtle. The effective tax rate on business profits depends on the rules defining the tax base and on the statutory (corporate) tax rate applied to taxable profits. If governments must raise a certain amount of revenue via taxes on corporate income, a rise in foreign direct investment will induce policy makers to lower the statutory tax rate and to broaden the tax base by reducing depreciation allowances and eliminating special investment incentives (see Haufler and Schjelderup, 1999a). The reason is that a lower *statutory* corporate tax rate makes government revenue less vulnerable to the profit-shifting activities of multinational corporations such as the practice of allocating taxable profits to low-tax jurisdictions by manipulating prices in intra-firm transactions (transfer-pricing), and the practice of allocating company debt and the associated deductions for interest payments to subsidiaries in high-tax countries (thin capitalization).

While it seems clear that transfer-pricing and thin capitalization will induce cuts in statutory corporate tax rates, it is less clear why governments faced with rising foreign direct investment would broaden the tax base to maintain the effective corporate tax rate, if they have access to other taxes on less mobile factors. Two facts may help us to understand this: (1) the return to direct investment often includes an element of location-specific pure profit; (2) economic integration increases the international cross-ownership of firms. The first fact means that capital owners cannot fully shift the burden of the source-based corporation tax onto other factors of production. The second fact means that a growing share of the domestic capital stock becomes foreign-owned. The corporate income tax then becomes a more effective tool for shifting the domestic tax burden onto foreigners, since the source-based corporation tax will fall to a larger extent on the pure profits accruing to foreign investors. As Mintz (1994) and Huizinga and Nielsen (1997) have emphasized, this opportunity for *tax exportation* provides an incentive for (nationalistic) governments to *raise* the effective corporate tax rate as a reaction to deepening economic integration.[4]

In summary, while growing capital mobility coupled with source-based taxation may be expected to drive down *statutory* tax rates on corporate profits and personal capital income, it will have two offsetting effects on *effective* corporate tax rates. On the one hand governments have an incentive to lower effective tax rates in an effort to attract increasingly mobile business activities. On the other hand increasing foreign ownership of domestic firms makes it more tempting to use the domestic corporation tax as a means of exporting part of the domestic tax burden. The net impact of these offsetting incentives on effective corporate tax rates is ambiguous, although most writers on tax competition seem to believe that the former effect will dominate. With these observations in mind, let us turn to the data.

Table 24.1 shows that statutory tax rates on capital income in the OECD area have declined significantly from the mid 1980s to the late 1990s, consistent with the hypothesis that the increase in capital mobility over this period has intensified tax competition. The theory of tax competition suggests that small countries will *ceteris paribus* set a lower tax rate on capital income than large countries, because the smaller countries face a higher elasticity of capital supply from the world capital market (see Bucovetsky, 1991; Wilson, 1991). For the same reason an increase in capital mobility over time should cause a larger drop in capital income tax rates in the smaller countries. On average, the data in Table 24.1 are seen to be consistent with this prediction.

Table 24.2 considers the evolution of the *average effective tax rate* on capital income, defined as total revenue from the taxation of capital, property and wealth as a percentage of the estimated total income from capital. To put these figures in perspective, the table also shows the change in the total average effective tax rate on labour income from the first half of the 1980s to the first half of the 1990s, accounting for the fact that consumption taxes are really indirect taxes on labour, since they contribute to the total wedge between the gross real labour cost to the employer and the real after-tax wage rate received by the employee. The *total* average effective tax rate on labour income reported in Table 24.2 thus includes indirect as well as direct taxes (see the formula in the note to the table).

According to Table 24.2 the recent drop in statutory tax rates on capital income has not translated into a similar drop in the effective tax rate. This reflects the fact that recent tax reforms in the OECD area have combined cuts in statutory tax rates with measures to broaden the capital income tax base. Indeed, on average the effective tax rate on capital has been roughly constant for all the country groups in Table 24.2. An alternative grouping into small and large countries did not reveal any systematic effect of country size on the evolution of tax rates.

The estimates in Table 24.2 are based on a methodology developed by Mendoza *et al.* (1994). Like all calculations of effective tax rates, they may

Table 24.1 Statutory tax rates on capital income

	Tax rate on retained corporate income (%) [a]			Top personal tax rate on interest income (%) [b]		
	1985	*1999*	*Change 1985–99*	*1985*	*1998*	*Change 1985–98*
Small countries (<20 mill.)						
Denmark	50	32	−18	73.2	60	−13.2
Finland	57	28	−29	71	28	−43
Norway	51	28	−23	40.5	28	−12.5
Sweden	52	28	−24	50	30	−20
Belgium	45	40.2	−4.8	25	15	−10
Netherlands	42	35	−7	72	60	−12
Luxembourg	45.5	37.5	−8.0	57	50	−7
Ireland	50(10)	28(10)	−22	60	27	−33
Portugal	50	34	−16	15	20	5
Austria	61.5	34	−27.5	62	25	−37
Switzerland	35.0	25.1	−9.9	45.8	45	−0.8
Australia	50	33	−17	60	47	−13
Average for small countries	49.1[c]	31.9[c]	−17.2[c]	52.6	36.3	−16.4
Larger countries (>40 mill.)						
Spain	33	35	2	66	31	−35
Italy	47.8	37	−10.8	12.5	12.5	17.5
France	50	40	−10	26	20.9	−5.1
Germany	61.7	52.3	−9.4	54.5	53	−1.5
UK	40	30	−10	60	40	−20
USA	49.5	38	−11.5	54	39.8	−14.2
Japan	55.4	48	−7.4	20	20	0
Average for large countries	48.2	40.0	−8.2	41.9	31	−10.9

Sources: The figures for 1985 were taken from the Ruding Report (1992), tables 8.5 and 8.6. The figures for 1998 and 1999 were taken from Andersson (1999).

Notes:

[a] Including local taxes.

[b] Many countries have special savings incentives with lower tax rates. These are not reflected in the table.

[c] For manufacturing corporations in Ireland a low 10% corporate income tax applies (as indicated in parentheses). If this rate is used in computing the average for small countries the figures would be 45.8, 30.4 and −15.4 respectively.

suffer from measurement problems (see Volkerink and de Haan, 1999). Yet the alternative measures of effective tax rates presented in Chennells and Griffith (1997) tend to confirm the impression that – averaging across different asset types and different modes of investment finance – the average as well as the *marginal* effective tax rates on capital income in the most important OECD countries have been roughly constant between the mid 1980s and the mid 1990s.

However, this cannot be taken as evidence that tax competition is absent. First of all, the increase in the overall tax burden over time has tended to be concentrated on labour, as indicated by the rising effective tax rates on labour

Table 24.2 Average effective tax rates on labour and capital income

	Total effective tax rate on labour income (%) [a]		Effective tax rate on capital income (%)	
	1981–85	1991–95	1981–85	1991–95
Nordic countries				
Denmark	55.64	59.74	47.82	40.04
Finland	45.23	49.51	35.20	45.20
Norway	53.83	54.06	42.60	30.30
Sweden	57.44	59.80	47.40	53.10
Average	53.03	55.78	43.26	42.16
Continental Europe				
Austria	54.62	55.74	21.48	22.74
Belgium	52.90	54.71	39.50	36.00
France	52.53	56.98	28.40	24.80
Germany	47.07	50.23	31.00	26.50
Italy	43.75	52.76	25.30	34.50
Netherlands	57.25	59.84	29.70	31.90
Spain	37.71	40.92	13.90	20.30
Average	49.41	53.02	27.04	28.11
Anglo-Saxon countries				
Australia	24.90	25.51	44.50	44.40
Canada	33.02	38.89	37.90	49.50
United Kingdom	37.51	35.55	66.50	45.30
United States	32.14	31.12	40.90	41.10
Average	31.89	32.77	47.45	45.08
Japan	27.86	31.74	39.70	43.90
Average for all countries	44.59	47.32	36.99	36.85

Source: The estimates of effective tax rates on labour income, capital income and consumption are based on the methodology developed by Mendoza, Razin and Tesar (1994); the figures were taken from Daveri and Tabellini (2000) and Volkerink and de Haan (1999).
Note:
[a] The total effective tax rate on labour income (t) is given by the formula $t = (t^l - t^c)/(1 + t^l)$, where t^l = effective direct tax rate on labour income and t^c = effective tax rate on consumption.

documented in Table 24.2. This shows that governments do in fact try to shift the tax burden towards the more immobile factor of production. Secondly, the sharp recent drop in statutory tax rates on capital income suggests an increasingly intense tax competition for foreign portfolio investment and for the taxable 'paper profits' of multinational corporations.

4 MODELLING TAX COMPETITION

4.1 The spillovers from capital income taxation

The case for international co-ordination of capital income taxes rests on the fact that such taxes have international spillover effects. When one country changes its source-based capital income tax, it will affect the welfare of other countries via an investment reallocation effect, a saving effect, a tax exporting effect, and an intertemporal terms-of-trade effect. I will now explain these fiscal externalities, dividing the world economy into the domestic economy ('Home') and the rest of the world ('ROW').

4.1.1. The investment reallocation effect

Under source-based capital income taxation, a rise in Home's capital income tax rate will reduce the relative attractiveness of domestic investment, inducing a capital flow from Home to ROW. With a positive capital income tax in ROW, the social (pre-tax) rate of return on the extra investment in the foreign economy will exceed the after-tax rate of return required by private investors. The difference between the social and the private return to the extra capital imports represents a net social gain to ROW which takes the form of an increase in foreign capital income tax revenue, as shown by Wildasin (1989). The inflow of capital to the foreign economy will also tend to drive up the foreign wage rate, thereby stimulating foreign labour supply and employment. If the initial employment level is distorted by a labour income tax, this rise in foreign employment generates a further increase in foreign welfare, reflected in an increase in foreign labour tax revenue. The welfare gain is amplified if initial employment is also distorted for non-tax reasons so that involuntary unemployment prevails in the initial equilibrium. In the absence of co-ordination, the Home government will not take these positive spillovers on the foreign economy into account. Hence the investment reallocation effect implies that capital income tax rates will tend to be inefficiently low under tax competition.

4.1.2. The saving effect

When Home raises its capital income tax rate, the resulting fall in the domestic after-tax rate of return may reduce the volume of domestic saving, thus reducing the outflow of capital to ROW and the concomitant rise in foreign welfare. If the negative effect on domestic saving is sufficiently strong and the international mobility of capital is sufficiently low, it is even conceivable that the net impact on investment in ROW will be negative (see Bettendorf and Heijdra, 1999). The saving effect thus generates a negative international spillover effect of a rise in the domestic capital income tax rate.

4.1.3. The tax exporting effect

Under perfect capital mobility and source-based taxation, investors may escape a domestic tax on the normal return to capital by reallocating investment from the domestic to the foreign economy. However, if part of the return to domestic investment represents pure rents, and if some of these rents accrue to foreign owners of domestic firms, a rise in Home's capital income tax will have a direct negative impact on the after-tax income of foreign owners. *Ceteris paribus*, this negative international spillover implies that capital income taxes tend to be too high under tax competition where national tax policies do not account for the welfare effects on foreigners (see Mintz, 1994; Huizinga and Nielsen, 1997).

4.1.4. The intertemporal terms-of-trade effect

A rise in Home's source-based capital income tax will reduce the domestic demand for capital. If the domestic economy is large, this will depress the global level of interest rates. By lowering the cost of foreign debt service, the lower world interest rate will benefit foreign countries if ROW is a net debtor to the Home economy. On the other hand, the spillover on ROW will be negative if foreigners have positive net claims on the Home economy (for an elaboration of this intertemporal terms-of-trade effect, see Sinn, 1987, section 7.4; and Depata and Myers, 1994).

Since a higher capital income tax in one country will generate positive as well as negative international spillover effects, it is not clear *a priori* whether source-based capital income taxes will tend to be too high or too low under tax competition. To judge whether there is a need for a co-ordinated rise or a co-ordinated fall in the level of capital income taxation, a quantitative analysis like the one presented in Section 5 is needed.

4.2 Other fiscal spillovers

The capital income tax rate is not the only fiscal instrument with the potential to generate international spillovers. By raising its spending on infrastructure, a government can attract mobile capital because a better infrastructure increases the profitability of domestic investment. Since the resulting reallocation of capital from the foreign to the domestic economy will reduce foreign welfare, the global level of infrastructure spending will tend to be inefficiently high under fiscal competition. One of the purposes of the model set up below is to investigate whether the potential gains from co-ordination of capital income taxation will be nullified by more aggressive infrastructure spending when governments can no longer attract mobile capital by undercutting each other's rates of capital taxation.[5]

4.3 TAXCOM: a model of tax competition and tax co-ordination

To estimate the welfare gains from tax co-ordination, one needs a general equilibrium model of the world economy to allow for the interaction of national tax policies. In this section and in the technical appendix I sketch such a model, called TAXCOM. The model is static, describing a stationary long-run equilibrium. Figure 24.1 illustrates the structure of the model. In each national economy firms combine internationally mobile capital with immobile labour and a fixed factor to produce a homogeneous internationally traded good. The fixed factor may be thought of as land and natural

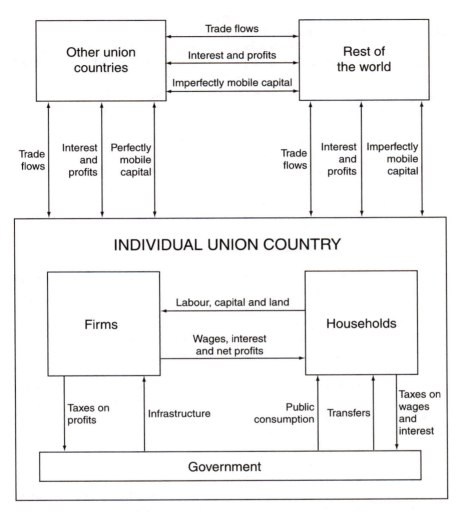

Figure 24.1 Structure of the TAXCOM model

resources and is supplied in proportion to the exogenous population of the country. This assumption of identical population densities means that small countries have no inherent productivity advantage over large countries, and vice versa. All markets are competitive, and profit maximization implies that labour and capital are paid their marginal products. National income is divided into the wages of labour, the interest on capital, and the pure profits accruing to the owners of the fixed factor.

Consumers have identical preferences, and each individual consumer is endowed with a predetermined stock of human as well as non-human wealth. These initial endowments are *unevenly distributed*, providing governments with a motive for redistributive taxation. A consumer may consume his initial non-human wealth right away, or he may invest it in the capital market at a rising marginal transaction cost. In the latter case he accumulates a capital stock earning an interest which may be consumed along with the principal at the end of the period. The transaction cost may be thought of as the cost of financial intermediation; its role is analogous to the role played by consumer time preference in an explicitly intertemporal model. Weighing the transaction cost against the return to capital, the utility-maximizing consumer chooses to increase his capital supply ('savings') as the after-tax real rate of interest increases. In other words, although *endowments* are exogenous, the supply of productive *capital* is endogenous. Because of rising marginal disutility of work, utility maximization also implies that labour supply rises with the after-tax real wage rate per unit of human capital.

An exogenous fraction of domestic firms is owned by foreign residents, so a similar fraction of domestic profits accrues to foreigners. At the same time domestic residents receive a share of the profits generated in other countries. Within each country, the individual consumer's share of total profits equals his share of initial wealth.

Governments impose a tax on labour income which may be interpreted to include personal income taxes, social security taxes, payroll taxes, and a uniform VAT. In addition, governments levy a proportional tax on interest and profits. Interest and profits are taxed at the same rate because of administrative problems of distinguishing pure profits from the normal return to capital. Tax revenues are used to finance public consumption generating consumer utility; spending on infrastructure serving to raise total factor productivity, and lump sum transfers paid out in an equal amount to all consumers. Since the unequal distribution of initial wealth implies that factor incomes are unequally distributed, the government transfer evens out the distribution of disposable incomes. The combination of the lump sum transfer with the flat tax rate on labour income is equivalent to assuming that labour income is subject to a progressive linear income tax.

The TAXCOM model is designed to highlight the effects of regional tax co-ordination among a subgroup of countries. This region is referred to as the 'union' and may be thought of as the EU. Regional tax co-ordination may be motivated by the fact that the co-ordinating countries are economically more integrated with each other than with the rest of the world. In the context of Economic and Monetary Union in Europe it seems reasonable to assume that the EU countries are particularly deeply integrated. For example, the econometric study by Devereux and Griffith (1998) found that the decisions of US based multinationals to locate production in Europe rather than in the US have not been significantly affected by taxation, whereas differences in effective tax rates across European countries have had a significant impact on the location of American-owned firms *within* Europe, once the decision to invest in Europe has been made. More recently, Portes and Rey (2000) have found strong evidence that cross-border equity flows decrease with the geographical distance between national markets, and that distance is a proxy for the information and transaction costs of investing abroad. These empirical studies are consistent with the view that the degree of capital mobility is higher within Europe than across the Atlantic. The TAXCOM model therefore assumes that capital is perfectly mobile within the union area whereas capital mobility between the union and the rest of the world is *imperfect*. Technically this is modelled by specifying the stock of capital owned by individual households as a CES-aggregate of assets located in the union and assets located in the rest of the world, with a finite elasticity of substitution between the two asset types. This captures the idea that households face rising marginal transaction costs when they switch assets between the union and the non-union area in their efforts to maximize the net income from their total capital stock. The limiting case where capital becomes perfectly mobile between the union and the rest of the world is obtained when the elasticity of substitution between union and non-union assets approaches infinity.

A general equilibrium in the TAXCOM model is achieved when all firms maximize their profits, all consumers maximize their utilities, and all markets are clearing. In the absence of international exchange of information, the governments of residence countries cannot enforce taxes on foreign-source interest and profit income. The source principle of capital income taxation therefore prevails under pure tax competition. In equilibrium, perfect capital mobility then implies that the *after-tax* interest rate is equalized within the union whereas imperfect capital mobility vis-à-vis the rest of the world implies a different after-tax rate of return on non-union assets.

4.4 Social welfare and political economy

The fiscal policy instruments in the TAXCOM model are endogenously determined by optimizing government behaviour. This may be given a conventional welfare-theoretic interpretation in which the policy maker maximizes a social welfare function of the following form:

Social welfare = average utility − $a \cdot$ (standard deviation of
individual utilities) (1)

The policy maker is seen to be concerned about the *average* level of individual welfare and about the *dispersion* of individual utilities around this mean. In the special case where the parameter $a = 0$, the policy maker is a classical utilitarian striving to maximize the sum of individual utilities, which is equivalent to maximizing average utility when population size is exogenous. In the general case the policy maker is averse to inequality, implying a positive value of the parameter a. The optimal national policy is found by maximizing (1) with respect to the domestic fiscal policy instruments, subject to the government budget constraint plus the constraints implied by optimizing private sector behaviour. In the absence of co-ordination, the outcome is a non-cooperative (Nash) equilibrium in which each national government has optimized its own fiscal instruments, given the policies chosen by other governments.

Traditional welfare economics is often criticized for failing to specify a democratic political process through which the 'optimal' policy can be implemented. The TAXCOM model is not vulnerable to this criticism. As demonstrated in the appendix, the social welfare function (1) is identical to the indirect utility function of the consumer with an initial wealth endowment of $1 - a\sigma$, where σ is the standard deviation of individual wealth levels around their normalized mean value of unity. Following Osborne and Slivinsky (1996) and Besley and Coate (1997), we may therefore imagine that fiscal policy in the TAXCOM model is made by a 'citizen candidate', that is, an ordinary citizen who is voted into office and simply implements the policy which will maximize his own individual utility. Each consumer's preferred policy depends on his initial wealth endowment, and simulations with the TAXCOM model have shown that the individual voter's utility will always be higher, the closer his wealth level is to the wealth level of the elected citizen candidate determining policy. With simple majority voting, this means that the citizen with the *median* level of wealth will be able to win any election in which candidates campaign on the basis of their own preferred policies. We may therefore interpret the policy maker's objective function (1) as the indirect utility function of the voter endowed with the median level of wealth. This conforms with the democratic norm that any policy maker elected through majority voting has the right to define 'social welfare'.

Apart from capturing the equity-efficiency trade-off in a simple manner, the objective function (1) thus allows a synthesis of traditional welfare-theoretic policy analysis and modern political economy analysis.

To understand the policy simulations below, it is important to note that public consumption goods will never be underprovided in the TAXCOM model. At the margin, the policy maker may always choose to reduce the uniform lump sum transfer by one unit in order to provide one more unit of public consumption goods. In this sense it is as if public consumption is financed by a lump sum tax. Moreover, in the TAXCOM model all consumers have the same marginal utility from private as well as public consumption. The combination of lump sum finance and identical preferences implies that all voters will want the government to provide the first-best level of public consumption goods. By contrast, because there are international spillovers from public infrastructure spending and from the capital income taxes financing (part of) the redistributive transfer, government spending on infrastructure and transfers will be distorted in the absence of international cooperation.

4.5 Calibration and world equilibrium with tax competition

Let us now consider the quantitative properties of the general equilibrium emerging under tax competition. The TAXCOM model relies on simple functional forms, allowing calibration of key elasticities and income shares by appropriate choice of a few structural parameters. Descriptive realism has been subordinated to the goals of simplicity and transparency. The model should therefore be seen only as 'theory with numbers'; it attempts to estimate the rough order of magnitude of the welfare gains from tax co-ordination, assuming reasonable values of those key parameters which according to theory should be crucial for the effects of co-ordination.

The model is calibrated such that the initial model equilibrium with tax competition roughly replicates the level and structure of taxation in Western Europe and the United States. Based on the estimated effective tax rates in Table 24.2, Western Europe is divided into three subregions: the Nordic countries with high taxes on capital as well as labour; Continental Europe with high labour taxes but relatively low taxes on capital, and the UK with low labour taxes but high taxes on capital. The rest of the world is represented by the US where labour taxes are lower than anywhere else while capital taxes correspond roughly to the level in the Nordic region and in the UK.

Countries within each subregion are assumed to be symmetric. The parameter values for each region are given in the upper part of Table 24.3 where the symbols in brackets refer to the parameters introduced in the appendix. The resulting tax rates etc. implied by the model are reported in the lower part of Table 24.3 where the corresponding empirical estimates are indicated in brackets.

To replicate the observed level of capital income taxation within the framework of the TAXCOM model, it is necessary to assume a fairly high pure profit share of GDP, giving governments an incentive to maintain positive capital income taxes despite high capital mobility. Pure profits are interpreted to include all quasi-rents in addition to conventional natural resource rents. While quasi-rents in any given firm or sector are wiped out by competition in the long run, new quasi-rents keep popping up as a result of continuing technological and structural change. Hence quasi-rents are never eliminated at the macro level in a real-world dynamic economy. The fairly high pure profit share in the static TAXCOM model is a pragmatic way of accounting for this.

To explain the higher level of capital taxation in the Nordic countries and in the UK compared to Continental Europe, I assume that the two former subregions have slightly higher profit shares and higher foreign ownership shares, as shown in Table 24.3. The relatively low foreign ownership share in the US reflects that foreign ownership is less prevalent in the large US economy. For the US the degree of capital mobility vis-à-vis Europe is an important determinant of the level of capital taxation. The elasticity of substitution between European and US assets is chosen so as to generate a realistic value for the US capital income tax rate.

Because factor incomes are unevenly distributed, they count for less than the evenly distributed transfer incomes in the egalitarian social welfare function. The weight given to factor income relative to transfer income (the parameter $1 - a\sigma$ mentioned in Section 4.4) is therefore less than one. If the relative social weight of factor income is, say, 0.8, the policy maker will

Table 24.3 Benchmark calibration of the TAXCOM model

	Nordic countries[a]	Continental Europe[b]	UK	Western Europe	US
Wage share of GDP (α)	0.70	0.70	0.70	0.70	0.70
Capital income share of GDP (β)	0.13	0.15	0.13	0.145	0.12
Pure profit share of GDP ($1 - \alpha - \beta$)	0.17	0.15	0.17	0.155	0.18
Foreign ownership share (δ)	0.32	0.22	0.34	0.26	0.13
Social weight given to factor income relative to transfer income ($1 - a\sigma$)[c]	0.7	0.73	0.80	0.74	0.89
Wage elasticity of labour supply ($1/\varepsilon$)	0.25	0.25	0.33	0.26	0.25
Interest elasticity of capital supply ($1/\phi$)	0.5	0.5	0.5	0.5	0.5
Elasticity of factor productivity w.r.t. infrastructure spending (μ_1)	0.1	0.1	0.1	0.1	0.1
Elasticity of substitution between union and non-union assets (ζ)	6	6	6	6	6
Degree of home bias[d] ($\psi/(1 - \psi)$)	75/25	75/25	75/25	75/25	75/25
Share of world population[e] (s)	0.04	0.42	0.10	0.56	0.44
Scale parameter affecting total factor productivity (μ_2)	1.22	0.98	1.09	1.02	1.16
Model equilibrium with tax competition[f]					
Tax rate on labour income (%)	54.5 (55.8)	51.9 (53.0)	37.5 (35.6)	49.8 (52.5)	30.6 (31.1)
Tax rate on capital income (%)	41.0 (42.2)	32.0 (28.1)	41.0 (45.3)	33.8 (34.22)	40.2 (41.1)
Ratio of GNP to GDP	100.0 (97.0)	99.9 (99.5)	100.0 (99.5)	99.9 (98.7)	100.1 (100.4)
Transfers in percent of GDP	33.3	26.4	21.3	26.0	16.3
Infrastructure spending in percent of GDP	10.0	10.0	10.0	10.0	10.0
Public consumption in percent of GDP	7.2	9.5	7.2	8.9	7.2

Notes: The Greek letters refer to the parameters introduced in the appendix.

[a] Denmark, Finland, Norway and Sweden.

[b] Defined here as Austria, Belgium, France, Germany, Italy, Netherlands and Spain.

[c] The magnitude $1 - a\sigma$ may also be interpreted as the median level of individual wealth relative to the mean wealth level.

[d] A degree of home bias equal to 75/25 means that union (non-union) residents will invest 75% (25%) of their capital within the union and the remaining 25% (75%) in the rest of the world if the after-tax rate of return is the same in the two regions.

[e] The Nordic region is divided into 4 equally large countries each comprising 1% of world population. Continental Europe is divided into 7 countries each including 6% of world population.

[f] The figures in parentheses are empirical estimates. The average effective tax rates were calculated on the basis of the data for 1991–95 in Table 24.2.

impose redistributive factor income taxes up to the point where the last euro of revenue raised (the last euro of transfers paid out) causes a total fall of $1/0.8 = 1.25$ euros in disposable factor income. To achieve a more equitable distribution of income, the policy maker is thus willing to tolerate an 'excess burden' of $1.25 - 1 = 0.25$ euros arising from the fall in economic activity caused by distortionary taxes. Given the assumed labour supply elasticities, the relative social weights imputed to factor income are chosen such that the model roughly reproduces the effective labour income taxes observed in the various regions. This implies that policy makers in the Nordic countries and in Continental Europe are taken to be more egalitarian than policy makers in the Anglo-Saxon countries, in accordance with popular perceptions.

In the TAXCOM model total factor productivity is determined by an exogenous technological scale parameter and by endogenous government spending on infrastructure. The elasticity of total factor productivity with respect to public infrastructure spending was estimated by Aschauer (1989) to be in the range of 0.3, but other writers have found this to be too optimistic, so I chose the more conservative value of 0.1 for this parameter. The technological scale parameter affects the profitability of domestic investment and may therefore be used to calibrate the country's net foreign asset position which influences its gain from a co-ordinated rise in capital income taxes, as explained in Section 4.1. A positive (negative) net foreign asset position implies that the ratio of GNP to GDP is greater (smaller) than one. For each region in the model the technological scale parameter was chosen so as to produce the empirically observed sign of the net foreign asset position. To generate a negative net foreign asset position for the UK without imputing an unrealistically high level of factor productivity to that country, it is necessary to assume a relatively high UK elasticity of labour supply. With a high labour supply elasticity, the relatively low level of labour taxation in the UK ensures an ample labour supply which attracts foreign capital by increasing the marginal productivity of investment in Britain.

The elasticity of capital supply with respect to the after-tax interest rate is set at 0.5 for all regions. Although Summers (1981) argued that the interest elasticity of savings could be much higher than this figure, most empirical studies have found considerably lower savings elasticities. However, the elasticity of capital supply in the TAXCOM model must capture not only the effect of taxation on aggregate saving, but also the distorting effects of capital income taxation on the *allocation* of capital. In practice it is impossible to ensure a uniform treatment of all types of investment, because of the difficulties of measuring true economic depreciation, and because of the well-known problems of taxing capital gains. Hence the returns to different forms of saving and investment are inevitably subject to different effective tax rates generating differences in capital's pre-tax marginal value product across sectors. When the average level of capital income taxation is raised, these intersectoral distortions reducing capital's aggregate productivity are typically exacerbated. Setting a high value of the after-tax interest elasticity of aggregate capital supply is a rough way of accounting for this effect of taxation on the *effective* supply of capital.

By calculating population-weighted averages of parameter values across the three subregions, we obtain the picture of the average Western European country given in the fourth column of Table 24.3. This 'synthetic' country will serve as a benchmark for an analysis of tax co-ordination within a tax union of symmetric countries.

5 THE GAINS FROM TAX CO-ORDINATION

As we have seen in Section 4.2, fiscal competition generates fiscal externalities and is therefore likely to be inefficient. This part of the paper applies the TAXCOM model to illustrate the potential welfare gains from international co-ordination of capital income taxation. In accordance with recent proposals in the European policy debate, coordination takes the form of an international agreement on a minimum source-based capital income tax rate which is binding for all the co-ordinating countries. This minimum tax rate is chosen so as to maximize the population-weighted sum of the social welfare for the co-ordinating countries, accounting for the fact that national governments will set their remaining fiscal instruments to maximize their own welfare.[6]

5.1 Regional versus global tax co-ordination

Table 24.4 shows the simulated effects of a minimum capital income tax rate. The table assumes that all Western European ('union') countries are symmetric, with parameter values equal to those stated in the fourth column of Table 24.3. This unrealistic symmetry assumption is made deliberately to isolate the effect of capital mobility on tax policies in a world without policy co-ordination. By considering the tax competition effects of capital mobility within a group of identical countries, we may gain a better understanding of the implications of the various cross-country asymmetries to be considered in the next section.

The third and the fourth columns of Table 24.4 assume that tax co-ordination only involves the Western European countries and that the rest of the world (the US) does not change its fiscal policy in response to the policy change in Europe. The union authority sets a common minimum capital tax rate with the purpose of maximizing the population-weighted sum of national welfare levels within the union, taking the fiscal policies of the US as given. Under tax competition the individual union country may use its capital income tax to export part of the domestic tax burden to other union countries. Under regional co-ordination, the union authority internalizes this tax exporting effect. *Ceteris paribus*, this works in favour of lower capital income tax rates under co-ordination. However, regional co-ordination also eliminates the downward pressure on capital income tax rates exerted by intra-European capital mobility, as the union authority exploits the collective

Table 24.4 Effects of a minimum capital income tax rate

	Tax competition		Regional co-ordination (no policy response from the US)		Regional co-ordination (optimal policy response from the US)		Global co-ordination	
	Western Europe	US	Western Europe	US	Western Europe	US	Western Europe	US
Policy variables								
Tax rate on capital income and profits (%)	33.8	40.1	46.2	40.1	46.5	42.4	52.2	52.2
Labour income tax (%)	49.8	30.6	48.3	30.6	48.2	30.6	47.5	29.5
Transfers	100	100	107	102	107	104	111	115
Infrastructure spending	100	100	102	100	102	104	104	105
Other variables								
Capital stock per capita	100	100	88	107	89	105	87	96
Employment	100	100	100.3	100.2	100.4	100.2	100.7	100.3
GDP per capita	100	100	99	101	99	101	98.9	100.2
Ratio of GNP to GDP	99.9	100.1	100.5	99.5	100.4	99.6	100.0	100.0
Welfare gain from co-ordination (% of GDP)	—	—	0.16	0.16	0.19	0.16	0.32	0.10

Source: Simulations with the TAXCOM model, based on the benchmark calibration in columns 4 and 5 in Table 24.3.

market power of European countries in the international capital market, accounting for the fact that the elasticity of capital supply to the union as a whole is much lower than the elasticity of capital supply to the individual union country. This effect of co-ordination outweighs the effect of the internalization of tax exporting and leads to a substantial increase in the level of capital income taxation in Europe, as shown in the third column of Table 24.4. With a higher capital income tax rate, it becomes optimal for individual union countries to lower their labour income tax rates, because a stimulus to domestic investment brought about by higher labour supply will now generate more revenue from capital taxation. The neutralization of capital income tax competition within the union also induces member states to raise their expenditure on infrastructure in an effort to attract mobile capital. Despite the slightly lower labour income tax rate and the rise in infrastructure spending, the higher capital tax rate suffices to finance an increase in redistributive transfers in the union. The higher taxes on investment in Western Europe induce a reallocation of capital towards the rest of the world which increases economic activity, tax revenue and public transfers outside the union. As a result of these positive fiscal externalities, social welfare increases just as much in the US as in Europe. The welfare gains are fairly modest, amounting to less than 0.2% of GDP. Note that the welfare gain for Europe arises despite a slight drop in European GDP. Hence the gain for Europe is generated by an improved distribution of income, as will be elaborated in Section 5.4.

The fifth and sixth columns in Table 24.4 show the effects of regional tax co-ordination within Europe when the US reacts optimally to European co-ordination rather than remaining passive. To understand the US policy response, note that under source-based taxation a lower interest rate raises domestic welfare by raising domestic activity. A large country like the US can drive down the interest rate by lowering the demand for capital through a rise in its capital income tax rate. In the TAXCOM model, the rise in domestic welfare generated by a fall in the interest rate is larger, the lower the initial interest rate.[7] Thus, when the union countries generate a capital inflow to the US lowering the US interest rate, they increase the incentive for the US to raise its capital tax in order to benefit from a further fall in the interest rate. The resulting rise in the US capital income tax in turn generates a positive fiscal externality effect on union countries and induces the union to undertake a further slight increase in its capital tax. Through this *strategic complementarity* of capital income tax rates, the level of capital income taxes is raised a bit further towards the level which would be second-best optimal for the world as a whole. According to the theoretical analysis of Konrad and Schjelderup (1999), regional co-ordination of capital income taxation is sure to improve the welfare of all countries in the world if capital income taxes are strategic complements in the sense explained above. The simulations presented here indicate that such strategic complementarity will indeed prevail.

The scenario with regional co-ordination is of particular interest since co-ordination is more likely to occur within a subgroup of countries like the EU member states with close economic and political links. For comparison, the last two columns of Table 24.4 show the simulated effects of *global* co-ordination taking the form of a common binding minimum capital tax rate for the US and Europe set so as to maximize the population-weighted average global welfare level. The qualitative effects are similar to those of regional coordination, but the co-ordinated capital income tax rate is now higher, since global coordination eliminates capital income tax competition across the Atlantic. The rise in the US capital income tax rate mitigates the reallocation of capital from Europe to the US and almost doubles the European welfare gain, compared to the scenario with regional co-ordination. By contrast, for the US the welfare gain is *smaller* than the gain occurring when coordination only involves Europe, suggesting that the US would not want to commit to global co-ordination. The fact that the US gains so little from global coordination is crucially dependent on the assumption that the low observed level of labour taxation in the US reflects a weak social preference for redistribution in America. Because of the stronger preference for redistribution in Europe, the globally co-ordinated capital income tax rate ends up at a suboptimally high level from the American viewpoint. If the US had the same preference for redistribution as Europe, simulations with the TAXCOM model imply that global tax co-ordination would generate a substantial welfare gain for the US. This finding motivates a further analysis of the implications of cross-country asymmetries for the distribution of the gains from tax co-ordination.

5.2 Regional co-ordination among asymmetric countries

To isolate the effects of regionalization, the previous section assumed that countries within the co-ordinating region had identical tastes, technologies and population sizes. However, even within a fairly homogeneous group of nations like the present EU member states, countries differ in several important respects. In Table 24.5 I start out from the assumption in Table 24.4 that all union countries are symmetric. In successive steps, I then consider the effects of each of the asymmetries which were introduced in Table 24.3 to explain the observed differences in tax rates across the three subregions of Western Europe, adding each additional asymmetry onto the others. Table 24.5 indicates how each type of asymmetry affects the size and distribution of the welfare gain from introducing a minimum capital income tax rate in Europe. When all of the asymmetries are added together in the bottom row of Table 24.5, I arrive at the asymmetric equilibrium with tax competition summarized in Table 24.3. The bottom row of Table 24.5 then shows the effects of regional tax co-ordination on tax rates and welfare when all asymmetries are taken into account. Given the stylized nature of the TAXCOM model and the fact that the calibration of the asymmetries is not based on careful empirical estimates of parameter values for each country, the figures in Table 24.5 should not be interpreted literally as an estimate of the effects of tax co-ordination for any specific country. Table 24.5 should rather be seen as

Table 24.5 Asymmetries and the distribution of the gains from regional tax co-ordination

	Tax competition						Regional co-ordination								
	Nordic countries		Continental Europe		UK		Nordic countries			Continental Europe			UK		
	t	τ	t	τ	t	τ	t	τ	W	t	τ	W	t	τ	W
All union countries symmetric[a]	49.8	33.8	49.8	33.8	49.8	33.8	48.2	46.5	0.19	48.2	46.5	0.19	48.2	46.5	0.19
1: Differences in population	49.8	33.1	49.8	34.1	49.8	34.8	48.1	46.5	0.18	48.3	46.5	0.18	48.4	46.5	0.19
2: 1 + differences in preference for redistribution	53.4	34.5	50.8	34.3	43.3	32.7	52.0	46.5	0.28	49.3	46.5	0.21	41.5	46.5	0.03
3: 2 + differences in pure profit share	53.4	39.1	50.8	33.2	43.3	36.0	52.6	46.4	0.30	49.1	46.4	0.19	42.0	46.4	0.09
4: 3 + differences in total factor productivity	53.4	39.2	50.8	33.0	43.3	36.5	52.6	46.6	0.54	49.1	46.6	0.13	42.1	46.6	0.20
5: 4 + differences in labour supply elasticity	54.5	39.2	51.9	33.0	37.5	37.1	53.7	46.6	0.52	50.3	46.6	0.10	36.2	46.6	0.30
6: 5 + differences in foreign ownership share = asymmetric equilibrium in Table 24.3	54.5	41.0	51.9	32.0	37.5	41.0	53.9	46.8	0.53	50.1	46.8	0.07	36.7	46.8	0.35

Source: Simulations with the TAXCOM model.

Notes: t = tax rate on labour income. τ = tax rate on capital income and profits. W = welfare gain from co-ordination in percent of GDP. The differences in parameter values across regions are equal to those stated in Table 24.3.

[a] All union countries have identical parameter values equal to the population-weighted averages of the parameters for the union countries stated in the fourth column in Table 24.3.

an estimate of the likely effects of the particular types of asymmetries considered.

In theory small countries should be less motivated to undertake a co-ordinated rise in capital income taxes than large countries, because small countries face a higher elasticity of capital supply from the world capital market. The estimates presented in the second row of Table 24.5 suggest that, in practice, cross-country differences in population size of the magnitude found in Europe would not significantly affect the distribution of the welfare gains from regional tax co-ordination.

In contrast, the third row of Table 24.5 shows that asymmetries in the social preference for redistribution shift the welfare gains from co-ordination away from less egalitarian countries like the UK towards the more egalitarian regions in Northern and Continental Europe (assuming that observed differences in labour tax rates mainly reflect differences in the preference for redistribution). This is in line with the popular view that the Nordic and continental high-tax countries have a stronger interest in protection from the forces of tax competition.

Introducing differences in pure profit shares will shift the gains from co-ordination in favour of those countries where a larger part of the return to capital takes the form of pure profits and where the distortionary effect of the rise in capital income tax rates will therefore be smaller. In the TAXCOM model these countries are represented by the Nordic region and by the UK, but the inter-regional distribution effects of this asymmetry are seen to be minor.

When exogenous differences in total factor productivity are introduced, the stocks of foreign debt are shifted towards the high-productivity countries which are now offering improved investment opportunities. To explain the observed pattern of foreign debt, the TAXCOM model assumes a higher level of factor productivity in the Nordic region and in the UK than in Continental Europe. *Ceteris paribus*, the more indebted countries will reap a larger gain from co-ordination because they will benefit more from the fall in net interest rates induced by higher capital income taxes.

In Section 4.5 I explained that, to generate foreign debt in the UK without postulating an implausibly high productivity level in that country, it is necessary to assume a relatively high UK labour supply elasticity. Since this asymmetry shifts net foreign assets away from the UK, it also shifts the gains from co-ordination in favour of Britain. Finally, because it is assumed to have a relatively large foreign ownership share, the UK also benefits from this type of asymmetry, since the co-ordinated rise in the capital income tax will fall to a smaller extent on domestic residents when a larger share of profits accrue to foreigners.

In summary, Table 24.5 suggests that cross-country asymmetries in economic structures may imply a rather uneven distribution of the gains from tax co-ordination. Conceivably, some countries may even lose and may hence try to block efforts at co-ordination.

5.3 Sensitivity analysis

Studying the effect of asymmetries in parameter values across countries is one form of sensitivity analysis. To gain further understanding of the role played by the various parameters, this section investigates the effects of varying specific parameters across *all* countries.

Table 24.6 illustrates the sensitivity of the effects of a regional minimum capital tax rate to changes in the key parameters, returning to the assumption that all union countries are symmetric. As a benchmark, the first row restates the union's equilibrium under tax competition and under regional co-ordination, given the original parameter values for the 'average' European country reported in the fourth column of Table 24.3.

In the benchmark scenario the after-tax interest elasticity of effective capital supply is assumed to be 0.5. The second row in Table 24.6 shows the effects of switching from tax competition to regional co-ordination on the assumption made in much of the tax competition literature that this elasticity is zero so that capital is inelastically supplied to the world economy as a whole. With this assumption the elasticity of capital supply to the union area is also reduced, making it optimal for the union to co-ordinate on a higher level of capital taxation. When capital is inelastically supplied to the world as a whole, the distorting effects of higher capital taxes are smaller, and the welfare gain from a co-ordinated rise in capital income taxes is considerably higher than before. Yet the scope for regional co-ordination remains constrained by the possibility of capital flight to the rest of the world. Thus, under global co-ordination the optimal capital income tax rate would be 100%, because a harmonized tax on the fixed world supply of capital would be non-distortionary, but under regional co-ordination the union's optimal capital income tax rate is only 56%.

The third row of Table 24.6 shows the effect of lowering the labour supply elasticity from about 0.25 in the benchmark scenario to a value of 0.15 which has been used in many other simulation studies. While a more inelastic labour supply induces governments to set a higher tax rate on labour income, it has no noticeable effect on the gain from co-ordination of capital income taxes. In the fourth row of Table 24.6 I investigate the role of the elasticity of factor productivity with respect to infrastructure spending. A doubling of this elasticity from 0.1 to 0.2 (which is more in line with the estimates of Aschauer, 1989) induces governments to spend more on infrastructure at the expense of transfers, but hardly affects the choice of tax rates and the welfare gain from co-ordination.

In the benchmark equilibrium governments use the capital income tax as an indirect means of taxing pure rents. If no such rents exist, this motive for capital income taxation vanishes. Under tax competition the only remaining motive for taxing capital is a desire to reduce the international level of interest rates by lowering the world demand for capital, since a lower interest rate causes a welfare-improving rise in domestic activity which outweighs the direct income loss to domestic owners of capital. However, since the

Table 24.6 Effects of a regional minimum capital tax rate: sensitivity analysis

	Tax competition		Regional co-ordination between symmetric union countries		
	Labour income tax (%)	Capital income tax (%)	Labour income tax (%)	Capital income tax (%)	Welfare gain from co-ordination (% of GDP)
Benchmark scenario	49.8	33.8	48.2	46.5	0.19
Sensitivity to factor supply elasticities					
Zero interest elasticity of capital supply	49.8	34.4	47.1	56.2	0.85
Low wage elasticity of labour supply[a]	63.4	33.8	62.2	46.5	0.20
Higher productivity effect of infrastructure[b]	49.8	33.8	48.3	46.2	0.17
Sensitivity to profits and foreign ownership					
Zero pure profits share[c]	49.8	0.9	46.6	15.9	0.12
Zero foreign ownership share	49.8	23.0	47.9	41.0	0.35
Sensitivity to capital mobility					
Low capital mobility between union and rest of the world[d]	49.8	34.4	46.6	60.4	0.48
Perfect capital mobility between union and rest of the world[e]	49.8	33.5	49.0	39.9	0.08
Sensitivity to other factors					
Stronger preference for redistribution[f]	60.5	38.9	58.6	56.7	0.62
Lower weight of the union in the world economy[g]	49.8	33.8	48.3	45.6	0.17

Source: Simulations with the TAXCOM model.

Notes: The figures in the table refer to the symmetric countries forming a tax union. The rest of the world is assumed to undertake an optional policy response to co-ordination within the union.

[a] The wage elasticity of labour supply is 0.15.

[b] Elasticity of factor productivity with respect to infrastructure (μ_1) = 0.2.

[c] Wage share of GDP = 0.7; capital income share = 0.3.

[d] Elasticity of substitution between union and non-union assets = 1.

[e] Elasticity of substitution between union and non-union assets $\rightarrow \infty$.

[f] Social weight given to factor income = 60%.

[g] Union population = 40% of world population.

452   Peter Birch Sørensen

individual union country is small, its ability to influence the union interest rate is very limited. Hence its optimal capital income tax rate is close to zero in a tax competition equilibrium with no pure profits, as shown in the fifth row of Table 24.6. As a group the union countries have a larger impact on the interest rate, inducing them to raise the capital income tax rate under regional co-ordination. The tax increase is almost the same as in the benchmark scenario, but the welfare gain is smaller, since there is no longer any fixed factor to absorb part of the tax increase.

In the benchmark scenario the incentive for countries to lower their source-based capital taxes below the international optimum is counteracted by the incentive to impose tax on the foreign owners who are entitled to about one fourth of the profits of domestic firms. As shown in the sixth row of Table 24.6, if there is no foreign ownership of domestic firms, the level of capital income taxation will be much lower under tax competition. Since the absence of foreign ownership intensifies the fiscal competition induced by capital mobility, the welfare gain from regional tax co-ordination is significantly larger, compared to the benchmark simulation.

The elasticity of substitution between union and non-union assets determines the degree of capital mobility between the two regions. In the seventh row of Table 24.6 this substitution elasticity is lowered from 6 to 1.[8] With such a low degree of capital mobility vis-à-vis the rest of the world, a co-ordinated rise in capital income taxes within the union generates much less capital flight to the non-union area. Compared to the benchmark scenario, regional co-ordination therefore causes a much larger increase in capital taxation and welfare in the union. In contrast, when the substitution elasticity approaches infinity, implying perfect capital mobility between Europe and the US, the welfare gain from regional tax co-ordination is significantly reduced by a larger outflow of capital from Europe, as shown in the eighth row of Table 24.6.

According to the ninth row the social preference for redistribution is also an important parameter. When the social weight given to unevenly distributed factor income relative to evenly distributed transfer income is 60% rather than the 74% assumed in the benchmark case, the equity gain from a co-ordinated rise in capital income taxation is valued more highly, raising the welfare gain from co-ordination by a factor of more than three.

In the TAXCOM model the world economy includes only Europe and the US. In accordance with relative population size, Europe is assumed to comprise 56% of 'world' population. If the non-union area were assumed to include all the OECD countries outside Western Europe, the latter region would only represent about 40% of 'world' population. The bottom row of Table 24.6 shows that such a change in the relative size of the tax union would have little effect on the welfare gain from regional tax co-ordination.

Table 24.6 leaves the impression that, even under conditions which would seem to imply a strong case for tax co-ordination, the welfare gains from regional co-ordination within a subgroup of countries like the EU are likely to be less than 1% of GDP. Indeed, a gain of 0.5% of GDP may seem an optimistic estimate.[9] As we shall see below, tax co-ordination may nevertheless have significant welfare effects for some groups in society.

5.4 Distributional effects of tax co-ordination

Even if the median voter's gain from tax co-ordination may be small, making tax co-ordination politically difficult to implement unless the political process functions very smoothly, the gains for the poorer sections of society may be quite large. This is the message of Table 24.7 which divides the population of the representative union country in the TAXCOM model into five quintiles on the basis of their share of total initial wealth. The wealth shares have been proxied by the empirical income shares of the five quintiles of the Danish population, as recorded by Statistics Denmark, since 'wealth' in the TAX-COM model includes human as well as non-human wealth. Fiscal policy is assumed to be made by an individual from the third quintile which includes the median voter. As explained in Section 4.3, this individual acts as a domestically elected 'citizen candidate', implementing the policy which he prefers, given his place in the wealth distribution.

The welfare gains of each quintile are measured relative to the quintile's disposable income under tax competition. In the benchmark calibration of the TAXCOM model, regional tax co-ordination raising the level of redistributive capital taxes would raise the welfare of the poorest 20% of the population by more than 2.2% of disposable income, at the cost of a fairly modest loss to the richest 40% of the population.

Of course this is nothing but a stylized numerical example. But given that the wealth distribution of many countries (and particularly the distribution of capital income) is much more unequal than the one shown in Table 24.7, the example does suggest that tax competition could have a non-trivial effect

Table 24.7 Effects of regional tax co-ordination on the distribution of welfare in a union country

Quintile	Share of total wealth (%)[a]	Welfare gain from introducing a regional minimum capital tax rate[b]
1	2	2.22
2	7	1.15
3	14	0.37
4	24	− 0.20
5	53	− 0.85

Source: Simulations with the TAXCOM model.
Notes: Fiscal policies are decided by a policy maker representing the 3rd quintile (the median voter), implying that the social weight given to factor income relative to transfer income is equal to $14/20 = 0.7$ within the tax union. The other parameter values are equal to those stated in columns 4 and 5 in Table 24.3.
[a] Estimated on the basis of the distribution of factor incomes in Denmark (data provided by Statistics Denmark).
[b] Welfare gain for residents in the representative union country. The welfare gain is measured in percent of the quintile's disposable income under tax competition.

454 Peter Birch Sørensen

on income distribution and that the poor could have a strong interest in tax co-ordination. The simulations also help to explain why countries have internal political disagreements over tax co-ordination.

5.5 Limitations and caveats

I have already stressed that the simulations presented above should be seen only as 'theory with numbers', giving at best a rough idea of the order of magnitude of the gains from international tax co-ordination. Let me end this paper by discussing some limitations of my analysis.

5.5.1. Endogenous growth

The TAXCOM model describes a long-run equilibrium, so the simulated effects of tax co-ordination on economic activity and welfare should be interpreted as changes in the equilibrium *levels* of these variables in the context of exogenous steady-state growth. If long-run growth is endogenous, a co-ordinated rise in capital income tax rates may permanently depress the growth rate, potentially with large negative implications for welfare. However, the fact that taxes have manifestly trended upwards whereas growth rates do not trend anywhere suggests that taxes do not matter much for long-run growth, as argued by Jones (1995). Analysing alternative models of endogenous growth, Stokey and Rebelo (1995) also find that taxes have little effect on long-run growth rates for realistic parameter values, confirming the claim by Lucas (1990) and Mendoza *et al.* (1997) that capital taxation does not matter significantly for long-run growth. Surveying the literature on taxation and economic growth, Engen and Skinner (1999) and Myles (2000) likewise point out that empirical studies have not been able to identify strong permanent growth effects of capital income taxation. These studies suggest that the implicit assumption of exogenous growth is not a serious limitation of the present paper.

5.5.2. Imperfect competition

In line with the bulk of the tax competition literature, the TAXCOM model assumes perfect competition in all markets. In a model with imperfect competition, Janeba (1998) has shown that tax competition may play an efficiency-enhancing role when borders are opened to capital mobility. In the absence of capital mobility imperfect competition will induce national governments to subsidize their own firms to enable them to compete more aggressively in the world market, thereby increasing domestic profits at the expense of the profits of foreign firms. When free capital mobility is allowed, Janeba finds that competition among governments will drive the negative tax rates upwards to zero. No country will offer a tax rate below zero, since this would attract foreign firms and imply a transfer of domestic revenue to foreigners. Thus tax competition combined with capital mobility will tend to eliminate globally inefficient subsidies under imperfect competition. This suggests that the usual assumption of perfect competition may bias the analysis in favour of tax co-ordination. Yet, in a European context where the EU Commission imposes limitations on state aids to industry (see Besley and Seabright, 1999), the beneficial effect of tax competition pointed out by Janeba is likely to be minor.

5.5.3. Time inconsistency

This paper implicitly assumes that governments can credibly commit not to raise taxes on capital, once it has been accumulated. As emphasized by Kehoe (1989), such credibility may be difficult to achieve, since a rise in the tax rate on pre-exisiting capital will work like a non-distortionary tax on a fixed factor, giving governments a strong *ex post* incentive to exploit this source of revenue. Fearing that governments will succumb to this temptation, the private sector may end up saving too little. By offering an escape route from domestic taxation, capital mobility and international tax competition may then provide a healthy incentive for private saving in a setting where capital accumulation is hampered by government credibility problems. However, rather than resorting to tax competition, it may be possible to solve this time consistency problem by electing a 'conservative' (wealthy) policy maker to neutralize the government's incentive to overtax capital, as suggested by Persson and Tabellini (1999, pp. 49–51).

5.5.4. Political distortions

As I explained in Section 4.4, the TAXCOM model assumes a well-functioning fiscal policy process respecting individual preferences. In practice, political distortions and rent-seeking may imply a tendency for governments to spend too much. Proponents of tax co-ordination argue that such problems should be addressed through institutional reforms aimed directly at correcting the relevant distortions in political decision-making. In this view tax competition is an odd second-best means of reducing the scope for rent-seeking, since fiscal competition generates its own (economic) distortions. On the other hand, if the required institutional reforms are politically infeasible, the case for co-ordinated rises in the level of capital income taxation is clearly weakened.

5.5.5. Defining and harmonizing the tax base

Inspired by the current tax policy debate in the EU, a large part of this paper has studied the effects of introducing a binding minimum capital income tax rate levied at source. I have assumed the possibility of establishing a floor for the *effective* tax rate on capital income. As pointed out by the Ruding Committee (1992) and recently emphasized by Fuest and Huber (1999), this would require constraints on the ability of governments to define their capital income tax bases as well as constraints on their choice of statutory capital income tax rates. If only statutory rates are constrained, competing governments could still reduce effective tax rates on capital by offering generous depreciation allowances, by exempting certain types of income or activities from tax, or by introducing direct subsidies to capital. Investment subsidies could also take the form of targeted infrastructure spending. Hence it may be necessary to supplement a regime of tax co-ordination by tighter EU controls on state aids to industry. Another assumption of this paper is that income at source is a well-defined concept. In practice the source of income is becoming ever more difficult to determine as the scope for income-shifting across countries increases due to growing intra-firm trade within multinational conglomerates, financial innovations, and the growing importance of electronic commerce and hard-to-value intangible assets. These developments create an increasing need for governments to co-ordinate their transfer-pricing rules and other rules delineating national tax bases, and perhaps a need to resort to so-called 'formula apportionment' in order to allocate the profits tax base of multinationals across national tax jurisdictions, as discussed by Mintz (1998).

5.5.6. Residence taxes versus source taxes

Like most of the literature, I have assumed that residence countries cannot enforce taxes on foreign-source capital income in the absence of international co-operation. This view may be too pessimistic, since most of foreign portfolio investment is channelled through financial intermediaries which may be easier to monitor than private households. On the other hand, foreign direct investment is subject to the corporate income tax which is mainly based on the source principle, as explained in more detail in Sørensen (1993). Hence, it might be relevant to study tax co-ordination within a framework where portfolio investment is subject to residence-based taxation whereas foreign direct investment is taxed according to the source principle. Ideally such an analysis should account for the fact that portfolio investment is typically more mobile than direct investment. Developing such a framework would be a complicated but interesting challenge for future research.

6 SUMMARY AND CONCLUSIONS

In an integrated world economy the attempts of governments to attract mobile capital may drive capital income tax rates to inefficiently low levels, because capital mobility raises the elasticity of capital supply to the individual country far above the elasticity of capital supply to the world as a whole. On the other hand foreign ownership of domestic firms may tempt national governments to raise corporate tax rates in order to export part of the domestic tax burden to foreigners. This paper has tried to explain and to quantify the fiscal externalities from tax competition and the gains from international co-ordination of capital income taxation.

The potential for tax competition arises because the governments of residence countries have difficulties enforcing taxes on the foreign-source investment income of their citizens. In practice domestic capital income taxes thus tend to fall only on domestic-source income. In an era when capital markets are liberalized, the theory of tax competition suggests that we should observe a fall in the statutory tax rates on interest income, as governments try to avoid an export of highly mobile portfolio investment to foreign tax havens. Theory also suggests that governments would react to growing volumes of foreign direct investment by lowering their statutory corporate income tax rates, to make themselves less vulnerable to the transfer-pricing practices of multinationals. In Section 3 we saw that statutory corporate and personal capital income tax rates have indeed fallen substantially in the OECD area from the mid 1980s to the end of the 1990s, a period in which capital mobility increased. At the same time the *effective* capital income tax rates appear to have been roughly constant, due to a broadening of the tax base, but rising effective tax rates on labour income indicate that governments have in fact tried to shift the tax burden towards the more immobile factor of production.

Against this background I presented an applied general equilibrium model (TAXCOM) describing the allocation and distribution effects of tax competition and tax co-ordination within a unified framework. Synthesizing several recent contributions to the tax competition literature, the TAXCOM model incorporates internationally mobile capital combined with immobile labour and a local fixed factor to produce an internationally traded good; endogenous labour supply and an endogenous global supply of capital; international cross-ownership of firms and the existence of pure profits accruing partly to foreigners; productive government spending on infrastructure as well as spending on public consumption goods; an unequal distribution of human and non-human wealth providing a motive for redistributive taxation; and a social welfare function which may be given a political economy interpretation as the indirect utility function of the median voter. The model is intended to serve as 'theory with numbers', offering a rough estimate of the likely magnitude and distribution of the gains from tax co-ordination.

The TAXCOM model is designed to highlight the differences between regional tax co-ordination within Western Europe and global co-ordination involving all countries in the world. Allowing for deeper economic integration within the EU, the model assumes perfect capital mobility within Western Europe, whereas capital mobility between Europe and the rest of the world is taken to be imperfect. The model is calibrated so as to reproduce the observed level and pattern of taxation in Western Europe and the US as an equilibrium with tax competition.

The analysis focused on the effects of an international agreement on a binding minimum tax on capital income, levied at source and chosen so as to maximize the population-weighted average of national welfare levels. When the agreement only involves the European countries, the welfare gain from co-ordination is estimated to be roughly 0.2% of GDP for the average European country in the benchmark scenario. Since co-ordination raises the level of capital taxation, there is a slight fall in European economic activity, but social welfare nevertheless increases due to an improvement in the distribution of income. The welfare gain is limited by the fact that countries use infrastructure spending and labour taxes more aggressively to attract mobile capital when capital income tax competition is neutralized through co-ordination. The gain for Europe is further limited by the fact that higher European capital taxes drive capital out of Europe, thus benefiting the rest of the world.

If co-ordination involves the US as well as Europe, the TAXCOM model suggests that the welfare gain for Europe increases to more than 0.3% of GDP, since the rise in the US capital tax will limit the outflow of capital from Europe. However, the analysis also suggests that the US would not be motivated to engage in tax co-ordination, since the harmonized level of capital income taxation would be too high from the American perspective, given that the US appears to have a lower social preference for redistribution than Europe.

A sensitivity analysis reveals that the welfare gain from regional tax co-ordination within the EU could be larger than the 0.2% of GDP reported in the benchmark scenario, especially if the interest elasticity of capital supply is very low, as is often assumed. However, even under assumptions most favourable to tax co-ordination, the gains from regional co-ordination are likely to remain below 1% of GDP, according to the TAXCOM model. The model also suggests that the gains from tax co-ordination would be unevenly distributed across European countries, due to asymmetries in economic structures and preferences. For example, the analysis indicated that the Nordic countries would gain disproportionately from tax co-ordination, assuming that the high level of taxation in the Nordic region reflects a relatively strong social preference for redistribution.

Finally, the TAXCOM model indicates that even if the median voter's gain from regional tax co-ordination may be modest, making tax co-ordination politically difficult to implement, the poorer sections of society deriving a large part of their incomes from public transfers are likely to gain significantly. The flipside of this coin is that unfettered tax competition may have a strong negative impact on income distribution.

APPENDIX: KEY SPECIFICATIONS IN THE TAXCOM MODEL

The TAXCOM model described in Section 4.3 of the main text is documented in detail in Sørensen (2000). This appendix presents the key specifications in the model. The equations below refer to an individual (potential) union country j, but the country subscript j is omitted to simplify notation when no misunderstanding is possible.

Firms

In all countries the representative firm produces the same composite good Y by means of capital K, effective labour input L, and a fixed factor. The supply of the fixed factor to each country is proportional to the country's exogenous population N, with a proportionality factor b. This ensures that large countries have no inherent productivity advantage over small countries, or vice versa. Adopting a Cobb–Douglas production function with multifactor productivity A and constant returns to scale, we thus have

$$Y = AK^{\beta}L^{a}(bN)^{1-a-\beta}, \qquad 0 < a < 1, \quad 0 < \beta < 1, \quad 0 < a + \beta < 1 \qquad (A1)$$

Worker i is endowed with a fraction θ_i of the total stock of human wealth which is normalized to equal total population size N. The working hours of worker i – the rate at which his human capital is utilized – are h_i. Hence the effective labour input supplied by worker i is $\theta_i N h_i$, and aggregate effective labour input is

$$L = \sum_{i=1}^{N} \theta_i N h_i, \quad 0 < \theta_i < 1 \quad \text{for all } i, \qquad \sum_{i=1}^{N} \theta_i = 1 \qquad (A2)$$

The competitive firm chooses the inputs of capital and all of the N types of labour to maximize its profits. With the output price normalized at unity, this yields the following first-order conditions, where τ is the capital income tax rate, ρ_u is the after-tax interest rate, $k \equiv K/N$ is capital intensity, $l \equiv L/N$ is average effective labour input per worker, $w \equiv (1/L)\sum_i w_i h_i$ is the average return to human capital, and $\tilde{A} \equiv Ab^{1-a-\beta}$ is adjusted multifactor productivity:

Demand for capital: $\quad \beta\tilde{A}k^{\beta-1}l^{a} = \dfrac{\rho_u}{1-\tau} \qquad\qquad$ (A3)

Demand for labour: $\quad a\tilde{A}k^{\beta}l^{a-1} = w \qquad\qquad$ (A4)

Real wage of worker i: $\quad w_i = \theta_i N w \qquad i = 1, 2, \ldots, N \qquad$ (A5)

Consumers

The utility of worker/consumer i is given by the additive utility function

$$U_i = C_i - \theta_i N \cdot \frac{h_i^{1+\varepsilon}}{1+\varepsilon} + \frac{\gamma_2}{\gamma_1} G^{\gamma_1} \qquad (A6)$$

$$\varepsilon > 0, \quad 0 < \gamma_1 < 1, \quad \gamma_2 > 0$$

where C_i is his private consumption and G is public consumption per capita. The specification of the consumer's disutility from work assumes that his opportunity cost of time spent in the labour market various varies positively with his productivity, proxied by his stock of human capital $\theta_i N$. As we shall see below, this implies a negative wealth effect on individual labour supply.

At the beginning of the period, the economy is endowed with a total stock of *non-human* wealth normalized to equal its population N. The fraction of aggregate non-human wealth owned by consumer i is θ_i (equal for simplicity to his share of human wealth). The consumer may consume his non-human wealth directly, or he may invest it in the capital market at a transaction cost c_i, thereby building up a capital stock k_i^s earning an average after-tax return ρ. In addition to capital income, labour income and a government transfer T, the consumer receives profit income from domestic and foreign firms. An exogenous fraction δ of domestic firms is owned by foreigners. At the same time consumers in domestic country j receive a fraction $s_j \delta_z/(1 - s_z)$ of the profits generated in foreign country z, where s_v $(v = j, z)$ is country v's share of total world population so that $1 - s_z$ is the fraction of world population residing outside country z. The profits paid out from each country are thus allocated across all the other countries in proportion to their population shares. Consumer i receives a fraction θ_i of all profit incomes earned by domestic residents, whether from domestic or from foreign sources. Under pure tax competition governments cannot tax capital income and profits from foreign sources, but they tax all domestic-source capital and profit income at the domestic rate τ_v $(v = j, z)$. With these assumptions one can show that consumer i in country j will be subject to the budget constraint

$$C_i = w_i h_i (1 - t) + \rho k_i^s + \theta_i N - c_i + T + \theta_i N (1 - \delta)(1 - \tau) \pi + \theta_i N$$

$$\sum_{z = 1, z \neq j}^{m} \left(\frac{s_z \delta_z}{1 - s_z} \right) (1 - \tau_z) \pi_z \qquad (A7)$$

where t is the labour income tax rate, π and π_z are pre-tax profits *per capita* in the domestic country j and in foreign country z, respectively, and m is the total number of countries in the world.

When the consumer transforms (part of) his initial non-human wealth $\theta_i N$ into business capital k_i^s, his transaction costs c_i relative to his stock of wealth increase more than proportionally with his investment rate $k_i^s/\theta_i N$:

$$\frac{c_i}{\theta_i N} = \frac{1}{1 + \sigma} \left(\frac{k_i^s}{\theta_i N} \right)^{1 + \sigma}, \qquad \sigma > 0 \qquad (A8)$$

The consumer chooses h_i and k_i^s to maximize utility (A6) subject to the constraints (A7) and (A8). The first-order conditions for the solution to this problem imply that

$$h_i = \left[\frac{w_i (1 - t)}{\theta_i N} \right]^{1/\varepsilon} = [w(1 - t)]^{1/\varepsilon} \qquad (A9)$$

$$k_i^s = \rho^{1/\sigma} \cdot \theta_i N \qquad (A10)$$

where the last equality in (A9) follows from (A5). Note that $1/\varepsilon$ is the net wage elasticity of labour supply, while $1/\sigma$ may be interpreted as the net interest elasticity of savings.

The total capital stock supplied by consumer i in the representative union country is a CES-aggregate of capital supplied to the union area, k_i^{su}, and capital supplied to the non-union area, k_i^{sn}, where ζ is the finite elasticity of substitution between the two asset types:

$$k_i^s = [\Psi^{-1/\zeta}(k_i^{su})^{(\zeta+1)/\zeta} + (1 - \Psi^{-1/\zeta}(k_i^{sn})^{(\zeta+1)/\zeta}]^{\zeta/(\zeta+1)}, \quad \zeta > 0,$$
$$0 < \Psi < 1 \qquad \text{(A11)}$$

The consumer's total income from capital is $\rho k_i^s = \rho_u k_i^{su} + \rho_n k_i^{sn}$, where ρ_u is the after-tax interest rate prevailing within the union (which is common to all union countries because perfect capital mobility within the union), and ρ_n is the after-tax interest rate in the non-union area, and where ρ is the 'average' net rate of return on capital. Having optimized his aggregate capital stock k_i^s in accordance with (A10), the consumer allocates this stock between union and non-union locations so as to maximize his total net income from capital $\rho_u k_i^{su} + \rho_n k_i^{sn}$, subject to (A11). The first-order conditions for the solution to this problem imply that

$$\rho = [\Psi\rho_u^{\zeta+1} + (1 - \Psi)\rho_n^{\zeta+1}]^{1/(\zeta+1)} \qquad \text{(A12)}$$

$$k_i^{su} = \left(\frac{\rho_u}{\rho}\right)^\zeta \Psi k_i^s, \quad k_i^{sn} = \left(\frac{\rho_n}{\rho}\right)^\zeta (1 - \Psi)k_i^s \qquad \text{(A13)}$$

The portfolio allocation of non-union residents is described by similar equations.

Government

Governments spend their tax revenues on public consumption G, on 'infrastructure' Q and on a redistributive transfer paid out in an identical amount T to all citizens. Under pure tax competition, taxes are levied according to the source principle, and the government in a union country is subject to the budget constraint

$$T + G + Q = twh + \tau\left(\frac{\rho_u}{1-\tau}\right)k + \tau\pi \qquad \text{(A14)}$$

where all variables are measured on a per capita basis. Note from (A9) that all workers will supply the same number of work hours $h_i = h = [w(1-t)]^{1/\varepsilon}$, so h is the average working time per worker. The amount of productive government spending per capita (Q) does not yield direct utility, but it increases factor productivity, albeit at a diminishing rate:

$$\tilde{A} = \mu_2 Q^{\mu 1}, \quad \mu_2 > 0, \quad 0 < \mu_1 < 1 \qquad \text{(A15)}$$

Welfare and government policy

Inserting (A7) through (A10) into (A6), we may write the indirect utility of consumer i in country j as

$$U_i = T + \frac{\gamma_2}{\gamma_1} G^{\gamma_1}$$

$$+ \theta_i N \left\{ \frac{\varepsilon h^{1+\varepsilon}}{1+\varepsilon} + 1 + \frac{\varphi \rho \frac{1+\varphi}{\varphi}}{1+\varphi} + (1-\delta)(1-\tau)\pi \right.$$

$$\left. + \sum_{z=1,\,z\neq j}^{m} \left(\frac{s_z \delta_z}{1\; s_z} \right)(1-\tau_z)\pi_z \right\} \qquad \text{(A16)}$$

The government in each country is concerned about the *average* level of individual welfare $\overline{U}$ and about the *dispersion* of individual utilities around this mean, as reflected in the following social welfare function,

$$SW = \overline{U} - a\sqrt{\frac{1}{N}\left[\sum_{i=1}^{N}(U_i - \overline{U})^2\right]}, \; a \geq 0 \qquad \text{(A17)}$$

where the square root measures the degree of inequality by the standard deviation of individual utilities, and where the parameter a indicates the degree of government aversion to inequality. Since $\overline{U} \equiv 1/N\Sigma_i U_i$ and $\Sigma_i \theta_i = 1$, it follows from (A16) and (A17) that

$$SW = T + \frac{\gamma_2}{\gamma_1} G^{\gamma_1}$$

$$+ (1-a\sigma)\left[\frac{\varepsilon h^{1+\varepsilon}}{1+\varepsilon} + 1 + \frac{\varphi \rho \frac{1+\varphi}{\varphi}}{1+\varphi} + (1-\delta)(1-\tau)\pi + \sum_{z\neq j}\left(\frac{s_z \delta_z}{1-s_z}\right) \right.$$

$$\left. (1-\tau_z)\pi_z \right] \qquad \text{(A18)}$$

$$\sigma \equiv \sqrt{\frac{1}{N}\sum_i (\theta_i N - 1)^2}$$

where σ is the standard deviation of individual wealth levels around the mean value of unity, reflecting the degree of inequality of the initial distribution of wealth. I assume that $a\sigma < 1$ to ensure that an increase in private factor income will always increase social welfare (for given levels of T and G).

From (A16) and (A18) we see that social welfare coincides with the individual welfare of the consumer with an initial wealth endowment $\theta_i N = 1-a\sigma$. Hence maximization of (A18) for different values of $a\sigma$ corresponds to a situation where an elected citizen with endowment $\theta_i N$ is allowed to determine fiscal policy.

For given government policy instruments, a general equilibrium is attained when all private agents optimize their objective functions and national labour markets as well as the union and the non-union capital markets are clearing. Under tax competition the government (the median voter) chooses the policy instruments t, τ, G and Q to maximize the objective function (A18), subject to (A14), (A15) and all the constraints implied by private sector behaviour. If governments choose a common minimum capital income tax rate, the private and government budget constraints are modified in a straightforward manner, and the common capital income tax rate is found by maximizing a population-weighted sum of the social welfare functions of the individual cooperating countries. Sørensen (2000) derives the optimal policy rules under the different policy regimes described in this paper.

NOTES

1 There is ample evidence that tax policy affects the location of economic activity. See Hines (1999) for a survey of the empirical literature.
2 See Devereux (1996) and Wilson (1999) for recent surveys of the theory of tax competition.
3 Sørensen (1993) offers a more detailed account of the practical difficulties of implementing consistent residence-based taxation of capital income.
4 When residence countries offer a credit for taxes paid to the foreign-source country, source countries can levy taxes without deterring inward foreign investment and will therefore wish to impose source taxes up to the maximum limit on the residence country's tax credit (see Sørensen, 1990; Gordon, 1992). Gordon suggests that large residence countries offer foreign tax credits to encourage source taxation abroad so that residence countries can maintain positive levels of tax on *domestic* investment without provoking a capital flight.
5 Labour taxes may also give rise to spillovers. If the domestic government lowers its labour income tax rate, domestic labour supply may increase, causing a rise in the marginal productivity of domestic investment which will attract capital from abroad. Since national tax policies do not internalize this spillover, it is tempting to conclude that there is a need for an internationally co-ordinated rise in labour tax rates. However, in the TAXCOM model (discussed in Section 4.3) the incentive for governments to keep the labour tax rate too low is held in check by the fact that the capital income tax rate is *also* too low under tax competition. A low capital income tax wedge implies a low efficiency cost of a drop in investment. Given that a higher labour tax discourages domestic investment, the lower efficiency cost of reduced investment under tax competition induces governments to keep labour taxes at an 'appropriate' level even though they neglect the positive international spillover effect of a higher labour tax.
6 In game-theoretic terms, the co-ordinating world tax authority plays the role of a Stackelberg leader, with national governments acting as followers in the fiscal policy game.
7 The TAXCOM specifications of tastes and technology imply that each country's demand for capital is isoelastic. Hence, if K is the capital stock and r is the real interest rate, the capital demand curve is convex to the origin in (K,r)-space. When the interest rate falls, the welfare-improving rise in domestic investment will therefore be larger the lower the initial level of the interest rate.
8 For comparison, the benchmark scenario in the simulation study by Thalman *et al.* (1996) assumed a substitution elasticity between US and European assets equal to 4.

9 A more systematic sensitivity analysis is presented in a set of tables available at the internet address http://www.econ.ku.dk/pbs/default.htm (see under 'Recent working papers').

REFERENCES

Andersson, K. (1999). 'Skatternes Betydelse för den Finansielle Sektorns Konkurrenskraft', Report to the Swedish Committee on Financial Markets (Finansmarknadsutredningen).

Aschauer, D. (1989). 'Is public expenditure productive?', *Journal of Monetary Economics*, vol. 23, no. 2, pp. 177–200.

Bacchetta, Ph. and M.P. Espinosa (2000). 'Exchange-of-information clauses in international tax treaties', *International Tax and Public Finance*, vol. 7, no. 3, pp. 275–94.

Besley, T. and S. Coate (1997). 'An economic model of representative democracy', *Quarterly Journal of Economics*, vol. 99, no. 2, pp. 207–40.

Besley, T. and P. Seabright (1999). 'The effects and policy implications of state aids to industry: an economic analysis', *Economic Policy*, **28**.

Bewley, T.F. (1981). 'A critique of Tiebout's theory of local public expenditures', *Econometrica*, vol. 49, no. 3, pp. 713–40.

Bettendorf, L.J.H. and B.J. Heijdra (1999). 'International co-ordination of capital income taxes and the degree of asset substitution', mimeo, Erasmus University and University of Groningen.

Brennan, G. and J.M. Buchanan (1980). *The Power to Tax: Analytical Foundations of a Fiscal Constitution*, New York: Cambridge University Press.

Bucovetsky, S. (1991). 'Asymmetric tax competition', *Journal of Urban Economics*, vol. 30, no. 2, pp. 167–81.

Chennells, L. and R. Griffith (1997). *Taxing Profits in a Changing World*, London: Institute for Fiscal Studies.

Daveri, F. and G. Tabellini (2000). 'Unemployment, growth and taxation in industrial countries', *Economic Policy*, no. 30 (April), pp. 97–104.

Depata, J. and G. Myers (1994). 'Strategic capital tax competition: a pecuniary externality and a corrective device', *Journal of Urban Economics*.

Devereux, M.P. (1996). 'Tax competition and the impact on capital flows', in H. Siebert (ed.), *Locational Competition in the World Economy*, Tubingen: J.C.B. Mohr.

Devereux, M.P. and R. Griffith (1998). 'Taxes and the location of production: evidence from a panel of US multinationals', *Journal of Public Economics*, vol. 68, no. 3, pp. 335–67.

Devereux, M.P. and M. Pearson (1989). *Corporate Tax Harmonisation and Economic Efficiency*, IFS Report 35, London: Institute for Fiscal Studies.

Edwards, J. and M. Keen (1996). 'Tax competition and the Leviathan', *European Economic Review*, vol. 40, no. 1, pp. 113–34.

Engen, E. and J. Skinner (1999). 'Taxation and economic growth', in J. Slemrod (ed.), *Tax Policy in the Real World*, Cambridge: Cambridge University Press.

Fuest, C. and B. Huber (1999). 'Can tax co-ordination work?', *Finanzarchiv*, 56 (3/4), 443–58.

Giovannini, A. (1989). 'National tax systems versus the European capital market', *Economic Policy*, no. 9 (October), pp. 345–86.

Gordon, R.H. (1986). 'Taxation of investment and saving in a world economy', *American Economic Review*, vol. 76, no. 5, pp. 1086–1102.

Gordon, R.H. (1992). 'Can capital income taxes survive in open economies?', *Journal of Finance*, vol. 47, no. 3, pp. 1159–80.

Haufler, A. and G. Schjelderup (1999a). 'Corporate tax systems and cross-country profit shifting', *Oxford Economic Papers*, 52 (2), 306–25.

Haufler, A. and G. Schjelderup (1999b). 'Corporate taxation, profit shifting, and the efficiency of public input provision', *Finanzarchiv*, 56 (3/4), 481–99.

Hines, J.R. (1999). 'Lessons from behavioral responses to international taxation', *National Tax Journal*.

Huizinga, H. and S.B. Nielsen (1997). 'Capital income and profit taxation with foreign ownership of firms', *Journal of International Economics*, vol. 42, no. 1–2, pp. 149–66.

Janeba, E. (1998). 'Tax competition in imperfectly competitive markets', *Journal of International Economics*, vol. 44, no. 1, pp. 135–53.

Jones, C.I. (1995). 'Time series tests of endogenous growth models', *Quarterly Journal of Economics*.

Keen, M. and M. Marchand (1997). 'Fiscal competition and the pattern of public spending', *Journal of Public Economics*, vol. 66, no. 1, pp. 33–53.

Keen, M. and S. Smith (1996). 'The future of value added tax in the European Union', *Economic Policy*, no. 23 (October), pp. 373–420.

Kehoe, P. (1989). 'Policy cooperation among benevolent governments may be undesirable', *Review of Economic Studies*, vol. 56, pp. 289–96.

Konrad, K.A. and G. Schjelderup (1999). 'Fortress building in global tax competition', *Journal of Urban Economics*, vol. 46, no. 1, pp. 156–67.

Lockwood, B. (1999). 'Tax competition and coordination under origin and destination principles: a synthesis', mimeo, Department of Economics, University of Warwick.

Lucas, R.E., Jr (1990). 'Supply-side economics: an analytical review', *Oxford Economic Papers*, vol. 42, no. 2, pp. 293–316.

Mendoza, E.G., A. Razin, and L.L. Tesar (1994). 'Effective tax rates in macroeconomics: cross-country estimates of tax rates on factor incomes and consumption', *Journal of Monetary Economics*, vol. 34, no. 3, pp. 297–324.

Mendoza, E.G., G.M. Milesi-Ferretti and P. Asea (1997). 'On the ineffectiveness of tax policy in altering long-run growth: Harberger's superneutrality conjecture', *Journal of Public Economics*, vol. 66, no. 1, pp. 99–126.

Mintz, J.M. (1994). 'Is there a future for capital income taxation?', *Canadian Tax Journal*.

Mintz, J.M. (1998). 'The role of allocation in a globalized corporate income tax', IMF Working Paper 98/134.

Musgrave, P.B. (1969). *United States Taxation of Foreign Investment Income: Issues and Arguments*, Cambridge, MA: Harvard Law School.

Musgrave, R.A. (1969). *Fiscal Systems*, New Haven and London: Yale University Press.

Myles, G.D. (2000). 'Taxation and economic growth', *Fiscal Studies*, vol. 21, no. 1, pp. 141–68.

Oates, W.E. (1972). *Fiscal Federalism*, New York: Harcourt Brace Jovanovich.

OECD (1977). *Model Double Taxation Convention on Income and Capital*, Paris: Report of the OECD Committee on Fiscal Affairs.

Osborne, M.J. and A. Slivinsky (1996). 'A model of political competition with citizen-candidates', *Quarterly Journal of Economics*, vol. 61, no. 1, pp. 65–96.

Persson, T. and G. Tabellini (1992). 'The politics of 1992: fiscal policy and European integration', *Review of Economic Studies*, vol. 59, no. 4, pp. 689–702.

Persson, T. and G. Tabellini (1999). 'Political economics and public finance', NBER Working Paper No. 7097, Cambridge, MA: National Bureau of Economic Research.

Portes, R. and H. Rey (2000). 'The determinants of cross-border equity flows: the geography of information', working paper.

Razin, A. and E. Sadka (1991). 'International tax competition and gains from tax harmonization', *Economics Letters*, vol. 37, no. 1, pp. 69–76.

Richter, W.F. (1994). 'The efficient allocation of local public goods in Tiebout's tradition', *Regional Science and Urban Economics*, vol. 24, no. 3, pp. 323–40.

Richter, W.F. and D. Wellisch (1996). 'The provision of local public goods and factors in the presence of firm and household mobility', *Journal of Public Economics*, vol. 60, no. 1, pp. 73–94.

Ruding Committee (1992). *Report of the Committee of Independent Experts on Company Taxation*, European Commission, Brussels.

Sinn, H.-W. (1987). *Capital Income Taxation and Resource Allocation*, Amsterdam: North Holland.

Sinn, H.-W. (1997). 'The selection principle and market failure in systems competition', *Journal of Public Economics*, vol. 66, no. 2, pp. 247–74.

Sørensen, P.B. (1990). 'Optimal capital taxation in a small capital-importing economy', in V. Tanzi (ed.), *Public Finance, Trade and Development*, Proceedings of the 44th Congress of the International Institute of Public Finance, Wayne State University Press.

Sørensen, P.B. (1993). 'Co-ordination of capital income taxation in the Economic and Monetary Union: what needs to be done?', in F. Giavazzi and F. Torres (eds), *Adjustment and Growth in the European Monetary Union*, CEPR and Cambridge University Press.

Sørensen, P.B. (2000). 'TAXCOM – a model of tax competition and tax coordination', technical working paper, Economic Policy Research Unit, University of Copenhagen.

Stokey, N.L. and S. Rebelo (1995). 'Growth effects of flat-rate taxes', *Journal of Political Economy*, vol. 103, no. 3, pp. 519–50.

Summers, L.H. (1981). 'Taxation and capital accumulation in a life cycle growth model', *American Economic Review*, vol. 71, no. 4, pp. 533–44.

Thalmann, P., L.H. Goulder and F. Delorme (1996). 'Assessing the international spillover effects of capital income taxation', *International Tax and Public Finance*, vol. 3, no. 4, pp. 449–78.

Tiebout, C.M. (1956). 'A pure theory of local expenditures', *Journal of Political Economy*.

Volkerink, B. and J. de Haan (1999). 'Tax ratios: a critical survey', working paper, Faculty of Economics, University of Groningen.

Wildasin, D.E. (1989). 'Interjurisdictional capital mobility: fiscal externalities and a corrective subsidy', *Journal of Urban Economics*, vol. 25, no. 2, pp. 193–212.

Wilson, J.D. (1986). 'A theory of interregional tax competition', *Journal of Urban Economics*.

Wilson, J.D. (1999). 'Theories of tax competition', *National Tax Journal*, vol. 52, no. 2, pp. 269–304.

Zodrow, G.R. and P. Mieszkowski (1986). 'Piegou, Tiebout, property taxation and the underprovision of local public goods', *Journal of Urban Economics*.

Questions

1 'Globalisation has provided companies and individual investors with new opportunities to avoid taxes and induced governments to divert the flows of mobile capital.' Do you agree?

2 'The investors in as well as governments and residents of harmful preferential tax regimes are free-riders.' Discuss.

3 'Tax competition is a disciplining device that ties the hands of governments that would be inclined to tax capital excessively once the latter has been invested.' Discuss.

4 'Capital income taxes will vanish altogether in small open economies faced with perfect capital mobility.' Discuss.

5 'The case for or against tax policy co-ordination is an empirical rather than theoretical issue. It can be decided only on the basis of quantitative analysis.' Discuss in the light of international taxation externalities.

6 'The multinational corporations' location decisions are not affected by taxation when the decision involves a choice between two large countries, but the opposite holds when the countries are small.' Discuss.

7 'The case for intra-EU tax policy co-ordination is strengthened by the deepening of the intra-EU financial integration and the size of the EU member states.' Discuss.

8 'Tax policy co-ordination yields unimpressive results in terms of welfare gains. Therefore, the case for tax policy co-ordination rests on equity rather than efficiency considerations.' Do you agree?

9 'Tax policy co-ordination is made difficult if not impossible by the high degree of capital ownership concentration.' Discuss.

Further reading and references

FURTHER READING

The recent debate on tax policy co-ordination has been closely related to globalisation, which makes taxing capital income highly difficult. On this, see Chennells and Griffith (1997); Tanzi (1995); OECD (1991); and Ruding Committee (1992). On tax reforms in developed countries, see OECD (1990). For an assessment of tax reforms, see Frenkel and Razin (1989). For a detailed study of externalities associated with tax competition, see Thalman et al. (1996). For a review of the literature on international tax competition, see Janeba (1997), ch. 1. The classical paper on strategic interaction in capital income taxation is Hamada (1966). On strategic interaction between European taxation policies, see Persson and Tabellini (1992).

REFERENCES

Chennells, L. and R. Griffith (1997) *Taxing Profits in a Changing World*, London: Institute for Fiscal Studies.
Frenkel, J.A. and A. Razin (1989) 'International effects of tax reforms', *Economic Journal* 99, 38–58.
Hamada, K. (1966) 'Strategic aspects of taxation on foreign investment income', *Quarterly Journal of Economics* 80, 361–75.
Janeba, E. (1997) *International Tax Competition*, Tübingen: Mohr Siebeck.
OECD (1990) *Taxation and International Capital Flows: A Symposium of OECD and Non-OECD Countries*, Paris: OECD.
OECD (1991) *Taxing Profits in a Global Economy: Domestic and International Issues*, Paris: OECD.
Persson, T. and G. Tabellini (1992) 'The politics of 1992: fiscal policy and European integration', *Review of Economic Studies* 59, 689–701.
Ruding Committee (1992) *Report of the Committee of Independent Experts on Company Taxation*, Brussels: European Commission.
Tanzi, V. (1995) *Taxation in an Integrated World*, Washington, DC: The Brookings Institution.
Thalman, P., L.H. Goulder and P. Delorme (1996) 'Assessing the international spillover effects of capital income taxation', *International Tax and Public Finance* 3(4), 449–78.

Part IX

Labour market policy and institutions

A comparative assessment

Introduction

Traditionally, labour market policy has been treated as a closed economy issue. This approach has been justified on the grounds that labour mobility between countries is very low due to cultural and linguistic barriers and legal restrictions on labour migration. In fact, with the exception of migratory flows into the New World in the second half of the nineteenth century and the regulated importation of 'guest workers' into Europe in the 1960s, immigration controls have been the norm. As a result, labour market policy has been seen as a 'national issue' because of the perceived lack of spillover effects.

Yet it would be a gross error to assume that interdependence does not exist between national labour market policies. On the one hand, we know that the spillover effects of other macroeconomic policies (such as monetary, fiscal or exchange rate policies) or the effects of external shocks are – at least partly – mediated through the labour market. For example, under a flexible exchange rate regime, monetary expansion at home may well lead to export of unemployment abroad. On the other hand, we have been observing increasingly convergent labour market policy choices across countries. The international tendency to emphasise labour market de-regulation since the 1980s is a clear example. This tendency suggests that it is possible to speak of a labour market policy arbitrage, implying that the policy choice in one country is no longer isolated from what is going on in the rest of the world. This is the main reason for including labour market policy in this book.

The two articles in this part provide a clear account of the developments in the literature on labour market policy. The clarity of the account, however, should not be taken as an indication of agreement on what the policy choices should be. In fact, the findings of the articles occupy the opposite ends of the spectrum. The article by Elmeskov *et al.* in Chapter 25 represents the mainstream view (shared and supported by the OECD) that the increase in and persistence of unemployment in OECD countries have been due to labour market rigidities. Therefore, the cure for unemployment lies in labour market de-regulation, which should increase the flexibility of the labour market. The article by Gregg and Manning in Chapter 26 challenges the conventional view by arguing that unemployment is essentially due to the monopsonistic position of the firms in the labour market. Therefore, labour market de-regulation is ineffective in ensuring labour market flexibility and it is highly likely to exacerbate income inequalities.

The article by Elmeskov *et al.* builds upon previous work by one of the authors and draws on OECD unemployment data. The data presented enable the authors to distinguish between three groups of countries in terms of their success in reducing structural unemployment: success stories, failures and those with stagnant levels of unemployment. This setting then leads to a pertinent but predictable question: how can one account for different labour market performance in these countries? Elmeskov *et al.* use a reduced-form unemployment equation to estimate the impact on unemployment of labour market institutions (i.e. the degree of co-ordination/centralisation in wage bargaining, union density, etc.) and labour market policies (e.g. generosity of unemployment benefit, active labour market policy, employment protection legislation).

Pooling data for nineteen countries over the period 1983–95, Elmeskov *et al.* establish that unemployment benefits, employment protection legislation and taxes are conducive to an increase in structural employment. This is in line with the findings of the de-regulation school. Their findings concerning labour market institutions, however, contradict the policy recommendations of the de-regulation school. For example, a high degree of co-ordination between and within employee and employer organisations and centralisation of the collective bargaining are found to be conducive to lower structural employment. Union density is also found to be negatively related to unemployment, but the relationship is not statistically significant. The policy implication is that officially imposed or voluntary regulation should be defended to the extent that it leads to co-ordination as well as centralisation of the collective bargaining.

Despite this contradiction, however, Elmeskov *et al.* are essentially in the tradition that focuses on labour market rigidities – which may be caused either by labour market policies or by the institutional set-up. Therefore, they are in favour of comprehensive labour market reforms. To demonstrate the relevance of labour market reforms, they disaggregate the impact of policy and institutional variables on the performance of the successful and unsuccessful countries. Their estimates show that these variables have contributed to the fall in structural unemployment in successful countries whereas they have contributed to the increase in unsuccessful countries. Having demonstrated that the successful countries are those that have embraced the OECD reform package, Elmeskov *et al.* conclude that structural unemployment can be reduced significantly if governments embark on comprehensive reforms and carry them through without hesitation.

The article by Gregg and Manning in Chapter 26 takes issue with this view. Their intervention is highly significant because it injects some clarity into the debate on labour market policy (or unemployment). This is done in two ways. First, Gregg and Manning classify the literature on the basis of the assumptions about the source of labour market rigidities. In other words, are the rigidities in the labour market caused by monopolistic behaviour of the employees (and their organisations) or by monopsonistic behaviour of the employers? Second, they describe those who assume monopolistic employee behaviour as proponents of labour market de-regulation and those assuming monopsonistic employer behaviour as proponents of labour market regulation. The limitation of Gregg and Manning is that they demonstrate the shortcomings of the de-regulation school convincingly, but the evidence they cite in favour of regulation remains tentative.

In their criticism of the de-regulation school, Gregg and Manning point to methodological as well as empirical problems. In terms of methodology, they criticise the use of time series analysis because the latter tends to contain a time trend or suitably chosen dummy variables that perform a convenient function. With respect to evidence, they put forward two qualifications. First, unemployment continued to increase in OECD countries for a long time after labour market de-regulation had been introduced in the early 1980s. Second, the cross-section evidence on the link between labour market regulation and various measures of labour market performance is not consistent. While some studies suggest a negative effect of regulation on performance, some studies point in the opposite direction. A cross-section test presented by the authors is a graphic proof of this inconsistency.

The crescendo in Gregg and Manning's criticism of the de-regulation school is reached when they cite some research findings suggesting that labour market de-regulation can be both inefficient and inequitable. The thrust of their argument is that the monopsony power of the employers enables them to pay wages that are below the marginal products of the employees. The more de-regulated the labour market is, the higher is the probability that employers will exercise this power. Therefore, de-regulation is highly likely to generate heterogeneity in reservation wages of workers with similar productivity levels. The end result, then, is a move away from efficiency and an increase in inequality. In addition, the de-regulation school overlooks the negative impact of this combination on the search intensity of the workers.

As can be seen from the summary above, the two articles in this part reflect the state of the art in the research on labour market policy. It is true that consensus is still elusive, but the way in which the controversy is generating new breakthroughs cannot be ignored. In the brief introduction above, we have deliberately set the two articles against each other in order to highlight the differences. Yet the relative strengths and weaknesses of each point out another dimension: the need for further research on the extent to which employer behaviour can and should be incorporated into the analysis of labour market performance. We hope that the reader, by making these articles accessible, will contribute to the search in that direction.

25 Key lessons for labour market reforms

Evidence from OECD countries' experiences

Jørgen Elmeskov, John P. Martin and Stefano Scarpetta*

Swedish Economic Policy Review, vol. 5, no. 2 (1998), pp. 207–52

High and persistent unemployment has been a major blot on the economic and social record of most OECD countries during the past two decades or more. In 1992, OECD ministers gave the organisation a mandate to analyse the causes and consequences of high and persistent unemployment and propose effective remedies to tackle the problem. The first fruits of this work, published in 1994 under the title *The OECD Jobs Study*, included a list of more than 60 detailed policy recommendations backed by two volumes of research; see OECD (1994a, 1994b). Ministers then mandated the organisation to continue its analytical work in certain areas. They also asked the organisation to flesh out detailed policy recommendations for each OECD country (considering each country's historical, institutional and political contexts) and to monitor progress in the implementation of these recommendations and their impacts on labour market performance.[1]

The OECD work since 1994 has produced a series of additional publications; see OECD (1996a, 1996b, 1997a). This work culminated in a major report in 1997, *Implementing the OECD Jobs Strategy: Member Countries' Experience*.[2] And it enabled the organisation to identify several country success stories and failures in terms of implementing OECD recommendations and the resulting labour market outcomes. In assessing needs for reform, the work relied heavily on the econometric analysis in Scarpetta (1996) that quantified the role of a range of labour market policies and institutional factors in explaining differences in unemployment rates across OECD countries.

The aim of this paper is to distil the main lessons for labour market reforms from the successes and failures revealed by recent OECD research. In short, the paper tries to answer this question: Why did a few OECD countries succeed in the task of significantly reducing structural unemployment during the past decade while most have failed so far?

The paper has three main sections. Section 1 presents estimates of the structural unemployment rate indicator that the OECD used to identify

* We acknowledge helpful comments from Lars Calmfors, the referee, and participants at the Stockholm conference. We are grateful to Martine Levasseur for statistical assistance and to Léa Duboscq for secretarial assistance. The views expressed in this paper are our own and should not be held to represent those of the OECD or its member governments.

successes and failures and briefly discusses its pros and cons. This is followed by a review of the main determinants of unemployment rates across countries, which is essentially an update and extension of the cross-country results in Scarpetta (1996). In particular, it focuses on possible interactions between labour market policies and institutional features of the collective bargaining system. Section 3 highlights some key lessons for labour market reforms revealed by OECD research. The final section contains concluding remarks.

1 IDENTIFICATION OF COUNTRY SUCCESSES AND FAILURES

1.1 Structural unemployment rates

Because the ultimate goal of policy is to reduce high and persistent unemployment, it is natural to use an unemployment-rate measure as the criterion to distinguish success from failure. To abstract from business-cycle effects, the OECD opted for a measure of the structural or equilibrium unemployment rate as its criterion. Table 25.1 presents estimates of the *non-accelerating wage rate of unemployment* (NAWRU) that indicate the possible level and evolution of non-cyclical unemployment in OECD countries over the past decade; see Appendix A.

Estimates of the NAWRU are used to split the OECD countries into three groups consisting of countries where structural unemployment has: (1) increased during the 1990s; (2) shown little change; and (3) decreased. (A change in the structural unemployment rate between 1990 and 1997 is considered significant, and hence determines which of the three groups a country is assigned to, if it exceeds one standard deviation).

These estimates suggest that structural unemployment rates significantly increased in the 1990s in 10 countries, including Sweden, remained stable in another six, and significantly declined in the remaining six countries. This latter group, designated the success stories for the purposes of this paper, consists of Australia, Denmark, Ireland, the Netherlands, New Zealand, and the UK. Note that the success stories are not confined to English-speaking countries but also include two continental European countries: Denmark and the Netherlands. Several countries in the second group in Table 25.1 also managed to maintain structural unemployment rates at relatively low levels. This group includes Japan, Norway, Portugal, and the US. OECD (1997b) argues that some of these countries managed to maintain low structural unemployment because their policies in important respects followed the main thrust in the *Jobs Strategy*, though with clear differences of emphasis among countries. Also note that some of the countries in the first group, e.g., Austria, Iceland, and Switzerland, while experiencing rising structural unemployment in the 1990s, managed to maintain relatively low levels of unemployment.

Table 25.1 Structural unemployment in the OECD countries as a per cent of the total labour force[a]

In the 1990s, the structural unemployment rate has . . .			
. . . *increased in*	*1986*	*1990*	*1997*
Finland	5.5	7.0	12.8
Sweden	2.1	3.2	6.7
Germany	7.3	6.9	9.6
Iceland	0.8	1.5	4.0
Switzerland	0.7	1.3	3.0
Greece	7.8	8.2	9.8
Italy	8.4	9.7	10.6
France	8.9	9.3	10.2
Belgium	11.7	11.0	11.6
Austria	4.1	4.9	5.4
. . . *remained fairly stable in*			
Japan	2.5	2.5	2.8
Norway	3.1	4.2	4.5
Spain	19.1	19.8	19.9
Portugal	7.8	5.9	5.8
US	6.2	5.8	5.6
Canada	8.3	9.0	8.5
. . . *decreased in*			
Denmark	8.6	9.2	8.6
Australia	7.9	8.3	7.5
New Zealand	4.7	7.3	6.0
UK	9.5	8.5	7.2
Netherlands	8.0	7.0	5.5
Ireland	14.6	14.6	11.0
OECD structural unemployment rate[b]	6.9	6.8	7.1
OECD actual unemployment rate[b]	7.7	6.0	7.5

Source: OECD Secretariat.
Notes:
[a] Structural unemployment data are based on estimates of the NAWRU made for the *OECD Economic Outlook*, 63, 1998. A change is considered significant (in absolute terms) if it exceeds one standard deviation. The latter was calculated for each series and country during the 1986–97 period.
[b] Weighted averages of the countries reported in the table.

1.2 The pros and cons of using estimates of structural unemployment rates as an indicator of success or failure

Because by definition the structural unemployment rate is an unobservable variable, serious questions can be raised about its use in this way to classify cross-country performance. And many economists question the analytical usefulness of the concept itself—witness the different views expressed on the concept in a symposium in the *Journal of Economic Perspectives*, Winter 1997.

Because differing views on the use of the concept for analytical and empirical purposes are well known, we do not rehearse the case again. All we are saying is that the OECD Secretariat has found the concept to be a useful one in its analyses of the unemployment problem, and the relevant OECD bodies that oversee work on implementing the OECD *Jobs Strategy* largely share this view.[3] Even if one accepts that the concept is a useful analytical device, there still remains the issue of deriving satisfactory empirical proxies for it. The previously cited OECD work has opted to proxy the structural unemployment rate by estimates of the NAWRU. Of course these time-varying estimates of NAWRUs are somewhat fragile, but similar concepts based on the unemployment rate that is associated with some average vacancy rate or some average capacity-utilisation rate, tend to give broadly similar numerical estimates (Elmeskov, 1993). The OECD NAWRU estimates are broadly aligned with those of other studies.[4] We also examined the correlations between changes in estimated structural unemployment rates during the 1990–97 period with corresponding movements in a range of *observable* labour market indicators, such as long-term unemployment, unemployment rates for low-skilled workers, and employment rates (OECD, 1997b). In all cases, relatively high correlation exists between movements in the different series. Figure 25.1 illustrates the correlation between changes in structural unemployment and changes in the cyclically adjusted employment rate.

In sum, while OECD estimates of structural unemployment rates are

Change in structural unemployment rate

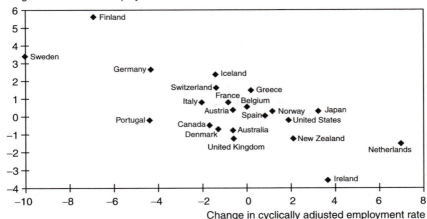

Figure 25.1 Change in the structural unemployment rate plotted against the change in the employment rate, 1990–97

Note: Correlation coefficient = −0.7. t-statistic = −5.0. The cyclically adjusted employment rate was estimated by regressing the actual employment/population ratio against an estimate of the output gap based on the proportional difference between actual and trend output. The latter has been estimated using a Hodrick–Prescott filter.

subject to conceptual and numerical uncertainties, the evidence suggests that changes in estimated structural unemployment rates in the 1990s matched real changes in labour market conditions in OECD countries. This, in turn, suggests that the three-way classification of countries in Table 25.1 permits a meaningful identification of successes and failures.

2   DETERMINANTS OF STRUCTURAL UNEMPLOYMENT IN OECD COUNTRIES

The preceding section identifies several countries that have either maintained low structural unemployment rates during the past decade or have managed to significantly reduce them. This section explores the possible determinants of the significant cross-country disparities in structural unemployment rates, drawing on the Scarpetta (1996) approach. Our empirical analysis extends Scarpetta's work in three main directions by:

- Considering a larger number of countries (from 17 to 19) and extending the time period.
- Exploiting recent information on the evolution of collective bargaining structures and employment protection legislation (EPL).
- Focusing on potential interactions between labour market policies and institutional factors.

2.1   A reduced-form unemployment equation

The theoretical framework for the analysis follows the familiar Layard-Nickell-Jackman (1991) model characterised by an upward sloping *wage-setting* schedule, based on the assumption that real wages are the results of a bargaining process between employers and employees, and a downward-sloping *labour-demand* schedule. Product market conditions, including the price mark-up over marginal costs, influence the latter, while a range of wage-push factors influence the wage-setting schedule.

It can be easily shown that the intersection of the labour demand curve and the wage-setting schedule identifies the structural (or equilibrium) unemployment rate and the equilibrium level of real wages. In this framework, structural unemployment is a function of wage-push factors, price-push factors, and the elasticities of real wages and price mark-ups to unemployment.

In our empirical analysis of the determinants of structural unemployment, we tested several potential wage- and price-push factors, including income-support schemes for the unemployed; active labour market policies; the tax wedge; EPL; the structure of collective bargaining; and minimum wages.[5] To quantify the relative importance of these policy and institutional variables in determining the wide disparities in structural unemployment across OECD countries, we estimated a static model over the 1983–95 period. The period corresponds, more or less, to a full business cycle, over which structural unemployment has changed only moderately in most OECD countries, at least compared with the sharp increases of the 1970s and early 1980s. This is also the period for which most of the information is available on labour market institutions and labour market policies.

Pooling data for 19 countries[6] over the 1983–95 period and adding an explanatory variable to account for the effects of aggregate demand fluctuations over the cycle,[7] the determinants of the actual unemployment rate were modelled by a reduced-form equation with this structure:

$$u_{it} = \mu_0 + \mu_i + \Sigma_k \beta_k x_{kit} + \gamma z_i + \phi g_{it} + v_{it} \tag{1}$$

where i indexes countries, t the years, u is the unemployment rate, x denotes a set of time-varying explanatory variables, z is our measure of public spending on active labour market policies per unemployed person,[8] g is the output gap included to account for changes in the business cycle,[9] μ_0 is a constant, μ_i is the country-specific effect not accounted for by the available explanatory variables, and v is the usual error term.[10] Table 25.B1 shows the key characteristics of the data set (see Scarpetta, 1996 for more details).

Table 25.2 presents the results of estimating different specifications of the reduced-form, unemployment-rate equation. The first three columns of the table focus, in turn, on key features of collective bargaining arrangements—namely, the degree of co-ordination in bargaining (column 1), the predominant bargaining level at which wages are negotiated (centralisation/decentralisation) (column 2), and a summary measure that combines the degree of centralisation/co-ordination (column 3).[11] Column 4 introduces the tax wedge in the analysis, while column 5 replicates the same specification on a sample that excludes Sweden to test for changes in the estimated parameter for active labour market policy (ALMPU).[12] Finally, equation 6 tests for the possible influence of statutory minimum wages on aggregate unemployment rates. Statutory minimum wages exist in only nine of the 19 countries considered in our analysis. So the coefficients for the other explanatory variables in column 6 are not necessarily comparable with those in the other columns.

There is clear evidence in Table 25.2 that different collective bargaining arrangements affect labour market outcomes. A high degree of co-ordination on employer and employee sides (HGCOOR) can significantly reduce structural unemployment insofar as such co-ordination provides a mechanism by which economy-wide labour market conditions can be internalised in the wage-setting process, increasing the sensitivity of real wages to shocks. There is also some evidence (see column 2) that highly centralised (HGCENTR) and fully decentralised bargaining systems lead to somewhat lower structural unemployment compared with intermediate (sectoral) systems (INTCENTR).

The summary measure of collective bargaining structures (INTCORP and HGCORP) brings together the different features of co-ordination and the bargaining levels into a single indicator. For example, the summary measure allows us to consider cases where cross-industry co-ordination between

Table 25.2 Reduced-form unemployment rate equations, 1983–95[a] (random effects, FGLS)

	1	2	3	4	5[b]	6
ALMPU	−0.11*	−0.11*	−0.09	−0.11*	−0.53**	..
	0.06	*0.06*	*0.06*	*0.06*	*0.21*	
UB	0.11***	0.08***	0.10***	0.09***	0.10***	−0.01
	0.02	*0.02*	*0.02*	*0.02*	*0.02*	*0.05*
EPL	0.32*	0.34*	0.38**	0.33*	0.37**	0.68***
	0.17	*0.19*	*0.18*	*0.19*	*0.19*	*0.24*
UDENS	0.01	−0.01	−0.02	−0.02	−0.01	−0.06**
	0.02	*0.02*	*0.02*	*0.02*	*0.02*	*0.03*
INTCOOR	−0.40					
	0.48					
HGCOOR	−1.91***					
	0.48					
INTCENTR		0.66*				
		0.39				
HGCENTR		−0.79*				
		0.43				
INTCORP			0.61*	0.58*	0.35	..
			0.35	*0.35*	*0.36*	
HGCORP[c]			−1.39***	−1.48***	−1.25***	−1.69***
			0.34	*0.34*	*0.35*	*0.45*
TWEDGE				0.10**	0.14***	0.12*
				0.04	*0.04*	*0.06*
GAP	−0.46***	−0.50***	−0.50***	−0.51***	−0.49***	−0.62***
	0.03	*0.03*	*0.03*	*0.03*	*0.03*	*0.05*
MINWAGE						−0.02
						0.03
Observations	238	238	238	238	226	112
Countries	19	19	19	19	18	9
F-test[d]	11.3***	125.4***	146.3***	136.6***	123.5***	86.3***
B&P LM[e]	1001.4***	1050.6***	1119.1***	1086.4***	1043.8***	172.4***
Hausman[f]	8.5	7.1	8.0	11.6	9.0	6.0

Notes: Each coefficient represents the expected change in the unemployment rate in response to a unitary change in the independent variable.

*   = Statistically significant at 10% level

**   = Statistically significant at 5% level

*** = Statistically significant at 1% level

[a] All regressions include a constant term, standard errors in *italic*.

[b] Sweden is excluded from the panel data set for this regression.

[c] Due to the limited number of countries in the HGCORP group in the equation 6 specification, HGCORP includes low & high centralisation/co-ordination countries.

[d] F-test of the hypothesis of absence of country-specific fixed effects.

[e] Breusch and Pagan LM test of the hypothesis of randomness of country-specific effects. The statistic is distributed as an χ^2 (1).

[f] Hausman (1978) structural test, distributed as χ^2.

employers and unions in an industry bargaining setting (e.g., Germany and Austria and more recently, Ireland and the Netherlands, with centralised income policy agreements) may be an alternative or functionally equivalent to centralised systems.

The estimated coefficients for the measures of centralisation/co-ordination (decentralised countries are the reference group) give some support to the hump-shaped hypothesis (Calmfors and Driffill, 1988), whereby highly centralised/co-ordinated systems and fully decentralised systems help to restrain the insiders' wage claims and thereby serve to lower structural unemployment.

It is also interesting to note that union density (UDENS), per se, does not help to explain cross-country differences in structural unemployment, once other features of the collective bargaining system are considered. Moreover, the empirical analysis did not detect a statistically significant impact of statutory minimum wages (relative to the average wage) on aggregate unemployment.[13]

Turning to the role of labour market policies, there is strong evidence that more generous unemployment benefits (UB) lead to higher structural unemployment. The implicit average elasticity of unemployment with respect to the OECD summary measure of benefit entitlements is around 0.4, a value that is close to those often found in the microeconometric literature (Holmlund, 1998).

The econometric evidence is mixed concerning the role of active labour market policies. The results in the first four columns of Table 25.2 show that our measure of spending on active labour market policies always has a negative coefficient; however, it is only marginally significant. But as Scarpetta (1996) has demonstrated, the presence of Sweden in the panel is crucial for this inconclusive result: if Sweden is excluded on the grounds that it is an outlier in the panel data set, the magnitude and statistical significance of the estimated coefficient for ALMPU increases sharply (the estimated coefficient becomes −0.53 in equation 5 in Table 25.2).

For employment-protection legislation (EPL), our results point to a positive impact of strict regulations on firing on structural unemployment. These results are somewhat more robust than those previously found by Scarpetta (1996). A possible explanation for this is that the measure of EPL used in Table 25.2 accounts for recent changes in regulations.

Finally, the tax wedge (TWEDGE) is statistically significant in all equations. The estimated elasticity of unemployment with respect to the tax wedge is moderate (around 0.5), which implies that the observed reduction in the OECD average tax wedge of 7 percentage points during the 1983–95 period could have contributed to reduce structural unemployment by about 0.7 percentage points.

It is of interest to compare our results with those of Layard and Nickell (1997) for 20 OECD countries based on two cross-sections for 1983–88 and 1989–94. The first point to note is that there is quite a high concordance between the two sets of results regarding the determinants of unemployment rates across OECD countries. Both studies assign significant roles to unemployment benefits, collective bargaining structures, active labour market policies (allowing for the caveat about the exclusion of Sweden), and the tax wedge—even if the variables in question are defined somewhat differently between the two studies. There are also some notable differences. For example, Layard and Nickell (1997) do not find a significant effect from EPL on the total unemployment rate. Their equation also includes the owner-occupier rate that is not included in our regressions, and they use changes in inflation to account for cyclical fluctuations of the unemployment rate, while we use the output gap.

2.2 Structural unemployment and reforms in the successful countries

How do these results help to explain the role of labour market and institutional reforms on the estimated changes in structural unemployment? To answer this question we do not use the NAWRU estimates in Table 25.1. Instead, we proxy structural unemployment by adjusting the actual unemployment rate by the estimated cyclical component based on the coefficients of the output gap in Table 25.2. Then, Table 25.3 breaks down the estimated changes in structural unemployment into the contributions of the main determinants, namely changes in unemployment benefits, the tax wedge, and institutional settings (i.e., the joint impact of collective bargaining systems and EPL) plus a residual that accounts for changes in unobserved country-specific factors.[14] For each country, the estimated parameters of equation 4 in Table 25.2 were used to compute the expected changes in unemployment that result from the observed changes in each of the explanatory variables. The calculations were made for two time periods, the full 1983–95 sample period and the 1990–95 sub-period. In Ireland, the Netherlands, and the UK—which began introducing reforms in the early to mid-1980s—structural unemployment fell over the entire period covered in the empirical analysis (Table 25.3a). In New Zealand, Australia, and Denmark, where most reforms were introduced somewhat later, falls in structural unemployment were recorded in the 1990s. For the latter countries, the decomposition over the 1990–95 period (Table 25.3b) is more meaningful.

An important fraction of the estimated change in structural unemployment cannot be accounted for by changes in the explanatory variables included in our analysis. Other omitted factors probably played important roles. And possible interactions between labour market policies and institutional factors, albeit difficult to identify (see below), have not been considered in the decomposition of Table 25.3. Bearing these caveats in mind, we can see that reforms in the key policy areas in the six *success* countries have generally gone in the direction of reducing structural unemployment, although there are noticeable differences between them in the contribution that can be assigned to each of the policies and institutional reforms.

To draw some lessons from the success stories, it is of interest to specify in somewhat greater detail what policy reforms were undertaken in these

Table 25.3a. Accounting for the changes in structural unemployment, 1983/85–1993/95

	Estimated change in structural unemployment[a]	UB	TWEDGE	Institutional factors[b]	Country-specific effect
Australia	0.9	0.4	0.1	−0.2	0.7
Austria	1.3	−0.1	0.1	0.2	1.2
Belgium	−0.4	−0.3	−0.1	0.0	0.0
Canada	−0.4	−0.2	0.4	0.0	−0.7
Denmark	−0.5	1.3	−0.1	0.0	−1.7
Finland	10.2	1.1	0.2	1.9	7.0
France	2.6	0.4	0.1	0.6	1.5
West Germany	1.2	−0.1	0.3	0.1	0.9
Ireland	−3.1	0.5	−0.2	−2.0	−1.4
Italy	5.5	1.6	−0.1	−1.5	5.5
Japan	0.7	0.1	0.1	0.1	0.4
Netherlands	−3.5	−0.4	−0.5	−2.1	−0.5
New Zealand	1.7	−0.3	−0.3	−0.1	2.3
Norway	1.6	0.5	−0.5	0.0	1.6
Portugal	−0.4	1.9	0.2	0.2	−2.7
Spain	4.7	−0.3	0.1	−0.2	5.1
Sweden	4.3	0.0	−0.4	1.9	2.8
UK	−1.6	−0.3	−0.4	−0.4	−0.5
US	−1.6	−0.2	−0.3	0.1	−1.2

Notes:
[a] Structural unemployment is proxied by actual unemployment minus the cyclical component estimated from the coefficient of the output gap in col. 4 of Table 25.2.
[b] The degree of centralisation/co-ordination and the index of employment protection legislation (EPL).

countries. Evidently, policy settings in many areas, including importantly product markets, have the scope to affect labour market outcomes, but the focus here is restricted to policies that impinge directly on labour markets.

During the past 15 years, while several OECD countries have increased the generosity of *unemployment benefits* by altering one or other of the central parameters of the system (i.e., replacement rates and duration of benefits), five of the six success countries either kept them unchanged or curtailed them.[15] As an illustration, in countries such as Ireland, New Zealand, and the Netherlands, the estimated impact of changes in benefits during the 1990s on structural unemployment is in the order of 0.2 to 0.6 percentage points. Moreover, the six countries (like several others) tightened up on various aspects of eligibility and job-availability conditions for receipt of unemployment benefits that are not accounted for in the OECD summary measure of benefit generosity.[16]

Measured relative to GDP, spending on *active labour market programmes* shows large variations across the six countries. But three of them, Denmark, Ireland (in the 1990s), and the Netherlands, are well above average regarding spending on active policies. These countries also managed to shift more of their spending on labour market policies toward active policies and away

Table 25.3b Accounting for the changes in structural unemployment, 1990–95

	Estimated change in structural unemployment[a]	UB	TWEDGE	Institutional factors[b]	Country-specific effect
Australia	−0.3	0.1	0.0	−0.3	−0.2
Austria	0.2	−0.4	0.1	0.1	0.4
Belgium	1.7	−0.3	0.5	0.0	1.6
Canada	0.2	−0.1	0.3	0.0	0.0
Denmark	−0.7	1.4	−0.1	0.0	−2.0
Finland	9.6	0.6	0.3	−0.2	8.8
France	0.9	0.0	0.3	0.2	0.5
West Germany	1.1	−0.1	0.3	0.1	0.9
Ireland	−2.1	−0.2	−0.1	0.0	−1.8
Italy	1.8	1.5	0.1	−1.5	1.7
Japan	−0.3	0.0	−0.2	0.0	−0.2
Netherlands	−0.7	−0.6	−0.1	0.0	0.1
New Zealand	−1.4	−0.4	0.1	−0.1	−1.0
Norway	0.7	0.0	−1.6	0.0	2.3
Portugal	−0.3	0.2	0.0	0.0	−0.5
Spain	2.2	−0.2	0.2	−0.2	2.4
Sweden	4.2	−0.2	−0.4	1.9	2.8
UK	−0.5	0.0	0.0	0.0	−0.5
US	−0.8	0.1	0.0	0.0	−0.8

Notes:

[a] Structural unemployment is proxied by actual unemployment minus the cyclical component estimated from the coefficient of the output gap in col. 4 of Table 25.2.

[b] The degree of centralisation/co-ordination and the index of employment protection legislation (EPL).

from unemployment benefits during the 1985–97 period. In Australia, New Zealand, and the UK, there has also been a shift in the orientation of spending on active policies toward job-search assistance and counselling for groups with particular disadvantages in the labour market. In Denmark, this shift in emphasis was a key element of the 1994 labour market policy reform, which laid down that individual action plans must be prepared for all people with more than three months of unemployment.

The overall *tax wedge on labour use* has been reduced in several OECD countries over the past decade, including the six success stories. The tax burden was reduced by more than 5 percentage points in the UK, Ireland and New Zealand, and by almost 8 percentage points in the Netherlands (albeit from an extremely high level in the early 1980s). According to our econometric estimates, these reductions could have lowered structural unemployment by about 0.2 to 0.5 percentage points. Australia recorded a decline in the tax wedge in the late 1980s that was subsequently reversed.

Because of their direct effect on labour costs, employer social security contributions were cut in recent years in several countries, sometimes targeted to encourage the hiring of low-wage workers. Thus, the Netherlands, Ireland, and to a minor extent the UK, reduced these contributions together with

France and Sweden. But in the latter two countries, the tight fiscal position meant that other taxes had to be raised to offset the revenue loss.

Though there are marked differences in the strictness of EPL across OECD countries, there has been a tendency toward less constraining hiring and firing practices in several of them, including some of the six success cases. In particular, there has been some relaxation of EPL in the case of individual and/or collective dismissals in the UK (1993), and in Italy (1991), Portugal (1989, 1991), Spain and, more recently, in Germany and the Netherlands. In Australia, in response to employers' concerns about the 1993 tightening of regulations, new legislation was introduced in 1994 and 1995 to reduce legal costs to employers and to simplify procedures for dismissal in justified circumstances. But France moved in the opposite direction, with some easing of dismissal procedures (abolition of the administrative authorisations) in 1986 being followed by tightening in 1989 and 1993 for collective redundancies (the introduction of social plans).

As previously stressed, there are several relevant dimensions to *wage formation* that make it difficult to characterise a country as having done better or worse over time in this field. In addition, many aspects of wage formation are only indirectly amenable to policy influence, resting principally on private-sector decisions. Notwithstanding these difficulties, the six countries seem to have moved away from uncoordinated, sectoral, wage bargaining to either higher co-ordination or full decentralisation, both leading to greater wage moderation and lower structural unemployment, at least according to our empirical results (see Table 25.3). Widespread decentralisation of wage bargaining has been the result of a deliberate policy aimed at reducing union power in the UK and New Zealand. Wage bargaining has also been substantially decentralised in Denmark, though employers maintain a significant element of co-ordination, and Australia has also moved toward decentralisation since the late 1980s, if from a very particular starting point. By contrast, Ireland (since 1988) and the Netherlands (since 1983) have conducted wage bargaining with close co-ordination among the government, employers' associations, and trade unions.

At the end of the day, what appears to set apart the six success stories from those countries that have failed to prevent a rise in structural unemployment in the 1990s is that they have implemented policy reforms across most of the key policy areas identified in the empirical analysis. Indeed, the six countries stand out as a group more in terms of the *comprehensive* coverage of reforms than in terms of their having taken particularly bold steps in specific areas— with industrial relations reform in New Zealand and to some extent in the UK, standing out as exceptions. To this comprehensive approach must be added the effects of relatively successful macroeconomic policies (see below).

Comprehensiveness seems indeed to be a crucial feature of any successful strategy to reduce unemployment because reforms in different areas can reinforce each other's effects. Conversely, policies that tend to drive up unemployment may also be mutually reinforcing. An example is that an increase in payroll taxes may have a larger effect on unemployment if introduced in a context of a high minimum wage, which prevents backward shifting of the tax hike into wages.[17]

2.3 Are there significant interactions between labour market policies and institutions?

Labour market policies may have a different impact on the functioning of the labour market depending upon the institutional framework within which they operate. Interaction mechanisms are generally complex and may not be fully accounted for by the analytical approach used in this study. But to shed some preliminary light on this issue, Table 25.4 presents the results of reduced-form unemployment rate regressions in which some policy parameters are allowed to vary across different policy and institutional settings. The results reported refer to those interactions that were statistically significant.

Column 1 in Table 25.4 suggests that unemployment benefits probably have different effects on structural unemployment depending on the intensity of public spending on active labour market policies. In countries that spend a lot on active programmes, per person unemployed, unemployment benefits have a slightly stronger impact than they do in the intermediate group of countries.[18] This result has intuitive appeal: the joint effect of generous benefits and high spending on active programmes serves to raise the reservation wage of the unemployed over and above what each policy in isolation would have done and thus leads to an even stronger aggregate impact on unemployment. But given this reasoning, one would expect to find the largest interaction effect for the countries with the highest spending on ALMPs, followed by the group of intermediate and low-spending countries in that order. The fact that our estimates do not match this pattern is a finding for which we have no satisfactory explanation.

Buti *et al.* (1998) argued that strict EPL may act as a substitute for unemployment insurance benefits. Under this hypothesis, countries might opt for either generous unemployment benefits and lax EPL or *vice versa*, and a combination of generous benefits with strict EPL could lead to higher structural unemployment. But the evidence in column 2 of Table 25.4 does not support this hypothesis: the estimated effect of unemployment benefits is not statistically different in countries with either strict or lax EPL.

Table 25.4 suggests that different collective bargaining arrangements influence the way in which EPL and the tax wedge affect unemployment. In both cases, the positive impact on aggregate unemployment is stronger and statistically significant in countries with an intermediate degree of centralisation/co-ordination, i.e., where sectoral wage bargaining predominates with limited co-ordination, while neither EPL nor the tax wedge are statistically significant in either highly centralised/co-ordinated or decentralised countries.[19] These results are consistent with the hypothesis that when insiders have strong bargaining power, they may more easily resist employers' attempts to reflect higher payroll taxes and/or high turnover costs (due to strict EPL) in lower wages, even if this works to the detriment of outsiders.

Table 25.4 Reduced-form unemployment rate equations, 1983–1995: interactions between explanatory variables

	1	2	3	4
ALMPU	−0.30	−0.11*	−0.04	−0.06
	0.23	*0.07*	*0.07*	*0.06*
UB			0.10***	0.09***
			0.02	*0.02*
UB*LWalmpu	0.21***			
	0.04			
UB*INTalmpu	0.05**			
	0.02			
UB*HGalmpu	0.11**			
	0.05			
UB*LWepl		0.09***		
		0.03		
UB*HGepl		0.10***		
		0.03		
EPL	0.28*	0.31		0.26
	0.17	*0.20*		*0.17*
UDENS	−0.01	−0.02	−0.02	−0.01
	0.02	*0.02*	*0.02*	*0.02*
INTCORP	0.25	0.55	0.53	0.46
	0.35	*0.36*	*0.34*	*0.35*
HGCORP	−1.65***	−1.49***	−1.46***	−1.42***
	0.38	*0.34*	*0.33*	*0.34*
EPL*HGCORP			−0.12	
			0.29	
EPL*INTCORP			0.50**	
			0.21	
EPL*LWCORP			0.35	
			0.33	
TWEDGE*HGCORP				0.06
				0.05
TWEDGE*INTCORP				0.15***
				0.05
TWEDGE*LWCORP				0.12*
				0.06
TWEDGE	0.15***	0.10**	0.10**	
	0.04	*0.04*	*0.04*	
GAP	−0.49***	−0.51***	−0.50***	−0.50***
	0.03	*0.03*	*0.03*	*0.03*
Observations	226	238	238	238
Countries	18[a]	19	19	19
F-test	89.7*** 890.0*** 124.6***		114.1***	101.0***
B&P LM test	12.1	1034.0***	956.5***	853.7***
Hausman test		36.1***	12.4	11.1

Notes: See the notes for Table 25.2.

Acronym	**Dummy for countries with . . .**
LWalmpu	= Low levels of ALMPU: Australia, Canada, Italy, Japan, Spain, UK, US
INTalmpu	= Intermediate levels of ALMPU; Austria, Belgium, Denmark, France, Ireland, the Netherlands, New Zealand, Portugal
HGalmpu	= High levels of ALMPU; Finland, Germany and Norway
LWepl	= Low levels of EPL: Austria, Canada, Denmark, Ireland, Japan, New Zealand, UK, and US
HGepl	= High levels of EPL: Austria, Belgium, Finland, France, Germany, Italy, the Netherlands, Norway, Portugal, Spain, and Sweden
HGCORP INTCORP LWCORP	= High, intermediate, low degree of centralisation/co-ordination. For the list of countries in each group and changes over time, see Table 25.B2.

[a] Sweden is not included in the sample.

Bearing in mind the tentative nature of these results, they may have some implications for the understanding of the determinants of changes in structural unemployment discussed above. In particular, the impact of significant changes in the tax wedge may have been less marked in countries with either a high degree of centralisation/co-ordination (i.e., Austria and Germany) or decentralised wage bargaining systems (i.e., Canada and Japan). Conversely, the impact could have been stronger in countries with intermediate wage bargaining settings (e.g., Belgium, Finland, France, and Spain). Similarly, the tightening of EPL in France in 1989 and 1993 might have produced a more important increase in structural unemployment than that calculated in Table 25.3, while the loosening of EPL in Portugal in the 1990s might have contributed more strongly to the estimated reduction in structural unemployment.

2.4 The role of macroeconomic policies

Sound macroeconomic policies are an important element in any comprehensive strategy to combat high and persistent unemployment. This is in part because large macroeconomic fluctuations are likely to contribute to rising structural unemployment as increases in unemployment, which are initially cyclical, tend, over time, to become structural.[20]

Across countries, a positive correlation exists between the degree of annual volatility of unemployment and the extent of the rise over time in structural unemployment (Figure 25.2). Thus, stable conditions may help to maintain low structural unemployment. As a corollary, countries with macroeconomic room for manoeuvre to counteract prolonged slumps in macroeconomic conditions (e.g., Norway) have often avoided strong increases in actual unemployment.

There are also potentially important interactions between macroeconomic and structural policy settings. Thus labour market policies can help determine to what extent cyclical unemployment increases are translated into higher structural unemployment.[21] The policy implications of this include:

- For countries with very rigid labour markets, macroeconomic instability carries a particularly high price in terms of structural unemployment, whereas countries with flexible labour markets, most notably the US, have experienced large cyclical fluctuations in unemployment around a rather stable level of structural unemployment.[22]
- Moves toward medium-term macroeconomic targets will often be less costly in terms of unemployment if the appropriate structural policies have been implemented first (Ball, 1996). Conversely, a sequencing that involves moving toward macroeconomic targets before implementing structural reform may be expensive in terms of unemployment.

The medium-term orientation of macroeconomic policies will probably also be important. This is mainly due to the effects over the longer term of

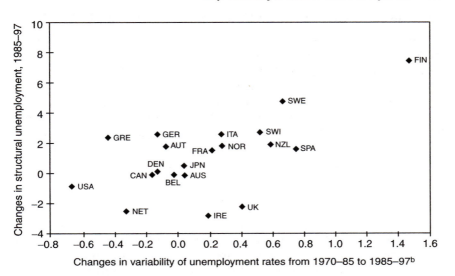

Figure 25.2 Cyclical variability and a structural unemployment,[a] 1985–97 (percentage points)

Source: OECD.
Notes:
[a] Structural unemployment data are based on estimates of the NAWRU made for the OECD *Economic Outlook*, 63, 1998.
[b] Measured by the standard deviation of yearly changes in unemployment rates.

sound public finances and price stability on unemployment *via* the channel of real interest rates:

- A fall of real interest rates may lower production costs in much the same way that lower payroll taxes or energy prices would do, and it may raise capital accumulation and thereby labour productivity. Where wage earners do not receive a corresponding increase in real wages, unemployment might fall.
- In some cases, lower real interest rates may affect: the bargaining attitudes of workers and the labour-demand behaviour of enterprises, leading to the end result of lower unemployment.[23]
- Lower real interest rates could also favourably affect productivity growth, either temporarily—while the capital-intensity of production responds, or more long lastingly—if the rate of innovation and its diffusion are affected. Increased productivity growth again might cause unemployment to fall. This would be the case to the extent it reduced the incidence of downward wage stickiness or facilitated wage bargaining by increasing the scope for real-wage gains.[24]

Empirical estimates of the effects of real interest rates on cross-country differences in unemployment yielded results that are variable but suggestive of significant impacts in some countries.[25]

3 OVERCOMING RESISTANCE TO LABOUR MARKET REFORM

The analysis in the previous section treats a range of institutional and labour market policies as exogenous factors. On this view, unemployment is basically the result of misguided policies. But an alternative view sees the policy settings that influence unemployment as determined by political-economy considerations. This may also explain why it is so difficult to introduce policy reforms that will reduce unemployment. This section discusses the role that resistance by labour market insiders may have played as a hindrance to effective labour market reform; the role of equity considerations in shaping policies; and some evidence on the role of crises in overcoming resistance to reforms.

3.1 Insider resistance as a hindrance to reform

There can be little doubt that the insider–outsider distinction is an important one. Figure 25.3 shows a cross-country breakdown of employment rates by age and gender. What sets countries apart in terms of overall employment/ population rates is largely the extent to which *outsider* groups are employed. The young, older workers, and adult women represent outsiders in Figure 25.3. By contrast, the employment/population rates of prime-age males, a group dominated by *insiders*, are much more similar across countries.

Arguments why insiders may oppose reforms that would produce higher employment for outsiders come in different forms. One such argument is that insiders are virtually unaffected by the unemployment consequences of labour market rigidities, but that the same rigidities may enhance their bargaining power in wage negotiations.

In these circumstances, insiders will have an interest in raising rigidities to the point where the extra gain in terms of higher real wages is offset by the loss in terms of added risk of unemployment and related income loss.[26]

Some empirical observations are consistent with such an insider–outsider view of policy determination:

- Across countries, there is a positive correlation between strictness of EPL for permanent workers and *excess coverage of wage contracts*, which is a measure of the extent to which union wage agreements are extended to non-union members (Figure 25.4). This suggests that the insiders, who benefit from strict EPL, may press for administrative extension of wage agreements as a protection against underbidding of their wages by outsiders.
- Spending on active labour market policies should empower labour market outsiders to compete more effectively with insiders. It may be no coincidence that Figure 25.5 shows a positive correlation between the extent of such spending (per unemployed and relative to per capita GDP) and the extent of union density. Where large parts of the labour market (including those with an outsider or near-outsider status) are organised, there may be greater internalisation of the gains from integrating out-siders and greater pressure to do so.

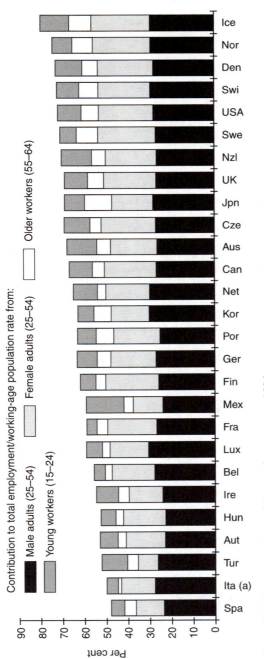

Figure 25.3 Decomposition of the employment rate, 1996

Source: OECD Labour Force Statistics, Analytical Data Base.

Notes:

[a] Italy 1997. Adults = 25–59 years of age.

The contributions of individual demographic groups to the overall employment/working-age population rate were calculated as the group-specific employment rates multiplied by the share of individual groups in the population of working age. The countries are ordered from left to right in ascending order of the total employment population rate.

Index of the strictness of employment protection legislation

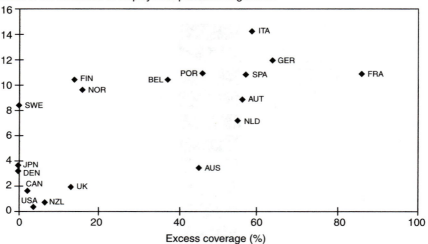

Figure 25.4 Employment protection legislation and coverage of wage agreements

Note: The excess coverage index is the difference between the coverage rate (proportion of workers covered by the terms of wage agreements) and union density rate.

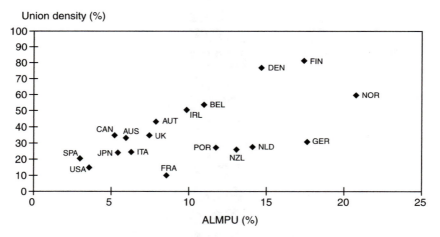

Figure 25.5 Union density and active labour market programmes

Note: ALMPU is spending on active labour market programmes per unemployed relative to GDP per capita.

Evidence in OECD (1997b, 1998a) suggests that successful countries may have succeeded where others failed, in part, because their reform efforts to a greater extent were directed at reducing the bargaining power of insiders:

- Many countries have tightened up the eligibility conditions of their unemployment benefit schemes—a move that is unlikely to affect the insiders who, by definition, enjoy high job tenure. By contrast, central parameters of unemployment and related welfare benefit systems such as replacement rates and duration of benefits, which may affect the bargaining positions of insiders, were left relatively untouched in most countries outside the group of success stories.

- In a similar vein, many countries have eased up on the regulation of fixed-term contracts that expanded the supply of temporary jobs for outsiders, but it has typically been much more difficult to lower employment protection for permanent workers. In this context, Bentolila and Dolado (1994) argue that the existence of a group of temporary workers, who are easy to lay off, effectively reduces the unemployment risk of the secure insiders, and thus strengthens their position in wage bargaining.

This raises the question why successful countries could introduce policy reforms that affected insiders whereas other countries could not. Initial weakening of insider power may be part of the answer.

Thus in some of the successful countries, in particular the UK and New Zealand, governments took determined action at the outset of the reform process to weaken the bargaining power of insiders, notably through curbs on union rights and privileges. In other success countries, including Ireland, the Netherlands and Australia (at least in the initial phase of reform in the 1980s), there were moves toward increased centralisation of wage bargaining and a more corporatist attitude toward the setting of labour market policies, which may have led to a greater internalisation of outsider interests. But these are only proximate answers, because they do not explain why the weakening of insider power occurred in the first place.

In some cases, insider resistance may also have been reduced because individual reforms were seen as part of a comprehensive strategy of structural reforms. The argument would be that any individual reform might hurt the insiders who will therefore resist it. But when individual reforms are part of a much wider strategy, affecting all groups, they may be seen as more fair, the losses suffered by any particular group may not appear excessive, and there may be a stronger likelihood of economy-wide gains that may compensate some of the losses.

3.2 Equity concerns as a hindrance to reform

A reason often cited by countries to account for slow and sporadic implementation of the *OECD Jobs Strategy* recommendations is the perception that undertaking reform of, in particular, wage formation, EPL and social transfer systems involves conflict with policy objectives concerning income distribution.

Reflecting the many complicated mechanisms operating in this area, OECD research as to the nature and magnitudes of any potential trade-offs has provided no conclusive evidence. Nevertheless, it has been suggested that equity and efficiency objectives do not necessarily conflict, or at least that the terms of the trade-off may change, when they are seen in a dynamic perspective. Three reasons have been quoted for this:

1   Increased employment, because of policy reform, will tend to offset, at least partly, the impact of increased wage dispersion and restricted social transfers on income distribution. Thus, a wider distribution of wage rates is likely to enhance the employment prospects of workers at the bottom of the qualifications scale. But little agreement exists about the magnitude of such employment effects, with econometric estimates of elasticities between relative wage rates and demands for different categories of labour being highly uncertain and variable across studies.[27]

2   There is evidence of considerable mobility of individuals over time within the earnings distribution, showing that in some cases low-paid jobs are a stepping-stone to good careers. Across countries, with large differences in the static distribution of earnings, the degree of mobility seems remarkably similar.[28] OECD (1997c, Chapter 2) shows that, as a rule of thumb, after a period of five years only about one-third of those full-time workers initially receiving low earnings (belonging to the lowest earnings quintile) do so at the end of the period. A large part of the workers who left low-paid employment had moved up in the earnings distribution, though in some countries a significant fraction had also moved out of employment (in particular, this was the case in the US).

3   Lower relative incomes at the bottom of the scale may raise incentives for investment in human capital by groups who would otherwise have made little such investment; the existence of this kind of linkage is supported by evidence that, across countries, university graduation rates tend to be higher where the financial reward to such education is higher (Figure 25.6).[29] Such an effect, in turn, could reduce income dispersion over the longer run and assist the adaptation of the workforce to changing skills requirements.

Nevertheless, there are also arguments that might suggest that the equity-efficiency trade-off is even starker. For example, there is concern about the effectiveness of relative wage signals in influencing human-capital investment, not least because increased inequality of income, in a context of imperfect capital markets, may prevent those at the bottom of the income distribution from investing in their own or their children's education.[30]

In the context of the conflicting evidence on the strength, and perhaps even the sign, of the equity-efficiency trade-off, the Nordic countries have tended to take a strong position against wider dispersion of wage rates as a means of reducing unemployment. Instead, policies are directed toward validating the existing, relatively compressed earnings distributions in these countries by creating a similarly narrow distribution of individual productivities. The emphasis is put, in particular, on education and active labour market policies to achieve this latter goal. But beyond a certain level of spending, active labour

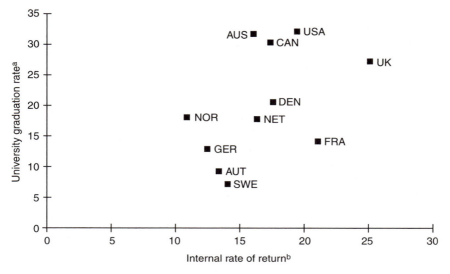

Figure 25.6 Internal rate of return and university graduation rates

Sources: OECD, *Education at a Glance*, Paris, 1996; OECD, *The OECD Jobs Study*, Vol II, Paris, 1994.

Notes:

[a] Ratio of graduates from short first university degree programmes to population at the typical age of graduation in 1994 [long first university degree programmes where short first degree programmes are not available (Austria, France, and Germany)].

[b] Based on university wage *premia* in the early 1990s, theoretical length of study and assumed retirement at age 65.

market policies may suffer from declining returns to scale. Even abstracting from this consideration, the results in Section 2 suggest that quite sizeable public spending in this area, with accompanying effects on taxes, could be required to validate relatively compressed earnings distributions. Moreover, there is a question as to how effective government subsidies to education, through near-free provision and generous grants, can be as an instrument to offset the disincentives arising from compressed wages and progressive taxes.

3.3 The role of crises in facilitating reform

OECD (1988) argued that crisis conditions are often necessary to change the general orientation of macroeconomic policies. In a similar vein, crises may help to overcome resistance to labour market reforms, be it based on insider intransigence or equity considerations. Indeed, it has been argued that many of the successful countries embarked on reform programmes because "existing policies could no longer be sustained" (OECD, 1997b).

Taking a more systematic view on the role of crises should begin with an attempt to date the beginning of the reform process. For the six successful countries, this produces the following picture:

- In Australia, the re-orientation of policies has been a gradual process, beginning with trade liberalisation and tri-partite wage Accords after the new Labour government took office in 1983. This process gathered speed in the late 1980s and early 1990s with moves toward decentralisation of wage bargaining and an increasingly medium-term orientation of macroeconomic policies.
- In Denmark, the 1982 change of government marks a relatively clear break, with an immediate shift toward a medium-term orientation for macroeconomic policies, based on a fixed exchange rate vis-à-vis the DM and fiscal consolidation, and the abolition of indexation of private and public-sector wages and income transfers.
- For Ireland, the shift in policy stance also dates back to the early 1980s when the incoming coalition government embarked on a major shift in the orientation of fiscal policies, emphasising the imperative need to halt the debt spiral. The 1987 change in government led to a strong focus on wage moderation achieved through tri-partite national agreements, and with a tax-based element as government finances improved. The 1990s have seen sustained attempts to raise work incentives via reforms to the tax/benefit system, cuts in the tax wedge, and increased spending on ALMPs.
- In the Netherlands, 1982 is also a watershed year, with a change of government, a shift toward fiscal consolidation (eventually to be followed by tax cuts) and deregulation, and the conclusion of the tri-partite so-called Wassenaar agreement on wage moderation.
- In New Zealand, the change of government in 1984 marks a clear shift in economic philosophy toward one of stability-oriented macroeconomic policies and market deregulation—a series of reforms to the collective bargaining system culminated in the Employment Contracts Act in 1991.
- In the UK, the change in government that occurred in 1979 also led to increased emphasis on market deregulation and macroeconomic stability—even if the latter proved to be rather elusive, at least until recently.

One notable lesson from this dating exercise is the role that changes in government seem to have played in the context of radical shifts in policy orientation. Not surprisingly, it is easier for a new government to break with past policies and strike out on a new path. A second lesson is that it can take a long time for a radical shift in policy orientation to bear fruits in terms of making significant inroads into structural unemployment. In most cases, the reform process in the successful countries got underway in the early or mid-1980s, but it took up to a decade before this was translated into success.

Even if a change of government was involved at the start of the reform process in the success countries, this does not explain why shifts in government in other countries did not lead to sustained reforms capable of reducing structural unemployment. We tried to examine whether particular features of economic developments might explain why reform programmes were enacted. The main results are:

- Major hikes in unemployment occurred in the years before the beginning of the reform process in Australia, Denmark, Ireland, and the Netherlands (Table 25.5). But for the other two success countries, it is difficult to argue that a sharp rise in unemployment was a major trigger of reform. And, some other countries experienced periods of significant rises in unemployment without embarking on sustained reforms. In other cases, though, sharp hikes in unemployment may have prompted a change in policy orientation that has not yet had sufficient time to work.
- A misery index, constructed by summing unemployment rates, government budget deficits, and external deficits relative to GDP, is not suggestive of crisis as a major common factor among the six countries. Denmark and Ireland are the only countries with a sharp rise in the misery index just before reform; Australia and the Netherlands had recorded a steady,

Table 25.5 Unemployment developments and policy reform 1961–96[a]

Country[b]	Change in unemployment preceding policy reform		Maximum rise in unemployment over[c]	
	2 years	*3 years*	*2 years*	*3 years*
Australia (1983)	4.2	3.9	4.2 (83)	4.6 (92)
Denmark (1982)	2.8	3.6	4.5 (75)	4.5 (76)
Ireland (1982)	4.0	4.1	4.0 (84)	6.5 (83)
Netherlands (1982)	4.5	4.9	5.2 (83)	7.0 (83)
New Zealand (1984)	0.9	1.1	3.2 (91)	4.7 (91)
UK (1979)	−0.6	−0.3	4.5 (81)	5.9 (82)
US			3.6 (75)	3.9 (82)
Japan			0.7 (94)	1.0 (95)
Germany			3.4 (83)	4.7 (83)
France			2.3 (93)	2.8 (94)
Italy			2.5 (94)	3.1 (95)
Canada			4.3 (83)	4.4 (83)
Austria			1.8 (83)	2.2 (83)
Belgium			4.0 (82)	5.3 (83)
Finland			10.2 (93)	14.4 (93)
Greece			3.8 (83)	5.1 (83)
Iceland			2.9 (93)	3.3 (94)
Norway			2.8 (89)	3.1 (90)
Portugal			3.8 (76)	5.2 (77)
Spain			6.4 (93)	7.9 (94)
Sweden			5.3 (93)	6.6 (93)
Switzerland			3.4 (93)	4.0 (93)

Notes:
[a] Data availability restricts the period for some countries.
[b] Year when policy reform began in parentheses.
[c] End-year of rise in parentheses.

but fairly slow, rise in the index; and, if anything, the index had tended to decline in the UK. Several other countries also recorded increases in the misery index that match those of the successful countries.

- Exchange-rate pressures are capable of precipitating or exacerbating crises, and they were strong at the time of policy change in Denmark, Ireland, and New Zealand. Moreover, while pressures may not have been as strong, the Netherlands actually devalued in 1982, and the UK exchange rate declined significantly through 1978 and into 1979 (the winter of discontent). But Australia did not really experience exchange-rate pressures before 1986, that is, after the reform programme had been launched.

Overall, it is difficult to argue that the existence of a crisis, in the narrow sense of a sharp rise in unemployment, or in the misery index or in exchange-market pressures, was a common factor triggering policy reform in the success countries and setting them apart from other countries. Clearly, other countries went through crises without introducing policies sufficient to reduce structural unemployment. But the success countries generally began their policy reforms against a background of either full-blown crisis or, at least, critical developments. In sum, while the evidence is not very conclusive, it might tentatively be argued that crises tend to create a groundswell of support for reforms, though the ability to harness such support and translate it into actions depends on political factors, such as shifts in government.

4 CONCLUDING REMARKS

Recent OECD work on remedies for the unemployment problem has highlighted an important message: countries can reduce high and persistent unemployment significantly if they implement the right policies in a determined fashion.

This message is important because it runs counter to the sense of pessimism about tackling the unemployment problem that pervades much of the debate in the media and general public in many OECD countries today, especially in Europe. Hence, there is nothing inevitable about high unemployment, even if the evidence suggests that it can take quite some time for a successful strategy to bear its fruits.

It is also important to add that the six country successes highlighted by recent OECD research span a wide range of social, economic, and political models that include four EU countries.

When one reviews the experiences of the country successes and failures, one is struck by the great diversity in their experiences. There is no unique golden road to implement the policies required for success.

This paper identifies several policy settings and institutional features of the labour market that are associated with high structural unemployment. At the same time, it tries to highlight some important common features across those countries that were successful in reducing structural unemployment. In particular, we emphasise the importance of opting for a *comprehensive* set of reforms to all the policies and institutional factors that are the main determinants of structural unemployment, and to exploiting the synergies between these reforms and macroeconomic policies. We also draw attention to the important role played by changes of government, often against the backdrop of crises, in implementing effective reforms.

We also discuss some of the obstacles to implementation of the OECD *Jobs Strategy*. Some of the medicine prescribed under the OECD recommendations is bitter and hard for many countries to swallow, especially insofar as it appears to raise concerns about equity and appears to threaten some of the rents and privileges of insiders. As a result, there is natural tendency in many countries to delay needed reforms in certain areas and/or to search for alternative, sweeter remedies.

It requires strong political will and leadership to convince electorates that it is necessary to swallow all the medicine, and that it will take time before this treatment leads to improved labour market performance and falling unemployment. But the success stories show that it can be done.

APPENDIX A: OECD INDICATOR OF STRUCTURAL UNEMPLOYMENT

The OECD indicator of structural unemployment is based on the notion of a non-accelerating wage rate of unemployment, NAWRU. Estimates are derived under the assumption that changes in wage inflation are proportional to the gap between actual unemployment and the *NAWRU*:

$$D^2 \log W = -a \cdot (U - NAWRU), a > 0, \tag{A1}$$

where D is the first-difference operator, and W and U are levels of wages and the unemployment rate, respectively. Using consecutive observations, and assuming the *NAWRU* to be constant between two consecutive years, an estimate of a can be calculated as:

$$a = -D^3 \log W/DU \tag{A2}$$

which yields an estimate of the *NAWRU* as

$$NAWRU = U - ((DU/D^3 \log W) \cdot D^2 \log W). \tag{A3}$$

Conceptually, the *NAWRU* estimated in this way is a short-run concept, i.e., it indicates the unemployment rate which, in a given year and based on the *actual* history of unemployment, would be associated with a constant rate of nominal wage increases.[31] In practice, the OECD indicator of structural unemployment takes into account not only the (suitably smoothed) mechanical estimates based on the above method but also the views of country experts (Giorno *et al.*, 1995).

APPENDIX B: THE EMPIRICAL ANALYSIS

Table 25.B1 shows basic characteristics of variables used in the regression analysis in Tables 25.2 and 25.4. More details are in Scarpetta (1996).

Table 25.B1 Basic characteristics of the variables used

Averages of values over the 1983–95 period

Variables	Mean	Standard deviation	Minimum	Maximum	No. of countries
UR	7.96	4.23	1.46	22.60	19
ALMPU	14.03	16.29	3.11	78.94	19
UB	29.77	12.92	0.35	70.97	19
EPL	6.88	4.34	0.36	14.25	19
UDENS	41.44	20.09	8.83	91.00	19
GAP	−0.29	2.50	−7.88	8.72	19
TWEDGE	38.39	9.40	17.70	54.51	19
MINWAGE	47.57	10.12	29.33	65.34	9

Acronym	Explanation
UR	For all countries but Denmark (administrative data), the OECD standardised unemployment rate.
ALMPU	Public expenditures for active labour market programmes per person unemployed relative to GDP per capita (in per cent).
UB	The OECD summary measure of benefit entitlements that is computed as the average of unemployment benefit replacement rates for two earnings levels, three family situations, and three duration categories.
EPL	Index of the strictness of employment protection legislation (see below).
UDENS	The proportion of workers who are members of a trade union (in per cent).
GAP	Output gap = [(Ao/To) − 1] · 100; where Ao is actual output and To is trend output computed by applying the Hodrick-Prescott filter to actual output.
TWEDGE	The total value of employers' and employees' social security contributions and personal income tax paid divided by gross earnings plus employers' social security contributions.
MINWAGE	Gross statutory minimum wage relative to the average wage.

Negotiating levels and co-ordination in collective bargaining arrangements

The collective bargaining structure of each OECD country was assessed on the basis of the union density index (the proportion of workers who are members of a trade union) and indicators of the predominant level of wage bargaining and the level of co-ordination among employers, on the one hand, and among trade unions, on the other hand. Moreover, we also used a summary measure that considers both the degree of centralisation and the degree of co-ordination in bargaining.

Three dummies were created to capture the level of centralisation, co-ordination or the summary measure (1 = low; 2 = intermediate; 3 = high).[32] The reference group in the tables of the main text includes countries with low levels of centralisation and co-ordination. The summary measure of centralisation/co-ordination was computed on the basis of the values assigned to the two individual indexes, considering the degree of centralisation first, and then the degree of coordination. In countries with decentralised wage bargaining, it was assumed that different degrees of co-ordination did not significantly modify the potential labour market outcomes: wages were still considered to be predominantly determined by firms' conditions. But coordination was considered crucial in the case of intermediate (sectoral) wage bargaining: each bargaining unit could generate disemployment effects if the decisions of employers' associations and sectoral trade unions are not well co-ordinated. Finally, high centralisation is generally accompanied by a high degree of co-ordination and countries in this group were considered as highly centralised/co-ordinated.

The distribution of countries according to the three measures and the changes over the period covered by our data are in Table 25.B2. It should be stressed that the indicators in Table 25.B2 are intended to summarise the broad trend in the degree of centralisation and/or co-ordination in each country and cannot fully account for repeated changes in a short time period, such as the zigzag path toward decentralisation observed in some Nordic countries.

Changes in employment protection legislation (EPL)

The summary measure of EPL is the average of two indices measuring the strictness of EPL rules for regular and fixed-term contracts, as presented in Tables 6.5 and 6.6 in OECD (1994b). In particular, the two indices are country rankings based on the average of scores assigned to several key elements characterising regular and fixed-term contracts, respectively. Since this classification was made, there were significant changes in the EPL of several OECD countries, including Germany, France, the UK, Australia, Denmark, Portugal and Spain (see OECD, 1997b). These changes were considered, using the following procedure: (1) the country scores for each of the key elements of regular and fixed-term contracts were re-evaluated on the basis of the observed changes; (2) the overall country scores for regular and fixed-term contracts were re-calculated; and, (3) the summary EPL indexes were recalculated taking into account (for the countries with changes in EPL) how their new summary scores compared with those of countries that had no changes.

In other words, the original ranking presented in OECD (1994b) was used as a benchmark; each country whose EPL had changed was assigned a position in the new ranking similar to the country with the closest summary score. Along these lines, Germany had only a marginal change that did not modify its position in the overall country ranking. France moved gradually to a more restrictive EPL from 1989 (the index rose from 9.5 to 11.5 in 1995). The UK moved to a slightly less-restrictive EPL (the index fell from 2.25 to 2 in 1993). Australia moved firstly to a more restrictive EPL in 1993

Table 25.B2 Country groupings—according to degree of centralisation/co-ordination (1 = low; 2 = intermediate; 3 = high)

Country	Centralisation	Co-ordination	Summary measure of centralisation/ co-ordination	Comments
US	1	1	1	
Japan	1	3	1	
Germany	2	3	3	
France	2	2	2	
Italy	1; 3 since 1992	2; 3 since 1992	1; 3 since 1992	Income policy accords of July 1992 and July 1993
UK[a]	2; gradually to 1	1	2; gradually to 1	
Canada	1	1	1	
Australia	2; 1 since 1988	2; 1 since 1988	2; 1 since 1988	Industrial Relations Act of 1988 followed by the Industrial Reform Act of 1993, that created a formal system of enterprise bargaining
Austria	2	3	3	
Belgium	2	2	2	
Denmark	3; gradually 2	3	3	Move toward decentralised bargaining but with a strong degree of co-ordination
Finland[b]	3; gradually to 2	2	3; gradually to 2	Tripartite three-year national pay agreements since 1988
Ireland	2	2; 3 since 1988	2; 3 since 1988	Wassenaar Agreement, 1982, which set tripartite negotiations at national level on pay increases
Netherlands	2	2; 3 since 1982	2; 3 since 1982	
New Zealand	2; 1 since 1991	1	2; 1 since 1991	Employment Contracts Act of 1991
Norway	3	3	3	
Portugal	2	2	2	
Spain	2	3; 2 since 1987	3; 2 since 1986	Up to 1986 national tripartite accords
Sweden	3; gradually 2	3; gradually 1 in the 1980s and back to 2 in 1991–95	3; gradually 2	In 1983, the engineering industry employer association and metal workers broke away from economy-wide negotiations; 1989 last central agreement for non-manual workers (SAF-PTK); 1991 and 1993 tripartite agreements.

Notes:

[a] In the UK, there has been a gradual move toward company-level pay setting. In the empirical analysis, it was assumed that by the end of the 1980s the UK was among the decentralised group of countries.

[b] In Finland, economy-wide bargaining agreements set guidelines rather than binding provisions, and sectoral unions have often, and increasingly over time, deviated from these guidelines. In the empirical analysis, it was assumed that in the second half of the 1980s, Finland was among the intermediate group of countries.

(from 3.26 to 4) and then in the opposite direction in 1994 (from 4 to 3.5). Denmark moved to a somewhat more restrictive EPL in 1994 (from 3.25 to 3.5). Portugal moved to ease its very strict EPL slightly in 1989 and 1991 (from 12.5 to 11.5 and 11).

Testing for reverse causality

To explore the possibility of reverse causality, Granger causality tests were run between, on the one hand, unemployment and, on the other hand, the generosity of unemployment benefits and the size of the tax wedge. The tests obviously had to be restricted to the variables that vary over time. Keeping this caveat in mind, the results in Table 25.B3 do not give strong backing to the hypothesis of reverse causation. But there are a few exceptions. Thus, unemployment may have led changes in benefit generosity in Belgium, France and Italy.

The hypothesis that unemployment does not lead benefit generosity is

Table 25.B3 Testing for reverse causality (F-statistics of the Granger causality tests, 1970–95)[a]

| Country | Test of the hypothesis that unemployment does not Granger-cause | |
	Benefit generosity	Tax wedge
Australia	0.47	0.58
Austria	0.59	4.90**
Belgium	8.29***	1.32
Canada	0.95	0.53
Denmark	0.91	0.49
Finland	0.54	2.42
France	5.98***	0.68
West Germany	1.13	1.45
Ireland	0.74	5.23**
Italy	9.47***	1.51
Japan	2.43	0.75
Netherlands	3.11*	0.16
New Zealand	0.18	1.63
Norway	0.07	3.89**
Portugal	0.93	1.98
Spain	0.48	0.74
Sweden	0.14	0.74
UK	3.62**	0.17
US	3.56**	0.02

Notes:
* = Statistically significant at 10% level
** = Statistically significant at 5% level
*** = Statistically significant at 1% level
[a] F-statistics of the relevant hypotheses. Different lag structures of the dependent and independent variables were used to maximise the efficiency of the estimates and obtain white-noise residuals.

also rejected for the UK and the US; in the latter, this result may reflect the regular practice of extending benefit duration from 26 to 39 weeks during periods of recession. Similarly, the hypothesis that unemployment does not lead changes in the tax wedge is rejected for Austria, Ireland, and Norway. Here, rejection does not necessarily imply a political-economy link, but could just reflect the normal economic mechanism that as unemployment changes, government budgets are affected and tax changes may be enacted in response.

NOTES

1 The results of this monitoring exercise were published in OECD Economic Surveys of individual countries.
2 OECD (1998a) presents a short update of the 1997 report.
3 Here, it is interesting to note the trenchant defence of the concept by Stiglitz (1997). He was formerly chairman of the OECD's Economic Policy Committee.
4 See the set of country studies on "The NAIRU: Concept, Measurement and Policy Implications" in the *OECD Economics Department Working Papers* series. However, Holden and Nymoen (1998) argue that estimates of rising NAWRUs for the Nordic countries may be misleading. While some of their conclusions may reflect conceptual differences in the definition of structural unemployment, and the strength of their evidence may be assessed differently, it must be acknowledged that estimates of structural unemployment are particularly uncertain where economies were subject to large shocks, as was the case in Finland and Sweden in the early 1990s.
5 The OECD has produced quantitative indicators for each of these factors (see Scarpetta, 1996, for definitions and sources for all the variables except statutory minimum wages, which are described in OECD, 1998b). We used these data as regressors in our reduced-form unemployment equation.
6 The set of 19 countries includes: Japan, Western Germany, France, Italy, Canada, Australia, Austria, Belgium, Denmark, Finland, Ireland, Netherlands, New Zealand, Norway, Portugal, Spain, Sweden, the US and UK.
7 Different variables are used in the literature to proxy aggregate demand effects. Layard and Nickell (1997) and Phelps (1994) used changes in inflation, while Coe (1990) used changes in capacity utilisation, as did Sargent and Sheikh (1996) who also included the output gap in their equation. We used the latter variable but also tested for the effects of replacing it by the change in inflation. The results were less satisfactory, most likely because in some countries factors other than aggregate demand (e.g., changes in macroeconomic policy regimes or income policy agreements) affected inflation.
8 By construction, active spending per unemployed relative to GDP per worker (ALMPU) is highly endogenous and must be instrumented. We used the average of ALMPU over the entire sample period as the instrument. We also experimented with using government spending (less net interest paid and labour market spending) as the instrument: first active spending as a share of GDP was instrumented with government spending, and then the instrumented variable was normalised with a smoothed employment/unemployment (E/U) ratio. The approach was not pursued because of the limited power of government spending in explaining the variations in active spending in some countries, and because the explanatory power of the overall instrument variable in the reduced-form unemployment equation was extremely sensitive to the choice of the smoothing factor for the E/U ratio.
9 The gap variable is defined as the proportional difference between actual and trend

output, where the latter is estimated by applying the Hodrick–Prescott filter to GDP. To minimise possible problems in estimating trend output at the two extremes of the series (1983 and 1995), we used a longer time series from 1970 to 1998 (the latter based on the latest OECD projections). Note that the assumption of an identical parameter for the gap variable across all cross-sectional units does not significantly affect estimated coefficients for the other explanatory variables.

10 The conventional F-test was used to check for unobservable, country-specific effects and when the null hypothesis was rejected at conventional significance levels, random-effects models were considered. The assumption that country-specific effects are random was tested using the Breusch–Pagan test, and Hausman's (1978) orthogonal test was used to test for the correlation between the random country-specific effects and the other regressors. Finally, the following observations were removed from the sample because the diagnostic analysis revealed that they severely affected the standard error of the regression and/or the estimated coefficients: 1983 and 1984 for Portugal; 1993, 1994, and 1995 for Finland; 1983 and 1994 for New Zealand; 1995 for Sweden and for Spain. See Scarpetta (1996) for details on the tests used to identify outliers in the data set.

11 In Tables 25.2 and 25.3, the reference group includes countries with either decentralised wage bargaining, low co-ordination or a low index of centralisation/co-ordination. Thus the estimated coefficients on the other two groups refer to the performance of these systems *relative to* decentralised/uncoordinated bargaining systems. A positive coefficient implies, other things being equal, a positive effect on the unemployment rate of the bargaining system relative to the decentralised system, and *vice versa*. In the table, the INT acronym represents *intermediate*, HG represents *high*. Appendix B discusses changes in these country groupings over time.

12 Sweden has been characterised by extremely high expenditures on active labour market programmes (four times the OECD average) in the 1983–95 period and by levels of unemployment which, albeit low (until the early 1990s), are comparable with those of countries that spent much less on ALMPs.

13 But econometric analysis for the same panel of nine OECD countries, reported in OECD (1998b), shows that high levels of the minimum relative to average earnings reduce youth employment.

14 A positive value of the country-specific effect means that other (omitted) factors have contributed to raise structural unemployment, while a negative value suggests that omitted factors have contributed to reduce structural unemployment.

15 Australia is the exception. For Denmark, the OECD summary measure does not pick up the fact that the abolition in 1993 of the possibility of renewing benefit eligibility through participation in ALMPs effectively implied a cut in maximum duration, which has been followed by further cuts and recently, by a combined cut in duration and the replacement rate for young workers. For Ireland, the abolition of the earnings-related benefit in 1995 implied a significant cut in replacement rates. In the UK, the recent introduction of the Job-Seekers Allowance implied a halving in the duration of unemployment insurance benefits to six months. The Netherlands reduced the maximum duration of benefits (from 2.5 years to 1.5 years), and benefits were not raised in line with increases in earnings. In New Zealand, several changes were made since the late 1980s, which cut the average replacement rate from a peak of 33% in 1987 to the current 27%

16 See Martin (1996) for a review of the OECD summary measure. An international overview of various dimensions of availability and eligibility does not suggest that the levels of these requirements deviate in any systematic manner between the six countries and other OECD countries (Danish Ministry of Finance, 1998).

17 Such interaction effects have recently received theoretical backing in Coe and

Snower (1997). At the practical level, the OECD's reviews of individual countries' progress in implementing the *Jobs Strategy* have thrown up many examples of such interactions between policies in different fields—for details, see OECD (1997b).

18 The Wald test rejects the restriction that the coefficients of UB are equal for the three groups of countries according to their spending on ALMPs.

19 Daveri and Tabellini (1997) obtained a similar result for the differentiated impact of the tax wedge on unemployment, although they included a smaller number of countries in their analysis and used a slightly different classification of countries according to the collective bargaining system.

20 This would also occur if the impact of unemployment on wage inflation is non-linear (the Phillips curve). For example, if the difference between the log of unemployment and the log of the natural rate drives changes in inflation, the average level of unemployment will be larger, the greater the variance of unemployment, even if the log of unemployment is on average equal to the log of the natural rate. Indeed, if $(\log U - \log U^*)$ is normally distributed with mean zero and variance $\sigma 2$, then the expected value of U is: $E(U) = \exp(\log U^* + \frac{1}{2}\sigma 2)$. Turner (1995) presents estimation results that suggest that, for three of the G7 countries, the inflationary effects of a positive output gap (output being above trend) are much bigger than the disinflationary effects of a corresponding negative output gap.

21 Scarpetta (1996) links slow adjustment of unemployment to strict employment protection, generous unemployment benefits, and aspects of wage bargaining systems. Layard (1989) finds that long benefit durations slow adjustment whereas centralised bargaining and expenditure on active labour market policies speed it up.

22 Bean (1997) provides some empirical evidence of the long-lasting effect of a demand shock in EU countries compared with the US.

23 Phelps (1992) argues that real interest rates affect the value that firms put on their customer base and their stock of employees familiarised with the firm, and thereby labour demand. Similarly, in a context where current employment raises the chances of future employment, a lower real interest rate may soften the bargaining stance of wage earners because the discounted value of future earnings associated with having a current job will increase.

24 Manning (1992) argues that higher productivity and real-wage growth increase the incentives to set wages so that a job is retained.

25 Scarpetta (1996) finds that the rise in real interest rates accounted for between 1 and 3 percentage points of the rise in the unemployment rate across 17 OECD countries during the 1971–93 period. Manning (1992), in a study of 19 OECD countries, finds effects suggesting that a 1 percentage point increase in real interest rates may increase unemployment by between 0 and 1 percentage point. In a study of 17 OECD countries, Phelps (1994) finds an impact of 0.1 to 0.4 percentage points on unemployment. Cotis *et al.* (1996) report estimates suggesting that rising real interest rates accounted for about half of the rise in the French equilibrium unemployment rate between 1974 and the mid-1990s.

26 Seeing policy settings as endogenously determined has potential implications for the Section 2 analysis. In principle, it could raise questions about the direction of causality of the links between unemployment and policy settings and about the extent to which coefficients in Table 25.2 may be estimates of the impact of policy settings on unemployment. To spotlight this issue, we ran some Granger causality tests to explore the possibility of reverse causality (see Appendix B). The results mostly tend to support interpretations of the empirical results in Section 2.

27 For example, estimates of elasticities of substitution between different categories of labour substantially above one were found by Bound and Johnson (1992) and

Katz and Murphy (1992) for the US, and by Risager (1992) for Denmark. In contrast, Machin *et al.* (1996) find an elasticity of around one for the US and less than one-half for the UK, Denmark and Sweden.

28 This is based on the comparative data on earnings mobility in several countries presented in OECD (1996c, 1997c). Aaberge *et al.* (1996) also supported the finding of broadly similar mobility patterns across countries.

29 The rates of return in Figure 25.6 do not account for the effects of tax-transfer systems, including support for students or different unemployment risks across education categories.

30 Benabou (1996) presents a model that illustrates this point.

31 In the presence of speed-limit effects or slow adjustment, a lower (or higher) unemployment rate may be associated with stable wage inflation in the long run, but this unemployment rate cannot be reached in the short term without setting off changes in inflation.

32 The classification proposed is based on recent OECD' publications, including the 1995 and the 1997 issues of the OECD *Employment Outlook* (chapter 5 and chapter 3, respectively) and the special chapters on implementing the *Jobs Strategy* in the OECD Economic Surveys.

REFERENCES

Aaberge, R., A. Björklund, M. Jäntti, M. Palme, P.J. Pedersen, N. Smith and T. Wennnemo (1996), 'Income Inequality and Income Mobility in the Scandinavian Countries Compared to the United States', Statistics Norway Discussion Paper No. 168.

Ball, L. (1996), 'Disinflation and the NAIRU', NBER Working Paper No. 5520.

Bean, C.R. (1994), 'European Unemployment: a Survey', *Journal of Economic Literature*, 32, 573–619.

Bean, C.R. (1997), 'The Role of Demand-Management Policies in Reducing Unemployment', in: D.J. Snower and G. de la Dehosa (eds), *Unemployment Policy: Government Options for the Labour Market* (CERP, Cambridge University Press).

Benabou, R. (1996), 'Inequality and Growth', NBER Working Paper No. 5658.

Bentolila, S. and J.J. Dolado (1994), 'Labour Flexibility and Wages: Lessons from Spain', *Economic Policy* 18, 53–99.

Bound, J. and G. Johnson (1992), 'Changes in the Structure of Wages in the 1980s: An Evaluation of Alternative Explanations', *American Economic Review* 82, 371–392.

Buti M., L.R. Pench and P. Sestito (1998), *European Unemployment: Contending Theories and Institutional Complexities*, Economic and Financial Reports, BEI/EIB, Report 98/01.

Calmfors, L. and J. Driffill (1988), 'Bargaining Structure, Corporatism and Macroeconomic Performance', *Economic Policy* 6, 14–61.

Coe, D. (1990), 'Structural Determinants of the Natural Rate of Unemployment in Canada', *IMF Staff Papers* 37, 95–115.

Coe, D. and D. Snower (1997), 'Policy Complementarities: The Case for Fundamental Labour Market Reform', *IMF Staff Papers* 44, 1–35.

Cotis, J.P., R. Méary and N. Sobczak (1996), 'Le Chômage d'Equilibre en France: Une Evaluation'. French contribution to the OECD WP1 Meeting on The NAIRU: Concept, Measurement and Policy Implications, 10–11 October.

Danish Ministry of Finance (1998), 'Availability Criteria in Selected OECD Countries', Working Paper No. 6, Copenhagen.

Daveri, F. and G. Tabellini (1997), 'Unemployment, Growth and Taxation in Industrial Countries', Brescia University, Discussion Paper No. 9706.

Elmeskov, J. (1993), 'High and Persistent Unemployment: Assessment of the Problem and its Causes', OECD Economics Department, Working Paper No. 132, Paris.

Giorno, C., P. Richardson, D. Roseveare and P. van den Noord (1995), 'Estimating Potential Output, Output Gaps and Structural Budget Balances', OECD Economics Department, Working Paper No. 152, Paris.

Hausman, J. (1978), 'Specification Tests in Econometrics', *Econometrica* 46, 1251–1271.

Holden, S. and R. Nymoen (1998), 'Measuring Structural Unemployment: Is There a Rough and Ready Answer?' mimeo, University of Oslo, June.

Holmlund, B. (1998), 'Unemployment Insurance in Theory and Practice', *Scandinavian Journal of Economics* 100, 113–142.

Katz, L.F. and K.M. Murphy (1992), 'Changes in Relative Wages, 1963–1987: Supply and Demand Factors', *Quarterly Journal of Economics* CVII, 35–78.

Layard, R. (1989), 'European Unemployment: Cause and Cure, London School of Economics', Centre for Labour Economics, Discussion Paper No. 368.

Layard, R., S. Nickell and R. Jackman (1991), *Unemployment: Macroeconomic Performance and the Labour Market* (Oxford: Oxford University Press).

Layard, R. and S. Nickell (1997), 'Labour Market Institutions and Economic Performance', Oxford University, Centre for Economic Performance, Discussion Paper No. 23.

Machin, S., A. Ryan and J. van Reenan (1996), 'Technology and Changes in Skill Structure: Evidence from an International Panel of Industries', London School of Economics, Centre for Economic Performance, Discussion Paper No. 297.

Manning, A. (1992), 'Productivity Growth, Wage Setting and Equilibrium Rate of Unemployment', London School of Economics, Centre for Economic Performance, Discussion Paper No. 63.

Martin, J.P. (1996), 'Measures of Replacement Rates for the Purpose of International Comparisons: A Note', *OECD Economic Studies* 26, 99–115.

OECD (1988), *Why Economic Policies Change Course—Eleven Case Studies* (Paris: OECD).

OECD (1994a), *The OECD Jobs Study: Facts, Analysis, Strategies* (Paris: OECD).

OECD (1994b), *The OECD Jobs Study: Evidence and Explanations*, Vols. I & II (Paris: OECD).

OECD (1996a), *The OECD Jobs Strategy: Enhancing the Effectiveness of Active Labour Market Policies* (Paris: OECD).

OECD (1996b), *The OECD Jobs Strategy: Technology, Productivity and Job Creation* (Paris: OECD).

OECD (1996c), *Employment Outlook* (Paris: OECD).

OECD (1997a), *The OECD Jobs Strategy: Making Work Pay* (Paris, OECD).

OECD (1997b), *Implementing the OECD Jobs Strategy: Member Countries' Experience* (Paris: OECD).

OECD (1997c), *Employment Outlook* (Paris: OECD).

OECD (1998a), *Implementing the OECD Jobs Strategy: Progress Report* (Paris: OECD).

OECD (1998b), *Employment Outlook* (Paris: OECD).

Risager, O. (1992), 'Substitutionselasticiteten mellem faglærte og ufaglærte mænd i Danmark: Resultater og implikationer', in: Ministry of Finance, *Bilag til Finansredegørelse 92* (Copenhagen: Ministry of Finance).

Phelps, E.S. (1992), 'Consumer Demand and Equilibrium Unemployment in a

Working Model of the Customer-Market Incentive-Wage Economy', *Quarterly Journal of Economics* CVII, 1003–1032.

Phelps, E.S. (1994), *Structural Slumps: The Modern Equilibrium Theory of Unemployment, Interest and Assets* (Cambridge, MA: Harvard University Press).

Sargent, T.C. and M.A. Sheikh (1996), 'The Natural Rate of Unemployment: Theory, Evidence and Policy Implications', Department of Finance, Canada, contribution to the OECD WP1 Meeting on The NAIRU: Concept, Measurement and Policy Implications, 10–11 October.

Scarpetta, S. (1996), 'Assessing the Role of Labour Market Policies and Institutional Settings on Unemployment: A Cross-Country Study', *OECD Economic Studies* 26, 43–98.

Stiglitz, J. (1997), 'Reflections on the Natural Rate Hypothesis', *Journal of Economic Perspectives* 11, 3–10.

Turner, D. (1995), 'Speed Limit and Asymmetric Inflation Effects from the Output Gap in the Major Seven Economies', *OECD Economic Studies* 24, 57–87.

26 Labour market regulation and unemployment

Paul Gregg and Alan Manning
Dennis J. Snower and Guillermo de la Dehesa (eds), *Unemployment Policy: Government Options for the Labour Market*, Cambridge University Press (1997), pp. 395–424

1 INTRODUCTION

There is understandable concern about the stubbornly high level of unemployment in OECD countries, and a strong desire to find policies that can reduce it. It is no longer fashionable to blame a shortfall in aggregate demand for this situation, as such an explanation is generally thought to be unable to address the progressive rise in unemployment over the last 25 years. Among economists, the most common current view has been to identify the problem as being on the supply side of the economy and in the labour market in particular. 'Interference' in the free workings of the labour market which keep real wage costs above market-clearing levels is seen as one of the main causes of unemployment. The proposed cure for unemployment generally involves removal of these interferences or what we will call labour market de-regulation.[1]

In this chapter we argue that this faith in the merits of labour market de-regulation is misplaced. We argue that economists have seriously over-emphasised the gains in terms of unemployment or more general measures of labour market efficiency to be obtained from de-regulation, and under-estimated the costs. If one asks someone who believes in the ability of labour market de-regulation to reduce unemployment about the source of their beliefs, they would probably cite various pieces of empirical evidence in support of their view. We consider this empirical evidence below and argue that it is much less persuasive than is commonly believed. We argue that the evidence is regarded as persuasive because of the touching faith that many economists have in the view that the de-regulation of the labour market moves it towards the perfectly competitive ideal in which everyone who wants a job can find one at a wage equal to the value of their contribution to society. We argue that a close examination of the behaviour of de-regulated labour markets suggests that they bear little relationship to the perfectly competitive model.

We do not want to argue that all labour market regulation is necessarily good for unemployment. But we do want to argue that the relationship between labour market regulation and unemployment is more complex than is generally suggested and that there are instances where increased de-regulation actually leads to increased unemployment or some other form of inefficiency in the operation of the labour market. Of course, the interesting question is then the optimal amount of labour market regulation: on this, we outline some general principles but have little to say about details.

The plan of this chapter is as follows. In section 2 we consider the broad framework of analysis which covers a range of economic opinion which places regulation as a key factor in rising unemployment. Section 3 considers the empirical evidence that is used to justify the case that labour market de-regulation leads to reduced unemployment and argues that it is much less persuasive than it might at first seem. We also consider some other pieces of evidence that are less rarely considered but also suggest that the link between regulation and unemployment may not be straightforward. We then try to provide some explanation for why deregulation may not always reduce the unemployment problem, and we argue that the reason is that de-regulated labour markets contain important elements of monopsony, so that making jobs attractive to workers is at least as important as encouraging job creation by firms in determining the level of unemployment. Labour market regula-tion is necessary to give workers some countervailing power against employers. We conclude by considering what principles should determine the optimal amount and form of labour market regulation.

2 THE CONVENTIONAL ANALYSIS OF REGULATION IN THE LABOUR MARKET

The most important interferences in the workings of the labour market that are normally mentioned in discussions on unemployment are the following (some of which are of more importance in some countries and at some times more than others):

- Social security systems which provide a safety net for the living standards of those out of work and which reduce the gap in living standards between those in or out of work and are thought to reduce the incentives to find or keep jobs. Where the safety net is paid by taxes on wages it will also raise total labour costs.
- Minimum wages which are thought to price workers out of jobs if set at levels above those prevailing in an unregulated labour market.
- Employment protection legislation such as restrictions on the ability of employers to hire and fire at will also raise labour costs and are thought to lead to reduced flexibility and possibly reduced employment.
- Trade unions which are thought to raise wages to levels which destroy jobs and perhaps to reduce productive efficiency through restrictive practices.

In this chapter, we will use the term 'labour market de-regulation' (or simply 'de-regulation') to refer to the type of policies which have as their aim the reform of social security system to make benefit provision less generous, the reduction or abolition of minimum wages, the removal of employment protection and reductions in the power of trade unions. Using a single term to refer to a collection of policies which, at least in some aspects, may have very different effects on the labour market, is potentially dangerous but we believe that the basic ideas behind all these policy recommendations is essentially the same and that they have enough in common to be usefully discussed in the same terms.

There are a number of different attitudes to the relationship between labour market regulation and the behaviour of OECD unemployment. According to one view (for example, the views of Minford and Riley, 1994, in the UK), the rise in OECD unemployment since the 1950s and 1960s is itself caused by the increased scope of labour market regulation that occurred in many countries in the 1960s and 1970s and in some cases continued into the 1980s. According to another view (the influential insider–outsider view popularised by Blanchard and Summers, 1986 and Lindbeck and Snower, 1989), it was labour market regulation combined with a number of adverse but temporary shocks like the oil price rises in the 1970s that caused unemployment to remain high long after the original impetus for the rise in unemployment had disappeared. A third view, becoming increasingly popular (for example, Juhn, Murphy and Topel, 1991), is that technological change that is biased in favour of skilled labour, perhaps combined with globalisation of the world economy, has led to a deterioration in the economic position of the unskilled in OECD countries and that labour market regulation has hindered the required adjustment in the wage structure, with the consequence of high unemployment concentrated on the less skilled.

But although these analyses differ in their views of the fundamental origins of the rise in unemployment, they all tend to emphasise that labour market de-regulation should be part of the solution. This type of analysis is well summarised by the OECD *Jobs Study* (OECD, 1994, p. 22) which concluded that

> wages have significant consequences for employment and unemployment. The process of wage determination is strongly influenced by labour market pressures, social perceptions, legislation and industrial relation systems.

This study represents the culmination of two years' intense effort. As would be expected from a mainstream transnational body, it represents a synthesis of collective wisdom derived from the last five years or so of the analysis of the functioning of the labour market. The report is permeated with the notion of the 'flexible labour market', but 'flexibility' is a word open to numerous interpretations.

The OECD is clear about the flexibility it seeks as a result of policy reform – that wages should be highly sensitive to unemployment and that the unemployed should enter work frequently, so as to avoid a build-up of long-term unemployment. 'Wage flexibility' should mean that as unemployment rises, real wage costs should fall relative to productivity. This, it is argued, raises profitability, stimulates growth and encourages employment. Just as wages should be sensitive to unemployment at the aggregate level, they should also be sensitive to concentrations of unemployment in society, so that if unemployment is higher for young people, their wages should fall relative to older workers. This would in turn induce employers to recruit young people. The second aspect of flexibility should be that the pool of the unemployed should turn over rapidly to avoid the development of a large stock of long-term unemployed. The long-term unemployed are envisaged as not only suffering greater deprivation but as losing usable skills and motivation, which becomes part of the structural unemployment problem.

From these notions of flexibility, the OECD suggests nine principles of policy which should, in their view, combine to ensure that employment grows in line with the population wanting to work with a reasonable level of unemployment:

1   Macroeconomic policy should be set to encourage sustainable growth.
2   Technical development should be encouraged, as should its diffusion into the economy.
3   Flexible working time, both in current hours and amount of lifetime in the labour force, should be encouraged.
4   A positive entrepreneurial climate to encourage business start-ups should be generated.
5   Wages and non-wage labour costs should be made more flexible across groups in the workforce, especially for the young.
6   There should be reform of employment security provision.
7   Active labour market expenditure should be increased instead of passive benefit provision.
8   Workforce skills should be improved through education and training programmes.
9   Unemployment benefit systems (and tax) should be reformed to encourage positive incentives to go into work.

Many (but not all) of these proposals are designed to lessen the impact of the labour market regulations of the sort described earlier. A crude summary of the conventional view would be that it is necessary to reduce labour costs (broadly defined) to increase employment, and to the extent that this means reductions in wages paid to workers, the incentive to work can only be maintained by a reduction in welfare payments to the unemployed. The policy option advocated is not complete labour market de-regulation, but the case for retaining some regulation is normally in terms of equity rather than efficiency. So, for example, in its discussion of the role of minimum wages, the OECD study (p. 46) said that OECD countries should if it is judged desirable to maintain a legal minimum wage as part of an anti-poverty strategy, consider minimising its adverse employment effects.

It is taken for granted that minimum wages are bad for employment and only equity considerations may justify their retention.

3 EMPIRICAL EVIDENCE ON THE RELATIONSHIP BETWEEN LABOUR MARKET DE-REGULATION AND UNEMPLOYMENT

In this section, we review the empirical evidence for the case that labour market regulation can be held responsible for unemployment. This literature is voluminous, and a complete survey is impossible (see for example, Bean, 1994, for a survey of European experience), but what follows is, we believe, a fair representation of the work that has been done.

3.1 Time-series evidence

First, there is a considerable amount of econometric work on macro-economic data designed to shed light on the determinants of unemployment (in Europe the so-called 'Chelwood Gate' conference papers being good examples – see Blanchard, 1990, for a summary). Typically these studies involve a regression of the unemployment rate on a set of variables thought to influence unemployment, or the estimation of a system of equations from which the determinants of unemployment can be inferred. The sort of variables thought to influence unemployment include some measures of labour market regulation and also some other variables thought to be relevant. These models are generally dynamic, so can be used to explain the behaviour of unemployment in both the short run and the long run. It may be invidious to single out individuals, but a good example of this sort of work is the book by Layard, Nickell and Jackman (1991) which ends up estimating an equation for the unemployment rate in 19 countries for the period 1956–88. The variables included as determinants of the unemployment rate are the duration and generosity of unemployment benefits (measured as the replacement ratio), some measure of collective bargaining structure and the proportion of employees with job tenure less than two years (which is designed to proxy job security legislation).

If one reads this sort of study, one often comes away with the impression that these models are really rather successful in explaining the changes in unemployment both across countries and over time. But appearances are deceptive. If one examines these models closely one generally finds that within them they contain a time trend, suitably chosen dummy variables or some variable that behaves something like them (but is itself implausible as an explanation of the rise in unemployment) that does a very large part of the work in explaining changes in unemployment over time. So, for example, Layard, Nickell and Jackman (1991) contains a dummy variable which implies that, for some reason, there was a permanent jump in the unemployment rate in 1970.

So these models do not provide a very coherent explanation of the time-series behaviour of the unemployment rate. The reason why these models are unable to explain the rise in unemployment in terms of increased labour market regulation is a simple one. From the late 1960s unemployment throughout the OECD has been on a rising trend. In the 1960s and 1970s labour market regulation was increased in most countries. So if one was writing about unemployment in the first half of the 1980s, it is not surprising that there seemed to be a connection between increased unemployment and increased labour market regulation. But this analysis was not ignored by policy makers, and from the early 1980s the labour market policies adopted in most countries (although some more than others) have ended to favour de-regulation; yet, unemployment continued to rise. A striking example of this is the UK, where the Conservative government that took power in 1979 pursued a very aggressive policy of labour market de-regulation. Yet at no point in the 1980s and 1990s has the unemployment rate been below the highest level experienced in the period from 1945 to 1979. Another good example is the USA, where the labour market has always been relatively unregulated and, if anything, has become less so. But there has still been a rise in unemployment which it has been thought necessary to explain, as is evidenced by the title of Juhn, Murphy and Topel (1991), 'Why has the natural rate of unemployment increased over time?' Furthermore, since the 1979 oil price rise no serious external shock has hit the developed markets and if anything the shocks have been positive (e.g. the collapse of raw material prices).

In the mid-1980s, this realisation that economists were at a loss in explaining the rise in unemployment led to the popularity of insider–outsider and hysteresis models (Blanchard and Summers, 1986; Lindbeck and Snower, 1989) which emphasised the importance of unemployment persistence after temporary shocks. These ideas were attractive when they were invented in the mid-1980s as it was then relatively plausible to believe that the high unemployment was the result of a very slow adjustment after temporary shocks like the 1970s oil price shocks. But we are now in the mid-1990s and there has been no noticeable reduction in unemployment and there seems to be something permanent about it, so these models come to seem much less plausible. All the empirical studies which try to explain the rise in unemployment find that the rise is permanent, not just a very drawn-out response to some temporary shocks.

The inability of our econometric models to explain the rise in unemployment in terms of increased labour market regulation or any other commonly included shock-type variable has inevitably led to a search for a new 'answer'. A number of candidates are available. Phelps (1994) has argued that real interest rates are important (see Malinvaud, 1997; Phelps, 1997); elsewhere we have argued (Manning, 1991) that the rate of productivity growth may be important. But the most fashionable current explanation is that the labour market opportunities for the less skilled relative to the more skilled have been declining. This type of argument has its origins in the USA, where it seems to fit the data very well. For example, Juhn, Murphy and Topel (1991) document that the unemployment-population ratio for the top 60 per cent of prime-age men (in terms of predicted wages) hardly changed between 1967 and 1990 while the unemployment-population ratio for the bottom 10 per cent rose from something over 4 per cent to about 12 per cent. In terms of non-employment the changes are more dramatic, the rates for the bottom 10 per cent tripling to about 35 per cent. At the same time the real hourly wages of the bottom 10 per cent have fallen by 30 per cent since 1970 while the real hourly wages for the top 60 per cent are essentially constant. This evidence is very strongly indicative of a shift in demand against the less skilled. Why there has been a shift against the unskilled is less clear. The two most favoured explanations are competition with low-wage labour in developing countries and technical progress that is biased against the unskilled (the studies by Berman *et al.*, 1994 and Murphy and Welch, 1993, suggest that the former explanation cannot be the whole story). These are long-term trends rather than temporary shocks, and we would expect both these mechanisms to be at work in all industrialised countries.

The argument then continues that countries which have institutions which maintain the living standards of those at the bottom end of the wage distribution (like welfare states, minimum wages and trade unions) avoid the extreme falls in living standards for less able workers but at the cost of preventing relative wage adjustment and, as a consequence, high unemployment. So, while labour market regulation is not the fundamental cause of the labour market problems currently being experienced, it does determine the form that those problems take. Yet whilst the rise in unemployment in the USA has been entirely among the least able, it has been in spite of the large falls in real wages that these individuals have had. If the European countries have not had enough real wage adjustment because of labour market regulation, then we would expect the divergence in unemployment rates to be much larger in Europe than in the USA. But there is little evidence that this is the case (see, for example, the evidence provided on a number of countries by Nickell and Bell, 1997).

Take the example of the UK. While it is true that the absolute gap between the unemployment rates of the skilled and unskilled has widened, it is not true that the relative unemployment rates have widened. Figure 26.1 reports the results for the UK of the Juhn *et al.* (1991) decomposition in which the unemployment and non-employment rates of prime-aged men are computed for various deciles of the predicted wage distribution. Although there is a widening in the absolute unemployment differentials between the top and bottom of the earnings distribution there is no very obvious movement in the relative unemployment rates. One can debate whether it is the absolute or relative unemployment rates that are more relevant (see Layard *et al.*, 1991, chapter 6; Manning *et al.*, 1995), but the important point is that it does not matter which measure is used for the USA while it does for the UK. The relative deterioration in the employment prospects of the least skilled does

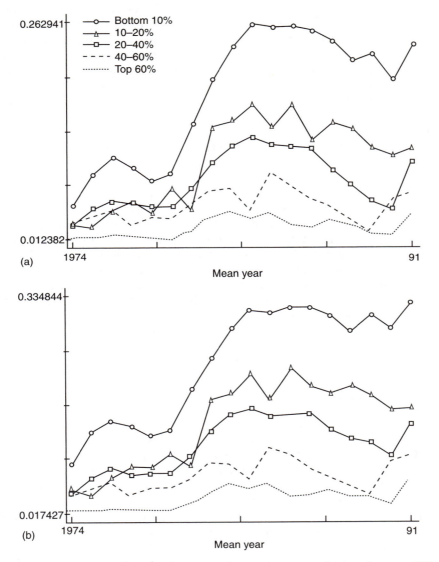

Figure 26.1 Unemployment and non-employment rates, prime-aged men, UK, 1974–91, by deciles of the predicted wage distribution
(a) Unemployment rates.
(b) Non-employment rates.

Source: Juhn *et al.* (1991).

not seem to be greater in the UK than the USA, which is a strong prediction of the theory that blames labour market regulation and skill-biased change for current labour market problems. Indeed, on the basis of these figures the non-employment rates for the bottom 10 per cent of workers in the UK and the USA seem to be very similar (at about 35 per cent) although the break-down into inactivity and unemployment is rather different with two-thirds of non-employment in the UK being measured as unemployment but only one-third in the USA. What that suggests is that the bottom 10 per cent of the prime-aged male population in the USA may be doing substantially worse in terms of relative wages and no better in terms of employment than the bottom 10 per cent in the UK.

One possible explanation for these findings is the following. Skill-biased change is not a new phenomenon. The shift towards the use of more skilled labour has been occurring since at least the beginning of industrialisation and it is not clear that it is currently at a faster rate (a study by Berman *et al.*, 1994, warns against assuming we are living in a period with uniquely fast change). If, in the past, this did not lead to such dramatic changes in relative wages and unemployment rates, that was because the relative supply of skilled labour increased roughly in line with relative demands. The failure of this supply-side mechanism to work in the USA today may be the cause of the deteriorating position of those who find themselves at the bottom end of the skill distribution, and this may have something to do with the way in which the education system and general social environment for the most disadvantaged in the USA is probably worse than it is in Europe.

3.2 Cross-section evidence

The view that all developed countries have been faced with a deteriorating labour market situation and that labour market regulation affects the form that the problems take is consistent with the fact that where the econometric model of Layard *et al.* (1991) discussed above does appear to be more successful is in explaining differences in unemployment across countries by differences in labour market regulation.

However, there are problems with this cross-section evidence as well. For example, Burda (1988), among others, reports that the generosity of unemployment benefits is correlated with unemployment, but the study in OECD (1991) finds no relationship. Lazear (1990) finds that job security provisions are associated with unemployment but Bertola (1990) finds no such relationship. And there seems to be no very simple relationship between the power of trade unions and unemployment, as is shown by Calmfors and Driffill (1988) and the papers that have followed from it.

To illustrate these types of problems Table 26.1 presents single variable regressions of a variety of measures of labour market performance on a variety of measures of labour market regulation based on the available data for 16 OECD countries (the data is presented in the appendix). Although multivariate regressions would be desirable, the small sample sizes combined

Table 26.1 Single variable correlations

	Mean tenure	Bertola index	TU density	Coverage rate	Benefit duration	Replacement ratio	Minimum wage
Change in unemployment rate	-0.080	-0.281	-0.053	0.039	0.078	-0.054	0.111
	(0.534)	(0.296)	(0.037)	(0.024)	(0.035)	(0.034)	(0.050)
No. of countries	10	10	14	14	16	16	9
R^2	0.00	0.06	0.12	0.11	0.24	0.12	0.49
Unemployment rate in 1990	-0.438	-0.183	-0.059	-0.01	0.035	-0.068	0.015
	(0.333)	(0.244)	(0.023)	(0.024)	(0.040)	(0.028)	(0.032)
No. of countries	10	10	14	14	16	16	9
R^2	0.17	0.17	0.26	0.00	0.07	0.26	0.02
Long-term unemployment (%)	1.75	-4.40	-0.25	0.30	0.17	-0.22	0.82
	(2.54)	(1.69)	(0.21)	(0.17)	(0.34)	(0.30)	(0.32)
No. of countries	10	10	12	12	14	14	9
R^2	0.05	0.33	0.07	0.16	0.02	0.04	0.33
Male non-employment rate	-0.21	0.056	0.042	0.015	0.088	-0.059	-0.090
	(0.642)	(0.211)	(0.045)	(0.056)	(0.053)	(0.029)	(0.036)
No. of obs.	9	9	11	11	13	13	8
R^2	0.33	0.00	0.04	0.01	0.23	0.10	0.29
Changes in male non-employment rate	-0.660	-0.199	0.029	0.035	0.120	-0.061	-0.074
	(0.622)	(0.209)	(0.033)	(0.037)	(0.035)	(0.036)	(0.081)
No. of obs.	9	8	10	10	11	11	7
R^2	0.13	0.03	0.03	0.07	0.48	>0.14	0.12

with the fact that few countries have a complete set of regulation variables makes this impossible. We start with three of the most common measures of labour market performance: the unemployment rate in 1990, the change in the unemployment rate (the difference between the 1985–9 average and the 1960–4 average), and the percentage of the unemployed who are classed as long-term unemployed (defined as being unemployed for a year or more). As measures of labour market regulation, we use benefit duration and the replacement ratio as measures of the generosity of the social security system, trade union density and the collective bargaining coverage rate as measures of the bargaining power of workers, the minimum wage relative to the average wage as a measure of the strength of minimum wage legislation and the average job tenure and the Bertola index of job security as measures of the strength of employment protection legislation (note that low values of the Bertola index mean high employment protection).

If the conventional analysis of labour market regulation is correct, we would expect to find labour market performance to be negatively correlated with benefit duration, replacement ratios, trade union density, coverage, the minimum wage, job tenure and positively correlated with the Bertola index. Yet, when one looks at the results in Table 26.1, the most striking thing is that it is very rare to find any significant relationship at all. Those relationships that are significant at the 10 per cent level or less are summarised in Table 26.2. Consistent with the conventional analysis is the relationship between the change in unemployment between the 'golden age' years and the 1980s and the minimum wage and benefit duration, and between the proportion of long-term unemployed and the Bertola index and the minimum wage. But against this needs to be set the fact that the replacement ratio is negatively correlated with both the level and change in unemployment, and the same is true of the relationship between trade union density and the level of

Table 26.2 Significant relationships between regulation and performance

	Consistent with conventional view	*Not consistent with conventional view*
Unemployment rate		Trade union density Replacement ratio
Change in unemployment rate	Benefit duration Minimum wage	Replacement ratio
Proportion long-term unemployed	Bertola index Minimum wage coverage rate	
Non-employment rate	Benefit duration	Mean job tenure Replacement ratio Minimum wage
Change in non-employment rate	Benefit duration	Replacement ratio

unemployment. There is simply no strong evidence for the conventional view that regulation is associated with poor unemployment performance.

There are also reasons why one should be cautious even in interpreting these regressions, as comparing unemployment rates across countries is fraught with dangers. The unemployment rates that are most commonly used in comparisons across countries are the standardised ones produced by the OECD which are based on a common definition and so, in theory, should be comparable. The standardisation is based on the ILO definition which counts someone as unemployed if they are not currently doing any paid work, if they have looked for a job in the recent past and if they are ready to start work within a specified time period. The problem is that whether someone is classed as 'unemployed' on this definition is not likely to be invariant to the system of unemployment insurance. For example, potential recipients of unemployment benefit or income support in the UK are only eligible if they are actively looking for work and ready to start work, i.e. if they can be classed as unemployed on the ILO definition. On the other hand, in countries with less extensive welfare states or in countries which do not tie benefit provision to a similar condition, there is no incentive for someone without a job to have themselves classed as unemployed on the ILO definition.

This means that we would like to have some measure of the lack of work which is not sensitive to the institutional details of labour market regulation. In recent years, there has been increasing attention paid to rates of non-employment, i.e. to include those classed as inactive with those convention-ally measured as unemployed. Traditionally, those people without a job but classed as inactive have not been seen as a cause for concern as it has been assumed that their classification as inactive means that they do not want a job. While this may be true for some of those classed as inactive (and there is good evidence that unemployment and inactivity are different states), there are very good reasons for thinking that this is not true of all those classed as inactive. For example, many countries (the USA, the UK, the Netherlands and possibly others) have seen a large increase in the number of workers classed as inactive because of sickness. In the UK, the numbers of men on Sickness and Invalidity Benefits have doubled from about 600,000 in 1979 to 1.4 million in 1992 (see Layard, 1997). In addition around 450,000 have been added to those claiming Income Support but unable to search for work due to illness. It is simply incredible to think that an epidemic has been sweeping these countries making millions too sick to work. A more plausible explan-ation is the following. In many countries there are monetary incentives to be classed as sick rather than unemployed as benefit provision tends to be more generous for the sick, does not suffer time limitations, and requirements to seek work are less onerous. On the other hand, those classified as sick may have less access to state employment agencies. Given a choice, individuals may choose sickness benefit, particularly at times when jobs are scarce and, as a result, they are classed as inactive. But there is a strong suspicion that these are people who would be in work if the labour market were more favourable.

So, at least some of the inactive should almost certainly be classed together with the unemployed as a source for concern about labour market performance, and certainly when one is concerned about the social distress and benefit dependence associated with the absence of available employment. But once one does this, countries that appear to be successful on one measure of labour market performance may no longer appear to be so successful on another. For example, consider the figures in OECD (1993). If we consider men aged 25–54 (for the reason that we think their attachment to the labour market should be very strong) the average of the unemployment rate over the 1980s for the USA is 5.2 per cent, which is slightly lower than the reported (unweighted) average over most OECD countries of 5.3 per cent. But once one looks at non-employment rates, the USA no longer appears so attractive as its average non-employment rate of 12.1 per cent is above the reported average of 11.2 per cent. One should not make too much of this comparison as one should not simply judge labour market performance by what it provides for prime-aged men, as some countries have institutions which effectively protect this group at the expense of women and/or young workers. But it does illustrate the point that comparisons of labour market performance across countries can be sensitive to the measures used.

To investigate whether there is any evidence for this, the last two rows of Table 26.1 present regressions of the male non-employment rate and its change against the measures of labour market regulation discussed above. The relationships that are significant at the 10 per cent level or less are presented in Table 26.2. The correlation between benefit duration and non-employment remains consistent with the conventional view.

But the main change from the results obtained using the unemployment rate is that the minimum wage is now no longer associated with poor labour market performance; indeed, it is significantly negatively related to the non-employment rate. This is consistent with recent microeconomic work in the USA and UK on the effects of minimum wages on employment. Studies in the USA by Card (1992a, 1992b), Card and Krueger (1994) and Katz and Krueger (1992) and studies in the UK by Machin and Manning (1994a) and Dickens *et al.* (1994) have all found zero or positive effects of minimum wages on employment. Our findings in Table 26.1 are consistent with the view that a minimum wage raises employment but also attracts more workers into the labour market, possible because the labour market is offering better opportunities.

3.3 'Experimental evidence': labour market de-regulation in the UK

Another way of considering whether de-regulation improves labour market performance is to closely examine the experience of countries that have shifted policy explicitly to follow this route. In the 1980s and 1990s, the UK is probably the clearest example. Since 1979, welfare benefits have been made much less generous. This has been achieved by removing the link with past wages (abolishing the Earnings Related Supplement, see Booth, 1997) and pegging benefits to prices rather than wages. Hence, average replacement rates have fallen from around 25 per cent in the 1970s to around 18 per cent currently (OECD *Jobs Study*, 1994). Trade union power and membership has been reduced. Membership has fallen from around 13 million in 1979 to 9 million in 1993. Coverage of bargaining over wages has ceased for about 10 per cent of those in work and the wage mark-up has probably fallen marginally (see Metcalf, 1994, for details and other supporting information). Job security provisions have been reduced or abolished. The qualifying period for employment protection against unfair dismissal (except discrimination) has risen progressively from six months to two years (five years for part-time workers). Finally, minimum wages disappeared (save in agriculture) in 1993 when the Wages Councils which set industry minima were abolished. Prior to abolition, their influence had also been reduced through the 1980s (see Dickens *et al.*, 1993).

On wages, these policies have had the desired effect. The UK has seen the most rapid increase in wage inequality of any OECD nation over the last 15 years (see, for example, Schmitt, 1993 or Gregg and Machin, 1994). But despite the flexibility in relative wages which is all or more than many advocates of the policy wanted, the predicted reduction in unemployment that was supposed to be associated with this wage flexibility has not happened. Blanchflower and Freeman (1995) found that the annual entry rate into work for unemployed men fell from 46 per cent in 1979 to 32 per cent in 1990 at the top of the last upswing. For women these numbers were the same, at 43 per cent in both periods. Furthermore, large numbers of people, especially less educated men, have become inactive. These men (and a smaller number of women) are not even bothering to search for work but are accepting semi-enforced retirement or long-term sickness (see Schmitt and Wadsworth, 1993). Blanchflower and Freeman sum it up (1995, p. 75):

> the observed outcomes raise the disheartening possibility that the reforms in fact brought the UK a mixture of the worst of two possible worlds: the massive wage inequality of the decentralised US labour market together with high and lengthy spells of unemployment, European-style.

4 WHY MIGHT LABOUR MARKET DE-REGULATION NOT ALWAYS REDUCE UNEMPLOYMENT?

We have argued so far that the empirical evidence for the benefits of labour market de-regulation in reducing unemployment is not as persuasive as is sometimes made out. The reason that it is regarded as persuasive by many economists is that they have a strong *a priori* belief that regulation increases unemployment. The source of this belief is that the models that most economists use to analyse regulation and unemployment assume that de-regulation will move labour markets towards the perfectly competitive ideal in which all individuals can get a job if they want it at a wage equal to the value of the output they produce (their marginal product). This is not to say that these economists believe that unregulated labour markets will be market-clearing; most probably believe that there will be some involuntary unemployment in completely de-regulated labour markets (perhaps because of efficiency wage considerations or frictions in market operation). But the analysis suggests that regulation moves the economy even further from market-clearing.

But even though many economists would not profess to believe in the perfectly competitive model, its pernicious influence implicitly pervades much analysis. A good example is the literature on the effects of unemployment benefits on unemployment durations (see Devine and Kiefer, 1990 or Atkinson and Micklewright, 1991, for a summary of this literature). Commonly cited in support of the view that increasing unemployment benefits will inevitably increase unemployment is microeconomic evidence that is predominantly cross-sectional in nature. This evidence shows that, other things being equal, individuals who have higher receipts of unemployment benefits have, on average, longer spells of unemployment than those individuals who receive lower benefits. Can we conclude from this evidence that raising the general level of benefits will raise unemployment? This is a reasonable conclusion if one thinks of the labour market as basically competitive, as one could then argue that the distribution of wages reflects the distribution of marginal products, that the productivity of a worker is (at least to a first approximation) unaffected by the level of unemployment benefits and hence raising benefits must reduce the gap between income in work and income out of work, and that this will tend to raise unemployment.

But if the labour market is not basically competitive, this type of reasoning does not necessarily hold. We will give two examples. First, suppose, for the sake of argument, that the number of jobs is fixed independent of the level of benefits and that the unemployed compete among themselves for those jobs. It is plausible to believe that those individuals with lower benefits will be more desperate to find work, so will compete harder to get a job and hence will tend to have shorter spells of unemployment, thus explaining the cross-sectional evidence. What this implies is that an individual's spell of unemployment will be influenced by their search intensity relative to the average which will itself be influenced by their level of benefits relative to the average level. The size of the effect of the average level of benefits on an individual's unemployment duration is of crucial importance in determining the effect on unemployment of a general increase in unemployment benefits, yet cannot be identified from cross-sectional evidence alone. The assumption that the labour market is perfectly competitive allows one to assume that the effect of average benefits is zero, but that is not more than an assumption.

For a second example, consider the following argument. The theoretical search and matching models used to justify the empirical analysis of the effects of benefits on unemployment durations is a model of a labour market with frictions in which workers cannot move instantaneously to a job that pays their marginal product. The implications of these models are generally only discussed from the point of view of the behaviour of workers. But if one considers their implications for the behaviour of firms, one realises that labour market frictions give employers some monopsony power in setting wages. We would expect firms to use this market power to pay wages that are below marginal products and are, in part, determined by the wage that workers are prepared to work for (their reservation wage), which will be influenced by unemployment benefits. If we raise unemployment benefits this will raise the reservation wages of workers, which will tend to lead to a rise in wages but this will not necessarily lead to a reduction in employment as firms were paying wages below marginal products.

What this type of analysis would suggest is that it is important to avoid a situation in labour markets where there is considerable heterogeneity in reservation wages of workers with similar productivity. For example, the current system in the UK provides very little in the way of welfare support for young people and individuals with a working partner. This only encourages firms to create low-paying jobs with the aim of employing these workers in them, but this has the effect of making those jobs unattractive to, for example, middle-aged workers who have recently lost their jobs or those in families dependent on means-tested welfare benefits. There is evidence for the UK that the vacancies open to those not in work are now dominated by part-time and temporary jobs. Further, there is strong evidence that those not in work but who have a working partner are much more able to take these jobs than those with no partner (e.g. single parents) or those families where all adults are not in work. What is more, this distinction has worsened considerably since 1979. Thus, the incentives for the unemployed to take available work are poor, mainly because of the collapse of vacancies for full-time work (see Gregg and Wadsworth, 1994). Consequently, on all these criteria the labour market appears to be functioning less well than before.

The main argument that we would advance here is that the conventional analysis of the labour market makes the mistake of assuming that the only important deviation from perfect competition is the monopoly power possessed by some groups of workers. It completely ignores monopoly power on the other side of the labour market, i.e. that possessed by employers. We would argue that the monopsony power of employers is important and becomes more important the greater the degree of labour market de-regulation.

Theoretical developments have almost universally been aimed at assessing the sources of monopoly power of workers, i.e. why workers can maintain wages above market-clearing levels. Jobs are then seen as being in short supply and the constraint on employment in the economy is the supply of jobs by employers. So most policy analysis focuses exclusively on the need to increase the incentives to employers to hire labour, even if that means making jobs less attractive to workers. The elements of de-regulation described above are all aimed at reducing possible sources of monopoly power of workers, even if they raise the monopsony power of employers.

A good example of this bias is the analysis of severance costs. There is a voluminous literature on how the presence of firing costs that must be paid by the firm acts as a disincentive to the hiring of workers, and how workers (known as 'insiders') may be able to exploit these turnover costs to raise wages and hence further hinder job creation. Yet one will look in vain for a single analysis of the quitting cost imposed on workers in all countries which is the result of entitlement to welfare benefits being reduced or withdrawn if a worker leaves a job voluntarily (in a number of countries including the USA there is a complete disqualification). We might expect these quitting costs to make workers more cautious in taking jobs and they might enable employers to reduce wages as workers find it costly to quit. Atkinson and Micklewright (1991) state that 8–10 per cent of new claimants in the UK are disqualified for this reason and the data in Murphy and Topel (1987) would suggest that a similar proportion in the USA could be affected, so the proportion of workers involved is not negligible.

Most economists probably think that one can ignore monopsony in thinking about labour markets and hence that there are good reasons for holding the view that 'only firms matter' for job creation. In labour economics textbooks, the case of monopsony is generally treated as being synonymous with the company town and hence extremely rare. But labour markets will be to some extent monopsonistic as long as the labour supply to a firm is not perfectly elastic, i.e. as long as a firm that cuts wages by an infinitesimal amount does not find that all their workers instantaneously disappear. It seems impossible to claim that monopsony does not exist in this sense. A second reason why many economists are extremely sceptical about the relevance of monopsony is that they think that most unemployment is involuntary and that this is inconsistent with monopsony models in which employment is supply-determined. But the existence of monopsony power and involuntary unemployment are not incompatible. Monopsony power will exist whenever the supply of labour to a firm is not perfectly elastic. Involuntary unemployment will occur whenever the supply of workers who want to work in the firm is greater than the number of workers that the firm is prepared to hire. It is perfectly possible to have both these conditions satisfied, as is shown in more formal models by Manning (1994, 1995).

The existence of monopsony power in the labour market suggests that it should be possible to raise wages through appropriate labour market regulation without necessarily jeopardising employment. But if one wants to argue that certain labour market regulation can raise employment, one needs to argue that the supply of labour to the market as a whole is not inelastic, i.e. that increases in the attractiveness of jobs cause more workers to participate, unemployed workers to search harder, or increase the incentives for workers to invest in human capital, or some combination of these. While it would be commonly agreed that the labour supply of women is elastic, the conventional view has been that the labour supply of prime-aged men is virtually inelastic and hence one cannot expect to reduce their unemployment rates by appropriate labour market regulation. But recent evidence suggests that this might not be the case.

For the case of the USA, Juhn *et al.* (1991) have argued that the rising unemployment (or non-employment) rates and declining real wages for the less skilled over the period 1967–90 can be interpreted as a move down a labour supply curve that is not inelastic. This interpretation is not without its problems as it is not clear that it can explain the movements of wages and employment over the period 1945–67 when real wages for this type of worker rose substantially but employment rates were approximately constant, but it does suggest that employment outcomes for this group of workers are determined as much by supply as by demand. Of course, the authors interpret the demand curve facing these workers as being a competitive one, but if it came from a monopsonistic labour market one could then raise employment by appropriate labour market regulation.

To the extent that this is recognised in conventional thinking, it is normally put in terms of the reservation wages of these workers being high in relation to the wages in the jobs open to them. In the conventional analysis of this situation, the reservation wage is thought to be strongly (if not exclusively) influenced by the level of welfare benefits and the wage available by their marginal product so that it is labour market regulation itself that is seen as making the supply curve elastic. The conclusion drawn is that to reduce unemployment for this group one needs to reduce their benefits or (perhaps more kindly) increase their marginal product through training programmes. A policy like a minimum wage can only price these workers out of jobs. But as Juhn *et al.* (1991) and Topel (1993) emphasise, most of these workers receive very little in the way of benefits (they rely instead on savings, loans, friends and families) so that one cannot really blame welfare systems for making the supply curve elastic.

The view that there are important frictions in the labour market and that this gives firms potential monopsony power seems very reasonable. But the frictions which make job mobility costly for workers also tend to make it costly for firms to replace workers. This means that there are important elements of bilateral monopoly in the relationship between employer and worker. Monopsony will only be the outcome if the firm has unilateral power to set wages: one could argue that this is not the case, i.e. that workers are able to exercise their potential bargaining power even in de-regulated labour markets so that it is not *a priori* obvious that wages will be too low in these markets. We would not want to deny that some workers do manage to exploit the bargaining power that labour market frictions give to them. But we would argue that the ability of workers to do this is greater where that person has scarce skills, firm-specific information or their effort and cooperation are important to the functioning of the firm. Then the more educated, skilled and senior in the firm's hierarchy the person is, then the more individual power they possess. But these are not the workers on whom unemployment is concentrated, and we would argue that in de-regulated markets for unskilled labour it is a very close approximation to the truth to say that employers set wages: it is simply not accurate to think of workers in fast food restaurants and supermarkets as having substantial power to negotiate their wages. We would provide two pieces of casual evidence for the view that employers set wages in unregulated unskilled labour markets. First, we are all familiar with advertisements for job vacancies which provide information on the wage to be paid: any potential worker has obviously had no say in determining this wage. Yet we never see advertisements from unemployed workers advertising their labour at a fixed wage to potential employers. And the study of Machin and Manning (1994b) of the unregulated market for labour in UK residential homes for the elderly found that there is incredibly little wage dispersion within firms, with a third of firms having no wage dispersion at all. This simply could not be the outcome of bargaining of the employer with workers who are heterogeneous.

As legal regulation of minimum standards and most union organisation is about protecting or supporting the position of the economically vulnerable not reinforcing the position of the powerful groups (although there are exceptions), we would expect such regulation to be protecting groups which would otherwise have no bargaining power. The agenda of de-regulation outlined earlier in this chapter undermines the position of the weak but makes no assault on the sources of the bargaining power of more privileged workers. As such, it will serve to raise inequality in society, but not efficiency. Indeed, one often gets the impression that the only important aspects of monopoly power are among the disadvantaged. The popular 'insider–outsider' model with its assumptions that replacement of workers is costly and workers set wages seems most appropriate to the analysis of managerial labour markets, but is more commonly used to analyse unskilled labour markets.

So far, we have argued that de-regulated labour markets are not likely to be efficient. If one takes a historical view, one should not be surprised at this conclusion. The de-regulated labour markets of, say, late Victorian London, were not thought of by contemporaries as models of efficiency (although, disturbingly, they seem to satisfy many of the criteria laid down for a well functioning labour market by many modern commentators), and the origins of labour market regulation lay in widespread dissatisfaction with the operation of these labour markets. They were felt to provide only short-term menial jobs at low wages which gave workers little or no incentive to acquire skills and encouraged the entry of bad employers. However, one should not conclude from this that all labour market regulation (including the seemingly very restrictive job security provisions of some Southern European countries today) will lead to an improvement in labour market performance. Rather it is that there is some optimal level and form of regulation which strengthens the position of workers in the labour market. It is obviously of crucial importance to say something more precise about what this form may be. Doing this is made rather difficult because extraordinarily little attention has been paid by economists to this possibility and so there is little existing work to cite on the subject. So, we are unable to go much beyond suggesting some broad principles.

5 THE OPTIMAL AMOUNT AND FORM OF LABOUR MARKET REGULATION

Let us start by considering a variety of existing models to consider what they say about the optimal amount of power that workers should have in wage-setting. For the moment, we will equate labour market regulation with policies to strengthen the power of labour relative to employers, although later we will try to take a more discriminating approach as different types of labour market regulation will generally have different effects. We assume (which, as we have argued above, seems reasonable for the labour market for less skilled workers) that, in an unregulated labour market, it is employers who set wages and workers have no bargaining power.

In the matching model of Pissarides (1990), it is the respective importance of unemployed workers and vacant jobs in determining the number of matches that determines the optimal amount of bargaining power that workers should have. In the simplest version of this model, which assumes a perfectly elastic supply of jobs and a totally inelastic supply of workers to the market, fixed search intensity and no investments in human capital, increases in worker bargaining power always increase unemployment although it is possible that unemployment can be inefficiently low (in this case the labour market is filled up with too many low-quality jobs which one can think of as a casual labour market). But in versions of the model where worker search intensity is a choice variable unemployment may not be monotonically related to worker bargaining power. In this framework, the view that all labour market de-regulation is good is (crudely) consistent with the view that only the behaviour of firms matters for job creation. However, there is no empirical evidence for this position; estimates of matching functions suggest that it is not just vacancies alone that determine the outflows from unemployment (see Blanchard and Diamond, 1990, for the USA and Pissarides, 1986, for the UK).

In the model of Lockwood (1986) the model of Pissarides is generalised to allow for (exogenously given) variation in worker quality. In this case, it is optimal to give workers all the bargaining power, as if firms extract any share of the rents they have a private incentive to try to find a high-quality worker, an activity that is socially wasteful. The model of Acemoglu (1994) modifies the matching model to allow both workers and firms to make investments in human and physical capital. Crudely, the efficient level of worker bargaining power is determined by the relative sensitivity of these investments to the expected rewards. In the models of Albrecht and Axell (1984) and Burdett and Mortensen (1989), which assume an inelastic supply of firms and an elastic supply of workers, it is optimal to give all the bargaining power to workers. Eckstein and Wolpin (1990) relax the assumption that jobs are inelastically supplied and find that the optimal power of labour is lower.

One could add almost endlessly to this list of studies. The important point is that the optimal bargaining power of workers in search and matching models is not zero, so that complete labour market deregulation should not be expected to lead to efficiency. One might wonder whether any general principles emerge about the factors that are likely to determine the optimal amount of labour market regulation. Generally, increasing wages will increase the incentives of workers to undertake activities like job search, investment in human capital and make them more likely to accept jobs. On the other hand, it reduces incentives for firms to engage in recruitment, investment and makes them more wary in hiring workers. The optimal amount of labour market regulation will be higher the more important are the actions of workers relative to the actions of firms in determining labour market outcomes and the more sensitive are those actions to economic incentives.

This says nothing about the form that labour market regulation should take, as the different forms of intervention that we have discussed are likely to have different effects. For example, we would expect both the payment of unemployment benefits and minimum wages to raise wages for those in work, but they have opposite effects on the incentives of the unemployed to seek work which we would expect to be greater with minimum wages. On the other hand, minimum wages may be hard to enforce, while raising wages by universally raising welfare payments may be more self-enforcing, as no individual will have an incentive to work for low wages. On the other hand, benefits are often paid at very different rates to different groups which also have important consequences. We would also expect trade unions to have similar effects to minimum wages as they raise wages without reducing incentives for the unemployed to seek work and collective bargaining has the advantage that the negotiated wage can take into account local circumstances in a way which it is difficult for minimum wages to do. However, it may be very difficult to establish effective trade union organisation in some sectors so that some form of minimum wage legislation would be needed.

So the appropriate form of regulation is likely to depend on the particular circumstances of the labour market. Each aspect of regulation will have limits beyond which it no longer serves to counter monopsonistic power, and all policy needs to be geared to understanding these limits and how policy design can minimise any other costs. But equally there is a regulation agenda that can be used to limit the monopolistic power of elite workers, which limits the availability of such jobs and intensifies job competition in other sectors of the labour market. Controls which shareholders can use to control company directors are one obvious area, as is opening up professional closed shops in areas such as accountancy, the legal professions, etc. If skills are a source of limiting monopsony power then avoiding the presence of a large pool of low-skilled people with limited education again may help.

6 CONCLUSION

Because of their upbringing, in which perfectly competitive models are given exaggerated emphasis, economists are too easily persuaded that labour market regulation reduces the efficient workings of labour markets and can only be justified on equity grounds. What is staggering is that only sources of inefficiency which give market power to workers have received serious analysis. This strong *a priori* belief colours the reading and interpretation of empirical evidence and leads to one-sided policy analysis that emphasises only the need to increase the incentives for employers to hire workers while neglecting the need to make these jobs attractive to workers (except in so far as welfare benefits are thought to reduce the incentives to work). We have argued that totally deregulated labour markets are not likely to be efficient, primarily because they are likely to be monopsonistic in nature for those groups of workers who are most prone to unemployment. These workers are those who benefit most from such regulation. We believe that one can make a perfectly respectable economic case that some degree of labour market regulation is necessary for an efficient labour market. Working out the amount and form that this regulation should take then obviously becomes a crucial matter for economic research, but it is an issue that barely makes an appearance in most policy analyses at present.

NOTE

1 This is something of an ugly term, as not all the 'interferences' in the labour market that we will consider are naturally thought of as regulation, e.g. trade unions may emerge spontaneously without any government intervention. But it is very convenient to have a single term to describe a package of policies, and the term we use is quite common.

REFERENCES

Acemoglu, D., 1994. 'Search in the labour market, incomplete contracts and growth', Cambridge, MA: MIT, unpublished.

Albrecht, J. and B. Axell, 1984. 'An equilibrium model of search unemployment', *Journal of Political Economy*, 92, 824–40.

Atkinson, A.B. and J. Micklewright, 1991. 'Unemployment compensation and labour market transitions: a critical review', *Journal of Economic Literature*, 29, 1679–1727.

Bean, C.R., 1994. 'European unemployment: a survey', *Journal of Economic Literature*, 32, 573–619.

Berman, E., J. Bound and Z. Griliches, 1994. 'Changes in the demand for skilled labor within US manufacturing industries: evidence from the Annual Survey of Manufacturing', *Quarterly Journal of Economics*, 109, 367–97.

Bertola, G., 1990. 'Job Security, employment and wages', *European Economic Review*, 34, 851–86.

Blanchard, O., 1990. 'Unemployment: getting the questions right – and some of the answers', in J. Drèze and C. Bean (eds.), *Europe's Unemployment Problem*, Cambridge, MA: MIT Press.

Blanchard, O. and P. Diamond, 1990. 'The aggregate matching function', in P. Diamond (ed.), *Growth, Productivity, Unemployment*, Cambridge, MA: MIT Press.

Blanchard, O. and L. Summers, 1986. 'Hysteresis and the European unemployment problem', in S. Fischer (ed.), *NBER Economics Annual*, 1, Cambridge, MA: MIT Press, 15–77.

Blanchflower, D. and R. Freeman, 1993. 'Did the Thatcher reforms change British labour market performance?' in R. Barrell (ed.), *The UK Labour Market: Comparative Aspects and Institutional Developments*, Cambridge: Cambridge University Press.

Booth, A.L., 1997. 'An analysis of firing costs and their implications for unemployment policy', chapter 12 in Snower and de la Dehesa (1997).

Burda, M., 1988. 'Wait unemployment in Europe', *Economic Policy*, 7, 391–416.

Burdett, K. and D.T. Mortensen, 1989. 'Equilibrium wage differentials and employer size', University of Essex, unpublished.

Calmfors, L. and J. Driffill, 1988. 'Centralization of wage bargaining and macroeconomic performance', *Economic Policy*, 6, 13–61.

Card, D., 1992a. 'Using regional variations in wages to measure the effects of the federal minimum wage', *Industrial and Labor Relations Review*, 46, 22–37.

—— 1992b. 'Do minimum wages reduce employment? A case study of California, 1987–89', *Industrial and Labor Relations Review*, 46, 38–54.

Card, D. and A. Krueger, 1994. 'Minimum wages and employment: a case study of the fast food industry in New Jersey and Pennsylvania', *American Economic Review*, 84, 772–93.

Devine, T. and N. Kiefer, 1990. *Empirical Labor Economics: The Search Approach*, Ithaca, NY: Cornell University Press.

Dickens, R., S. Machin and A. Manning, 1993. 'The effect of the Wages Councils on employment', London School of Economics, unpublished.

Eckstein, Z. and Wolpin, 1990. 'Estimating a market equilibrium search model from panel data on individuals', *Econometrica*, 58, 783–808.

Freeman, R., 1994. 'Minimum wages again!', *International Journal of Manpower*, 2, 1–19.

Gregg, P. and S. Machin, 1993. 'Is the rise in UK inequality different?', in R. Barrell (ed.), *The UK Labour Market: Comparative Aspects and Institutional Developments*, Cambridge: Cambridge University Press.

Gregg, P. and J. Wadsworth, 1994. 'More work in fewer households?', NIESR, for the Joseph Rowntree Trust, mimeo.

Juhn, C., K. Murphy and R. Topel, 1991. 'Why has the natural rate of unemployment increased over time?', *Brookings Papers on Economic Activity*, 2, 75–142.

Katz, L. and A. Krueger, 1992. 'The effect of the minimum wage in the fast food industry', *Industrial and Labor Relations Review*, 46, 6–21.

Katz, L. and K. Murphy, 1992. 'Changes in relative wages, 1963–1987: supply and demand factors', *Quarterly Journal of Economics*, 107, 35–78.

Layard, R., 1997. 'Preventing long-term unemployment: an economic analysis', chapter 11 in Snower and de la Dehesa (1997).

Layard, P.R.G., S.J. Nickell and R.A. Jackman, 1991. *Unemployment: Macroeconomic Performance and the Labour Market*, Oxford: Oxford University Press.

Lazear, E., 1990. 'Job security provisions and employment', *Quarterly Journal of Economics*, 55, 699–726.

Lindbeck, A. and D.J. Snower, 1989. *The Insider–Outsider Theory of Employment and Unemployment*, Cambridge, MA: MIT Press.

Lockwood, B., 1986. 'Transferable skills, job matching and the inefficiency of the "natural" rate of unemployment', *Economic Journal*, 96, 961–74.

Machin, S. and A. Manning, 1994. 'Minimum wages, wage dispersion and employment: evidence from UK Wages Councils', *Industrial and Labor Relations Review*, 47, 319–29.

—— 1994b. 'The structure of wages in what should be a competitive labour market', London School of Economics, unpublished.

Malinvaud, E., 1997. 'Edmund Phelps' theory of structural slumps and its policy implications', chapter 5 in Snower and de la Dehesa (1997).

Manning, A., 1991. 'Productivity growth, wage-setting and the equilibrium rate of unemployment', Discussion Paper, London School of Economics, Centre for Economic Performance.

—— 1994. 'Labour markets with company wage policies', London School of Economics, unpublished.

—— 1995. 'How do we know that real wages are too high?', *Quarterly Journal of Economics*, 60(4), 1111–25.

Manning, A., J. Wadsworth and D. Wilkinson, 1994. 'Making your mind up: mismatch in Britain', London School of Economics, unpublished.

Metcalf, D. 1994. 'Transformation of British Industrial relations?', in R. Barrell (ed.), *The UK Labour Market: Comparative Aspects and Institutional Developments*, Cambridge: Cambridge University Press.

Minford, P. and J. Riley, 1994. 'The UK labour market: micro rigidities and macro obstacles', in R. Barrell (ed.), *The UK Labour Market: Comparative Aspects and Institutional Developments*, Cambridge: Cambridge University Press.

Murphy, K. and R. Topel, 1987. 'The evolution of unemployment in the United States', *NBER Macroeconomic Annual 1987*, 11–57.

Murphy, K. and F. Welch, 1993. 'Industrial change and the rising importance of skill', in S. Danziger and P. Gottschalk (eds.), *Uneven Tides: Rising Inequality in America*, New York: Russell Sage.

Nickell, S.J. and B. Bell, 1997. 'Would cutting payroll taxes on the unskilled have a significant impact on unemployment?', chapter 10 in Snower and de la Dehesa (1997).

OECD, 1989, 'Educational attainment of the labor force', *Employment Outlook*, Paris: OECD.

—— 1991. 'Unemployment benefit rules and labour market policy', *Employment Outlook*, chapter 7, Paris: OECD.

—— 1993. *Employment Outlook*, , Paris: OECD.

—— 1994. *The OECD Jobs Study: Facts, Analysis, Strategies*, Paris: OECD.

Phelps, E.S., 1994. *Structural Slumps: The Modern Equilibrium Theory of Employment, Interest, and Assets*, Cambridge, MA: Harvard University Press.

—— 1997. 'Wage subsidy programmes: alternative designs', chapter 7 in Snower and de la Dehesa (1997).

Pissarides, C., 1986. 'Unemployment and vacancies in Britain', *Economic Policy*, 3, 499–599.

—— 1990. *Equilibrium Employment Theory*, Oxford: Basil Blackwell.

Schmitt, J., 1993. 'The changing structure of male earnings in Britain, 1974–1988', Discussion Paper, London School of Economics, Centre for Economic Performance, 122 (March).

Schmitt, J. and J. Wadsworth, 1993. 'Why are two million men in Britain inactive?', London School of Economics, unpublished.

Snower, D.J. and G. de la Dehesa, 1997. *Unemployment Policy: Government Options for the Labour Market*, Cambridge: Cambridge University Press.

Topel, R., 1993. 'What have we learned from empirical studies of unemployment and turnover?', *American Economic Review, Papers and Proceedings*, 83, 110–15.

DATA APPENDIX

Table 26.A1

Netherlands	Change in average unemployment rate: 1960/4– 1985–9	Unemployment rate: 1990	Average unemployment rate: 1985–91	Percentage of unemployment with duration >1 year	Male non-employment rate: 1992	Change in male, non-employment rate: 1973–92
Australia	5.4	6.9	7.7	21.6	15.9	11.8
Austria	1.5	3.2	3.4	na	na	na
Belgium	7.8	7.2	8.3	69.9	na	na
Canada	2.3	8.1	8.9	5.7	18.1	10.2
Denmark	7.1	8.3	7.2	33.7	13.2	na
Finland	3.3	3.4	4.9	6.9	na	na
France	8.8	8.9	9.8	38.3	11.5	7.3
Germany	5.9	4.8	5.8	48.3	13.1	8.5
Greece	na	na	7.4	na	na	na
Italy	6.8	10.3	10.4	71.2	14.2	6.6
Japan	1.3	2.1	2.5	19.1	3.8	0.5
Netherlands	8.4	7.5	8.9	48.4	10.5	3.2
New Zealand	4.8	7.7	6.5	na	15	na
Norway	1.2	5.2	4.5	19.2	13.7	5.0
Spain	na	na	18.6	na	na	na
Sweden	0.6	1.5	2.1	4.8	12.2	6.6
UK	7.9	6.8	9.1	36	18.7	12.2
USA	0.5	5.4	6.1	5.6	13.8	5.4

Sources: Unemployment rates (levels and changes), non-employment rate (levels and changes), long-term employment: OECD, *Labour Force Statistics* (1971–1991); OECD, *Employment outlook*.
Note: na Data not available.

Table 26.A2

	Median job tenure: 1991	Bertola index (job security)	Trade union density	Trade union coverage	Max. benefit duration (months)	Initial replacement ratio: 1988	Min. wage as percentage of av. wage
Australia	3.5	na	40	80	Indef	43	35
Austria	na	na	46	98	Indef	41	na
Belgium	na	2	51	90	Indef	60	66
Canada	4.1	na	36	38	Indef	37	na
Denmark	na	9	na	na	Indef	35	69
Finland	5.2	na	72	95	Indef	26	na
France	7.5	3	10	92	Indef	26	61
Germany	7.5	5	32	90	Indef	52	69
Greece	na	na	na	na	na	50	na
Italy	na	1	na	na	6	15	50
Japan	8.5	6	25	23	6.9	48	na
Netherlands	3.1	8	26	71	36	70	72
New Zealand	na	na	45	67	Indef	40	na
Norway	6.5	na	56	75	18.5	62	na
Spain	na	na	na	na	na	50	na
Sweden	na	4	83	83	13.8	90	na
UK	4.4	7	39	47	Indef	26	52
USA	3	10	16	18	4.6	50	33

Sources: Median job tenure: OECD, *Employment outlook* (1989, 1992, 1993).
Job security provision: Bertola (1990).
Trade union density and coverage: OECD.
Replacement ratio and benefit duration: OECD.
Minimum wage: Freeman (1994).
Notes: na Data not available. Indef Benefits are of potentially unlimited duration.

Questions

1 'High levels and persistence of structural unemployment can and should be explained by labour market rigidities.' Discuss.
2 'Labour market flexibility is essential for attaining low levels of unemployment, but the problem is how to ensure flexibility in the labour market.' Discuss.
3 'The problem faced by the de-regulation school in labour economics is that weak unions and de-centralised collective bargaining are conducive to high levels of unemployment.' Do you agree?
4 'The existing evidence suggests that some countries have succeeded in reducing employment because their reforms were directed at reducing the bargaining power of the insiders.' Discuss.
5 'There is little or no evidence indicating that the efficiency–equity trade-off is a significant obstacle to labour market reforms.' Discuss.
6 'The faith in the merits of labour market de-regulation is misplaced because it is based on overestimation of the benefits and underestimation of the costs.' Discuss.
7 'De-regulation of the labour market does not encourage competition. On the contrary, it fosters anti-competitive behaviour by reducing the bargaining power of the weak and increasing the bargaining power of the strong.' Do you agree?
8 'For success in the fight against unemployment, making jobs attractive for workers is as important as providing incentives for job creation by the firms.' Discuss.

Further reading and references

FURTHER READING

The OECD's *Employment Outlook* is an annual publication that can be consulted for trends in employment as well as policy developments. OECD (1994) is a major source of information on the mainstream approach to labour market reforms. This was followed by OECD (1997), which examines the extent to which the OECD's guidelines for reform have been adopted and what results have been achieved.

For a political economy approach to rigidities in the labour market, see Saint-Paul (1997). For a review of the literature on European labour market rigidities, see Bean (1994) and Blachard (1990). On the significance of collective bargaining institutions and a review of the literature on this issue, see Calmors (1993). On the impact of hysteresis and the insider–outsider divide on unemployment, see Blanchard and Summers (1986) and Lindbeck and Snower (1989).

The literature on the consequences of monoponistic employer behaviour is less developed compared to that focusing on anti-competitive behaviour of labour organisations. However, Manning (1995) can be consulted on the existence of monopsony power. Atkinson and Micklewright (1991) demonstrate that a reduction in benefits is conductive to higher unemployment. On rising unemployment in the presence of falling real wages, see Juhn *et al.* (1991).

REFERENCES

Atkinson, A.B. and J. Micklewright (1991) 'Unemployment compensation and labour market transitions: a critical review', *Journal of Economic Literature* 29, 1679–1727.

Bean, C.R. (1994) 'European unemployment: a survey', *Journal of Economic Literature* 32, 573–619.

Blanchard, O. (1990) 'Unemployment: getting the questions right – and some of the answers', in J. Drèze and C. Bean (eds) *Europe's Unemployment Problem*, Cambridge, MA: MIT Press.

Blanchard, O. and L. Summers (1986) 'Hysteresis and the European unemployment problem', in S. Fischer (ed.), *NBER Economics Annual* 1, Cambridge, MA: MIT Press, pp. 15–77.

Calmors, L. (1993) 'Centralisation of wage bargaining and macroeconomic performance – a survey', *OECD Economic Studies*, no. 21 (Winter), 161–91.

Juhn, C., K. Murphy and R. Topel (1991) 'Why has the rate of natural unemployment increased over time?', *Brookings Paper on Economic Activity* 2, 75–142.

Lindbeck, A. and D.J. Snower (1989) *The Insider–Outsider Theory of Employment and Unemployment*, Cambridge, MA: MIT Press.

Manning, A. (1995) 'How do we know that real wages are too high?', *Quarterly Journal of Economics* 60(4), 1111–25.

OECD (1994) *Jobs Study: Facts, Analysis, Strategies*, Paris: OECD.

OECD (1997) *Implementing the OECD Jobs Strategy: Member Countries' Experience*, Paris: OECD.

Saint-Paul, G. (1997) 'High unemployment from a political economy perspective', in D.J. Snower and G. de la Dehesa (eds), *Unemployment Policy: Government Options for the Labour Market*, Cambridge: Cambridge University Press.

Index

Page numbers in italic, e.g. *115*, signify references to figures. Page numbers in bold, e.g. **31**, denote references to tables.